Information Sources in
Politics and Political Science:
A Survey Worldwide

Butterworths Guides to Information Sources

A series under the General Editorship of
D. J. Foskett, MA, FLA
and
M. W. Hill, MA, BSc, MRIC

This series was known previously as 'Information Sources for Research and Development'. Other titles available are:

Information Sources in Agriculture
  edited by G. P. Lilley

Information Sources in Economics
  edited by J. Fletcher

Information Sources in Education and Work
  edited by E. H. K. Dibden and J. C. Tomlinson

Information Sources in the History of Science and Medicine
  edited by P. Corsi and P. Weindling

Information Sources in Management and Business
  edited by K. D. C. Vernon

Information Sources in the Medical Sciences
  edited by L. T. Morton and S. Godbolt

Use of Chemical Literature (Third edition)
  edition by R. T. Bottle

Use of Engineering Literature
  edited by K. W. Mildren

Use of Mathematical Literature
  edited by A. R. Dorling

Use of Physics Literature
  edited by H. Coblans

Use of Reports Literature
  edited by C. P. Auger

Use of Social Sciences Literature
  edited by N. Roberts

Information Sources in
Politics and Political Science:
A Survey Worldwide

Editors
Dermot Englefield
Deputy Librarian, House of Commons, Westminster

Gavin Drewry
Reader in Social Administration, Bedford College,
University of London

Butterworths
London Boston Durban Singapore Sydney Toronto Wellington

© **Butterworth & Co (Publishers) Ltd 1984**

British Library Cataloguing in Publication Data

Information sources in politics and political science.—
(Butterworth's guides to information sources)
1. Political science—Information services
2. Political science—Bibliography
I. Englefield, Dermot J. T.   II. Drewry, Gavin
320'.07   JA74

ISBN 0-408-11470-3

Library of Congress Cataloging in Publication Data

Main entry under title:
Information sources in politics and political science.
(Butterworths guides to information sources)
Includes index.
1. Political science—Bibliography—Addresses,
essays, lectures. 2. Political science literature—Addresses,
essays, lectures. I. Englefield, Dermot J. T.
II. Drewry, Gavin, III. Series.
Z7161.1544 1984   [JA71] 016.32   84-2819

ISBN 0-408-11470-3

Photoset by Butterworths Litho Preparation Department
Printed in Great Britain by Butler & Tanner Ltd, Frome and London

Series Editors' Foreword

Daniel Bell has made it clear in his book *The Post-Industrial Society* that we now live an age in which information has succeeded raw materials and energy as the primary commodity. We have also seen in recent years the growth of a new discipline, information science. This is in spite of the fact that skill in acquiring and using information has always been one of the distinguishing features of the educated person. As Dr Johnson observed, 'Knowledge is of two kinds. We know a subject ourselves, or we know where we can find information upon it'.

But a new problem faces the modern educated person. We now have an excess of information, and even an excess of sources of information. This is often called the 'information explosion', though it might be more accurately called the 'publication explosion'. Yet it is of a deeper nature than either. The totality of knowledge itself, let alone of theories and opinions about knowledge, seems to have increased to an unbelievable extent, so that the pieces one seeks in order to solve any problem appear to be but a relatively few small straws in a very large haystack. That analogy, however, implies that we are indeed seeking but a few straws. In fact, when information arrives on our desks, we often find those few straws are actually far too big and far too numerous for one person to grasp and use easily. In the jargon used in the information world, efficient retrieval of relevant information often results in information overkill.

Ever since writing was invented, it has been a common practice for men to record and store information; not only facts and figures, but also theories and opinions. The rate of recording accelerated after the invention of printing and moveable type, not because that in itself could increase the amount of recording but because, by making it easy to publish multiple copies of a document and sell them at a profit, recording and distributing information became very lucrative and hence attractive to more people. On the other hand, men and women in whose lives the discovery of the handling of information plays a large part usually devise ways of getting what they want from other people, rather than from books, in their efforts to avoid information overkill. Conferences, briefings, committee meetings are one means of this; personal contacts through the 'invisible college' and members of one's club are another. While such people do read, some of them voraciously, the reading of published literature, including in this category newspapers as well as books and journals and even watching television, may provide little more than 10% of the total information that they use.

Computers have increased the opportunities, not merely by acting as more efficient stores and providers of certain kinds of information than libraries, but also by manipulating the data they contain in order to synthesize new information. To give a simple illustration, a computer which holds data on commodity prices in the various trading capitals of the world, and also data on currency exchange rates, can be programmed to indicate comparative costs in different places in one single currency. Computerized data bases, i.e. stores of bibliographic information, are now well established and quite widely available for anyone to use. Also increasing are the number of data banks, i.e. stores of factual information, which are now generally accessible. Anyone who buys a suitable terminal may be able to arrange to draw information directly from these computer systems for their own purposes; the systems are normally linked to the subscriber by means of the telephone network. Equally, an alternative is now being provided by information supply services such as libraries, more and more of which are introducing terminals as part of their regular services.

The number of sources of information on any topic can therefore be very extensive indeed: publications (in the widest sense), people (experts), specialist organizations from research associations to chambers of commerce, and computer stores. The number of channels by which one can have access to these vast collections of information are also very numerous, ranging from professional literature searchers, via computer intermediaries, to Citizens' Advice Bureaux, information marketing services and information brokers.

The aim of the Butterworths Guides to Information Sources is to bring all these sources and channels together in a single convenient form and to present a picture of the international scene as it exists in each of the disciplines we plan to cover. Consideration is also being given to volumes that will cover major interdisciplinary areas of what are now sometimes called 'mission-oriented' fields of knowledge. The first stage of the whole project will give greater emphasis to publications and their exploitation, partly because they are so numerous, and partly because more detail is needed to guide them adequately. But it may be that in due course the balance will change, and certainly the balance in each volume will be that which is appropriate to its subject at the time.

The editor of each volume is a person of high standing, with substantial experience of the discipline and of the sources of information in it. With a team of authors of whom each one is a specialist in one aspect of the field, the total volume provides an integrated and highly expert account of the current sources, of all types, in its subject

D. J. Foskett
Michael Hill

Preface

Within the covers of *Information Sources in Politics and Political Science* the reader will find a critical assessment of a large English-language library on both the study and the practice of this vital subject. Its coverage is not just of the UK, but is worldwide, partly because English today is probably the most international language there has been in history and is therefore an excellent medium for such a multicountry guide, and partly because even the most superficial reading of a newspaper quickly shows how seamless the subject itself is: even the most ethnocentric little Englander cannot ignore the international environment of UK politics. To keep the chapters to manageable length, the editors have had to introduce some seams!

The book has not been compiled to gather dust on library shelves labelled 'Bibliography'. Politics and government have always been practical arts (leaving aside the continuing dispute about whether the study of them justifies the description of a 'science'), but never more so than today, when both ideas and actions can be so easily and widely communicated. We believe, of course, that the book will be of help to a teacher at various levels, whether he or she is sketching out a new course or advising a student who needs a literature survey in what is, for that teacher, an uncharted area. And we hope that students themselves will browse in these pages, not just to find sources for essays and dissertations, but also to cultivate an interest in a world which will so clearly affect their future. We hope also that it will be of service to librarians and other brokers of information, not just in academic institutions but more generally.

But in addition, today, following several decades of lavish publishing in this subject area (an intellectual product of our growing need to cross both geographical and mental frontiers), there are many others whom we hope will find the book useful. The journalist whom is suddenly given the assignment of an election in a distant country; the administrator wishing to push back the frontiers of his or her own knowledge; the local or federal politician wanting to step back a little and assess the political world in which he or she operates. Finally, there is something in it for all of us as armchair critics of the contemporary scene, for both politics and administration are very much a part, for better or for worse, of our day-to-day world. In the last analysis, as Aristotle recognized more than two millennia ago, we are 'political animals', humanized by civic association in the State. The bibliographical needs and interests of all these categories have been borne in mind in planning this book.

'Politics' has been defined in a wide variety of ways, not all of them flattering, ever since people began thinking seriously about the subject. The editors take the view, for the purposes of this book, that politics is concerned with the accretion and expression of power in a society, whereby a particular group, normally called a government, can develop the society on the basis of an agreed set of priorities. These may be agreed only between members of a small group, such as with a military or one-party dictatorship, or they may be agreed between the majority of members of society, in which case we may call it a democracy (the terminology associated with different types of regime is fraught with dangerous ambiguity and emotively tainted usage). But in any case the society shapes and is shaped by its politics, the mechanisms by which priorities are ordered. Administration is that very important complement, the means of carrying out agreed priorities.

The start of this book was a telephone call from the publisher to Dermot Englefield, inviting him to consider the need for and the possibility of editing such a volume. He submitted a draft outline at the beginning of 1980. The publisher then suggested an 'academic co-editor', an idea quickly accepted, as it offered the chance to bridge the practice of politics at Westminster with its study in university departments. Gavin Drewry accepted Dermot Englefield's invitation to join him and work started on selecting and inviting a group of contributors.

We set out to recruit a team which would include a number of entrepreneurs in the marketplace of information, subject-specialist librarians, and also a group of users and creators of information (not to mention teachers), namely practising academics. If the book leads to better communication and understanding between these two selected groups, then so much the better.

We were fortunate in securing the help of experienced library staff from the Bodleian (Oxford), the British Library, the Foreign and Commonwealth Office, the London School of Economics, the Royal Institute of International Affairs (Chatham House) and the School of Oriental and African Studies. Academics joined us from England, including Exeter, Leicester and Southampton Universities and Bedford and Goldsmiths Colleges in London, and from Scotland, including Aberdeen, Edinburgh and Stirling Universities. Finally, a third group joined us from the House of Commons Library, where they undertake information and non-academic research work for politicians at Westminster, and where the practical atmosphere surrounding politics and government contrasts with that of academic institutions. We firmed up the plan of the work and decided to give our contributors a reasonably free rein.

This follows the well-tried policy of choosing experts of good reputation and asking them to write in their own way about aspects of their respective specialist fields. A different group of equally reputable contributors would certainly have produced a different book, albeit with a core of consensus about what is important and what is not, but not necessarily a better book. The decision to mix the expertise of academics and librarians caused the editors some initial anxiety: most lecturers would admit to blushing at the ill-concealed despair with which professional library staff are wont to survey the well-meaning muddle of references on students' reading lists. But in practice the chemistry has worked very well – to an extent where, in some cases, it would be hard to be sure merely by reading a chapter to which category its author belongs. Librarians need a working knowledge of the scholarly substance underlying their catalogues and bibliographies; academics cannot get far without cultivating some bibliographical skills. Herein lies a major part of the rationale of this volume.

Nevertheless, this editorial strategy has yielded chapters of considerable variety and individuality. Some authors (not all of them librarians) have given greater weight to the bibliographical products of their subject areas than to its substance; others (not all of them academics) have chosen to say rather more about substance than bibliography. Only in very few cases have we found it necessary to apply a corrective.

The tendency towards variety has, in any case, been accentuated by the absence of a definitional consensus about the boundaries of the subject as a whole and of its component subareas. Thus many of the contributors – particularly the authors of chapters in Part 2, 'Approaches to the Study of Politics and Government' – remind us that there is a wide variety of different, though interconnected, ways of approaching the subject. For one thing, academic fashions are liable to undergo rapid and substantial change: witness the 'behavioural revolution' in post-war political science in the United States (Chapter 3); successive shifts in the emphasis and methodology of pressure-group studies (Chapter 6) and of public administration and policy studies (Chapter 10); the eclipse and subsequent partial revival of constitutional and legal approaches to the study of British government (Chapters 7 and 11). And the study of politics concerns a *living* subject in a constant state of motion. Its literature reflects changing circumstances and momentous episodes of life in a real world – the various conflicts in the Middle East (Chapter 23), the coming and going of International Organizations (Chapters 17 and 18), the changing relationship between Congress and the Presidency since Watergate (Chapter 14).

We must remember also that an understanding of such an elusive and emotive subject as politics requires two things. First, it requires us to detach ourselves as far as possible from our own prejudices, or at least to recognize those prejudices and acknowledge them in what we say and write. There may be no hope of a truly value-free social science, but we can at least strive for maximum self-awareness and analytical rigour. We reocognize, for instance, that this book has a strong bias towards UK government and towards Western–democratic traditions of politics and political science.

The second requirement is that we approach the subject from as many angles as possible. There may be no 'truths' in politics, but the nearest approximations to the truth will be found in intellectual territory located by the intersection of numerous disciplines. Political science is an eclectic field of study and not a monolithic discipline in its own right. This eclecticism is clearly brought out by Jeffrey Stanyer (Chapters 2 and 3) in his wide-ranging analysis of 'The Quest for a Science of Politics'. This traces the complex relationship between political science and other social sciences, and also touches upon its intellectual links with 'the established sciences' such as biology and cybernetics.

Indeed, most of our contributors venture widely into cognate fields in their search for bibliographical material: the literature of history, sociology, geography, philosophy, economics, law, anthropology and psychology flows into the deep reservoir from which this book has drawn information and inspiration. The mixing of intellectual traditions adds to the underlying variety and richness of the subject and its literature.

A word must be said about the geographical and ethnic emphasis of the book and about decisions that have been taken about boundaries. Our centre of gravity is the UK: this is immediately apparent from the fact that a block of UK chapters forms a separate section, though several chapters in Part 3 do incorporate overseas comparative material. Although the coverage is global (or almost so – for reasons beyond the editors' control a section on South-east Asia could not be included, though the deficiency will be remedied in future editions), the geographical and cultural bias is clear. There is almost exclusive emphasis on English-language sources. China is given less space than UK local government and no more than New Zealand.

Hard choices have had to be made about the grouping of countries: does Canada really belong with Australia (as in Chapter 16), or with the United States in a 'North America' chapter; is Yugoslavia 'Eastern Europe' (Chapter 19), as we decided it was, or 'Western Europe'; does it really make sense to group China with Japan? Our approach was essentially pragmatic. Chapters were conceived, and the boundaries between them adjusted, with the interests and expertise of particular contributors in mind. If this has perpetuated anomalies or begged political questions, so be it. Alternative configurations were in many cases carefully considered, but were generally found to be no less problematical, and in many cases more so, than the ones eventually chosen.

The editors and (as many of the chapters make clear) the various contributors are well aware of the underlying problems, discussion of which is an important part of the book. Our task has been to hold up a mirror to the world as it is commonly conceived to be, at least by Western scholars, and not to pretend that it is as we and others might like it to be. This is not an exercise in intellectual imperialism, but, as we said at the beginning of this introduction, the book is meant to appeal to a diverse but predominantly English-speaking readership, with a variety of needs and interests.

What, then, does it contain? Chapter 1 opens the door with the aid of an experienced professional to the main library tools of the trade. It stands like a well-staffed enquiry desk, until recently so lacking in university libraries, and we would expect the reader to return to it at intervals to get his bearings. It is a catch-all chapter of interest to all.

Chapter 2–6, which are written by academics, look at the study of politics from various angles. Contributors have been invited not only to discuss sources but also to reflect on writings about political thought, comparative politics, political behaviour and, an expression of the latter, pressure groups.

Following this generalized academic approach, Chapters 7–12 sharpen the focus on the UK, where, after a general chapter on textbooks, there follow two chapters on the practice of politics, which cover parties and elections and then Parliament and Ministers and two chapters on administration, which cover public administration and policy studies, the judiciary and government, and then local government.

The second half of the book in terms of length, is concerned with the world outside the UK. The sources are virtually all in English. Once again, we start off (Chapter 13) in the hands of an experienced librarian, appropriately enough that of the Royal Institute of International Affairs (Chatham House), and again we would expect readers to need to return to this chapter at intervals. The next three chapters are by academics, and cover the continent of America in Chapters 14, 15 and part of 16, Australia (Chapter 15) and South Africa (also Chapter 15). The grouping has a traditional geographical or historical logic about it which we see no reason to disturb. Chapters 17–19, contributed by members of the staff of the House of Commons Library, cover Europe, with acceptance of the contemporary political fact that the continent is divided. Chapter 18 deals with the latest important grouping within Western Europe, namely the European Communities. Chapters 20 and 21 similarly deal with a continent in two parts, our colleague in the Bodleian covering China and Japan and our colleague in the British Library covering South Asia. Chapter 22, by an academic, covers Africa south of the Sahara and obviously pairs with Chapter 23, by a professional librarian, which covers North Africa as well as the Middle East. We conclude with a chapter on that twentieth-century phenomenon labelled Inter-Governmental Organizations, which is written by a librarian.

It must be stressed that while the editors have tried to eliminate obvious areas of duplication between chapters and have inserted signposts to assist with cross-referencing there is a certain amount of overlap. Indeed in some areas of the subject – e.g. international relations (see Chapters 4, 13 and 24) – we have encouraged the tackling of identical and closely related subjects from more than one bibliographical and intellectual standpoint. The diversity of the subject, discussed earlier, makes this inevitable. Readers are therefore advised to look beyond the contents of a single chapter, bearing an obviously relevant title, in order to get a complete picture. An index is provided to assist in this.

Contributors

Chris Allen
Lecturer, Department of Politics, University of Edinburgh

Carole Andrews
Senior Library Clerk, International Affairs Section, House of Commons Library, Westminster

Rohan Bolton
Research Officer, London Information Office of the European Parliament

R. L. Borthwick
Senior Lecturer in Politics, University of Leicester

Ivor Burton
Professor of Social Policy, Bedford College, University of London

Tony Butcher
Senior Lecturer in Government, Department of Social Science and Administration, University of London Goldsmiths' College

Peter Butler
Lecturer, Department of Politics, University of Exeter

Janet Coleman
Lecturer in Political Theory, Department of Politics, University of Exeter

Peter Colvin
Assistant Librarian, Islamic Near and Middle East Department, School of Oriental and African Studies Library, University of London

Gavin Drewry
Reader in Social Administration, Department of Social Policy and Social Science, Bedford College, University of London

Dermot Englefield
Deputy Librarian, House of Commons, Westminster

Nicole M. Gallimore
Librarian, Royal Institute of International Affairs, London

Peter D. Griffiths
Librarian in Charge, Overseas Development Administration, Foreign and Commonwealth Office, London

Qazi Mahmudul Haq
Assistant Keeper, Department of Oriental Manuscripts and Printed Books, British Library, London

Dilys M. Hill
Reader in Politics, University of Southampton

Grant Jordan
Lecturer, Department of Politics, University of Aberdeen

Kenneth N. Medhurst
Professor of Political Studies, University of Stirling

Jenny Pearce
Executive Secretary of the Latin American Bureau

A. D. S. Roberts
Keeper of Oriental Books at the Bodleian Library, Oxford

Michael Rush
Senior Lecturer, Department of Politics, University of Exeter

Janet Seaton
Higher Library Executive, Home Affairs Section, House of Commons Library, Westminster

Jeffrey Stanyer
Senior Lecturer, Department of Politics, University of Exeter

Richard Ware
Senior Library Clerk, International Affairs Section, House of Commons Library, Westminster

Jacqueline Whiteside
Head of Bibliographic Services, British Library of Political and Economic Science, London School of Economics and Political Science, University of London

Contents

PART 1
Resources

1
Library and bibliographical aids to the study of politics

Jacqueline Whiteside

Introduction

The bibliographical sources for the study of politics are as varied as the literature of the discipline itself, and no single approach to these sources can be said to be in itself superior, since it is the object and the nature of the search which determine the most appropriate procedure.

The basis of a productive search in the literature of any subject is the identification and precise definition of the question which is really being asked. Once this has been done, the search strategy must be established. For example, is the searcher interested only in recent materials, or is a systematic retrospective search required? Are any specific types of publication (books, journal articles, theses, government publications, conference papers, etc.) needed or, indeed, are any to be excluded? It is important to have this clear, since the following bibliographical resources approach their subjects very differently, offering a variety in both breadth and depth of access to a range of materials. More and more political science literature is being produced, and forms of production are changing. Appropriately, the tools that give bibliographic access to the literature are also growing in number and changing in format to meet current needs.

General bibliographies

The general national bibliographies can be used for both a systematic retrospective search and a current check on what is being published on a particular subject. The details of their arrangement have been discussed in many sources, but it is worth mentioning two major tools appropriate for any subject search.

The *British National Bibliography (BNB)* (Council of the British National Bibliography, 1950–1974; British Library Bibliographic Services Division, 1975–) lists new British publications submitted to the Copyright Receipt Office and includes Cataloguing In Publication entries supplied by an increasing number of publishers in advance of publication, which give access to current British book publishing by natural language subject headings, Dewey Decimal class number and author/editor and title. *BNB* is published weekly, with a cumulated monthly index. Cumulations appear every four months and then annually. Larger cumulations have appeared, covering 1950–1954, 1955–1959, 1960–1964, 1965 –1967, 1968–1970 and 1971–1973 so that retrospective searching is greatly facilitated.

The Library of Congress *Subject Catalog*, sometime *Library of Congress Catalog – Books: Subjects* (Library of Congress, 1950–) is published quarterly, with annual and quinquennial cumulations. The Library of Congress's aim, to acquire as much as possible of the world's publishing output of 'significant' books and journals, means that the *Subject Catalog* gives up-to-date (very current for the US and usually no more than a year's delay for foreign publications) access by subject to an unparalleled range of materials in all subjects. The arrangement is alphabetical by natural language subject headings, as established in the *Library of Congress Subject Headings* (Library of Congress, 9th (latest) edn, 1981) and its cumulative supplements. These headings are, however, usually all within the range of American usage, but topical and geographical headings are not treated consistently. For example, certain subjects relating to a particular country are displayed as subdivisions under the country name (e.g. Great Britain – Politics and government, 1945–), while other subjects stand in their own right and are subdivided by place (e.g. Political parties – Great Britain). Further changes made over the last few years have resulted in varities of form of place name, and in variations on the approach to more detailed localities and subdivisions. These may appear minor in isolation, but when searching through this and other sources using *Library of Congress Subject Headings*, it is important to know that one would no longer find items helpfully grouped together under, say, Political parties – United States – (Illinois, Indiana, Iowa, etc.), but that Political parties – Illinois would now come before Political parties – India. This use of direct and indirect geographical subdivisions necessitates searching under all conceivable names of localities under a particular subject, should one wish to find an example of a UK or US case study within that topic.

General social science bibliographies: current

The bibliographical tools for the social sciences as a whole divide into those that are current and continue to examine publishing output, and those that are retrospective and review existing literature from a given date. Most of the current sources deal mainly with periodical articles, but *A London Bibliography of the Social Sciences (LBSS)* (London School of Economics and Political Science, 1931–1932, + Supplements, 1934–) deals only with books and pamphlets. Originally covering additions to nine libraries in all, from Volume 7 onwards coverage is restricted to the holdings of the British Library of Political and Economic Science (BLPES) and the Edward Fry Library of International Law (held at BLPES). From Supplement 6, *LBSS* has been published by Mansell Publishing, and since Supplement 9 the photo-typesetting tapes have been computer-produced. Arrangement of the *Bibliography* is by Library of Congress subject headings in alphabetical sequence, then in chronological order of publication under subjects or country/topic subdivisions. BLPES is recognized as the largest single library devoted exclusively to the social sciences, and has aimed at comprehensive coverage of significant works in the 'core' social sciences (politics, sociology and economics), in languages in the Roman and Cyrillic alphabets. Although financial concerns may have limited the amount of foreign-language material acquired, it continues to provide an excellent and increasingly current record of significant publishing in these areas. Now published annually, the 1983 volume appeared in March 1984. Each volume currently contains entries for over 13 500 bibliographical items, each item usually being entered under more than one subject heading. The limitation of the *LBSS* is that it excludes periodical articles, and it is increasingly in this journal literature that the political scientist looks for the results of research, information and analysis.

General and social sciences

Indexing services

The most effective tools for the identification of articles are periodical indexes and abstracts. The most basic provision of indexes is the self-index, i.e. the part, volume, and possibly cumulative indexes produced by a journal itself. One might, for example, look through the indexes of *Political Science Quarterly* to discover what articles and book reviews had appeared in this authoritative journal. However, many self-indexes are not arranged by subject, and such searching may be time-consuming and unproductive, especially if a very specific subject is sought. Notable exceptions to the usual pattern of self-indexing are those for newspapers. *The Times Index*, formerly *The Official Index to The Times*, previously *An Index to The Times* (The Times, 1906–), is now published monthly with annual cumulations from 1977 onwards. From 1973 the *Index* has also covered the *Sunday Times* and its magazine, and *The Times Literary, Educational* and *Higher Educational Supplements*. It is very current, with the January 1984 index published in March 1984. The *Monthly Index to the Financial Times* (Financial Times Business Information Ltd, January 1981–) is equally up-to-date. The first *Annual Index to the Financial Times*, that for 1981, was published in mid-1982.

These are all extremely detailed subject and proper name indexes to the wealth of information contained in these newspapers. Extensive articles on the political and economic conditions of particular countries, information and opinion on current events and political developments are resources that should not be ignored, and in consequence indexes to these newspapers and others like them, for example, the *New York Times* and *Wall Street Journal* (Part 2 of the *Index*), are appropriate for inclusion in many searches.

The many indexing services available give subject access to information in a range of journals and other sources. These may be very general, for example, the *British Humanities Index* (The Library Association, 1963–), one of the successors to the *Subject Index to Periodicals* (1915–1961). This appears quarterly with annual cumulations, using its own natural language subject headings to index articles from sources as varied as the *Sunday Times* and *Local Government Chronicle*. It is generally more 'popular' in coverage than its closest American counterpart, the *Humanities Index* (H. W. Wilson, 1874–), which is one of the two indexes superseding *Social Sciences and Humanities Index* (H. W. Wilson, 1965–1974), formerly *International Index* (H. W. Wilson, 1916

-1965, covering articles published 1907-). Appearing quarterly with annual cumulations, it covers a broad subject area. Author and subject entries are arranged in one alphabetical sequence. The other index springing from *Social Sciences and Humanities Index* and *International Index* is *Social Sciences Index* (H. W. Wilson, 1974-). The arrangement follows that of the *Humanities Index*, with book reviews listed in a separate section following the main author/subject alphabetical sequence. They both cover about 260 English-language journals, including most journals regarded as significant in the field of political science, and appear quarterly with annual cumulations.

One of the most current and useful general social science sources, which nonetheless has a strong bias towards the literature of politics, public administration and international relations, is *Public Affairs Information Service Bulletin* (Public Affairs Information Service, 1915-). This covers over 1000 English-language periodicals, as well as books, pamphlets, reports of public and private agencies and some government documents, aiming to identify public affairs information for the benefit of legislators, policy researchers and students, as well as the business and financial community. Unlike many services, it defines a selection policy: to index material on subjects relating to contemporary public issues and to public policy making and evaluation, all with an emphasis on factual and statistical information. Publications are not indexed if no new contribution is made in subjects on which much has already been written. The entries are arranged alphabetically by subject heading, close to those used by the Library of Congress. The *Bulletin* appears twice a month, with three quarterly cumulations and an annual bound volume. A serious limitation until 1977 was the lack of an author index. Newly computerized production meant that the 1980 annual cumulation was produced nearly a year ahead of the old schedule. The publication of the 15-volume *Cumulative Subject Index to the Public Affairs Information Service Bulletin, 1915–74*, edited by Ruth Matteson Blackmore (Carrollton Press, 1977), has speeded up retrospective subject searching enormously. With its advantages of currency, broad coverage and use of natural language subject headings the *Bulletin* and its separate *Foreign Language Index* (Public Affairs Information Service, 1972-) have a justifiably high reputation in the social sciences, especially for coverage of political science. Nonetheless, partly because of its selectivity, a student of international relations may find it less valuable than one investigating, say, voting behaviour.

A simple and up-to-date form of indexing is to present tables of contents of recently published journals. Such an index is *Current Contents/Social & Behavioral Sciences*, formerly *Current Contents/ Behavioral, Social and Educational Sciences*, which superseded *Current Contents/Behavioral, Social and Management Sciences* and *Current Contents/Education* (Institute for Scientific Information, 1969–). Issued weekly, it reprints the tables of contents of over 1300 journals (mainly English-language) in the social and behavioural sciences. These are arranged under various subject headings, including political science and history. In a separate section are reprinted tables of contents of recent monographs, symposia and conference proceedings. Each issue contains a subject index based on keywords in article titles and an author index. A further service offered, the Original Article Text Service, provides reprints of articles listed. Since it lacks cumulating indexes it cannot be used for a systematic retrospective search, but it effectively fulfils its main purpose, to give up-to-date information on current publications.

A further current general social sciences index, but of a very different nature, can yield much bibliographic information, as long as it is used carefully – the *Social Sciences Citation Index (SSCI)* (Institute for Scientific Information, 1973–). The tri-annuals and annuals index cover 4400 journals, of which about 1500 are fully covered and over 2900 selectively. The total number of citations for the last complete year (1982) was over 1 590 000. Cumulations for 1966–1970 and 1971–1975 were published in 1979, and the 1976–1980 cumulation was published at the end of 1983. This extensive source gives access to the current literature of the social sciences by listing all works that have been referred to in other documents during the period covered. If one knows the author and title (and date) of a book or article which is relevant to the search topic, by looking in the *Citations Index* of *SSCI* one can discover who has referred to it and where. The value of this approach is based on the assumption that a given piece of writing in a specific subject area will have been known to others working in similar or related areas, and will have been quoted or mentioned by them in their own writings. Thus, (in the *Citation Index*) under the author's name and initials, the reference year, the publication name, volume and page number are listed the source articles citing this work, giving only brief information but indicating the type of source item, whether article, book review, biographical item (e.g. an obituary), editorial, etc. Citations of government publications, etc. are listed in the *Corporate Author Citation Index*, and of anonymous items in the *Anonymous Citation Index*. For full bibliographical information about the source (i.e. where the original work was cited, not the work itself), the user must turn to the *Source Index* and the *List of Books Covered.*

Citation searching is not totally reliable, since an article citing a work which one knows to be relevant may be referring to it very peripherally, but in many cases the full title information obtained from the *Source Index* indicates whether the reference is worth pursuing or not. It is possible to extend the search if one is confident in the citation references, by searching in the *Citation Index* under the citing authors just discovered in order to find who has cited the citers themselves. The further approach which *SSCI* offers is by subject, in the *Permuterm Subject Index.* Every significant word in the title of all source items listed in *SSCI* is indexed, and under each significant word, other significant words which appeared with that word in a title are listed. The citation index principle was established originally for the natural and physical sciences in which the (usually) unequivocal terminology makes such references of undoubted value. In the *Social Sciences Citation Index* the ambiguity and variation in usage of terms within a subject like political science may result in such searches being less productive or potentially misleading. Nonetheless, in a subject search it is likely that the terms in which a researcher conceptualizes his problem will coincide more exactly with those in current use by scholars in his field than with those subject headings used in conventional indexes. On a more prosaic level, *SSCI* may also be useful when information is only half-remembered, since one or two significant words in the title can lead to the full bibliographic identification of a work.

Two interrelated sources give information on the literature of the methods and techniques of empirical social research, essential for the student of, say, voting behaviour: *Social Research Methodology Bibliography* (SRM-Documentation Centre, Erasmus University, Rotterdam, 1978–) and *Social Research Methodology Abstracts* (SRM-Documentation Centre, 1979–). *SRM-Bibliography* is a quarterly index of recent social methodology publications. Intended as a very current source, it indexes not only from publications themselves but also from abstracts and mere title information. In all cases the basis of the index is indicated. Using its own classification scheme, with 318 categories available, the bibliography is divided into twelve sections, which are followed by an alphabetical list of descriptors based on the *SRM-Thesaurus*, edited by C. van de Merwe (Rotterdam University Press, 1974; SRM-Documentation Centre, 1979). This list of descriptors is also used used in the annual publication, *SRM-*

Abstracts which includes both abstracts that the SRM-Documentation Centre indexers have created themselves and those that have appeared in other published sources. (This information is also accessible on the SRM data base, which contains records from 1970 onwards.)

Abstracting services

Abstracting services give even more subject information to the researcher than indexes. Not only are bibliographical items identified by subject through the use of subject headings, title keywords or classification marks, but a short summary of the contents of the item is provided. This is likely to give a reasonable indication of whether a reference is worth pursuing or not, and may therefore save time. For the social sciences as a whole, the *Bulletin Analytique de Documentation Politique, Economique et Sociale Contemporaine*, formerly *Bulletin Bibliographique de Documentation Internationale Contemporaine*, 1926–1940 (Fondation Nationale des Sciences Politiques, 1946–) contains about 4500 abstracts per year of articles selected from approximately 2300 journals. These are not restricted to standard Western European and North American sources, but include a number from Asia and Africa. The abstracts are arranged in individual country and international relations and comparative studies sections, each subdivided into political studies, etc., with further detailed subdivisions. The emphasis is on contemporary problems, and the historical and theoretical aspects of politics are not covered. There are no indexes in the monthly issues, but an annual alphabetical subject index is published as a supplement to the first issue of the following year. Although the abstracts are in French, this should not deter prospective users, since the abstracts are short, clear and informative, and the journals include a number not usually scanned.

The above indexing and abstracting services provide bibliographical information in the social sciences generally. Detailed discussion is appropriate, since they provide substantial and expert coverage of the literature of political science itself, and at the same time do not exclude material on the related social sciences, such as sociology, economics, social psychology and cultural anthropology. The lines of demarcation between political science and other social sciences are no longer distinct, and such 'umbrella' social science bibliographical information sources do not limit a search by too rigid definitions.

Political science

Indexing services

To turn to the more specifically political science bibliographical sources, *ABC POL SCI*, or, more fully, *A Bibliography of Contents: Political Science and Government: Indexed Article Titles; a Guide to Periodical Literature*, formerly *Advance Bibliography of Contents, etc.* (ABC–Clio Press and EBC–Clio Press, 1969–) is published five times a year, plus an annual cumulated index. It reproduces (not photographically) the tables of contents of over 300 journals published worldwide in political science and related disciplines. They appear in their original language, and are arranged in alphabetical order of journal title. This makes it essential to use the subject profile indexes that are formed by rotating the subject, geographic and biographic descriptors assigned to each article listed in the main bibliography of contents. Each issue contains both subject and author indexes, and the sixth issue of each year contains the annual cumulations of these.

More international, but much less current, is the *International Bibliography of the Social Sciences: Political Science*, prepared by the International Committee for Social Science Information and Documentation (UNESCO, now Tavistock Publications and Aldine Publishing Company, 1954–). This is probably the broadest political science index, containing over 4500 references per year to books, pamphlets, book reviews and articles from more than 1500 social science journals published worldwide. However, in attempting fair worldwide coverage, items appear to be selected partly for their country of origin, rather than entirely on the significance of the contribution to the literature of the subject, and the delay in items appearing in the one issue per year is considerable. Entries are arranged according to a detailed subject classification scheme in English and French, with six main headings: political science (general studies, methods and research techniques, etc.); political thought; government and public administration; governmental process (political influences, parties, political behaviour); international relations; area studies. These are further subdivided by topic and by country. Titles in languages other than English or French are translated into English. In each volume an author index and an alphabetical subject index in English and in French are provided. Items for which abstracts appear in *International Political Science Abstracts* are indicated.

Abstracting services

International Political Science Abstracts is the central abstracting service in the discipline. It is prepared by the International Political Science Association, in cooperation with the International Committee for Social Sciences Documentation, and with the support of UNESCO (Blackwell and Presses Universitaires de France, 1951–1972, then International Political Science Association, 1973–). It contains about 5000 abstracts per year in either English or French from about 650 periodicals in political science and related disciplines, such as law and sociology, published worldwide. These 150–200-word abstracts are arranged by a classified subject scheme which relates very closely to that of the *International Bibliography of the Social Sciences: Political Science:* methods and theory; political thinkers and ideas; governmental and administrative institutions; political process (public opinion, attitudes, parties, forces, groups and elections); international relations (including international law, organization and administration, foreign policy); national and area studies. Published six times a year, each issue has an alphabetical subject index, and the final issue for each year contains cumulated subject and author indexes.

United States Political Science Documents (University of Pittsburgh, University Center for International Studies, in conjunction with the American Political Science Association, 1976–) is the published form of a computer-based information system for political science developed at Pittsburgh. Although all journals indexed (150 scholarly periodicals in political science and related disciplines) are published in the US, the subject matter is not restricted to that country but is predominant. This annual bibliography appears in two parts. Part I consists of author, alphabetical subject, geographical area, proper name and journal indexes, giving full bibliographical information at each entry, together with an accession number. This number locates the entry in Part II, document descriptions, which is arranged in accession-number order. Here also the full bibliographic citation is given, together with an abstract, the names of authors cited in the article, proper names discussed there, geographical area descriptors and key subject descriptors.

Part of a far more ambitious project is the *Universal Reference System: Political Science, Government and Public Policy Series* (IFI/Plenum, 1965–). This was originally published in ten volumes covering international affairs (2nd edn, 1969); legislative process, representation and decision making; bibliography of bibliographies in political science, government and public policy; administrative management – public and private bureaucracy; current events and problems of modern society; public opinion, mass behaviour and political psychology; law, jurisprudence and judicial process; economic regulation – business and government; public policy and the management of science; and comparative government and cultures. The Universal Reference System itself, devised by Alfred de Grazia, the general editor, is a computerized information-retrieval service, attempting to give multi-faceted access to the literature of the social and behavioural sciences. The editor states that he is aiming at the large middle group of scholars, falling between the general public on the one hand and the highly specialized researcher on the other. Instructions for use of the system are as complex as the system itself. If it were accessible online, the complexity and detail of the indexing and the use of truncated terms would pose no obstacles, but in a 'fixed' printed form, where a considerable amount of eye-scanning and physical manipulation of pages is involved, the system's value is reduced. The classification system is awkward, and requires ingenuity and precision from the reader. It is almost entirely confined to American materials, foreign titles forming only about 5 per cent of the 8000 references to be found in the annual supplements, which cover all subject areas of the original ten volumes in a single bibliography. About 1300 journals are scanned. From the same data base is produced the *American Political Science Research Guide* (IFI/Plenum, 1977–), a classified bibliography with abstracts covering the various branches of government, together with review articles examining the current state of political research.

Neue politische Literatur: Berichte über das internationale Schrifttum (Franz Steiner Verlag, 1956–) appears quarterly. As well as shorter reviews of new books, it contains long articles that are surveys of the international literature on a particular topic. Regrettably, the language of the publication may limit the readership of this thorough and detailed source of bibliographical information.

Another publication of similar approach, intended as a continuing yearbook, is the *Political Science Annual,* edited by James Robinson (Bobbs-Merill, 1966–). This five-volume set contains excellent systematic bibliographical essays on subjects like political socialization, legislative institutions and processes, public opinion and opinion change.

Book review sections

The book review sections of important journals in the subject area are a further regular source of information on recent publications, although substantial reviews frequently appear in such sources rather late. In the US, *American Political Science Review (APSR)* (American Political Science Association, 1906–) is the most highly regarded for its extensive critical review essays and book reviews. *Political Science Quarterly* (Academy of Political Science, 1886–) is the oldest established political science journal, and contains nearly as many lengthy book reviews as *APSR*. Large sections of book reviews and briefer notices are also contained in the American serial, *Journal of Politics*, formerly *Proceedings of the Southern Political Science Association* (Southern Political Science Association, 1939–), although practically all of the American regional political science associations' journals include substantial review sections. In the UK, politics journals began publication very much later, but *Political Quarterly* (Macmillan, then TPL Magazines, 1930–) and *Political Studies* (Oxford University Press, 1953–) have always provided significant coverage of recent publications in their reviews. A further discussion of journals can be found later in this chapter.

Retrospective services

In addition to current coverage of periodical and other literature in regularly published sources, retrospective indexes have been compiled, either cumulating and consolidating earlier current bibliographies, or specifically compiled. *C.R.I.S.: the Combined Retrospective Index Set to Journals in Political Science, 1866–1974* (Carrollton Press, 1977–1978) has six volumes of subject index and two of author index. The subject index uses both keywords and subject categories, and this combined approach greatly assists retrieval. The 95 alphabetical subject categories have been grouped together in the arrangement of volumes, one covering law and relations, one methodology, political behaviour and process, political systems, etc., and volumes three to six covering public administration. The predominance of US references is naturally due to the earlier publication of journals in the subject area in that country.

A source much more closely defined in scope, *The Essex Reference Index: British Journals on Politics and Sociology, 1950 –1973*, edited by K. I. Macdonald (Macmillan, 1975), is a comprehensive index by subject to articles to articles and research notes published in that period. In order to keep the index concise, after careful selection only eleven major British journals in politics and sociology were covered in this compilation by the Department of Government at the University of Essex. Within this restriction, the index is full, running to 397 pages. It is a KWIC (keywords in context) index, i.e. the title of each of the 5145 articles is listed separately under every non-trivial word appearing in it. At each entry, a full bibliographic citation is given.

Administration, central and local

Many indexing and abstracting services exist for special aspects of political science. For example, in the field of public administration, *Sage Public Administration Abstracts* (Sage, 1974–) appears quarterly, each issue containing about 250 abstracts of books, pamphlets, government publications, significant speeches, legislative research studies and periodical articles from about 200 English-language periodicals in a wide range of subject fields related to public administration. The abstracts, many of which are 'self'-abstracts, i.e. they have been prepared by the author of the article itself, are arranged under about thirteen subject groupings. These include organizational theory and behaviour; policy analysis; decision making; budgeting and finance; planning and forecasting; foreign policy making; local administration; etc. In addition to the author and alphabetical subject indexes (which are cumulated in the fourth issue of each year), a 'related citations' section lists articles and books which are not abstracted. The journals covered and their subject matter are predominantly North American.

A source particularly strong in coverage of public administration in European countries is the *Bulletin Signalétique 528: Science Administrative*, superseding in part *Bulletin Signalétique: Philosophie. Sciences Humaines*, formerly *Bulletin Analytique* (Centre National de la Recherche Scientifique, Centre de Documentation Sciences Humaines, 1974–). Each quarterly issue contains entries arranged according to a subject classification scheme which includes the history, methods, structure and control of administrations, with annotations in French, together with alphabetical subject, geographical and author indexes. A separate issue cumulating these indexes is published annually. In all, the *Bulletin* contains over 2000 references per year to reports, pamphlets and articles from about 300 periodicals published worldwide.

In the field of local government, *LOGA: Local Government Annotations Service*, issued on behalf of the Association of London Chief Librarians, in cooperation with many borough libraries, and currently produced and edited at the Reference Library of the London Borough of Havering (1966/1967–), covers every aspect for the UK. It is primarily intended for local government officers, but it offers useful current-awareness information to students of the subject. Some 87 journals are scanned (including *The Stage* and *The Chartered Surveyor*), and the varied selections arranged under 44 subject headings. It has no index.

The publications and bibliographies emanating from government departments are also a valuable source of information both on local and central government. For example, the Departments of the Environment and Transport *Library Bulletin* (DoE/Tp, Library Services, 1972–), which appeared formerly as its *Monthly Index to Periodicals,* appears twenty-three times a year. Not all entries contain abstracts, and where they appear they are brief. This is an admirably up-to-date source: for example, December 1983 publications are abstracted in the 1 March 1984 issue. The *Monthly Supplement* to the *Library Bulletin* lists legislation, circulars, Departmental standards and advice notes, and other publications issued or sponsored by the Departments of the Environment and Transport. A consolidated *Annual List of Publications* has been published each year since 1973 (which covered 1971 publications), arranged by type of publication and then by subject. Indexes are provided to authors and issuing agents, and to subjects. Speed of publication has increased, the volume for 1982 being published in April 1983.

To identify foreign material particularly useful for comparative study of local administration, the library of the International Union of Local Authorities, which aims to promote cooperation and consultation between local authorities throughout the world, produces a current bibliography bi-monthly: *Bibliographia* (IULA, 1958–). This is annotated in the language of the original publication, and arranged in broad subjects alphabetically. It has no index.

The publications of central government provide essential source material and comment on its workings. Bibliographical control of such publications has traditionally been regarded as difficult and complex, and information on guides to their retrieval and use will be discussed later. However, while examining current serial bibliographical tools it is appropriate to mention those regular listings of interest to the student of central government, restricting this to the UK. Those dealing solely with British Parliamentary publications are here excluded, since they will be covered in Chapter 10. Whereas before 1921 most British government publication was in fact printed for or by the direct order of Parliament, the pattern of official publishing significantly altered, and from 1922, the standard sequence of sales lists of Her Majesty's Stationery Office publications, which form the basis of current searching, became established. From 1922 to 1935, the *Consolidated List of Government Publications* was published twice a year, cumulating the *Monthly Lists* which have appeared regularly since January 1923 under a variety of titles. The annual cumulations which started in 1936 have also changed title frequently, and are now usually referred to as the 'Annual Catalogue', rather than the present cover title, *Government Publications*. Since the Second World War, titles sold but not published by HMSO have been included in these lists, for example, the publications of the nationalized industries and of intergovernmental organizations. Although the latter are still included in the daily and monthly listings, since 1955 there has been a separate annual publication, *International Organisations' and Overseas Agencies' Publications*. The style of entry in these several sources has varied, perhaps the most dramatic change arising with the production of the 1976 annual and the February 1977 monthly lists, which were compiled from a machine-readable data base. This latest revision has increased the number of cross-references for agency headings, altered the previous usage of inverted headings (e.g. Department of Employment, no longer Employment, Department of), but, most significantly, substantially increased the number of subject entries in the index. The problem of late production of both the monthly and annual lists remains, the annual volume often appearing at least six months after the end of the year covered. The *Daily List of Government Publications* gives up-to-date notification of what HMSO is publishing. Retrospectively, every five years a *Consolidated Index to Government Publications* is generated from the annual catalogues, the first that for 1936–1940, but the most extensive tool is the *Cumulative Index to the Annual Catalogues of Her Majesty's Stationery Office Publications, 1922–1972*, compiled by Ruth Matteson Blackmore (Carrollton Press, 1976). A helpful 'subject' approach to the wealth of HMSO publications is found in the series of *Sectional Lists* which are updated irregularly and cover material available in print from a given department or collect together material on a given topic emanating from a number of departments. Increasingly, material is being published by government departments themselves; fewer than 45 per cent of all British official publications now come from HMSO. Control therefore becomes more disparate, and the researcher looks to individual government department library services for the production of annual or more frequent guides to their own documents.

Most helpfully, a commercial publisher has supplied an overall approach to this potentially unfathomable mass of material by producing a *Catalogue of British Official Publications not Published by HMSO* (Chadwyck-Healey, 1981–). This appears six times a year, with an annual cumulation, and is arranged by issuing body, but with good indexing. Chadwyck-Healey microfilm all the material appearing in their index, and microfiche copies of documents may be obtained from them. It is not yet comprehensive.

By no means uncomplicated, the literature of official bodies forms both primary and secondary sources for the study of political science. British government publications are well served by the many well-structured and clear guides to their use. (For guides to parliamentary publications, see Chapter 10.) J. E. Pemberton, *British Official Publications* (2nd rev. edn, Pergamon, 1973), is one of the most comprehensive and comprehensible guides, including useful facsimile reproductions of title-pages, etc., of many types of publication. His definitions are admirable, especially for such as the elusive 'Green Paper'. J. G. Ollé, *An Introduction to British Government Publications* (2nd edn, Association of Assistant Librarians, 1973), is much shorter, but reliable. Two more recent sources are S. Richard, *Directory of British Official Publications: a Guide to Sources* (Mansell Publishing, 1981), which examines official organizations as publishers, a particularly important matter in view of the move away from HMSO's monopoly of official publishing; and F. Rodgers, *A Guide to British Government Publications* (Wilson, 1980), which covers not only the usual range of statutory bodies but also nationalized industries, etc., incorporating parliamentary publications of departmental origin with the non-parliamentary material from the same department. Under each agency, a brief account of its origins, history and changes in function is given. A. F. Comfort and C. Loveless, *Guide to Government Data: a Survey of Unpublished Social Science Material in Libraries of Government Departments in London* (Macmillan, 1974), indicates access to data unrecorded elsewhere.

International relations

In the field of international relations, *Foreign Affairs* (Council on Foreign Relations, 1921–) contains in each quarterly issue a classified annotated bibliography of recent books on international relations, based on which is the *Foreign Affairs Bibliography: a Select and Annotated List of Books on International Affairs*

(Bowker, for Council on Foreign Relations, 1933–). This source has a high reputation. It contains only books, and generally excludes government publications, and is, in fact, rather limited in the extent of its coverage in comparison with the number of books published in the field each year. It is divided into three sections: general international relations; the world since 1914; and the world by regions. Author and title indexes appear in each volume. Byron Dexter, *The Foreign Affairs 50 Years Bibliography: New Evaluations of Significant Books on International Relations, 1920 –1970* (Bowker, for Council on Foreign Relations, 1972), is a new selection of over 2000 items, under very broad subject definitions, with longer reviews than those for *Foreign Affairs Bibliography* itself. Title and author indexes are included.

The Canadian Peace Research Institute is responsible for compiling and publishing *Peace Research Abstracts Journal* (1964–). This monthly service contains about 7500 abstracts a year of books, reports and articles from about 1000 periodicals published all over the world. Titles covered include general magazines, international affairs journals and professional journals in a variety of disciplines. The abstracts are arranged into ten main classes, e.g. military situation; limitation of arms; international law; economics and diplomacy; etc., each with many subclasses. Each issue has an author index, an alphabetical subject index using broad subject headings and a 'primary code index'.

One of the most important library collections for the study of international politics is that of the Royal Institute of International Affairs, at Chatham House in London. Consequently its *Classified List of Books and Pamphlets Added to the Library* (RIIA Library, 1976–) is a valuable source of information on current monographic publication in this wide subject area. Originally appearing fortnightly, twelve issues a year are now published. Chatham House Library also establishes its own index of periodical articles held there, and these records have been cumulated and published as follows: *Index to Periodical Articles, 1950–1964, in the Library of the Royal Institute of International Affairs* (G. K. Hall, 1964); *Index to Periodical Articles, 1965–1972, in the Library of the Royal Institute of International Affairs* (G. K. Hall, 1973); and *Index to Periodical Articles in the Library of the Royal Institute of International Affairs, 1973–1978* (G. K. Hall, 1979). These are photographic reproductions of catalogue cards, arranged by the Institute's own classification scheme, A–H (general and subject) and J–T (regions), to which a guide precedes the index itself in each cumulation. In addition there are a geographic index, a subject index and a list of the principal periodicals indexed.

Area listings

Current serial bibliographies covering individual geographic areas are also produced: details will appear in other chapters.

Related social sciences: current bibliographies

As has been mentioned earlier, it is impossible to view political science in isolation from the other social sciences, and the researcher will find useful and essential references in such current sources for other disciplines as *Abstracts in Anthropology* (Baywood Publishing, 1970–), especially the section on political structure and process; *Psychological Abstracts* (American Psychological Association, 1927–); and *Sociological Abstracts* (Sociological Abstracts, 1952–), co-sponsored by the American Sociological Association, the Eastern Sociological Society, the International Sociological Association and the Midwest Sociological Society.

Guides to bibliographical sources

As must by now be obvious, some guidance is necessary to provide access to the existence of such current bibliographies. A clearly arranged and helpful tool is *Periodical Indexes in the Social Sciences and Humanities: a Subject Guide*, by Lois A. Harzfeld (Scarecrow Press, 1978), which is arranged in alphabetical order of subject (some 48 divisions). Each bibliography is thoroughly described, but listing is not comprehensive, being confined to the 'key' indexing sources on a particular subject. The section on political science examines eight services; that on public administration, two; and for the social sciences generally, six. An earlier source, similar in concept, is *Serial Bibliographies in the Humanities and Social Sciences,* compiled by R. A. Gray (Pierian Press, 1969). This is arranged by the Dewey Decimal Classification Scheme, and although without annotations, entries include codes for language, policy of inclusion, frequency, arrangement, indexes, etc. Coverage in both these sources is incomplete, since certain categories are deliberately excluded, such as book review sections of journals, library accessions lists and bibliographical bulletins. For serial and other types of bibliography, much more detailed guides are required.

Bibliographies of bibliographies, however remote-sounding, can in fact be a vital first step to the retrieval of useful references. The standard source has been T. A. Besterman, *A World Bibliography of Bibliographies and of Bibliographical Catalogues, Calendars, Abstracts, Digest, Indexes, and the Like* (4th edn, Societas Bibliographica, 1965–1966. 5 vols). This, however, is limited to bibliographies which are separately published. *Bibliographic Index: a Cumulative Bibliography of Bibliographies* (Wilson, 1838–) has the advantages of being a continuing publication, therefore more current, and of including bibliographies published as parts of books, pamphlets and periodical articles. Much less extensive than Besterman is R. L. Collison, *Bibliographies: Subject and National: a Guide to their Contents, Arrangement and Use* (3rd edn, Crosby Lockwood, 1968). Although this contains only a few hundred references, they have been carefully chosen and are fully annotated. References to subject bibliographies are arranged in nine broad divisions. A bi-monthly international source is *Bibliography, Documentation, Terminology* (UNESCO, 1961–), which includes useful references.

The above are all of a general nature. A bibliography of bibliographies in political science is *Hjelpemidler for Litteratursøking i Statsvitenskap: en Annotert Bibliografi*, compiled by B. Berntsen (Universitet i Oslo, 1977). This is a useful listing even for those unable to read the annotations in Norwegian, but it deserves translation in order to make the full value of this bibliography more accessible.

Guides to political science literature

Guides to the literature of political science are not merely bibliographies: they aim to introduce the reader to the subject and to present the literature in such a way as to direct him towards and to encourage him in the use of materials. They are selective and usually critical. Of the many guides to political science literature, a recent and comprehensive example is *Foundation of Political Science*, edited by D. M. Freeman (Free Press, New York; and Collier–Macmillan, 1977). This work surveys the literature in detail, examining not only the traditional fields of political science, but also newly developing areas, such as political socialization, small-group theory, etc. A remarkably well-researched bibliographical listing compiled by I. Freeman occupies the final 140 pages but regrettably there is no subject approach, either by subject grouping or by indexing.

Political Research Methods: Foundations and Techniques, by B. Leigh Smith *et al.* (Houghton Mifflin, 1976), provides a reliable introduction to the classic general guides to the literature, indexes, abstracts, bibliographies and bibliographical essays. However, the publication date is misleading, since most of the works listed appeared in the 1960s, and the most recent publication cited is one of 1973.

The duplication contained in the five-volume first edition (1975) of one of the most thorough of politics guides, that by F. L. Holler, *The Information Sources of Political Science*, has disappeared with the publication of the one-volume 3rd edition (ABC–Clio, 1981). As the editor acknowledges the difficulty of arriving at a universally acceptable definition of political science, he has cast his net very wide. He also discusses the problems and limitations of political reference literature, identifying them as gaps in coverage, duplication, delays in availability, poor definition (overlapping boundaries in the subject matter), instability of publication (i.e. failures to maintain a projected continuing source) and quantity.

A guide which makes no comment, but lists the contents of its references as well as the titles is D. F. La Barr and J. D. Singer, *The Study of International Politics: a Guide to the Sources for the Student, Teacher, and Researcher* (Clio Books, 1976). All sources are English-language but extensive nonetheless.

A further guide from the US is by C. Brock, *The Literature of Political Science* (Bowker, 1969). An extensive annotated guide aimed at students, librarians and teachers, it is well structured, with still-valid information on starting a literature search, followed by detailed treatment of types of publications such as indexes and abstracts, book reviews, US and State government publications, international organizations publications and guides to bibliographies.

Still older, but a classic of its kind, is L. R. Wynar, *Guide to Reference Materials in Political Science: a Selective Bibliography* (Libraries Unlimited, 1968). It covers general reference sources in the social sciences, political science general reference sources, political theory, international relations, public administration, political behaviour, comparative political systems, government documents and reference sources in law.

Political Science: a Bibliographical Guide to the Literature (Scarecrow Press, 1965), with *Supplements* in 1968, 1972 and 1974, compiled by R. B. Harmon, maintains much the same structure throughout the publications: general and social sciences in general; the structure and development of political science; political planning; practical politics; etc. In the latest supplement, part of the Subject Bibliography is arranged by Library of Congress Subject headings, rather than merely by broad grouping. The annotations are rather too brief to be effective.

Guides to general social science literature

The number of up-to-date 'monographic' bibliographies and guides to the literature of political science can be seen to be few. The same is true of such guides to the social sciences as a whole, but the quality of those produced more recently tends to be higher and their coverage of political science is good. One of those produced in the last few years is by Tze-chung Li, *Social Science Reference Sources: a Practical Guide* (Greenwood Press, 1980). While biassed towards North American sources, this has wide appeal, setting out the nature of the social sciences in general, the bibliographical needs and usage of social scientists, research resources, access to materials, sources of information, statistical sources, periodicals, government publications (US), unpublished materials and data archives and data base bibliographic services. In the subdiscipline sections, over 40 pages are dedicated to political science. Regrettably, not a single UK publication is mentioned in this detailed evaluative selection of the key sources.

The Use of Social Science Literature, edited by Norman H. Roberts (Butterworths, 1977), is aimed much more at a UK audience. Its contributors are either librarians or academic experts in a given field. Since, generally speaking, only one chapter is allocated to each aspect of the social sciences, style, coverage and approach vary enormously from one contribution to another. For example, the chapter on politics (and data archives), by Richard Rose, is primarily about methodology, whereas that on public administration, by Maurice Wright, covers the literature and sources of the subject.

The standard guide in the social sciences has an appropriately broad definition of scope. C. M. White, *Sources of Information in the Social Sciences* (2nd edn, American Library Association, 1973), contains in each area a bibliographic review by a specialist in the field, in which are given references to basic monographic works, followed by an annotated listing of reference works, many of which are bibliographies. Bibliographical essays also form the basis of B. F. Hoselitz, *A Reader's Guide to the Social Sciences* (2nd edn, Free Press, New York, and Collier–Macmillan, 1970). A useful bibliography and author index enhance the value of this publication. A very selective guide, also using bibliographical essays, is T. Freides, *Literature and Bibliography of the Social Sciences* (Melville Publishing, 1973). To each chapter is attached a selected list of works arranged by subject. Indexes are provided to subject, author and title.

A briefer British guide is unfortunately now rather dated: *The Literature of the Social Sciences: an Introductory Survey and*

Guide, by Peter R. Lewis (Library Association, 1960). It is thorough and clearly written, concentrating on British sources. Subjects such as anthropology and psychology are not covered.

Individual topic bibliographies

These general introductions to the literature of the social sciences in general and to political science in particular are complemented by the more specific individual bibliographies. Like the guides to their use, 'one-off' bibliographies are limited by their dates of publication. Always, by the time the bibliography or guide is published, new material of interest has appeared, and it is only continuing sources or frequently updating editions that can hope to keep up with the constant outpuring of new publications. Individual titles are not here included since detailed descriptions are the responsibility of the authors of appropriate chapters.

Theses, research and conference proceedings

All the publications listed above deal mainly in material which is obviously 'published', such as books and journal articles. Much valuable information is, however, to be found in rather less 'hard' publication form, and is more difficult to trace. A category of material which technically is 'unpublished' is the dissertation. It is important for any researcher to establish what research has been completed and what is still in progress in a given subject area. (For the new research student this is not only to ensure that he is not embarking on a M.Phil. topic which is already being researched elsewhere, but also to enable him to contact those working in related areas.) This is much less closely controlled than published output, but there are now an increasing number of tools available to assist identification. To begin historically, a useful finding-list is the *Retrospective Index to Theses of Great Britain and Ireland, 1716–1950*. Volume 1 (of 5) is *Social Sciences and Humanities*. The work is edited by R. R. Bilboul and E. H. Boehm (European Bibliographical Center/Clio Press, 1975), and contains some 13000 theses in these disciplines which were produced before the start of systematic bibliographical coverage of theses in the Aslib annual *Index to Theses* (see below). Each thesis title (and its bibliographical details) appears not only under author but also, on average, under two subject headings of a quite specific nature. These subject headings have been assigned from a strictly controlled thesaurus based on that of the *British Humanities Index*.

For North America, the *Comprehensive Dissertation Index, 1861–1972* (Xerox University Microfilms, 1973) lists most of the theses accepted for academic doctoral degrees by US educational institutions, together with some from foreign universities, over 417 000 in all. Volume 27 of the 37-volume set covers Law and Political Science (the social sciences generally are to be found in Volume 17), with political science, including public administration and international law and relations, taking up 656 of the 710 pages of entries. Arrangement is by very general subject headings. At the beginning of each section there is a list of cross-references, designed to help locate theses in related subjects and in disciplines which have changed over time. In the next cumulation, that for 1973–1977 (University Microfilms International, 1979), Political Science is grouped with History and Law in Volume 13 (of 19). The indexing is here enhanced by the introduction of key-phrasing. Both the cumulations and the subsequent annual indexes refer to entries in *Dissertation Abstracts International (DAI)*, formerly *Dissertation Abstracts* (Xerox University Microfilms, then University Microfilms International, 1938–). This monthly publication contains short abstracts written by the authors of doctoral dissertations from over 200 Canadian and American universities. Divided into two sections, the humanities and the sciences, it is indexed annually by subject and author, with some cross-classification to other relevant subjects. Copies of all dissertations are available from University Microfilms International. However a number of significant institutions, such as Harvard and MIT, do not contribute, nor is coverage complete even for those universities which normally cooperate. *American Doctoral Dissertations*, formerly *Doctoral Dissertations Accepted by American Universities* (Wilson, 1934–1956; then *Index to American Doctoral Dissertations*, 1957–), has much fuller coverage than *DAI*, containing in one listing all thesis titles for a particular year in the US and Canada, whether microfilmed or not.

In the UK, current coverage of university dissertations is provided, although with some delay, in *Index to Theses Accepted for Higher Degrees by the Universities of Great Britain and Ireland and the Council for National Academic Awards*, edited by G. M. Paterson and J. E. Hardy (Aslib, 1950–). Originally annual, the *Index* has since 1972 been produced twice per year. It does not contain dissertations accepted in only partial fulfilment of requirements for a higher degree. Entries are arranged by broad subject according to the Universal Decimal Classification, followed by author and subject indexes. The terms in the subject index offer a more specific level of search, since they have been abstracted from the titles themselves. From Volume 26, Part 1 onwards, for nearly every thesis a date has been given, usually the year of award, thus assisting inter-library loan requests, and the abstracts received by Aslib in connection with the preparation of the *Index* were made available on microfiche as *Abstracts to Theses*, each issue of which corresponds to an issue of the *Index*. From Volume 28 photocopies of individual abstracts may be obtained from the Aslib Library. Not all universities participate in the abstracts scheme, however.

Research in progress on the social sciences in the UK is listed in *Research in British Universities, Polytechnics and Colleges, Government Departments and other Institutions: Volume 3: Social Sciences* (British Library Lending Division, 1980–). This supersedes the publication *Scientific Research in British Universities and Colleges: Volume 3: Social Sciences* (HMSO, 1952–1972, then BLLD, 1973–). This three-volume annual is effectively the national register of research. The main sequence is arranged by broad subject grouping, then alphabetically by institution. Section J covers political science and international relations. Name and alphabetical subject indexes appear at the end of the volume. Another annual listing is the register of *Research Supported by the Social Science Research Council* (SSRC, 1973–), which, although arranged by type of grant awarded, etc., contains indexes of investigators and titles of projects, giving some subject access. A list of reports deposited at the British Library Lending Division, and one of SSRC publications, are also included.

Apart from these general listings, guides to more specific research areas are produced. *Political Science Theses: an Annual Register of Research Theses, supported from all Sources, and being Prepared for British Higher Degrees in all Aspects of Political Science* was published by the Social Science Research Council (UK) in 1973, with a supplement for 1973/1974 in 1975. With a change of title and a new editor, A. Barker, *Political Science Theses Register: a Register of Research Theses, supported from all Sources and being Prepared for Higher Degrees in the United Kingdom on Topics of Interest to Scholars of Political Science* appeared in 1976, covering 1974–1976, with a further edition in 1977. Arranged by broad subject areas, it includes both completed and uncompleted theses.

Area studies are well served for theses listings. The Institute of Latin American Studies of the University of London has published annually since 1966 *Theses in Latin American Studies at British Universities In Progress and Completed*. An irregular directory is published by Durham University Centre for Middle East and Islamic Studies, *Current British Research in Middle Eastern and*

Islamic Studies (1969–). The third listing was published in 1977. The Standing Conference on Library Materials on Africa has prepared cumulations of listings on Theses on Africa Accepted by Universities in the United Kingdom and Ireland for 1920–1962 (Heffer, 1964), and for 1963–1975 (Mansell, 1976). B. C. Bloomfield, *Theses on Asia Accepted by Universities in the United Kingdom and Ireland, 1877–1964* (Cass, 1967) is arranged by seven geographical areas, with an author index. Annual lists of research on Russia and the Soviet Union are published in the journal *Slavic Review*, and a substantial survey has appeared in J. J. Dossick, *Doctoral Research on Russia and the Soviet Union, 1960–1975: a Classified List of 3150 American, Canadian and British Dissertations, with some Critical and Statistical Analysis* (Garland Press, 1976). *Theses in Progress in Commonwealth Studies: a Cumulative List* was issued by the Institute of Commonwealth Studies of the University of London, listing by area 'all titles believed to be still in progress noted during the period January 1970 to October 1979', and now appears annually. However research 'in progress' may represent aspiration rather than reality.

An example of a thesis listing on a specific topic is by J. P. Siemers and E. H. Siemers-Hidman, *European Integration: Select International Bibliography of Theses and Dissertations, 1957–1980* (2nd rev. and enl. edn, Martinus Nijhoff, 1981). Well over 2000 references are given for this period, arranged under the headings of European integration in general, and various aspects of the European Communities' institutions and activities. The subject index is in French, with German and English indexes referring to the appropriate French term.

Another elusive form of contribution to knowledge is the conference paper. However, *Index to Social Sciences and Humanities Proceedings* (Institute for Scientific Information, 1976–) now provides detailed indexes by author of paper, subject of paper, place of conference, name of conference and sponsoring body, and is rapidly extending its coverage. It appears quarterly with annual cumulations. *Proceedings in Print* (Proceedings in Print, 1964–) is published six times a year with a separate annual cumulative index. This has an alphabetical arrangement by title of conference, followed by a single alphabetical index, interfiling corporate authors, sponsoring agencies, editors and subject headings. A chronological arrangement is followed in *Directory of Published Proceedings. Series SSH: Social Sciences/Humanities* (InterDoc, 1968–). This appears quarterly. Editor, location and subject/sponsor indexes are to be found in the four-yearly cumulations.

Library catalogues

The institutions which house and make accessible all kinds of information, whether published, unpublished or in machine-readable form, are libraries. In the UK, specialist libraries include the Marx Memorial Library, the Library of the Royal Institute of International Affairs, the Libraries of the Foreign and Commonwealth Office, Overseas Development Administration, and Management and Personnel Office (formerly Civil Service Department), and the British Library of Political and Economic Science. The published record of some of these libraries' holdings has been mentioned above, but also important are the *Catalogue of the Foreign Office Library, 1926–1968* (G. K. Hall, 1972), covering not only British official publications in the relevant subject areas but also those of the Commonwealth governments; and the *Catalogue of the Marx Memorial Library, London* (G. K. Hall, 1979), with its obvious specialization, divided into books (by authors, reference books, foreign-language books and subjects) and pamphlets (unbound by title, and bound by author), but with a disappointing degree of subject approach. The enormous *Library Catalogs of the Hoover Institution on War, Revolution and Peace, Stanford University: Catalog of the Western Language Collections* (63 vols, G. K. Hall, 1969) and its *First Supplement* (5 vols, G. K. Hall, 1972) provide a very detailed subject bibliography in terms of the holdings of one of the most extensive libraries in the world in the field of international relations.

Organizations and journals

Libraries and their catalogues are visible: the information communicated via the so-called 'invisible college' is harder to identify. Specialists in the field inevitably pass information about new publications, work in progress, current thinking, through less formalized channels than the tools discussed above. Nonetheless, associations exist to promote the passage of such knowledge and should be considered in the identification of bibliographical data. The oldest of the political science associations were formed in the US. The American Academy of Political and Social Science was created in 1889 and the American Political Science Association in 1903. These were responsible for publication of the *Political Science Quarterly* (1886) and the *American Political Science Review* (1906), both of which carry extensive book review sections.

Annual meetings, seminars, newsletters and publications on the literature of the subject, especially by the latter organization, have greatly enhanced bibliographical awareness among the growing political science community in the US. In addition, eight regional associations have been established, six of which publish journals with book review sections and hold annual meetings. In the UK, a formal organization of specialists was much later in formation. Only after the establishment of the International Political Science Association (IPSA) (very much at the instigation and under the auspices of UNESCO in 1949), and indeed resulting effectively from the invitation to attend the conference which led to the founding of IPSA, was the movement to form the Political Studies Association (PSA) of the United Kingdom accelerated. IPSA aimed to advance political science throughout the world by promoting research, communications and contacts among political scientists, and also to establish national political associations. IPSA itself has been responsible for valuable sources of bibliographical information such as *International Political Science Abstracts, International Political Science Review*, and in initiating the *International Bibliography of Political Science*. The continuous programme of meetings, seminars, etc. promotes such communication less formally. The PSA, since its formation in 1950, has similarly established patterns of meetings and seminars, and initiated publication of *Political Studies* in 1953, an essential part of which was to disseminate bibliographical information to its members. Subsequently further political studies journals were founded, all with useful review or listing sections, such as *Government and Opposition* (1966), *British Journal of Political Science* (1971) and *Policy and Politics* (1972). A new journal has now been started by the Association itself: *Politics* (1982), containing shorter articles than *Political Studies*, and aiming to pass on research findings faster and more succinctly, together with material useful for teaching. Members of PSA have been very much involved in the founding of the European Consortium for Political Research (ECPR) in 1970, modelled very closely on the Inter-University Consortium for Political and Social Research (ICPSR) at the University of Michigan. Like ICPSR, ECPR not only publishes on a regular basis and organizes meetings and workings, it also has formed a research data base, which provides the occasion and opportunity for an unprecedented degree of cooperation between European politicists.

Data banks and data bases

The purpose of the Inter-University Consortium for Political and Social Research is to maximize the availability and utilization of social science resources. It works in close cooperation with organizations such as the European Consortium, the International Social Science Council, UNESCO, the International Federation of Data Organizations, and the Council of European Social Science Data Archives. The data archive of ICPSR receives, processes and distributes machine-readable data on social phenomena from over 130 countries. These data have been produced by surveys of mass and elite attitudes, census records, election returns, international interactions and legislative records. It is nonetheless primarily a US resource, and the British contact institution is the Social Science Research Council Survey Archive. The latter has been establishing banks of such data at the University of Essex since 1967, inputting time series data such as national political polls, cross-national studies (for example, on attitudes to European integration in EEC nations) and surveys and censuses carried out by the Social Survey Division of the Office of Population Censuses and Surveys. Copies of sets of data are also available in magnetic tape form for local mounting. All over Europe the number and variety of data banks has grown to such an extent that the European Community Host Organization (ECHO) is establishing EUROFILE, a data base forming an inventory of data bases and banks available in Europe. CIRCE is the Information and Documentary Research Centre of the European Communities, and provides for the Commission a number of data bases, including two files which are accessible by other users: CELEX, which is intended eventually to cover the whole of the law of the European Communities in full text in all the official languages, and CRONOS, the EC Statistical Office data bank. The data in such banks as these are primary, i.e. they give access to facts. A large number of data bases have been formed to provide access to bibliographical information in the social sciences since the early 1970s, i.e. they provide information on where to find information.

To conduct a thorough literature search using all the relevant bibliographical sources mentioned earlier would require a substantial commitment in time. An increasing amount of such information is now available in computer-held files, which may be searched in a fraction of the time required to check the same data manually. These online files have usually been derived from the machine-readable form of production file for an abstracting journal, although as access to data bases becomes more commonly available, many are being constructed specifically for online retrieval, without the intention of regular published output.

Apart from the advantage of speed which such facilities afford, the user has the opportunity to modify, refine and redefine his search in the light of the references he retrieves, and where necessary can recover easily from any mistakes in the original formulation of the search strategy. The speed of the operation means that it is possible to repeat searches of certain files in the light of discoveries made in the course of a search (something rarely feasible in a manual search), and access is possible to an extremely wide range of indexes which might not normally be available in any one library. Not only is the number of access points to each item greater than that usually provided in printed sources but the facility is usually present for the combination of search terms by Boolean operators ('and', 'or', and 'not'), automatically narrowing down the retrieval to those items which most specifically cover the question asked, by effectively eliminating from the retrieval the numerous references not precisely related to each other in the way the searcher requires. To achieve the same result manually, all references bearing a certain descriptor would have to be scanned, and in each case an intellectual decision taken whether or not to discard it. Printed sources have not the flexibility for such combinations and exclusions: probably the closest they come is in the rotation of terms in KWIC (keyword in context) indexes. Most data bases now offer the facility of searching both free text and by thesaurus descriptors, a further example of the flexibility of machine-held information. The need to make notes of the references retrieved is eliminated, since references can be printed out either online or offline or a combination of the two.

The bibliographical data bases for the pure and applied sciences, medicine and agriculture are by far the largest and longest established, but the references searchable online in the social sciences are no longer inconsiderable, and the number of bases is growing rapidly. Many of the sources mentioned earlier in their print forms are accessible online. The most current of all such data bases is *Social Scisearch*, the online source of *Social Sciences Citation Index*, which is updated monthly. The Institute for Scientific Information claims that turn-round time for publications reaching them and being indexed is never more than 12 days. Remarkably comprehensive in its coverage of core journals, it offers, as has already been mentioned, the opportunity for retrieval of very relevant materials from sources not covered by single-discipline indexes or abstracts, whether online or in print, together with the unique facility of citation searching detailed earlier. Slightly less current than *Social Scisearch*, *PAIS International* corresponds to *Public Affairs Information Service Bulletin* and its *Foreign Language Index*. The file is updated monthly for the former and quarterly for the latter. Index entries appear between two and six months after publication of the original. The changes in its controlled vocabulary over the years complicate the search strategy, and the stated but not always clearly comprehensible selection policy (described earlier) produces rather idiosyncratic and erratic coverage for anyone attempting to use it as a general political science data base. *United States Political Science Documents (USPSD)* corresponds to the published index of the same title. The data base is updated irregularly about three times per year. Each entry has 10–12 descriptors from the *American Political Science Thesaurus* (APSA, 1979), and these are given either major or minor status, to assist in the closer definition of searches. An uncommon facility offered in *USPSD* is the ability to search on cited authors' names although references to their publications are not retrievable. Unlike *PAIS* and *Social Scisearch*, it carries lengthy descriptive abstracts, covering a much smaller range of journals, but in much greater depth. Emphasis is on the US.

Urban information, including local government, references are available via *ACOMPLINE*, which has grown out of the Greater London Council's internal ACOMPLIS data base. It covers not only journal articles, reports, legislation, conference papers and books, but also a large number of unpublished documents from local authorities and the GLC's own internal reports and minutes, material which is difficult to trace and obtain through the usual sources. *POLIS* covers UK and European Parliamentary information: it is referred to in Chapter 10.

The number of such data bases useful to the political scientist grows rapidly. Of significance are: *NTIS*, the National Technical Information Service, which covers US Government-sponsored research; UNESCO's *Data Retrieval System for Social Sciences* (DARE), covering not only UNESCO documents but also journals and books received at the UNESCO library; *FRANCIS* (French Retrieval Automated Network for Current Information in Social and Human Sciences), a merged data base containing current information in the social and human sciences drawn from some 16 journals; and the online equivalents of the USGPO *Monthly Catalog of US Government Publications* (GPO Monthly Catalog), of Congressional Information Service *Index (CIS/INDEX), Sociological Abstracts, Psychological Abstracts (PSYCHINFO),* etc.

As the literature of political science expands, the need for effective bibliographical control and retrieval increases. Fortunately there is every indication that, both in print and machine-readable form, tools are being developed and improved to ensure the researcher access to current information in the discipline.

PART 2
Approaches to the study of politics and government

2
The quest for a science of politics: comparative politics
Jeffrey Stanyer

Comparative politics and political behaviour are well-established fields within political studies which have been strongly affected by the twentieth-century search for a science of politics. To understand both it is necessary to have an awareness of the nature of science in general and of the interdisciplinary developments that have occurred and are occurring on the frontiers of the two subjects.

Most of the general introductions to the study of politics deal with these developments, with questions about what is involved in the search for a science of politics and with the implications the adoption of such an aim has for methods of research and analysis. Among the volumes that may be consulted are H. V. Wiseman, *Politics the Master Science* (Routledge and Kegan Paul, 1969); J. Blondel, 'Government' in N. Mackenzie (ed.), *A Guide to the Social Sciences* (Weidenfeld and Nicolson, 1966); H. Eulau, 'Political Science' in B. F. Hoselitz (ed.), *A Reader's Guide to the Social Sciences* (Free Press, Collier–Macmillan, New York, 1959); and W. J. M. Mackenzie, *The Study of Political Science Today* (Macmillan, 1971). The reader is also recommended to look at two books of essays. Interdisciplinary subjects are discussed in S. M. Lipset (ed.), *Politics and the Social Sciences* (Oxford University Press, 1969), whilst concepts, methods and techniques are the subject of J. C. Charlesworth (ed.), *Contemporary Political Analysis* (Free Press, Collier–Macmillan, New York, 1967). A more personal analysis is presented in W. J. M. Mackenzie, *Politics and Social Science* (Penguin, 1967), now unfortunately out of print.

No serious student should be unaware of both the twentieth-century history of the subject and developments in the philosophy and sociology of science. The argument about a science of politics has been strongly influenced by the rise of interpretations of natural science popularized by Karl Popper in *The Logic of Scientific Discovery* (first published in Vienna, 1934; English edn, Hutchinson, 1959) and carried further by philosophers such as Carl Hempel in a series of papers, now collected together as *Aspects of Scientific Explanation* (Free Press, Collier–Macmillan, New York, 1965), and Ernest Nagel in *The Structure of Science* (Routledge and Kegan Paul, 1961). A shorter version is to be found in C. Hempel, *Philosophy of Natural Science* (Foundations of Philosophy Series, Prentice-Hall, Englewood Cliffs, NJ, 1966). The best direct examinations of the nature of social science are to be found in R. Rudner, *Philosophy of Social Science* (Foundations of Philosophy Series, Prentice-Hall, Englewood Cliffs, NJ, 1966), which is, partly for linguistic reasons, a difficult text, and A. Ryan, *Philosophy of the Social Sciences* (Macmillan, 1970), which should be on the bookshelves of all serious students of politics.

The evolution of the sciences has been analysed in general terms by Thomas Kuhn, and his book *The Structure of Scientific Revolutions* (International Encyclopaedia of Unified Science, Chicago University Press, first published 1962, 2nd edn, 1970) has been very influential in the sociology and history of science. The condition of political studies in the twentieth century seems to fit very well into his analysis, and serious students of politics should consider carefully its relevance to what they themselves hope to achieve. Though there is no real substitute for the book itself, there have been several attempts to interpret its approach in terms of political studies. Examples of this include J. Stephens, 'The Kuhnian Paradigm and Political Inquiry: An Appraisal', *American Journal of Political Science*, **17/3** (1973); T. Ball, 'From Paradigms to Research Programs: Towards a Post-Kuhnian Political Science', *American Journal of Political Science*, **20/1** (1976); and D. Ricci, 'Reading Thomas Kuhn in the Post-Behavioural Era', *Western Political Quarterly*, **30/1** (1977).

A sense of the urgency and emotion involved in the evolution of twentieth-century political studies can be obtained from several different sources. Since the beginning of the twentieth century the main drive for a science of politics has occurred in America, and this can be followed in A. Somit and J. Tanenhaus, *The Development of American Political Science* (Allyn and Bacon, Boston, 1967; enl. edn, Irvington Publications, New York, 1981). A shorter account is contained in R. Jensen's chapter – 'History and the Political Scientist' – in S. M. Lipset (1969, work cited). The general attitudes of those who experienced 'the behavioural revolution' at first hand are best expressed by R. A. Dahl in 'The Behavioural Movement in Political Science; Epitaph for a Monument to a Successful Protest', *American Political Science Review,* **55/4** (1961). The work of H. Eulau is also very useful; see for instance, *The Behavioural Persuasion in Politics* (Random House, New York, 1963). Another influential writer was David Truman, whose book *The Governmental Process* (Knopf, New York, 1951) signalled a remarkable growth in research that was both behavioural and comparative in the 1950s. For a time 'pressure groups' occupied a central place in the drive for a better political analysis. A good short account of developments up to the mid-1960s is to be found in an article 'Politics, Comparative' by G. A. Almond – himself a protagonist in methodological controversies since the 1950s – in *The International Encyclopaedia of the Social Sciences,* edited by D. Sills (Macmillan, New York, 1968). This also illustrates the tendency to treat comparative politics as almost synonymous with political studies as a whole. But perhaps the most important work, and one that should still be read by all students of politics, is *The Political System* by David Easton (Knopf, New York, 1953). Most of the major issues relating to the evolution of political studies in the twentieth century and to the problems of a science of politics are better described and discussed in this work than any other. The reverberations of Easton's work continue to the present day, and will be mentioned in succeeding chapters. In particular, his concern about the relationship between political theory and political research and the extent to which a science of politics needs to combine the two is still a central issue.

Direct inspiration from the established sciences is much rarer. A. Somit, *Biology and Politics; Recent Explorations* (Mouton, Paris–La Haye, 1976), and W. J. M. Mackenzie, *Biological Ideas in Politics* (Penguin, 1978), are examples of one approach. Occasionally attempts to imitate physics appear as in R. Taagepera, 'A Physics-inspired Introduction to Political Science', *Teaching Political Science,* **3/2** (1976), and D. Fairlie and I. Budge, 'Newtonian Mechanics and Predictive Election Theory', *British Journal of Political Science,* **7/3** (1977). R. A. Hinde's *Ethology* (Fontana, 1982) has implications for the study of political behaviour but this subject is better known for its popularizations in R. Ardrey, *The Territorial Imperative* (Collins, 1967) and *The Social Contract* (Collins, 1970), and controversial works such as R. Dawkins, *The Selfish Gene* (Oxford University Press, 1976). Cybernetics is potentially a very important contributor to a future science of politics. It is, of course, present in an undeveloped form in systems analysis, but more ambitious examples are K. Deutsch, *The Nerves of Government* (Free Press, Glencoe, Ill., 1st edn, 1963) and a work in the management and public administration field by Stafford Beer, *Cybernetics and Management* (English Universities Press, 1959). Norbert Wiener's own work in *The Human Use of Human Beings* (Sphere Books edn, 1968) is also highly political.

The pressures for a science of politics have been felt in every subject area. Public administration has been influenced by management science and organization theory, for instance through the work of Herbert Simon in *Administrative Behaviour* (Macmillan, New York, 1945) and in collaboration with D. W. Smithburg and V. A. Thompson, *Public Administration* (Knopf, New York, 1950). International politics reflects developments in economics through games theory, as in T. C. Schelling, *The Strategy of Conflict* (Harvard University Press, Cambridge, Mass., 1960), and political thought by linguistics and linguistic analysis, as, for instance, in the controversial work *The Vocabulary of Politics* by T. D. Weldon (Penguin, 1953).

In a similar way, developments in technical methods that are relevant to many different types of empirical material have been extended to politics. Both comparative politics and political behaviour as contemporary subjects are marked by the use of statistics, mathematics, survey methods, computing and non-verbal means of presentation – charts, maps, diagrams and tables. Books and articles within the scientific tradition of political studies are easily recognizable because their analyses and results are offered to the reader in distinctive forms. Students of politics now need to keep at hand the volumes on technical research methods that are used by other social sciences. Reference to these is made in Chapter 3.

The most striking examples of attacks on the idea of a science of politics are to be found in H. J. Storing (ed.), *Essays on the Scientific Study of Politics* (Holt, Rinehart and Winston, New York, 1962) but in addition reference may be made to the sources cited in the 'Anti-Behaviouralism' section of Chapter 3.

Both comparative politics and political behaviour have played a central role in general movements for a science of politics and in the more specific episodes involving political sociology and the like. By the late 1960s the study of politics was established as an independent subject in most universities and, within the curriculum, both comparative politics and political behaviour were to be found – sometimes under different names – as central parts of the 'scientific' side of political studies.

In view of the similarities between the two, how can comparative politics and political behaviour be distinguished? Is Anthony Downs' *An Economic Theory of Democracy* (Harper and Row, New York, 1957) a comparative analysis of liberal democracies or of democratic political behaviour? Is *Political Change in Britain* by David Butler and Donald Stokes (Macmillan, 1st edn, 1969, 2nd edn, 1974) an empirical study of one political system or of British political behaviour?

The major difference between the two can best be explained with the aid of a distinction imported from economics – between macro- and microanalysis.

Macroanalysis deals with collectivities such as the economy and investigates large-scale phenomena such as the level of unemployment, the rate of inflation, the growth of national income, the balance of trade and the size of the public sector. Microanalysis deals with the behaviour of individuals, such as workers and capitalists, and basic units such as firms and households. Comparative politics is macroanalysis, its subject matter being the political system as a whole – including the constitution, the party system, the distribution of political opinions and attitudes and the territorial pattern of administration – which are characteristics of the whole country – whilst the study of political behaviour focuses on the individual – the voter, activist and legislator, or on small groups such as the local party, the legislative committee and the specific pressure group.

But as with economics, macro and micro factors are indissolubly linked in practice; the most interesting developments towards a science of politics, in fact, embrace both levels of phenomena. Typical system-level characteristics, such as political change through elections, involve the behaviour of the mass of individuals; the interaction of national pressure groups is in practice the relationships between small numbers of political leaders; and political culture is interpreted by each citizen in a personal way. The reason why the contributions of Downs (work cited) and Butler and Stokes (work cited) belong to both comparative government and political behaviour is that they incorporate both macro and micro elements in a general analysis. They involve generalizations about individual and systemic behaviour.

The ideas and concepts discussed in these chapters have a wider scope than those dealt with in most of the other chapters. As 'movements' and 'persuasions', comparative politics and political behaviour embrace other branches such as international politics and public administration, and the separate aspects of UK politics are subsumable under the behavioural heading whilst overseas governments are typically treated as area studies within comparative politics. Comparative analysis and behavioural methods have produced more specialized fields within the main areas of political studies. Comparative public administration, comparative foreign policy making, comparative local government and comparative policy studies all have their experts and are recognized through headings in general bibliographies. Likewise, administrative behaviour, international decision making and local political behaviour are expressions used by those who see themselves as adopting modern approaches within their fields of study.

Introduction

Comparative politics and its counterpart *comparative government* are phrases with two distinct meanings; sometimes they are virtually equated with political science itself and on other occasions given a more specific meaning which will be called *cross-national analysis* in this chapter. Related expressions, including *comparative public administration, comparative constitutional law* and *comparative public policy*, are also usually cross-national in conception; that is, they take the state or the country as the basic unit and build their analyses on two or more examples.

How has this distinction come about and why is it important? Why are these subjects generally seen as difficult spheres in which to attain a high degree of rigour in analysis? Why is it that much of what passes for comparative politics does not meet conventional intellectual standards – of proof and accuracy – and is often forcefully rejected? It is not sufficient for an author to set him or herself higher standards by attempting something ambitious, as Duverger did in his effort at 'a valid description of the comparative functioning of political parties' in M. Duverger, *Political Parties* (Methuen, 1954). This merely creates an industry out of criticism and refutation. Perhaps a testimony to its difficulty can be found when journals with the titles *Comparative Politics* and *Comparative Political Studies* have whole issues devoted to single-country studies, and when commentators have noted that for a long time many were willing to grant the title 'comparative' to such studies if they had a perspective that was somewhat general.

For an appreciation of the variety contained under this heading and the difficulties that beset systematic comparison of political systems, the reader might well begin by looking at the books of readings that contain some of the best work in the field: R. C. Macridis and B. E. Brown (eds), *Comparative Politics* (Dorsey

Press, Homewood, Ill., 1961); H. Eckstein and D. E. Apter (eds), *Comparative Politics* (Collier–Macmillan, London, 1963); J. Blondel (ed.), *Reader in Comparative Government* (Macmillan, 1969); R. J. Jackson and M. B. Stein, *Issues in Comparative Politics: a Text with Readings* (St Martin's Press, New York, 1971); and *The Practice of Comparative Government* (Longman, 2nd edn, 1978) edited by P. G. Lewis *et al.* There are many competing general textbooks and overviews of the subject. Early developments are reflected in K. Loewenstein, 'Report of the Research Panel on Comparative Government', *American Political Science Review,* **38/4** (1944), R. C. Macridis, *The Study of Comparative Government* (Random House, New York, 1955) and G. Hecksher, *The Study of Comparative Government and Politics* (Allen and Unwin, 1959). After a period of acute controversy in the late 1950s and 1960s, two substantial attempts were made in Britain to provide a synthesis of previous work and a basis for future developments: S. E. Finer, *Comparative Government* (Penguin edn, 1970) and J. Blondel, *An Introduction to Comparative Government* (Weidenfeld and Nicolson, 1969). Blondel has followed this with two shorter books, *Comparing Political Systems* (Weidenfeld and Nicolson, 1973) and *Comparative Government* (Macmillan, 1969). A more detailed and technical survey is provided by R. L. Merritt in *Systematic Approaches to Comparative Politics* (Rand-McNally, Chicago, 1970).

The importance of comparison in the study of public administration is shown in the following books: F. Heady and S. L. Stokes (eds), *Papers in Comparative Public Administration* (Ann Arbor, Michigan, 1962); W. J. Siffin (ed.), *Toward the Comparative Study of Public Administration* (Department of Government, Indiana University, Bloomington, Indiana, 1957); N. Raphaeli (ed.), *Readings in Comparative Public Administration* (Allyn and Bacon, Boston, 1967); and F. Heady, *Public Administration: A Comparative Perspective* (Marcel Dekker AG, 2nd edn, 1979).

However, it has always been easier to review the problems of the subject and identify the difficulties that have prevented progress than to provide answers to the basic dilemma described below. The mid-1950s saw a flood of articles either proposing radical changes in approaches to cross-national analysis or objecting to the innovations of others. The reader should look at some of the more general articles which raise methodological and philosophical problems and which are thus part of the argument about the possibility of a science of politics. There are, for instance: G. A. Almond, 'Comparative Political Systems', *Journal of Politics,* **18/3** (1956); D. E. Apter, 'A Comparative Method for the

Study of Politics', *American Journal of Sociology*, **64/3** (1958);
A. L. Kalleberg, 'The Logic of Comparison', *World Politics*, **19/1**
(1966); S. Verba, 'Some Dilemmas in Comparative Research',
World Politics, **20/1** (1967); G. Sartori, 'Concept Misformation in
Comparative Politics', *American Political Science Review*, **64/4**
(1970); A. J. Gregor, 'Theory, Metatheory and Comparative
Politics', *Comparative Politics*, **3/4** (1971); G. Loewenberg, 'New
Directions in Comparative Political Research', *Midwest Journal of
Political Science*, **15/4** (1971); R. E. Ward, 'Culture and the
Comparative Study of Politics', *American Political Science Review*,
68/1 (1974); A. Lijphart and J. A. Caporaso (eds.), 'Symposium
on Comparative Methodology', *Comparative Political Studies*, **8/2**
(1975); I. A. Gilbert, 'Comparative Politics – a Retreat from
Grand Theory', *Polity*, **7/3** (1975); and R. W. Benjamin, 'Strategy
versus Methodology in Comparative Research', *Comparative Political Studies*, **9/4** (1977).

Implicit and explicit comparison

It is necessary to distinguish between implicit and explicit comparison because comparison in general is the fundamental activity of
all intellectual endeavours. When political analysis compares the
behaviour of different types of individual – for instance, supporters of different parties or members of different occupational
groups – it is simply following the scientific principles enunciated
by J. S. Mill in *A System of Logic* (Parker, London, 1st edn, 1843)
over a century ago. The importance of comparison in this most
basic sense is highlighted by the fact that it occurs in all other
subjects, including the arts, law, history, sociology, economics and
psychology. Therefore when students of politics analyse local
government, they are implicitly comparing it with field administration; when they investigate the House Committee on Ways and
Means, they remind readers that there are other kinds of legislative committees – sometimes through the words of its members.
The use of implicit comparison never ends.

But when the word 'comparative' is used in political studies, it
does not normally refer to implicit comparison of the above type.
It is important to realize and always remember that *comparative
politics* usually means something more than the use of the comparative method. The reasons for this are not hard to find and have
been canvassed by commentators – for instance, Blondel in his
cited works – for a considerable time. On the one hand it is hard to

avoid attempting *explicit* comparison for the combination of the nature of the data and the aims of the investigation presses the researcher in that direction. On the other hand, when it is attempted it is usually, almost invariably, found that there are insuperable difficulties. The problems have led A. MacIntyre to ask 'Is a Science of Comparative Politics Possible?' in *Against the Self-Images of the Age* (Duckworth, 1971), reprinted in P. Laslett *et al.* (eds), *Philosophy, Politics and Society*, 4th series (Cambridge University Press, 1972).

What reasons, then, force students of politics to attempt explicit comparison and why do efforts always seem to end in an unsatisfactory manner?

The basic reason lies in the fact that those who give a positive answer to MacIntyre's question find themselves forced to try to increase the number of cases in their analyses. As the logic of understanding national systems of government is the same as understanding any phenomena, the analysis will come to a full stop unless one can find evidence from outside the country. Explicit comparison is thus the deliberate search for evidence from other political systems in order to throw light on or explain an individual state's behaviour, or to find cross-national generalizations applicable to a number of countries; in fact, generalizations about behaviour at the system level.

Though comparative politics has dealt primarily and largely with states, the same activity is to be found when individual, regional and local political systems, alliances and economic communities are directly compared. For examples, there is the policy output literature on British local government reviewed by K. Newton, 'Community Performance in Britain', *Current Sociology*, **22/1** (1974), and the study of community power in the US analysed in N. W. Polsby, *Community Power and Political Theory* (Yale University Press, New Haven, 2nd edn, 1980).

The significance of this distinction is confirmed when it is discovered that an identical one operates in many other subjects. Not only do literature, law, history, sociology and economics contain implicit comparison, but they also recognize as branches the subdivisions of *comparative literature, comparative law, comparative history, comparative sociology* and *comparative economic systems* – and in each case the comparison is deliberate and systematic.

Over the centuries awareness of the need for explicit comparison has risen and fallen. For instance, Aristotle's *Politics* (Penguin version, trans. by T. A. Sinclair, rev. edn, 1981) clearly fits into the category of 'cross-polis analysis', and Montesquieu is generally regarded as representing another high point in its history. It is only, however, in the last forty years that students of politics have regularly undertaken systematic comparison of two or more named political systems. After an undistinguished evolution in the 1930s, comparative government was seen as a major line of development, particularly after the Second World War, when political science was being organized on an international scale. The early general works cited above usually include an account of its history up to the 1950s.

The realization of the significance of systematic cross-national analysis arose from the perception of several general defects in political studies.

Ethnocentrism

First, there is the problem of ethnocentrism. The study of politics in general is bedevilled by this. Many writers about politics and government came from, and still do come from, the world of practice; they are participants rather than observers. But a politician or public servant can only experience one major political system; in relation to all others they are as removed or detached as the academic student. Few are totally unaware of the distinguishing characteristics or main features of other systems, but it is difficult for one whose credentials depend on 'knowledge by acquaintance' to analyse a foreign country. Ethnocentrism has been identified at all levels in the political system, from the state down to the locality and ward. Other social sciences experience this problem. Even if there is no built-in bias from the political system itself, there is the problem of 'travellers' tales' and the attitude of mind that accompanies them. Admiration or distrust of foreign countries is a fact of national politics; the Cold War systematically distorted many people's views of the Soviet Union and the People's Republic of China. Comparisons by the Left of bourgeois regimes with those in the socialist bloc are uniformly unfavourable, whilst the Right and Centre consistently denigrate everything about members of the Warsaw Pact. The bias is apparent in the popular and 'quality' press, in works written by emigrés and in research done for the defence and foreign affairs establishments.

The attempts described below to produce an agreed universal framework of analysis equally applicable to all countries of the world are in part attempts to escape from the insidious and pervasive influence of ethnocentrism.

Unbalance

Ethnocentrism is related to another problem in political studies – that of unbalance. This is caused in the first instance by the fact that researchers and analysts usually have a detailed knowledge of their own system but it is compounded by the fact that different degrees of understanding and levels of research have been achieved for different types of foreign country. Because political science is overwhelmingly a phenomenon of the English-speaking world, a large part of our knowledge is of the American and British political systems; when students of politics in those countries have turned to the outside world they have looked at Canada, Australia and the former British Empire; for instance, India, Nigeria and Ghana. For UK students France has traditionally been the most popular overseas country after the US. The problem is not entirely one of language; the level of development in a country strongly influences the extent to which its nationals have been able to study their own system. Thus the Scandinavian states have a thriving political (and social) science of their own – much of it published in English – but francophone Africa – which includes some of the poorest countries of the world – is *terrae incognitae*.

Even if a society can easily sustain a thriving and autonomous study of politics and government, there may be other factors which have inhibited home-grown contributions. It is difficult for Western-type social sciences to thrive in socialist systems, and in some Western European countries the educational system, by subordinating politics to other subjects, retards its intellectual development.

Clearly, there is no way in which a satisfactory science of politics can develop if its subject matter is regarded as hopelessly unrepresentative. The growth of international organizations, such as the United Nations, drew attention to the fact that the US and the UK were not typical of the world's political systems. In particular, the foundation of the International Political Science Association in 1949, under the auspices of UNESCO, made 'equality of evidential status' a major goal for political scientists; every country had an equal 'right' to contribute towards an understanding of politics and government.

Redressing the balance

The first step in redressing the unbalance created by a north Atlantic perspective has therefore been to draw up lists of states with as much general information about each as can be gathered at a central point. In the early days of enthusiasm for new approaches in the subject even a list of names and their twentieth-century history as states was found to be useful. The nominalist approach is well illustrated by B. M. Russett *et al.*, 'National Political Units in the Twentieth Century', *American Political Science Review*, **62/3,** (1968), whilst the systematic collection of facts about all countries is illustrated by the data bank movement described below.

Once a nominalist approach had been adopted, evidence quickly accumulated about the untypicality of the US and UK. The comparative perspective has fed back into the study of individual countries by highlighting their special features; each state is to the non-ethnocentric observer a mixture of familiar and unfamiliar. It was striking that British students ignored Northern Ireland, yet its politics are much more like those of the rest of world than are the politics of England. In the US the 'melting pot' theory of assimilation made political scientists underestimate the importance of social differences such as religion and ethnic origins. Thus the attitudes involved in studies of individual political systems have changed considerably under the influence of the cross-national analysis movement.

The 'all-states-of-the-world' approach can be criticized on grounds of superficiality and it does not by itself remedy the natural disparities in the amount of information available about different continents and regions. The alternative approach may be referred to as 'area studies'. Intellectual imperialism suffered the same fate as political imperialism. States not belonging to the Anglo-American and Western European traditions demanded 'positive discrimination' to put right the neglect of decades.

The first group to escape for this reason were the developing areas – a general name for South-east Asia, Africa and Latin America – in the 1950s. Some of the most impressive work is to be found in the monographs on individual countries – for instance, Ghana, Nigeria, Burma, India, Morocco – but the existence of case studies also increased the demand for comparative frameworks which would transcend the particular instance – an element in the pressure for a science of politics. Influential articles were published by G. Kahin *et al.*, 'Comparative Politics of Non-Western Countries', *American Political Science Review*, **49/4** (1955) and L. Pye, 'The Non-Western Political Process', *Journal of Politics,* **20/3** (1958), but much of the main thrust came from the work of G. A. Almond, the high point of whose endeavours is the collection of studies, with a lengthy introduction and conclusion, published as *The Politics of the Developing Areas* (Princeton

University Press, Princeton, NJ, 1960) and jointly edited with J. S. Coleman. Although many of the details of the 'new' approaches have been discredited or remain controversial, the Third World has become a main subdivision of cross-national analysis.

The 1960s saw the need to integrate the study of socialist countries into general comparative government. The reduction of international tension led to more personal interactions between individuals and organizations in the 'First' and 'Second' Worlds. The general political importance of the Soviet Union and the People's Republic of China encouraged the growth of language skills outside the emigré communities, which had tended to dominate research and writing about these and other socialist regimes. As with the Third World, the first step was to apply standard political science concepts and methods to the individual countries, examples of which are to be found in R. Kanet (ed.), *The Behavioural Revolution and Communist Studies* (Free Press, New York, 1971), which deals with the Soviet Union. For general discussion, the reader should look at the 'Symposium on Comparative Politics and Communist Systems', *Slavic Review,* **26/1** (1967), particularly the articles by Armstrong, Meyer, Kautsky, Jacobs and Sharlet. Many of the best pieces are included in F. J. Fleron (ed.), *Communist Studies and the Social Sciences* (Rand-McNally, Chicago, 1969). More recent studies include D. E. Powell and P. Shoup, 'The Emergence of Political Science in Communist Countries', *American Political Science Review,* **64/2** (1970); S. R. Lieberman, 'Comparative Communist Studies or Area Studies?', *Polity,* **4/3** (1972); R. Lowenthal, 'On "Established" Communist Party Regimes', *Studies in Comparative Communism,* **7/4** (1974); J. La Palombara, 'Monoliths or Plural Systems: Through Conceptual Lenses Darkly', *Studies in Comparative Communism,* **8/3** (1975); and the bibliography by L. L. Whetten, *Current Research on Comparative Communism* (Praeger, New York, 1976). There was also growth of interest in the comparative analysis of non-ruling Communist parties; for instance, in G. W. Rice, 'The Electoral Prospects for Non-Ruling Communist Parties', *American Journal of Political Science,* **17/3** (1973) and 'Non-Ruling Parties and the "Peaceful" Path', *Problems of Communism,* **22/4** (1973) and T. H. Greene, 'Non-Ruling Communist Parties and Political Adaptation', *Studies in Comparative Communism,* **6/4** (1973).

In the 1970s smaller regions of the world, such as the Middle East and South America, began to hive off from the wider category of the 'Third World'. Part of the reason for this is to be found in pressure generated by the demands of foreign policy by the governments of the major powers. The special place of Latin America was recognized relatively early; for instance, in J. D. Martz, 'The Place of Latin America in the Study of Comparative Politics', *Journal of Politics,* **28/1** (1966), and D. E. Stansfield, 'The Study of Latin American Politics in British Universities', *Latin American Research Review,* **9/2** (1974). Similar claims have been made for many other parts of the world.

Methods of cross-national analysis

States can be guaranteed 'equality' in the contribution that they make to knowledge and understanding in cross-national analysis either by the way in which instances are selected or by the adoption of an all-embracing neutral framework or scheme of analysis in advance of the choice of countries.

Once countries have been chosen – the minimum is two and the maximum a census of the states of the world – the analyst still faces the problem of how to describe each. All methods experience the tension between holism and methodological individualism. Should a start be made with the whole system or should particular aspects be picked out for special study? Many comparative studies do not attempt to present a picture of the whole system but begin by picking out a dimension of politics, such as interest groups, political parties or the legislature, and then make this the foundation of the investigation.

When one of the modern methods is chosen it is usually in deliberate reaction to and rejection of the traditional method, which may be labelled 'the comparative reference'. This is the most elementary form and one which dominated the study of states and governments until the 1950s.

The comparative reference

Students of politics have always recognized the existence of a great variety of political systems, but this is not by itself sufficient to solve the problems of how to deal with the range of evidence that they provide. Traditionally, when politics within the student's own country was described and analysed, material from other states was incorporated by means of the 'comparative reference'. This phrase is used to indicate the subordinate and illustrative nature of foreign experience when the major thrust of political studies is self-centred. For instance, elementary factual knowledge relating to other countries is cited in relation to a theme such as reform of the electoral system and its effects on political parties.

The comparative reference continues to be widely used but its weaknesses are more often in evidence than its strengths. Even when it is well done it is unsatisfactory in rather obvious ways. The fleeting reference to another political system often gives the reader pause to wonder whether the latter has been properly understood. It is a common complaint in comparative studies that they usually give offence to specialists in the countries entering into the comparison – and the shorter the reference, the greater the offence. And once the admissibility of evidence from the rest of the world has been granted, it is hard to refuse to look at other countries. What sort of explanation is it that is deliberately restricted to one country and an aspect of another?

The comparative reference also lends itself to the iteration of examples; having looked at two countries the researcher might go on to look at fourth, fifth, . . . , examples, one supporting and the next throwing doubt on the conclusion. The way in which unsystematic comparison can run into trouble is well illustrated by Duverger's work on political parties (work cited). This is rightly regarded as a very important work of comparative analysis, but its methods demonstrate how necessary it is to be careful in order to achieve ordinary standards of intellectual rigour. Amongst many articles following on from Duverger's 'conclusions' are S. E. Finer, 'Duverger Reconsidered', *Political Studies*, **2/3** (1954); A. Wildavsky, 'A Methodological Critique of Duverger's "Political Parties" ', *Journal of Politics*, **21/2** (1959); C. T. Leys, 'Models, Theories and the Theory of Political Parties', *Political Studies*, **7/2** (1959); D. V. Smiley, 'The Two Party System and One-Party Dominance', *Canadian Journal of Economics and Political Science*, **24/3** (1958); and D. W. Rae, *The Political Consequences of Electoral Laws* (Yale University Press, New Haven, rev. edn, 1967).

From this point onwards the comparative reference will be ignored. It belongs to a gentlemanly tradition of political analysis which has long been discredited.

Choosing countries to be studied

The problem with the comparative reference is that it puts the object of the reference in a secondary position. The essence of acceptable methods in cross-national analysis is the creation of equality – of knowledge, understanding and 'weight' – between the systems entering into the comparison. The criteria used to choose the cases are therefore crucial, and the student of comparative politics must give special attention to the question of the representativeness of the states entering into any particular analysis.

THE WORLD CENSUS APPROACH

Including all the states of the world in one's cross-national analysis is heroic but rarely succeeds; descriptive 'equality of contribution' cannot be achieved for a number of reasons. Political scientists rely on material gathered by governments and private organizations, but where public statistical services are undeveloped or unreliable and private organizations rudimentary there is no way in which the researcher can fill in the gaps. A similar problem is faced by the economist dealing with the world economic system; enormous efforts have to be made in relation to Third World and socialist regimes. One should note also the problems of 'regime-specific' material and the impact of the political system itself on the data that can be collected.

Nonetheless there have been important efforts to develop systematic ways of describing and measuring the important features of all political systems and to publish catalogues or profiles of every country. Many of these have occurred within programmes to create lists of political indicators and are associated with American data banks and survey centres. Among researchers who have attempted to include all the states or major political systems of the world within their analysis are A. S. Banks and R. Textor in *A Cross-Polity Survey* (MIT Press, Cambridge, Mass., 1963), and this book should be consulted – but not read! – first. The latter also applies to publications of handbooks of social, economic and political indicators, such as B. M. Russett *et al., World Handbook of Social and Political Indicators* (Yale University Press, New Haven, 1964). The 'census of states' programmes sparked off some controversies about the usefulness of standardized quantitative data in comparative politics, as, for instance, in R. Retzlaff, 'The Use of Aggregate Data in Comparative Political Analysis', *Journal of Politics,* **27/4** (1965); T. R. Gurr, 'The Neo-Alexandrians: a Review Essay on Data Handbooks in Political Science', *American Political Science Review,* **68/1** (1974); and R. Rose, 'The Dynamics of Data Archives', *Social Science Information,* **13/6** (1974).

SAMPLING THE UNIVERSE OF STATES

It is clear that unless the selection is done logically the end result will remain unsatisfactory. But unfortunately both random and quota samples of the sort regarded as standard in behavioural research are almost never used, and if they were, the researcher would encounter the problems of lack of data met by those who use the census method. In both methods the use of replacement strategies to overcome what are in effect problems of nonresponse defeats the object of the process – equality of evidential status for all political systems – because eventually the researcher ends up with the countries that would have been chosen anyway by non-systematic methods.

Hence much cross-national analysis which takes as its starting point named political systems is only marginally better than the comparative reference. The minimum number of countries that can be compared is two, but this option will rarely be thought to be satisfactory. The two-country approach is rightly suspect because it is very easy to choose on non-academic grounds – familiarity, convenience, knowledge of the language, antiquarian interest or quaintness. The problem does not disappear if three countries are chosen, as in H. Zink *et al., Rural Local Government in Sweden, Italy and India* (Stevens, for the International Political Science Association, 1957) or four – Australia, Britain, Canada and the US – as in R. R. Alford, *Party and Society* (John Murray, 1964), or five – Britain, Italy, Mexico, the US and West Germany – as in G. A. Almond and S. Verba, *The Civic Culture* (Princeton University Press, Princeton, NJ, 1963).

In each of the cases quoted, and in many others, reasons are given by the authors for their particular choices. But even if these are acceptable in the particular instance, their total impact may be unsatisfactory because quantitatively some countries and some types of country may be grossly overrepresented, and the problem of 'unbalance' remains. Ethnocentric political studies can, in fact, be continued under the guise of cross-national analysis when non-random methods of selecting countries are used.

Area studies

Area studies constitute an attempt to approach the subject from a different perspective. If the world is divided up into major regions (the Middle East, Latin America, etc.) and each is studied by a group of specialists the total effect will be to produce a range of analyses covering the whole world spectrum.

Area studies are popular for several reasons. Such factors as level of development are often held constant and language problems reduced. For reasons of international politics and economics, governments come to feel that they need to have a much better understanding and knowledge of a particular part of the world; research funds are therefore made available, centres and institutes set up and projects funded. In these there is a recognition that comparative politics is essentially an interpersonal subject – one which depends on the cooperative effort of many individuals with special knowledge and skills. The strategy is thus one of 'division of labour' and the extent to which it will succeed depends on two factors: how extensive the examination of individual systems is within each area (equality of evidential status in each region) and how equal the effort in total is for each area. Unfortunately the tendency to overrepresent certain countries applies to area specialisms as well as to the world as a whole. Thus students of the socialist state have done much less on Bulgaria and Albania than on the Soviet Union and the People's Republic of China, students of Latin America have not given as clear a picture of Paraguay as of Brazil and Israel outweighs all other Middle Eastern countries in academic attention.

The dilemma of cross-national analysis

From the above it will be clear that the student of comparative government encounters a dilemma. As the number of countries studied increases so do the problems of comparability. Do words denote the same thing in different countries? Or are there different words in each country that in fact have the same meaning? There are also specific problems arising from the ways in which governments do – or do not – collect data, from the idiosyncrasies of the writers of monographs on individual countries, from the language problem and from the fact that data have been collected, from a global perspective, non-systematically by social scientists. The fewer the number of countries entering into the analysis, the easier the task of comparing.

But the logic of scientific research points in the opposite direction. In order to use the techniques that are of general importance and relevance in the social sciences it is necessary to draw evidence from a considerable number of cases – the more the better. There is thus a trade-off: the number of countries and the comparability of the data available for the set are inversely related. If the number of cases is increased, the comparability is reduced; if high standards of comparability are adopted, then the smaller the number of cases that can be included.

The use of analytical frameworks

The type of cross-national analysis described so far takes the individual named political system as its foundation and works towards its conclusions by systematically comparing two or more cases. To undertake this operation it is necessary to have an intellectual framework or a set of general ideas to guide the research. In many examples, particularly those with a traditional orientation, the assumptions and concepts are intuitive, unsystematic and implicit. For ambitious students of politics such approaches were not acceptable – they contributed little or nothing towards the creation of a legitimate science of politics – and since the 1950s, the study of comparative government has been dominated by arguments about the claims of universal analytical frameworks and theoretical perspectives.

Analytical frameworks may be evaluated under a number of headings. The minimum level that they must achieve is clarity of definition and a degree of simplification and standardization, but much more should be expected of those that aim at a high degree of penetration and acceptability within the subject.

Simplification and standardization are two widely used processes by which analysts attempt to bring the variety and complexity of the world they study under control, making it intelligible and predictable. 'Cases', that is, the elements that are being investigated, differ from instance to instance, sometimes only slightly and sometimes substantially. The student is faced with either treating each case as *sui generis* or devising a scheme which applies to all within the universe of discourse. The 'scientific' response to this choice is to try to bring all the diversity into a common focus by creating a conceptual framework to embrace all the relevant empirical material.

The methods by which simplification and standardization, as a prelude to analysis, are achieved, however, are themselves diverse. The most elementary is *definition*, followed by the use of *typologies* or *classification*, then *ideal-type analysis, paradigm cases* and *syndromes*. Examples of all of these can be found in systematic cross-national research, but in methodological discussion they have been overshadowed by more complex approaches, which are usually called *conceptual frameworks*.

Conceptual frameworks are more complex because they usually contain elements of definition, classification, ideal-types and positive assertions that function as axioms or premises. Both using and assessing a conceptual framework are more difficult than the same operations with the simpler analytical devices.

Structural–functionalism

One of the best examples of an elaborate conceptual framework for comparative politics is to be found in the work of G. A. Almond. His 'introduction' to *The Politics of the Developing Areas* (work cited, p.3) argued that traditional approaches had steadily lost their competence to deal with even the phenomena of Western European politics and could never cope with the developing countries, where sociological and anthropological theories were the most relevant. He therefore proposed to replace the conventionally accepted terminology with new concepts: 'the state' was to become 'the political system', 'powers' were replaced by 'functions', 'offices' by 'roles', 'institutions' by 'structures', 'public opinion' by 'political culture' and 'citizenship training' by 'political socialization'.

The next step was to clarify the meaning of each of the new terms, starting with 'politics' and 'political system'. This has an essentially comparative purpose: to provide a 'sharp' definition of *politics* and to separate out analytically the structures which perform political functions in all societies, regardless of scale, degree of differentiation and culture. The process is then repeated for all the other major elements in the conceptual framework. Almond claimed that in his approach there was 'an intimation of a major step forward in the nature of political science as science' – towards a 'probabilistic theory of politics'.

From the very beginning structural–functionalism evoked strong emotions and generated lengthy controversies. Almond himself wrote many defences of it and encourated others to undertake empirical work using it as the basis. For a considered later statement see G. Almond and G. B. Powell, *Comparative Politics* (Little, Brown, 2nd edn, 1978).

The heyday of structural–functionalism is now well past and for reasons why it did not establish itself more strongly as a method in cross-national analysis, the reader should look at some of the critical evaluations of it in journal articles. There is, for instance, R. E. Dowse, 'A Functionalist's Logic', *World Politics*, **18/4** (1966); A. J. Gregor, 'Political Science and the Uses of Functional Analysis', *American Political Science Review*, **62/2** (1968); J. Stephens, 'The Logic of Functional and Systems Analyses in Political Science', *Midwest Journal of Political Science*, **13/3** (1969); and S. E. Finer, 'Almond's Concept of the "Political System": a Textual Critique', *Government and Opposition*, **5/1** (1969–1970), with Almond's reply – 'Determinacy–Choice' – in the same issue.

Systems analysis

Though structural–functionalism is often referred to as 'systems analysis', it should be carefully distinguished from the type of approach discussed below. Outside the fields of political studies systems analysis is regarded as an interdisciplinary subject in its own right – 'general systems theory' – with important branches in cybernetics and information theory, and applications in ecology, biology and related subjects, operational research, automation and other branches of applied science. In politics the general ideas underlying the above are to be found in the conceptual framework and diagrammatic models created by David Easton in the early 1950s and since elaborated and defended on many occasions.

The essence of this type of systems analysis is the creation of a logical model, framed in terms of abstract symbols, whose behaviour exhibits the phenomenon of *self-regulation*. When the model is interpreted, by replacing the symbols with theoretical and empirical terms, there is created a distinction between the system itself and its environment, the latter being the source of 'inputs' and the destination of 'outputs'. Self-regulation occurs when the outputs 'feedback' to the sources of the inputs and produce changes in the system itself. These in their turn affect the outputs which again modify the environment and therefore the inputs; the process is never-ending.

For students of comparative government, the most interesting form of self-regulation has been 'negative feedback', whereby disturbances in an environment are successively damped down and eventually the system reverts to the state it was in before the environment changed. Such 'mechanisms' appear to account for the persistence of political systems and the continuity of detailed behavioural patterns shown within many of them over long periods. The student feels instinctively that Eastonian systems analysis is on the right lines because it indicates that established political systems such as states should exhibit a degree of ruggedness and a capacity to adapt to changing circumstances without turning into something quite different. There is, however, no logical necessity for a system to reproduce the pre-existing state of affairs. It may produce regular oscillations around an equilibrium state or it may produce positive feedback in the form of ever-increasing deviations from stability until a 'catastrophe' occurs.

The original source for this approach is to be found, along with much of great interest, in D. Easton, *The Political System* (A. A. Knopf, New York, 1953), but perhaps the best first introduction is 'An Approach to the Analysis of Political Systems', *World Politics,* **9/3** (1957). More elaborate presentations are *A Framework for Political Analysis* (Prentice-Hall, Englewood Cliffs, NJ, 1965) and *A Systems Analysis of Political Life* (Wiley, New York, 1965). An edited volume – *Varities of Political Theory* (Prentice-Hall,

Englewood Cliffs, NJ, 1966) – illustrates a wider range of applications. Readers should also consult Easton's replies to his critics in 'Reflections on Criticisms', *Social Science Information,* **12/3** (1973), and 'Systems Analysis and its Classical Critics', *Political Science Reviewer,* **3** (1973).

Some of the criticisms of Easton's approach are to be found in the articles on structural–functionalism, but more direct reviews are found in M. Evans, 'Notes on David Easton's Model of the Political System', *Journal of Commonwealth Political Studies,* **8/2** (1970); C. Campbell, 'Current Models of the Political System', *Comparative Political Studies,* **4/1** (1971); P. Leslie, 'General Theory in Political Science', *British Journal of Political Science,* **2/2** (1972); and A. W. Penn, 'Toward a New Generation of Systems Models in Political Science', *Polity,* **4/3** (1972).

It is fair to say that the main influence of Eastonian analysis has been felt in the study of political behaviour rather than cross-national comparison. This is because of the complexity of the concept when interpreted and applied holistically, that is, at the level of the state itself. In practice there are few countrywide systems analyses, though many writers have subscribed in principle to the programme for using the approach in relation to individual states. The approach, however, does not by itself explain any particular examples of persistence and resilience or of revolution and catastrophe; to account for detailed behavioural patterns of these kinds requires much more than is contained in a framework and elementary model.

Models and theories

The words 'model' and 'theory' also occur frequently in cross-national analysis. In other subjects such as the natural sciences and economics they have specific meanings which have been expounded and analysed by philosophers of science, but they are often used indiscriminately in comparative government for any systematic approach, including those discussed above. The use of models and theories is described and illustrated in J. Stanyer, 'Electoral Behaviour in Local Government: A Model of a Two-Party System', *Political Studies,* **18/2** (1970); 'Social and Rational Models of Man; Alternative Approaches to the Study of Local Elections', *The Advancement of Science,* **130** (1970); and 'Irresistible Forces: the Pressures for a Science of Politics', *Political Studies,* **24/3** (1976). These are concerned with cross-national analysis by implication; the latter is an important field where this type of intellectual method ought to be used.

The best example of a theoretical approach in comparative politics is to be found in A. Downs, *An Economic Theory of Democracy* (Harper and Row, New York, 1957). This has stimulated many efforts at theoretical refinement, many attempts to test conclusions empirically and the formulation of models of liberal –democratic political systems. Downs' work is only partly comparative politics; it is significant also in the field of political behaviour and political theory, and thus is doubly attractive to students who look forward to a 'science of politics'.

Conclusion

Cross-national analysis remains intellectually one of the most important fields of political studies. But there is a general feeling of dissatisfaction with much of what is claimed to be comparative. The dilemma remains; the more countries involved in the comparison, the less the comparability of the material, and the fewer the countries, the less the acceptability of the conclusions. Only better theoretical analysis will in the long run provide a solution to the problems that face the serious student of politics in this area of the subject.

There are signs that the mechanistic comparison of 'Atlantis and Lyonesse' – by listing the features of their political systems side-by-side – is in decline. Cross-national analysis is becoming more general in scope, more theoretical and more behavioural.

As has been mentioned already, cross-national research is essentially a cooperative effort. This implies interpersonal interactions both in organizational and intellectual terms. In response to the exhortations of the leaders of the profession in articles and books, national associations have formed committees and sponsored cooperative research, official and unofficial grant-giving bodies have looked with favour on proposals which have an interstate basis, those studying relatively unknown countries have tried to relate their work to the body of accumulated knowledge and there has been a rapid growth in data banks and survey archives.

The greater emphasis on theory has led to wide-ranging studies which draw their evidence from every country in which it can be found. Many of these are in the general field of political economy and some take their original inspiration from Marxist social science. The roles of racial, ethnic and national minorities, for example, have formed the subject of many recent studies that start from the general problems in this field and use evidence, as far as this is possible, from the whole world. Examples include C. Enloe, *Ethnic Soldiers* (Penguin, 1980); A. D. Smith, *The Ethnic Revival* (Cambridge University Press, 1981); and M. Banton, *Racial and Ethnic Competition* (Cambridge University Press, 1983). The studies are also behavioural in that they draw on empirical material gathered and processed according to the standards of social science in general.

Comparative politics as a field of political studies has changed considerably in the last three decades. It is much less ethnocentric and unbalanced, it is better integrated with work in other fields such as political theory and behavioural research and it is supported by a stronger framework of institutions. The result is that the differences between implicit and explicit comparison are declining in importance, and the student may look forward to a time when the comparative analysis of individual political systems is fully integrated into general political science.

3
The quest for a science of politics: political behaviour
Jeffrey Stanyer

Introduction

In contrast to the titles 'comparative government' and 'cross-national analysis', whose meaning can be sensed by any intelligent person, the words that comprise the name of this branch of political studies – 'political' and 'behaviour' – in combination produce a phrase that can only be understood as a term of art or as a technical expression.

Behaviour is essentially a social concept and, when qualified by any one of a range of adjectives, such as 'moral', 'polite' and 'sexual', produces immediately recognizable forms of words whose connotations and denotations will be widely understood. But *political behaviour* is not such a form of words. Rather it is an esoteric expression whose use is largely restricted to specialists in the subject, including both supporters and critics of what it stands for. It was not used to identify a separate part of political studies until the 1920s and thus its meaning and significance can only be properly appreciated in the light of its recent history.

If it is regarded as a movement it is a set of ideas adopted by a few leading members of the 'profession' in the mid-1920s and vigorously prosecuted by example, preaching and through influence on post-graduate education, and eventually extended to all branches of political studies. It was also a protest against the state into which political studies had fallen immediately after the First World War; its leaders were intellectual revolutionaries and they inspired the 'young Turks' of the profession in the next decades. It can also be seen as an ideology; that is, as a weapon in the struggle for the acceptance of political studies in the eyes of established university subjects. It arose from the need for a science of politics in the battle for funds, status, jobs, professional autonomy and self-respect. To achieve legitimacy it is necessary to justify to others what is being done, to show that the methods used are reasonable and acceptable because they are identical with those used by established disciplines. If necessary, the 'intruder' in the list of academic subjects will copy the work of other more prestigious ones in its own subject-matter. Legitimacy also requires the establishment of an identity in theoretical terms by showing that there are distinctive concepts – theoretical terms, axioms, etc. – as well as adequate working tools and techniques. The study of politics also faced a problem of identity; what exactly was its subject matter? Behaviouralism answered this question in wide empirical terms. Politics was not the study of great ideas and great thinkers; it was what politicians of all types do, the activities of citizens when involved in politics, the decisions of public servants in internal and international affairs and the activities of groups and organizations that attempted to influence the actions of the state. Local politics was as important a source of evidence as 'the great affairs of state'. Hence behaviouralists thought in terms of different types of political behaviour – 'elite behaviour', 'mass behaviour', 'voting behaviour', 'committee behaviour', etc.

According to behaviouralists, political studies should start with research into matters of fact – what actually happens – and not only strive for accurate and complete description but also examine it for patterns, relationships, sequences, trends and cycles. The study of 'behaviour', therefore, contrasts with the 'institutional' and 'legal' approaches and to philosophical ways of analysis in terms of 'principles' and 'essences'. The new leaders of the profession were therefore also much concerned with the relationships between *politics* the subject and *politics* the activity – between doing and knowing, knowledge by description and knowledge by acquaintance and between 'practical' and 'theoretical' knowledge.

A superb illustration of early behaviouralism in political studies is given in H. F. Gosnell, *Machine Politics: Chicago Style* (originally Chicago University Press, 1937; now reprinted by Greenwood Press, New York, 1968). Students investigating the movement for a science of politics can hardly do better than look at this as an example of how an individual was inspired to undertake a massive piece of research and to persevere until the study was complete.

The main emphasis of this chapter will be on behaviouralism as a method of research in politics and its application to diverse subject matters. The reader should, however, first look at the general background to the behavioural movement.

Most of the general introductions to the study of politics deal with these developments, but the reader is recommended to look at three books of essays. Interdisciplinary subjects are discussed in S. M. Lipset (ed.), *Politics and the Social Sciences* (Oxford University Press, 1969), whilst concepts, methods and techniques are the subject of J. C. Charlesworth (ed.), *Contemporary Political Analysis* (Free Press, Collier–Macmillan, New York, 1967). A range of subjects is represented in A. Ranney (ed.), *Essays on the Behavioural Study of Politics* (University of Illinois Press, Urbana, Ill., 1962). As behaviouralism in its early years was largely American, the reader should refer to the works cited in the introductory section to Chapter 2 by A. Somit and J. Tanenhaus (1967), R. Jensen (1969), R. A. Dahl (1961) and H. Eulau (1963). A British view is given in D. E. Butler, *The Study of Political Behaviour* (Hutchinson, 1958).

Some appreciation of the range of distinct topics generally included under the heading of 'political behaviour' can be gained from the following books of readings: H. Eulau and others (eds.), *Political Behaviour* (Free Press, Glencoe, Ill., 1956); R. A. Dahl and D. E. Neubauer (eds.), *Readings in Modern Political Analysis* (Prentice-Hall, Englewood Cliffs, NJ, 1968); J. D. Barber (ed.), *Readings in Citizen Politics* (Markham Publishing Company, Chicago, 1970); and J. H. Kessel *et al.* (eds), *Micro-Politics* (Holt Rinehart and Winston, New York, 1970).

The interdisciplinary nature of the behavioural movement can be seen in the following rather personal selection from a wide range of works. Political sociology is represented by S. M. Lipset, 'Sociology and Political Science', *American Sociological Review*, **29/5** (1964), and in several books of readings: L. Coser (ed.), *Political Sociology* (Harper Torchbooks, New York, 1966); E. A. Nordlinger (ed.), *Politics and Society: Studies in Comparative Political Sociology* (Prentice-Hall, Englewood Cliffs, NJ, 1970); and E. Allardt and S. Rokkan (eds.), *Mass Politics: Studies in Political Sociology* (Free Press, New York, 1970). Controversies about the sociological method in politics have been pursued in a large number of articles; for instance, I. L. Horowitz, 'Sociology and Politics: The Myth of Functionalism Revisited', *Journal of Politics*, **25/2** (1963), and G. Sartori, 'From the Sociology of Politics to Political Sociology', *Government and Opposition*, **4/3** (1969) (reprinted in S. M. Lipset (1969, work cited). The best

general text, which adopts a very wide definition of the subject, is
R. E. Dowse and J. A. Hughes, *Political Sociology* (Wiley, 1972).

The change in inspiration for ambitious students of politics
during the 1960s is foreshadowed in W. C. Mitchell, 'The Shape of
Political Theory to Come: from Political Sociology to Political
Economy', *American Behavioural Scientist*, **11/2** (1967–1968) (re-
printed in S. M. Lipset (1969, work cited). An overview is also
provided by N. Frolich and J. A. Oppenheimer, *Modern Political
Economy* (Prentice-Hall, Foundations of Political Science series,
Englewood Cliffs, NJ, 1978). It is probably better, however, for a
student to read the original innovatory works in the tradition of
bourgeois economics. These include A. Downs, *An Economic
Theory of Democracy* (Harper and Row, New York, 1957); J.
Buchanan and G. Tullock, *The Calcalus of Consent* (Michigan
University Press, Ann Arbor, Michigan, 1962); C. E. Lindblom,
The Intelligence of Democracy (Free Press, New York, 1965);
R. A. Dahl, *A Preface to Democratic Theory* (Chicago University
Press, Chicago, 1956); and Mancur Olson, *The Logic of Collective
Action* (Harvard University Press, Cambridge, Mass., 1965). A
systematic comparison of pre-1970s work which favours economics
rather than sociology is B. M. Barry, *Sociologists, Economists and
Democracy* (Collier–Macmillan, 1970).

Political psychology has had periods of popularity with the work
of Harold Lasswell (*Psychopathology and Politics*, Viking Press,
1960, originally 1930), in the early 1950s with work on the
authoritarian personality (T. W. Adorno *et al.*, *The Authoritarian
Personality*, Harper and Row, New York, 1950) and R. Christie
and M. Jahoda (eds), *Studies in the Scope and Method of the
Authoritarian Personality* (Free Press, Glencoe, Ill., 1954) and in
the work of H. J. Eysenck, *Psychology and Politics* (Routledge
and Kegan Paul, 1954), some of which appears in his popular
paperbacks *Uses and Abuses of Psychology* (Penguin, 1953) and
Sense and Nonsense in Psychology (Penguin, 1957). Overviews are
provided by F. I. Greenstein, *Personality and Politics* (Markham
Publishing Company, Chicago, 1969); J. N. Knutson (ed.), *Handbook of Political Psychology* (Jossey-Bass, San Francisco, 1973);
A. C. Elms (ed.), *Personality in Politics* (Harcourt Brace Jovano-
vitch, New York, 1976); and L. N. Rieselbach and G. I. Balch
(eds), *Psychology and Politics* (Holt Rinehart and Winston, New
York, 1969).

The classic studies in political anthropology are M. Fortes and
E. E. Evans-Pritchard (eds), *African Political Systems* (Oxford
University Press, 1940) and E. R. Leach, *The Political Systems of
Highland Burma* (Bell, 1954). General surveys of interest are L.

Mair, *Primitive Government* (Penguin, 1962), M. J. Swartz, *Political Anthropology* (Aldine, Chicago, 1967) and G. Balandier, *Political Anthropology* (Penguin, 1972).

Political geography seems set to be a fashionable subject in the late 1980s with the recent foundation of a new journal with that title. The Fascist episode which threw the subject into disfavour is the subject of A. Gyorgy, *Geopolitics* (University of California Press, 1944, now available as a Johnson Reprint). Amongst more recent volumes are C. A. Fisher (ed.), *Essays in Political Geography* (1968), which deals largely with decolonization, R. K. Kasperson and J. V. Minghi, *The Structure of Political Geography* (Aldine, Chicago, 1969); J. R. V. Prescott, *Political Geography* (Methuen, 1972); R. Muir, *Modern Political Geography* (Macmillan, 1975); M. Glassner and H. J. de Blij (eds.), *Systematic Political Geography* (Wiley, New York, 3rd edn, 1980); and R. Muir and R. Paddison, *Politics, Geography and Behaviour* (Methuen, 1981).

The methodology of behavioural research

The original inspiration of behaviouralism involved a deliberate attempt to develop in the manner of the established sciences. One striking feature of the latter is their concern with standards of empirical investigation – with factual accuracy and completeness – and with standards of analysis – logical coherence. Science is also essentially a collective venture; the work of individuals must be capable of repetition and development by others. Idiosyncratic and personalized contributions cannot fulfil this function unless they have a minimum of compatibility with the work of others. Getting matters exactly and interpersonally right was therefore a major aim of the behavioural movement. Research in this tradition is characterized by deliberate connections with previous work, by precise definition and by a stress on methodology – often reflected in the inclusion of an 'appendix on methods'.

Students of politics are well advised to have on their bookshelves some of the general books on social research, such as F. Kerlinger, *Foundations of Behavioural Research* (Holt Rinehart and Winston, New York, 1964); C. A. Moser and G. Kalton, *Survey Methods in Social Investigation* (Heinemann, 2nd edn, 1972); B. H. Erickson and T. A. Nosanchuk, *Understanding Data* (Open University Press, 1979); and H. Blalock, *Social Statistics* (McGraw-Hill, New York, 1960). A new series – *Contemporary Social Research* – published by Allen and Unwin also includes helpful volumes as, for instance, M. Bulmer, *The Uses of Social Research* (No.3, 1982) and C. Hakim, *Secondary Analysis in Social Research* (No.5, 1982). These, and many similar volumes, not only provide help in dealing with matters of detail but also offer introductions to the activity of empirical research in general.

There are fewer books that are specifically aimed at a political studies readership, but mention may be made of T. R. Gurr, *Politimetrics: an Introduction to Quantitative Macropolitics* (Prentice-Hall, Englewood Cliffs, NJ, 1972) and E. R. Tufte, *Data Analysis for Politics and Policy* (Prentice-Hall, Englewood Cliffs, NJ, 1974). Some of the popular paperbacks on statistics include political examples; for instance, D. J. Bartholomew and E. E. Bassett, *Let's Look at the Figures* (Penguin, 1971) and R. L. Meek, *Figuring out Society* (Fontana, 1972).

The data of political behaviour

Behavioural research in politics involves data of two main types; individual and aggregate. Though the basic unit of analysis is the individual, the forms in which the facts are collected and published often destroy the information relating to named persons, and thus the data are available only for some aggregate – a constituency, a locality, even a state. Facts relating to collections of individuals are less than ideal for the political scientist but this is compensated for by the low cost, great variety and temporal and geographical range that published statistics exhibit. The tradition of aggregate analysis – for instance, in electoral geography and policy outcomes research – draws on nineteenth-century intellectual developments in demography, economic and social statistics, and more remotely on developments in the applied sciences of agricultural zoology and botany and environmental medicine.

The word 'individual' in 'individual level data' is systematically ambiguous, and care must be taken to distinguish between data which relate to persons (voters, activists, legislators, cabinet ministers, etc.) and those which relate to other entities, such as committees, boards, groups, etc, when they are considered as units that 'behave'. In this respect politics follows economics which operates with individuals – consumers and workers – and entities – households and firms – as part of the same theoretical framework.

The higher the status of the persons or groups studied, the more likely that there will be public information available about individual behaviour. Thus members of executives and legislatures have their actions and activities scrutinized and recorded for all to analyse. Legislative committees are also generally and automatically publicized so that their behaviour is also open to inspection.

But for the most part the behaviour of people in mass politics – for instance, elections – is concealed by the process of aggregation. For this reason, students have had to turn to the methods pioneered by sociologists and social psychologists for finding out about citizens as electors, voters, party members, protestors and demonstrators, 'consumers' of public services, etc. Methods of studying the individual in mass politics range from the large-scale social survey to the in-depth psychological interview. More than anything else, political behaviour has been associated with the use of interviews and questionnaires administered to separate individuals.

Two final points must be made about the data of political studies. First, students of political behaviour have to rely heavily on government statistical publications, but these are not necessarily prepared in forms that are appropriate for researchers and easily obtainable by outsiders. The publication of volumes of 'political facts' mirrors the collection of historical and economic statistics. There are, for instance, D. E. Butler and J. Freeman, *British Political Facts* (Macmillan, 1st edn, 1963) and the series of *British Political Reference Publications*, edited by F. W. S. Craig (Chichester, continuing). Comparative Government as a subject has also felt the need for systematic statistical series published in convenient forms. Second, because of the cost of obtaining sophisticated data – whether aggregate or individual – the political studies profession has joined with other social sciences in creating data banks, survey archives and other ways of making available to other people engaged in related research the information collected in individual projects. The Social Science Research Council Archive at the University of Essex is part of an international network of information storage centres and provides UK political scientists with access to national and foreign data of many different kinds. For advice on using its facilities the reader should contact it directly at The University.

Behavioural research procedure

Because it attempts to be scientific, particularly interpersonal and cumulative, the study of political behaviour has tended to approximate to an easily recognizable pattern. Research procedures derive from the paradigms of science outlined in the introduction to Chapter 2 and embody the methodological principles that are described in the section on 'methodology' above. Individual research projects, though not necessarily undertaken in a given historic order, tend to embody a standard sequence of stages.

Their technicalities can best be understood by referring to the standard works on social science research methods mentioned above.

The main stages are: clarification of the issues involved in the problem under investigation; the choice of empirical material for investigation; consideration of a range of explanatory factors; the postulation of hypotheses to be tested; the use of technical methods to test the said hypotheses; and the assessment of the whole process, particularly of causal relations and the extent to which the research has answered the questions originally posed.

Applications of behavioural methods

The behavioural revolution has had an impact on all the major divisions of political studies, but some show its influence more clearly and more substantially than others. Its roles in international politics and public administration are less substantial than in 'political behaviour' narrowly defined. The major areas in which the approach has been used are elections, legislatures, the courts, parties and other political organizations; where it has been used elsewhere, the author is often regarded as an innovator or 'deviant'.

Electoral behaviour

The study of elections was one of the earliest substantial developments in the behavioural movement. It is also one of the best for illustrating both the major concerns of protagonists of a 'science of politics' and the variety of methods and techniques that behaviouralists use. The connections between traditional and new approaches can also be clearly seen, as the study of political behaviour involves defining a role for law, history and normative philosophical considerations. In particular, behavioural research has contributed substantially to the evolution of the concept of democracy in Western societies.

There are many collections of articles and essays on electoral behaviour including E. Burdick and A. J. Brodbeck (eds), *American Voting Behaviour*, (Free Press, Glencoe, Ill., 1959); A. Campbell *et al.* (eds), *Elections and the Political Order* (Wiley, New York, 1966); M. K. Jennings and L. H. Zeigler (eds), *The Electoral Process* (Prentice-Hall, Englewood Cliffs, NJ, 1966); R. Rose (ed.), *Electoral Behaviour* (Macmillan, 1974); and R. G.

Niemi and H. F. Weisberg (eds), *Controversies in American Voting Behaviour* (W. H. Freeman & Co., San Francisco, USA, 1976).

AGGREGATE STUDIES

Election results constitute the most elaborate type of political statistics that can be found, partly because they are inherently quantitative and partly because they are systematically collected by public authorities, including the state itself. The extent to which they are aggregated varies from country to country and from electoral system to electoral system. If statistics are available for the smallest areas – polling districts – then the research will be more sophisticated and informative than if the ballot papers are taken to some central place for counting.

Perhaps the earliest use of aggregate electoral statistics was by politicians attempting to gerrymander constituencies in their own interest, but the French, in their development of electoral geography, must be regarded as the academic pioneers of this type of behavioural research. The most useful book for this aspect is P. J. Taylor and R. J. Johnston, *The Geography of Elections* (Penguin, 1979). The early American behaviouralists made many attempts to use election results in rigorous analysis and extended their interest to Europe. The tradition has continued to produce small pieces of research since that time, often based on state or local elections, such as J. Kim *et al.*, 'Voter Turnout among the American States', *American Political Science Review,* **69/1** (1975). In Britain an early interest was shown in the study of local election results, and the original work has been repeated on several occasions. Many of the references are cited in P. Davies and K. Newton, 'An Aggregate Data Analysis of Turnout and Party Voting in Local Elections', *Sociology,* **8/2** (1974). At the national level the analysis of general election results is an integral part of the British approach, and some of the most interesting work is still based on constituency statistics, which are easily available and provide a reliable time series. Examples of this are to be found in Appendices in the series of Nuffield General Election Studies, now edited by David Butler and an associate and published by Macmillan.

Aggregate election results usually include the following data for each electoral area: total number of electors; number of seats at stake; total number of votes cast; number of valid candidates; number of votes cast for each candidate; sex and party affiliation of each candidate; and whether an incumbent or not. They therefore provide information on important subjects for politicians, political journalists and political theorists on, for instance,

turnout, competitiveness, partisanship and changing party fortunes and on candidate performance and political recruitment.

For the would-be political scientist aggregate election statistics
have several major advantages. As they are often available on a
uniform basis for the whole country and for a long period of time
they enable the researcher to give a comparative and historical
dimension to his or her work which is usually lacking in the
'snapshot' survey research. They are also easily available and
cheap to use, and therefore replication and cumulation of research
is feasible. There are, however, serious difficulties with aggregate
data. There are undoubtedly vagaries of collection which are
outside the control of the researcher, and if series are incomplete
because of government policy, there is nothing that can be done.
More fundamental, however, is the problem of relating aggregate
statistics to political *behaviour* itself. Ultimately its study must
make reference to what people do – to the activities of electors,
workers, candidates, to electioneering through the expenditure of
money, doorstep canvassing, the publication of leaflets, press,
radio and television advertising, the spread of opinion by word of
mouth; to individual voting decisions about whether to vote and
who to vote for; to factors affecting the result via their impact on
individuals, such as death and coming of age, immigration and
emigration, which affect the composition of the electorate in
individual terms, and salient political issues and personalities,
which affect existing electors. The relationship between aggregate
and individual electoral behaviour is usually discussed under the
heading of 'the ecological fallacy'. This problem was originally
popularized by W. S. Robinson in 'Ecological Correlations and the
Behaviour of Individuals', *American Sociological Review,* **15/3**
(1950), and since that time both sociologists and geographers have
given much thought and effort to avoiding its implications.

STUDIES OF INDIVIDUALS

Aggregate statistics are net figures; for instance, they obliterate all
the gross changes that take place between elections and present
one measure only – a number which has resulted from the
summation of a variety of movements. It is not surprising that
students of political behaviour have felt impelled to study individuals directly in order to obtain the sort of information that is
concealed by published figures.

Serious research into individual electoral behaviour began with
the study of Erie County, Ohio, 1940, by Paul Lazarsfeld *et al.*,
and published originally as *The People's Choice* (Columbia University Press, New York, 1944). This began a tradition which was

continued by A. Campbell *et al., The Voter Decides* (Row-Peterson, Chicago, 1954), B. Berelson *et al., Voting* (University of Chicago Press, 1954) and culminated in *The American Voter* by A. Campbell *et al.,* (Wiley, New York, 1960). The methods perfected by the authors of the latter study have been used again and again in the US and extended to other liberal democracies. The most important British study at the time of writing is D. E. Butler and D. Stokes, *Political Change in Britain* (Macmillan, 1st edn, 1969) but reports on the elections of the 1970s are expected shortly.

As the title of the Butler and Stokes book indicates, the main focus of academic electoral research has been on explaining change between one election and the next. By 'political change' is meant change in any one of the dimensions of political behaviour, such as turnout, competition, voting decisions and party support. Thus turnout rises and falls, competitiveness increases and declines, the electorate becomes more or less volatile, new parties are formed and the social composition of existing ones evolves in various ways. Much of this literature is based on the concepts of 'party identification' and 'political generation'. For a discussion of the bases of political allegiance there is S. M. Lipset and S. Rokkan (eds.), *Party Systems and Voter Alignments* (Free Press, Glencoe, Ill., 1967) and for the use of party identification as a component of electoral decision, I. Budge (ed.), *Party Identification and Beyond* (Wiley, 1976). Factors such as the level of inflation or unemployment, controversies about candidates and the need for new policies can cause a change in vote without a change in basic allegiance, and sway 'independents', that is, those who claim to have no party identification. Academic analysis on this approach concludes that events in the week up to and including election-day, therefore, can have only a minor effect on a few electors because most people have firmly made their decision well before then.

Legislative behaviour

The study of legislatures ranks second to elections in historical and contemporary importance in behavioural studies, and there have been times when it has seemed to be the most dynamic and innovative field of research. Like elections, it has been criticized for overemphasis on the measurable, for instance, roll-call votes, but the nature of the material relating to parliaments, assemblies, councils, boards and committees has given the subject its special character. Aggregate quantified data are much less generally available on legislatures, as they vary tremendously in the extent to which they create, in the course of their ordinary functioning, statistics of interest to the student of politics. But behaviour within the legislature is much more open to inspection than is behaviour within the electorate. Elected bodies also tend to be small, certainly when compared with the mass electorate, and thus the individual political actor is not totally submerged in units of thousands or millions. Thus with hard work it is possible to describe and analyse the working of a legislature in a detail which is impossible for the electorate. What legislative behaviour loses in terms of official statistics it more than gains in its potential for direct measurement by the students themselves.

Unlike 'elections', there is no single straightforward definition of 'legislature'. The tradition has developed, however, of referring to elected bodies and to bodies created by appointment from them by this title. It thus denotes indiscriminately parliaments, houses, senates, congresses, assemblies, councils, commissions, soviets, boards and, by extension, committees and subcommittees. There is no need for a tight definition, but marginal cases may be treated on merit. The concept of a *legislature* is appropriate wherever a body has a definite membership charged with specific tasks of collective decision making. The word 'behaviour' is systematically ambiguous in this context. Sometimes it refers to the activities of collectivities such as the legislature itself or one of its parts, such as a committee, and at other times it refers to the actions of individual legislators. Both are equally 'legislative behaviour'.

Each legislature has its own distinctive characteristics which give it a personality of its own separate from those of its parts and its individual members. There are two widely used general approaches to legislatures in themselves. First, they may be treated as formal organizations, that is, as a special category of a general social type which includes firms, trade unions, churches, government departments, political parties, prisons, hospitals, schools and universities. An example of this approach is to be found in L. A. Froman, 'Organisation Theory and the Explanation of Important Characteristics of Congress', *American Political Science Review,* **62/2** (1968). Second, they may be treated as social institutions (of which formal organizations are, of course, a category). This is done by N. W. Polsby in 'The Institutionalisation of the US House of Representatives', *American Political Science Review,* **62/1** (1968).

It is widely believed that legislative behaviour is strongly influenced by a number of general characteristics of the body. K. C. Wheare explores some of these, in a largely non-behavioural spirit, in his book *Legislatures* (Oxford University Press, 1963).

Among the potentially important factors are size, composition, constitutional position, internal structure and procedures. Even the shape and size of the meeting place has been thought to be significant – compare the continental semi-circular chamber with the adversarial House of Commons pattern.

The two most influential and interesting case studies are of American state legislatures: J. C. Wahlke *et al., The Legislative System* (Wiley, New York, 1962), and J. D. Barber, *The Lawmakers* (Yale University Press, New Haven, 1965). There are few equivalent studies from other political systems but the reader should be aware of the work of D. Macrae, Jr, *Parliament, Parties and Society in France, 1946–1958* (Macmillan, 1967), and P. Norton, *Dissension in the House of Commons, 1945–74* (Macmillan, 1975).

Much of the best work on legislative behaviour is in the form of case studies published as articles. The reader should first consult the early basic collection of readings edited by J. C. Wahlke and H. Eulau, *Legislative Behaviour* (Free Press, Glencoe, Ill., 1959). There are also many books of readings on congressional behaviour; such as R. K. Huitt and R. J. Peabody (eds), *Congress – Two Decades of Analysis* (Harper and Row, New York, 1969); R. J. Peabody and N. W. Polsby (eds), *New Perspectives on the House of Representatives* (Rand-McNally, Chicago, 1969); and J. Cooper and G. C. Mackenzie (eds), *The House at Work* (University of Texas Press, Austin, Texas, 1981). Comparative legislative behaviour is also the subject of several useful books of readings: H. Hirsch and D. M. Hancock (eds), *Comparative Legislative Systems* (Free Press, New York, 1971); S. C. Patterson and J. C. Wahlke (eds), *Comparative Legislative Behaviour* (Wiley, New York, 1972); and A. Kornberg (ed.), *Legislatures in Comparative Perspective* (David McKay, New York, 1973).

LEGISLATIVE DECISION MAKING

The analysis of legislative decision making has proved to be a fertile field for the development and use of advanced behavioural methods. How do legislatures make up their collective minds? A legislative decision is the product of processes which may be lengthy and of individual contributions, which may themselves be products of other processes and other individual contributions. The basic problem for the rigorous student of political behaviour is how to identify the exact part played by each member of a legislature at each stage of the relevant process.

The early 'scientific' students of politics leapt at the hard evidence provided by those legislatures that insist on recording in the official proceedings exactly how each member has behaved – 'for', 'against', 'abstained', 'absent'. The lists of names in *Hansard* or an equivalent document are snapshots of behaviour printed for ever, to be analysed at leisure and with a feeling of security in the immutability of the facts. The use of roll-call vote analysis is another good example of the way in which political behaviour as a field of study is driven on by the desire for accuracy, completeness and objectivity. The original behavioural enthusiasm has eventually given way to a more considered and balanced judgement. Where they exist in large numbers, they are invaluable as evidence about legislative decision making, but they need very careful interpretatation and assessment.

If the student remembers all the problems involves in this type of analysis, roll-call votes can provide important evidence relating to those legislatures that use them frequently. In particular, they can be used to investigate problems with a historical dimension – for instance, trends, cycles and erratic variation – to identify groups within the legislature – blocs, coalitions, alliances and cliques – and to assess the contributions of individuals. Among the phenomena that have particularly interested students of legislative behaviour are log rolling, the pork barrel and vote trading, leadership, bargaining over time and, in relation to individual decisions, the effects of constituency opinion and interest groups, the extent of party discipline in the legislature and the participation rates of different types of individual member.

Despite articles expressing some doubts about the method, such as W. Crane, 'A Caveat on Roll-Call Studies of Party Voting', *Midwest Journal of Political Science,* **4/3** (1960), and F. I. Greenstein and E. F. Jackson, 'A Second Look at the Validity of Roll Call Analysis', *Midwest Journal of Political Science,* **7/2** (May, 1963), it has been a standard technique for over thirty years. For examples, there are W. H. Riker, 'The Paradox of Voting and Congressional Rules for Voting on Amendments', *American Political Science Review,* **52/2** (1958); S. C. Patterson, 'Dimensions of Voting in a One-Party State Legislature', *Public Opinion Quarterly,* **26/2** (1962); L. A. Froman, 'The Importance of Individuality in Voting in Congress', *Journal of Politics,* **25/2** (1963); J. T. Murphy, 'Political Parties and the Pork Barrel', *American Political Science Review,* **68/1** (1974); and H. B. Asher and H. F. Weisberg, 'Voting Change in Congress', *American Journal of Political Science,* **22/2** (1978).

ORGANIZATIONAL DECISION MAKING

There are also organizational decisions that have to be taken by legislatures. These create the internal institutional structure of the legislature and the allocation of personnel to positions so created. The multiplicity of different lines of research makes it impossible to do more than choose one topic to illustrate this dimension of legislative behaviour.

Legislative behaviour is structured by the working of very general processes within the body's boundaries. The general name for those that affect individual members or the personnel of the legislature is 'recruitment', which is often also held to include organizational 'socialization'.

Political recruitment in general is the process by which individuals achieve a public office – by election in the case of parliamentarians and congressmen and by systematic selection procedures in the case of civil servants and federal executives. Persuading individuals to join a political party and firms a trade association is sometimes called 'recruitment', but this phenomenon lacks an important element of the total picture of the process – the fact that public offices are finite in number and few in relation to possible incumbents.

The main stages are: candidature, screening, socialization, re-recruitment and promotion (and their opposites) and 'exit'. The study of recruitment to an established legislature should start with the incumbents, because their decisions form a basic stage in the recruitment cycle. The final selection may result from an elaborate set of activities, including those within political parties and other groups, and at the end the voters have the last word.

Once elected, the individual undergoes a process of socialization, that is, a process of learning the 'rules of the game' and the ritual forms in which activities take place, of acquiring factual knowledge about the system and deciding what part he or she would like to play.

During service in a legislature the member undergoes a large number of experiences, some pleasant and others unpleasant. These are part of the learning process, but they also contribute to the extent to which the individual becomes committed to the organization. In some cases he or she will be so alienated that mid-term resignation will occur; in others involvement is so intense that the individual acquires a lifelong attachment to it, leaving only with great reluctance or through death. Of the events experienced by the legislator, probably the most significant are those of promotion and demotion. As legislatures are normally internally differentiated in a complex manner, they provide, through the hierarchy of roles of different degrees of status and power, a career structure.

The distinct stages in the process may be illustrated by the following selection of articles, most of which are case studies: H. Jacob, 'Initial Recruitment of Elected Officials in the United States – a Model', *Journal of Politics*, **24/4** (1962); L. G. Seligman, 'Political Recruitment and Party Structure', *American Political Science Review*, **55/1** (1961); A. L. Hunt and R. E. Pendley, 'Community Gatekeepers', *Midwest Journal of Political Science*, **16/3** (1972); R. J. Tobin and E. Keynes, 'Institutional Differences in the Recruitment Process', *American Journal of Political Science*, **19/4** (1975); S. Merritt, 'Winners and Losers', *American Journal of Political Science*, **21/4** (1977); S. E. Frantzich, 'De-Recruitment', *Western Political Quarterly*, **31/1** (1978); A. D. Cover, 'One Good Term Deserves Another', *American Journal of Political Science*, **21/3** (1977); and D. D. Kincaid, 'Over His Dead Body', *Western Political Quarterly*, **31/1** (1978).

The political career and its relationship to the internal structure of legislatures has been investigated in a large number of case studies. One of the most influential, which also deals with other factors, is N. W. Polsby, 'The Institutionalisation of the US House of Representatives', *American Political Science Review*, **62/1** (1968). Case studies include S. Kernell, 'Towards Understanding 19th Century Congressional Careers', *American Journal of Political Science*, **21/4** (1977); C. S. Bullock, 'House Careerists', *American Political Science Review*, **66/4** (1972); C. S. Bullock, 'Committee Transfers in the United States' House of Representatives', *Journal of Politics*, **35/1** (1973); and all the literature on the role of seniority within legislatures, an early study of which is G. Goodwin, 'The Seniority System in Congress', *American Political Science Review*, **53/2** (1959).

OTHER TYPES OF BEHAVIOURAL RESEARCH

Elections and legislatures have constituted by far the largest sources of materials for behavioural research, but the approach has had a noticeable impact in a number of other fields.

The field of judicial behaviour has been of special interest because it connects directly to traditional concerns of students of liberal democracies – the rule of law and justice within the state. What factors influence judges when they make judicial decisions? Is there a difference between a judge sitting alone and a body of judges operating through majority decision? Are judicial attitudes determined by the individual's personal history and social background? Are judges consistent in their decisions, showing a persistent and predictable bias towards liberal or conservative arguments? Concern with these questions has led those who study constitutional law to the use of a whole range of behavioural techniques – scaling, interviews, content analysis, even algebra. There have been controversies about the use of quantitative methods in this field; some have felt that research is itself a threat to judicial institutions and inappropriate in the context of liberal democracy.

The range of techniques is illustrated in G. Schubert (ed.), *Judicial Decision-making* (Free Press, Glencoe, Ill., 1963), and G. Schubert and D. J. Danelski (eds), *Comparative Judicial Behaviour* (Oxford University Press, 1969).

Most aspects of politics have been studied from a behavioural perspective, and the literature on political parties will, for reasons of space, have to represent a wide range of specific studies. There are, for example, S. J. Eldersveld, *Political Parties: a Behavioural Analysis* (Rand-McNally, Chicago, 1964); W. J. Crotty *et al.* (eds), *Political Parties and Political Behaviour* (Allyn and Bacon, Boston, 1966); and W. J. Crotty (ed.), *Approaches to the Study of Party Organisation* (Allyn and Bacon, Boston, 1968).

Public administration, international politics and local government studies all have examples of behavioural literature within them, but in general they have been less affected by the behavioural movement than has the study of elections, legislatures and the courts.

Anti-behaviouralism

It is important for the student of political behaviour to be aware of the range of criticisms that have been made of the whole of the literature within this tradition of research and analysis. Some of the important ones are to be found in C. McCoy and J. Playford (eds), *Apolitical Politics: a Critique of Behaviouralism* (Crowell, New York, 1967); and there is C. Bay, 'Politics and Pseudo-Politics', *American Political Science Review*, **59/1** (1965); K. Y. Kim, 'The Limits of Behavioural Explanation in Politics', *Canadian Journal of Economics and Political Science*, **31/3** (1965); F. D. Wormuth, 'Matched-Dependent Behaviouralism', *Western Political Quarterly*, **20/4** (1967); B. Susser, 'The Behavioural Ideology', *Political Studies*, **22/3** (1974); E. J. Meehan, 'Sheep, Goats and Roses', *Polity*, **1/4** (1969); E. Berndtson, 'Political Science in the Era of Post-Behaviouralism; The Need for Self-Reflection', *Scandinavian Political Studies*, **10** (1975); and M. E. Kirn, 'Behaviouralism, Post-Behaviouralism and the Philosophy of Science: Two Houses, One Plague', *Review of Politics*, **39/1** (1977).

Conclusion

It would be wrong to end on a pessimistic note. Despite the criticisms of the anti-behaviouralists, the pressures for a science of politics remain as strong as ever. It is to be expected that research in the behavioural tradition will continue to flourish and to exert an influence on all other fields of political studies. As Dahl says (1961, work cited), 'The behavioural mood will not disappear, then, because it has failed. It will disappear rather because it has succeeded'.

4
International politics and international relations
Peter Butler

'International politics' and 'international relations'

The terms in the title of this chapter are often used interchangeably. The presence of one rather than the other in the title of a textbook or the name of an academic department or course is no guide as to what will be offered there. For the sake of brevity, the present writer will use the term 'international politics' to refer to the academic study of what is sometimes also known as 'international relations', 'world politics', 'global politics' or some other cognate term. However, we will suggest, later on, that there are sometimes good reasons for making more fundamental distinctions between the meanings of such terms

International politics and international history

Popularly, students of international politics are thought to be interested in recent and contemporary goings-on in the relations between states. Such subject matter does indeed receive considerable treatment. This chapter should be read in conjunction with Chapter 13. Journals such as *International Affairs* (Oxford University Press, for the Royal Institute of International Affairs), *Foreign Affairs* (The Council on Foreign Relations), *Foreign*

Policy (The Carnegie Endowment for International Peace) and *Orbis* (the Foreign Policy Research Institute, in association with the Graduate Program in International Relations, University of Pennsylvania) offer informed comment on and analysis of recent and current events and issues in international politics. *The World Today* (The Royal Institute of International Affairs) offers a monthly analysis of various topics of contemporary significance. The International Institute for Strategic Studies publishes a large amount of material dealing with contemporary military and defence matters, including the series of *Adelphi Papers* and the annual issues of *The Military Balance* and *Strategic Survey*. Cumulative works such as *Keesing's Contemporary Archives* provide a useful collection of continuously updated information about world affairs. Peter Calvocoressi's *World Politics since 1945* (4th edn, Longman, 1982) attempts a longer-term analysis of recent international history.

Even though a distinction between international politics and international history is sometimes evident in the existence of separate departments in an academic institution ('international relations' and 'international history' at the London School of Economics, for example), international historians are commonly found in departments of international politics, and courses offered by such departments will often include extensive coverage of recent history and current affairs. Conversation between international historians and other students of international politics is maintained in the very full review section of *International Affairs* and in the pages of journals such as the *Review of International Studies* (Butterworths, for the British International Studies Association), *International Relations* (The David Davies Memorial Institute for International Studies), *World Politics* (Princeton University Press) and *International Studies Quarterly* (Butterworths, for the International Studies Association).

However, a distinction between international history and international politics is justified. The skills of the international historian are not, in general, different from those of other historians, even though the nearness of the events studied poses its own problems and provides its own opportunities for the acquisition of data. However, whereas the international historian is mainly concerned to elucidate a distinct happening, sequence of events or period of time, the student of international politics is more concerned to attain a general understanding of the kinds of happenings and issues with which international politics confronts us. This is not to say that the international historian makes no use of general understandings in order to cast light on particular occurrences or issues; nor that the student of international politics makes no recourse to history as an aid to the attainment of general understanding. The difference is one of emphasis. For the international historian, general understandings usually play a secondary role, subsidiary to the main task of giving an account of a happening, series of events or a period of time. For the student of international politics, the pursuit of general understanding is the primary task.

International politics and political science

Many aspects of the study of international politics have close links with well-established branches of the study of politics within states. The investigation of the reasons for different national styles of foreign policy can be part of the study of comparative government. International organizations experience problems in reaching and giving effect to decisions that would be familiar to students of public administration. Political sociologists would not have to move far from their main concerns in order to find material for study in the public acceptance of, and participation in, the foreign policies of states. Historians of political thought and political philosophers will find authors who have sought to apply general ideas about domestic politics, including ideas about political obligation, to the international level.

That much of the study of international politics involves what may be regarded as extensions to the international level of topics familiar to political scientists raises the question as to why international politics has a distinct identity. Why is there not simply an effort to extend those topics to include their international aspects? There is a variety of reasons for this: some to do with the nature of the subject matter; and some to do with contingent historical circumstances.

Politics within the state occurs within a framework of government, and this is reflected in the study of domestic politics. The various branches of the study of domestic politics are concerned with the machinery of government. Sometimes, the concern is an immediate one: with aspects of the process of government, such as legislation; or with the morality or rightness of certain types of government action. At other times, the concern with government is less obvious. The study of the ways in which children acquire certain attitudes towards politics, for example, does not seem to be closely linked with a concern with government. But such a study derives its significance from the importance of the knowledge gained for a more general understanding of life within a governed political setting: how such a life may continue, change or collapse.

International politics, by contrast, is not conducted within a governed political setting. There is no world government that possesses or claims the kind of jurisdiction over states that governments always claim and often possess over their citizens. Article 2 of the Charter of the United Nations states that that organization, which comes closest to being a 'world government', is 'based on the principle of the sovereign equality of all its members'; and its members are states, not individuals. And in Western political thought, we find it asserted that a government's responsibilities to its citizens impose upon it a duty not to place those citizens under an alien authority over which they may have little or no control. This was the view of, for example, the Swiss jurist Emeric de Vattel, whose book, *The Law of Nations* (Carnegie Institute of Washington, 1916), first published in 1758, provides a useful statement of this kind of understanding of the relationship between sovereign and subject. The better-known Thomas Hobbes in his *Leviathan*, first published in 1651, saw, for different reasons, no necessity for a government to be set over states. Although states existed in a condition akin to that which men inhabited prior to the formation of government – 'a state and posture of gladiators' – he noted that states, unlike men, could arm themselves successfully and defend themselves against attack.

Among the reasons, then, for the distinctiveness of the study of international politics are the absence of government from the relations between states, and the way in which the submission of states to international control has been seen as neither necessary nor appropriate. In passing, we should note the view that such an absence of government disqualifies the relations between states from being described as political. Bernard Crick, in *In Defence of Politics* (Wiedenfeld and Nicolson, 1962), puts forward this kind of view.

Other reasons have contributed to the distinctiveness of the subject. The absence of government over states has led to an acceptance by many that international politics is conducted in a manner that must reflect the interests of states in their survival and aggrandizement rather than the wellbeing and progress of the community of states and humanity in general. The debate between representatives of Melos and Athens that Thucydides, writing in the fifth century BC, portrays in *The Peloponnesian War* (Penguin, 1954) is a classic description of the tension between the claims of justice and the concern for power and security. The view that Thucydides attributes to the Athenians – 'that in fact the strong do what they have the power to do and the weak accept what they have to accept' – is close to that of Hans Morgenthau in the most influential Western textbook published since the Second World War: Morgenthau's *Politics Among Nations* (Knopf, 5th edn, 1978), which first appeared in 1947. Morgenthau states that 'domestic and international politics are but two different manifestations of the same phenomenon: "the struggle for power"'; but there are more competitors to his view of domestic politics than to his assessment of international politics.

While the separateness of international politics has to some extent been a product of the belief that a struggle for power is much more central to relations between states than is the case in domestic politics, the distinct identity of the subject has also been promoted in a different, though related, way. In a struggle for power amongst states, war is a means of seeking or preserving power. Indeed, the classic statement of the role of war – Karl von Clausewitz's *On War*, first published in 1832; (abridged edn, Penguin, 1968) – condemns war as meaningless unless it serves political ends in this way. In domestic politics, by contrast, the recourse to violence, whether by a government, a people or a group, is most commonly seen as indicating a collapse of politics, rather than its continuance by other means. Whereas the domestic polity is only exceptionally confronted with the possibility of collapse into violence, the potentiality of such a collapse in international order is much greater. The claim that war makes to be a part of international politics is, then, another reason for the distinctiveness of international politics. Indeed, the concern to prevent war was the driving force behind the separate development of the subject after the First World War. The first Chair of International Politics, at Aberystwyth, was endowed in 1919, and given the name of the Woodrow Wilson Chair, in optimistic recognition of Wilson's peace efforts. In the inter-war years, the study of the international legal order and proposals for its improvement occupied much of the effort of students of international politics. Morgenthau's 'realism', as set out in *Politics Among Nations* (work cited) was offered as an alternative to this so-called 'idealism'. The subtitle of Morgenthau's book is, interestingly, 'the struggle for power and peace'. Peace is seen as a product not of legal schemes but of the watchfulness and skill of diplomats and statesmen in noticing and remedying dangerous alterations in the global power structure. As we will see, 'realism' in this sense still exerts a powerful influence in the study of international politics, even though the general concern with patterns of global power has been joined by more scientific writing on various topics, and by a re-emergence of writing concerning international morality and the preconditions of peace.

More detailed accounts of the history of the development of the subject, setting out the chronology of concerns which have predominated – from the 'idealism' of the inter-war years, through post-war 'realism', scientific and behavioural approaches of the 1960s and 1970s, to present concerns about policy, peace and morality – are to be found in a number of places. Two of the chapters in *The Aberystwyth Papers*, edited by Brian Porter (Oxford University Press, 1972), are especially good: William Olson's on 'The Growth of a Discipline' and Hedley Bull's on 'The Theory of International Politics, 1919–1969'. Bull deals with attempts to contribute to 'the body of general propositions that may be advanced about political relations between states, or more generally about world politics'. Other useful accounts of the development of the subject are provided by Richard Little's chapter, 'The Evolution of International Relations as a Social Science' in *The Study and Teaching of International Relations*, edited by R. C. Kent and G. P. Nielsson (Frances Pinter, 1980), and in the entries for 'International Relations' in the *International Encyclopaedia of the Social Sciences* and the current edition of the *Encyclopaedia Britannica*.

A variety of approaches

A very large number of distinct approaches to the study of international politics has been identified. James Rosenau, in his collection *International Politics and Foreign Policy* (Free Press, 2nd edn, 1969) identified four kinds of concern with the international system as a whole, fourteen kinds of theories and approaches to studying the action and interaction of states and thirteen 'research techniques and orientations'. Other works that seek to identify different approaches and perspectives include Joseph Frankel's *Contemporary International Theory and the Behaviour of States* (Oxford University Press, 1973), Robert Lieber's *Theory and World Politics* (George Allen and Unwin, 1973) and Trevor Taylor's collection, *Approaches and Theory in International Relations* (Longman, 1978). A more compendious survey which attempts to introduce students to the whole field is *Contending Theories of International Relations*, by J. E. Dougherty and R. L. Pfaltzgraff (Lipincott, 1971).

In an attempt to manage this complexity, we shall use a simpler categorization of approaches, with three main headings. First, one major concern has been with the attainment of a satisfactory appreciation of the nature of international politics as a whole. Second, we can find investigators who have operated at what have been called different 'levels of analysis': some have been concerned with the international system as a whole; some with the state as an actor in international politics; and others with the roles of individuals, organizations and other kinds of entity that seem to play distinct parts in international politics. Third, we must notice that different writers have pursued different kinds of method in their search for understanding, the major difference being between those who claim to pursue a 'scientific' method and those who have been referred to as more 'traditional' in their approaches, using the techniques of the lawyer, historian and philosopher. Obviously, these are three overlapping categories, in the sense that an assertion about the general nature of international politics may be the product of investigation at a variety of levels of analysis, conducted according to a variety of methods. To categorize a writer according to the level of analysis at which he operates is to say nothing of his general understanding of the nature of international politics, nor of the method he uses.

Modes of understanding the general nature of international politics

The notion of 'an understanding of the general nature of international politics' is not an easy one. Machiavelli, in *the Prince*, written in 1513 (Penguin, 1970) offers, from the standpoint of Renaissance politics, a set of prescriptions for rulers that is plainly based on a general view of the politics of princedoms as occurring in an arena in which the strong take what they can and the weak give what they must. It is a general understanding that is derived from Machiavelli's view of men as 'fickle, lying and deceivers', by whom it is better to be feared than loved. Applied to the level of international politics, such a perspective has been called 'realism'. 'Political Realism', writes Morgenthau in *Politics Among Nations* (work cited), 'believes that politics, like society in general, is governed by objective laws that have their roots in human nature'. And human nature is such that the conduct of men bears out the assumption that 'statesmen think and act in terms of interest defined as power'. For realists, the dominant motif in international politics is the search for power by governments. It is a search which takes priority over efforts to attain moral goals. Indeed, to pursue such goals to the detriment of his state is, for realists, an abrogation of the statesman's moral responsibilities to his citizens. 'Realism' in this sense was a product of disenchantment with academic contributions to the discussion of international politics in the inter-war years, with its concentration on refining legal and organizational forms intended to strengthen international order.

An important early statement of the realist critique is E. H. Carr's *The Twenty Years' Crisis* (Macmillan, 1939; rev. edn, 1946), written shortly before, but published shortly after, the outbreak of war, with the purpose of remedying 'the almost total neglect of the factor of power' in inter-war writing on international politics. Carr's book remains in print, and is a valuable starting point for the discussion of the general nature of international politics.

'Realism' has informed the work of many writers who have focused on particular aspects of international politics, as well as those who have sought to put forward an understanding of international politics as a whole. Underlying the speculations of many authors who have considered the appropriate means of deterring a nuclear attack has been the view that those actors engaged in a relationship of nuclear deterrence cannot be trusted not to take any opportunity of increasing their power, even to the extent of launching a first strike, if this can be done with sufficient impunity to outweigh the retaliatory damage likely to be incurred. John Garnett's collection, *Theories of Peace and Security* (Macmillan, 1970), provides a good introduction to post-war strategic theory in this vein. *Contemporary Strategy*, by John Baylis *et al.* (Croom Helm, 1975), is a more recent account of strategic theory.

A succinct critique of 'realism' is offered by Robert Rothstein in 'On the Costs of Realism', *Political Science Quarterly*, **87** (1972). The predominance of the concern with power leads to an ignoring of important differences between types of states. Instead, all states are treated as 'billiard balls, interacting within a specific arena and according to established rules'. While such a perspective may be adequate for considering a world of similar states, it is less helpful in a world where international occurrences can be attributed to the totalitarian, revolutionary, underdeveloped or unstable natures of particular states, or to the activities of non-state actors. The assumption of a world of separate but similar power-seeking states is, Rothstein suggests, at variance with the growing importance of economic, social and cultural determinants of political behaviour, and the inseparability of security issues from these matters.

While 'realism' emerged as a response to a discredited 'idealism' of the inter-war period, the philosophical basis for that 'idealism' shows signs of exerting influence afresh. This philosophical basis is to be found in the writings of those such as Grotius, who sought, in the seventeenth century, in *The Laws of War and Peace* (Hyperion Press, 1980), to apply natural-law ideas to the relations between nations. There is a refusal to accept that the 'desire for power after power' is either a natural characteristic of man, or one which circumstances must always force upon him. The conduct to which such a desire gives rise is at variance with the real nature of man, which is sociable. The task in international politics is to extend the province of law and organization from the state to the international level, by means of argument and legal and organizational innovation. Hedley Bull in *Diplomatic Investigations*, edited by Martin Wight and Herbert Butterfield (Allen and Unwin, 1966), provides a chapter on 'The Grotian Conception of International Society' and examines critically this perspective. Among recent attempt to explore the possibility of a beneficial extension of the roles of law and organization are those of the contributors to *The Strategy of World Order*, edited by R. A. Falk and S. H. Mendlowitz (4 vols, World Law Fund, 1966), and *The Future of the International Legal Order*, edited by C. E. Black and R. A. Falk (4 vols, Princeton University Press, 1969–1972).

The main division amongst Western students of international politics, at the level of general understanding, has been between the realists and those who see the possibility of improvement through attention to law, organizations and a consideration of moral obligations in international politics. However, a third general perspective requires identifying, and is exemplified by a Marxist understanding that the problems of international politics can be solved only by a radical transformation of the international system. What may appear as a search for power by states is but the facade of a different kind of struggle: amongst capitalists, and consequently between capital and labour, where owners of the means of production use the machinery of the state as a means of retaining or acquiring markets, raw materials, cheap labour and, above all, profit. Attempts to improve international politics by means of legal and institutional change will founder, since they do not alter the essential class basis of states. Marxist theory of international politics has not been prominent in Western journals. Tony Thorndike's chapter, 'The Revolutionary Approach: the Marxist Perspective' in *Approaches and Theory in International Politics* (work cited) provides a useful introduction and bibliography. *Marxism–Leninism and the Theory of International Relations*, by V. Kubalkova and A. A. Cruikshank (Routledge and Kegan Paul, 1980), is the most substantial recent contribution.

The above categorization of modes of generally understanding international politics follows that of Martin Wight, who identified, in his lectures at the London School of Economics, three kinds of approaches or paradigms: 'realist', 'rationalist' and 'revolutionary'. Wight's categories have received recent attention in Brian Porter's chapter, 'Patterns of Thought and Practice: Martin Wight's "International Theory"' in *The Reason of States*, edited by Michael Donelan (Allen and Unwin, 1978) and in Hedley Bull's second Martin Wight Memorial Lecture: 'Martin Wight and the Theory of International Relations', *British Journal of International Studies*, **2** (1976).

Levels of analysis

In addition to distinguishing amongst students of international politics with regard to their general understanding of the nature of international politics, we can also identify different levels of analysis at which they have operated. J. D. Singer's article, 'The Level of Analysis Problem in International Politics', in *The International System: Theoretical Essays*, edited by Klaus Knorr and Sidney Verba (Princeton University Press, 1961), has been reprinted in a number of collections, and his identification of levels of analysis has been reflected in various textbooks. K. J. Holsti's *International Politics: a Framework for Analysis* (Prentice-Hall, 3rd edn, 1977) distinguishes between material dealing with 'International Systems' and that covering the 'foreign policy outputs' of states. John Spanier, in *Games Nations Play* (Holt Rhinehart and Winston, 3rd edn, 1978), provides an early chapter on 'three levels of analysis': 'the systemic level'; 'the nation-state level'; and 'the decision-making level'. Kenneth Waltz's *Man, the State and War* (Columbia University Press, 1954) is an important discussion of accounts of the causes of war that have been offered at the levels of the international system, the internal structure of states and the nature of man.

For a number of writers, the level of analysis that has been seen to offer the most important contribution to our understanding of international politics has been that of the international system as a whole. Whatever states or men may wish to do, the inescapable fact remains that the main political units – states – exist in a world that is not hierarchically ordered in any formal sense. The society of states is anarchical, and Hedley Bull's book, *The Anarchical Society* (Macmillan, 1977), explores the implications of this fact in a number of areas: with regard to the maintenance of order in international politics; the balance of power; international law; diplomacy; and the great powers. Kenneth Waltz, in *Theory of International Politics* (Addison-Wesley, 1979), also analyses the consequences of anarchy, and offers a powerful critique of the work of other writers on international systems.

Other writers have concentrated their attention on the state as an actor in international politics. The determinants of foreign policy have been considered. William Wallace's *Foreign Policy and the Political Process* (Macmillan, 1971) is a good introduction.

Kenneth Waltz's *Foreign Policy and Democratic Politics* (Longman, 1968) studies the relationship between internal and external aspects of foreign policy with reference to Britain and the US. Roy E. Jones's *Principles of Foreign Policy: the Civil State in its World Setting* (Martin Robertson, 1979) is a recent attempt to explore the problems and nature of foreign policy.

An important development in the study of foreign policy has been the move toward a consideration of what may be called its organizational and bureaucratic aspects. R. C. Snyder, H. W. Bruck and B. Sapin, in *Foreign Policy Decision-Making: An Approach to the Study of International Politics* (The Free Press, 1962), explored the factors influencing foreign policy decision makers. Although their call for a new approach was largely ignored, Graham Allison's important article, 'Conceptual Models and the Cuban Missile Crisis', *American Political Science Review*, **53** (1970) and his book *The Essence of Decision: Explaining the Cuban Missile Crisis* (Little, Brown, 1971) consider the impact of particular organizational and bureaucratic factors on decision making. Morton Halperin's *Bureaucratic Politics and Foreign Policy* (Brookings Institution, 1974) also exemplifies this concern.

Apart from the international system and the state, there are other levels that may occupy the attention of students of international politics: the individual, for example, either as leader or as led. Otto Klineberg's *The Human Dimension in International Relations* (Hot Rhinehart and Winston, 1964) provides a good starting point for general discussion. Various studies of leaders exist, and especially interesting are a number of works on Woodrow Wilson: Alexander and Juliet George's *Woodrow Wilson and Colonel House: a Personality Study* (John Day, 1956); *Thomas Woodrow Wilson: a Psychological Study*, by Sigmund Freud and Thomas E. Bullitt (Weidenfeld and Nicolson, 1967); and *Woodrow Wilson: a Medical and Psychological Biography*, by Edwin A. Weinstein (Princeton University Press, 1981).

Methods of study

An appreciation of the general nature of international politics, or an understanding obtained at a particular level of analysis, can be reached by a variety of methods of study, of which we will identify three: 'interpretative description'; scientific investigation; and philosophical speculation.

The writer uses the term 'interpretative description', rather than simply 'history' for two main reasons. First, it is an approach to the study of the present, as well as the past. Second, it involves more than the reconstruction of events or as accurate as possible a description of happenings; in addition, it seeks to draw from an investigation of happenings, utterances, writings and other manifestations of international politics a more general assessment of the causes of things. Its mode of argument is persuasive rather than conclusive, and can be found operating at each of the levels of analysis identified. Hans Morgenthau, operating at the level of the international system, and seeking to show that it is an arena for the play of power, claims that 'history bears out the assumption' that 'statesmen think and act in terms of interest defined as power'. He provides some examples to persuade us of this. Graham Allison uses interpretative description to persuade us that the decisions taken by US leaders at the time of the Cuban missile crisis are best explained by reference to the structure of organizations and competition amongst office holders. Adda B. Bozemann's *Politics and Culture in International History* (Princeton University Press, 1960) is a masterly examination of the relationship between ideas and practice from the earliest times. F. H. Hinsley's *Power and the Pursuit of Peace* (Cambridge University Press, 1967) considers the ideas of various thinkers on the topic of schemes for peace, and the relationship of these ideas to the real world of international politics. Maurice Keens-Soper, in his chapter 'The Practice of a States-System' in *The Reason of States* (work cited), interprets the ideas underlying the history and diplomatic forms of international politics in Europe. The recent publication of Martin Wight's *Systems of States* (Leicester University Press, 1977) and the republication in an enlarged form of his *Power Politics* (Leicester University Press, for the Royal Institute of International Affairs, 1978) have made available particularly fine examples of interpretative description in international politics.

Since the method of interpretative description involves persuasion rather than conclusive proof, there is an obvious lack of finality in such accounts. For some, this lack of finality may seem unsatisfactory. It may be suggested that such a dissatisfaction prompted attempts to develop more scientific approaches to the study of international politics, although the search for scientific understanding in international politics was also part of the more general development of the social sciences after the Second World War.

The main supposition that underpins the scientific enterprise is that reality is not chaotic; that it can be explained in terms of the operation of laws which it is the business of the scientist to discover. Amongst the earliest proponents of a scientific approach to the study of international politics was Morton Kaplan, whose book *System and Process in International Politics* (Wiley, 1957) still commands much attention in the literature. Kenneth Waltz's recent *Theory of International Politics* (work cited), for example, devotes considerable space to an attack on Kaplan.

Kaplan operates at the level of the international system. He is interested in the conditions under which systems of states may collapse, survive or change. The kinds of question he is interested in concern the alterations in the values of certain variables, such as the number of states in the system, the nature of the regimes in the states or the ease of access by states to information about the system, that can be tolerated by a system. He is also interested in the kinds of system that may emerge when the values of certain variables pass critical limits. Kaplan works by constructing what he calls 'models' of international systems. These are, in part, defined by 'rules' of behaviour that are followed by the component parts (e.g. the states). He considers, in abstraction, whether adherence to the rules would lead to a continuation of the system, or to its changing and the relationship between the likelihood of continued rule-adherence and the values of other variables.

What, though, is the aim of positing and investigating such hypothetical international systems? Kaplan sees it as a step on the way to a science of international politics:

> By shifting the focus of analysis from the particular event to the pattern of events, seemingly unique or accidental occurrences become part of a meaningful pattern of occurrences. In this way the historical loses its quality of uniqueness and is translated into the universal language of science. (*System and Process in International Politics*, p.25).

The key here is the idea of 'the historical' losing its 'uniqueness'. If we could discover, for example, those characteristics of actors in a system that led them to behave as if in conformity to certain rules, such as 'act to oppose any coalition or single actor which tends to assume a position of predominance with respect to the rest of the system', or characteristics which led to deviance from such rules, then this abstract knowledge could be applied to the real world. Kaplan himself explores the relative likelihood of hierarchically organized and democratic regimes, and 'system dominant' and 'sub-system dominant' actors obeying rules such as that mentioned above.

One of Waltz's major criticisms of Kaplan points to Kaplan's concentration on the impact of changes in the characteristics of the actors within a system. Kaplan, Waltz suggests, fails to explore fully the effects of there being an international system of separate states, and is rather engaged in a reductionism which conceives of the international system as, in the main, the product of its components. For Waltz, the anarchical nature of the international system is what is significant. While, in such a system, there may be collective agreement about the desirability of a chosen goal, no actor can take the risk of participating in a collective effort, lest another pursue and attain an individual goal in a way that frustrates the collective efforts of the others and leaves them, relatively, worse off than before. Waltz's exploration of the likely consequences of anarchy in international politics for the attainment of collective goals is akin to the work of M. Olson and R. Zeckhauser in their article 'An Economic Theory of Alliances', *Review of Economics and Statistics,* **48** (1966). There, the topic of alliances is dealt with in a way that shows how, in a situation where central direction is absent, the individual interests of states run counter to, and prevent the attainment of a collective goal which would, if attained, be of benefit to all.

Olson and Zeckhauser exemplify a trend in the 'scientific' study of international politics, which is away from efforts to comprehend the whole international system and toward the investigation of less general topics. The collection, *Quantitative International Politics*, edited by J. D. Singer (Free Press, 1968), provides an introduction to the use of quantifiable data to test hypotheses. Nazli Choucri and Robert North in *Nations in Conflict: National Growth and International Violence* (Freeman, 1975) seek correlations between various factors and the violent behaviour of states in the period immediately prior to the First World War. *The Correlates of War*, edited by J. D. Singer (2 vols, Free Press, 1980), and *Peace, War and Numbers*, edited by Bruce M. Russett (Sage, 1972), also exemplify the quantitative approach to the study of war. The general problem of hypothesis testing in the study of international politics is dealt with in *Contemporary Research in International Relations* by Dina A. Zinnes (Free Press, 1976). Zinnes also provides a useful overview and critique of recent work within the scientific mould in international politics.

While the construction of models of international systems, and the search for quantitative data that can be used to test hypotheses have been very significant aspects of the scientific approach, two other aspects also deserve mention. The first is game theory, which seeks to provide accounts of how actors will behave in certain abstract situations where choices of courses of action must be made in such a way that the benefits accruing to one actor as a result of his choice will depend on the choice of other actors. Thomas Schelling's *The Strategy of Conflict* (Oxford University

Press, 1963) provided an early exposition and critique of such a concern. The *Journal of Conflict Resolution* is a major source of articles on the subject. Second, and more complicated, is the development of mathematical models of international processes, such as arms races, and the attempt to investigate the 'fit' between such models and reality. Much of this work is inspired by that of Lewis F. Richardson, a meteorologist, whose work was post-humously published in *Arms and Insecurity* (Boxwood Press, 1960) and *The Statistics of Deadly Quarrels* (Boxwood Press, 1960). Zinnes (work cited) provides an account of more recent developments in this field.

Finally, in connection with the scientific approach, mention should be made of simulation. Various efforts have been made to simulate international systems and processes. Sometimes this has involved the use of role-playing individuals; at other times, more complex computer-based explorations. *Simulated International Processes*, by H. Guetzkow and J. J. Valdez (Sage, 1981), offers a recent account.

The scientific enterprise in international politics is aimed at providing increased understanding of the causes of happenings. While such knowledge may obviously be of use in the pursuit of particular objectives in international politics, science cannot, in itself, offer guidance as to what, morally, ought to be done. The approach to the study of international politics which I have called 'philosophical speculation' includes the consideration of the con-nection between moral ideas and international action, whether by state or individuals. In many of the major textbooks of the 1950s and 1960s, the consideration of 'international morality' commonly occupied a chapter or two toward the end of the book, and included an assessment of the impact of 'values' on the conduct of statesmen. More recently, there appears to have been an increase in the attention given to international morality in the literature. The present writer does not mean only the concern to elucidate the relationship between the ideas held by actors in international politics and the conduct of those actors – the kind of enterprise in which Bozemann (work cited) engages. In addition to the 'history of international thought' in that sense, there has also been a growth in interest shown in the discussion of international morality in the more straightforward sense of right and wrong, good and evil. J. E. Hare and Carey B. Joynt's *Ethics and International Affairs* (Macmillan, 1982) is a useful introduction. Charles Beitz's *Political Theory and International Relations* (Princeton University Press, 1979) is also valuable. Andrew Linklater explores both the history of thought concerning international politics, and the more general validity of various ideas in *Men and Citizens in the Theory of International Relations* (Macmillan, in association with the London School of Economics, 1982). The moral issues raised by war have also begun to receive further discussion. Michael Walzer's *Just and Unjust Wars* (Basic Books, 1977; Penguin Books, 1980) attempts to extract from human practice an account of what may be considered morally allowable and morally obnoxious in the conduct of war. Barrie Paskins and Michael Dockerill in *The Ethics of War* (Duckworth, 1979) also provide a mix of historical illustration and philosophical argument.

It is, perhaps, surprising that in the study of international politics, there has been a separation between the pursuit of a knowledge of the causes of happenings, whether by scientific or other methods, and the consideration of what is morally appropriate conduct in the relations between states. One possible reason for this is the extent to which the 'realist' perspective dominated the study of international relations after the Second World War. Not only was its acceptance shown in the popularity of Morgenthau's textbook. 'Realism' was also the underlying perspective or 'paradigm' of many of the 'scientific' authors. Kaplan's models of international systems deal, in the main, with states hypothesized as being primarily concerned to maximize 'capabilities'. Game theory investigates rational choices for value-maximizing actors. In a world where the pursuit of power and security seems predominant, there can appear little point in discussing matters unrelated to this fact. One exception to this may be found in what has become known as 'peace research' or 'peace science'. Here, a close relation between scientific investigation and a belief in the value of peace is found. John Galtung's *Essays in Peace Research* (5 vols, Christian Ejlers, 1975–1980) bring together the work of one of the best-known authors in this field. The *Journal of Peace Research* (Universitetsforlaget, ed. at the International Peace Research Institute, Oslo) and *Peace Science Society – Papers* (Peace Science Society (International), University of Pennsylvania) are leading journals.

International politics or international relations?

We mentioned earlier that there may sometimes be good reasons for distinguishing between international politics, international relations and other like terms more carefully than has been done in this chapter. Sometimes, a concentration on international politics can lead to an ignoring of the impact of non-political factors on the behaviour of governments in international affairs. John Burton, in *World Society* (Cambridge University Press, 1972), provides a useful corrective to this tendency. More specifically, the impact of economic factors has been dealt with at length in Joan E. Spero's *The Politics of International Economic Relations* (Allen and Unwin, 2nd edn, 1981). Susan Strange's article, 'The Study of Transnational Relations', *International Affairs*, **52** (1976), argues for the value of the development of international political economy as a subject.

International politics, then, is a many-faceted subject. Its subjects may have different overall appreciations of the nature of international politics. They work at different levels. They use different methods. The literature mentioned in this chapter is meant to reflect these differences.

5
Political thought
Janet Coleman

The nature of the beast:

From the Enlightenment until the present day, certain questions about the nature of man and the social conditions in which he normally lives have been posed in a distinctive way: what is the object of our investigation, how do we proceed to study it and what is the nature of a satisfactory explanation? We are heirs to this distinctive mode of investigating societies and the people who live in them, inheriting it from Hume and Kant. But from classical antiquity onwards it was assumed that man was a polis-living animal. Some believed this to be a natural rather than an artificial state, and political thought was developed as a manner of discoursing about the human animal in social conditions. What we say about social man and how we say it, and the manner in which we justify our statements, are the concerns of the academic discipline we call political thought.

How we talk about societies and people has changed during the two and a half thousand years during which politics has been a distinct subject of discourse. What kind of things then are societies and the people who live in them? There are *a priori* statement we can make about societies and persons that tell us what some believe are universally recognized features of social living. Other statements indicate that people are material objects capable of acting with intentions regarding the world, a world compromising other material objects, and that their special feature is that they can communicate their intentions, as well as the results of their activity, to others. For this latter neo-realism viewpoint see Roy Bhaskar, *A Realist Theory of Science* (Harvester Press, 2nd edn, 1978) and Roy Bhaskar, *The Possibility of Naturalism* (Harvester Press, 1979) p.18. One issue that has especially taxed thinkers of the nineteenth century to the present concerns whether it is possible to study past and present societies and people thus generally defined and, if so, whether it can be in some scientific way. How far are men and societies proper objects of inquiry, they ask, and what is the appropriate method by which to conduct the inquiry? The question for Aristotle in classical antiquity, however, was not whether a social and political science is possible but rather what kind of science politics is.

The focus of political thinkers today is on human action or 'behaviour' and the manner in which men intentionally describe and consciously or unconsciously 'understand' their own and others' actions. We ask of our own time and of earlier times how men implicitly and explicitly gain rational, critical perspectives on the quality of their social and political lives. We attempt to describe and understand how they altered their political lives, institutions and legal systems. The study of political thought, then, tries to describe and evaluate how men have lived, how they thought or saw themselves as living, and how they thought they ought to live. Political thought confronts the past and analyses the continuity and discontinuity in what where believed to be traditions of social and political living. It also confronts the present. Consequently it is a large, interdisciplinary field of study and we shall be referring selectively to a very wide range of current literature to show how contemporary students of political thought treat their subject. (An attempt at defining the field by a selective but extensive bibliography is made by Cary J. Nederman in 'A Bibliography of Articles in Political Theory 1974–78', *Political Theory*, **7**, 563–580 (1979); this is a supplement to Nederman's 'Bibliography of Political Theory articles: 1970–73', *Political Theory*, **2**, 468–78 (1974). The reader should also consult Cary Nederman and James Wray Goulding, 'Recent Books in Political Theory 1977–79', *Political Theory*, **9**, 121–142 (1981). There is no uncontested definition of political theory or political thought since its use varies with the epistemology, ethics, philosophical method, political interest and social location of the thinker: see Fred. I. Greenstein and Nelson W. Polsby, *Handbook of Political Science*, Vol. I: *Political Science: scope and theory* (Addison-Wesley, Reading, Mass., 1975), especially Chapter 2 by J. Donald Moon, 'The Logic of Political Inquiry: a Synthesis of Opposed Views'.

It is not enough to say that something has happened in the past and is, therefore, meaningful. Man's capacity to interpret what is 'known' to have happened and the various manners of evaluting it is what matters. Because man is historically conditioned in large part through learning a language, being educated and by experiencing a social world with a certain configuration of rules and laws into which he is born, he 'knows' and expresses his knowledge in ways that are specific to his culture at a specific time. But at the same time some have argued that there remains an 'absolute' common sense which is common to all men at all times, a core common way of experiencing the world and conceptualizing it, in virtue of which we are recognizably human, an idea dealt with in J. L. Gorman, *The Expression of Historical Knowledge* (Edinburgh University Press, 1982) p.113. We 'know' what we are like in a way that can transcend the sceptical or solipsist view, which argues that each person has only a private view of his world, unshared and unsharable by others. This presumed shared understanding of social experience supplies the epistemological foundations on which to construct a theory of human nature. But even at present, a theory of how men know, organize their knowledge and then evaluate present and past acts may not be sufficiently explicit to clarify the nature of human capacities of assessment. This is made especially plain in the debates between Noam Chomsky and Jean Piaget: Massimo Piatelli-Palmarini (ed.), *Théories du langage, théories de l'apprentissage, le débat entre Jean Piaget et Noam Chomsky* (Editions du Seuil, 1979).

At university the study of political thought is an intensely self-reflective discipline concerned to clarify the nature of what is studied and the various methods by which such studies yield significant organized knowledge. As such it draws on studies pursued in other disciplines like history, philosophy, sociology, economics, linguistics, law and psychology. Only a limited bibliography for each of these fields can be provided here. Many political theorists and those concerned with the history of political thought see theirs as the complex task of reflecting on the relation of philosophy and politics, of thinking to action, of being with oneself and being with others and of making a variety of judgments consequent on more general descriptions of these states of being and acting displayed in Western history. Andrew Gamble, in *An Introduction to Modern Social and Political Thought* (Macmillan, 1981), treats the meaning of the Western tradition, and it is the Western tradition with which political thought is largely concerned. A structured description, explanation and evaluation of human actions raises the question of whether and to what extent there is a conceptual confusion in the nineteenth and twentieth centuries' attempts to 'force' such descriptions and explanations into a grid that had been established for the empirical natural sciences. The work of Robert K. Merton, *Social Theory and Social Science* (The Free Press, rev. edn, 1968), is only one example of many in the behaviourist/positivist tradition in the social sciences, that draws logical parallels between biological and social science systems, proposing laws and elaborating theories that explain events in both as evidence of 'functional adaptations to the environment'. We shall return briefly to this.

The study of political thought is more than just a historical survey of grand political theories and political systems of the past: such histories include R. N. Berki, *The History of Political Though, a Short Introduction* (Dent, 1977); John Plamenatz, *Man and Society: a Critical Examination of some Important Social and Political Theories from Machiavelli to Marx* (2 vols, Longman, 1963); Dante Germino, *Machiavelli to Marx: Modern Western Political Thought* (Chicago University Press, 1979); George H. Sabine and Thomas C. Thorson, *A History of Political Theory* (Dryden Press, 4th edn, 1973); Sheldon S. Wolin, *Politics and Vision: Continuity and Innovation in Western Political Thought* (New York, 1960); and D. Thomson (ed.), *Political Ideas* (Penguin, 1966). Thus we study aspects of the political thought of the 'greats' as expressed in the traditional canon of texts of political thought: Plato (*Republic, The Laws*); Aristotle (*Ethics, Politics*); Cicero (*Republic, The Laws*); Augustine (*The City of God*); Thomas Aquinas (selections from his *Summa Theologiae*); Dante (*On Monarchy*); Marsilius of Padua (*Defender of Peace*); Machiavelli (*The Prince* and *The Discourses*); Hobbes (*Leviathan*); Locke (*Two Treatises of Government*); Hume (*An Essay Concerning Human Understanding*); Burke (*Reflections on the French Revolution*); Rousseau (*The Social Contract* and *The Discourses*). Also important are selections from the utilitarian –liberals Bentham, James and John Stuart Mill and Hegel (*Philosophy of Right*) together with selections from the works of Marx and Engels. We may also group political theorists in categories like idealists, realists, monarchists, republicans, civic humanists, liberals and utilitarians, socialists, communists, utopians, and study their thought schematically and synchronically. There is also an attempt to distinguish utilizable theories of the past from a mere narrative of the history of acknowledged great theories. In drawing this distinction we are affirming that the study of political thought concerns, in part, questions such as what is specifically human, what is not, and why the range of possibilities is limited in the way it is. Are there categories such as belonging to a group (and behaving differently in that group from the way one behaves individually), or obeying and following rules and sets of laws, categories that are indispensable to our understanding of what men are? Isaiah Berlin, in 'Does Political Theory Still Exist', in P. Laslett and G. Runciman (eds), *Philosophy, Politics and Society*, 2nd series (Blackwell, 1962), an occasional series with extremely relevant articles on current issues of debate in political theory which tackles this question. What are the historical contingencies that determine the range within which social communication and action take place is another question to be asked. The study of political thought therefore, deals not only with the source and the scope but also with the validity of certain human goals and the means to achieve them.

Some have argued that what men are and have been, rather than what they ought to be, is determined by the interpretative structures, the models, like language, inherited concepts of law, rules, games, institutions, that penetrate the thought and action of human actors at different historical times, and that these structures, whatever their content, which precede men's actions, show them how to act and shape their behaviour. Men do not act or speak randomly but within already existing structures that enable them both to constrain action and give meaning to it. Some think it is important, therefore, to study the historical conditions as well as the linguistic conventions amidst which political thinkers lived, thought and wrote. This is the aim of the journals, *History of Political Thought* (1981–): and also *Political Theory* (1973–).

In order to maintain social cohesion and to give meaning to their world, men often validate the present order of things and their ways of thinking and acting by reference to tradition, a complex network of concepts, some of which assume the form of laws, institutions and rules of acceptable behaviour. This is examined in Edward Shils, *Tradition* (London, 1981). Whether such structures are themselves universal and natural, or whether they are necessary but artificial, is debated both in texts of the past (Aristotle, Cicero, Hume, Hobbes) as well as today. The assertion that men act within traditions of understanding, behaviour and institutions is taken further when we consider that men interpret traditions, as explaining their current attitudes and behaviour. Take, for instance, Terry Coleman's interview in the *Guardian*, 13 September 1982 with John Nott, the retiring Secretary of Defence. Mr Nott described himself and Mrs Thatcher's Government as follows: 'I am a nineteenth-century liberal. So is Mrs Thatcher. That's what this government is all about'. He went on to say that he found the nineteenth-century political novels by Trollope a great relaxation during the Falklands war. One of the tasks of political thought might be to determine if it is possible to be a nineteenth-century liberal in the 1980s.

To see oneself as acting within a tradition (see Burke's *Reflections on the Revolution in France*) involves a certain degree of reinterpretation of the past to suit the present. The way we read and understand political texts is conditioned by who we are, where we are, what has happened to us, how we use our language and how we evaluate political actions, events and contexts, and these conditions exist prior to our confronting and interpreting political situations, whether past or present. This raises an increasingly urgent problem for those concerned to study past political thought. They must either understand it in the conditions of its own time or call upon it in support of current attitudes and policies. Recently, it has been argued that when we read the later seventeenth-century tracts by John Locke, his *Two Treatises of Government*, we must realize that what makes his theory political is simply 'the relevance of Locke's arguments about the exercise of political power to an existent [seventeenth-century] political movement within his society'. A theory is political in other words, only in relation to the maintenance or the furtherance of the social, political and economic objectives of a specifically identifiable group within society': this aspect is covered in Richard Ashcraft, 'On the Problem of Methodology and the Nature of Political Theory', *Political Theory*, **3**, 20 (1975); and Ashcraft, 'Revolutionary Politics and Locke's *Two Treatises of Government:* Radicalism and Lockean Political Theory', *Political Theory*, **8** (1980).

We know that some political theories were consciously constructed to suit a particular political situation and to sustain a point of view, a platform or ideology for the maintenance of the *status quo* or for change, and that nevertheless the theory has been invoked by later thinkers and actors in new conditions, who believe they see a programme suitable to their needs. An interesting example of this is the notion of property discussed throughout the history of political theory in differing ways as in Anthony Parel and Thomas Flanagan (eds), *Theories of Property, Aristotle to the Present* (The Calgary Institute for the Humanities, Wilfred Laurier University Press, 1979) and C. B. Macpherson (ed.), *Property, Mainstream and Critical Positions* (University of Toronto Press, 1978). There is indeed an aspect of the study of political thought which concerns itself with the often wilful misreadings of political theories where a subsequent age reads it eclectically with current

concerns uppermost in mind. A methodological dilemma, therefore, has been recognized.

How did past men communicate to one another and conceive of
their specific social identities, and what is the means by which we
may realistically and accurately allow ourselves to believe we
understand what they said about themselves and how they described their acts? Furthermore, to what extent did men of the
past, and we in the present, describe situations as they really are?
The extent to which we can grasp different conceptions of reasonableness that are culturally and temporally specific, that are
different from what we believe to be our own, is itself a debated
issue. But insofar as we may believe we can understand the past
and determine from past assertions what people believed, we tend
to draw more general lessons from their assertions. Later we shall
return to some of the methodological procedures called upon by
modern students of past political thought which presume the past
is knowable.

At the same time it follows for many that knowledge of specific
interests and beliefs is not, cannot and ought not to be an uncritical
and non-evaluative enterprise. Otherwise we cannot recognize
'forms of life' that are dehumanizing and alienating or we abdicate
our responsibility from doing so. The study of political thought is,
therefore, not only descriptive and explanatory but also evaluative
and critical: see Richard J. Bernstein, *The Restructuring of Social
and Political Theory* (Blackwell and Methuen, 1976), p.74. It is
both impossible and undesirable that it be value-free and
'objective'. It would be meaningless to us even were we able,
which we are not, to make value-free and 'objective' assertions
about political thought.

Political *thinking* itself is important because discourse is an
aspect of social behaviour which describes and explains the ways in
which men behave towards each other through the institutions of
their society. Political thinking may be considered on an even
more abstract level as an aspect of intellectuality, a distinct,
rational, contemplative mode by which men alone can gain an
understanding of their experience and environment, and thereby
make themselves 'at home in their world'. Abstracting from a
tradition of social behaviour, men thereafter tend to think about
social relations in terms less of concrete, observable, even material
experiences, than in terms of political persuasion or in terms of
abstract arguments that are mental, internal acts of knowing and
understanding. Reference should be made to J. C. A. Pocock,
'The History of Political Thought: a Methodological Inquiry' in
Laslett and Runciman (eds), *Philosophy, Politics and Society,* 2nd

series (work cited). Thus we have a tradition in political thought that deals with notions like obedience, rights, justice, duty, liberty and their interrelationship. There are numerous books treating these concepts mainly ahistorically such as Anthony de Crespigny and Alan Wertheimer (eds), *Contemporary Political Theory* (Nelson, 1970); L. J. Macfarlane, *Modern Political Theory* (Nelson, 1970); Norman J. Barry, *An Introduction to Modern Political Theory (St Martin's Press, New York, 1981);* and Michael Freeman and David Robertson (eds), *The Frontiers of Political Theory, essays in a revitalised discipline* (Harvester, 1980). Well-known arguments that have inspired controversy in modern analytical political theory include John Rawls, *A Theory of Justice* (Oxford University Press, 1972) and Robert Nozick, *Anarchy, State and Utopia* (Blackwell, 1974).

When such notions are interrelated and a structure emerges which appears unified, the world of sensually experienced behaviour is replaced by a more general *theory* of behaviour, and what were once questions about specific acts and how to understand them, become an ideology, that men in certain generalized conditions always behave in a particular manner. This kind of political analysis tries to establish an autonomy distinct from the material world of specific experiences and seeks to find room for ideas to be studied as events. In effect, this limits our study to the more abstract thought of theorists and leaves behind the world of pre-conceptualized historical events and contexts.

Those students, influenced by Marxian methods of historical analysis or by the historicist school, consider such acontextual abstract theory reductionist and falsifying of the wider material basis of historical concepts. The Marxist doctrine of historical materialism asserts that the factors determining historical development are ultimately economic. Changes in the state organization, in law, religion, morality, are a function of changes in the economic mode of production, and their doctrine is especially directed at those theories that emphasize the independent influence of ideas in the determination of historical change. Readers should consult E. P. Thompson, *The Making of the English Working Class* (Penguin, 1968) and his *The Poverty of Theory and Other Essays* (Merlin Press, 1978), criticizing Louis Althusser, and for a substantial bibliography there is Perry Anderson, *Arguments Within English Marxism* (New Left Books, 1980) as well as Richard Johnson *et al.* (eds), *Making Histories; Studies in History-Writing and Politics* (Centre for Contemporary Cultural Studies, University of Birmingham; Hutchinson, 1982).

The purely analytical, abstract discussion of concepts means that all we can deal with are ideas abstracted through the thinking process from experiences of a behavioural tradition, but where reference to that pre-conceptual level of experience is omitted. There is, thus, a debate whether any historical individual's actions must be understood by reference to the determining influence of the specific historical situation in which they were carried out, rather than by reference to theoretical principles on which they were said to be founded. Since expression of principles are themselves acts, even if we may dismiss them as propaganda, rationalizations or myths, it is argued by some that they form at least part of and indeed modify actual behaviour by their belief and utterance: as shown in Pocock (1962, work cited), p.192, and his 'Languages and their Implications: the Transformation of the Study of Political Thought', in J. G. A. Pocock, *Politics, Language and Time* (New York, 1971).

We cannot deny that men generalize about their specific, individual conditions, and that such theorizing bears both a logical and causal relation to action. But it tells only half the story. This point is made with force by Marxian and historicist political theorists. Rather, the historian of political thought and the theorist should see his task as threefold: an investigation of ideas, beliefs, arguments, rationales, and how they help us to understand men's actions in specific situations (a bibliography here would list books about the history of ideas; and a study of the activity of thinking, conceptualizing, abstracting ideas from particular situations and traditions (a bibliography here would list books on the psychology of learning and philosophical epistemology). The third aspect of the study would be concerned with the material world inhabited by thinkers and actors and which is only in part reproduced linguistically and conceptually in political theory texts (a bibliography here would list books on history and economics). Unless we see the task of political thought as threefold, we run the risk of reducing the study to one of both great and lesser political theory texts responding to texts. It is not enough to study the range of vocabularies that any stable, articulate society possesses in which to express concepts and in which to discuss political affairs. Often what is as important, if not more so, is what is *not* so expressed, those experiences which have no official vocabulary but which nonetheless shape men's worlds, constrain their motivations and intentions. Political thought is only, at its most obvious level of analysis, the language of political discussion, and events experienced by social men in a given context are not all converted into that kind of ideational construct which lends itself to systematic political discourse. Much of what a tradition is and transmits can be called inarticulate, unorganized and unspoken. A good deal of

French research coming from the *Annales* school (see their journal of the same name) tries to deal with inarticulate groups in societies when literacy was not anywhere near universal.

The study of political thought of the past to the present is only in part a study of the emergence of and the role of organizing concepts – e.g. the state. For this, see Gianfranco Poggi, *The Development of the Modern State* (Hutchinson, 1978).

The study of a particular political theory text is a study of both what is stated and what is left out; it may also be a study of men's delusions concerning their actual experiences, and it is important to realize that such a text may not be a reflection of the actual social structure which served as the context for its composition. Utopian political thought, from Thomas More's *Utopia* to the present science fiction mode, are cases in point: they are treated in Barbara Goodwin and Keith Taylor, *The Politics of Utopia* (Hutchinson, 1982).

One of the major questions for students of political thought is, therefore, how and to what degree is there a congruence between a society and its interests with the political theory of the time, in other words, to what extent is a given political theory a mirror of men's experiences or a mediation of their experiences which turns them into an aspiration. To what extent is much political theorizing a utopian enterprise?

Because the activity of interpreting a political theory is pursued in the present, one of its central tasks arises from the radically incomplete and impermanent bases of present political legitimacy: see Douglas Rae, 'Political Theory and the Division of Labour in Society', *Political Theory*, **9** (1981). The present shape of political society, the current organization of the state, its law, the ways it executes legislation and adjudicates, are outcomes of a tradition that is in constant motion. But to operate prudentially in the everyday world there is neither patience nor time for seeking reasons of accepted behaviour and unexamined premisses. Shared prejudices and habitual social behaviour militate against the disruption of the unexamined and shared patterns of seemingly fixed rules of social living. The political theorist or student of political thought, however, occupies an estranged if not alienated position both within and on the margins of society, if only because of a heightened awareness of those continuous recreations and reinterpretations of traditions which shape and sustain social institutions as they respond to an imperceptibly changing world. His job is to offer critically reasoned assessments of alternative bases and prescriptions for legitimate political practice and, in the footsteps of Socrates, to act as the gadfly prodding the sluggish beast, the society which is wrapped in its own dogmatism, to reassess its ways in order to survive. Put in another way, the political theorist asks why a man should obey, and he is asking for the explanation of what is normative in his society, in regard to authority, sovereignty, liberty and the justification of the use of such notions as valid in political arguments: there are various essays on these issues in Anthony Quinton (ed.), *Political Philosophy* (Oxford University Press, 1967), and Norman Barry (1981, work cited). A political theorist points to the discovery that many of these concepts do not even evoke wide agreement as to their meaning in the same society, and that there are differences expressed by men of the same society on what constitutes recognized authority for deciding questions of legitimacy. 'The history of thought and culture is, as Hegel showed with great brilliance, a changing pattern of great liberating ideas which inevitably turn into suffocating straitjackets and so stimulate their own destruction by new, emancipating and at the same time enslaving conceptions': Berlin (1962, work cited), p.19; see also D. Germino 'The Contemporary Relevance of the Classics of Political Philosophy' in Greenstein and Polsby (1975, work cited). But we must note that it is men, in certain conditions, who conceive these ideas, who analyse their situations by means of conceptualizing their experiences. Ideas themselves do not work their own will through willing, intending men. Thus it is argued that a major preoccupation of political thought is the formulation of models of man in order to understand the species in certain social conditions: as in Martin Hollis, *Models of Man* (Cambridge Univeristy Press, 1977). The writing of political theory and its subsequent analysis by readers, contemporary and in later ages, is concerned with an awareness of the categories and models that are socially, physiologically and materially determined, in which men necessarily think, and this in any age can be a disquieting activity with disrupting results. We are asking ourselves how we know our own views, how they knew theirs, of what man is like or what he could be in other circumstances. This has particular relevance to how we judge conditions in America, the Soviet Union, Latin America, Africa, the Far and Middle East. How do we know or evaluate what is or is not an adequate programme for human beings in given historical conditions, and to what extent do these material conditions motivate men to be what they would not be in other situations? This teaches us that our own unexamined or acknowledged opinions on, say, civil obedience are not at all the only legitimate or logically viable options.

To some it also indicates that being human is not a fact as facts are conceived by the natural sciences, and it can also point to a conclusion, which satisfies only some today, namely that the conscious ideas of man involve uninvestigatable categories. To ask what these categories are is to ask whether there are permanent and generalized ways in which men think, decide, perceive, judge; it is not a question about the data of experience itself, that is, of *what* men think, decide, judge. If one holds that an adequate model of man is conceivable, and in fact necessary (and most political theorists provide such models, although different ones), then political categories and values are a part of this web of ways of living, acting and thinking at a particular moment in history. This network or model is liable to change for many reasons, not least as a result of radical changes in reality or through dissociation from reality on the part of individuals, that is, madness. But how any age or culture actually decides what is mad, labelling 'mad' what may be politically and ethically dangerous to the existing order of things, is itself a contextual and political problem as much recent writing has shown: for instance, Michel Foucault, *Madness and Civilization* (Tavistock Press, 1971) and his *Mental Illness and Psychology* (Harper and Row, 1976), and his *L'archaeologie du Savoir* (Gallimard, 1969).

What is sought is some means of recognizing that models of men are not fixed through the course of time and we require means to transpose ourselves into states of mind other than our own, states of mind that were dominated by what we believe to be discarded or archaic social and psychological models of the past. We must be able to come to terms with other ways of looking at the 'facts' of social existence, without positing at the same time a total and abrupt discontinuity in the two millenia of the Western moral, philosophical and political consciousness. The classics here are R. G. Collingwood, *The Idea of History* (Oxford University Press, 1946) and W. H. Dray, *Perspectives on History* (Routledge and Kegan Paul, 1980).

One of the stable categories of political thought as studied through the ages is therefore seen to be that of man's rationality, defined in terms of his belief in and desire for justifications, explanations in terms of motives, causal factors and reasons for the social and political world being as it is. With this approach accepted, there are those who assert that even without the benefit of a belief in God, humans can discover what is intrinsically good and what are the practical standards for realizing this good. The role attributed to God in the Western political tradition is, of course, immense, as described in John Finnis, *Natural Law and Natural Rights* (Oxford University Press, 1980). There is established by these writers a continuity between Greek and Roman political theories and the political philosophy of the later Middle

Ages, the Renaissance and early modern political thought, where reason illuminates men in all these periods so that they come to certain unchanging, fundamental principles of moral social behaviour which serve as the basis for positive legal enactments. This continuity allows us to discuss the requisites of justice, the scope of human rights, the benefits and the limits of authority, the nature of law, the source of legal obligation, the status of unjust laws. For our own time this is well illustrated in T. Honderich and M. Burnyeat (eds), *Philosophy As It Is* (Penguin, 1979), and for an earlier period Richard Tuck, *Natural Rights Theories, their Origin and Development* (Cambridge University Press, 1979) and de Crespigny and Wertheimer (eds), *Contemporary Political Theory* (work cited).

The continuity of ethical categories in the history of political theory makes social ethics a primary concern for the student of political thought who is also concerned to develop principles of practical reasonableness for man as he recognizably is. Social ethics are also fundamental facts of life for the ordinary citizen. It is not surprising, therefore, that during the last two decades there has been a revival of the concept of rights seen as natural, human and moral. Since the 1948 Universal Declaration of Human Rights, rights terminology has played a significant part in the rhetoric of domestic and international politics: minority rights, womens' rights, homosexuals' rights, childrens' rights, animals' rights. The philosophical and legal literature here is extensive including, for instance, Ronald Dworkin, *Taking Rights Seriously* (Duckworth, new impression, 1978); and the classic, H. L. A. Hart, *The Concept of Law* (The Clarendon Press, 1961).

The spectrum of approaches to men's social and political ways of being in their world is evident in a survey of current journals dealing with the scope of political thought: see, for instance, *Political Studies, Political Theory, History of Political Thought.* The current literature divides the enterprise into three overlapping concerns: political philosophy, political theory and political ideology, each with its distinctive purpose.

Political philosophy seeks to see the world of man as a whole in hopes of discovering one coherent and articulate system that uncovers universal organizing principles in terms of which individual experiences have significance; an explanation of men in the universe, linking political life with the values and purposes pertaining to it within the larger cosmology that belongs to a given civilization. This is treated in works such as, Michael Oakeshott, *Experience and its Modes* (Cambridge University Press, 1933) and Nannerl O. Keohane, 'Philosophy, Theory, Ideology – an

Attempt at Clarification', *Political Theory*, **4** (1976). Thus it treats the highest good, the best state, as the ultimate criteria of justice.

The political theorist has a somewhat narrower focus, observing the 'game' of politics in the political arena, attempting to understand the rules and explain them. As such he is most often providing a conceptualization in summary form and through symbolic representation of what a given political order is about, providing meaning to a given political reality.

Political ideology is what we all know in both acknowledged and unacknowledged form – the habitual system of beliefs which is implicit knowledge for actors or participants in the political game, our 'portable intellectual equipment', our 'short-hand guide to action' in the world we inhabit. As such, political ideology is a system of emotional commitments habitually reinforced by acting in our social and political situations, and because it includes unexamined acceptance of the rules, it is open to bias and is value-laden – that is, normative. These are not mutually exclusive domains, nor is each unproblematic. Political philosophies encompass theories about the rules of politics and political theories presuppose philosophical ideas about models of human nature, epistemology and language. Many of the great political thinkers were concerned to incorporate philosophy, theory and ideology in their systems, Plato is a prime example, and perhaps the most important question a student of political thought can ask is how the ideology of each thinker at his moment in history relates to his work, or how his philosophical model of man leads to certain theoretical consequences as opposed to others.

Methods of study

Currently, there are two competing and often overlapping frameworks for socio-political analysis which try to answer questions about the 'mechanisms' of recurrent reproduction of political traditions: the liberal–rationalist tradition, which argues that human behaviour is a constant and is typified by rule-following, and the Marxist tradition, which sees human nature as a product of historical forces and social conditioning. The current debate is inextricably rooted in epistemological assumptions which are part of the longer enduring debate over the nature of investigative methods in the social sciences generally. The reader should consult Anthony Giddens, *Studies in Social and Political Theory* (Hutchinson, 1977) and his *New Rules of Sociological Method* (London, 1976). Weber and Marx helped to set the contours of the debate.

Is political thought more accurately classed as a study employing scientific or philosophical methods? Are science and philosophy mutually exclusive endeavours? To what extent is the history of political thought separate from analytical political theory? To what extent should the social sciences, of which political thought comprises an aspect, be dealing with a normative (fact/value) or a non-normative (empirical) approach to the language of description of social acts? Some of these issues have already been touched on above. There is a most elaborate division into 'camps' with differing and exclusive methodologies (see Greenstein and Polsby, work cited). Each differs in its attempts to elucidate 'the nature of explanation' which, we noted at the beginning, was one of the three post-Enlightenment categories within which questions have been distinctively posed with regard to the nature of man and the social conditions in which he normally lives. Are we to focus on the individual and the individualizing acts of human agents, or on general systems and structures, using functional and biological analogies for the operations of societies and states? And what is the form of our account? To what extent is prose narrative the best vehicle for describing and explaining social and political patterns, or should we be only interested in the statistical, the quantifiable aspects of social conduct and thereby hope to provide ourselves with the means of 'predicting' social conduct? Is politics to be equated only with the political speech of a society and is the appropriate approach to political theory texts one which only sees them within the philosophical framework of the problem of knowledge? Does one, can one, proffer *substantive* political recommendations to the present on the basis of a reading of past political speech? Only a few of the above issues can be dealt with in what follows.

Today social scientists and philosophers no longer believe that political theory and its history have nothing to contribute to their respective subjects. Twenty-five years ago this was not the case because of the then-current behaviourist and positivist orthodoxy. In the 1950s logical positivism was the basis for all methodology in the social sciences. Among its tenets were the verification theory of meaning, an assertion that all normative judgments are arbitrary and thus neither true nor false, together with the adoption of a programme of empirical inquiry that made politics into a natural science of behaviour. Political scientists were seen as neutral, value-free observers, their aim being law-like incontestable verification and accurate behavioural prediction. See, for instance, Melvin Richter (ed.), *Political Theory and Political Education* (Princeton University Press, 1980). It has now become clear to many that the so-called objective neutrality, even of the natural sciences, is itself an illusion, since all statements based on observation are theory-impregnated: see the radical statements of Paul Feyerabend, *Realism, Rationalism and Scientific Methods: Problems of Empiricism: philosophical papers* (2 vols, Cambridge University Press, 1981). For the social sciences this is even more serious, because it means that all theories concern a pre-interpreted world of ordinary language-meanings and use; a social world of already formed social categories, and the language of social scientists is not different from that used by all men in their daily, practical life. Consequently, when professional social scientists describe behavioural patterns their language can be and often is taken over by non-professionals to explain the daily, practical aspects of their culture. Note the influence of Freud's language on our own. This mutual knowledge separates the social sciences from biology and other natural sciences that have been seen as their model. And unless there is a sustained communication between social scientists and those whose conduct is studied, some have argued that social science will be turned into a social technology, a technical rationality that supports whatever is the dominant system as the only legitimate one: Jürgen Habermas, *Knowledge and Human Interests* (Beacon Press, 1971); and *Towards a Rational Society* (Beacon Press, 1970). The Frankfurt School in general has been interested in these issues, one member being Herbert Marcuse, *Reason and Revolution* (Oxford University Press, 1941). This would reduce the plurality of worlds, the multiple realities men confront daily (which enable them, for example, to disagree over questions of legitimacy and authority), to a single ideology. An 'objective' social science following empirical methods, would hardly be free from being ideological itself. Furthermore, language, itself a social structure, is not merely descriptive of behaviour; it is a way of being in the world peculiar to social, interacting humans. The internal consistency of language is that of grammar and syntax, and even these rules are broken and changed with altering social functions of language, alterations which active men themselves effect. Giddens (works cited) has useful up-to-date discussions of these issues.

Observed 'facts', especially in social studies, insofar as they have a human observer, are not only theory-laden but shaped and given meaning by the perceptual and conceptual schemes which are neither universal nor unchanging. Just as there are no hard empirical facts without a background theory by which to endow them with meaning in the natural sciences, even more so social and political 'facts' include intentions, motives, a subject matter that is not always publicly observable and thus not empirically verifiable, and these can only have meaning when referred to a pre-existent conceptual scheme and a historical context: see David Thomas, *Naturalism and Social Science – a Post-Empiricist Philosophy of Social Science* (Cambridge University Press, 1979). Scientific language is seen as a dynamic system growing by metaphorical extension of ordinary, natural language: see Mary Hesse, *The Structure of Scientific Inference* (London, 1974). If the central role of learning by analogy and the use of metaphor is accepted, it means a rejection of the positivism that has previously held sway in all the social sciences because 'truth' is no longer based merely on justifying an independent existence of a world of objects. An account of a concept of truth does not have to entail sensory experiences, it can deal with beliefs. Rather, social science focuses on the 'understanding' of human action. Some have seen this in part, as a process of re-experiencing or re-enacting the inner experience of others through an empathic identification with others. There has been a renewed emphasis on what 'understanding' is, what 'observable behaviour' is and *means*, and thereafter evaluating the 'subjective' elements of social conduct: see Hans-Georg Gadamer, *Truth and Method* (London, 1975). This has been the problem set by current proponents of hermeneutic phenomenology, and their approach has greatly influenced historians of political thought like Quentin Skinner and his followers, as in Skinner, 'Hermeneutics and the Role of History', *New Literary History*, 7 (1975–1976) and, for a wider discussion of hermeneutics and other modern approaches, there is Fred R. Dallmayr, *Twilight of Subjectivity, contributions to a post-individualist theory of politics* (University of Massachusetts Press, Amherst, 1981). There is only room to refer to some of the more influential hermeneutic and ordinary language theory approaches to political thought. There is Q. Skinner, 'Meaning and Understanding in the History of Ideas', *History and Theory*, 8 (1969) and J. L. Austin, *How To Do Things With Words* (Oxford University Press, 1962). On the recovery of the subjective intentions of authors of political theory texts, and on the attention paid to linguistic contexts and conventions of political theorists see Q. Skinner, 'Conventions and the Understanding of Speech Acts', *Philosophical Quarterly*, 21 (1970) and 'Social Meaning and Social Action' in Laslett *et al.* (eds), *Philosophy, Politics and Society* (4th series, series cited). Quentin Skinner has attempted to put his theory to use in his *The Foundations of Modern Political Thought* (2 vols, Cambridge University Press, 1978), a valuable and informative history of early modern political theory but where the purported methodology often gives way to a more traditional kind of history-writing. In general, Skinner *et al's* methodology, at least in theory, does not cover real acts, other than linguistic acts; but, as we previously noted, political thought is not only a matter of understanding contemporary linguistic conventions but is also an account of pre-linguistic, material experiences for which discourse is often an inadequate representation.

One final difficulty in the current literature deals with the degree to which historical narrative is itself a verbal fiction, 'the contents of which are as much invented as found and the forms of which have more in common with their counterparts in literature than they have with those in the sciences' (Hayden V. White, 'The Historical Text as Literary Artifact', in Robert H. Canary and Henry Kozicki (eds), *The Writing of History: Literary Form and Historical Understanding*, University of Wisconsin Press, Madison, 1978, p.42). It may be too radical to suppose that authorial intention is completely irretrievable and that meaning is only that which readers and audiences *give* to texts. But the distinction between history and fiction is now seen by some to be blurred. It has been suggested that one of the ways men make themselves at home in their world is by constructing narratives. 'We do not live stories even if we give our lives meaning by retrospectively casting them in the form of stories' (Hayden White, p.43). This view argues that the success of an historical narrative lies, in part, in its explanatory roles, achieved by making stories out of mere chronicles of 'facts'. The historian provides a plot structure which is recognized by his generation of readers. History is, therefore, no more than a plausible story forged from a congeries of 'facts' which, in unprocessed form, make no sense at all. What a historian of political thought or of historical events brings to his consideration of the historical record is a culturally conditioned notion of types of configurations of events that can be recognized as stories by an audience for which he is writing. The genre therefore provides the structure which endows meaning. Historical, political situations have no intrinsic meanings; plots provide the meaning.

In sum, the study of political thought is many things to many people. It treats the questions and answers proposed by the past about the nature of man and his necessarily social experience, and examines these as related to our own society as an inheritance. But as we all know, inheritances are at the mercy of custodial interpretors of our past tradition, be they magistrates, or the contemporary orthodoxy in the historical discipline as it is taught in school, or presented by journalists (previously educated in those schools), or by civil servants and ministers. New histories of some of our institutions, like Parliament, are ever being written. They tell us *something* about how it was but also a great deal about how it is. We are engaged in reconstructing continuities, but we must ourselves expect our interpretations to be passed over in the future, not unlike the great Victorian histories by Stubbs, Macaulay and Froude. Nonetheless, we live amidst the monuments of our past. In a sense we *are* past monuments through our inherited language and unquestioned roles of social behaviour. What we are, perceive, say and then do, institutionally, grows from our conscious and unconscious understanding of activities which have a past and which the study of political thought encourages us to reflect upon.

6
Group approaches to the study of politics
Grant Jordan

Groups and pluralism

The group approach to the study of politics is not, strictly speaking, synomymous with the pluralist approach. However, comparison of definitions by important authors in the two approaches suggest that there is considerable overlap. The most influential group book is D. B. Truman's *The Governmental Process* (Knopf, 1951 and 1971, references to 1st edn). He defined his key concept as follows:

> an interest group is a shared-attitude group that makes certain claims upon other groups in society. If and when it makes its claims through or upon any of the institutions of government, it becomes a political interest group (p.37).

In his *A Preface to Democratic Theory* (University of Chicago Press, 1956) Robert Dahl defined the normal (American pluralist) political process as one in which there is a high probability that an active and legitimate group in the population can make itself heard effectively at some crucial stage in the process of decision (p.145).

Most group and pluralist works share assumptions that a multiplicity of interests interact in policy making and that there are multiple points of access to the political system. It is possible to study the operation of various groups in the policy process and come to the non-pluralist conclusions (e.g. M. Ryan, *The Acceptable Pressure Group*, Saxon House, 1978), but this is an unusual combination. Comparison of Truman's work with that of Dahl shows that both were operating in the same area of intellectual life. If one looks at Dahl's *Pluralist Democracy in the United States* (Rand-McNally, 1967) one discovers that he is dealing with conflict – and the same undercurrent of consensus–identified by Truman. Dahl's argument is wider than Truman's – putting less emphasis on the group – but the same mechanism of 'over-lapping cleavage' is stressed (Chapter 14). It is something of a puzzle why Truman (1951) is not cited. The group and pluralist traditions are thoroughly intertwined.

Although the group/pluralist approaches are often said to dominate political science in Britain, there are remarkably few explicit adherents in the literature. The theoretical writing is mainly American, but below British versions of the ideas – which pre-dated their import from the US in the 1950s – are described.

The lack of much theoretical discussion in Britain can be linked to the empiricism that goes hand-in-hand with the approach. In 1928 R. Spencer produced what can be seen as a Hippocratic oath of the pressure-group school: 'It is the function of political scientists to observe political phenomena and to tell us what he sees'. (Quoted by G. D. Garson, *Group Theories of Politics*, Sage, 1978, p.36.) Related to this instinct for the empirical is a temperamental disinclination to define. A. F. Bentley, in the *Process of Government: A Study of Social Pressures* (University of Chicago Press, 1908; references to P. Odegard (ed.) edition, Belknap Press, 1967), captured that mood,

> Many a child, making paper toys has used his scissors too confidently and cut himself off from the materials he needs. That is an error to avoid, instead we shall plunge into any phenomena or set of phenomena belonging to the roughly recognised field of government . . . Who likes may snip verbal definitions in his old age, when his world has gone crackly and dry. (A new edition of Bentley, edited by L. A. Dexter, is due to be published in 1983 by Transaction Books.)

Even reviewing the literature sympathetically, one is struck by the relative absence of definitions, the unsatisfactory nature of some definitions and the unexplored consequences of such different definitions that appear. Most group writers would accept Truman's conception of society – 'a sort of mosaic of groups', 'a bewildering array of groups' (p.32). But his definitions (for example, see above) are not illuminating on key questions. Are 'the poor' a group, or can their interest be represented by a self-defined and self-selected grouping of individuals not themselves necessarily poor? Is all political activity interest group activity? How formally organized need a group be to be 'a group'?

Yet reading the work there is little doubt what Truman is discussing; it is his attempt to define his field in theoretical terms that is unsuccessful. He is discussing the work of lobbyists, groups such as the United Mineworkers of America, Arkansas State Medical Society, National Rifle Association, etc. It is the old story of the elephant, easier to recognize than define. Few group theorists would in practice baulk at incorporating in their studies the work of government agencies canvassing for funds, departments vying for administrative territory, companies seeking governmental favour and perhaps even wealthy individuals using funds to influence policy.

A wider definition reflecting this more indiscriminate approach is given by C. E. Lindblom in the *Policy Making Process* (Prentice-Hall, 2nd end, 1980): . . . 'We mean by interest group activities all interactions through which individuals and private groups not holding government authority seek to influence policy, together with these policy-influencing interactions of government officials that go well beyond the direct use of their authority'. It could be argued that this 'if it moves, its a pressure group' approach has so stretched the term to undermine its utility, but at least (as Bentley would have said) it is better to be over-generous than to begin with the assumption that only a limited set of interactions (say, between classes) is of significance. It seems true (as Lindblom suggests, p.86) that there is a trade-off between conceptual precision and consequentiality: precision tends to be at the cost of interest and relevance.

The study of group pressures has a lengthy pedigree and the appropriate role of sectional interests in society is a central element in political theory, but one doubts if the springs of contemporary pressure group study are to be found in Plato, or de Toqueville or the *Federalist Papers* – even though they contain much to interest the group-minded reader. Some authorities have identified a continuity between the pressure-group studies and the so-called English or classical pluralists of the nineteenth and early twentieth centuries. Earl Latham, in 'The Group Basis of Politics: Notes for a Theory', *American Political Science Review* (1952), explores these connections. The work of E. Barker, H. J. Laski, G. D. H. Cole and others is reviewed in Kung Chuan Hsiao, *Political Pluralism* (International Library of Psychology, Philosophy and Scientific Method, 1927). Stanislaw Ehrlich has also recently reviewed these precursors of contemporary pluralism in an intimidatingly well-footnoted study – *Pluralism: On and Off*

Course (Pergamon, 1982). In the early pluralist writing there is certainly a stress on associational life, a denial of the sovereignty and automatic legitimacy of the state, but the continuity to modern pluralism is more remarked upon by critics such as Garson (1978) or H. Kariel, *The Promise of Politics* (Prentice-Hall, 1966) than those themselves writing in the pressure-group pluralist tradition.

Significantly, Truman's first page refers not to political theory but the US muckraking tradition of journalism which had repeatedly published evidence of sinister 'special interests'. Arguably, the prime source of pressure-group studies is the observable volume of group activity. As Truman says (p.11), 'the fairly observant citizen sees various groups slugging it out with one another in pursuit of advantages from the Government'. Rightly or wrongly, the group-oriented writer is less likely to start with a conspectus of political theory than with a file of press clippings.

Truman is, beyond argument, a central figure in the development of pressure-group study, but he himself built upon three major sources in the development of the modern subject. These influences were A. F . Bentley, E. P. Herring and, to a lesser degree, P. Odegard.

Bentley (work cited) wrote boldly on the flyleaf, 'This Book is an Attempt to Fashion a Tool'. His preferred 'unit of analysis', the 'rough hewn tool', was the group. Equally important is his emphasis on pressure and process indicated by the title and subtitle. The existing state of society is presented as temporary – perpetually changing to reflect a new balance of group pressures. It is this conception of politics as a dynamic process that has encouraged the repeated rediscovery of Bentley – not the detail of the argument.

Bentley is a powerful advocate of empirical study, but he made little effort to measure the strength of pressures in practice. His appendix discussing municipal-ownership interest groups in Chicago is brief and unconvincing. For Bentley, all activity is to be translated into its underlying group significance. For example, he considers the significance of the President of the United States putting a paragraph in his annual message (to Congress) regarding legislation on the regulation of railroads. He argues, the issue is not what the President says or thinks but how the major interests 'stack up' on the matter: the policy will reflect that arithmetic.

There is little doubt that a close reading will yield inconsistencies. For example, he has a passage which pre-empts 'the second face of power' argument of Bachrach and Baratz (see below) '. . . vast mass of the matter of government is not what appears on the surface in discussion, theories, congresses or even in wars, but what is persistently in the background' (p.348). But earlier Bentley had advised us against assuming that groups exist, or will exist, merely because an interest has been identified. What is worth studying, he says, is the group in action, 'It is first, last, and at all times strictly empirical. There is no way to find it except by observation' (p.214).

Bentley conceded the difficulty of picturing the nation as made up of groups of men, each group cutting across very many others, each individual man a component of very many groups (p.204). There is a 'limitless criss cross of the groups' (p.206). He distinguishes between discussion groups (or idea activities) and organization groups. Legitimately, he argues that any distinction is likely to be artificial, but his demarcation seems unnecessarily blurred. Pure discussion groups he argues can be no more that 'a bit of decoration' in the governing process rather than as 'an important part of the moving process'. However, he fails to follow through the categorization systematically.

Another definitional issue is more fundamental. Bentley appears to have a much wider conception of the group than many of his successors. For Truman, the group was what is usually implied in non-technical discussion. In an article in the *American Political Science Review*, in 1969, Truman disclaims the description 'group theorist' and states that his purpose was simply to examine interest groups and their role. He starts from a position – more or less – of asking, 'What kind of power does (say) the American Medical Association have in policy making?' This differs from Bentley's assumption that only groups are significant, as Bentley's group very often lacked the formal organization of the AMA-type body.

Though Bentley is not widely followed on this point, it seems that his looser interpretation is needed if some of the later group arguments are to be sustained. It grew to be a tenet of the group approach that there was an overwhelmingly complex pattern of group membership and that conflict was only mediated by the fact that individuals had overlapping memberships in groups.

Critics have complained that empirical study does not confirm cross-cutting memberships, but this would not have bothered Bentley who, for example, identifies a consumer group (p.429) long before opponents of pluralism objected to the lack of consumer groups. From Bentley's viewpoint the consumer group was 'real' even if it was unorganized. The cross-cutting argument can thus be valid even without formal memberships. These points hint at what R. E. Dowling makes explicit: 'What, then, is [Truman's] avowed debt to Bentley? It is, I suggest, little more than a realization that interest groups are "very important in the political process . . ."' (Pressure Group Theory, *American Political Science Review*, 1960, **54**, No.4).

Compared with Bentley with his complex social psychology, works by P. Odegard, *Pressure Politics* (Columbia University Press, 1928) and E. Pendelton Herring, *Group Representation Before Congress* (Johns Hopkins Press, 1929), are far more orthodox attempts to describe and weigh the impact of groups. Herring's second book, *Public Administration and the Public Interest* (McGraw-Hill, 1936), was particularly significant for the themes developed later in this chapter.

Unlike Bentley, Herring values a concept of 'the public interest'. This issue permeates the literature, and not all those who advocate the term are critics of the group approach. Herring's preface establishes that the issue for him is the fairness of the contest to determine public policy. He suggested that

> In theory our government should strike a balance among these conflicting forces so as to promote the welfare of all. In fact some groups are placed more advantageously than others within our governmental structure and under our industrial system. The government draws its strength from the very elements it is supposed to regulate. Its officials both elective and appointive are subjected to constant pressure from these powerful interests.

Such a point could well have come from the critics of pluralism at any time from the 1960s to 1980s – as could his approving quotation from a more ephemeral work of 1932: 'The bureaucracy of a department is keenly attentive to the supposed wishes of the members of the committee, having in charge its department and it is no unusual situation for a member of such a legislative committee to believe that it is his right and duty to support the demands of the bureaucracy of the department under his charge with little or no investigation' (p.15). By no means, then, is Herring the complacent defender of this group system. He writes: 'Is the scope and development of our administrative service to be determined by the urging of special groups . . . ? How can interests that are socially important but politically weak be given a place in the federal administration?' (1936, work cited, p.5).

Truman himself (p.47) uses a quotation from Herring's study of Congress to set the scene for his own work: 'There has developed in this government an extra-legal [group] machinery of as integral and of as influential a nature as the system of party government . . .' Beer (see below) also found in Herring (1936, p.192) an apt phrase summing up an important proposition: 'The greater the degree of detailed and technical control the government seeks to exert over industrial and commerical interests, the greater must be their degree of consent and active participation'.

Given the obvious relevance of Bentley and Herring and others – cited and not cited in this account – it might seem capricious to claim that modern pressure-group study begins with Truman's *The Governmental Process*, but Truman deals with the system of interaction rather than particular cases. He provides general arguments about the origin of groups, the internal politics of groups, the tactic of groups. E. Latham's *The Group Basis of Politics* (Cornell, 1952) emerged at much the same time, but it was Truman's broader approach which had the more lasting impact.

Truman does not assume that groups are, by definition, pernicious in their effects, but at the same time he sees the need to limit adverse features. There is not the assumption of a self-correcting system. For example, he writes that we cannot hope to protect a government system from the results of group organization unless we have an adequate understanding of the process of which they are a part (p.12). He recognizes that a 'pathogenic (p.523) or 'morbific' (p.516) form of politics could result from group interaction. It would be fair, however, to acknowledge that he is prejudiced in favour of the group system; the first chapter is on 'The Alleged Mischiefs of Faction'; the concluding paragraph argues that the effects of overlapping membership will provide stability and peaceful change – 'a dynamic stability that permits gradual adaption' (p.535).

As Truman is so central to the group approach it is worth delineating some of the main themes – each of which has sponsored a sub-literature.

(1) He draws attention to the need for a theory to explain group-generation. He posits that new groups will be spawned from old when the internal equilibrium of the latter is disturbed in the balance of groups. His second argument on the creation of groups uses the idea of the 'potential group' (pp.34–35). He suggests that an interest can be examined even though no group has yet been formed. Truman needs this concept as part of his defence of the group system; where a point of view is not advanced by the current system, it can be assumed that the potential group will be mobilized to remedy this defect. One detects here, however, unease that he is moving from the empiricism of Bentley – that what is worth studying is what is to be found in practice, observable. Bentley

(1967, p.214) claimed that 'From the interest as a thing by itself no conclusion can be drawn'.

(2) Truman rejects the concept of the 'public interest' and the 'state' as being unhelpful, but in what was, perhaps equivocation, he says 'We cannot account for [the] system by adding up in some fashion the National Association of Manufacturers, the Congress of Industrial Organisations, the American Farm Bureau Federation, the American Legion, and the other groups that come to mind when "lobbies" and "pressure groups" are mentioned' (p.51). Truman is forced to concede a role for ideals and values, but the resolution of these to the rest of his scheme is weak. (See also pp.351, 512.)

(3) The most mechanistic point in Truman is probably where he writes that a viable administrative project 'requires a positive balance of political support over political opposition' (p.440). This kind of arithmetical policy studies is akin to Bentley's discussion of balance of interests (see Bentley, 1967, p.264.) Truman was in fact citing Simon, Smithbury and Thompson, *Public Administration* (Knopf, 1950).

(4) Truman picks up Bentley's point about overlapping membership of groups and claims that it is a fundamental fact whose importance for the process of group politics *through its impact on the internal politics of interest groups* can scarcely be exaggerated (p.158). Multiple membership is presented as the brake on incipient conflict. 'Without the notion of multiple memberships in potential groups, it is literally impossible to account for the existence of a viable polity . . .' (See p.514 onwards.)

(5) Particularly in Chapter 14, 'The Web of Relationships in the Administrative Process', Truman discusses at length, and explicitly, a pattern of politics that is at odds with the open group competition that critics often claim is Truman's position. He discusses 'What determines effective access to executive agencies?' (p.438); the development of 'stable relationships' (p.441); the process whereby the 'relationship [of an agency] to the surrounding interests become routinized' (p.444): he speculates that the problems faced by administrators in arriving at stable patterns of interaction makes them 'pawns of the dominant organized groups' (p.446); he observes 'the notion of the administrator as a neutralized public servant . . . is an illusion' (p.450); he discusses 'the inflexibility of the established web' (p. 467).

In other words, Truman, like Herring and others, knew perfectly well that open competition was not the sole type of group process.

(6) A final major dimension is the recurrent stress on complexity. This proliferation of groups is linked to the specialization in complex societies (p.57). For example, there is a 'bewildering array of groups'. The picture is of group diversity and governmental complexity; the image is of 'multiple access points'. Some such conception of disorder is needed to correspond to the box file of clippings.

In the late 1950s and early 1960s other important sources are better described as 'pluralist' than 'group' – but the distinction is fine. They include W. Kornhauser, *The Politics of Mass Society* (Free Press, 1959) which had at its heart the argument that groups weakened the potentially totalitarian power of the state. E. C. Banfield, *Political Influence* (Free Press, 1961), reached pluralist conclusions about the politics of Chicago – 'compromises patched up among competing parochial interests'. But Banfield's failure (again) to relate to Truman, or even Dahl, makes the identification of a coherent pluralist camp difficult. Another of the ambivalent corps of pluralists is H. Zeigler, *Interest Groups in American Society* (Prentice-Hall, 1964). He commends Bentley and Truman, and his chapter on 'Administrative Policy Making Under Pressure' is a particularly fruitful source, but he, too, qualifies his position, and in his Preface claims that his is not a theory of politics, but a theory of the role of organized groups in politics. This is more Truman than Bentley.

In the work of R. Dahl, C. E. Lindblom and D. Braybrooke (in various permutations) the merit of group interaction as a problem solving methodology is developed (see e.g. D. Braybrooke and C. E. Lindblom, *A Strategy of Decision*, Free Press, 1963). The ideas of disjointed incrementalism and partisan mutual adjustment are part of a debate on 'rationality', but are also important supporting concepts for group adherents.

British discussions

British post-war interest in group activity dates back to the mid 1950s – a date which allows the ripples of Truman's work to set off responses in Britain. It is noticeable that many of the important contributors in Britain in the 1950s/1960s were Americans – e.g. Beer, Potter, Storing, Eckstein, Christoph. But in fact it is difficult to establish a firm connection between the voluminous American literature and the British material on similar lines. Admittedly, W. J. M. Mackenzie was explicitly discussing Truman as early as

1955 in the *British Journal of Sociology* (VI, No.2) but elsewhere Truman was seldom mentioned. For example, S. Beer's *Modern British Politics* (Faber and Faber, 1965, 1969 and 1982 edns) is distinguished by its use of rich supporting material, sources and quotations, but it nonetheless again fails to index Truman or Bentley.

Two further reservations with regard to the assumption that British writing was American-inspired can be made. The first is that an indigenous literature existed. Richard Crossman's *How Britain is Governed* (Labour Book Service, n.d., *c.* 1938) presents a surprisingly well-developed consciousness of the importance of group politics. This shows that the analysis of the 1950s (and 1980s) is not so novel as it sometimes considered itself. Crossman described how public opinion was not a homogeneous mass but 'a complicated network of groups and interests'. He saw electoral participation alone as inadequate and went on: 'One doctor by himself is defenceless, but as a Member of the BMA he becomes part of a pressure group which every Government and party must fear'. He claimed that 'nowhere in the world are there such effective pressure groups as those which British lawyers, doctors, industrialists, financiers, landlords, architects, chartered accountants and so on have made'. He concluded that the real basis of successful political democracy is not to be found in (electoral) politics at all, 'but below the surface is the organization of a whole network of popular interests into pressure groups'.

Reading between the lines of Crossman one suspects that he was echoing Sidney and Beatrice Webb, who had argued similarly – and certainly not any American theory. Moreover, American theory itself used British material as support for the introduction of group ideas into the US. Bentley (cited above) discusses Britain in passing and Herring (*Virginia Quarterly Review,* 1930, **6,** No.3) is particularly explicit. He draws attention to the similarity between US and British groups, but also notes that in the US the emphasis is upon the legislature, but in Britain the Ministry and the administrative departments are of outstanding importance in the eyes of the reformer and the special-interest spokesman. Truman briefly examines the UK, basing his analyses on Ivor Jenning's *Parliament* (Cambridge University Press, 1957). If Truman was using an established British source as evidence of US group importance, it hardly required the power of post-war American theory to uncover British groups. The original Appendix II of the Jennings book sets out 'Who Made the Laws in 1936–7'. In this he gives the source of legislation – very frequently pressure groups. He unreservedly claims that the national interest is an amalgam of hundreds of group interests (p.190).

The above implies that Samuel Beer did not invent the study of British pressure groups, but his work in the mid-1950s certainly popularized it. Like Truman, however, Beer has denied parentage for too simple a pressure-group view. In 1980 (*Public Administration Bulletin*, No.32) Beer complained that 'No more than in the past do I believe that pressure groups are the sole or even the principal explanation of what happens in politics'. Yet, in 1956, he undoubtedly thought them important when he asked 'Where are your pressure groups?' (*American Political Science Review*, **L**, No.1 (1956)). In 1955 ('The Future of British Politics: an American View', *Political Quarterly*, **26**) where he argued that the main lines of domestic policy would be the same irrespective of party in power (p.33), he noted 'not a politics of class or of social philosophy, but a kind of pressure politics' (p.38). He did go on to qualify this image and said that policy was more than the result of groups pushing an inert government, but the qualification was that it is government which often – seeking electoral support – stimulates group activity. Beer's various articles lead up to *Modern British Politics* (Faber and Faber, 1965, new edn, 1982) in which he labelled the British system one of 'new group politics'.

In the original 1955 article, a single passage conveys two vital arguments. He said he wanted to focus not on 'noisy threats and loud, demanding claims' or 'mass demonstrations', but 'The civil servants of the organised interest groups . . . countless trade unions, trade associations and professional organizations . . . [who] deal directly and continually with civil servants in government'. Yates (see below) calls this kind of professionalized negotiation 'silent politics', as it is usually not the stuff of newspaper headlines, but group adherents would generally claim that such negotiations are the important type of politics. Second, Beer argued, 'While the outright corporatism of the war period, when organized bodies were . . . taken directly into administration, has been dismantled, a quasi-corporatism remains which leaves no important group without a channel of influence' (p.39).

The propositions worth noting are (1) that one type of group (producers) had a different mode of relations with the government than others (protest groups, value changing groups, consumers), and (2) that the systematic involvement of select groups in the process could be presented as quasi-corporatism. These two ideas – multiple modes of interaction and the concept of corporatism – stand out in works of the succeeding twenty-five years. In 1957 (*American Political Science Review*, **L1**, No.3) Beer claimed that 'Vocational pressure groups do not merely advise: they are regularly at the heart of the policy-making process'. Again Beer was pre-empting a major interest in later studies.

Of the volumes that quickly answered Beer's question, Finer's *Anonymous Empire* (Pall Mall, 1966) is certainly the most readable and has lasted well. A. Potter (*Organised Groups in British National Politics*, Faber and Faber, 1961) also follows Beer's advice to discuss the civil servant/group officer interaction rather than that of parliament and public protest. He claims that the 'public campaign has been replaced largely by informal and unostentatious contacts between officials' (p.22). Despite the subtitle, J. D. Stewart's *British Pressure Groups: Their Role in Relation to the House of Commons* (The Clarendon Press, 1958) has a valuable discussion of group–government–department consultations. Of the single case-based studies, H. Eckstein's *Pressure Group Politics: The Politics of the BMA* (Allen and Unwin, 1960) is also of general interest – for example, his discussion of a negotiation–consultation continuum (p.23). A particularly important feature of P. Self and H. Storing, *The State and the Farmer* (Allen and Unwin, 1960) was their refusal to reject the concept of the public interest. Their conclusion was that 'Government cannot, consistently with its responsibility to the public interest, bind itself by such a partnership with any sectional interest'.

Other early case study-based British works include studies of the introduction of commercial television (H. H. Wilson, *Pressure Group*, Secker and Warburg, 1961; penal reform (G. Rose, *The Struggle for Penal Reform*, Stevens, 1962); capital punishment (J. B. Christoph, *Capital Punishment and British Politics*, Allen and Unwin, 1962); and ex-servicemens' associations (G. Wootton, *The Politics of Influence*, Routledge and Kegan Paul, 1963).

A feature of the literature of the period was the interest in classification – a discussion which did not reach very stimulating conclusions. For example, Finer distinguished between 'interest groups' and 'promotional groups' (p.34), and found that the former had more access to Whitehall. The principal argument was that the department and the interest group have mutual needs of each other. He offers the law of inverse proportion, 'The closer and the snugger the Lobby's consultative status, the more exclusive its relationship with its ministry, the less use will it come to make of parliamentary methods'. Potter (1961, pp.25–32) uses a sectional or spokesman/promotional group distinction; Stewart uses a sectional/cause group categorization (1958, p.25).

As R. Kimber and J. J. Richardson describe (*Pressure Groups in Britain*, Dent, 1974, pp.12–14), groups will attempt to use multiple channels in pursuit of their ends but, nonetheless, there is a strong tendency for the sectional-type group to be more interested in long-term, close bureaucratic relations, while the promotional group is involved in public/parliamentary campaigning.

Amending pluralism

It is a cliché to say that pluralism is the ruling intellectual orthodoxy of political science (see, for example, T. R. Dye and L. H. Zeigler, *The Irony of Democracy*, 3rd edn, Duxbury Press, 1975). But it seems paradoxical that quite so many authors reject a so-called dominant paradigm. From about 1960 onwards the popular position was to reject (or at least amend) pluralism. Among the important qualifications are those listed below.

The non-decision issue

P. Bachrach and M. Baratz's book *Power and Poverty: Theory and Practice* (Oxford University Press, 1970), stems from articles in the *American Political Science Review* in 1962 and 1963. Joining in the pluralist's criticism of the alternate elitist concept, Bachrach and Baratz nonetheless contend that the pluralist focus on participation in decisions neglects the possibility that some person or association could exercise its power by preventing important issues from emerging. (See also E. E. Schattsneider, *The Semi-Sovereign People*, Rinehart and Winston, 1960.) This is certainly a logical possibility – which is not to say that in practice it is important. Given the temperamental inclination of the pressure groups students to observe and test, there is something disconcerting about the Bachrach and Baratz argument that power is not necessarily revealed in studies of conflict. Although the phenomenon has now been firmly labelled 'non-decision', it might have been better had it been called 'non-issue'. Evidence of no-decision, or indecision, is not at all the same as non-issue emergence. The Bachrach and Baratz type argument has been extended by others including S. Lukes (*Power: A Radical View,* Macmillan, 1974).

Distorted pluralism

A second type of criticism has been labelled neo-pluralism (E. Nordlinger, *On the Autonomy of the Democratic State*, Harvard University Press, 1981, p.265). In the broad neo-pluralist camp the image is of a 'distorted liberal state' (Nordlinger, p.157). The putative distortion is on two related dimensions. The first is a broader version of the non-decision point – the pluralist competitive policy-making model is normatively unsatisfactory because effective resources are not reasonably equally distributed. This allows certain privileged groups undue influence in public decisions.

Dahl himself has recently observed that he is puzzled by these assertions by critics of pluralist theory that such a theory contends, or assumes, that all groups, interests, interest groups and so on are equal or even substantially equal in organizational capacities and access or resources, or power, or influence, or the like (see R. Dahl, *Dilemmas of Pluralist Democracy*, Yale University Press, 1982, p.208). Dahl cites passages both from Truman's and his own work to indicate that precisely the opposite assumptions were made – e.g. 'In American politics, as in all other societies, control over decisions is unevenly distributed; neither individuals nor groups are political equals' (from *A Preface to Democratic Theory*, pp.145–146).

Nonetheless though Dahl is correct to point out that critics of pluralism have invented weaknesses in the pluralist case, there is a real point of difference between the pluralists and their critics. The pluralist world view can be indicated by several remarks by Dahl; for example, 'Virtually no-one, and certainly no group of more than a few individuals, is entirely lacking in some influence resources' (*Who Governs*, Yale University Press, 1961, p.228), or 'Thus the making of governmental decision is not a majestic march of great majorities. It is the steady appeasement of relatively small groups' (*A Preface to Democratic Theory*, p.146). Critics of pluralism reject this presentation of the political process.

The second distortion was identified by critics such as T. Lowi, *The End of Liberalism* (Norton, 1969); G. McConnell, *Private Power and American Democracy* (Knopf, 1966); H. Kariel, *The Decline of American Pluralism* (Stanford University Press, 1961); Wright Mills, *The Power Elite* (Oxford University Press, 1959); and W. Connolly (ed.), *The Bias of Pluralism* (Atherton Press, 1969). This distortion related to a specific manifestation of the imbalance of group resources – the difficulty of some types of group in getting *access* to the policy process. This point has been developed in Britain by J. Dearlove, *The Politics of Policy in Local Government* (Cambridge University Press, 1973) and R. Benewick in *Knowledge and Belief in Politics*, edited by R. Benewick *et al.* (Allen and Unwin, 1973). The most noteworthy critic on this point is Charles Lindblom's redefinition of his position in *Politics and Markets* (Basic Books, 1977), which argues that there is a privileged position for business in that corporations actively manipulate the public consensus.

However, as the quotations from Herring and Truman above make clear, the tendency for departments and agencies to develop favoured clienteles had long been recognized by those in the pluralist tradition. Departments do not sit back adjudicating group conflict but themselves enter partnerships with interested groups in 'policy communities' (see J.J. Richardson and A.G. Jordan, *Governing Under Pressure*, Martin Robertson, 1979). Truman discusses this at some length in his chapter entitled 'The Web of Relationships in the Administrative Process'. He describes how these departmental/group relations can become 'inflexible' – ruling out consideration of new points of view. The agency is seen as a 'regulator of access'.

There are, in fact, two models of group–departmental relations implicit in much group-orientated writing. There is an *ad hoc*, open competition model but there is a model of sectorized policy making in sub-governments where departments reach accommodations with constituencies of like-minded groups. Many have been able to discuss these 'private governments' (where access is an issue) without denying the utility of the group approach. For example, Murray Edelman, *The Symbolic Uses of Politics* (University of Illinois Press, 1964) draws attention to the mutual benefits of group–department symbiosis. J. LaPalombara, *Interest Groups in Italian Politics* (Princeton University Press, 1964), in a book of wider interest than the title suggests, managed to disagree with Bentley (p.13) and Truman (p.14) but still writes in the general pluralist vein while stressing 'clientela' relations.

The rationality of group action?

A more specific objection (and directly on pressure groups rather than pluralism) is contained in M. Olsen, *The Logic of Collective Action* (Harvard University Press, 2nd edn, 1971). The main Olsen thesis concerns Truman's assumption that individuals will become active in groups merely because they value a particular output. Olsen stressed the 'rational free-rider' proposition that 'unless there is coercion or some other special device to make individuals act in their common interest, rational self-interested individuals will not act to achieve their common or group interests' (p.2). He suggested that this accounts for the frequent group goal of compulsory membership (closed shop) and the supply of by-product incentives by organizations (e.g. cheap insurance as an incentive to join).

Olsen has been influential, but his work has recently been subject to two important criticisms. The first was a book by Terry Moe, *The Organisation of Interests* (University of Chicago Press, 1980); the second an article by R. Kimber, 'Collective Action and the Fallacy of the Liberal Fallacy', *World Politics*, **XXX111**, No.2 (Jan. 1981).

Another dimension on the emergence of groups is put forward by R. H. Salisbury ('An Exchange Theory of Interest Groups', *Mid-West Journal of Political Science* (1969) in his discussion of the group entrepreneur. This has prompted its own specialist sub-literature. (See, for example, P. R. Jones, *Doctors and the BMA*, Gower, 1981, which includes a lengthy bibliography.)

There has been a related discussion on the inner democracy of groups. Work such as G. Wilson, *Special Interests and Policymaking* (Wiley, 1977) suggests that internally democratic processes deny the leadership flexibility in negotiations and that some of the most effective groups are relatively oligarchical.

From pluralism to corporatism?

The debate on pluralism–group theory ran on throughout the 1950s and 1960s – particularly in the context of community power studies. The work which had explicit theoretical concerns came out mainly as anti-pluralist.

The pluralist response has included the second edition of Truman's *The Governmental Process* (1971) and W. Kelso's *American Democratic Theory* (Greenwood Press, 1978). In the general tradition there are useful books by D. R. Hall, *Co-operative Lobbying* (University of Arizona Press, 1969) and Carol S. Greenwald, *Group Power* (Praeger, 1977), J. Berry, *Lobbying for the People* (Princeton, 1977) and G. Wilson, *Interest Groups in the U.S.A.* (Clarendon, 1981). On the whole these books emphasize the growing complexity of making policy in the overcrowded environments which result from the mobilization of more and more groups – rather than extend the theoretical discussion. Douglas Yates, however, in *Bureaucratic Democracy* (Harvard University Press, 1982) valuably focuses on the role of bureaucracy in a pluralist democracy. It might be expected the most significant of all the pluralist responses would be Dahl's *Dilemmas of a Pluralist Democracy* (Yale University Press, 1982), but Dahl chooses to respond to critics obliquely – save for Appendix A – and thus the significance of the book in the context of the long debate on pluralism is not self-evident.

In fact, the orientation of the debate changed in the course of the lengthy gestation of the Dahl book: when N. Polsby and K. Newton had a lengthy, acerbic exchange in *Political Studies, (XXVII* (Dec. 1974)) the discussion was surprising not because the issues had been settled, but because the discussion in these terms had slipped out of common academic currency. The focus of discussion has changed and concerns how (accepted) group departmental relations are to be characterized.

For some time a dual system of politics has been recognized; for example, Schattsneider (work cited) distinguished between 'pressure politics' and 'party politics' (see also Crossman, work cited). In 1966, Stein Rokkan differentiated between 'numerical democracy' and corporate pluralism. (See his chapter in R. Dahl, *Political Opposition in Western Democracies*, Yale, 1966.) In proposing that 'the crucial decisions on economic policy are rarely taken in the parties or in Parliament: the central area is the bargaining table where the government authorities meet directly with the trade union leaders, the representatives of the farmers, the small holders and the fishermen, and the delegates of the Employers' Association. These yearly rounds of negotiations have in fact come to mean more in the lives of rank and file citizens that formal elections', Rokkan seemed to highlight, and make sense of, a downgrading of electoral democracy that was apparently taking place in Western societies. As mentioned above, corporatism was a label that had periodically been used to describe regularized group-involvement in policy making. Variants were Beer (1965) 'quasi-corporatism', Andrew Shonfield (*Modern Capitalism*, Oxford University Press, 1965) 'corporatist formula', J. B. Christoph (1962) 'persistent corporativism', etc. W. Grant and D. Marsh's study of The CBI (Hodder and Stoughton, 1977) discusses the related 'tripartism'. The 'corporate bias' observed by Keith Middlemass in *Politics in Industrial Society* (André Deutsch, 1979) was thus extensively foreshadowed.

From a different intellectual terrain, in 1974 Phillippe Schmitter asked 'Still the century of corporatism?' in a special issue of the *Review of Politics* (Vol.36). In his influential definition, Schmitter claimed 'Corporatism can be defined as a system of interest representation in which the constituent units are organized into a limited number of singular, compulsory, non-competitive, hierarchically ordered and functionally differentiated categories . . .'

Although Schmitter lists a number of basic features which he said were common to both the corporatist and pluralist models – and which were required for 'any realistic model of modern interests politics' – nonetheless much of the new corporatist writing has been explicitly anti-pluralist, such as P. Schmitter and G. Lembruch, *Trends Toward Corporatist Intermediation* (Sage, 1969); G. Lembruch and P. Schmitter, *Patterns of Corporatist Policy-Making* (Sage, 1982); and O. Newman, *The Challenge of Corporatism* (Macmillan, 1981). Other less aggressive sources include R. J. Harrison, *Pluralism and Corporatism* (Allen and Unwin, 1980) and Alan Cawson, *Corporatism and Welfare* (Heinemann Education, 1982).

In 1981 S. Berger edited *Organizing Interests in Western Europe* (Cambridge University Press) which was presented as the successor to H. Ehrmann (ed.), *Interest Groups on Four Continents* (University of Pittsburgh Press, 1958). Whereas the Ehrmann volume had included Beer, Finer, Herring, etc. with their pressure group focus, the Berger volume, including Offe and Schmitter, saw a definite theme of corporatism. The volumes record a shift in academic interests.

In a thorough review of this more recent group-based writing, J. P. Olsen has used the broad concept of 'integrated organizational participation in government' (in P. C. Nystrom and W. H. Starbuck (eds), *Handbook of Organizational Design* (Vol.2, 1981)). Olsen skilfully discusses the influences that lead to the development of these regularized relations. His conclusion is that the fluctuating, *ad hoc* relationships emphasized by Bentley and his followers have been replaced by the idea of stable intimate relationships, a symbiosis of governmental authority and organized interests (p.493). This important point needs to be qualified in two ways. The novelty of this observed symbiosis can be overstated (see above) and not all group/governmental relations are of the symbiosis type.

Schmitter has presented the corporatist approach as a 'strong criticism . . . of the hithertofore dominant ways of conceptualizing the activities of interest groups, the pluralist model' (Schmitter and Lembruch, work cited, p.3). The corporatist literature – with almost no exceptions – fails to link the new emphasis on structured, segmented relations between groups and the government with the similar ideas in the pluralist texts (and even more so in the works of critics of pluralism).

Whereas the corporatists appear to offer a relatively simple model of politics, an alternative image of a growing disorder in policy making is made in Hugh Heclo's article, 'Issue Networks and the Executive Establishment', in A. King (ed.), *The New American Political System* (American Enterprise Institute, 1978). Commonsense and cursory examination of the diversity of groups and issues that exist suggests that a range of modes of interaction will ultimately be required. It is precisely because of the complexity that a corporatist model seems particularly inadequate.

What is not at issue between pluralists and corporatists is that there are regularized, routinized relations between departments and groups. This stress on one of the pluralist models identified above has been labelled 'corporate pluralism' (see M. Heisler, 'Corporate Pluralism Revisited', *Scandinavian Political Studies,* **2** (New Series), No.3 (1979)). The corporate pluralist approach concentrates on describing the segmentation of policy making and the active role of groups in policy development – without the ambitious theoretical claims of corporatism. Good examples of this empirically based approach include M. O. Heisler (ed.), *Politics in Europe* (David McKay, 1974); R. B. Kvavik, *Interest Groups in Norwegian Politics* (Universitetsforlaget, 1976); and J. P. Olsen, *Organized Democracy* (Universitetsforlaget, 1983).

From pluralism to policy studies

Recent British material explicitly on the pressure-group theme is limited, and more commonplace is the related policy studies literature (see Chapter 9). Kimber and Richardson, however, edited two readers in the early 1970s – *Campaigning for the Environment* (Routledge and Kegan Paul, 1974) and *Pressure Groups in Britain* (Dent, 1974). The second is particularly useful as an introduction to general issues. Other collections of case studies have come from B. Frost, *The Tactics of Pressure Groups* (Galliard, 1975), and P. Rivers, *Politics of Pressure* (Harrap, 1974). D. Marsh (ed.), *Pressure Politics* (Junction Books, 1983) contains recent examples, as does G. Alderman, *Pressure Groups and Government in Great Britain* (Longman, 1984). Ryan (1978, work cited), Grant and Marsh, *The C.B.I.* (Hodder and Stoughton, 1977), Dearlove (1973, work cited), and K. Newton, *Second City Politics* (The Clarendon Press, 1976) have all contributed (critically) to group writing. Recent case study-based works include D. Marsh and J. Chambers, *Abortion Politics* (Junction Books, 1981) and E. Ashby and M. Anderson, *The Politics of Clean Air* (Oxford, 1981). There have been some (but still not many) useful works focusing on single interests – such as Grant and Marsh (1977, work cited), R. M. Martin, *T.U.C.: The Growth of a Pressure Group* (The Clarendon Press, 1980).

More fruitful and fashionable than pressure group studies in recent years has been the 'policy studies' movement, which has produced work by K. G. Banting, *Poverty, Politics and Policy* (Macmillan, 1979); K. Ovenden, *The Politics of Steel* (Macmillan, 1978); M. Moran, *The Politics of Industrial Relations* (Macmillan, 1977); B. Hogwood, *Government and Shipbuilding* (Saxon House, 1979); G. Donges, *Policymaking for the Mentally Handicapped* (Gower, 1982); D. Barnes and E. Reid, *Governments and Trade Unions* (Heinemann Educational, 1980); and Martin Holmes, *Political Pressure and Economic Policy* (Butterworths, 1982). Perhaps we owe more to Bentley (1967) for the 'process' noted in his title and 'pressure' in his subtitle, than the concept of the group, which has proved so elusive in use.

PART 3
Politics and government: UK

7
General textbooks on British politics and government

Ivor Burton

The best advice today for a student of British politics and government wanting to buy a textbook is 'Don't'. Nevertheless, there are important works, including some that may properly be described as textbooks, which cannot be classified under one of the areas that form the subject matter of subsequent chapters in this section; it is the object of this chapter to identify them. Textbooks often have a long life, going through several editions and even more impressions: where the data of the original edition is important as an indication of its approach and value today, it will be given, as well as the date of the most recent edition.

Introduction

Textbooks are books prescribed for students to study. They have an important place in the professional education of persons such as lawyers, doctors and priests who are expected to take a mass of factual information into the examination room and to refer to it subsequently in their professional practice. Textbooks also have a role for students of the natural sciences when they provide a preliminary general foundation for later specialized study. Textbooks are similarly encountered as student aids in the social sciences, although many academics deplore their use, arguing that they deceive students into believing that there exists a body of unchallenged knowledge which will be sufficient for them to acquire an understanding of their subject. Textbooks in the narrow sense are directed in political science most commonly at students on low-level courses: British Constitution and its successors for GCE A/level examinations or Public Administration for HNC/D or BEC. The information in them is geared strictly to the requirements of the examination. It will rarely prove of much value in the student's subsequent career, even should he enter the civil or local government service, partly because it rapidly becomes out of date and partly because much of the information relates to a level of government far above that at which the student will operate.

Outside this restricted field, textbooks on British politics and government hardly exist in the true definition of the term. General works covering this subject, as distinct from monographs on particular topics within it, nevertheless abound, many of them important and others useful. A market for them clearly exists, to judge by the number of times many of them are reprinted. In part, this market consists of social science students taking a course on British government and politics as part of a degree in politics, or public administration, or social administration, or sociology, or some other combination of social studies. However, it is important to recognize that the genre existed before that market developed, and that it arose from two sources quite distinct from the needs of social science undergraduates.

England was admired in the nineteenth century for its successful development of representative institutions and responsible government. Some academics looked to constitutional history, and in particular to the medieval foundations of parliament, to explain this achievement, but others wrote, with journalists and politicians, for the general public and used the emerging discipline of political science, both to enlighten and to persuade. At the same time, there was one profession, that of law, which, because it had to practise its arts in dealing with the operations of government itself, discovered a need to educate its students in those operations as well as in the law which related to them. Both types of work, what may usefully be described as 'Essays on the British Constitution' and what may less elegantly be termed 'Works based on Constitutional History and Law', were well established by the Second World War. The first remains a recognizable type, though the emphasis has come to be on the need for reform rather than upon the working of the constitution. The second category has disintegrated. Books on constitutional law, now usually incorporating administrative law into their title (see Chapter 11), have come to be used almost exclusively by lawyers. With important exceptions, they have abandoned the needs of political science students. Books on constitutional history are not even used by students of history despite the growth of studies in nineteenth-century administrative history.

Academic political scientists in the 1950s made a determined attempt to break what they considered to be the constricting mould of 'British Constitution' and to develop alternative analyses of both British politics and British government, two overlapping but not identical fields. The 1960s saw this development result in a number of one-volume books with the title 'British Government and/or Politics'. These have had an impact on the textbooks for low-level examinations, and while the two types remain recognizably different, they overlap at the boundaries. Finally, in the 1970s, the wheel appeared about to come full circle: books were again written whose authors were not ashamed to include the word 'constitution' in the title, and two works demonstrated the continuing value of law in providing a firm foundation for the study of British government.

Works based on constitutional history and law

Books on constitutional and administrative law

The Law and Custom of the Constitution, by W. R. Anson (vol. I, *Parliament*, 1886, subsequently re-edited by Sir Maurice Gwyer, 1922; vol. II, *The Crown*, 1892, subsequently re-edited by A. B. Keith, 1935), established the format for these books. *Constitutional Law*, by E. C. S. Wade and G. G. Phillips (Longman, 1931; 9th edn by A. W. Bradley, under title *Constitutional Law*, 1977) was for long a standby for teachers of British Constitution and a recommended text for their students. In its original editions it was perhaps the epitome of what was wrong with the British constitution approach to British government and politics: an overemphasis upon the role of the courts, an uncritical acceptance of the views of A. V. Dicey (see below), the absence of discussion of the function of political institutions such as parties and groups and an overpowering dullness for students not interested in the law as such. Even so, the criticism was overdone. The advantage of a textbook is that it can be kept up to date, and the later editions of the work incorporated the findings of post-Dicey writing on the constitution. *Constitutional and Administrative Law*, by O. Hood Phillips (Sweet and Maxwell, 1952; 5th edn, 1973), had the advantage of being first written much later. It is essentially a lawyers' book, of use to political science students, but in no way a substitute for a general textbook. *Constitutional and Administrative Law*, by S. A. de Smith (Penguin, 1971; 4th edn by H. Street and R. Brazier, 1981), has probably superseded both works for political scientists. It recognizes, in the words of Professor Street, the General Editor of the series of which it forms part, the need to depart from 'Dicey-as-subsequently-amended-or-doubted' and to incorporate 'the vast and disparate sources of constitutional law: Hansard, Blue Books, White Papers, recent political biography, and periodical literature in the political sciences'. There is a proper emphasis on recent developments in the field of administrative law.

Books deriving from constitutional and administrative law

Introduction to the Study of the Law of the Constitution, by A. V. Dicey (1885, 10th edn with an introduction by E. C. S. Wade, Macmillan, 1959), was not intended to be a textbook, the author disclaiming any pretence of providing 'even a summary, much less a complete account of constitional law'. Dicey wanted to teach his students 'two or three guiding principles which pervade the modern constitution of England'. One of these was the absence in English law of what the French know as *droit administratif*. Dicey's views, based on Whig principles which emphasized the restricted role and powers of government in a free society, were distorted subsequently by later authorities, notably Lord Chief Justice Hewart, and insofar as they were used to deny the possibility of collectivism within the law were opposed by politicians as much as by political scientists. The latter should nevertheless at some stage read Dicey in the original. Not all constitutional lawyers followed Dicey uncritically, and one such, Ivor Jennings, planned an ambitious work in three volumes in the 1930s which aimed to set constitutional law in its wider political context. The work was interrupted by the Second World War and ceased to be a single work, so much as three separate works. The first two, *Cabinet Government* (Cambridge University Press, 1936; 3rd edn, 1959; re-issued in paperback, 1969) and *Parliament* (Cambridge University Press, 1939; 2nd edn, 1957; new paperback edn, 1969), remain standard works, although out of date, because of their comprehensiveness: they provide an authoritative answer on questions totally neglected by one-volume introductions to British politics and government. The third work, *Party Politics* (Cambridge University Press, 1960–1962 in 3 volumes: *Appeal to the People*, 1960; *The Growth of the Parties*, 1961; and *The Structure of Politics*, 1962), was much less successful, and the failure of

Jennings-inspired constitutions in the Commonwealth added to a lack of confidence in his political analysis.

Jennings inspired many popularizers, and himself operated in that area with *The British Constitution* (Cambridge University Press, 1941; 5th edn, 1966). It is perhaps sufficient to mention the best examination text for British Constitution, *The British Constitution* by J. Harvey and L. Bather (Macmillan; 4th edn, 1977), strenuously opposed by political scientists because of its very success, for which the nature of the examination was the real culprit. Academic works in this category have been few since Jennings but it is too soon to say that the category is obsolete. *The British Constitution*, by H. R. G. Greaves (Allen and Unwin, 1938; 2nd edn, 1948 o.p.), in fact covers much the same ground as later books with the title of 'British Government and Politics', including chapters on the central and local administration, the education system, the political opposition and democracy. *Government and the Law: an Introduction to the Working of the Constitution in Britain*, by T. C. Hartley and J. A. G. Griffith (Weidenfeld and Nicolson, 1975; 2nd edn, 1981), sets out to 'treat students of law and of politics as a single audience'. Parts of the book reflect Professor Griffith's own contribution to political science; it is comprehensive, dealing with political, administrative and legal institutions and with such recently arising issues as police powers and the European Communities; it is too soon to say whether it has succeeded in reuniting political science with constitutional and administrative law (see Chapter 11). *Parliamentary Government in Britain*, by Michael Rush (Pitman, 1981), the most recent work in the tradition of Jennings, appears to revert to a conventional treatment, and perhaps to fall between the categories of general introduction and constitutional essay.

Constitutional histories

The Constitutional History of England, by F. W. Maitland (Cambridge University Press, 1908, but consisting of lectures delivered in 1887/1888; re-issued in paperback, 1961), is notable for the fact that this great lawyer recognized the very developments that Dicey denounced. Thus, the scheme for the lectures circulated to his students says under the heading 'Social Affairs and Local Government': 'Only possible to hint at the existence of this great field of law which constantly grows wider; but at least its existence should be known'. A very different work, deservedly successful, is *The Constitutional History of Modern Britain, 1485–1937*, by D. L. Keir (Adam and Charles Black, 1938; 5th edn, 1953). It contains a useful, but now outdated, outline of modern administrative as well as of modern constitutional developments. Quite unique (alas) is *A Hundred Years of English Government*, by K. B. Smellie (Duckworth, 1937; 2nd edn, 1951 o.p.): the material here, organized around three themes, The State and Society, Government and Parties and The Machinery of Administration, with a chapter on the 'Interregnum' of 1914–1918, is available in one volume nowhere else and the absence of a more modern work covering the same field is to be deplored, though G. H. L. le May, *The Victorian Constitution* (Duckworth, 1979), goes some way towards filling the gap. *The British Cabinet*, by J. P. Mackintosh (Stevens, 1962; 3rd edn paperback, 1981) is, despite the title, an historical work dealing with the working of the constitution, and its success emphasizes the essential contribution of history to the study of contemporary British politics and government.

Works by modern political scientists

This category blossomed in the 1960s with the paperback revolution and the expansion of degree courses in the social sciences. Up to that time, academic political scientists wishing to provide their students with a sound introduction to British government, based on a political science analysis and including material on political institutions and processes and on the British social structure and political culture, had to rely upon their own lectures. Two substantial general works which properly fall into this category, *The Government of England*, by A. L. Lowell, 2 vols, Macmillan, 1908), and *The Government of England*, by S. Low (Unwin, 1904), had been the standby of journalists and political commentators up to the 1930s, but nothing succeeded them. In the 1960s, academics began to publish shortened versions of their lectures. Almost invariably, the word *government* replaced *constitution*, as in *The Government of Great Britain*, by G. C. Moodie (Methuen, 1964; 3rd edn, 1971). The bibliography listed nearly two hundred works for a book of only two hundred pages dealing with the historical background, the social background, the electoral and party system, cabinet government, parliament, the administration and the civil service, the judicial system, local government, the administration of the welfare state and foreign relations, ending with a final overview. It was an impressive sweep, which dispelled the notion that British government was a dull and narrow subject. But it cannot be regarded as a textbook: five and a half pages on local government will not suffice even for the needs of a first-year undergraduate in a tolerant department.

Others have succeeded, in what must be regarded as an impossible task, no better than Professor Moodie. *The British System of Government*, by A. H. Birch (Allen and Unwin, 1967; 4th edn, 1980), is longer and less comprehensive. It concentrates upon explaining how the total system works rather than upon analysing the component structures. Professor Birch employs two useful distinctions, between the development of the constitution and the survival of medieval institutions and between the governmental and political institutions and the administrative and policy-making processes. Each chapter has a guide to further reading but there is no bibliography. The book is a good introduction in that it provides an understanding of British government in political science terms, but it lacks information and so cannot be regarded as a real textbook.

The Government of Modern Britain, by F. Stacey (Oxford University Press, 1968), consists of 405 pages, again without a bibliography. The structure of the book is somewhat eccentric. It begins with three chapters on voting and elections followed by five on the House of Commons and one on the House of Lords. Only one chapter, xv, deals with the machinery of administration (followed by one on administrative tribunals) and there is nothing on local government. The author confessed that the origin of the book lay in the lectures he gave to first- and second-year students, and no doubt they had other opportunities of learning about the missing material which was virtually the whole field of public administration. The book also bears the stamp of its time: three pages on the Department of Economic Affairs, abolished soon after the book was published, and one line on the Home Office (set in a chapter on pressure groups). It was written at the very moment when the institutional framework it described was being transformed. The late Professor Stacey therefore produced a further volume, *British Government 1966–1975: Years of Reform* (Oxford University Press, 1975), partly as a supplement, but also as a volume in its own right. Again, priority is given to electoral and parliamentary reform (and the concept of 'reform' is not always useful as a way of analysing change), but there is much more space than in the previous volume given to public administration, including chapters on local government reform and health service reform, and there are 8 pages of bibliography. *British Government and Politics*, by R. M. Punnett (Heinemann, 1968; 4th edn, 1980), has 412 pages of text and 66 pages of bibliography. The author states his purpose as being 'to give a more detailed and all-embracing account of government and politics in Britain than is to be found in the various general works that already exist'. The book is organized into three main parts, political institutions, parliamentary government and public administration, with a short introduction on the social context of British politics and a final conclusion analysing the political system in Britain. There is no doubt that this is the book that students will find most useful and least harmful. The bibliography alone is sufficient to justify its being recommended. Nevertheless, there are imbalances, and in general there is very little description of the substantive activities of government. *Government in Britain*, by C. T. Popham (Pergamon, 1969), is valuable for that very purpose, dealing with economic affairs, foreign and defence policy and social policy. There is also by way of conclusion a short introduction to public administration as an academic discipline. All this, however, is at the expense, in a book of 268 pages, of a reduced treatment of other areas, and because of its character, the book suffers even more than most from becoming rapidly out of date.

Governing Britain: a Guide-Book to Political Institutions, by A. H. Hanson and M. Walles (Fontana/Collins, 1970; 3rd edn, 1980) has some claim to be 'a text for students of politics', especially when viewed in the context of the paperback series on Public Administration by the same publishers which includes *Administering Britain* by Jeffery Stanyer and Brian Smith (Fontana/Collins, 1976). It is, however, refreshingly different from other such students' texts. Employing the concept of 'new wine in old bottles', the authors draw attention to an often-neglected feature of British government, the contradiction between age and innovation. The authors thereby emphasize that British politics and government are not presently established on secure foundations but under great strain while attempting to adapt their institutions to the demands imposed by the establishment of a welfare state, the loss of empire and the loss of markets. When its omissions are filled in by what its title suggests is a kind of companion volume, Hanson and Walles can serve as a textbook; it is also a thought-provoking constitutional essay, a category considered below.

These works do not exhaust the list of textbooks on British Government and Politics; there are many texts for low-level examinations, just as there used to be on British Constitution. These books have a purpose, but they cannot be counted as fulfilling a need for academic students in higher education, still less for the general public. There are, however, books on British public administration, in addition to *Administering Britain* already referred to, such as *British Public Administration*, by J. A. Cross (University Tutorial Press, 1970) which in many ways operate more successfully as textbooks than more ambitious works covering all of government and politics. An extended discussion of the literature in this area can be found in Chapter 10, Public Administration and Policy Studies.

There are also general works on British politics which include sufficient material on government institutions and processes for them to be reviewed in this chapter. There are, in particular, the works of Richard Rose: *Politics in England* (Faber, 1965; new edns under the title *Politics in England Today*, Faber, 1974 and *Politics in England: an Interpretation for the 1980s*, Faber, 1980) which incorporate chapters on the constitutional machinery and on the policy-making processes. They are perhaps the most successful attempt to fuse government and politics as areas of study, but they do not incorporate the public administration sector as successfully.

'Readers', collections of reprinted papers and extracts from longer works, were, like one-volume texts on British government and politics, a product of the 1960s. There are some useful works in this category that can provide an introduction for students to the findings of political science on this subject. *Crisis in British Government: The Need for Reform*, edited by W. J. Stankiewicz (Collier–Macmillan, 1967), reproduces 32 papers and extracts grouped into sections on constitutional principles, parliament, government and the administration, the electoral system and the political process, local government and regionalism and the Commonwealth. *British Government in an Era of Reform*, edited by the same person (Collier–Macmillan, 1976), reproduces 26 items similarly arranged. *Readings on British Politics and Government*, edited by Robert Benewick and Robert E. Dowse (University of London Press, 1968), reproduces 15 items, all, except for two on the cabinet, on politics rather than on government. *Policy Making in Britain: A Reader in Government*, edited by Richard Rose (Macmillan, 1969), includes 24 items and a bibliography of articles; at the time it was compiled, a valuable addition. There were also two readers dealing exclusively with British politics: *Studies in British Politics*, edited by Richard Rose (Macmillan, 1966; 3rd edn, 1976), which has remained in print, and *British Politics: People. Politics and Parliament*, edited by Anthony King (Heath & Co., Boston, USA, 1966), which has not. Readers are not textbooks and perhaps they are evidence that good textbooks on a subject do not, for some reason, exist. They have largely gone out of fashion, perhaps rendered redundant by the illegal use of a photocopier. The works listed above have no special virtues save convenience.

Documents on Contemporary British Government and Politics: Vol. 1: British Government and Constitutional Change; Vol. 2:

Local Government in Britain, edited by Martin Monogue (Cambridge University Press, 1977), contains commentary as well as documents and also a bibliography, and should be noticed in the context of this chapter. In some ways it might constitute a better textbook than most of the works so far considered, but it also repeats the failings of readers in that it reproduces as documents what are only extracts from academic commentaries. The second volume, where there are abundant documents in the shape of official reports, White Papers and statutes, is less open to this criticism. *British Government since 1918*, by Lord Campion *et al.* (Allen and Unwin, 1950), is in a category of its own, being a symposium of essays by Lord Campion on Parliament, D. N. Chester on the Cabinet, W. J. M. Mackenzie on the Central Administration, W. A. Robson on Administrative Law, Sir Arthur Street on Quasi-government Bodies and J. H. Warren on Local Government. It is to be recommended for the detail to be found in it that is not readily accessible elsewhere.

Essays on the British constitution

The English Constitution, by Walter Bagehot (1867; republished with an introduction by R. H. S. Crossman, Fontana, 1963; available in the original format, Oxford University Press, 1928), has deservedly become a classic. Bagehot set out, originally in a series of articles in *The Fortnightly*, to explain how the constitution really worked, as distinct from how it might appear to an outsider examining how its formal institutions operate. He relegated the monarchy to a decorative role which he called 'dignified', and identified the cabinet as playing the effective role in politics and government by resolving conflicts between the representative institutions and the executive government. His analysis has had a strange fate: rendered obsolete almost at once by the 1867 Reform Act which within less than a quarter of a century led to the subordination of the House of Commons to the executive government, it continued nevertheless to be accepted as embodying essential truths by the politicians themselves (and incidentally by at least one monarch, since George V's tutor accorded it the status of a true textbook, requiring it to be paraphrased, committed to memory and followed for subsequent constitutional actions), up to, and even beyond, R. H. S. Crossman's revision. Bagehot therefore remains essential reading, because his book enshrines some of the important myths that continue to bedevil both British constitutional development and its academic study in the second half of the twentieth century.

Bagehot's reputation continued undiminished until the successful working of the constitution itself began to be questioned between the wars. A variety of writing contributed to this change. *Thoughts on the Constitution*, by L. S. Amery (Oxford University Press, 1947; re-issued in paperback in 1964, o.p.), addressed itself particularly to the central issue of the function of the cabinet, repeating the views first advanced by the author as a practising statesman in the 1930s in favour of a small controlling cabinet of non-departmental ministers. *Government and Parliament: a Survey from the Inside*, by Lord Morrison of Lambeth (Oxford University Press, 1954; 3rd edn, 1964, o.p.), was wider in scope and less polemical. It contained much material indispensible for an understanding of government in the 1950s and thereafter. There has been nothing as good from a practising statesman since. *Parliamentary Government in England*, by H. J. Laski (Allen and Unwin, 1938, o.p.), was a polemic, of interest now because of the position the author held in the Labour Party. His later work, *Reflexions on the Constitution, the House of Commons, the Cabinet, the Civil Service* (Manchester University Press, 1951), was intended to justify rather than to promote. *The People and the Constitution*, by C. S. Emden (Oxford University Press, 1933; paperback 1962, o.p.), added a new dimension to Bagehot's analysis in discussing doctrines such as the mandate, as did *Government by Committee: an Essay on the British Constitution*, by K. C. Wheare (Oxford University Press, 1955), which analysed the different uses of committees in British government. *Some Problems of the Constitution*, by Geoffrey Marshall and G. C. Moodie (Hutchinson, 1959; rev. edn, 1967), dealt with a number of contemporary issues.

Essays on the British constitution suffered from the stigma attached to that term by the new post-war generation of political scientists who wished to emphasize the political dimension of government. Yet the genre has never died and may perhaps, in the context of Britain's membership of the European Communities, a possible break-up of traditional political allegiances, and proposals for devolution, be due for a revival. The baby may indeed have been thrown out with the bath water. *Representative and Responsible Government: an Essay on the British Constitution*, by A. H. Birch (Allen and Unwin, 1964), consists of an analysis of traditional British constitutional doctrines, emphasizing that there is more than one, followed by a discussion of modern theories of representation and of arguments for collectivism. The book then examines the machinery of responsible government and the nature of public opinion before advancing well-argued conclusions on the state of representative and responsible government in Britain. *The Government and Politics of Britain*, by John P. Mackintosh (Hutchinson, 1970; 5th edn, revised by Peter Richards, 1982), is, like the same author's *The British Cabinet*, not what it seems but, avowedly, an essay on the British constitution, concentrating upon a number of issues such as prime-ministerial power (from which the author was a sufferer), the effectiveness of parliament, the condition of the civil service, local government and the nationalized industries. *Britain's Developing Constitution: Studies in Political Science*, itself a significant title, by Peter Bromhead (Allen and Unwin, 1974), argues unequivocally that political issues can be understood only in the context of an understanding of constitutional development. *In Search of the Constitution*, by Nevil Johnson (Pergamon, 1977), is a forcefully argued example of the reform-biased analysis of the British constitution, expounding in particular the need for the development of public law.

Conclusion

The fact that the wheel appears to have come full circle, that not only are books again being published on the British constitution but that there are works on constitutional (and administrative) law again being directed at social scientists, while no new books on British government and politics appear likely to usurp the existing standbys, must confirm the advice to the student not to buy a textbook. It would seem that political scientists can no more produce a satisfactory single volume than constitutional lawyers and historians. The fact is that to make a success of studying British government and politics requires a knowledge of political science, constitutional and political history, sociology and public administration, not to speak of comparative government and politics. An attempt to do all this in a single volume, and usually an introductory volume at that, must be doomed to failure. Many of the books discussed here are important works, throwing light on British government and politics, but they are not textbooks in any meaningful sense of the term and are not to be recommended as such. The existence of so many different kinds of single-volume works confirms the conclusion that we have not yet mastered the subject sufficiently for it to be the subject of a textbook.

8
Political parties and elections
Janet Seaton

Political parties

Introduction

The literature concerning political parties is almost as diverse as the parties themselves, and as the old two-party political system becomes more complicated by the rise of new parties, it becomes increasingly necessary to have some framework within which to organize the field.

Definitions are not easy to formulate, but there are certain features which are generally accepted as a minimum statement of what constitutes a political party:

(1) It must have an organization.
(2) It must compete for positions of political power within the political system (i.e. contest elections) as one of its primary aims.
(3) It must have a distinctive label that distinguishes it from other political groups.

It is worth noting that you do not have to belong to a political party in order to stand as a candidate in UK elections, and in recent years there has been a proliferation of candidates, particularly at by-elections, who describe themselves on the ballot paper using curious party names. Concern over such 'freak' candidatures during the First World War led to the introduction of the deposit at parliamentary elections, but its present level is now widely regarded as being too low to have any deterrent value. Indeed, the Home Affairs Select Committee report on the *Representation of the People Acts* (HC 32, Session 1982–1983) recommended that the deposit should be increased to £1000 and periodically reviewed. The publicity surrounding by-elections and the 1969 change in the law which allowed candidates' descriptions on the ballot paper to include their political activities may have encouraged this trend, but eccentric independents do not fulfil the first requirement of having an organization. Even Independent Members standing for re-election must be disqualified on this count, and it could be argued that a party must seek (at least in theory) to fill more than one position of political power if it is to be taken seriously.

Parties are generally regarded, by their activists at least, as being useful because they 'organize the vote'. In pluralist societies a number of parties compete for support amongst the electorate by putting forward a distinct programme of policies, thus enabling people to choose between them. In single-party states the party machine is difficult to distinguish from the organs of executive power, so its functions differ substantially from the parties we are considering here. This underlines the fact that the literature of parties, and to some extent elections as well, is very closely bound up with the political ideas and the political system in which they operate.

Primary sources

The literature relating to political parties is dominated by the publications of the parties themselves. Only by studying these primary sources can the ideology and to some extent the organizational strategy of each party be accurately discovered. The party manifestos are the most important sources of the party's ideology. They may be published at any time, but they are always produced at the time of a general election, and can be found collected together in the *Times Guide to the House of Commons* for the Parliament returned at each election. F. W. S. Craig has also published a historical collection entitled *British General Election Manifestos 1900–1974* (Macmillan, rev. edn, 1975), which is mainly confined to Conservative, Labour and Liberal manifestos. The Conservative Research Department also publishes from time to time *The Campaign Guide*, which sets out detailed policy statements and criticizes the stance of the other parties on the major issues of the day. A similar publication was produced by the Labour Party before the 1979 General Election, called *Labour*

Party Campaign Handbooks, which appeared in twenty-three parts, each covering a major policy area, but this was not repeated in 1983.

Annual reports of each party's conference not only show the major issues of debate for the party but its organizational and personnel details as well. Labour Party Conference Reports go back to 1900, although the name Labour Party dates, strictly speaking, from 1906. The earliest reports can be found in a reprinted volume, *The Labour Party Foundation Conference and Annual Conference Report 1900–1905* (Labour Representation Committee 1900–1905; Hammersmith Bookshop reprint, 1967). From 1906 the series is simply called *Labour Party Conference Reports*.

Conservative Party conference reports date from 1867, but since 1978 they no longer publish a full report, although they do release the text of speeches by Ministers. This is much less satisfactory from an archival point of view, but it does perhaps reflect the different place of the party conference in Conservative Party politics. Once again, F. W. S. Craig has compiled and published a very useful work of reference: *Conservative and Labour Party Conference Decisions 1945–1981* (Parliamentary Research Services, 1982), which is arranged in broad subject areas. The Liberal Party has never published verbatim reports of its annual conferences (which it prefers to call Assemblies), although texts of the resolutions debated at each Assembly are available since 1976. The party was established as the National Liberal Federation in 1877, but the party conference only really became a forum for policy discussion in the mid-1960s. A subject index to Assembly resolutions since 1967 can be found in the Gladstone Club's *Directory of Liberal Party Resolutions 1967–1978*, with its annual supplements. The party also produces an annual report giving details of work and organization of the party during the previous year. The newest party of all, the Social Democratic Party, continuing its conscious attempts to break out of the old party system, does not hold a party conference in the traditional sense. The party's representative policy-making body, the Council for Social Democracy, meets three times a year to formulate policy. There is no report of proceedings although major policy papers are published. Once a year there are also Consultative Assemblies, at which rank-and-file party members can discuss party policy, but no publications will result from these. Most parties also publish weekly or monthly periodicals for their members which provide up-to-date statements of the party's position on current events as well as news of internal party developments. *Labour Weekly*

(1971–) and *Liberal News* (1936–) appear weekly; *Conservative Newsline* (September 1982–) is monthly and the Conservative Research Department's *Politics Today* (1975–) appears fortnightly. Confusingly, the Labour Research Department, which publishes the monthly *Labour Research* (1917–), has no connection with the Labour Party.

On a particular issue it is always advisable to check whether the party has published a pamphlet on the subject. The bigger parties aim to cover all major issues in their pamphlet series, smaller ones such as Plaid Cymru or the Communist Party may only publish one or two items a year, so their manifesto would be a better source of general policy. Sometimes smaller parties produce useful pamphlets about themselves and their history. A recent example is Ian Birchall's *The Smallest Mass Party in the World* (Socialist Workers Party, 1981). References can often be found in the bibliographies of secondary sources. Some interest groups and factions within the larger parties also produce newsletters and pamphlets to publicize their point of view, such as *YL Newsletter* (Young Liberals), which can provide useful additional detail on particular policy stances or on differences of opinion within the party. One of the most influential groups is Conservative Action for Electoral Reform, which represents a sizeable section of Conservative Party opinion in favour of proportional representation, and regularly publishes pamphlets on the subject. Equally significant to the Labour movement, and of much greater antiquity and prestige, is the Fabian Society, which was founded in 1884 and 'exists to further socialist education and research'. It is affiliated to the Labour Party, and publishes *Fabian News* (1891–) as well as the *Fabian Tracts* (1884–), *Fabian Research Series* (1932–) and *Young Fabian* series of pamphlets (1961–). Their archives are in Nuffield College, Oxford. The Bow Group, although not connected with the Conservative Party, is open only to those with Conservative views and serves as the Conservative equivalent of the Fabian Society in publishing a major series of policy pamphlets.

Turning from ideology to organization, each party's constitution and rules for constituency branches are printed either as part of the annual conference record or as separate pamphlets. The constitutions of the major parties are reproduced in J. D. Lees and R. Kimber, *Political Parties in Modern Britain* (Routledge and Kegan Paul, 1972); but since the party conferences usually have the power to amend the constitution, a new one tends to be printed after any changes have been made. Detailed party procedures on such matters as the selection of parliamentary candidates may also be found in the party's rules for constituency branches.

The Conservative Party, for example, has *Model Rules for Constituency and Branch* (rev. edn, Conservative Central Office, 1982) and the Labour Party publishes *Rules for Constituency Labour Parties & Branches* (1981). References to the constitution and rules of regional parties can be found in *United Kingdom Facts*, by R. Rose and I. McAllister (Macmillan, 1982).

Both the Labour and Conservative Parties have libraries at their London headquarters where researchers can consult their publications on request. Most of the Conservative Party archives have been deposited at the Bodleian Library, but the archives of the Labour Party can be consulted in London by appointment, subject to a fifteen-year closure rule on sensitive material. The other parties, suffering from a lack of resources, do not operate their own libraries as such.

Secondary sources

Works about political parties can best be considered under three main headings. They tend to focus on either the party system, party organization and finance or on studies of individual parties.

THE PARTY SYSTEM

A major theme of recent writings is the future of the system. Does the proliferation of parties mean the end of the two-party system? H. M. Drucker explores this theme in his *Multi-party Britain* (Macmillan, 1979), which includes chapters by contributors on major and minor parties, as well as a very useful section on extra-parliamentary parties which are not otherwise well documented. A more analytical approach is used by S. E. Finer in *The Changing British Party System, 1945–1979* (American Enterprise Institute, 1980), which also discusses party organization and the impact of the electoral system. Another study of the likely effects of the rise of 'minor' parties is David Butler's *Governing Without a Majority* (Collins, 1983), which discusses various types of possible future 'hung parliaments'. A thorough up-to-date survey is provided by Alan R. Ball's *British Political Parties: the Emergence of a Modern Party System* (Macmillan, 1981), which includes a good bibliography. Further historical detail can be found in the standard works: *The Growth of the British Party System*, by Ivor Bulmer-Thomas (2nd edn, John Baker, 1967) and *Party Politics: the Growth of Parties*, by Sir Ivor Jennings (Vol.2, Cambridge University Press, 1961). For many years accepted as the standard explanation of the rise of parties, *Democracy and the*

Organisation of Political Parties, by M. I. Ostrogorski (2 vols, Quartet Books, 1964) is still a classic work of reference in the field. S. H. Beer has just reprinted his *Modern British Politics* (Faber, new edn, 1982) in which he takes a historical view of the links between ideology and policy making, concentrating mainly on the Conservative and Labour parties.

PARTY ORGANIZATION AND FINANCE

The best modern study of political parties is Richard Rose's *The Problem of Party Government* (Macmillan, 1974). An important comparison of the internal policies of the Labour and Conservative parties is to be found in *British Political Parties*, by R. T. McKenzie (Heinemann, 2nd edn, 1963). Party organization is well analysed in Lees and Kimber's *Political Parties in Modern Britain* (Macmillan, 1972), and a detailed examination of the regional structure of the Labour and Conservative parties can be found in David J. Wilson, *Power and Party Bureaucracy in Britain* (Saxon House, 1975). An excellent historical study of the growth of party organization after the Reform Act of 1867 at both national and local level is H. J. Hanham, *Elections and Party Management: Politics in the Time of Disraeli and Gladstone* (Harvester Press, 2nd edn, 1978). It includes a useful bibliography. Studies of local constituency parties tend to focus on election campaigns, but *Constituency Labour Parties in Britain*, by E. G. Janosik (Pall Mall Press, 1968), is a good example of a study of constituency party leaders and activists. A more detailed analysis of political sociology and party membership is D. Berry's survey of attitudes in Liverpool: *The Sociology of Grass Roots Politics* (Macmillan, 1970). The subject of candidate selection is dealt with by two classic studies: A. Ranney, *Pathways to Parliament* (Macmillan, 1965) and M. Rush, *The Selection of Parliamentary Candidates* (Nelson, 1969). It is a tribute to their efforts that nobody has had much to say on the subject since their publication. The study of party finance should be much easier since the publication of Michael Pinto-Duschinsky's *British Political Finance 1830–1980* (American Enterprise Institute, 1981). Consideration of the arguments for state aid to political parties outside Parliament can also be found in one of the few official publications in this field, namely the *Report of the Committee on Financial Aid to Political Parties* (Chairman, Lord Houghton; Cmnd. 6601, HMSO, 1976), which recommended state aid at both central and local levels by a system of partial reimbursement of candidates' election expenses. This has never been implemented. The highly respected Hansard

Society for Parliamentary Government published a report on the subject in July 1981 entitled *Paying for Politics*, in which they recommended a system of state aid dependent upon matching contributions to party funds. This provoked little comment. Analysis of company donations (principally to the Conservative Party), appear every year in the August issue of *Labour Research* and in more detail in the Labour Party Research Department's regular Information Paper, *Company Donations to the Tory Party and other Political Organisations*, which is usually published in August or September.

Since 1975, state aid has been given to opposition parties in Parliament on the basis of the number of seats won and votes gained at the previous general election. It is designed to finance secretarial and research support mainly for opposition front-bench spokesmen.

The role of the party conference is thoroughly discussed by Lewis Minkin in his book *The Labour Party Conference* (Manchester University Press, 2nd edn, 1980). Unfortunately, there is nothing similar for the other parties.

INDIVIDUAL PARTIES

It is noticeable that more is being written about elections and voting behaviour than about parties as entities. There are very few studies of individual parties, apart from the minor parties whose increasing electoral success has brought them widespread attention; whereas many books concentrate on the party in power by discussing a particular administration, for example *Labour in Power?: A Study of the Labour Government 1974–79*, by D. Coates (Longman, 1980); or on a short historical period, for example, P. Adelman, *The Decline of the Liberal Party 1910–1931* (Longman, 1981); or on one aspect of the party such as *The Making of Conservative Party Policy: the Conservative Research Department since 1929*, by John Ramsden (Longman, 1980). Biographies of Ministers or prominent politicians should not be overlooked as they can provide valuable insights into particular incidents or periods.

The Conservative Party
An early bibliography of Conservatism is G. D. M. Block, *A Source Book of Conservatism* (Conservative Political Centre, 1964). There are many books discussing the history of the party at various periods, but among the best are *The Conservative Party from Peel to Churchill*, by Robert Blake (Eyre and Spottiswoode,

1970), which surveys the period from 1830 to 1955; *The Conservatives: a History from their Origins to 1965*, edited by Lord Butler (Allen and Unwin, 1977); and to bring the story up to date, *The Conservative Party from Heath to Thatcher*, by R. Behrens (Saxon House, 1980). The major work on ideology remains Ian Gilmour's *Inside Right: A Study of Conservatism* (Hutchinson, 1977), although Z. Layton-Henry's collection of conference papers, *Conservative Party Politics* (Macmillan, 1980), provides an interesting insight into the Conservative Party as a party in opposition. A critical look at more recent developments is taken by S. Hall and M. Jacques in *The Politics of Thatcherism* (Lawrence and Wishart, 1983), which is a collection of essays from *Marxism Today*.

The Labour Party

The early history is well set out in *The Emergence of the Labour Party 1880–1924*, by Roger Moore (Hodder and Stoughton, 1978). Details of the developing party organization are to be found in *A History of the Labour Party from 1914*, by G. D. H. Cole (Routledge and Kegan Paul, 1948). A good introduction which also studies the more recent period is *A Short History of the Labour Party*, by H. Pelling (Macmillan, 6th edn, 1978). Dennis Kavanagh has edited a useful collection of papers which discuss various aspects of current controversy within the party: *The Politics of the Labour Party* (Allen and Unwin, 1982). One of the best studies of ideology remains *Parliamentary Socialism*, by R. Miliband (Merlin Press, 2nd edn, 1972), although Anthony Crosland's thinking in *The Future of Socialism* (Jonathan Cape, 1956) and *Socialism Now*, essays edited by Dick Leonard (Jonathan Cape, 1974) is still considered a formative influence in socialist philosophy. A more recent account of ideological division in the party is S. Haseler's *The Tragedy of Labour* (Blackwell, 1980), and *The Battle for the Labour Party*, by David and Maurice Kogan (Kogan Page, 2nd edn, 1983), charts the recent power struggles within the party in a clear and structured way.

The Liberal Party

The Liberal Party is not so well documented as it might be, in spite of many discussions of its rise and fall at various periods. The most useful works are *The Formation of the British Liberal Party 1857–68*, by J. Vincent (Constable, 1966); *History of the Liberal Party 1895–1970*, by R. Douglas (Sidgwick and Jackson, 1971); and Chris Cook's more recent *Short History of the Liberal Party 1900–1976* (Macmillan, 1976), which includes a very useful bib-

liographic note. A more sociological study is *The Liberal Party*, by
J. S. Rasmussen (Constable, 1965). A thorough historical study of
ideology is P. Clarke's *Liberals and Social Democrats* (Cambridge
University Press, 1978), now a source of certain renewed interest.
Clarke's arguments also appear in a book edited by V. Bogdanor,
Liberal Party Politics (Oxford University Press, 1983), which
surveys Liberal Party fortunes since 1931. It is a similar work to
Layton-Henry's *Conservative Party Politics* and Kavanagh's *The
Politics of the Labour Party* (see above), which also resulted from
conferences sponsored by the Social Science Research Council
(now the Economic and Social Research Council).

The Social Democratic Party
Although a recent phenomenon, the formation and development
of the SDP has attracted considerable attention. Ian Bradley's
Breaking the Mould? (Martin Robertson, 1981) traces its emergence from the Labour Party, while Hugh Stephenson's *Claret and
Chips* (Michael Joseph, 1982) focuses on the leading personalities
and the central organization. The latter reprints as appendices
some useful documents such as the Limehouse Declaration.

Minor parties
The best starting point is *Minor Parties at British Parliamentary
Elections 1885–1974*, by F. W. S. Craig (Macmillan, 1975), which
lists which parties have stood, their candidates and results, and
gives a short list of sources on each. This should be supplemented
by *United Kingdom Facts* (see above), Chapter 3: Political Parties,
which covers parties in Wales, Scotland and Northern Ireland, the
latter being excluded from Craig. A short bibliography is given in
each case. An early study of small parties and pressure groups is
G. Thayer, *The British Political Fringe* (Anthony Blond, 1965).
Some of the material has been superseded by later works, but it is
still a useful survey of groupings who were then outside the
two-party system. Other studies of minor parties have concentrated on those of the Right, the Left or the various nationalist
viewpoints. One of the most useful is *Left, Right: the March of
Political Extremism in Britain*, by J. Tomlinson (John Calder,
1981). Blake Baker's recent 'exposé of the extreme Left in
Britain', *The Far Left* (Weidenfeld and Nicolson, 1981), also
contains some helpful information not available elsewhere. Right-
wing movements were not previously very well covered, but *The
British Right*, edited by N. Nugent and R. King (Saxon House,
1977) and Harvester Press' occasional series of limited but useful
bibliographical guides entitled *The Radical Right and Patriotic
Movements in Britain* (during 1975, published in 1978; and during

1978, published in 1982) have helped to fill the gap. They have also produced a similar publication dealing with left-wing political movements entitled *The Left in Britain: a Checklist and Guide* (Harvester Press, 1976) which covers groups that were active between 1904 and 1972. Single studies of individual small parties are too numerous to list here, and there is certainly room for a comprehensive bibliography in this area.

Elections

Introduction

The major purpose of any political party must be to contest elections. It is inevitable, therefore, that much of the literature relating to parties is also important to the understanding of elections. However, the electoral system within which parties have to operate, the election process itself and the political implications of both of these have each been studied separately and have generated a vast body of literature.

Primary reference sources

It is something of a curiosity that, unlike many other European countries, we do not have a handy volume which sets out the body of our electoral law. The nearest source is the current edition of *Halsbury's Laws of England*, whose volume on elections covers most electoral law, although other relevant provisions are scattered under different headings. Rules for the conduct of a parliamentary election are set out in the standard work *Parker's Conduct of Parliamentary Elections* (Charles Knight, new edn, 1983), which is now in a loose-leaf format. More procedural detail can be found in Chapter II of Erskine May's *Parliamentary Practice* (Butterworths, 20th edn, 1983). Local election rules differ slightly, and here *Little's Local Government Elections* (Shaw and Sons, 8th edn, 1979) can help.

Details of which areas are included in each constituency are contained in the schedules to the Act implementing the latest redistribution of seats. These are usually called Representation of the People Acts, and they put into effect the agreed reports of the Parliamentary Boundary Commissions. Since 1944 the four Boundary Commissions (for England, Wales, Scotland and Northern Ireland) have been required to report at ten to fifteen-year intervals. Previous reports were in 1947, 1954 and 1969. The latest reports are:

Boundary Commission for England (2 vols, Cmnd. 8797, 1983);
Boundary Commission for Wales (Cmnd. 8798, 1983);
Boundary Commission for Scotland (2 vols, Cmnd. 8794, 1983)
and
Boundary Commission for Northern Ireland (Cmnd. 8753, 1982).

The best source for maps of each constituency is the appropriate
Boundary Commission report. The tracing of boundary changes
over the years is a complex task, and although much can be done
by comparing maps and the Boundary Commission recommendations over the years, the non-specialist is better advised to use
F. W. S. Craig's helpful summary, *Boundaries of Parliamentary
Constituencies 1885–1972* (Political Reference Publications, 1972).
It is important to distinguish here the Parliamentary (PBC) from
the Local Government Boundary Commissions (LGBC). There
are four LGBCs matching the four PBCs. Their function is to draw
local government boundaries as the PBC's is to draw parliamentary constituency boundaries, but they operate under separate
legislation and separate rules. This section considers only the
Parliamentary Commissions.

Works concerned with election results are a basic source for any
further investigation. Parliamentary election results are fairly easy
to discover, largely thanks to the efforts of Fred Craig, who has
produced a number of indispensible works of reference in this
field. His series of *British Parliamentary Election Results* covers
the period 1832 to 1973: (*1832–1885:* Macmillan, 1977. *1885–1918:*
Macmillan, 1974. *1918–1949:* Macmillan, new edn, 1977. *1950
–1973:* Political Reference Publications, 1983). Thereafter *Britain
Votes 2* (Parliamentary Research Services, 2nd edn, 1980) and
Britain Votes 3 (1984) cover parliamentary election results from
1974 to 1983. For detailed analyses of different aspects of elections
and by-elections, his *British Electoral Facts 1832–1980* (Parliamentary Research Services, 1981) will answer most questions. Further
discussions of by-elections since 1918 are contained in *By-
Elections in British Politics*, edited by C. Cook and J. Ramsden
(Macmillan, 1973), which lists in an appendix the results of all
contested by-elections from 1919 to March 1973 (with a few
exceptions). Election results before 1832 are less easy to obtain,
but Fred Craig has edited an edition of Henry Stooks Smith's
Parliaments of England (Political Reference Publications, 2nd
edn, 1973), which gives the results from 1715 to 1847. Before 1715
there is no comparable reference book, apart from the original
Official Return of Members of Parliament (HC 69, Session 1877
–1878) which lists the Members elected to each Parliament as far

back as 1213, in chronological order of Parliament with an alphabetical index of names. This publication is not without errors and omissions, but it is the most comprehensive work available and always worth consulting. As far as Irish seats at Westminster are concerned, F. W. S. Craig does not include details of any before the creation of the Northern Ireland Parliament in 1921. They can, however, be found in *Parliamentary Election Results in Ireland, 1801–1922*, edited by B. M. Walker (Royal Irish Academy, Dublin, 1978).

The various parliamentary bodies in Northern Ireland are well covered. *Northern Ireland Parliamentary Election Results 1921 –1972*, by Sydney Elliott (Political Reference Publications, 1973) gives the results for all general elections and by-elections during the Stormont Parliament. Elections to the Northern Ireland Assembly in 1973 are summarized in *The Northern Ireland General Elections of 1973* (Cmnd. 5851, HMSO, 1975), and the results of the elections to the 1975 Convention are found in most detail in *The 1975 Northern Ireland Convention Election*, by Ian McAllister (University of Strathclyde Survey Research Centre, Occasional Paper No.14, 1975). The first elections to the present Assembly are listed and discussed in *The 1982 Northern Ireland Assembly Election*, by S. Elliott and A. Wilford (University of Strathclyde, 1983).

Local elections results are much more difficult to find, especially at ward level. The only local election results which have been compiled for elections before 1973 concern the GLC: *Greater London Votes 1: The Greater London Council 1964–1970*, by F. W. S. Craig (Political Reference Publications, 1971). No further works were published in this series. Since then, they are better documented for Scotland, Wales and Northern Ireland than they are for England – an unusual and difficult situation. As far as Scotland is concerned, since 1973 J. D. Bochel and D. T. Denver have been compiling the results after each election. Their two most recent publications are *The Scottish Regional Elections 1978: Results and Statistics* (with B. J. McHardy: Universities of Dundee and Lancaster, 1978) and *The Scottish District Elections 1980: Results and Statistics* (University of Dundee, 1980). For Wales some data are available in *A Political and Electoral Handbook for Wales*, by D. Balsom and M. Burch (Gower, 1980), although, unlike Bochel and Denver, individual results are not given.

Local election results for Northern Ireland are, like Scotland, contained in a variety of sources. This time the main contributor is Sydney Elliott. He was co-author of the Command Paper on the Northern Ireland elections of 1973 (see above) which includes a section on the local elections in that year. Unfortunately the detailed results are not included. He has also compiled jointly with F. J. Smith, *Northern Ireland Local Government Elections of 1977* (Queen's University of Belfast, 1977) and *Northern Ireland: the District Council Elections of 1981* (Queen's University of Belfast, 1981), both of which show individual transfers of votes at each stage of the count as well as the final figures.

The only results which are readily available for areas in England are those for the GLC. Fred Craig has compiled the results for GLC elections from 1964 to 1970 (see above), but since then the GLC itself has taken on the task of compiling and publishing results for both the GLC elections and the London Borough Council elections. The results for each election are published in separate volumes, the latest ones being *Greater London Council Election 7 May 1981* and *London Borough Council Elections 6 May 1982*. The detailed election results for any other area can only be found in local newspaper reports at the time or by contacting each local Returning Officer.

The results of national and regional referenda are important to the study of the political and electoral system, and are all included in *British Electoral Facts 1832–1980* (see above), where the references to the official publications containing the results of each can be found.

The main sources of statistics relating to elections which go further than the results themselves are *Electoral Statistics*, published annually by the Office of Population, Censuses and Surveys and supplemented periodically by the *OPCS Monitor*; and the *Annual Abstract of Statistics*, which also contains data on numbers of electors, votes cast, etc. for the last eleven elections. After each general election an official return of election expenses is published which includes details of polling stations, postal votes and spoilt ballot papers together with the expenses of each candidate. The return relating to the 1983 general election is *Election Expenses* (HC 130, Session 1983–1984: HMSO, 1983).

Secondary sources

There have been countless studies of different aspects of elections over the years, and to the student of electoral history contemporary accounts of the system and its operation at various periods are always valuable. Nevertheless some organization of the field is essential to avoid confusing readers unfamiliar with the complexities of the subject matter.

THE ELECTORAL SYSTEM

Although it is now slightly out of date, R. L. Leonard's *Elections in Britain* (Van Nostrand, 1968) gives one of the clearest accounts of the technicalities of the system as well as describing in detail what actually happens during an election. The best analysis of the workings of the electoral system remains D. E. Butler's *The Electoral System in Britain since 1918* (The Clarendon Press, 2nd edn, 1963) which discusses how the present system developed as well as how it operates. The extension of the franchise has always been a popular subject of study, and there are a number of useful sources which could be used to supplement Part 1 of Butler's book if more details were needed. The passage of the major electoral reforms of the nineteenth century can be traced in various works on each of the Acts. The 1832 Act is the subject of Michael Brock's *The Great Reform Act* (Hutchinson University Library, 1973) and J. R. M. Butler's *The Passing of the Great Reform Bill* (Frank Cass, 1964), which recounts the political controversy of the time through the accounts of the main participants. The consequences of these early reforms are dealt with in *Politics in the Age of Peel: a Study in the Technique of Parliamentary Representation 1830–50*, by Norman Gash (Harvester Press, 2nd edn, 1977). The next attempts at reform are charted in F. B. Smith's *The Making of the Second Reform Bill* (Cambridge University Press, 1966). A more detailed account of the effects of these reforms and those of the mid-1880s is contained in Charles Seymour's very thorough *Electoral Reform in England and Wales: the Development and Operation of the Parliamentary Franchise 1832–1885* (Oxford University Press, 1915; reprint, David and Charles, 1970). Another good account of the reforms of the second half of the century is Cornelius O'Leary's *The Elimination of Corrupt Practices in British Elections 1868–1911* (The Clarendon Press, 1962). Moving on to discussions of twentieth-century developments, H. L. Morris' *Parliamentary Franchise Reform 1885–1918* (Columbia University Press, 1921) is less analytical than Seymour or Butler, although he does discuss the campaign for women's suffrage in some detail, a topic surprisingly poorly treated in many sources. The best work devoted to this subject is Constance Rover's *Women's Suffrage and Party Politics in Britain, 1866–1914* (Routledge and Kegan Paul, 1967), which includes a useful appendix showing Private Members' Bills attempting to introduce the enfranchisement of women. Roger Fulford's *Votes for Women* (Faber, 1957), is a good readable study of the suffragette movement and its eventual success. Fulford covers the period up to

1918, and a chapter in J. F. S. Ross' *Elections and Electors* (Eyre and Spottiswoode, 1955) deals with the extension of the franchise from 1918 to 1951 (Chapter 16, *Women in Parliament*, pp.252 –268). A more detailed account of the passage of the 1918 Representation of the People Act is in Martin Pugh, *Electoral Reform in War and Peace 1906–18* (Routledge and Kegan Paul, 1978), which, despite its irritating typescript appearance, gives more of the flavour of the events than Morris' rather dry style.

The parliamentary franchise has unfortunately never been identical with the franchise for local elections. One of the very few sources on this subject is *The English Local Government Franchise*, by B. Keith-Lucas (Blackwell, 1952), which concentrates largely on nineteenth-century developments. A brief discussion of the twentieth century position is found in Chapter 2 of *A History of Local Government in the Twentieth Century*, by B. Keith-Lucas and P. G. Richards (Allen and Unwin, 1978, pp.18–23).

THE ELECTION IN PRACTICE

Sources range from relatively straightforward accounts of the conduct of the campaign nationally or locally to thoroughly researched post-mortems on the outcome and investigations into the behaviour of the electorate. Into the first category come the 'instant' guides to the next general election. A good example is the series of *Guardian/Quartet Election Guides*, which not only examine the performance of the incumbent administration, but give considerable background detail on the various issues to figure in the campaign. In 1983 a trio of books appeared, written by Members of Parliament, arguing the case for each of the three main parties by explaining their policy and ideology. Chris Patten put *The Tory Case*, Austin Mitchell *The Case for Labour* and Alan Beith argued *The Case for the Liberal Party and the Alliance* (all: Longman, 1983). They were published so near the 1983 general election that it is doubtful whether they swayed any voters, but they will be referred to as classic statements of each party's current philosophy for many years.

Into the category of post-mortems come studies of single general elections, an interesting genre which deserves more attention. Since 1945 Nuffield College, Oxford has sponsored a series of these, in which the biggest single contribution has been made by David Butler, who has been author or co-author of each one since 1951. His last three works have been written jointly with Dennis Kavanagh: *The British General Election of February 1974* (Macmillan, 1974); *The British General Election of October 1974*

(Macmillan, 1975); and *The British General Election of 1979* (Macmillan, 1980). Each of these goes far beyond a summary of the events of the election concerned. The 1979 study, for instance, includes a survey of the record of the previous administration, the performance of the opposition, major political events, re-selection struggles and the effect of media coverage. An American initiative has led to a series entitled *Britain at the Polls*, under the editorship of H. R. Penniman. Two studies have appeared so far – *Britain at the Polls: the Parliamentary Elections of 1974* (American Enterprise Institute, Washington, 1975) and *Britain at the Polls, 1979: a Study of the General Election* (American Enterprise Institute, Washington, 1981). Using a mixture of British and non-British contributors, Penniman gives an interesting comparative perspective on our own processes. There are a number of studies of earlier elections, such as A. K. Russell's *Liberal Landslide: the General Election of 1906* (David and Charles, 1973) and *Baldwin Thwarts the Opposition: the British General Election of 1935*, by T. Stannage (Croom Helm, 1980). A list of the major studies of this type is given in the bibliography to *The British Voter: an Atlas and Survey since 1885*, by M. Kinnear (Batsford, 2nd edn, 1981). Kinnear surveys the results of each election since 1885 and illustrates the voting with maps. He also has useful analyses of swings, turnout and voting behaviour.

A further type of election study focuses on a single constituency and analyses grass-roots political activity and organization, which usefully supplements the national perspective. Anyone interested in the history of a particular constituency might find useful a longitudinal study such as *The Parliamentary History of Glamorgan 1542–1976*, by R. Grant (Christopher Davies, 1978). (There is as yet no bibliography of sources in this field, although one is in compilation by the author.)

An increasingly popular aspect of election studies is the analysis of voting behaviour. Arguments about the extension of the franchise often turned on the dangers of entrusting the vote to the mass electorate, and although we now have universal education, the question of voter rationality is still an important issue. The parties themselves want to know which factors will encourage people to vote for them – policies, personalities, image or tradition – and academic studies have begun to concentrate on voting behaviour as an indicator of the success of the electoral system in producing the results that voters intend.

The most comprehensive study in the field is *Political Change in Britain*, by D. Butler and D. Stokes (Macmillan, 2nd edn, 1974). Besides attempting to explain the factors influencing an individual voter's choice, including the impact of major issues, Butler and Stokes also examine in detail the concept of party identification, which in turn helps to explain shifts in party support over the years. More recent work by Ivor Crewe has shown that the once-popular notion that there were 'floating voters' who regularly switched their allegiance from one party to another no longer describes voting behaviour. His theory of 'partisan dealignment' is that traditional party allegiances are breaking down, partly as a result of the rise of new parties. His *Decade of Dealignment*, written jointly with Bo Sarlvik (Cambridge University Press, 1983), analyses these trends in the 1970s. A more detailed social psychological study can be found in *How Voters Decide*, by H. T. Himmelweit and others (Academic Press, 1981), which re-analyses some of Butler and Stokes' data. Sadly, the 'swingometer' only worked when there were two main parties. A much more sensitive device is needed to portray the complexities of electoral choices when so many more candidates are involved. One interesting attempt to analyse the interaction between politicians and voters is Iain McLean's *Dealing in Votes* (Martin Robertson, 1982). McLean discusses voting behaviour in the context of the influences that may be exerted on an individual's choice, and links it to the attitudes of elected politicians. He includes comparisons with American experience. Another comparative study is Richard Rose's *Electoral Participation* (Sage, 1980), a collection of papers relating to different electoral systems, with attention focused on the analysis of voting turnout.

ELECTORAL REFORM

Pressures for reform of the electoral system are usually in three directions – the extension of the franchise, the operation of electoral procedures and the effect of the system itself. Since the achievement of universal suffrage there have only been minor alterations to the franchise, such as the recent enfranchisement of patients in mental hospitals. There is some pressure for Irish nationals living in the UK to be disfranchised, but this is unlikely to become a reality. On the question of electoral procedures, the level of the deposit and the provision of postal votes for people on holiday on polling day are two topics of current concern. By far the most persistent calls for reform, however, relate to the operation of the electoral system itself. Studies of how votes are translated into seats and comparisons with other voting systems have come to prominence mainly since the Second World War. This is due partly to the results of particular general elections in which parties obtained a majority of votes but a minority of seats, and partly to the consistent underrepresentation of smaller parties in Parliament in proportion to their support amongst the electorate.

The concept of representation has always been fundamental to the study of democratic systems, and one of the clearest presentations of the subject is A. H. Birch's *Representation* (Pall Mall Press, 1971), which includes an extensive bibliography. A thorough critique of the voting system, its effects and alternatives is J. F. S. Ross' *Elections and Electors* (Eyre and Spottiswoode, 1955). It also contains a useful section on the Speaker's Conferences on Electoral Reform. In spite of being written before many disparities between voting strength and seats had become obvious, this book is still a very valuable comprehensive survey. A more recent work which is a standard textbook for politics students is *Political Representation and Elections in Britain*, by P. G. J. Pulzer (Allen and Unwin, 3rd edn, 1975). Pulzer has a section on representation in theory, as well as discussions of the system in practice, including the place of political parties in the electoral process. It is readable and has useful footnotes and a good classified bibliography. Another well-written analysis of our electoral system is Iain McLean's *Elections* (Longman, 2nd edn, 1980), which also deals purely with Britain.

The works mentioned above are primarily critiques of the present system, but there is a sizeable body of literature which not only analyses what is said to be wrong with our electoral system, but advocates that some form of proportional representation should take its place. The classic work on the subject is by Britain's foremost campaigner for proportional representation (PR) – Enid Lakeman. It is *How Democracies Vote: a Study of Electoral Systems* (Faber, 4th edn, 1974). It is the most thorough and comprehensive account of not only our own voting methods, but those in other voting systems, and contains strong cogent arguments in favour of PR. The Electoral Reform Society, of which she was a director for many years, has a library with a good collection of books, pamphlets and newspaper cuttings which can be consulted by appointment. The next useful work to be published was *Adversary Politics and Electoral Reform* (Anthony Wigram, 1975), a collection of essays edited by S. E. Finer. These include pieces about the experience of European electoral systems, the effect of our electoral system on our economic life and the effect of electoral reform on the local Member of Parliament. This book is particularly interesting, because Professor Finer admits to having revised his former anti-PR opinions due to concern about the 'malfunctioning' of the political system, as demonstrated by the break-up of the two-party system. In 1975 the Hansard Society for Parliamentary Government set up a Commission to study the case for and against electoral reform and its possible impact on the British political system. Its report, published in 1976, is a masterly summary of the present system, alternative systems and the pros and cons of electoral reform. They were unanimous in recommending that there should be electoral reform (*Report of the Hansard Society Commission on Electoral Reform.* Hansard Society, 1976). A more technical discussion of the formulae involved in the various voting systems can be found in *The Political Consequences of Electoral Laws*, by D. W. Rae (Yale University Press, rev. edn, 1971). His final chapter contains a rather complex statistical refutation of some of the criticisms of PR, such as that it leads to a multiplicity of parties, or causes government instability. Very different styles are evident in two of the best pleas in favour of PR: Joe Rogaly's *Parliament for the People* (Temple Smith, 1976) is in simple language and is easy to read, whereas Enid Lakeman's latest book *Power to Elect* (Heinemann, 1982) is a sober, serious statement of the case for the adoption of PR by the single transferable vote method. Both are valuable, even if they appeal to different audiences. Finally, Vernon Bogdanor has produced a very useful book called *The People and the Party System* (Cambridge University Press, 1981). The first part argues for the extension of the use of the referendum, but the second advocates the introduction of the single transferable vote type of PR, and contains a very good historical survey of the attempts to introduce PR since 1831.

It is in these discussions of electoral reform that the two themes of parties and elections are combined. Analyses of how votes are translated into seats and whether we elect the government we deserve inevitably involve the political parties as intermediaries in this process. The two aspects are complementary, and should be studied together to achieve a full understanding of our electoral system.

9
Parliament and ministers
Dermot Englefield

Parliament

Unlike the broad subjects covered by many of the chapters in this book, this one is concerned with one specific institution, Parliament, the sharp focus of our national politics. From the majority party in the House of Commons, seldom more than some 400 persons, our Government is formed and this chapter concludes with mention of the modest literature concerning this aspect of Parliament's role. The wider issues of politics and constitutional history have been excluded. Political parties and elections, which generate the membership of the House of Commons, are treated in Chapter 8.

Bibliography

Considering the age and prestige of Parliament as a national institution, it is surprising how inadequate is the bibliography of the subject. For instance, it might be thought that the standard *Bibliography of British History* published by the Oxford University Press would offer sound support, but, as the following details show, comparatively short entries are offered:

A Bibliography of English History to 1485, edited by Edgar
    Graves, pp.503–524 (Oxford University Press, 1975)
Bibliography of British History 1485–1603, edited by Conyers
    Read, 2nd edn, pp.88–96 (Oxford Univeristy Press, 1959)

Bibliography of British History 1603–1714, edited by Mary Keeler, 2nd edn, pp.111–130 (Oxford University Press, 1970)

Bibliography of British History 1714–1789, edited by Stanley Pergellis and D. J. Medley, pp.55–65 (Oxford University Press, 1955)

Bibliography of British History 1789–1851, edited by Lucy Brown and Jan Christie, pp.62–70 (Oxford University Press, 1977)

Bibliography of British History 1851–1914, compiled and edited by H. J. Hanham, pp.50–60 (Oxford University Press, 1976)

In total then, a mere 70 pages including many duplicate entries, in a bibliography running to 5500 pages. And what is more important, a bibliography on Parliament that is decidedly patchy.

It is fortunate, therefore, that we can consult the entries under the heading ENGLAND–PARLIAMENT . . . which are to be found in vol. 63 of the *British Museum General Catalogue of Printed Books: photolithographic edition to 1955* (263 vols, British Museum, 1960–1966). The entry runs to 562 columns and to this must be added the entries in the Supplements covering *1956–65* (50 vols, 1968 (see vol. 7)); *1966–70* (26 vols, 1971–2 (see vol. 4)); *1971–75* (13 vols, 1978–79 (see vol. 4)). Together these offer a good start, although it takes time to get used to the arrangement of the subsections of the main entry ENGLAND–PARLIAMENT.

The second important source of bibliographical information on Parliament and one more clearly organized than the British Museum Catalogue is the American *National Union Catalogue: pre 1956 imprints* (754 vols, Mansell, 1968–1981). Here, under the heading GREAT BRITAIN Parliament, in vols 214, pp.441–697 and 215, pp.1–40, together with vol. 730, pp.361–387, will be found a list of the great collections on the subject Parliament in this massive work. Most of the material is arranged chronologically session-by-session and many of the entries have useful notes. The main catalogue continues with Supplements where additional entries are to be found under the same heading covering *1953–57* (26 vols, 1958); *1958–62* (50 vols, 1963); *1963–67* (59 vols, 1969); *1968–72* (104 vols, 1973); *1973–77* (135 vols, 1978) and the further annual volumes will be cumulated thereafter. While the British Museum Catalogue uses as its author subject heading ENGLAND – PARLIAMENT and the NUC uses GREAT BRITAIN – PARLIAMENT the catalogue of the Bodleian Library at Oxford uses just PARLIAMENT. The main pre-1922 catalogue has, until recently, been on slips in boxes – about four large boxes covered the subject. It is currently being thoroughly revised and transferred to a computer from which volumes are printed for use by students at the Library at Oxford. The volumes covering Parliament should be printed by the end of 1983 and it is to be hoped that in time they will be made available to others – possibly on microfiche. Also important is *A London Bibliography of the Social Sciences* (4 vols, British Library of Political and Economic Science, 1931–1932), together with Supplements every few years since, where, just to add variety, the heading chosen is UNITED KINGDOM Parliament. In 1980 the heading was changed to GREAT BRITAIN Parliament. This collection is especially strong in modern pamphlet material while the other major catalogues are strong on history. Finally, there is the standard work, *Writings on British History 1901–66* (In progress, Royal Historical Society and University of London). *Parliament of Great Britain: Bibliography* by R. V. Goehlert and F. S. Martin (Gower, 1983) is a pioneer work. Clearly, a lot of systematic examination of the more obvious periodicals has been undertaken and many of the most obvious secondary sources listed. But it does reflect the problems of undertaking the bibliography of a complicated institution from the outside, the most major gaps being the extensive bibliography of Parliament to be found in its own reports.

Articles on Parliament have to be sought in the obvious published indexes to periodicals, especially those covering history, law and the social sciences, but we are fortunate in having a duplicated memorandum *A Handlist of Articles in Periodicals and other Serial Publications Relating to the History of Parliament*, compiled by H. S. Cobb (House of Lords Record Office, 1973). A supplement to this memorandum updating it to 1980 is in preparation.

Records

In 1497 the then Clerk of the Parliaments, whose successor is still responsible for the records of the House of Lords (and of the Commons, on behalf of the authorities of that House), decided to keep thereafter the original Acts of Parliament at Westminster to which other records were subsequently added. This means that the records of Parliament prior to that date (and a few, such as the Rolls of Parliament, thereafter) are to be found in the Public Record Office, while most post-1497 records are to be found at the House of Lords Record Office in the purpose-built and recently renovated Victoria Tower. For the pre-1497 period, therefore, reference must be made to *Guide to the Contents of the Public Record Office* (3 vols, HMSO, 1963–1968), especially the first two volumes. For the post-1497 records there is the *Guide to the*

Records of Parliament by Maurice Bond (HMSO, 1971). It is an excellent account both of the very large collection of documents at Westminster and of the context within which they were prepared. Calendars of some of these manuscripts up until 1678 were included in the *Reports of the Royal Commission on Historical Manuscripts*, Vols 1–9 (HMSO, 1874–1884) and for the period 1678–1693 in the appendices of Vols 11–14 (HMSO, 1887–1894). Volumes 1–9 have been reprinted by the publisher Kraus and the separately available volume *A Companion to the Kraus Reprint Edition* (KTO Press Nendeln, Liechtenstein, 1977) should be consulted. This work has been continued more fully in the *Calendar of the Manuscripts of the House of Lords 1693–1718* (12 vols, HMSO, 1964–1977). This series has now ceased. However, the *Annual Report of the House of Lords Record Office*, published as one of their series of Memoranda, updates Bond's Guide by listing each year the Parliamentary records transferred by the various departments of the two Houses to the archive in the Record Office, together with other accessions from outside Parliament.

House of Commons proceedings (excluding debates)

Parliament, and especially the House of Commons, has for many generations ensured that many of its proceedings have been printed, partly for its own use and partly for general information. A certain number of proceedings and indeed papers were published during the period 1641–1660 and, apart from the catalogues already mentioned, reference should also be made to the heading ENGLAND in *A short title catalogue . . . 1641–1700*, compiled by Donald Wing, Vol. 1, pp.567–621 (2nd edn, 3 vols, Index Committee of the Modern Languages Association of America, 1972 –). The whole question of this mid-seventeenth-century Parliamentary printing has been examined in *The Beginning of Printing for the House of Commons 1640–42* by Sheila Lambert (In The Library; Transaction of the Bibliographical Society, 6th Series, Vol. 3, No. 1, March 1981).

Regular printing of proceedings did not start until 1680, when Mr Speaker was instructed by the House to print their Votes and Proceedings on a daily basis. The early history of this venture is covered in *Votes and Standing Orders of the House of Commons: The Beginning*, by Betty Kemp, (HMSO, House of Commons Library Document No. 8, 1971), and *The Printing of the Votes of the House of Commons 1730–1781*, by K. Maslen in (The Library,

5th Series, XXV, 1970). The printing of the Votes and Proceedings has continued until the present day, and these are the papers required to understand and conduct the work of the House of Commons. Over the centuries, as procedures have altered, extra sections have been added, Division lists since 1836, for instance, and occasionally sections have been withdrawn. Today the 'Vote Bundle', as it is colloquially called, runs to eight main sections which are unindexed. They are available from HMSO but only on subscription:

(1) Votes and Proceedings
(2) Private Business
(3) Private Bill Lists
(4) Public Petitions
(5) Public Bill Lists
(6) Division Lists
(7) Notices of Motion
(8) Supplement to the Votes and Proceedings

Section 1 of this series later forms the Journal of the House of Commons. Recently some of these series have been published on microfiche, namely *Division Lists 1836–1909, Appendices to the Votes and Proceedings 1817–1890* and also *Reports of the Select Committee on Public Petitions 1833–1900*, all edited by F. W. Torrington (Chadwyck-Healey, 1982).

The next important date in Parliamentary printing is 1742, when the first printing of the House of Commons Journal was authorized. This edition is rare, and it is more usual to have access to *Journals of the House of Commons from November the 8th 1547 . . .* reprinted by order of the House (1803). This is not just a reprint, more a new edition, and vols 56 (1801) to vol. 89 (1834) include important Appendices of accounts and papers for each session. The history of the Journal and, most importantly, its indexing is described in *Journal of the House of Commons: a Bibliographical Guide* by D. Menhennet (HMSO, House of Commons Library, Document No. 7, 1971). The current Journal is to be found in comparatively few libraries, although it is the one official record of both the work of the House of Commons and the information, i.e. papers laid before it. Individual volumes are indexed and eight volumes of index cover 1547–1878/1879. Since 1880 there are decennial indexes. The Minutes of Proceedings of House of Commons Standing and Select Committees are published as House of Commons papers.

House of Commons papers

The early printed papers of the House of Commons occasionally appeared as 'separates' and some of them, reports of Committes, were first collected together in the eighteenth century as *Reports from Committees of the House of Commons Printed by Order of the House* (4 vols, 1772–1773). A second updated collection appeared as *Reports from Committees of the House of Commons which have been Printed by Order of the House 1715–1801* (16 vols, 1803–1806). The final volume is a very detailed index to the whole set and includes a list of reports which had been printed in the Journals 1696–1800 and therefore excluded from the Reports of Committees . . . Another collection made at the beginning of the nineteenth century and known as the Abbot Collection covers 1731–1800, and includes Bills, Reports, and Accounts and Papers. It runs to 110 volumes. There are four nearly complete sets, including one in the British Library, one in the University of London Library and two at the Houses of Parliament and also one or two part sets; so they are very rare. The indexes to both these sets of papers have been reprinted as *Hansard Catalogue and Breviate of Parliamentary Papers 1696–1834* (reprinted, Blackwell, 1953) and *Catalogue of Papers Printed by Order of the House of Commons 1731–1800* (reprinted, Blackwell, 1954).

In recent years there has appeared *House of Commons Sessional Papers of the Eighteenth Century*, edited by Sheila Lambert (Scholarly Resources Inc., 145 vols, 1975–1976). The collection, which consists of facsimiles of Public Bills, Reports of Committees and Accounts and Papers, opens with Volume I *Introduction and List, 1715–1760* and Volume II *List, 1761–1800*. This introduction includes the most exhaustive and scholarly account of Parliamentary printing not only for the eighteenth century but also through until the mid-nineteenth century. As a collection it is the most complete and best-organized set of pre-1800 House of Commons Sessional Papers.

From 1800 onwards the House of Commons Sessional Papers have been regularly printed session by session, including Bills and House of Commons Papers and, from the 1830s, Command Papers. In 1806–1807 printed title pages were introduced and the arrangement of the series quickly stabilized into groups of Bills, Papers of Committees, Reports of Commissioners and Accounts and Reports. A list of these volumes is available in *A Checklist of the British Parliamentary Papers (bound set) 1801–1950*, compiled by K. C. Parsons (privately printed, Cambridge, 1958). It might be more accurately called a checklist of volumes of House of Commons Papers . . . There are official indexes to these papers, namely the *General Index to the Reports of Select Committees 1801–1852; General Index to the Bills 1801–1852*; and *General Index to the Accounts and Papers, Reports of Commissioners, Estimates, etc. etc. 1801–1852*. Less well known is an important and very comprehensive set of *Indexes to Reports of the House of Commons 1801–1834* (1837 HC paper 626; 1834 HC paper 498). For later papers there are the *General Alphabetical Index to the Bills, Reports, Estimates, Accounts and Papers . . . and to Command Papers 1852–1899; General Index to the Bills, Reports and Papers . . . 1900 to 1948–49* and those are followed by *General Alphabetical Index to the Bills, Reports and Papers . . . 1950 to 1958–59* and a similar volume covering *1959 to 1968–69.* These are based on individual Sessional Indexes which since 1979–1980 have been indexed using the House of Commons Library POLIS thesaurus (see Domestic Matters). These are all HMSO publications. Throughout the period 1800–1968/1969 the arrangement of papers did not change, but there was a change in 1969–1970 and from 1979–1980 onwards a further change, as now the papers are simply arranged by number of Bill or House of Commons Paper within the session and Command Papers by running number.

The post-1800 papers are included in three recent major republishing projects. First, the Irish Universities Press selected 1000 volumes of reports from the period 1801–1899 and brought them out as handsomely produced and bound facsimiles in broad subject groups. Details are to be found in the *Checklist of British Parliamentary Papers in the Irish University Press 1,000 Volume Series* by P. Ford (Irish University Press, 1972). Second, the firm of Chadwyck-Healey is well advanced with its project of bringing out a microfiche edition of the complete House of Commons papers 1801–1921, and in the future this is likely to be the most usual source. The title is given as *House of Commons Parliamentary Papers 1801–1900* and *House of Commons Parliamentary Papers 1901–1921* (64 500 microfiche, Chadwyck-Healey, 1980 –1984). This set is more complete than any collection in a library. Third, from the same source microfiche copies of the Irish University Press volumes mentioned above may be obtained, including the indexes already mentioned. When these projects are completed a bibliographical guide will be published listing documents added to the edition which are not recorded on the contents pages or in the older indexes of the bound Library sets. The Parliamentary Papers 1922–1972 are available in microfilm under the title *Controller's Library Collection of Her Majesty's Stationery*

Office Publications, 1922–1972 in 1700 reels (Historical Documents Institute, Inverness, 1976–1978). In connection with this is the separately published *Cumulative Index to HMSO Annual Catalogues, 1922–1972* (2 vols, Historical Documents Institute, 1976).

Apart from the official sessional indexes already mentioned there are a number of guides, lists, breviates, etc., prepared by or under Professor and Mrs Ford of the University of Southampton. First, there is their standard short work *A Guide to Parliamentary Papers: Where they are, How to find Them, How to use Them* by P. and G. Ford (3rd edn, Irish University Press, 1972). Then the papers of the nineteenth century are covered by their *Select list of British Parliamentary Papers 1833–99* (reprinted Irish University Press, 1970).

Also useful as a guide and summary of twentieth-century papers are the following volumes: P. and G. Ford, *A breviate of parliamentary papers 1900–1916* (Blackwell, 1957); *1917–1939* (Blackwell, 1951) – these two volumes were reprinted by the Irish University Press in 1969; *1940–1954* (Blackwell, 1961). After 1954 this work changed to a classified list with *Select list of British Parliamentary Papers 1955–64* (Irish University Press, 1970) and D. Marshallsay and J. Smith, *Ford List of British Parliamentary Papers 1965–74* (KTO Press, 1979).

These lists, which will be continued, seek to select the papers concerned with policy rather than routine administration. Finally, there is a useful finding list for Parliamentary Papers and Proceedings, *Access to Parliamentary Resources and Information in London Libraries*, APRILL (House of Commons Library, Public Information Office, 1982).

House of Lords proceedings (excluding debates)

The daily *Minutes of Proceedings of the House of Lords* (HMSO) are available by subscription and now appear in two parts covering past business and future business. They have been printed since 1825. From 1836 they have been included in the main series of the House of Lords papers (see below). The Minutes, like the Votes and Proceedings of the House of Commons are unindexed. The Journal of the House of Lords reports proceedings, starting in 1510. It was first ordered to be printed in 1767, and until 1980 included the text of Select Committee Reports. They are served by an index for each volume, six volumes of cumulated indexes covering 1510–1853 and decennial indexes thereafter. From the beginning of session 1981–1982 the relationship between the

Minutes and the Journal has been simplified, so the latter is now revised Minutes furnished with an Attendance Register and Index. The Proceedings of Select Committees are published as House of Lords Papers.

A recent publication *Divisions in the House of Lords . . . 1685 to 1857* compiled by J. C. Sainty and D. Dewar (HMSO, 1976) illuminates this aspect of House of Lords Proceedings. Of importance on this subject generally is *The Journals, Minutes and Committee Books of the House of Lords* (rev. edn, House of Lords Record Office Memorandum No. 13, 1957).

House of Lords papers

As with the House of Commons, the early printed papers of the House of Lords first appeared as rare 'separates', but recently, surviving papers were collected together and a facsimile was published as *House of Lords Sessional Papers 1714–1805*, edited by F. W. Torrington (60 vols, Oceana Publications, 1972–1978). The volumes include all the Bills and Reports available and this is the only significant collection of pre-1800 House of Lords papers outside the holdings of the House of Lords Library.

The same editor and publisher continued this series in microfilm from 1806 to 1859 as *House of Lords Sessional Papers* (Trans-Media Publishing Company Inc., 1976) and Mr Torrington was able to add a number of papers to this series (13 volumes) which are listed in an addendum to *A General Index to the Sessional Papers . . . of the House of Lords 1801–1859 Session I* (reprinted, 2 vols, Oceana Publications Inc., 1976). The reprint includes a checklist of House of Lords Sessional Papers, 1801–1859.

The original House of Lords printed Sessional Papers started in 1801 with volumes 1–XV covering 1801–1805 and volumes 1–*CCCXXIX* covering 1806–1834. Session 1835 has its own numbering and from 1836 the House of Lords Sessional Papers include the Minutes as volume 1 of each session and have printed title-pages. In 1900 Command Papers were dropped from the collection to avoid duplication with the House of Commons sets. The main indexes cover 1801–1859 Session I, reprinted in 1976 as mentioned above, 1859 Session II – 1870, 1871–1884/1885 and sessionally 1886–1921. Since 1921 there has been no published index to the House of Lords Sessional Papers. Reference should be made to a short but important article 'House of Lords Sessional Papers 1641–1859', by K. Mallaber (in *Journal of Librarianship,* **4,** No. 2 (April 1976)).

Debates

Before 1800, debates had been reported very selectively in early newsletters, then after the event in the commercial journals, and finally reports were collected together into publishers' sets. Another source for reports on debates was Members' published Diaries. *A Bibliography of Parliamentary Debates of Great Britain* (HMSO House of Commons Library, Document No. 2, 1956) (a new edition would be welcome) sets out to list these pre-1800 printed debates and diaries. There are a number of articles on pre-1800 debates, including 'The Beginning of Parliamentary Reporting in Newspapers 1768–1774' by P. Thomas (*English Historical Review,* **LXXIV** (1959)); *Sources for Debates of the House of Commons 1768–1774* by P. Thomas (Athlone Press, 1959); and 'The Reliability of Contemporary Reporting of the Debates of the House of Commons, 1727–41' by M. Ransome (*Bulletin of Institute of Historical Research,* **XIX** (1942–1943)). Also important is the introduction to *Samuel Johnson's Parliamentary Reporting* by B. B. Hoover (Cambridge University Press, 1953).

We start, at the beginning of the nineteenth century, with the *Parliamentary History* by Cobbett. This work purports to report debates going back to the earliest history of Parliament and is itself heavily dependent on the reports in the eighteenth century commercial journals listed in *A Bibliography of Parliamentary Debates of Great Britain* (previously cited). This was soon taken over by T. C. Hansard, and we reach the early series of *Hansard.* These fall into the 1st Series, 1803–1804 to 1819–1820, 41 vols; 2nd Series, 1820 to 1830, 25 vols; 3rd Series, 1830–1831 to 1890–1891, 356 vols; 4th Series, 1892 to 1908, 199 vols. By the late nineteenth century a Treasury subsidy was needed to publish these debates and in 1909 the *Official Report (Hansard)* was finally taken over by HMSO acting as an agent for Parliament.

There then started the 5th Series with different sequences of volumes for the House of Lords and the House of Commons. It is only since the beginning of the 5th Series that reports have been compiled by Parliamentary staff and have been verbatim. A 6th Series began in March 1980. Fortnightly, volume and sessional indexes are prepared and from 1984 this indexing has been undertaken in the House of Commons Library and based on POLIS (see Domestic Matters). Standing Committee debates of the House of Commons have been published since 1919 (HMSO). They have no indexes.

Procedure

The two Houses regularly publish official documents on their procedure. The House of Lords has *Standing Orders for Public Business* (HMSO), *Standing Orders for Private Business* (HMSO), *Companion to Standing Orders* (HMSO) and House of Lords *Form of Appeal (Criminal)* (HMSO) and *Form of Appeal (Civil)* (HMSO) to cover their judicial work. The House of Commons publishes *Standing Orders Private Business* (HMSO), *Standing Orders Public Business* (HMSO) and *Manual of Procedure* (HMSO). The last major review of procedure was the *First Report from the Select Committee on Procedure* 1977–1978 HC 588 I-III (HMSO, 1978) which 'considers the practice and procedure of the House in relation to public business'.

Since its first edition in 1844, the standard work on procedure has been T. E. May's *A Treatise on the Law, Privileges, Proceedings and Usage of Parliament* (Butterworths, 20th edn, 1983). The first edition of May has been reprinted (Irish University Press, 1971) and includes a collection of the prefaces from the first eighteen editions. Today Erskine May is prepared under the May Memorial Fund and is edited by the Clerk of the House of Commons with support from the Clerk of the Parliaments for House of Lords matters. It is a mine of information on the working of Parliament and is revised every few years. But to keep up to date with procedural matters it is also essential to read the reports of and any published evidence given to the Select Committees on Procedure. These appear as House of Lords or House of Commons papers. An occasional summary of changes is to be found in the journal *Parliamentary Affairs*. As its title suggests, *The House of Commons at work* by Eric Taylor (Macmillan, 9th edn, 1979) is a monograph which contains a lot of information on procedure.

There are a number of important historic works, including *Precedents of Proceedings in the House of Commons* by J. Hatsell (new edn, 5 vols, 1818; reprinted Irish University Press, 1971). Also important is *The Procedure of the House of Commons*, by J. Redlich (3 vols, 1908) and for a short historical survey *An Introduction to the Procedure of the House of Commons* by Lord Campion remains of interest (Macmillan, 3rd edn, 1958). In *Parliament at Work: a Case-book of Parliamentary Procedure* by A. H. Hanson and H. V. Wiseman (reprinted, Greenwood Press, 1975) the authors have set out 'to provide a case-book which will illustrate the use to which the House of Commons puts its various procedures', and under headings such as Questions, Financial Procedure, Select Committees, it works well, though as it was originally published in 1962 and so rapid is change in some of these areas, it is already rather dated.

Domestic matters

Since the mid-sixteenth century Parliament has met in the Palace of Westminster. In recent years growing interst has been shown by historians in Parliament's actual physical surroundings and their effect on its work. The dividing line is, of course, 1834, when the old Palace, with the important exception of Westminster Hall, burnt down. The old Palace has been fully described in *History of the King's Work*, edited by H. M. Colvin, Vols I and II, The Middle Ages (HMSO, 1963), Vols III and IV, 1485–1660 (HMSO, 1975), Vol. V, 1660–1782, pp.385–431 (HMSO, 1976) and Vol. VI, 1782–1851, pp.496–537 (HMSO, 1973). There is also *Views of the Old Palace of Westminster*, edited by H. M. Colvin (Society of Architectural Historians of Great Britain, 1966), *Westminster Hall* by Hilary St George Saunders (Michael Joseph, 1951) and Maurice Hastings, *St. Stephen's House* (Architectural Press, 1950). Essential is the standard pre-1834 Palace work, *The History of the Ancient Palace and Late Houses of Parliament*, by E. W. Brayley and J. Brittan (1836).

When we come to the new Palace of Westminster, so familiar to us all, apart from the numerous Select Committee Reports during the many years during which it was being built, there is the *History of the King's Work*, edited by H. M. Colvin, Vol. VI (HMSO, 1973); *Houses of Parliament*, edited by M. H. Port (Yale University Press, 1976), the standard work; *Works of Art in the House of Lords*, edited by Maurice Bond (HMSO, 1980); and two special articles, 'The Palace of Westminster after the Fire of 1834' by R. J. B. Walker (*Walpole Society*, **44** (1972–1974, 1974)) and 'Decoration of the New Palace of Westminster by T. S. R. Boase (*Journal of the Warburg and Courtauld Institutes*, **XVII**, Numbers 3–4 (1954)). The essential older work with its fine illustrations is Wright and Smith, *Parliament Past and Present* (Hutchinson, *c.*1902).

There has been a great deal of frustrated speculation and planning about future accommodation for the House of Commons, the current plan being set down in *New Parliamentary Building Bridge Street; Feasibility Study* (Casson Conder and Partners, 1979). Special attention should also be given to the flow of reports on accommodation from the House of Commons (Services) Committee.

Outside the Journals of both Houses which can occasionally be important sources for domestic matters, and obviously the relevant Select Committee Reports of both Houses, there is little monograph material. *The Clerical Organisation of the House of Commons 1661–1850*, by O. Williams (Oxford University Press, 1954) is a distinguished account of the Clerk's Department, and it is to be hoped that the last century will be covered. A brief general account of House of Commons Officials is to be found in *The Officers of the Commons 1363–1978* by P. Marsden (HMSO, 1979) and there is also a list, *Officers of the House of Lords 1485 to 1971* (House of Lords Record Office Memorandum No. 45, 1971).

Since 1966, domestic matters in the House of Commons have been the concern of the House of Commons (Services) Committee, chaired normally by the Leader of the House, with its four Sub-Committees covering Accommodation, Catering, Computer Matters and the Library. It meets in private but sometimes prints its evidence, and its reports always appear as House of Commons papers. Broadcasting is the responsibility of the Select Committee on Sound Broadcasting. Since the *House of Commons Administration Act 1978, cap 36* (HMSO, 1978) the staff of the House has been employed by the House of Commons Commission, and this group of Members, chaired by Mr Speaker, publish an *Annual Report of the House of Commons Commission*, again as a House of Commons Paper (HMSO). In the House of Lords it is the Offices Committee which plays the role of the Services Committee and with similar Sub-Committees takes evidence and publishes Reports on domestic matters as House of Lords Papers (HMSO).

There is only one general survey of facilities, etc., *The House of Commons: Services and Facilities*, edited by M. Rush and M. Shaw (Allen and Unwin, 1974), updated by *The House of Commons: Services and Facilities 1972–1982*, edited by M. Rush (Policy Studies Institute, 1983). It contains a full list of Select Committee Reports on the subject. A recent survey of the Library and its research and information services is *Parliament and Information: the Westminster Scene*, by D. Englefield (Library Association, 1981), which describes facilities in both Houses and also information on Westminster which is available to the public.

As a postscript to this section on domestic matters mention must be made of POLIS, standing for Parliamentary On Line Information System, a computer-based subject index to Parliament's proceedings since 1980–1981 and papers since 1979–1980, which the House of Commons Library compiles daily and which is available to outside subscribers. The system is described in 'How the Parliamentary On Line Information System at Westminster was Planned' by D. Englefield (*Inspel*, Official Organ of the IFLA Division of Special Libraries, **16**, No. 3 (1982)) and 'POLIS in Parliament . . .' by D. Menhennet and J. Wainwright (*Journal of Documentation*, **38**, No. 2 (1982)).

General works

In a chapter as short as this it is not possible to cover the long history of Parliament. For this, reference should be made to the bibliographies and lists already mentioned. This section is confined to the twentieth century.

The Study of Parliament, by Peter Richards (University of Southampton, 1972), and 'The British House of Commons as a Focus for Political Research', by S. C. Patterson (*British Journal of Political Science*, **3** (1973)), are useful starting points for Parliamentary studies. An elementary but very useful survey is the COI pamphlet *The British Parliament* (HMSO), which is regularly updated. *Parliament* by Sir Ivor Jennings (2nd edn, Cambridge University Press, 1957; reprinted 1970), although dated in arrangement and facts, remains a substantial work of historical interest. More recent in its focus, and concerned just with the House of Commons, R. Butt's *The Power of Parliament* (Constable, 2nd edn, 1969) is part of the mid-1960s movement for reform which was articulated in *The Reform of Parliament*, by B. Crick (Weidenfeld and Nicholson, rev. 2nd edn, 1970). *Parliamentary Reform: a Survey of Recent Proposals for the House of Commons* (Cassell, 2nd rev. edn, for the Hansard Society, 1967) is a summary of facts and gives the subject perspective. A recent political textbook is *Parliamentary Government in Britain*, by M. Rush (Pitman, 1981). The last two authors are members of the Study of Parliament Group formed in 1963, which is made up of academic and Parliamentary officials, some of whom contributed to *The House of Commons in the Twentieth Century*, edited by S. A. Walkland (The Clarendon Press, 1979), which covers the whole century, and *The Commons Today*, edited by S. A. Walkland and M. Ryle (Fontana, 1981), really concerned with the last ten years. (The earlier two editions of this work *Commons in Transition*, edited by A. H. Hanson and B. Crick (Fontana, 1970) and the *Commons in the 70s*, edited by S. A. Walkland and M. Ryle (Fontana, 1977) make interesting comparative reading with *The Commons Today*.) Both *The House of Commons in the Twentieth Century* and *The Commons Today* are focused on the workings of the House of Commons, while *The Commons in Perspective* by P. Norton (Martin Robertson, 1981) is a useful 'overview'. An important comparative study of both Chambers of the UK and the US is *Parliament and Congress*, by K. Bradshaw and D. Pring (Constable, 1972), with an updating chapter (Quartet, 1981).

The House of Lords has two roles, as a judiciary and a legislature. Literature on the House of Lords as part of the judiciary is in Chapter 11. As a legislature a number of the works mentioned in this chapter cover both Houses. However, a useful short bibliography is *Select List of Published Material on the House of Lords in the Twentieth Century*, House of Lords Fact Sheet No. 7 (House of Lords Information Office, 1980). It is especially strong in periodical articles and official papers. *The House of Lords and Contemporary Politics 1911–1957*, by P. Bromhead (Routledge and Kegan Paul, 1958) and *The House of Lords and the Labour Government 1964–1970*, by J. Morgan (Oxford University Press, 1975), are general studies of the Upper House. An interesting insider's view is *The Lords*, by Viscount Masserene and Ferrard (Leslie Frewin, 1973). Reform of the House of Lords has been a subject of interest for a number of years, and a handy starting point which lists most of the material available and contains a useful introduction is *House of Lords Reform: 1850–1970*, House of Lords Factsheet No. 1 (2nd edn, House of Lords Information Office, 1979).

Between the First World War and 1945, Select Committees were of small importance, except for the Public Accounts Committee and the Estimates Committee, surveyed in *The Control of Public Expenditure: Financial Committees of the House of Commons*, by B. Chubb (Oxford University Press, 1952). In *Parliament and Administration*, by N. Johnson (Allen and Unwin, 1966), the Estimates Committee 1945–1965 is further considered and *The Member of Parliament and the Administration*, by D. Coombes (Allen and Unwin, 1966), examines the first ten years of the work of the important Nationalised Industries Committee established in 1956. *Parliament and Public Ownership*, by A. Hanson (Cassell, 1961), also considered the subject. A new stage arrived in the mid-1960s with the 'Crossman Reforms' and the establishment of some 'Departmental' and some 'Subject' Select Committees, examined in *The Growth of Parliamentary Scrutiny by Committees*, by A. Morris (Pergamon, 1970), and in 1970 the Estimates Committee was replaced by the Expenditure Committee, which had wider terms of reference and which is the subject of *Parliament and Public Spending*, by A. Robinson (Heinemann, 1978). Her book is also an interesting study of the Select Committee system in general. *Called to Account: The Public Accounts*

Committee . . . 1965–66 to 1977–78, by V. Flegmann (Gower, 1980), is a disappointing supplement to the earlier work of B. Chubb. Following the *First Report from the Select Committee on Procedure 1977–78* HC 588 (HMSO, 1978), the new Departmental Select Committee system was established in late 1979. So far, preliminary consideration of this move has been made in *Reformed Select Committees*, by A. Davies (Outer Circle Policy Unit, 1980), and the *First Report for the House of Commons Liaison Committee: The Select Committee System, 1982–1983*, HC 92 (HMSO, 1983) together with Dilys M. Hill (ed.), *Parliamentary Select Committees in Action: a Symposium* (University of Strathclyde Discussion papers in Politics, 1983). *Commons Select Committees – Catalysts for Progress?*, edited by D. Englefield, (Longmans, 1984) is a series of papers by Members and witnesses with full details of the Committees' work; a further study edited by G. Drewry is to be published by Oxford University Press in 1985. Despite these important changes, many believe the problems of Parliamentary oversight, examined in *Parliament and Foreign Affairs* by P. Richards (Allen and Unwin, 1967) and *Parliament and Economic Affairs*, edited by D. Coombes and S. A. Walkland, Part II (Heinemann, 1980), remain.

Over the decades the process of legislative scrutiny has changed less than Committee work, so that *Parliamentary Scrutiny of Government Bills*, by J. A. G. Griffith (Allen and Unwin, 1974), though based on the period 1967–1968 to 1970–1971, remains important. A more recent important study is *Legislation and Public Policy: Public Bills in the 1970–74 Parliament*, by I. Burton and G. Drewry (Macmillan, 1981). It is not always the Government which introduces Public Bills, and *Private Members' Bills in the British Parliament*, by P. Bromhead (Routledge and Kegan Paul, 1956), covers the subject during the first half of the century. The first Committee on legislation for a long time published *The Preparation of Legislation*, Sir D. Renton, Chairman, Cmnd. 6053 (HMSO, 1975), which is an authoritative and lucid description of Public Bill Procedure. An unusual insight into the passing of a Bill is to be found in *The State of the Nation: Parliament* (Granada Television Ltd, 1973).

For private bills there are two distinguished historical works, F. Clifford's *History of Private Bill Legislation* (2 vols, reprinted, Cass, 1968), a reprint of the 1885–1887 edition, and O. Williams, *The Historical Development of Private Bill Procedure and Standing Orders in the House of Commons* (2 vols, HMSO, 1948–1949). Completed in 1945, this is the work of a distinguished parliamentary official. Also of interest in this context is D. L. Rydz, *The Parliamentary Agents: a History* (Royal Historical Society, 1979).

A further method of scrutiny is covered in *Questions in Parliament*, by D. N. Chester and N. Bowring (Oxford University Press, 1962), and also important for this subject is the report of the *Select Committee on Parliamentary Questions* 1971-1972, HC 393 (HMSO, 1972).

Finally on the subject of scrutiny there is the latest service for Members and their electorate – the Ombudsman. The reports of the Select Committee on the Parliamentary Commissioner for Administration are clearly essential reading, as are the Ombudsman's Annual Reports (HMSO) and his quarterly reports of Selected Cases (HMSO). As Health Service Commissioner the same official provides the same service for Members regarding the administrative aspects of the National Health Service. Also important are *The Parliamentary Ombudsman*, by R. Gregory and P. Hutchesson (Royal Institute of Public Administration, 1975), and *The British Ombudsman*, by F. Stacey (The Clarendon Press, 1971), which includes the legislative history of the establishment of the Parliamentary Commissioner in 1967. *Maladministration and its Remedies* (25th Hamylin lecture) (Stevens, 1973), by K. C. Wheare, includes an important chapter on Ombudsmen and F. Stacey, in *Ombudsmen Compared* (The Clarendon Press, 1978), includes a number of chapters on the UK Ombudsman which update his earlier book. A preliminary review of the first few years of the system working is to be found in *Our Fettered Ombudsman* (Justice, 1977).

The job of being a Member has been examined in *The Backbenchers*, by P. Richards (Faber, 1972), and various aspects in an anthology of printed pieces, *The Backbencher and Parliament*, edited by D. Leonard and V. Herman (Macmillan, 1972). *British Members of Parliament: a Self-portrait*, by A. King (in association with Granada Television, 1974), is mostly Members talking about their role and *Backbench Specialisation in the House of Commons*, by D. Judge (Heinemann, 1981), considers their work in the face of growing specialization. *Parliament and the Public*, by E. Marshall (Macmillan, 1982), is a Member's own view of his job both inside and outside the House. So also is A. Mitchell, *Westminster Man* (Methuen, 1982), and *Member of Parliament*, by J. Grant (Michael Joseph, 1974), which gives a diary of a year's work. *Using Computers to Analyse the Activities of Members of Parliament*, by M. N. Franklin (University of Strathclyde, 1971), is a more scientific approach to the same subject. Their influence is examined in *The Influence of the Backbencher . . .* , by J. P. Mackintosh (Manchester Statistical Society, 1971).

Women were first elected to the House in 1918 and *Women at Westminster . . . 1918–1966*, by P. Brookes (Peter Davies, 1967), and *Women in the House*, by E. Vallance (Athlone Press, 1979), a more academic study, cover the subject. *Women and Parliament 1918–70*, by B. Stobaugh (Exposition Press, Hicksville, 1978), and *The Divided House*, by M. Phillips (Sidgwick and Jackson, 1980), are more up-to-date studies, while *Women in National Legislatures*, by Walter Kohn (Praeger, 1980) puts the Westminster women MPs in the context of five other legislatures. A pioneering pamphlet covers women in the House of Lords, *The Impact of Women in the House of Lords*, by G. Drewry and J. Brock, Studies in Public Policy No. 112 (Centre for the Study of Public Policy, University of Strathclyde, 1983).

Within the House, voting is a key aspect of Members' work and *Dissension in the House of Commons 1945–1974*, compiled and edited by P. Norton (Macmillan, 1975), and *1974–1979*, by P. Norton (The Clarendon Press, 1980), are reference books of sources. Other works in this area are *Rebels and Whips . . . since 1945*, by R. Jackson (Macmillan, 1968); *Backbench Opinion in the House of Commons 1945–55*, by H. Berrington (Pergamon, 1978); and *Backbench Opinion . . . 1955–59*, by S. E. Finer *et al.* (Pergamon, 1961). The careers of Members of the House of Commons is examined in *Amateurs and Professionals in British Politics 1918 –1959*, by P. W. Buck (University of Chicago Press, 1963).

Reference works and periodicals

There is a short list of reference works and periodicals on Parliament but it is a pity that some of the former are growing a little out of date. An *Encyclopaedia of Parliament*, by P. Laundy (Cassell, 4th edn, 1972) gathers a lot of information together on the world Parliamentary scene, while *Parliamentary Dictionary*, by S. Hawtrey and H. M. Barclay (Butterworths, 3rd edn, 1970), concerned with Westminster, is accurate technically but dated. A lucid and up-to-date assembly of information on Parliament is to be found in *Halsbury's Laws of England* (Butterworths, 4th edn, Vol. 34, 1980). This was prepared by the Clerks of each House and is updated periodically.

Annually there appears *The Table, Being the Journal of the Society of Clerks-at-the-Table . . .* (1933–), and this is especially strong in articles on the minutiae of Parliament's working. While edited at Westminster, it covers all Commonwealth Parliaments. Also edited at Westminster is *The Parliamentarian* (1920– , Commonwealth Parliamentary Association, quarterly). Lively and authoritative articles are contributed and the editorial policy takes very seriously the dispersal of both technical and bibliographical information on Parliaments. *Parliamentary Affairs* (1947– , Hansard Society, quarterly) is also central to the subject and is strong on book reviews and articles. But, of course, much information on Parliament is to be found in reference works and periodicals covering law, history, public administration and, to some extent, politics. We mention two periodicals on current Parliamentary matters, namely the *House of Commons Weekly Information Bulletin* (1980– , HMSO, weekly during the Session), which covers the work of the current and previous week in Parliament, and keeps the reader up to date with the session's legislation, membership of committees, etc. and the *House Magazine* (1976– , Parlimentary Communications Ltd, weekly during the Session), which carries current information, analysis of important Reports, Bills, etc. and interesting articles on Parliamentary matters written by specialists. There is a new annual *Parliamentary History Yearbook* (1982– , Alan Sutton Ltd) which appeared with articles covering British Parliamentary history and includes commentaries on parliamentary electoral history as well as book reviews.

Until recent years the standard authority for membership of the House of Commons were lists prepared in response to a motion for a 'Return of the names of every member of the lower house of parliaments of England. . .' made in 1876 and 1877. These consolidated lists, which cover the ground from the year 1213, began to appear in (1878) HC 69, 69-I, 69-II, and continued until (1929–30) HC 56. More recently, The History of Parliament Trust is setting out to compile a biographical dictionary of the House of Commons 1386 to 1832, and has so far published *History of Parliament: Biographies of Members of the House of Commons 1439–1509*, by J. C. Wedgwood (HMSO, 1936), *The House of Commons 1509 –1558*, by S. T. Bindoff (3 vols, Secker and Warburg, 1982); *The House of Commons 1558–1603*, by P. W. Hasler (3 vols, HMSO, 1981); *The House of Commons 1660–1690*, by B. D. Henning (3 vols, Secker and Warburg, 1983); *The House of Commons 1715 –1754*, by R. Sedgwick (3 vols, HMSO, 1970); and *The House of Commons 1754–1790*, by L. Namier and J. Brooke (3 vols, HMSO, 1964). Other volumes to fill gaps are in preparation, and it should be noted that each set contains an important introduction. Today there are a number of important reference works covering the biography of Members. *Who's Who of British Members of Parliament 1832–1979*, compiled by M. Stenton (4 vols, Harvester Press, 1976–1981) has for biographies superseded the great runs of *Dod's Parliamentary Companion* (1832–). *The Times Guide to the House of Commons*, published after each election since the 1880s (Times Publishing Company), is also important. Finally, *Sources in British Political History*, 1900–1951, compiled by C. Cook (5 vols, Macmillan, 1977), covers the private papers of Members of Parliament in vols 2, A–K, and 4, L–Z. Members of Parliament frequently appear in standard reference works such as the *Dictionary of National Biography*, school and university registers, Boase, etc.

Mention has already been made of a certain number of Committee reports, and it must be emphasized that central to the bibliography of Parliament and its work are the reports and published evidence of its Select Committees. For the House of Lords these include the Special Reports of the *Committee on European Communities* concerning their work, the Reports, etc. of *House of Lords' Offices Committee, Privileges Committee, Procedure Committee* and also the *Sound Broadcasting Committee*. In addition there may be *ad hoc* Select Committees on domestic matters. For the House of Commons there are the Special Reports of the *European Legislation etc. Committee*, concerning their work, the Reports, etc. of the *House of Commons (Services) Committee, Members Interests Committee*, Special Reports of the *Parliamentary Commissioner for Administration Committee* and the Reports of the *Privileges Committee, Procedure Committee* and the *Sound Broadcasting Committee*. There are also Special Reports of the *Liaison Committee*, which is made up of the Chairmen of Select Committees. In addition to these regular Committees, the House of Commons also may set up *ad hoc* Select Committees on domestic matters.

Also published by the House of Commons are a number of Returns of information about its work covering *Public Bills, Select Committees* and *Standing Committees*, together with the *Register of Members' Interests*. In addition to these papers, all published by HMSO, there are also Returns not ordered to be printed for which recourse should be made to the House of Lords Record Office.

Ministers

One of Parliament's roles is to provide a majority group whose leader is invited by the Crown to form a Government, i.e. to appoint a Ministerial team. About one Member in eight of the House of Commons is a Minister and of these about one in six is in the Cabinet. Books on individual posts and Departments are not included.

It was only in 1916 that a Secretariat for the Cabinet was formed. For this reason, for the earlier period *The Prime Ministers' Papers 1801–1902*, Historical Manuscript Commission (HMSO, 1968) and *Papers of British Cabinet Ministers 1782–1900* Historical Manuscript Commission Guide . . . No. 1 (HMSO, 1981), which gives a comprehensive list of relevant family papers where many Cabinet papers still rest, together with their locations, are both vital. A continuation volume, *Guide to the Papers of British Cabinet Ministers, 1900–1951*, compiled by C. Hazlehurst and C. Woodland (Royal Historical Society, 1974), is also essential. The Public Record Office, which keeps later papers, has published *List of Cabinet Papers 1880–1914* Handbook No. 4 (HMSO, 1964), *List of Cabinet Papers 1915 and 1916* Handbook No. 9 (HMSO, 1966) and *Reports of the Cabinet Office to 1922* Handbook No. 11 (HMSO, 1966). No further volumes are planned but there is also an important monograph *The Cabinet Office to 1945* Handbook No. 17 (HMSO, 1975), which sets out the context of the records as well as lists of Cabinet documentation. The first Secretary to the Cabinet was Lord Hankey, Secretary from 1916 to 1938, and the distinguished biography *Hankey, Man of Secrets*, by S. Roskill (3 vols, Collins, 1970–1974), is important for understanding Cabinet matters, as is *Whitehall Diary* (of Thomas Jones), edited by K. Middlemass (3 vols, Oxford University Press, 1969–1971).

All this material has been published much later than earlier monographs such as *The British Cabinet System, 1830–1938*, by A. B. Keith (Stevens, 1939) and *Cabinet Government*, by Sir Ivor Jennings (Cambridge University Press, 3rd edn, 1959). This latter is a textbook which ranges far wider than the Cabinet itself. Two slim volumes add perspective to the subject, namely *Cabinet Government and War 1890–1940*, the Lees Knowles lectures of 1957, by J. Ehrman (Cambridge University Press, 1958) and his distillation, *Reflections on the Constitution*, by H. Laski (Manchester University Press, 1951), which covers both Parliament and Cabinet.

A modern survey, revised since Cabinet papers of only thirty years ago might be consulted, is *The British Cabinet* by J. P. Mackintosh (3rd edn, Stevens, 1977) and there is a useful collection of essays, *Cabinet Studies: A Reader,* edited by V. Herman and J. Alt (Macmillan, 1975). It covers subjects from 'The Cabinet and the Lobby' (also worth consulting on this is *The Westminster Lobby Correspondents*, by J. Tunstall (Routledge and Kegan Paul, 1970)) to 'Resignations', also treated in *The Tactics of Resignation: a Study in British Cabinet Government* by R. Alderman and J. Cross (Routledge and Kegan Paul, 1967). The job itself is examined in *British Cabinet Ministers: the Roles of Politicians in Executive Office*, by B. Headey (Allen and Unwin, 1974), and one aspect of their job, namely Ministerial patronage, is critically examined in *Patronage in British Government*, by P. Richards (Allen and Unwin, 1963). A more general survey of the institution is *Cabinet Reform in Britain 1914–1963*, by H. Daalder (Stanford University Press, 1964).

There are a number of inside views of a Minister's role, including his relationship with Parliament, and of these, *Government and Parliament* by H. Morrison (Oxford University Press, 3rd edn, 1964), which grew out of a fireside chat to Oxford dons, still remains the most important. Another view is *The Cabinet* by P. Gordon Walker (Cape, rev. edn, 1972), and there is an insider's introductory work, *The Governance of Britain*, by Sir Harold Wilson (Weidenfeld and Nicholson, 1978). After the excitement of keeping his diaries, R. Crossman delivered a reflective *Inside view . . . on Prime Ministerial Government*, Godkin lectures 1970 (Jonathan Cape, 1972), which revealed worried distinctions between Presidential and Cabinet Government. An interesting first attempt to unveil the relationship between Minister and Civil Servant, with a side-glance at Parliament, is H. Young and A. Sloman, *No, Minister* (BBC, 1982). The subject is treated broadly and authoritatively in four lectures *Parliament and the Executive* (Royal Institute of Public Administration, 1982).

The perspective on the Cabinet has been changed by two events in recent years. First, under *Public Records Act, 1967* (HMSO) the period for documents to be held before being opened to the public was reduced from fifty years to thirty years. Overnight, half a generation of Cabinet papers were revealed. A description of the method of passing Departmental papers to the Public Record Office is to be found in *Modern Public Records: Selection and Access*, Report of a Committee appointed by the Lord Chancellor, Chairman Sir D. Wilson, Cmnd. 8204 (HMSO, 1981). Second, *The Crossman Diaries 1964–70* (3 vols, Collins, 1975–1977) gave the most detailed account of the work of Ministers and the Cabinet yet available. A description of what happened concerning its publication and the implications is to be found in *The Crossman Affair* by H. Young (Hamish Hamilton and Jonathan Cape, 1976). Further detail on the working of the Cabinet and of a Minister's role is to be found in *The Castle Diaries 1974–76* (Weidenfeld and Nicholson, 1980) and Sir Harold Wilson himself wrote a detailed account of the recent past in *The Labour Government 1964–1970* (Weidenfeld and Nicholson, 1971) and *Final Term: the Labour*

Government 1974–76 (Weidenfeld and Nicholson, 1979). Cross-referring between these several works must illuminate uniquely these years of Ministerial life. Finally, there are two lighter works designed to take us behind the scenes, *The Secret Constitution*, by B. Sedgemore (Hodder and Stoughton, 1980) and *How to be a Minister*, by G. Kaufman (Sidgwick and Jackson, 1980).

To conclude this survey we would mention two books, one third of the text of each of which is devoted to lists and other data on the subjects of this chapter. These are *British Historical Facts 1830–1900*, edited by C. Cook and B. Keith (Macmillan, 1975), and the frequently updated *British Political Facts 1900–1979*, edited by D. Butler and A. Sloman (Macmillan, 5th edn, 1980). The latter especially has been honed to a high level of accuracy and both can save the grateful student many hours of devilling.

10
Public administration and policy studies
Tony Butcher

Introduction

Public administration is traditionally regarded as a subdivision of political science. Almost without exception, the founding fathers of the subject in the US were political scientists, including Woodrow Wilson, whose famous essay on 'The Study of Administration' (*Political Science Quarterly,* **2** (1887)) is generally regarded as the symbolic beginning of public administration as a self-conscious subject. The academic subject of public administration in Britain also has its roots in the study of politics. But while the subject grew up under the wing of political science, the study of public administration today draws many of its theories and concepts from other social science disciplines, including sociology, psychology and economics. Such is the movement of public administration away from its mother discipline, especially in the US, that F. F. Ridley maintains that it has become a true 'crossroads' science, so interdisciplinary that its links with political science are now outweighed by the range of its links with other disciplines ('Public Administration: Cause for Discontent', *Public Administration,* **50** (1972)).

For some American scholars the problem of identifying the subject's disciplinary core is so intractable that its academic study is said to be suffering from what Dwight Waldo has termed a 'crisis of identity' ('Scope of the Theory of Public Administration', in *Theory and Practice of Public Administration*, edited by J. C. Charlesworth, The American Academy of Political and Social

Science, 1968), and there has been an extensive literature of self-examination, a notable example being *Toward a New Public Administration*, edited by Frank Marini (Chandler, 1971). The American debate has been matched by a similar self-examination in Britain, of which Ridley (1972, work cited) and L. A. Gunn, 'Public Administration as Management' (*PAC Bulletin*, **11** (1971)) are examples. Ridley's views on the nature of public administration are developed in *The Study of Government* (Allen and Unwin, 1975).

Public administration's identity problem has undoubtedly been compounded by the debate on the purposes of the subject. Should public administration teaching provide a general education in the liberal arts tradition, with an emphasis on what Ridley has described as a concern with researching the *how* and theorizing about the *why*, or should it be primarily concerned with training practitioners and would-be-administrators, with an emphasis on the *how to* – the techniques of administration? Unlike the US, where the study of public administration has long been recognized as a formal body of knowledge accepted as the basis for a profession, British universities have traditionally aimed to offer 'education for public administration', with public administration being taught as part of wider courses on politics and government (see *Teaching Public Administration*, by R. A. Chapman, Joint University Council for Social and Public Administration, 1973). L. A. Gunn (work cited), however, emphasizes public administration as 'administrative studies' for future and practising administrators, arguing that any coherence that public administration possesses as an area of study derives from a notion of an identifiable clientele.

Despite these identity problems, for some writers the variety of approaches to the subject is one of public administration's main attractions. Thus R. A. W. Rhodes, in his review of developments in Britain and the US (*Public Administration and Policy Analysis*, Saxon House, 1979), concludes that the search for the 'holy grail' of disciplinary status will, in all probability, fail, defeated by the range and complexity of the subject matter. In Rhodes' view, the diversity of the subject should be regarded as its main defining characteristic rather than treated as a problem. For Ridley, however, public administration is growing in so many directions and has become involved with so many other disciplines at its periphery that it is in danger of disappearing as a recognizable focus of study, with the risk of overlooking the very aspect of public administration of which earlier political scientists were so aware: the importance of 'formal institutions and formal procedures' (1975, work cited).

Approaches to the study of public administration

There is much truth in Ridley's conclusion that public administration has advanced in so many directions 'that it is almost impossible to pattern the current literature' (1975, work cited, p.178). Thus R. G. S. Brown's outline of approaches to the study of the subject in *The Management of Welfare* (Fontana, 1975) deals successively with the formal structure of administration, the perspective of political sociology, organization theory, the sociology of professions, quantitative analysis and policy analysis. A recent Open University course on the subject was organized around the formal structural approach, the administrative process as a decision-making and goal-attaining process, incrementalism, history and law (*Social Sciences: A Third Level Course: Public Administration*, Open University Press, 1974). A distinction can be made between the traditional institutional and descriptive approaches which still characterize much of the study of the subject in Britain, and the organizational analysis and policy-oriented approaches primarily associated with the subject in the US.

Traditional approaches

One way of approaching the study of public administration is to concentrate on the formal machinery and processes of government. Historically, much of the work in this tradition has consisted of descriptions of the history, structure, powers and relationships of public bodies, and the methods of controlling them. Representative examples of this tradition are *A Primer of Public Administration*, by S. E. Finer (Frederick Muller, 1950), and the works of E. N. Gladden, which include *An Introduction to Public Administration* (Staples Press, 1961).

This institutional/descriptive approach still colours much of the writing on British public administration, and has rather unfairly earned the subject a reputation as the Cinderella of the political science family. But although this approach is largely descriptive, many studies in this tradition do have a prescriptive orientation, and the institutional/descriptive approach is often associated with what Rhodes (work cited) calls the approach of the 'social critic': i.e. a concern to describe institutions and/or policies with a view to affecting change in them, as represented in W. A. Robson's work on local government (see, for example, *Local Government in Crisis*, Allen and Unwin, 1966).

Public administration as the study of organizations

Another approach to the study of public administration is to treat its problems as ones of organizations and to relate them to the ideas of organization theory. There is a good general discussion of the subject, which is mainly American, in *The Theory of Organisations*, by David Silverman (Heinemann, 1970). *Administration: the Word and the Science*, by Andrew Dunsire (Martin Robertson, 1973), provides a useful overview of the literature in the context of a wider discussion of the development of 'administrative science', while the utility of this body of knowledge to the study of public administration is discussed by R. G. S. Brown, 'Public Administration and the Study of Administrative Organisations' (*PAC Bulletin*, **11** (1971)).

One way of studying organizations is to see them as hierarchies of formal and well-defined positions. This is the approach of the classical school of organization theory, which attempted to show that there are certain principles of administration to guide the structuring of organizations. Drawing much of its inspiration from F. W. Taylor's work on industrial management (*The Principles of Scientific Management*, Harper, 1911), the classical school is best represented in the *Papers on the Science of Administration*, edited by Luther Gulick and Lyndall F. Urwick (Institute of Public Administration, New York, 1937). The student of British public administration will find an excellent example of this approach in the Haldane *Report of the Machinery of Government Committee* (Cd. 9230, HMSO, 1918). Many of the ideas of the classical school are similar to the prepositions advanced by Max Weber in his work on bureaucracy (*The Theory of Social and Economic Organisation*, translated and edited by A. M. Henderson and T. Parsons, Free Press, 1947). In contrast to his ideal type bureaucracy, modern sociologists have concentrated attention on the unanticipated consequences of this form of organization. Particularly influential is R. K. Merton's 'Bureaucratic Structure and Personality' in *Reader in Bureaucracy*, edited by R. K. Merton *et al.* (Free Press, 1952), which declared that Weber's ideal bureaucracy had important dysfunctional consequences, a theme echoed by later sociological studies, notably *TVA and the Grass Roots*, by P. Selznick (University of California Press, 1949) and *Patterns of Industrial Bureaucracy*, by A. W. Gouldner (Free Press, 1954). Another influential contribution is that of the French sociologist, Michel Crozier, *The Bureaucratic Phenomenon* (Tavistock Publications, 1964).

The importance of informal patterns of group behaviour in organizations has been the subject of attention by writers in the human relations school, which examines organizations as social institutions. The beginnings of this school are usually identified as the 'Hawthorne' experiments of the late 1920s and early 1930s, reported in *Management and the Worker*, by F. J. Roethlisberger and W. J. Dickson (Harvard University Press, 1939). Although the term 'human relations' is now much less commonly used, research and literature continues to be focused upon the 'needs' of organizational members, in particular the work of such American organizational psychologists as C. Argyris (*Personality and Organisation*, Harper and Row, 1957), D. McGregor (*The Human Side of Enterprise*, McGraw-Hill, 1960) and R. Likert (*New Patterns of Management*, McGraw-Hill, 1961), who are much more sophisticated about the complexity of individuals' 'psychological needs'.

Other writers look at organizations as 'systems' which are continually interacting with their environment, one important application being that which describes organizations as 'sociotechnical systems', stressing the interrelationships of technology, environment, the sentiments of participants and organizational form. Of particular importance are the works of three leading British organizational theorists: *Industrial Organisation: Theory and Practice*, by Joan Woodward (Oxford University Press, 1965), and *The Management of Innovation*, by T. Burns and G. M. Stalker (Tavistock Publications, 1961), which introduces the famous distinction between 'mechanistic' and 'organic' management systems. More recently, several writers have developed the study of the internal characteristics and environment of organizations into 'contingency theory', British work in this field can be found in the Aston studies: *Organisational Structure in its Context*, edited by D. S. Pugh and D. J. Hickson (Saxon House, 1976), and *Organisational Structure: Extensions and Replications*, edited by D. S. Pugh and C. R. Hinings (Saxon House, 1976).

Another important branch of organization theory is that which discusses organizations as decision-making structures. Decision making is primarily associated with H. A. Simon, who, in an argument begun in *Administrative Behaviour* (Free Press, 3rd edn, 1976), which has become a classic, argues that while the pursuit of rationality is a desirable aim in decision making, decision makers will always be subject to 'bounded rationality', and obliged to 'satisfice' and search for solutions that are satisfactory or 'good enough'.

Simon's work has inspired a whole generation of writing on decision making, notably that of C. E. Lindblom, who argues that for complex policy problems no-one can approximate to Simon's synoptic ideal, and formulates the very important concept of 'incrementalism' to describe decision makers' reactions to complex problems. The origins of this work can be found in 'The Science of "Muddling Through" ', *Public Administration Review*, **19** (1959), but the most complete statement of his ideas is *The Intelligence of Democracy* (Free Press, 1965).

Other important contributions to the literature include A. T. Etzioni, who sees Simon and Lindblom's approaches as complementary ('Mixed Scanning: a "Third" Approach to Decision-making', *Public Administration Review*, **27** (1967)), and an important British contribution is *The Art of Judgement*, by Sir Geoffrey Vickers (Chapman and Hall, 1965), which, acknowledging a great debt to Simon, depicts policy making as being concerned with the regulation of systems through governing 'norms' or relations, and not in terms of the setting of goals.

Policy studies

Vickers' book is recognized as one of the foundations for a relatively new approach in public administration: the study of public policy, emphasis upon which has brought the subject of public administration much closer to political science. The origins of policy studies can be traced back at least as far as the writings of Harold Lasswell in the 1950s (*The Policy Sciences*, edited by D. Lerner and H. Lasswell, Stanford University Press, 1951), but the interest in policy as a central organizing concept only really began to emerge in the 1960s, partly as a reaction against what was seen as an excessive concern by political scientists with the inputs of the political system, and partly as an attempt to provide political science with an applied function (W. I. Jenkins and G. K. Roberts, 'Policy Analysis: a Wider Perspective on Public Administration', *PAC Bulletin*, **11** (1971)). The growing concern with policy studies has not, however, been accompanied by agreement on how such studies should be conducted, and there are many different approaches to the study of public policy, ranging from essentially descriptive and explanatory studies (such as studies of policy content, studies of the policy process and studies of policy outputs) to studies which are essentially prescriptive, such as the work of Y. Dror (see, for example, *Public Policymaking Re-examined*, Chandler, 1968). This distinction is discussed further by I. Gordon *et al.*, 'Perspectives on Policy Analysis' (*Public Administration Bulletin*, **25** (1977)). A useful *tour d'horizon* of the literature on policy studies will be found in *Policy Analysis*, by W. I. Jenkins (Martin Robertson, 1978).

For many writers the central focus of the study of public policy is the policy process. Some writers examine the policy process in terms of a systems framework derived from the writings of David Easton, a perspective favoured by Thomas Dye in *Understanding Public Policy* (Prentice-Hall, 1972). Another commonly presented framework suggests a number of stages through which issues proceed: agenda setting, problem definition, policy formation, policy implementation and so on. Typical of this approach is *Public Policy-Making*, by J. E. Anderson (Nelson, 1975). Analysis of the policy process draws heavily on the literature of decision making discussed in the previous section, especially Lindblom's discussion of incrementalism. There are also important links with the literature on power, a particularly important concept being that of 'non-decisions'; it being necessary, as P. Bachrach and M. Baratz point out in a famous article, not only to look at decisions, but also at how potential issues are kept off the policy agenda by those in political power ('Two Faces of Power', *American Political Science Review*, **56** (1962)).

Although the literature on the policy process has traditionally emphasized the policy-formation stage, and there are a vast number of what H. Heclo, in his discussion of the case study approach ('Policy Analysis', *British Journal of Political Science*, **2** (1972)), calls 'who did what' accounts, the policy process is being increasingly studied from a broader perspective. Following the publication of J. L. Pressman and A. Wildavsky's classic *Implementation* (University of California Press, 1973), there has been a developing interest in the implementation stage, the literature of which is reviewed by M. J. Hill *et al.,* 'Implementation and the Central–Local Relationship' (Appendix II in *Central–Local Government Relationships*, SSRC, 1979), and in *Implementation in a Bureaucracy*, by A. Dunsire (Martin Robertson, 1978). Studies of policy implementation need to be distinguished from policy impact studies, which attempt to evaluate policies by measuring the amount of change brought about by them. The literature on policy impact is reviewed by A. King, 'On Studying the Impacts of Public Policies', in *What Government Does*, edited by M. Holden and D. L. Dresang (Sage, 1975). There has also developed a literature on the termination of policies following evaluation, an overview of which is provided by Peter de Leon, 'A Theory of Policy Termination', in *The Policy Cycle*, edited by J. V. May and A. Wildavsky (Sage, 1978). The concept of policy succession, whereby existing policies are replaced by 'new' ones, is discussed in *Policy Dynamics*, by Brian Hogwood and B. Guy Peters (Wheatsheaf, 1983).

A different perspective on the policy process is provided by Theodore Lowi, who suggests that we should examine the outputs of policy making and then relate them back to policy processes. In a famous article, 'American Business, Public Policy, Case Studies and Political Theory' (*World Politics*, **16** (1964)), Lowi argues that each of three categories of a typology of policy outputs indicates a different kind of policy process. While accepting that all policies are not handled in the same way, others have suggested that it is equally true to say that policies are not so distinctive as to prevent them being accommodated in a basic simple typology of 'policy styles'. This is the theme of *Policy Styles in Western Europe*, edited by Jeremy Richardson (Allen and Unwin, 1982), which defines policy style as the interaction between the government's approach to problem-solving and its relationship with the other actors in the policy process. Such a definition enables societies to be categorized into four basic policy styles, the book concluding, on the basis of case studies of several Western European systems, that there appears to be a drift towards 'a consensus relationship between government and other actors combined with a reactive, rather than an anticipatory, approach to problem-solving'.

Richardson's book exemplifies the increasing awareness of the importance of comparative studies of public administration and public policy in broadening the critical appraisal of one's own system. An assessment of the state of the comparative study of public administration, together with bibliographical details of the literature, will be found in *Public Administration: A Comparative Perspective* by Ferrel Heady (Marcel Dekker, 2nd edn, 1979), and references to the literature of various overseas administrative systems will be found in the chapters in Part 4 of this book.

British public administration

Traditionally, the study and literature of public administration in Britain has been characterized by the institutional/descriptive approach, an emphasis which has been the subject of much criticism. Thus Ridley (1972, work cited), writing in the early 1970s, referred to 'a missing literature', and expressed dissatisfaction with the lack of theoretical contributions to the subject by British scholars. Increasingly, however, the study of public administration in Britain has begun to incorporate broader approaches, notably the organizational and policy perspectives discussed in the previous section. The literature has also seen the addition of several important theoretical contributions. Ridley himself refers to R. G. S. Brown's pioneering *The Administrative Process in Britain* (Methuen, 1970), which attempted to move away from a 'commonsense' approach to public administration to see whether organization theory could provide a more satisfying perspective, and this was soon followed by *Administrative Theories and Politics*, by Peter Self (Allen and Unwin, 1972), relating theories of the administrative process to the actual functioning of governmental systems. Other significant contributions include R. J. S. Baker's attempt to develop a theory of public administration in Britain in *Administrative Theory and Public Administration* (Hutchinson University Library, 1972), and *The Sociology of Public Administration*, by Michael Hill (Weidenfeld and Nicholson, 1972), suggesting ways in which modern developments in sociology can be applied to the study of British public administration. An important contribution by a serving civil servant is *Management in Government*, by Desmond Keeling (Allen and Unwin, 1972), which, although mainly about the use of resources in public administration, develops an interesting discussion of the characteristic features of administration.

Although the literature on British public administration now compares more favourably with the US in respect of theoretical contributions, unlike the US, there are few British textbooks which serve as an introduction to the whole subject. There are several introductory textbooks which are aimed at the level of professional courses and first-year undergraduates, but the only comprehensive account of the system is *Administering Britain*, by B. C. Smith and J. Stanyer (Martin Robertson, 1976), which attempts, *inter alia*, to discuss the interrelationships between the separate parts of the British administrative system. It is to the literature on the separate parts that we now turn.

Central administration

A major problem in discussing the British central administrative system is the absence of an up-to-date survey of the field. The standard work is *The Organization of British Central Government: 1914–1964*, by D. N. Chester and F. M. G. Willson (Allen and Unwin, 2nd edn, 1968), but this deals only with changes in departmental structure and functions up to 1964. As Christopher Hood and Andrew Dunsire point out in *Bureaumetrics* (Gower, 1981), Chester and Willson also belongs to an era when machinery of government problems were studied almost entirely historically and descriptively, and before the development of techniques of large-scale systematic comparison of organizations. *Bureaumetrics* pioneers the use of such methods in the examination of central administration, and argues for a well-developed set of analytical and measuring techniques for assessing and characterizing the organizational *status quo*.

Although Hood and Dunsire's book breaks new ground in the study of what they term the 'meso' level of central government, most of the literature on the 'micro' level is embedded firmly in the descriptive tradition, with the emphasis upon constitutional relationships, and saying little about the internal structure and functioning of government departments. A few authors have written about the working of departments from experience within them, including H. E. Dale's classic pre-war study, *The Higher Civil Service of Great Britain* (Oxford University Press, 1941), but this is now of historical interest only, and there are no comparable modern-day accounts. The New Whitehall Series, published under the auspices of the Royal Institute of Public Administration, and a successor to the inter-war Whitehall Series, covers (to date) some sixteen departments, including *The Treasury*, by Lord Bridges (Allen and Unwin, 1964), but the books in this series are essentially descriptions of the departments concerned and, inevitably, they are in many cases seriously outdated. One book that does move away from formal description is *Government Departments*, by D. C. Pitt and B. C. Smith (Routledge and Kegan Paul, 1981), which attempts to show how departments look when concepts of organizational analysis are applied to such issues as organizational environment, goals, structure and management.

Whilst Chester and Willson found it possible in the late 1960s to define 'central administration' as 'the government departments whose spiritual if not physical headquarters are to be found in Whitehall', the position today is much more complicated. Of particular importance has been the growth of central non-departmental bodies outside the traditional departmental structure. Various terms have been used to describe such bodies, but the word which has entered most popular usage is 'quango', originally an acronym for 'quasi-non-governmental organization'. Non-departmental bodies, in their various guises, have been part of the British administrative system since the nineteenth century, but their importance has grown dramatically since the end of the Second World War, as reflected in the substantial literature on the public corporation (see, for example, *The Nationalised Industries since 1960*, edited by L. Tivey, Allen and Unwin, 1973). This traditional area of study has broadened to include quangos, and several publications have followed on from the Anglo-American Carnegie Accountability Project, 1968–1972, including *Public*

Policy and Private Interests, edited by D. C. Hague and others (Macmillan, 1975), and several papers by Christopher Hood, including 'Keeping the Centre Small: Explanations of Agency Type' (*Political Studies*, **26** (1978)). Hood is also a contributor to a collection of valuable essays edited by A. Barker, *Quangos in Britain* (Macmillan, 1982), which also contains a substantial bibliography.

The 'functional' decentralization of central government functions to non-departmental bodies is only one aspect of a wider process of decentralization. Geographical decentralization is also an important feature of the British administrative system, but although there is a vast literature on local government (see Chapter 12 on this subject), and regionalism has been a recurring theme in the literature of British government (see, for instance, *The Case for Regional Reform*, edited by W. Thornhill, Nelson, 1972), there have been few detailed descriptions of how government operates at the regional level, a gap which has now been partly filled by a collection of essays on the main regional arms of central government: *Regional Government in England*, edited by Brian Hogwood and Michael Keating (The Clarendon Press, 1982). Regional administration in Scotland and Wales is discussed in J. G. Kellas and P. Madgwick, 'Territorial Ministries: the Scottish and Welsh Offices', in Peter Madgwick and Richard Rose (eds), *The Territorial Dimension in United Kingdom Politics* (Macmillan, 1982), while the 'Stormont' experience, together with the succeeding phase of direct rule, is discussed in *Policy and Government in Northern Ireland*, by D. Birrell and A. Murie (Gill and Macmillan, 1980). Useful information on regional administration in all four countries of the UK can be found in the evidence to, and reports of, the Kilbrandon Commission: *Royal Commission on the Constitution, 1969–1973* (Vols I–II, Cmnd. 5460, HMSO, 1973).

The growing complexity of the central administrative system underlines the need for coordination. *The British Cabinet*, by J. P. Mackintosh (Stevens, 3rd edn, 1977), remains the classic study of the major instrument of coordination at the centre of British government, whilst a useful 'insider' account is *The Cabinet*, by P. Gordon Walker (Jonathan Cape, rev. edn, 1972). Another 'insider' account, *The Diaries of a Cabinet Minister*, by Richard Crossman (Vols I–III, Hamish Hamilton and Jonathan Cape, 1975, 1976 and 1977), confirms the longstanding criticism that policy at the centre of British government is made through a process of departmental pluralism rather than through the imposition of consistent priorities by the Cabinet. Material on the most recent attempt to improve the strategic capacity at the centre, the Central Policy Review Staff (abolished in 1983), is sparse, but William Plowden, 'The British Central Policy Review Staff', in *Policy Analysis and Policy Innovation*, edited by P. R. Baehr and B. Wittrock (Sage, 1981), is an interesting overview by a former member.

One area where there is an expanding literature on the processes, as opposed to the structure, of coordination is that of public expenditure planning and control. Detailed discussion on the origins, mechanisms and problems of the PESC cycle introduced after the important Plowden Report (*Report of the Committee on the Control of Public Expenditure*, Cmnd. 1432, HMSO, 1961) can be found in C. Pollitt, 'The Public Expenditure Survey 1961–72', and Maurice Wright, 'Public Expenditure in Britain: the Crisis of Control' (both in *Public Administration*, **55** (1977)). Wright develops his study of PESC and the application of cash limits in 'From Planning to Control: PESC in the 1970's', in *Public Spending Decisions*, edited by Maurice Wright (Allen and Unwin, 1980). A mandarin's-eye view of the process can be found in *Getting and Spending: Public Expenditure, Employment and Inflation*, by Leo Pliatzky (Blackwell, 1982), while *Inside the Treasury*, by Joel Barnett (André Deutsch, 1982), is an account by an ex-Chief Secretary to the Treasury. But it takes two Americans, H. Heclo and A. Wildavsky, in one of the most important books on British public administration of the last decade, *The Private Government of Public Money* (Macmillan, 2nd edn, 1981), to tell us how Treasury officials, spending departments and Cabinet ministers actually interact with each other in the public expenditure 'community' to produce the pattern of public spending.

The civil service

At present no book provides a comprehensive introduction to the British civil service. *Central Administration in Britain*, by W. J. M. Mackenzie and J. W. Grove (Longman, 1957), describes in detail the structure of the service, its recruitment and training procedures, its conditions of employment, its tasks, its history and its relationship to other parts of British government, but is now mainly of historical interest. The only book that begins to cover the ground is *The Administrative Process in Britain*, by R. G. S. Brown and D. R. Steel (Methuen, 2nd edn, 1979), which contains chapters outlining the main features of the civil service as it was at the beginning of 1977. An up-to-date statistical profile can be obtained by reference to the latest volumes of *Civil Service Statistics* and *Annual Reports of the Civil Service Commission*.

There are several good surveys of the historical development of the modern civil service. The development of the service in the nineteenth century is discussed in *Constitutional Bureaucracy*, by H. Parris (Allen and Unwin, 1969), and *Treasury Control of the Civil Service 1854–1874*, by Maurice Wright (The Clarendon Press, 1969). The nineteenth-century civil service classic, the Northcote–Trevelyan *Report on the Organisation of the Permanent Civil Service* (C.1713, 1854), which had such an impact on the 'generalist' philosophy, is reprinted as an appendix to the Fulton Report (*Report of the Committee on the Civil Service, 1966–68*, Cmnd. 3638, HMSO, 1968). *Statesmen in Disguise*, by G. K. Fry (Macmillan, 1969), discusses the changing role of the Administrative Class up to Fulton.

As Parris reminds us, for many years the literature was almost unanimous in extolling the virtues of the civil service. Typical was Herman Finer's view in *The British Civil Service* (Allen and Unwin, 1937), that the service was 'rightly the envy of the world'. There were occasional criticisms, notably H. J. Laski's questioning of the political neutrality of the service in *Parliamentary Government in England* (Allen and Unwin, 1938), but it was 'almost always possible to show that the critics were either misinformed or that they had an axe to grind' (Parris, work cited, p.285). By the mid-1960s, however, the literature had become increasingly characterized by criticisms that the service was amateurish and incapable of dealing with the problems of a modern state, the classic indictment of the service's 'generalist' philosophy being provided by Thomas Balogh, who argued in 'The Apotheosis of the Dilettante', in *The Establishment*, edited by Hugh Thomas (Anthony Blond, 1959), that 'in a planned economy, the crossword puzzle mind, reared on mathematics at Cambridge or Greats at Oxford, has only a limited outlet'. Although an elegant 'insider' defence of the role of the 'generalist' was provided in *The Spirit of British Administration*, by C. H. Sisson (Faber, 1959), Balogh's theme was taken up by others, notably the polemical *British Government Observed*, by Brian Chapman (Allen and Unwin, 1963). These, and other, attacks were given official recognition in the report of the Fulton Committee (work cited).

Attacks on the service have not subsided with the publication of Fulton. In *The Civil Servants* (Macdonald Futura, 1980), Peter Kellner and Lord Crowther-Hunt (the latter a member of the Fulton Committee) continue the attack on the 'generalist' philosophy. The book's subtitle, 'An Inquiry into Britain's Ruling Class', indicates its general approach, which argues that the power of the civil service is substantial and that, like ruling classes in the past, it has constructed an elaborate system of defences to protect that power from erosion, as evidenced by the blocking of the Fulton reforms. Another account of what has (or rather what has not) happened since Fulton is *Managing the Civil Service*, by John Garrett (Heinemann, 1980). Garrett's earlier book, *The Management of Government* (Penguin, 1972), discusses 'the managerial revolution' in central government of the 1960s and early 1970s. In addition to being a member of the Management Consultancy Group which advised the Fulton Committee, Garrett later became a member of the House of Commons Select Committee which produced a critical report on developments in the civil service since Fulton (*The Eleventh Report from the Expenditure Committee, 1976–77*, HC 535, HMSO, 1977). The Minutes of Evidence and Appendices to this Report contain a wealth of information on the civil service.

The alleged sabotaging of the Fulton proposals by the civil service has been seen by Kellner and Crowther-Hunt as 'the insidious operation of civil service power at its most triumphant', and there has been much discussion as to whether it is ministers or their officials who control policy making. According to constitutional convention the position is clear: ministers decide policies and take responsibility for them; civil servants, who are anonymous, advise their ministers and execute their decisions. These traditional assumptions are being increasingly questioned. The validity of the traditional convention of ministerial responsibility has been challenged by several writers, notably S. E. Finer in his classic article 'The Individual Responsibility of Ministers' (*Public Administration*, **34** (1956)), and there are also signs that the related convention of civil service anonymity is being attenuated. A fuller discussion of the assumptions underlying the minister –civil service relationship is Maurice Wright, 'Ministers and Civil Servants: Relations and Responsibilities' (*Parliamentary Affairs*, **30** (1977)).

In recent years, various writers have questioned the view that ministers decide policies, maintaining that civil servants can actually obstruct policies of which they disapprove and push ministers into adopting policies that the departments want to adopt. Laski's misgivings about the political neutrality of the civil service have given way to the more sophisticated view of Tony Benn that the civil service 'sees itself as being above the party battle with a political position of its own to defend against all-comers, including incoming governments' ('Manifestos and Mandarins', in *Policy and Practice*, Royal Institute of Public Administration, 1980). Similar criticisms have been made by other former Labour ministers, notably Richard Crossman (work cited).

The arguments about civil service power are not, of course, one-sided. Former ministerial colleagues of Mr Benn question his thesis, with Shirley Williams rejecting both the traditional constitutional doctrine and the alternative thesis that the bureaucracy rules, concluding that 'power consists of intersecting rings: it resides in areas where people are able to come together between the civil service, ministers, and to some extent . . . pressure groups' ('The Decision-makers', in *Policy and Practice*, work cited). Other antidotes to the 'bureaucracy rules' thesis can be found in the discussions by ministers, ex-ministers and civil servants in *No Minister*, edited by Hugo Young and Anne Sloman (BBC, 1982). The view that civil servants actually prefer a decisive minister is one of the many valuable points to emerge from Bruce Headey's appraisal of ministerial roles in *British Cabinet Ministers* (Allen and Unwin, 1974).

Control of the administration

The control of the administration is an important and familiar part of the literature of British public administration. The main control of public administration in Britain is political, as enshrined in the constitutional convention of ministerial responsibility (see S. E. Finer, 1956, work cited), and enforced through the operation of various parliamentary procedures. Ministerial responsibility is complemented by legal responsibility enforced by the courts. There is a substantial literature on both these aspects of control, and detailed discussions can be found in Chapters 9 and 11.

Increasingly, however, many disputes between the citizen and the administration are heard and decided outside the traditional arenas of Parliament and the courts, by what H. J. Elcock terms 'the machinery of administrative justice' – administrative tribunals and public inquiries (*Administrative Justice*, Longmans, 1969). The procedures of tribunals have been the concern of lawyers since the publication in the late 1920s of W. A. Robson's classic *Justice and Administrative Law* (Macmillan, 1928; Stevens, 3rd edn, 1951) and the more dramatic *The New Despotism*, by Lord Hewart (Benn, 1929), which denounced tribunals as 'administrative lawlessness'. Although Robson's book remained the standard work for many years, the last edition was overtaken by the publication of the Franks Report (*Report of the Committee on Administrative Tribunals and Enquiries*, Cmnd. 218, HMSO, 1957), and *Administrative Tribunals*, by R. E. Wraith and P. G. Hutchesson (Allen and Unwin, 1973) is now the most comprehensive study. Although many of the most fruitful contributions in this area continue to be made by lawyers (for instance, H. Street's *Justice in the Welfare State*, Stevens, 2nd edn, 1975), there have been a number of important research-based studies by social policy specialists on the major (in terms of cases heard) social security tribunal, including the *Research Study on Supplementary Benefit Appeal Tribunals*, by Kathleen Bell (HMSO, 1975), which prompted important changes in the rules concerning these tribunals. The major piece of work on public inquiries is *Public Inquiries as an Instrument of Government*, by R. E. Wraith and G. B. Lamb (Allen and Unwin, 1971).

Although constitutionally separated from the courts and administrative tribunals, and operating as an extension of the apparatus of parliamentary scrutiny of the administrative process, the work of the Parliamentary Commissioner for Administration is generally recognized as falling within the ambit of administrative justice. The Parliamentary Commissioner has been the subject of a burgeoning literature since the establishment of the office in 1967, the major work being *The Parliamentary Ombudsman* by Roy Gregory and Peter Hutchesson (Allen and Unwin, 1975), now, sadly, out of print. Two books by the late Frank Stacey are also major contributions: *The British Ombudsman* (The Clarendon Press, 1971), which describes in detail the campaign for an Ombudsman in Britain and the drafting and passage of the Parliamentary Commissioner for Administration Bill, and *Ombudsmen Compared* (The Clarendon Press, 1978), which compares the operation of the British system with systems in Scandinavia, the Canadian provinces and France. Both books are examples of the survival of the 'social critic' approach to the study of British public administration, making clear Stacey's commitment to the Ombudsman concept and to the changes which he thought necessary in the terms of reference and organization of the British version. The Parliamentary Commissioner's two major *causes célèbres* are discussed by G. K. Fry, 'The Sachsenhausen Concentration Camp Case and the Convention of Ministerial Responsibility' (*Public Law* (1970)), and R. Gregory, 'Court Line, Mr Benn and the Ombudsman' (*Parliamentary Affairs*, **30** (1977)). The shortcomings of the Parliamentary Commissioner system have been thoroughly surveyed by a Committee of 'Justice' in the aptly entitled *Our Fettered Ombudsman* (Justice, 1977). The published reports of the Parliamentary Commissioner contain a wealth of material on the processes of administration and policy making in government departments.

The original exclusions from the Parliamentary Commissioner's jurisdiction have been partially corrected by the extension of the

Ombudsman model to local government and the National Health Service. Apart from a chapter in Stacey's *Ombudsmen Compared* (work cited), there is no substantial account of the Health Service Commissioner, although there is a growing literature on the Local Commissioners for Administration, notably the evaluation by 'Justice', *The Local Ombudsmen; A Review of the First Five Years* (Justice, 1980). The office of the Northern Ireland Commissioner for Complaints is the subject of K. P. Poole's 'The Northern Ireland Commissioner for Complaints' (*Public Law* (1972)). For the local government Ombudsman system, see Chapter 12.

Policy studies in Britain

One of the most exciting and significant developments in the study of British public administration in recent years has been the discovery of policy studies, and several useful books have appeared in this area. An introductory text is *Policy Making in British Government*, by Brian Smith (Martin Robertson, 1976), which employs the two dimensions of power and rationality in an attempt to relate political and administrative processes to the making of public policy. More ambitious in its conception is *Policy and Politics in Britain*, by Douglas Ashford (Blackwell, 1981), which analyses six major policy areas in an attempt to see how established political constraints have affected policy making in Britain.

In an earlier section we referred to the attempt by Jeremy Richardson *et al.* (work cited) to develop the concept of 'policy style'. An important book which attempts to describe the dominant style of policy making in Britain is *Governing under Pressure*, by J. J. Richardson and A. G. Jordan (Martin Robertson, 1979), which, heavily influenced by Lindblom's model of decision making, characterizes the British policy process as essentially incremental, with policy making reflecting arrangements between groups and government departments which are intended to minimize conflict. Throughout their book, Richardson and Jordan examine the policy process as not one process, but as a series of subprocesses which are closely linked: issue emergence, processing of issues, decision and implementation, and there is a growing British literature on each of these subprocesses. Richardson's own article, 'Managing the Political Agenda: Problem Definition and Policy-making in Britain', co-written with Joan Stringer (*Parliamentary Affairs,* **33** (1980)), provides an overview of agenda management in Britain, while W. Solesbury, 'The Environmental Agenda' (*Public Administration,* **54** (1976)), although specifically concerned with the emergence of environmental issues, is a valuable analysis of the tests which nascent issues must pass in order to invoke action. As Solesbury's analysis reminds us, issues are often helped on to the policy agenda by commissions and committees of inquiry, and there is a wide literature on this traditional area of British public administration. The classic discussion remains *Government by Committee*, by K. C. Wheare (Oxford University Press, 1955), now nearly thirty years old, but still full of insights. Some of Wheare's ideas are drawn upon in *Committees of Inquiry*, by Gerald Rhodes (Allen and Unwin, 1975), which is a general survey of the field, whilst *Social Research and Royal Commissions*, edited by M. Bulmer (Allen and Unwin, 1980), is a useful set of case studies.

Although, as Richardson and Jordan remind us, political scientists have tended to neglect the study of policy implementation and policy delivery because they have been almost totally absorbed in the study of the legislative process, there is a widening literature on policy implementation in Britain. Two major theoretical contributions are *The Limits of Administration*, by C. Hood (Wiley, 1976), which examines the factors which prevent the achievement of the 'perfect administration' required to produce perfect policy implementation, and A. King's discussion of the relationship between non-compliance and the popular thesis that central government is 'overloaded' in 'Overload: Problems of Governing in the 1970's' (*Political Studies*, **23** (1975)). A useful 'insider' case study by a serving civil servant is Dorothy Johnstone's study of the introduction of VAT, *A Tax Shall be Charged* (Civil Service College Studies, No.1, HMSO, 1975).

Less has been written on the impact of public policy. One well-known study is *The Politics of Legislation*, by M. J. Barnett (Weidenfeld and Nicholson, 1969), which goes beyond the origins and passage of the 1957 Rent Act to examine the political, economic and social consequences, but, as King points out (in M. Holden and D. L. Dresang (eds), work cited), Barnett's account is largely vitiated by the failure to 'factor-out' those observed changes which are government-specific. One study which does attempt to do this is H. A. Scarrow, 'The Impact of British Domestic Air Pollution Legislation' (*British Journal of Political Science*, **2** (1972)).

Our understanding of the nature of the policy process in Britain has also been enriched by the availability of a large number of case studies covering particular policy issues or legislative enactments (see, for example, Barnett, work cited). A good bibliography of case study material published in article form can be found in

British Government and Politics, by R. M. Punnett (Heinemann, 4th edn, 1980, pp.477–480), and references to the literature on pressure groups and policy making will be found in Chapter 6. Despite Heclo's pessimistic conclusion that the inheritance from the majority of case-studies 'is a series of isolated, episodic descriptions . . . which are apparently thought to be of intrinsic interest' (work cited, p.90), there are a growing number of case studies with a rigorous theoretical framework, which contribute to our understanding of policy-making in general. Two important books, both in the area of social policy-making, are *Change, Choice and Conflict in Social Policy*, by P. Hall *et al.* (Heinemann, 1975), and *Poverty, Politics and Policy*, by Keith Banting (Macmillan, 1979). Hall *et al.* apply a systems model based on the work of David Easton to six case studies of policy change in an attempt 'to formulate middle-range propositions about how and in what particular circumstances certain issues attain predominance over others and become the source of new policy', while Banting advances a general interpretation of the politics of social policy-making on the basis of three case studies, arguing that policy making is 'both an intellectual activity and an institutional process'.

Other literature and information sources

Current trends in academic research can best be traced through journals. The principal British journals are *Public Administration* (1923–), *Public Administration Bulletin* (1972–) (formerly the *PAC Bulletin*, 1964–1972), *Policy and Politics* (1972–) and the *Journal of Public Policy* (1981–), the latter two journals being particularly concerned with the development of public policy studies. Other journals which sometimes carry articles dealing with public administration include *Public Law* (1956–), *Political Quarterly* (1930–) and *Parliamentary Affairs* (1948–). The American perspective is provided by *Public Administration Review* (1940–), *Administrative Science Quarterly* (1965–) and *Policy Studies Journal* (1972–). Articles on various countries are published in *International Review of Administrative Sciences* (1957 –). Abstracts of these and other journals, together with newspapers and their indexes are discussed in Chapter 1. Abstracts of many books and articles are provided in *Sage Public Administration Abstracts*, and the *International Political Science Abstracts* contain a section on governmental and administrative institutions. *Policy and Politics* also contains an abstracts section. It is also possible to identify articles on public administration which have appeared in other journals by referring to the *British Humanities Index* (Library Association), which is published quarterly, and the American *Public Affairs Information Service Bulletin* (PAIS), which includes a selective list of the latest literature relating to public administration in English throughout the world.

Valuable information about, and the 'feel' of, administration and policy making can also be acquired through reading political biographies and memoirs. A useful bibliography of such works is provided by Jeremy Moon, 'Post-war British Political Memoirs: a Discussion and Bibliography', *Parliamentary Affairs,* **35** (1982). Although many such works claim to reveal the secrets of how administration and policy making really works (see, for instance, Richard Crossman, work cited), as Moon warns us, it should always be remembered that this kind of literature inevitably sees events and personalities from one particular point of view, and that the subjectivity of such works is different from that of a conventional political scientist or historian.

Although ministerial memoirs and biographies 'must remain the servants of analysis and not substitutes for it', this kind of literature does provide information and insights not normally available to academic researchers, who have found it notoriously difficult to surmount the barriers imposed by the 'closed' system of British central government. A fuller discussion of government secrecy in Britain, and the movement to 'open up' British government, is *The Politics of Secrecy*, by James Michael (Penguin, 1982). The relaxation in 1967 of the rule whereby public documents were closed to inspection for a period of fifty years to one of thirty years makes comparatively little difference to students of contemporary and recent history, although access to documents within the closed period is sometimes given to scholars. The circumstances and conditions of such access are contained in a Civil Service Department Memorandum of 1970 (reproduced in *PAC Bulletin,* **8** (1970)). Many government departments also have Academic Liaison Officers who can put researchers in touch with the appropriate sections of their department when researching unpublished information. Current details can be found in *Public Administration Bulletin,* **37** (1981).

Official publications are, of course, readily available, and constitute the most important class of primary material available to students of public administration. Their nature and use are discussed in Chapter 1, which contains guidance on departmental and other specialist libraries.

11
Judiciary and government
Gavin Drewry

Partial revival of a lost tradition?

A century ago the jurist Sir Frederick Pollock aptly observed that 'law is to political institutions as the bones to the body': the observation appears in an interesting essay (originally a lecture) with the portentous title, 'The History of English Law as a Branch of Politics', reproduced in his book, *Essays in Jurisprudence and Ethics* (Macmillan, 1882). It is not hard to find modern echoes of this view. It was recently suggested, for example, in a political science journal that the study of courts and judicial decisions lies 'at the very heart of political science': L. Johnston, 'A Defence of Public Law', *Political Studies,* **16,** 384–392 (1968).

But the fact remains that, somewhat along the line, the study of politics in Britain became detached from the study of law – see also Chapter 7. A careful perusal of current British political science journals reveals a dearth of items with a recognizably legal or juridicial flavour. The wide physical separation between 'law' and 'politics' sections in most libraries symbolizes the breadth of the chasm between two disparate fields of study. This is in stark contrast to the situation in the US, with its written Constitution and its overtly 'political' Supreme Court, where the operation of courts and the behaviour of judges are matters of major concern to students of politics; and to the situation in many other countries of Europe, where politics and (even more emphatically) public administration are taught, practised and written about very largely as facets of public law.

Appearances may be slightly deceptive, however. Many major figures in the history of political thought, as taught to British politics students, are also familiar figures in the literature and teaching of theoretical jurisprudence: Bentham, Mill and Marx are discussed by theorists of both law and politics. An article on aspects of the relationship between the judiciary and British politics – 'Judges and the Political Order', by Howard Elcock (*Political Studies,* **XVII,** 294–312 (1969)) – notes the prevalence of legal concepts in political science, instancing the discussion of justice in Plato's *Republic*, as well as the classical (and legally derived) concept of 'social contract', associated notably with the writings of Hobbes, Locke and Rousseau. The brilliant essay, *Legalism*, by Judith Shklar (Harvard University Press, 1964), is one modern instance of the theoretical cross-fertilization that can, and sometimes does, take place across the boundaries of legal and political theory. The truth is that the boundary is, in the nature of the subject, an artificial one, endowed with reality only by academic convention.

It is the case, too, that some of the major authors of works on British government have themselves had a legal training. Thus the late William Robson, Professor of Public Administration at the London School of Economics and author of the pioneering work, *Justice and Administrative Law* (see below), was a barrister; so, too, was Sir Ivor Jennings (he became a bencher of Gray's Inn), the author of so many standard texts on institutional and constitutional subjects in the years spanning the Second World War. Two leading contemporary figures whose published works demonstrate eloquently the value of interpreting government and politics from legal perspectives are Geoffrey Marshall and J. A. G. Griffith, both of whom we will encounter later in this chapter.

One reason for the apparent gulf between law and political science is that many post-war political scientists (on both sides of the Atlantic) have sought to develop their subject through devising sophisticated techniques for evaluating political behaviour and quantifying political phenomena. This has been accompanied by rejection of institutional and constitutional approaches to the subject as being old-fashioned and atheoretical. Adjectives like 'formalistic' and 'descriptive' are sometimes used, pejoratively, to describe such work. But whereas American political scientists have harnessed their behavioural methodology, for better or for worse, to the study of judicial behaviour (hence the branch of the subject known as 'jurimetrics' – see below), their British counterparts have chosen largely to ignore the judges as part of their subject matter. This is, in part, because law is seen as 'formalistic' and its study as antithetical to the quest for a 'science' of politics; it also stems from the undoubted fact that British judges have traditionally been regarded as far more detached from the world of politics and government than are American judges. But, whatever the explanation, it is this writer's belief that neglecting legal and constitutional dimensions of the subject has deprived political science of a source of potential enrichment: this does not, of course, imply that 'law' is the Holy Grail of political science, merely that the latter is necessarily eclectic and needs to draw upon as many kinds of approach as possible.

There has in fact been something of a backlash against this neglect, and some forceful advocacy of the need to re-emphasize constitutional and institutional approaches: see, for example, *In Search of the Constitution*, by Nevil Johnson (Methuen, 1977), and *The Study of Government*, by F. F. Ridley (Allen and Unwin, 1975), both of which make telling comparisons between the legal and constitutional awareness of academic students of government in countries like France and West Germany, and the lack of interest in such matters in Britain. The work, *Constitutional Theory*, by Geoffrey Marshall (The Clarendon Press, 1971), underlines how much the study of government can benefit from a constitutional approach; some years earlier the same author had expressed his own concern about the need for political science to draw upon the resources of public law – see his article, 'Political Science and the Judicial Process', *Public Law*, 139–152 (1957). *Some Problems of the Constitution*, by Geoffrey Marshall and Graeme C. Moodie (Hutchinson, 4th edn, 1967) is a good instance of 'constitutional' writing which is stimulating and lucid. It is encouraging, too, to note faint signs of a possible revival of interest in constitutional issues among a younger generation of writers: see, for instance, a basic textbook, *The Constitution in Flux* by Philip Norton (Martin Robertson, 1982).

Such a revival (if it is one) may simply be a product of the random ebb and flow of academic fashion. But it may also be connected with various recent events and developments – such as an apparent increase in the political significance of judicial decisions, revival of the debate about enacting a new Bill of Rights, the debate about devolution of government and the constitutional and legal impact of Britain's membership of the European Communities. We will consider aspects of such phenomena in due course.

Were this chapter to confine itself strictly to the political science literature concerning the relationship between government and the judiciary in Britain then it would be embarrassingly brief. On the other hand, it would be possible to go to the opposite extreme by digging out the legal elements that exist in almost *every* corner of political and administrative life. Clearly, some compromise is necessary. The remaining sections of this chapter discuss the literature on the judicial process, on judicial institutions and machinery of justice and on administrative law. It then considers some of the contemporary issues which have intensified the degree of interplay between law and government. The chapter concludes with some remarks about legal journals and law reports.

The judicial process

An informative review article by an American academic ('Research on the English Judicial Process' by Lawrence Baum (*British Journal of Politics Science,* 7, 511–527 (1977)) notes, as we have done, that 'political scientists thus far have virtually ignored the English courts as an object of study'. This, he says, 'reflects a belief that the courts' political roles are too limited to demand study' – a view from which he vigorously dissents. The article does, however, provide a useful survey of what literature was in existence at that time, and includes references to American material – mainly to illustrate the kinds of research that he considers British political scientists ought to be doing.

Some of the sources cited by Baum are more in the category of 'machinery of justice' than in that of 'judicial process'. These expressions are used in this chapter to denote a significant difference of emphasis between, on the one hand, works concerning the institutional structure within which judges transact their business and, on the other, the nature and the determinants of judicial behaviour itself. It must be admitted, however, that the distinction is somewhat arbitrary – as can be illustrated by reference to the doctrine of precedent, which needs to be considered as a major factor determining the formal relationships between different courts (e.g. the rules which render the decisions of 'superior' courts binding upon 'inferior' tribunals) *and* as a major factor underlying patterns of judicial decision making.

Behavioural methodology (see Chapter 3) has, in the US, spawned a large literature on 'jurimetrics', based upon various kinds of quantitative analysis applied to judicial decisions. Little of this has been attempted in Britain: one interesting exception can be found in an article, 'Judicial Ideology in the House of Lords: A Jurimetric Analysis' by David Roberston (*British Journal of Political Science*, 12, 1–25 (1982)), which contains references to other source material in this area.

Unlike the case of the US Supreme Court, only intermittent attention has been paid to the operation of particular British courts from a political science or policy studies standpoint. A lonely pioneer was *The Restrictive Practices Court: A Study in Judicial Process and Economic Policy*, by R. B. Stevens and B. S. Yamey (Weidenfeld and Nicolson, 1965). The House of Lords, that constitutional oddity that sits at the top of the hierarchy of courts in Britain, is one obvious target for research (e.g. David Robertson's article, work cited), though it does not, of course, have the explicit political relevance of a Supreme Court which is custodian of a written Constitution. One of its former members observed, rather unkindly, in a review article ('Judges, Government and Politics' by Lord Devlin, *Modern Law Review*, **41**, 501–511 (1978)) that 'compared with the Supreme Court, the House is a disorganised rabble'.

Nevertheless, the Appellate Committee of the House of Lords has attracted increased notice on the part of political scientists in recent years, partly because a number of politically significant *causes célèbres* have compelled such attention. One of several instances of commentaries upon recent appellate judicial decisions appearing in politics journals (they appear as a matter of course in legal journals, see below) is 'The Law Lords and the Needs of Contemporary Society', by David Pannick (*Political Quarterly*, **53**, 318–328 (1982)). The title is overambitious, but this is a workmanlike critical essay on the political/policy implications of the *London Transport fares case* and the *Harriet Harman* contempt case, both decided by the House of Lords in 1982.

Apart from such welcome, but essentially patchy, evidence of interest in the political aspects of particular cases, this area of the subject has been put onto a more secure scholarly footing by the publication of three substantial studies of the judicial functions of the House of Lords (two of them having appeared since Baum's survey). Quite different in their respective approaches, they may be regarded as usefully mutually complementary to one another.

Final Appeal: A Study of the House of Lords in its Judicial Capacity, by Louis Blom-Cooper and Gavin Drewry (The Clarendon Press, 1972), is a non-behavioural (but, in part, quantitative) study of the role of the House of Lords, based mainly upon an examination of procedures, personnel and the substance of decisions in the period 1952–68. *Law and Politics: The House of Lords as a Judicial Body, 1800–1976* by Robert Stevens (Heinemann, 1979) is an attempt, over a broad time frame, 'to describe and evaluate in policy terms the legal doctrines that the House developed'. Drawing upon a wealth of documentation (which makes it a valuable quarry for legal and political historians), it traces the impact and significance of judicial decisions in various areas, and arrives at some trenchant conclusions about the patchy quality of judicial decision making. The last member of the trio is *The Law Lords*, by Alan Paterson (Macmillan, 1982), which uses role analysis to examine the dynamics of judicial decision making in the Lords, with special reference to the period 1957–1973. The main feature of this study is its use of material gleaned from interviews with 28 judges, 26 QCs and seven junior counsel. British judges have not been as eager as some of their American counterparts to encourage social scientists to examine their innermost thoughts, but Paterson managed to persuade nine of the 15 serving Law Lords not only to be interviewed but also to be tape recorded. If some of his findings are a little less than startling, Paterson deserves credit none the less for his success in breaking down the barriers of judicial inscrutability.

A much broader perspective on the judicial process, and a more controversial one, can be found in *The Politics of the Judiciary*, by J. A. G. Griffith (Fontana, 2nd edn, 1981). The author's examination of selected items of case law, under chapter headings of Industrial Relations, Personal Rights, Property Rights and the Control of Ministerial Discretion, the Uses of Conspiracy and Students and Trade Union Members, leads him to some disquieting conclusions about the pervasiveness of a conservative judicial ideology, and hence to refute simplistic assumptions about the 'political neutrality' of British judges. Griffith absolves the judges of making 'a conscious and deliberate attempt to pursue their own interests or those of their class', but he suggests that our most senior judges have 'a strikingly homogeneous collection of attitudes, beliefs and principles, which to them represents the public interest'. This radical critique is founded upon its author's formidable legal scholarship and thus deserves to be taken more seriously than some critics have suggested; but it needs perhaps to be read in conjunction with more conservative interpretations, such as that of Lord Devlin (considered below).

In exploring the sociological and ideological undercurrents of the judicial process, Griffith considers, but quickly abandons, classical Marxism as a possible explanatory framework. This reminds us, however, that the body of literature on law and government contains a lot of items written from Marxian perspective. This is particularly the case with studies that emphasize aspects of the legal process as an instrument of social control. This material has been of somewhat variable quality. *Images of Law*, by Zenon Bankowski and Geoff Mungham (Routledge and Kegan

Paul, 1976), is perhaps as good an instance as any for readers to turn to in order to discover both the strengths and the weaknesses of such an approach.

It is often forgotten that judges are sometimes used to serve the ends of government, not just by acting as courtroom adjudicators but also by serving as members and chairmen of official inquiries into issues of current concern and controversy. Some of the most prestigious of such exercises are those held under the Tribunals of Inquiry (Evidence) Act 1921, and the origins and usage of this and comparable machinery are considered in *Trial by Tribunal*, by G. W. Keeton (Museum Press, 1960). There may indeed be public benefits in using the reputation for political neutrality (*pace* Griffith) and the interrogative and analytical skills of judges in such ways, but arguably there are also dangers of tainting the credibility of the judicial process if the practice is overdone – see 'Judges and Political Inquiries: Harnessing a Myth', by Gavin Drewry (*Political Studies,* **XXIII,** 49–61 (1975)).

What manner of men (use of the masculine gender is deliberate, for only a derisory number of professional judges in Britain are women) are British judges? Apart from some useful material to be found in some of the works already cited (e.g. Griffith, Stevens), the evidence is patchy, largely because judges prefer and are encouraged to eschew public exposure. Early work on the political backgrounds of the judiciary can be found in *Studies in Law and Politics*, by Harold Laski (Allen and Unwin, 1932). More up-to-date studies include 'Judges: A Political Elite', by Alan Paterson (*British Journal of Law and Society*, **1**, 118–135 (1975)); and there is useful material in the work by Fred Morrison (cited below). A very useful general sourcebook on the judiciary (though it is written in ponderous style, and suffers from rather slack editing) is *Judges on Trial*, by Shimon Shetreet (North-Holland, 1976). *Courts and Judges in France, Germany and England*, by R. C. K. Ensor (Oxford University Press, 1933), still retains some of the freshness of a pioneering and classical comparative essay, despite its antiquity.

One judge who certainly did not hide behind a cloak of anonymity was Lord Denning, whose retirement as Master of the Rolls in 1982, at the age of eighty-three, marked the end of an era: it was, however, a turbulent era, since Lord Denning's idiosyncratic views and his advocacy of an explicitly 'creative' approach to the judicial process did not meet with unqualified approval, particularly among some of his fellow judges, who saw in his efforts to 'repair' the legislative products of Parliament an unacceptable usurpation of parliamentary functions and a danger of introducing uncertainty into the lives of citizens seeking to order their legal affairs. Lord Denning himself has written a number of books about his judicial philosophy, one of which, *What's Next in the Law* (Butterworths, 1982)) – the absence of a question mark sums up his self-confidence in his own views – played a material part in accelerating his long-delayed retirement, since it was found in its original form (which was hurriedly withdrawn) to contain libellous and racially offensive remarks, for which Lord Denning had publicly to apologize.

Almost everyone who has written in recent years about the British courts has found himself obliged to single out Lord Denning for special attention, if only as an exception who underlines various rules about the judicial process. A group of young legal academics has produced a radical critique of Lord Denning's contribution to various areas of law: *Justice, Lord Denning and the Constitution*, edited by P. Robson and P. Watchman (Gower, 1981).

But perhaps the most eloquent (though implicit) riposte to Lord Denning is to be found in an anthology of lectures by one of his former colleagues, *The Judge* by Patrick [Lord] Devlin (Oxford University Press, 1979). Lord Devlin broadly approves of judges being 'activists', by which he means 'the business of keeping pace with changes in the consensus', but is hostile towards judges being 'creative' or 'dynamic' lawmakers, using their position to 'generate change in the consensus': in his view, 'the keepers of the boundaries [between rulers and ruled] cannot also be the outriders'. He strongly favours the jury system, and is against training judges in penology in the hope of making them into more effective sentencers. His view that judges are 'an epitome of the ordinary Englishman' and thus endowed with insight into the nature of the 'consensus' will be taken with a pinch of salt by many readers; but this book, like his other writings, has much intellectual merit, clothed in fine literary style.

Lord Devlin argues that judges simply are not qualified to take important decision about issues of public policy. This argument is developed, in much greater detail, in *The Courts and Social Policy*, by Donald L. Horowitz (The Brookings Institution, 1977); although the book is concerned primarily with the US, the arguments deployed have much relevance elsewhere. The lawyers' literature on judicial approaches to statutory interpretation and 'judicial law making' is vast, and really deserves a separate chapter: a taste of it, and indication of further sources, can usefully be obtained from Chapter 2 and 6 of a sourcebook, *The Lawmaking Process*, by Michael Zander (Weidenfeld and Nicolson, 1980).

Judicial institutions and the machinery of justice

Many competent books on the machinery of British justice (some of which also contain outlines of areas of substantive law – crime, contract, tort, family law, etc.) have been published to meet the needs of law students, but few have any special claims upon the attentions of those studying government and politics (works on the police, in the context of local government, are referred to in Chapter 12). The present writer discovered that an introductory book on aspects of law that he had written for pre-university politics students – *Law, Justice and Politics* (Longman, 2nd edn, 1981) – was also being used at university level, something that clearly underlines the shortage of cross-disciplinary literature in this area. One useful, but still quite elementary, book which tackles the subject from a recognizably political science perspective, using a 'systems' framework, was written (perhaps inevitably) by an American: *Courts and the Political Process in England*, by Fred L. Morrison (Sage, 1973). A new edition is overdue.

Those seeking a comprehensive and lucid text on the legal system need go no further than *The Machinery of Justice in England*, by R. M. Jackson (Cambridge University Press, 7th edn, 1977). This covers the civil and criminal courts (including magistrates' courts) and their procedures, the personnel of the law (including juries and such matters as legal education), administrative tribunals and the cost of the law (including legal aid). It nicely balances description with criticism and prescription, and includes valuable references to other sources – including an index of the numerous official publications cited in the text.

The latter point is important. Continuing efforts to reform, update and consolidate law and legal institutions have, over the years, produced numerous standing and *ad hoc* official inquiries (whose role and workings are themselves of potential interest to students of government, as is the part played in this and other contexts by the legal professions acting as lobbyists). The English and Scottish Law Commissions have produced a steady flow of working papers, reports and draft Bills since they were set up in 1965: their *Report on Remedies in Administrative Law* (Cmnd. 6407, 1976) is one example that is of interest to students of public administration (see next section).

Other noteworthy official reports of recent years have included *The Report of the (Beeching) Royal Commission on Assizes and Quarter Sessions* (Cmnd. 4153, 1969); *Report of the (James) Committee on the Distribution of Criminal Business between the Crown Court and Magistrates' Courts* (Cmnd. 6323, 1975); *Report* of the *(Benson) Royal Commission on Legal Services* (Cmnd. 7648, 1979); and *Report of the (Philips) Royal Commission on Criminal Procedure* (Cmnd. 8092, 1981). Those studying the machinery of justice should refer to such reports and, in particular, to the useful volumes of evidence that often accompany them.

The subject has generated a large historical literature. Rather than plunging into the 'heavyweight' material (such as Sir William Holdsworth's epic, multi-volume work, *A History of English Law*), a good place to start is *Lawyers and the Courts* by Brian Abel-Smith and Robert Stevens (Heinemann, 1967). Two specialized studies that are of relevance to students of government are *The Law Officers of the Crown*, by J. Ll. J. Edwards (Sweet and Maxwell, 1964); and R. F. V. Houston, *The Lives of the Lord Chancellors 1885–1940* (The Clarendon Press, 1964). All these works contain useful bibliographical references.

Administrative law

The present writer has discussed elsewhere the under-exploitation of public law aspects of the study of public administration: 'Public Law: 'What's in it for Us?' by Gavin Drewry (*Public Administration Bulletin*, **27**, 2–19 (1978)). The reasons for the tardy and still incomplete evolution of public law in Britain, in sharp contrast to the rest of Europe, make a fascinating story in their own right.

The story begins with the distinguished constitutional lawyer, A. V. Dicey, telling his readers and students at the turn of the century that any movement in Britain towards the French system of a *droit administratif* would threaten the 'rule of law'. His views, in the absence of any significant counter-arguments, and despite Dicey's own partial recantation of some of his earlier, more dogmatic assertions about Continental systems of administrative law, became the conventional wisdom on the subject for several generations. Dicey's major work on the subject is still worth consulting: *Introduction to the Study of the Law of the Constitution* by A. V. Dicey (Macmillan, 1885; 10th edn, with introduction by E. C. S. Wade, 1959). Those seeking to follow this story further might usefully begin with the excellent biography, *The Rule of Law: Albert Venn Dicey, Victorian Jurist*, by Richard C. Cosgrove (Macmillan, 1980); but see the critical review of this work, by D. Sugarman (*Modern Law Review*, **46**, 102–111 (1983)). An article, 'The Donoughmore Report in Retrospect' by D. G. T. Williams (*Public Administration*, **60**, 273–292 (1982)), usefully examines the impact of Diceyan dogma on subsequent events. Looking more broadly at the history of public law, there is a well-documented account of the divergent patterns of early development in the US, Britain and the Continent of Europe: 'Public Administration and Administrative Law' by John A. Fairlie, in *Essays on the Law and Practice of Governmental Administration*, edited by Charles G. Haines and Marshall E. Dimock (Johns Hopkins Press, 1935). A much more recent comparison between Britain and the US in this area can be found in *Legal Control of Government*, by Bernard Schwartz and H. W. R. Wade (The Clarendon Press, 1972); and the state of French *droit administratif* a century after Dicey first misinterpreted it is usefully outlined in *French Administrative Law*, by L. Neville Brown and J. F. Garner (Butterworths, 3rd edn, 1983).

So far as the literary history of the subject in Britain is concerned, suffice it to say that despite the appearance of two pioneering works in the late 1920s, administrative law found hardly any authors to advance its cause until the 1950s. Those works still repay some attention even today. They are *Justice and Administrative Law*, by W. A. Robson (Macmillan, 1928), and *Administrative Law*, by F. J. Port (Longman, 1929). Robson's book was subsequently updated (Stevens, 3rd edn, 1951), but the later editions lost more than they gained from the author's inclusion of understandable but over-lengthy complaints about his treatment at the hands of the Donoughmore Committee on Ministers' Powers, a body strongly moved by the spirit of A. V. Dicey (see Williams's article, work cited). Another early work that still merits study is a collection of lectures, delivered in the US by Sir Cecil Carr, *Concerning English Administrative Law* (Oxford University Press, 1941).

There are several reasons for the post-war resurgence of interest (mainly among lawyers) in administrative law, and they are outlined in the first chapter of *The British Ombudsman*, by Frank Stacey (The Clarendon Press, 1971). The 1950s were the era of the *Crichel Down case*, of the Franks *Report on Administrative Tribunals and Enquiries* (Cmnd. 218, 1957) and of the first stages in a debate leading up to the establishment of the Parliamentary Commissioner for Administration in 1967. The academic journal *Public Law* (see below) was founded in 1956, and the earliest editions of what soon became well-established textbooks on administrative (and usually constitutional) law also appeared at around this time. An early Hamlyn lecture (see below), *Executive Discretion and Judicial Control* by C. J. Hamson (Stevens, 1954), a cogent comparison between the forms of judicial review provided by the French Conseil d'Etat and those available in the English courts (a good deal of reform has taken place since then), helped to dispel the wilder images of Diceyan mythology. Over a decade or so, administrative law became 'respectable', even fashionable. In due course the ultimate accolade was bestowed, in the shape of a separate entry on the subject in the third edition of the multi-volume encyclopedia of conventional legal wisdom, *Halsbury's Laws of England* (Butterworths, 1973).

However, respectable or not, and despite a number of important reforms, English administrative law still retains a fragmented and unsystematic quality which has been the despair of many critics, some of whom have urged the establishment of a fully fledged administrative court, perhaps on the pattern of the French Conseil d'Etat. Prominent among such critics was the late J. D. B. Mitchell, whose essays on the subject include 'The Causes and Effects of the Absence of a System of Public Law in the United Kingdom', *Public Law*, 95–118 (1965), and 'Administrative Law and Policy Effectiveness' in *From Policy to Administration*, edited by J. A. G. Griffith (Allen and Unwin, 1976). See also *Administration Under Law*, by a Committee of 'Justice', chairman, Keith Goodfellow, QC (Stevens, 1971), and 'Thoughts on a British Conseil d'Etat', by Maurice H. Smith (*Public Administration,* **45,** 23–42 (1967)).

There is now almost an embarrassment of choice among textbooks of administrative law, together with a good range of more specialized works in the field. So far as textbooks are concerned, variety is largely a matter of style, presentation and emphasis, and choice is therefore a matter of personal tastes and requirements. As with all books on law, it is important to use an up-to-date edition, though all books in this area will have been overtaken by significant events even on the day they are published. Particularly useful and well-established texts include *Government and Law*, by T. C. Hartley and J. A. G. Griffith (Weidenfeld and Nicolson, 2nd edn, 1981); *Constitutional and Administrative Law*, by S. A. de Smith (Penguin, 4th edn, edited by Harry Street and Rodney Brazier, 1981); *Administrative Law*, by David Foulkes (Butterworths, 5th edn, 1982); and *Administrative Law*, by H. W. R. Wade (The Clarendon Press, 5th edn, 1982). Casebooks, which usefully bring together disparate source material (not just case law), include *A Casebook of Administrative Law*, by J. A. G. Griffith and H. Street (Pitman, 1964) – worth reading, if only for its material on the epic saga of the *Chalkpit case*; and *Cases and Materials on Constitutional and Administrative Law*, by Geoffrey P. Wilson (Cambridge University Press, 2nd edn, 1976). A readable monograph by an administrative lawyer, which manages to break out of the stereotypical 'textbook' mould is *Administrative Procedures*, by Gabrielle Ganz (Sweet and Maxwell, 1974).

The standard text on judicial review has long been the monumental *Judicial Review of Administrative Action*, by S. A. de Smith (Stevens, 4th edn, rev. by J. M. Evans, 1980). The latest edition takes account of a major procedural overhaul that occurred in the wake of a review by the Law Commission (see previous section). This is further discussed in 'The New Face of Judicial Review: Administrative Changes in Order 53' by Louis Blom-Cooper (*Public Law*, 250–261 (1982)). But procedural rules provide only the framework of judicial review; the substance develops incrementally through the accumulation of precedents, reflecting the prevailing outlook of the judiciary and the eagerness of litigants to bring their grievances before the courts. Anyone seriously intending to study this area must keep up with recent trends by examining law reports and case notes in legal journals (see below). One important facet of the subject is covered in *Natural Justice*, by Paul Jackson (Sweet and Maxwell, 1979).

A glance at the contents of any of the general textbooks on administrative law cited earlier makes it clear that the subject goes far wider than 'judiciary and government' – which is the title of this chapter. It is generally regarded as including quasi-judicial bodies, administrative tribunals, set up mainly because the courts are regarded as unsuitable (too formal and expensive) to resolve disputes in specialized areas; public planning inquiries, which are not 'judicial' in any real sense; and ombudsmen, who belong more in the realms of 'executive responsibility' than of 'judicial control'. Rather than attempting to provide a mass of references on these important subjects, the writer would suggest consulting the footnotes and bibliographies of the major textbooks already cited. This part of the subject is also in a constant state of change. Developments in the tribunal and inquiry systems can usefully be traced via the Annual Reports of the Council on Tribunals; and in the work of the Parliamentary Commissioner for Administration, via his annual and quarterly reports, and those of the Select Committee on the Parliamentary Commissioner – all published in the regular series of parliamentary papers (see Chapter 10).

The spread of 'administrative law' far beyond the boundaries of 'law' is even more marked than has been so far discussed. Serious students of the subject will need to relate their work to such matters as the scope of state control, public access to benefits in the welfare state, the uses and abuses of administrative discretion, the role of public bureaucracies and aspects of public participation in decision making: a most useful work to set the subject in its wider context is *The State, Administration and the Individual*, by Michael Hill (Fontana, 1976). Another, more explicitly concerned with the developing area of 'welfare law', is *Welfare Law and Policy*, edited by Martin Partington and Jeffrey Jowell (Frances Pinter, 1979); and see *Justice in the Welfare State*, by Harry Street (Stevens, 2nd edn, 1975), one of an excellent set of monographs, many of them with public law themes, in the annual series of Hamlyn Lectures, dating back to 1949. Another well-established work by the latter author links our subject to aspects of 'civil liberty' and State control: *Freedom, the Individual and the Law*, by Harry Street (Penguin, 5th edn, 1982). And see *The Protection of Liberty*, by I. N. Stevens and D. C. M. Yardley (Blackwell, 1982).

One area of government where law has, of necessity, loomed large in the literature is local government – see Chapter 12. A strict *ultra vires* rule makes it necessary for local authorities to find statutory authority for everything that they do, and an important body of case law has arisen from litigation over the nature of their statutory powers. Traditional approaches to this part of the subject can be found in *Principles of Local Government Law*, by Sir Ivor Jennings (University of London Press, 4th edn, by J. A. G. Griffith, 1960) – now badly out of date; *Hart's Introduction to the Law of Local Government*, by Sir William O. Hart and J. F. Garner (Butterworths, 9th edn, 1973); and *Principles of Local Government Law*, by C. A. Cross (Sweet and Maxwell, 6th edn, 1980). Probably the best source for keeping more or less abreast of this rapidly changing subject is to use the *Encyclopaedia of Local Government Law*, edited by C. A. Cross, 2 vols, loose-leaf form, regularly updated (Sweet and Maxwell, 1980–). But political scientists will probably find more of immediate interest in two recently published analytical essays, the first by a lawyer and the second by a political scientist, on the nature of the legal framework within which local government operates: *The Role of Law in Central–Local Relations*, by Michael J. Elliott (Social Science Research Council, 1981); and *Laws and Orders in Central–Local Government Relations*, by Edward Page (University of Strathclyde, Studies in Public Policy No. 102, 1982). The former includes some interesting reflections on the present state of public law.

Present trends in law and politics

The development of a literature on law and government has reflected shifts in academic fashion; and the latter has in turn reflected changes in the level of salience of 'legal' issues in the processes of politics and government. One obvious instance has been the increasing 'activism' of the courts in tackling issues of public law. This has given rise to discussion about the merits of entrusting adjudication upon matters of public policy to judges who are not democratically accountable for their actions and who may not be professionally equipped to tackle complex issues, presented to them in isolation, in a competent and rational way: the debate about Lord Denning's judicial philosophy has brought such arguments into sharper focus in recent years.

Related to this has been some disquiet about features of constitutional arrangements and assumptions, prompted by such developments as Britain's membership of the European Communities, the debate about devolution of power to Scotland and Wales and the prospective disintegration of the two-party system. Some of the stresses engendered by constitutional uncertainty are discussed in *Constitutional Fundamentals*, by H. W. R. Wade (Stevens, 1980) – another in the Hamlyn Lecture series.

Two specific areas may be singled out for attention here. The first (an extension of the issue of how far judges should take an active role in matters of public policy) is the debate about a Bill of Rights. The radical idea of legislating to 'entrench' human rights in a formal constitutional document, and making the judges custodians of such a document, with a power to declare even the legislative products of a hitherto 'sovereign' Parliament invalid as being in breach of fundamental rights, has been floating around for many years. It received a sharp revival in yet another Hamlyn Lecture – *English Law – The New Dimension*, by Lord Scarman (Stevens, 1974) – and has inspired a considerable body of literature. Two items (both of which contain useful references to further sources) may be singled out: *A Bill of Rights*, by Michael Zander (Barry Rose, 2nd edn, 1980); and *Enacting a Bill of Rights*, by Joseph Jaconelli (The Clarendon Press, 1980). The latter is a technical guide to legal problems of enacting such a measure; the former is a useful and balanced summary of the many conflicting arguments about the merits in principle of so doing.

A second area is Britain's membership of the European Communities (see Chapter 18), which has had the important effect of importing into British law the legislative products of an extra-territorial and supra-national body, and has assigned final powers of adjudication in matters of European Communities Law to an international court. The relevant literature is vast. Students of politics might usefully begin with broad statements of jurisprudential principle before venturing into the daunting morass of technicality. Inevitably, there is another Hamlyn Lecture: *The Euro-*

pean Communities and the Rule of Law, by Lord Mackenzie Stuart (Stevens, 1977); and a useful article 'Britain and the European Economic Community', by David Sugarman (*Texas International Law Journal*, **10**, 279–320 (1975)). Almost every issue of every mainstream law journal contains at least one article or case note on some aspect of European Communities Law, and a specialist series of law reports, *The Common Market Law Reports* (1962 to date) caters for those seeking to keep abreast of judicial decisions in this area.

Law reports and lawyers' journals

Law is a mobile commodity, and anyone trying to keep pace with it must use some of the basic tools of the lawyer's trade. Those intending to make significant use of legal materials and law libraries might usefully invest a day or so's work at the outset reading a lucid introductory guidebook, *Learning the Law*, by Glanville Williams (Stevens, 11th edn, 1982).

Judicial decisions and pronouncements regarded as having some innovative content worth recording as precedents (and this applies to virtually every appeal heard by the House of Lords, to a substantial minority of cases in the intermediate appeal courts and to hardly anything decided in courts of first instance) are published in one or more of the many series of law reports. Glanville Williams succinctly describes the nature and use of these and other materials in Chapter 3 of his book (above). The non-lawyer will probably obtain much of what he needs by following the daily law reports in *The Times*. Public law decisions will in due course appear, along with a lot of other things, in the two main 'general' series of reports: the semi-official *Law Reports*, divided into various subseries (published since 1865 by the Incorporated Council of Law Reporting); and the *All England Law Reports* (Butterworths, 1936 to date). There is no specialized public law series, but students of local government may usefully consult *Knight's Local Government Reports* (1903 to date).

Lawyers' journals contain a significant proportion of articles, case notes and reviews which are of potential interest to students of British government; perusal of the cumulative indexes of the major journals such as *Law Quarterly Review* (Stevens, quarterly, 1885 to date) and *Modern Law Review* (Sweet and Maxwell, six issues a year, 1937 to date) can yield unexpected dividends. Probably the most useful of the academic journals in this context is *Public Law* (Stevens, quarterly, 1956 to date); while a newer publication, the *Journal of Law and Society* (formerly *British Journal of Law and Society*) (Martin Robertson, twice-yearly, 1973 to date), is a social science journal rather than strictly a 'legal' one, and usefully bridge an interdisciplinary gap. Examples of articles published in both these journals can be found elsewhere in this chapter. The weekly *New Law Journal* (Butterworths, 1965 to date) and the more explicitly radical *LAG Bulletin* (the monthly bulletin of the Legal Action Group) are valuable sources of quick reference (spiced with critical commentary) on current issues.

12
Local government
Dilys M. Hill

Introduction

C. H. Wilson, writing in 1948, believed that although J. S. Mill had said 'almost everything that was fundamentally important' about the institution of local government, it was vital to restate its value if it were to survive: a point whose relevance has re-emerged in the 1980s with a vengeance. Over the past quarter of a century critiques of democratic viability, functions and boundaries have been tempered with reassertions of the value of local government. The research preoccupations of the 1960s have now given way, however, to a radical recasting in which there are four main themes: urban historical studies; a comparative analysis which has moved away from 'community power' to a broader approach reflecting European, as well as American, ideas; an interdisciplinary debate about the nature and role of theory (see D. M. Hill, review article, *Political Studies,* **32,** 2, June 1984)); and a substantial body of British institutional and policy studies.

These developments have had two revolutionary effects. First, 'local government' does not describe the area of study adequately, in that publications are informed by broader and more sophisticated concepts. Second, work aimed at the undergraduate or 'layman' level is now much more difficult to achieve satisfactorily: there is a long way to go before there is a working consensus about analysis at this synthesized, introductory level. What has been encouraging about the structuralist/pluralist, neo-Marxist/neo-Weberian debate, however, is the interdisciplinary way in which it has been conducted. This is due to the relatively small academic world of local studies and the opportunities which have existed for collaboration between European and American scholars. Sadly, reduced research facilities now threaten the ecletic nature of this work, though some projects continue to attract welcome support.

Theories and definitions

'Local government' only became common usage after 1836 when the term appeared in a *Times* leading article. Both theory and practice then attracted increasing attention, in works such as: Josef Redlich, *Local Government in England*, edited by F. W. Hirst (2 vols, Macmillan, 1903; Vol. I was reissued, edited by B. Keith-Lucas, as *The History of Local Government in England* (Macmillan, 1958)); W. Hardy Wickwar, *The Political Theory of Local Government* (Columbia, University of South Carolina Press, 1970); W. Thornhill (ed.), *The Growth and Reform of English Local Government* (Weidenfeld and Nicholson, 1971); and D. M. Hill, *Democratic Theory and Local Government* (Allen and Unwin, 1974). After 1945, concern for democratic local government was a strong theme: 'Administrator', 'the Democratic Content of Local Government'; P. Self and 'Administrator', 'Local Government and the Community', *Fabian Quarterly,* **47** (1945) and **53** (1947); C. H. Wilson (ed.), *Essays on Local Government* (Blackwell, 1948); G. D. H. Cole, *Local and Regional Government* (Cassell, 1947); W. A. Robson, *Local Government in Crisis* (Allen and Unwin, 1966) – a revised version of the Prologue of *The Development of Local Government* (G. Allen, 1931); W. J. MacKenzie, 'Theories of Local Government', *Greater London Papers No.2* (London School of Economics and Political Science, 1961); J. P. Mackintosh, *The Devolution of Power* (Penguin, 1968); and L. J. Sharpe, 'Theories and Values of Local Government', *Political Studies,* **18** (1970).

In the 1960s research increased and American work became influential. A defence and re-evaluation of this work is N. W. Polsby, *Community Power and Political Theory* (London, Yale University Press, 1980). For a critique, there is K. Newton, 'Community Politics and Decision-Making: The American Experience', in K. Young (ed.), *Essays on the Study of Urban Politics* (Macmillan, 1975). In the 1970s, research moved in a number of directions – sociological critiques, policy studies, inter-disciplinary approaches (including political geography and political economy). Urban sociology, associated with the work of Margaret Stacey, R. Pahl, C. Bell, H. Newby and others, currently emphasizes social theory and a radical critique: M. P. Smith, *The City and Social Theory* (Blackwell, 1980); B. Elliott and D. McCrone, *The City* (Macmillan, 1982); P. Saunders, *Urban Politics* (Hutchinson, 1979); and his *Social Theory and the Urban Question* (Hutchinson, 1981). The distributional concerns of both political scientists and political geographers are analysed in K. Newton and L. J. Sharpe, 'Local Outputs Research: Some Reflections and Proposals', *Policy and Politics*, **5** (1977); R. J. Johnston, *Political, Electoral and Spatial Systems: An Essay in Political Geography* (The Clarendon Press, 1979); and K. R. Cox, *Location and Public Problems: A Political Geography of the Contemporary World* (Blackwell, 1980).

The expansion of research brought a radical attack on the location of local government studies primarily within public administration. The theoretical perspectives of Castells and others were made available to English-speaking readers first in C. G. Pickvance (ed.), *Urban Sociology: Critical Essays* (Methuen, 1976) and then in M. Castells, *The Urban Question: A Marxist Approach* (Edward Arnold, 1977) and his *City, Class and Power* (Macmillan, 1978). For an appraisal of the ideas of Castells and others, see M. Harloe (ed.), *Captive Cities* (Wiley, 1977). A trenchant criticism of existing local government perspectives is C. Cockburn, *The Local State* (Pluto Press, 1977). The concept of the 'local state' has been widely debated, for instance, in M. Boddy and C. Fudge (eds), 'The Local State', *Working Paper 20* (School of Advanced Urban Studies (SAUS), University of Bristol, 1981). Critical reviews of the neo-Marxist and radical perspectives are M. Harloe (ed.), *New Perspectives on Urban Change and Conflict* (Heinemann, 1981); M. Goldsmith, *Politics, Planning and the City* (Hutchinson, 1980); P. Dunleavy, *Urban Political Analysis* (Macmillan, 1980); and his *The Politics of Mass Housing in Britain 1945–1975* (The Clarendon Press, 1981).

Historical works and texts

The twentieth-century history of local government stands on the works of the Webbs, Cole, Laski, Herman Finer and Robson. In recent years, however, there has been a great expansion in the study of urban history. As well as specialized journals, a number of publishers now produce urban history series, notably those by the Leicester University Press, Edward Arnold and Basil Blackwell.

Particular local government services also have their own histories. Bibliographies can be found in, for example, M. Bruce, *The Coming of the Welfare State* (Batsford, 4th edn, 1968) and G. E. Cherry, *The Evolution of British Town Planning* (Leonard Hill, 1974). J. B. Cullingworth's official history of environmental planning includes: the wartime history up to 1947; National Parks; New Towns; and Land Values, Compensation and Betterment (*Environmental Planning 1939–1969, Vols I–IV*, HMSO, 1975 –1980).

The history of local government has its genesis in the writings of Chadwick and Simon and the official publications of the nineteenth century and in the monumental writings of Sidney and Beatrice Webb: under the title *English Local Government from the Revolution to the Municipal Corporations Act*, published by Longmans, Green & Co. The work consists of three studies: *The Parish and the County* (1906); *The Manor and the Borough*, Parts I and II (2 vols, 1908); and *Statutory Authorities for Special Purposes* (1922). Other works include Redlich and Hirst (work cited); V. D. Lipman, *Local Government Areas 1834–1945* (Blackwell, 1949); H. J. Laski, W. I. Jennings and W. A. Robson (eds), *A Century of Municipal Progress* (Allen and Unwin, 1935); B. Keith-Lucas, *The English Local Government Franchise* (Blackwell, 1952); and his *The Unreformed Local Government System* (Croom Helm, 1979). For this century there is B. Keith-Lucas' and P. G. Richards', *A History of Local Government in the 20th Century* (Allen and Unwin, 1978), a successor to Redlich and Hirst. A major text of the inter-war period was Sir Ivor Jennings, *Principles of Local Government Law* (University of London Press, 1931). This went into many editions, latterly revised by J. A. G. Griffith. The current text on the law relating to local government is C. A. Cross, *Principles of Local Government Law* (Sweet and Maxwell, 6th edn, 1980) (see also Chapter 11).

After 1945 the Allen and Unwin New Town and County Hall series, edited by J. H. Warren, published a wide range of studies, including Warren's own *The English Local Government System* (1946). This work established a tradition of frequent revisions, subsequently carried out by P. G. Richards (in 1968 under the amended title of *The New Local Government System*), who became Editor of the series. The tradition has continued: P. G. Richard's *The Reformed Local Government System* is regularly revised and gives a comprehensive description of the functions, powers and progress of local government. Other texts include:

R. J. Buxton, *Local Government* (Penguin, 2nd edn, 1975); J. Stanyer, *Understanding Local Government* (Fontana, 1976); J. Gyford, *Local Politics in Britain* (Croom Helm, 1976); W. H. Cox, *Cities: The Public Dimension* (Penguin, 1976); and H. Elcock (with a chapter by M. Wheaton), *Local Government* (Methuen, 1982). For School 'A'-level purposes there is M. Cross' and D. Mallen's *Local Government and Politics* (Longman, 1978). Books for the general reader include: T. Byrne, *Local Government in Britain* (Penguin, 1981) and M. Minogue (ed.) *The Consumers' Guide to Local Government*, with a valuable gazetteer (Macmillan, 1977). Lexington Books (D. C. Heath, Lexington, Mass.) produce a series of comparative texts on local government including the UK. For a view from the centre there is Dame Evelyn Sharp, *The Ministry of Housing and Local Government* (Allen and Unwin, 1969); R. Crossman, *The Diaries of a Cabinet Minister, Vol. I, Minister of Housing 1964–66* (Hamish Hamilton and Jonathan Cape, 1975); and C. Mellors, 'Local Government in Parliament: Twenty Years Later', *Public Administration,* **52** (1975).

Area studies, including London

In the past Wales and Scotland have tended to be neglected or, in the case of Wales, subsumed in general texts on English institutions. Now, work in this area is expanding. For Wales, there is D. Balsom and M. Burch, *A Political and Electoral Handbook for Wales* (Gower, 1980); and P. J. Madgwick with N. Griffiths and V. Walker, *The Politics of Rural Wales* (Hutchinson, 1973). For Scotland, there is J. P. Mackintosh, in *On Scotland*, edited by H. Drucker (Longman, 1982) and M. Keating and A. Midwinter, *The Government of Scotland* (Mainstream Publishing, 1983). Official publications include: the *Royal Commission on Local Government in Scotland 1966–1969* (the Wheatley Commission) *Report*, Cmnd. 4150 (HMSO, 1969); the *Royal Commission on the Constitution 1969–1973* (The Kilbrandon Report), *Vol. I, Report*, Cmnd. 5460, and *Vol. II, Memorandum of Dissent* (HMSO, 1973); and *Our Changing Democracy: Devolution to Scotland and Wales*, Cmnd. 6348 (HMSO, 1975). J. M. Bochel and D. T. Denver produced a series on elections since reform in the 1970s, *The Scottish Local Government Elections, 1974* (Scottish Academic Press, 1974) and three volumes published by the University of Dundee, *The Scottish District Elections* (1977), *The Scottish Regional Elections* (1978) and the *Scottish District Elections* (1980). A local study of pre-1975 Peterhead is F. Bealey and J. Sewel, *The Politics of*

Independence (Aberdeen University Press, 1981). An earlier study of Glasgow in the 1960s is I. Budge *et al.*, *Political Stratification and Democracy* (Macmillan, 1972). A. Midwinter and E. Page examined the effects of reform in 'Remote Bureaucracy or Administrative Efficiency: Scotland's New Local Government System', *Studies in Public Policy No. 38* (Glasgow, Centre for the Study of Public Policy, University of Strathclyde, 1981); and A. Midwinter, *Management Reform in Scottish Local Government* (Department of Administration, University of Strathclyde, 1982).

Material relating to Northern Ireland can be found in P. Arthur, *The Government and Politics of Northern Ireland* (Longman, 1980). A guide to local government in Northern Ireland and the Irish Republic is D. Roche, *Local Government in Ireland* (Dublin Institute of Public Administration, 1982) and on the Irish Republic, see Basil Chubb, *The Government and Politics of Ireland* (Oxford University Press, 1971), and T. J. Barrington, *From Big Government to Local Government* (Dublin, Institute of Public Administration, n.d., *c.* 1976).

For London, B. Donaghue and G. W. Jones, *Herbert Morrison* (Weidenfeld and Nicholson, 1973) contains an invaluable bibliography. A critical analysis is contained in W. A. Robson, *The Government and Misgovernment of London* (Allen and Unwin, 1939; 2nd cdn, 1948). The Greater London Group at the London School of Economics and Political Science published the *Greater London Papers*. On the reformed system of London Government the fundamental publication is *The Royal Commission on Local Government in Greater London, 1957–1960* (The Herbert Report), Cmnd. 1164 (HMSO, 1961). Academic studies include G. Rhodes, *The Government of Greater London: The Struggle for Reform* (Weidenfeld and Nicholson, 1970); G. Rhodes (ed.), *The New Government of London* (LSE/Weidenfeld and Nicholson, 1972); and S. Ruck and G. Rhodes, *The Government of Greater London* (Allen and Unwin, 1970). More recently, the enquiry into the GLC, commissioioned by the then-controlling Conservative group, chaired by Sir Frank Marshall, is *The Marshall Inquiry on Greater London, Report* to the Greater London Council (GLC, 1978).

Planning, Housing and other services have generated specialized London studies, including D. V. Donnison and D. Eversley (eds), *London: Urban Patterns, Problems and Policies* (Heinemann, 1974); M. Harloe *et al.*, *The Organization of Housing* (Heinemann/Centre for Environmental Studies, 1974); and K. Young and J. Kramer, *Strategy and Conflict in Metropolitan Housing* (Heinemann, 1978).

Political parties and elections (see also Chapter 8) are treated in: L. J. Sharpe, 'A Metropolis Votes', *Greater London Paper No. 8* (LSE, 1962); K. Young, *Local Politics and the Rise of Party* (Leicester University Press, 1975); P. Cousins, 'Council Leaders – London's 33 Prime Ministers', *Local Government Studies*, **5** (1979); A. D. Glassberg, *Representation and the Urban Community* (Macmillan, 1981); J. Bartley, 'London at the Polls: A Review of the 1981 GLC Election Results', *London Journal* (1982); and I. Gordon, 'London at the Polls', *London Journal* (1982). A historical evaluation is K. Young and P. L. Garside, *Metropolitan London: Politics and Urban Change 1837–1981* (Edward Arnold, 1982).

Comparative studies

American literature on community power (see Chapter 6) and more recently on distributional analysis has influenced British studies (see above). Recent contributions include: W. D. Hawley *et al.* (eds), *Theoretical Perspectives on Urban Politics* (Prentice-Hall, 1976); D. S. Wright, *Understanding Intergovernmental Relations* (Duxbury Press, North Scituate, Mass., 1978); and L. J. Sharpe, 'American Democracy Reconsidered', Parts I and II, *British Journal of Political Science*, **3**, 1–28 and 129–167 (1973).

An encompassing description of reorganized local government is D. C. Rowat (ed.), *International Handbook of Local Government Reorganization* (Aldwych Press, 1980). For the problems of comparative urbanism there is: U. K. Hicks, *The Large City* (Macmillan, 1974); W. A. Robson and D. E. Regan (eds), *Great Cities of the World* (3rd edn, 2 vols, Allen and Unwin, 1972); and B. Roberts, *Cities of Peasants* (Edward Arnold, 1978). The Institute of Commonwealth Studies has published a work on new states: W. R. Morris-Jones and S. K. Panter-Brick (eds), *A Revival of Local Government and Administration? An Assessment of Recent Developments in Several New States* (Athlone Press/Institute of Commonwealth Studies, 1980).

Of increasing interest are those comparative studies with a West European (including Scandinavian) focus: these include D. E. Ashford, *British Dogmatism and French Pragmatism* (Allen and Unwin, 1982); J. Lagroye and V. Wright (eds), *Local Government in Britain and France* (Allen and Unwin, 1979); N. Johnson and A. Cochrane, *Economic Policy-Making by Local Authorities in Britain and Western Germany* (Allen and Unwin, 1981); and A. B. Gunlicks (ed.), *Local Government Reform and Reorganization*

(Kennikat Press, Port Washington, 1981). An important area is that of central–local relations treated in C. Hull and R. A. W. Rhodes, *Intergovernmental Relations in the European Community* (Saxon House, 1977).

K. Newton and L. J. Sharpe's comparative series (some published under the aegis of the European Consortium for Political Research (ECPR) include K. Newton (ed.), *Balancing the Books: Financial Problems of Local Government in Western Europe* (Sage, 1980); L. J. Sharpe (ed.), *The Local Fiscal Crisis in Western Europe* (Sage, 1981); L. J. Sharpe (ed.), *Decentralist Trends in Western Democracies* (Sage, 1979); and K. Newton (ed.), *Urban Political Economy* (Frances Pinter, 1981).

Representation and participation

The study of local politics has been dominated by a pluralist framework – but one which has been challenged by neo-Marxists, radical sociologists and political economists. The pluralist approach focuses on community, on pressure groups and participation and on party politics. A selection of writings would include A. H. Birch, *Small Town Politics* (Oxford University Press, 1959); W. Hampton, *Democracy and Community* (Oxford University Press, 1970); and K. Newton, *Second City Politics* (Oxford University Press, 1976). On participation, there is 'People and Planning', *Report* of the Committee on Public Participation in Planning (The Skeffington Report), HMSO, 1969), D. M. Hill, *Participating in Local Affairs* (Penguin, 1970); S. Humble and J. Talbot, *Neighbourhood Councils in England* (Inlogov, University of Birmingham, 1977); R. Darke and R. Walker (eds), *Local Government and the Public* (Leonard Hill, 1977); and A. Barker, *Public Participation in Britain: A Classified Bibliography* (Bedford Square Press, 1979). The work of N. Boaden, M. Goldsmith, W. Hampton and P. Stringer on participation in structure planning (their *Interim Research Papers* can now be obtained only from the Department of the Environment) has culminated in a more general study: *Public Participation in Local Services* (Longman, 1982). On the role of the local press and broadcasting, there is D. M. Hill (1970, work cited); I. Jackson, *The Provincial Press and the Community* (Manchester University Press, 1971); W. H. Cox and D. Morgan, *City Politics and the Press* (Cambridge University Press, 1973); D. Murphy, *The Silent Watchdog* (Constable, 1976); and A. Wright, 'Local Broadcasting and the Local Authority', *Public Administration,* **60** (1982).

The case for the citizen's redress against his local council was argued in *The Citizen and his Council: Ombudsmen for Local Government?, Report* by *Justice* (Chairman, J. F. Garner) (Stevens, 1969). Evaluations of the system are: *The Local Ombudsman: a Review of the First Five years, Report* by *Justice* (Chairmen, V. Moore and H. Sales) (*Justice*, 1980); N. Lewis and B. Gateshill, *The Commission for Local Administration* (RIPA, 1978); and P. Cook's autobiography, *Ombudsman* (BKT Publications, 1981).

Work in the field of electoral studies is still sparse. Reference should be made to J. M. Bochel and D. T. Denver, '1976 District Council Election Data for England and Wales', which is lodged with the SSRC Survey Archive (*Data Set 1498(A)*, 1981); D. M. Clarke, *Battle for the Counties* (Redrose Publications, Newcastle, 1977); F. W. S. Craig's material on London elections (see below); and that of the GLC Research and Intelligence Unit (see below); M. Stead's annual electoral review in the *Economist*; S. Bristow's analyses of results in the *Municipal Review*; and also for the 1960s, L. J. Sharpe (ed.), *Voting in Cities* (Macmillan, 1967).

For political parties themselves there is J. G. Bulpitt, *Party Politics in English Local Government* (Longman, 1967); W. P. Grant, *Independent Local Politics in England and Wales* (Saxon House, 1977); D. G. Green, *Power and Party in an English City* (Allen and Unwin, 1980); and J. Gyford, work cited; RIPA, *Party Politics in Local Government* (1980), which includes B. Wood's survey of member/officer relations.

The issues of representation raised by L. J. Sharpe, 'Elected Representatives in Local Government', *British Journal of Sociology*, **13** (1962) and 'Leadership and Representation in Local Government', *Political Quarterly*, **37** (1966), have continued to exercise researchers. Such work includes A. M. Rees and T. Smith, *Town Councillors: a Study of Barking* (Acton Society Trust, 1964); J. P. Hennock, *Fit and Proper Persons* (Edward Arnold, 1973), G. W. Jones *Borough Politics* (Macmillan, 1969); and R. V. Clements, *Local Notables and the City Council* (Macmillan, 1969). The Maud and Robinson Committees looked at councillors' characteristics in the 1960s and again ten years later. Also important are the Committee on the Management of Local Government (The Maud Committee), *Vol.I, Report* (5 vols, HMSO, 1967); the Committee of Inquiry into the System of Remuneration of Members of Local Authorities (The Robinson Committee), *Vol.I, Report*, Cmnd. 7010 (2 vols, HMSO, 1977); and the Prime Minister's Committee on Local Government Rules of Conduct (The Lord Redcliffe-Maud Committee) *Vol.I, Report*, Cmnd. 5636 (HMSO, 1974). The Maud Committee's work has been criticized, and J. Stanyer warned of the difficulties of collecting and analysing such data in 'Electors, Candidates and Councillors: some Technical Problems in the Study of Political Recruitment Processes in Local Government', *Policy and Politics,* **6** (1977). S. Bristow pioneered research on women councillors: 'Women Councillors – An Explanation of the Under-Representation of Women in Local Government', *Local Government Studies,* **6** (1980). Also of interest is J. Hills, 'Women Local Councillors: A Reply to Bristow', *Local Government Studies,* **8** (1982).

A number of studies deal with aspects of leadership. These include G. W. Jones (work cited); R. V. Clements (work cited); J. M. Lee, *Social Leaders and Public Persons* (The Clarendon Press, 1963); and its successor, J. M. Lee, B. Wood, B. W. Solomon and P. Watts, *The Scope of Local Initiative* (Martin Robertson, 1974). There is also G. W. Jones and A. Norton (eds), *Political Leadership in Local Authorities* (Inlogov, University of Birmingham, 1978); C. Game, 'Review Essay: 'On Local Political Leadership', *Policy and Politics,* **7** (1979); and D. E. Regan, *A Headless State: The Unaccountable Executive in British Local Government* (University of Nottingham, 1980).

Functions

The main coverage of functions appears in the journals and general texts. In Planning, a standard work is J. B. Cullingworth, *Town and Country Planning in England Wales* (Allen and Unwin, 8th edn, 1982). A book with a wide sweep, beyond questions of law itself, is M. Grant, *Urban Planning Law* (Sweet and Maxwell, 1982). Criticisms of planning have multiplied: for example, J. M. Simmie, *Citizens in Conflict* (Hutchinson, 1974), and critics have also developed a wider policy interest, as in A. Blowers, *The Limits of Power: The Politics of Local Planning Policy* (Pergamon, 1980).

The proliferation of works on Housing is even greater. Bibliographies can be found in P. Dunleavy, *The Politics of Mass Housing 1945–1975* (The Clarendon Press, 1981) and S. Merrett, *State Housing in Britain* (Routledge and Kegan Paul, 1979).

For the Police, a standard text is G. Marshall, *Police and Government* (Methuen, 2nd edn, 1967) while for a history there is T. A. Critchley, *A History of Police in England and Wales* (Constable, rev. edn, 1978).

Urban Policy and Policy making now ranges widely, beyond questions of land-use planning, with works such as N. P. Boaden,

Urban Policy-Making (Cambridge University Press, 1971) and J. Dearlove, *The Politics of Policy in Local Government* (Cambridge University Press, 1973). Recently, increasing attention has been paid to the problems of the inner city: J. Edwards and R. Batley, *The Politics of Positive Discrimination* (Tavistock, 1978); J. Underwood, 'Policy for the Inner Cities – A Review Article', *Policy and Politics,* **8** (1980); P. Lawless, *Britain's Inner Cities* (Harper and Row, 1981); and M. Loney and M. Allen (eds), *The Crisis of the Inner City* (Macmillan, 1979). The Social Science Research Council (SSRC) Working Party, chaired by Peter Hall, published its final Report, *The Inner City in Context* (Heinemann/ SSRC, 1981) together with a series of eleven specialist reviews. The SSRC has now commissioned the next phase of the programme (SSRC *Newsletter,* **48** (March 1983)). Recent work on economic regeneration includes: R. Minns and J. Thornley, *State Shareholding* (Macmillan, 1978); C. Miller's review article, 'Local Authority Involvement in Economic Initiatives', *Local Government Studies,* **7** (1981); and K. Young and C. Mason (eds), *Urban Economic Development* (Macmillan, 1982). A different aspect of inner-city issues has been in the area of race relations (see bibliography section). The Scarman Report is now available: *The Scarman Report* (Penguin, 1982). The Policy Studies Institute has also carried out research in this area: K. Young and N. Connelly, *Policy and Practice in the Multi-Racial City* (PSI, 1981).

Finance

Leading publications on finance include the Committee of Enquiry into Local Government Finance (The Layfield Committee), *Report*, Cmnd. 6453 (HMSO, 1976); and C. D. Foster, R. Jackman and M. Perlman, with the assistance of B. Lynch, *Local Government Finance in a Unitary State* (Allen and Unwin, 1980). The major textbook is N. P. Hepworth, *The Finance of Local Government* (Allen and Unwin, 6th edn, 1980). Current interest in financial constraints is reflected in R. Rose and E. Page (eds), *Fiscal Stress in Cities* (Cambridge University Press, 1982). A work of specific criticism is T. Burgess and T. Travers, *Ten Billion Pounds: Whitehall's Takeover of the Town Halls* (Grant McIntyre, 1980).

Management

Studies of officers and of officer–councillor relations remain scarce but there is T. E. Headrick, *The Town Clerk in English Local Government* (Allen and Unwin, 1962); A. Alexander, *Local*

Government in Britain since Reorganisation (Allen and Unwin, 1982); C. A. Collins, C. R. Hinings and K. Walsh, 'The Officer and the Councillor in Local Government', *PAC Bulletin* (December 1978); B. Wood in RIPA (1979, work cited); The Committee on the Staffing of Local Government, *Report* (The Mallaby Report), (HMSO, 1967). The standard text is K. P. Poole, *The Local Government Service in England and Wales* (Allen and Unwin, 1978).

The 1970s saw a notable change of direction. A seminal work was J. K. Friend and W. N. Jessop, *Local Government and Strategic Choice* (Tavistock, 1969). Management concerns are reflected in: DOE/Local Authority Associations Study Group *Report*, 'The New Local Authorities: Management and Structure' (The Bains Report) (HMSO, 1972); J. Bourn, *Management in Central and Local Government* (Pitman, 1979); R. Greenwood, K. Walsh, C. R. Hinnings and S. Ranson, *Patterns of Management of Local Government* (Martin Robertson, 1980); R. Hambleton, *Policy Planning in Local Government* (Hutchinson, 1978); S. Leach and J. Stewart (eds), *Approaches in Public Policy* (Allen and Unwin, for Inlogov, 1982); R. J. Haynes, *Organisation Theory and Local Government* (Allen and Unwin, 1980); and S. Barratt and C. Fudge (eds), *Policy and Action: Essays on the Implementation of Public Policy* (Methuen, 1981).

Central–local relations

The thinking behind the SSRC's central–local panel and the theoretical approaches are described in G. W. Jones (ed.), *New Approaches to the Study of Central–Local Government Relations* (Gower, 1980); R. A. W. Rhodes, *Control and Power in Central –Local Government Relations* (Gower, 1981); and E. Page, 'Why Should Central–Local Relations in Scotland be any Different from Those in England?', *Studies in Public Policy, 21* (University of Strathclyde, Centre for the Study of Public Policy, 1978). For an alternative view: there is P. Saunders, 'Why Study Central–Local Relations?' *Local Government Studies, 8* (1982). Concern over this issue has a long history; for example: D. N. Chester, *Central and Local Government* (Macmillan, 1951); J. A. G. Griffith, *Central Departments and Local Authorities* (Allen and Unwin, 1966); 'Relations between Central Government and Local Authorities', *Report* by the Central Policy Review Staff (HMSO, 1977). Two innovatory areas in this research are in law: M. Elliott, *The Role of Law in Central–Local Relations* (SSRC, 1981), and in the 'National Local Government Community': see the work by J. Gyford and

M. James (SSRC *Newsletter* and journal articles); R. A. W. Rhodes, B. Hardy and K. Pudney's, work on the Local Authority Associations in *Discussion Papers* (University of Essex, Department of Government, 1982).

Reform

The reforms of the 1970s generated a number of studies: J. Brand, *Local Government Reform in England, 1888–1974* (Croom Helm, 1979); and C. J. Pearce, *The Machinery of Change in Local Government 1888–1974: A Study of Central Involvement* (Allen and Unwin for Inlogov, 1980). Lord Redcliffe-Maud, Chairman of the Royal Commission on Local Government in England (Cmnd. 4040, *Vol.I, Report; Vol.II*, 'Memorandum of Dissent' (D. Senior); *Vol.III*, 'Research Appendices' (HMSO, 1969)) was responsible, with B. Wood, for *English Local Government Reformed* (Oxford University Press, 1974) and B. Wood published *The Process of Local Government Reform 1966–1974* (Allen and Unwin, 1976). See also L. J. Sharpe, ' "Reforming" the Grass Roots: An Alternative Analysis', in D. E. Butler and A. H. Halsey (eds), *Policy and Politics* (Macmillan, 1978); and P. G. Richards, *The Local Government Act, 1972: Problems of Implementation* (Allen andUnwin/PEP, 1975). Lord Redcliffe-Maud, in his autobiography *Experiences of an Optimist* (Hamish Hamilton, 1981), describes the evolution of ideas in the Royal Commission.

John Dearlove challenges these views in *The Reorganisation of British Local Government* (Cambridge University Press, 1979). Alan Alexander's work on reorganization has been referred to above; his book *The Politics of Local Government in the United Kingdom* (Longman, 1982) describes the movements for change since 1945. The question of reform is still an open one; the future of the GLC and the other metropolitan authorities is uncertain (see above, The Marshall Report on Greater London) and the general debate continues, as R. McAllister and D. Hunter's *Local Government: Death or Devolution* (work cited) and journal articles reveal.

Official material and bibliography

Local authorities have a statutory duty to publish some kinds of information (see, the Local Government, Planning and Land Act, HMSO, 1980 and the Local Government Act, HMSO, 1972). Local newspapers, political parties and interest groups carry some records. Nationally, the Local Authority Associations maintain records and publish data. The Commission for Local Administration, established in 1974, produces an *Annual Report*.

Since 1967 the British Library Lending Division has maintained a comprehensive collection of social science publications, and the Official Publications Section of the British Library is the deposit of British government publications. HMSO publishes a *Consolidated Index to Government Publications*. The Departments of the Environment and Transport publishes a monthly *Library Bulletin* (which includes the Scottish and Welsh Offices). The DOE/DT sub-library produces an *Annual List of Publications* of their non-HMSO material.

The SSRC *Newsletter* reports on research projects, and theses are reported in the SSRC annual register *Political Science Theses*, and in the annual *Vol. III Social Science* of the *Scientific Research in British Universities and Colleges*, published by the Department of Education and Science. The European Consortium of Political Research (ECPR) Workgroup on Local Government and Politics reports on research and on publications in its *Newsletter*. The Political Studies Association Urban Politics Group publishes a biannual *Newsletter* and in October 1982 published a *Research Register*.

Statistical data are published annually in the DOE/Welsh Office *Local Government Financial Statistics for England and Wales* and *Rates and Rateable Values in England and Wales*. The Scottish Office publishes *Local Government Financial Statistics* (1st edn for 1975–1976 to 1977–1978 published December 1981; 2nd edn for 1978–1979 published 1982). The Welsh Office publishes *Welsh Local Government Financial Statistics* annually from 1977 onwards; No.4 (1980) covers 1978–1979. Between 1974 and 1979 the Office of Population, Censuses and Surveys *Series EL* (*Electoral Statistics*) (HMSO) published an analysis of local elections for English Metropolitan and non-Metropolitan counties, and Welsh counties and districts. The data were discontinued after the analysis of local elections of 1979 as part of the government's cutback of the statistical services. For previous years there are the *Registrar General's Statistical Review of England and Wales, Part II* (HMSO); for Scotland: the *Annual Report of the Registrar General for Scotland* (HMSO); for Northern Ireland: *The Analysis of the Register of Electors*, issued by the Chief Electoral Officer for Northern Ireland (HMSO).

The Chartered Institute of Public Finance and Accountancy (formerly the Institute of Municipal Treasurers and Accountants) publishes *Local Government Trends; Financial, General and Rat-*

ings Statistics (both annually); and the journal *Public Finance and Accountancy*. The GLC's *Urban Abstracts* publishes eight issues a year, in two series, on local government services. *Urbandoc News* (Capital Planning Information, 44 Main Street, Empingham, Oakham, and also in Edinburgh) publishes a monthly *Digest of Documents and Developments*. *A London Bibliography of the Social Sciences*, published by the British Library of Political and Economic Science, includes a local government section.

The GLC Research and Intelligence Unit publishes details of GLC and Borough Elections; additional material is F. W. S. Craig, *Greater London Votes, 1*: 'The Greater London Council 1964 –1970' (1971) and *2*, 'The Greater London Council 1964–1971' (1972) (Chichester, Political Reference Publications). Two journals containing London material are *London Journal* and the *London Review of Public Administration*.

The United Nations Department of Economic and Social Affairs publishes data on urbanization and local government. The International Union of Local Authorities, IULA (The Hague), published *Studies in Comparative Local Government* from 1967 to 1974 and from that data *Planning and Administration*. The British Sections of both IULA and of the Council of European Municipalities publish *IULA/CEM News*, and the monthly *European Information Service*. The former *Journal of Administration Overseas* is now published by the RIPA as *Public Administration and Development*. The public administration institutes of different countries publish journals (for example, *Public Administration Review* (USA), *Canadian Public Administration* (Canada) and *Administration* (Eire). American and comparative material can also be found in the monograph series of Sage: *Urban Affairs Annual Review*.

The major local government journals include *Local Government Studies*, and the Local Authority Associations publications – *Municipal Review, County Councils Gazette, District Council Review, Local Council Review*. Current work can also be found in *Public Administration, Public Administration Bulletin, British Journal of Political Science, Political Studies, Policy and Politics, Policy Studies*, and in the discussion paper series *Studies in Public Policy* (Centre for the Study of Public Policy, University of Strathclyde). Related journals are *Public Law, Urban Law and Policy, Journal of Urban and Regional Research, Political Geography Quarterly* and *CES Review* (published between 1977 and 1980).

Information on current research is in *Register of Research Projects* (Inlogov; see also the Inlogov reports and papers) and M.

Goldsmith, *Register of Research on Central–Local Relations in Britain* (SSRC, 1982–), an updating of the 1979 (A. Barker) register. See also the discussion and working papers of the School of Advanced Urban Studies, University of Bristol. Publications of the Race Relations Institute include the journal *Race and Class*, while the SSRC Research Unit on Ethnic Relations, University of Aston, publishes the information and research brochure *Racial and Ethnic Relations in Britain*.

PART 4
Politics and government: overseas

13
International reference works
Nicole M. Gallimore

International reference works dealing with world politics and government vary in their form and coverage, with inevitable overlapping. Categories surveyed in this chapter include general surveys and chronologies of domestic and international events, almanacs, encyclopedias, yearbooks, biographical listings and who's whos, dictionaries and atlases. Some monographs have been included when their field and scope, authorship and form render them valuable as reference tools.

Surveys and chronologies

The Annual Register: a review of public events at home and abroad for the year (1758– , London, 1761–) is the longest established general survey of world events. Published annually for over two hundred years, initially by J. Dodsley and since 1890 by Longmans Green, the present title *The Annual Register: World Events in . . .* reflects its current global coverage. Editors vary from the original editor Edmund Burke (1758), who put forward the idea of providing a broad grouping of chief movements of each year, to Mortimer Epstein, 1921 to 1945, Ivison S. Macadam from 1947 to 1972 and, from 1973 to date, H. V. Hodson. The 1980 edition covers internal affairs, as well as the foreign policy and the role in world affairs of the countries of the world grouped by regions, except for the first lengthy chapter devoted exclusively to the UK.

A section dealing with the activities of major international political organizations, from the United Nations to the Non-Aligned Movement, precedes a series of reviews of achievements and developments in economic and social affairs, the sciences, the law, the arts and sport. Comparative basic statistics for some twenty-four countries are provided. The text of documents and communiqués of international nature such as the Report on the Independent Commission on International Development Issues (Brand Report) or the Universal Islamic Declaration, or of international importance such as the protocol of the Gdansk Agreement, form a separate section. There is an index which, however, does not refer to entries listed in the brief month-by-month chronology.

The Diplomatic History 1713–1933 (Hollis and Carter, 1946), and its companion volume, *Earlier Diplomatic History 1492–1713* (Hollis and Carter, 1949), by Sir Charles Alexander Petrie, chronicle both domestic affairs and international political involvement of the main powers. Accounts of campaigns have been cut to a minimum. Events are arranged in chronological order with a minimum overlapping of accounts. There are clear chapter headings and subheadings, indexes in each volume and maps are provided. The most comprehensive and authoritative news digest, *Keesing's Contemporary Archives; Weekly Diary of World Events* (Keesing, July 1931–), covers events from 1 July 1931, with a thirty-five-page *Synopsis of Important Events 1918–1931*, published in 1936 as a supplement to volume 1. National and international news, abstracted from the main newspapers, official sources and news agencies' reports are displayed by country and by international organizations under subheadings in a weekly loose-leaf summary. Sources of each report are given, without, however, details of date and pagination. Texts of documents such as economic plans, lists of government membership and speeches highlights are reproduced. There are maps and statistics from authoritative quoted sources. Each report is followed by a direct reference to the previous entry on the same subject. The Index, issued fortnightly, is cumulated regularly, to form eventually a volume index covering two years up to 1972, then accompanying each one-year volume from 1973. The majority of entries are under country and maps are indexed separately as well as by subject (since 1959). Since 1959 a separate index of names has been added, issued quarterly and cumulated bi-annually and annually. *Facts on File, the Index of World Events* (Facts on File, Inc., New York, 1940–), is a comparable weekly loose-leaf service with annual bound volumes. The early volumes are heavily biased towards the US, dealing particularly with the daily general background of events that forced that country into the war. Besides the daily chronology of events on the principal war fronts, major developments in US national affairs as well as an account of foreign affairs worldwide are provided with a special section on Latin America. The entries are very succinct, and no sources, newspaper or otherwise, are given. The cumulative quarterly indexes are alphabetical by names of countries with chronological sublistings by subjects and by personal names. From 1965, the format became easier to handle, with a clear division between US national affairs and world affairs. There is a short list of 'Headline News' inset at the beginning of each weekly section. The current edition (1982) displays the chronology of news within categories, US affairs, world affairs, other nations and miscellaneous. Sources are given for tables and diagrams but not for facts. The yearly cumulated index contains country entries, with subject subheadings. The five-year indexes covering the thirty years from 1946 onwards enable the user to check key events, or construct the chronology of a complex political event involving several countries through a system of parallel columns.

The *Survey of International Affairs 1920/23–1963* (Oxford University Press, for the Royal Institute of International Affairs, 1925–1973) deals with the situation in countries, by areas as well as with relations between states. The pre-war series 1920 to 1938 by A. J. Toynbee and others, published in seventeen volumes between 1925 and 1953, covers the period following the Paris Peace Conference, recording events from the peace settlement to the war in Spain and its repercussions. The Wartime series 1939–1946, edited by A. J. Toynbee, published between 1952 and 1958 in eleven volumes, deals with particular aspects of international politics and domestic affairs over a period of years, e.g. *Hitler's Europe 1939–1946* and *The War and the Neutrals 1939–1946*. The post-war series since 1947 are annual in their coverage of political events and were published from 1952 to 1973. The *Survey of International Affairs 1925 Supplement*, compiled by V. M. Boulter (Oxford University Press, 1928), is a chronology listing alphabetically agreements, conventions and treaties by country participating. There are references by names of major treaties or subject of treaties to the countries involved. The companion series, *Documents on International Affairs, 1928–1963*, edited by J. W. Wheeler-Bennett *et al.*, 1929–1973 (Oxford University Press, for the Royal Institute of International Affairs) and designed to accompany the Survey of International Affairs, provides source material relating to domestic and foreign affairs. A *Consolidated Index*, compiled by E. M. R. Ditmas (Oxford University Press, for the

Royal Institute of International Affairs, 1967), consolidates thirty
or so indexes of the *Survey of International Affairs 1920–1938* and
of *Documents on International Affairs 1928–1938*. Post-1938
volumes in each series have integral indexes. The *World Almanac
and Book of Facts* (World Telegram, New York, 1868–), an
annual suspended in 1876 which resumed publication in 1886
under the direction of Joseph Pulitzer, despite its US/Canada
slant, provides a month-by-month chronology of world events, as
well as a section on world history and a list of battles from
antiquity to the present day. A chronology of world events,
stressing the progress of Communism from the birth of Karl Marx
to 1955, can be found in *World Communist Movement, Selective
Chronology 1818/1957*, compiled by the USA Library of Congress
Legislative Reference Service (4 vols, USGPO, Washington,
1960–1965). The arrangement is by year, and includes extracts
from documents, highlights from speeches and statements. An
annual review of political world events is provided by *Chamber's
Encyclopaedia Yearbook: A Year of Your Life* (International
Learning Systems, 1973–). Events are arranged in chronological
order, each month being preceded by a brief commentary. A
series of illustrated articles on a large variety of topics, including
politics, is followed by an index of personalities and an index of
events. *Britannica Book of the Year* (Encyclopaedia Britannica,
1975–) similarly provides a chronology of the previous year's
political and other events in the world, both domestic and international, followed by a dictionary listing of reviews of affairs by
country, and of economic, political and international affairs topics.

The volume for 1977 of the *Political Handbook and Atlas of the
World* (Harper and Row, for Council on Foreign Relations, New
York, 1 January 1927–) is the first of the series to preface the
annual list of review of world governments by a review of political,
regional and world issues. The book of reference concerning the
League of Nations, the *League Year Book*, edited by Judith
Jackson and Stephen King-Hall (Nicholson and Watson, London,
1932–1934) chronicles the world's political problems in Part II,
which is entitled 'Proceedings of the League of Nations'. In this
can be found a chronological summary of the proceedings of the
political organs of the League and of autonomous organs such as
the Permanent Court of International Justice. Important questions
brought before the League are the subject of separate chronologies such as the Sino–Japanese dispute from 1931 onwards or the
1932 Disarmament Conference. A more comprehensive chronology of international news can be found in *The Bulletin of International News* (Vol.1, No.1, February 1925 to Vol.XXII, No.13, 23

June 1945), compiled and published fortnightly by the Information Group of the Royal Institute of International Affairs and succeeded by the *World Today,* and its supplement: *Chronology of International Events and Documents* (Vol.1, No.1, July 1945 to Vol.11, No.24, December 1955). The *Year Book of the United Nations* (UN, New York, 1947–) includes a chronology of world politics and the activities of member-nations. *World Politics since 1945,* by Peter Calvocoressi (Longman, 4th edn, 1982) covers the period since the end of the Second World War to 1980. Both important UK domestic and international political events are chronicled. The first chapter is devoted to the Great Powers and the end of the Alliance in Europe, and the onset and progress of the Cold War, the resurgence of China and Japan, the UN and world order, OPEC, EEC, OECD, North–South Confrontation are reviewed. An area-by-area account of political events is given, concentrating on a dominant set of events for each area, i.e. for the Communist bloc: Stalin's empire, the Yugoslav secession, the 'discontents within the bloc', and security in Western Europe. The Middle East, Asia, Asean countries, Africa and Latin American receive similar treatment. A detailed index allows this standard textbook to be used as a work of reference. *The Strategic Survey* (International Institute for Strategic Studies, 1967–) covers material on world politics and military world affairs and includes a chronology of political events by areas. The *Annual of Power and Conflict* (Institute for the Study of Conflict, 1972–) is a yearly survey of political violence and transnational terrorism. Part I is a country-by-country chronology of relevant political events and Part II consists of five essays which consider the evolving balance of the political influence of the superpowers and its repercussion on events in countries in Western Europe, the Mediterranean, the Middle East, Africa South of the Sahara and Latin America. Each essay is followed by a glossary of 'allusions' in which treaties are briefly analysed, acronyms explained and political parties defined. Section 2 of *The Times Yearbook of World Affairs* edited by Sir David Hunt (Time Books, 2nd edn, 1980–) contains a history of the year, chronologically arranged, set out under the heading of the different countries alphabetically arranged. Section 3 gives a narrative of events in the world classified under topic: wars, terrorism, revolutions and *coups d'état.*

Whitaker's Almanack (Whitaker, 1913–) in the current edition for 1982 contains a brief chronological review of the world's political events in countries of the Commonwealth, in the US, the Common Market, other countries, British and Irish political events being dealt with separately. Among the chronologies covering short periods, *A Diary of World Affairs, June 23rd 1940–December 11, 1941*, by M. Hoden, translated from the French by Mabel Hanck (2 vols, Penguin, 1941), is notable by the fact that the author was Head of the German Section of the Press Bureau of the French Department of Foreign Affairs during the First World War and Private Permanent Secretary to the Secretary-General of the League of Nations from 1930 to 1938. The description of the Second World War period political events until Pearl Harbour is in chronological order by areas, and is accompanied by the text of official documents such as the Berlin Pact between Germany, Italy and Japan.

International Politics since World War II: a Short History, by Charles Langner Robertson (Wiley, New York, 2nd edn, 1975), is a useful survey of world politics, summarized in chronological order under broad chapter headings labelling the main trend of the particular area dealt with. The world is seen in terms of blocs, a simplified but useful approach.

The Intelligent Man's Guide Through The World Chaos, by George Douglas Howard Cole (Gollancz, 1932), gives an outline of post-First World War economic problems and economic policies when general elections in Europe and the US were fought during the Recession. Capitalism and the alternatives to capitalism are examined in various scenarios of the world political outlook. The companion volume, *The Intelligent Man's Guide to the Post War World* (Gollancz, 1947), gives a committed socialist's view of post-war political and economic conditions with particular reference to the problems of employment in Britain and the rest of the world. Both domestic and international political issues are dealt with. An index and book list add to the scope of the study.

Government: types and structure of governments

The *Political Systems of Empires*, by Samuel Noah Eisenstadt (Collier–Macmillan, 1963), presents a comparative analysis of types of political structures as found in different societies from the earliest recorded times, in order to find patterns and formulate the laws of development of political systems. Greek city states, the Mongol Empire, European feudalism, Moslem Spain and absolutist Europe are reviewed. An analytical index and thirty pages of tables chart the organization of political and bureaucratic systems and enable the reader to use the volume as a work of reference.

International Politics, by Norman Llewellyn Hill (Harper and Row, New York, 1963), must be mentioned as a reference textbook which deals with the nature of states and of the international community, the actions of states and the manner in which they conduct their relations *vis-à-vis* one another. It deals with the nature of diplomacy and the concepts of international politics, war, force, law and the role of international organizations.

The Governments of Europe (Macmillan, New York, 4th edn, 1954) and *Major Changes in the Governments of Europe since 1930* (Macmillan, New York, 1937), by William Bennett Munro, describe the antecedents, organization and processes of government in the chief European countries, with reference also to Switzerland, Russia, Austria, Hungary and the succession states as well as Japan. *The Background of European Governments*, by Norman Llewellyn Hill and Harold Walter Stoke (Farrar, New York, 1935), is a collection of readings and documents displaying the structure and operation of the governments of the major countries of Europe. In *Comparative Major European Governments*, by John Gilbert Heinberg (Farrar, New York, 1937), the material is arranged by topics: administration, legislative processes, economic control, public finance. England, France, Germany, Italy and Russia are compared. *Governments in Europe*, edited by Raymond Leslie Buell (Nelson, New York, 1938), is a competent manual arranged for ready reference, covering the principal nations of Europe. This is a revised and combined edition of *New Governments in Europe* (1934) and *Democratic Governments in Europe* (1935), both edited by R. L. Buell and published by Nelson. *Governments of Continental Europe*, edited by James Thomson Shotwell (Macmillan, New York, 1940), gives the historical background and the current status of governments in France, the Netherlands, Germany, Central Europe, Italy, Switzerland, the Scandinavian countries and Soviet Russia. The second revised edition (Macmillan, New York, 1952) confines itself to France, Italy, Switzerland, West Germany and the USSR. The effects of the Second World War on the governments of Britain, Germany, France, Italy, the USSR, the Balkans and Scandinavia are described in *Governments in War Time Europe*, edited by Harold Zink and Taylor Cole (Reynal, New York, 1941). Post-war volumes include *Government and politics abroad*, edited by Joseph Rouček (Funk, New York, 2nd edn, 1948), which deals with the Turkish and Latin American governments as well as those of Europe, and *Contemporary Foreign Governments by Herman Beukema et al.* (Rinehart, New York, 3rd edn, 1953), which gives a schematic presentation of the governmental apparatus of Great Britain, France, Italy, West Germany, the USSR and Japan, with a chapter on the Vichy regime, Mussolini's Social Republic and the Military Occupation Governments in Germany and Japan. A study of a selection of governments can be found in *Modern Foreign Governments* by Frederick A. Ogg and Harold Zink (Macmillan, New York, 4th rev. edn, 1957). First published in 1934 under the title *European Governments and Politics*, the work includes studies of types of governments, from democratic to authoritarian, and their institutions. The emphasis is on current structures, functions and problems of governments, with an outline of their historical development. Countries included are Great Britain and France; Germany from Empire to post-Second World War government; Central western European countries; Norway and Sweden, because of their experience as democratic countries with the multiparty system; Canada to exemplify the government of a Commonwealth country; the USSR; Argentina 1810 onwards because of its relationship with the US resulting from the 'Good Neighbour Policy'; and Japan, from early times. *Modern Governments* by Harold Zink (Van Nostrand, 3rd edn, 1966) presents a historical account of constitutional development of the political systems of Great Britain, France, West Germany, Scandinavia, the Soviet Union, the Americas, India and Japan. Additionally, the civil service, judiciary and local government are described. A selective bibliography precedes each chapter, and there is an index. An analysis of the systems of government adopted by Asian, African and Caribbean countries after independence can be found in *Politics and Government at Home and Abroad*, by William Alexander Robson (Allen and Unwin, 1967), as well as a chapter on various types of metropolitan government. There is an index.

Non-State Nations in International Politics: Comparative System Analyses, edited by Judy S. Bertelsen (Praeger, New York, 1977), is a chronological analysis of their role divided by headings such as goals, resources, environment and impact on international arena. The impact of non-state groups (Palestinian Arabs, Kurds) and non-state nations (Basques, Welsh) is included. *Communist Regimes in Eastern Europe*, by Richard Felix Staar (Hoover Institution Press, Stanford, 3rd rev. edn, 1977), deals individually in the first eight chapters with the countries of Eastern Europe under Communist rule. Governmental structure, constitutional framework, the electoral system, the ruling party, domestic policies and foreign relations are described. The last three chapters discuss relations between the various groupings of nations.

Marxist Governments, a World Survey, edited by Bogdan Szajkowski (3 vols, Macmillan, 1981), describes the governments and politics of these states. The collection of essays by specialists is organized alphabetically by country, and is preceded by two theoretical chapters which follow the history and development of the study of the Marxist–Leninist regimes, with an analysis of the nature of Marxist government. Each country section provides a short history of the movement, the resulting government, constitution, local government, party organization and membership, party/state and party/religious leaders relationships. A map showing provincial boundaries accompanies each chapter. The countries covered run from Albania through Mongolia to Yugoslavia, and include Kampuchea, Mozambique and Angola. The Democratic Republics of Afghanistan and Madagascar have been omitted for reasons of insufficient data. The Communist government of San Marino was voted into office too late to be included in this collection. In the preface the author expresses his hope to include in subsequent editions chapters on the Communist-led state governments in India, the Communist Parties' experiences in post-war West European governments and the Communist-led local councils in Italy, France, the Federal Republic of Germany and Portugal.

Freedom in the World, Political Rights and Civil Liberties, edited by Raymond D. Gastil (G. K. Hall, Boston, Mass., September 1978–), provides a country-by-country review with comparative tables of the percentage of people taking part in political activities within the existing constitutional structure, of opposition groups and of the media's relationship to the established government. There are also tables of political and economic systems by categories (by country).

Government directories

European Political Facts 1918–1973, by Chris Cook and John Paxton (Macmillan, 1975), lists the heads of state, prime ministers, foreign ministers and finance ministers of thirty-five European states (members of the League of Nations and of the United Nations), with dates of taking office, complemented retrospectively by *European Political Facts 1848–1918* by Chris Cook (Macmillan, 1977) and by *European Political Facts 1789–1848*, by Chris Cook (Macmillan, 1980). *The Times Survey of Foreign Ministries of the World*, edited by Zara Steiner (Times, 1982) combines an authoritative survey of the histories and present make-up of the world's leading foreign ministries with a study of the foreign policy process in the chancelleries of all EEC nations, the US and the USSR, Canada, Switzerland, Japan and China. Each chapter is followed by structural charts and a bibliography. *Bidwell's Guide to Government Ministers*, compiled and edited by Robin Bidwell (Vol.1– , Cass, 1973–), deals respectively with the major powers and Western Europe 1900–1971 (Volume I), the Arab World (Volume II) and the British Empire and successor states 1900 –1972 (Volume III). In Volume I the names of heads of state and of holders of principal ministerial posts are displayed by groups of countries labelled: World Powers, the Countries which link the Powers of Western and Northern Europe, Central and South Eastern European countries and Countries without Independent Ministers in 1900. The chronological arrangement in parallel columns for each group enables the user to consult a full vertical listing for one country for the period covered or to read transversally the ministerial representation in five or six countries at a given date. A similar pattern is followed in Volumes II and III. *Keesing's Contemporary Archives* (1931– , work cited) notes ministerial and governmental changes as they occur, then publishes a listing of the new cabinet with ministers' former office shown in brackets; similarly, *Facts on File* (1940– , work cited) lists the composition of new administrations in its fortnightly review of the world's political events. Annual publications which provide information on the background, the constitution, the government and politics, as well as lists of cabinet members for countries of the world A to Z include the *Political Handbook and Atlas of the World* (1927– , work cited), the *Europa Year Book* (2 vols, Europa Publications, 1959–), which replaced the loose-leaf encyclopedia *Europa* (1926–1958) and *Orbis* (1938–1958), *The Statesman's Yearbook*, edited by John Paxton (Macmillan, 1864 –) and *The International Yearbook and Statesmen's Who's Who* (Burke's Peerage, 1953–). *Countries of the World and their Leaders* (2 vols, supplement, Gale, Detroit, 1980–) is a compilation of the US Department of State reports on countries of the world which contains extensive listings of leaders and public officials. *The World Fact Book* (1982 edn, Central Intelligence Agency, Washington, 1982), until 1980 entitled *National Basic Intelligence Factbook*, gives a very brief description of the type of government, political subdivisions, government leaders of sovereign countries and non-independent countries of the world. *The Handbook of the Nations* (Gale, Detroit, 2nd edn, 1981) is a reprint of *The World Fact Book 1981* (see above). A very comprehensive reference source of information on the leadership of every national government and intergovernmental organization in the world is *Lambert's Worldwide Government Directory with Intergovernmental Organizations*, edited by Diane E. Hrabak (Lambert, Washington, DC, 1981), which includes besides address, telephone, telex and cable information for each office, the form of address for the head of state, the chief executive and ministers. The 1982 edition will incorporate a bi-monthly update service, compiled by computer.

The Current History Encyclopedia of Developing Nations, edited by Carol L. Thompson and others (McGraw-Hill, New York, 1982), covers the political history of ninety-three developing nations. Six regional sections cover Africa, the Middle East, East and South-east Asia and the Pacific, Mexico, Central America and the Caribbean, South America. The centrally planned Eastern European countries are specifically excluded. The country articles are arranged in alphabetical order preceded by a short statistical table, and sketch the recent main political, ethnic, social and economic events which are shaping each nation's development. *The Encyclopedia of the Third World*, by George Thomas Kurian (3 vols, Mansell, 2nd rev. edn, 1982), provides a description of the political economic and social systems of 122 'politically nonaligned and economically developing' countries of the world including a recent list of the members of the executive body of each country. Following this definition, some Communist-ruled countries are included in the survey; China and Taiwan are not. Newly independent countries such as Dominica, Kiribati and Zimbabwe fall within the scope of the 2nd edition, which has a cut-off date of 1 January 1981. There is a twenty-year chronology of political events and an up-to-date bibliography. *Great Cities of the World: Their Government Politics and Planning*, edited by William Alexander Robson (Allen and Unwin, 3rd rev. and enl. edn, 1972), deals with the government, politics and planning of a selected group of twenty-four major cities in Europe, America, Asia and Australasia. Part I describes the administrative framework, and the problems of large city government. Part II deals with the incidence of these problems in the circumstances peculiar to each metropolis. There is a bibliography arranged by cities and an index. Similar information can be found in *Cities of the World* (4 vols, Gale, Detroit, 1982): a compilation of revised US State Department *Post Reports* for one hundred and sixty-nine cities located throughout the world divided into five regions: Europe, Asia, Australasia, Africa and the Americas. *The Book of World Rankings*, by George Thomas Kurian (Macmillan, 1979), which covers some three hundred and twenty-five subjects from politics and defence to consumption, aims to display in rank order within each category figures relating to various countries of the world so as to show strengths and weaknesses. Chapter V is devoted to Politics, where countries are ranked on the basis of the relative stability and

capabilities of political systems. Subheadings include 'Most Power-
ful Nations', 'Registered Voters', 'Age of Nations', 'Size of
Cabinet', 'Political Opposition Index', 'Civil Disorder Index' and
'Communist Party Membership'. Sources are given.

Constitutions

Modern Constitutions since 1787, by John Arkas Hawgood (Macmillan, 1939), is a systematic treatise arranged topically rather
than by country, which places political constitutions both in their
historical perspective and in their relationship to each other. The
evolution of the constitutions of France, the US, Germany,
Belgium, Italy, Switzerland, countries of Central and Eastern
Europe and the USSR from the late eighteenth century is followed
chronologically. An index is provided. *Modern Political Constitutions*, by Charles Frederick Strong (Sidgwick and Jackson, 8th rev.
edn, 1972), is a similar historical sourcebook first published in
1930. The text in English of constitutions of sovereign states of the
world in effect at 1 September 1964 can be found in *Constitutions
of Nations*, prepared by Dorothy Peaslee Xydis (4 vols, Nijhoff,
The Hague, 3rd rev. edn, 1965–). The arrangement differs from
the alphabetical listing of texts A–Z chosen by Amos Jenkins
Peaslee for the 1st and 2nd editions of the compilation. The 3rd
edition lists Constitutions by continent: Vol.I Africa, Vol.II Asia,
Australasia, Oceania, Vol.III Europe, Vol.IV Americas. For each
country there is a brief summary discussing its international status
and form of government. A brief statement on the constitution in
force can be found by country A–Z in the *Statesman's Year Book*
(1864– , work cited), the *International Year Book and Statesmen's
Who's Who* (1953, work cited) and the *Political Handbook of the
World* (work cited). *Constitutions of the Countries of the World*,
edited by Albert P. Blaustein and Gisbert Flanz (Oceana, New
York, 1971–), issued in loose-leaf form, held in sixteen binders,
contains the text of the constitution in English translation, and a
brief resumé of the constitutional history for each nation. A
companion set of six binders with releases issued periodically
provides the text of the *Constitutions of Dependencies and Special
Sovereignties*, edited by Albert P. Blaustein and others (Oceana,
New York, 1975–). Coverage includes Northern Ireland, Jersey,
Sark, the Cayman Islands, The Faroe Islands and Spitzbergen.
The full text in English translation of the constitutions of the
Union of Social Socialist Republics, the People's Republic of
China and the Somali Democratic Republic can be found in the

annual volumes of *Documents in Communist Affairs*, edited by Bogdan Szajkowski (Cardiff Press, 1978–) for 1978, 1979 and 1980, respectively.

Parliaments

The organization, procedure and activities of fifty-six parliaments, as at 1 September 1974, are exhaustively examined in *Parliaments of the World: a Reference Compendium*, by Valentine Herman and Françoise Mendel (Macmillan, 1976). The volume, sponsored by the Interparliamentary Union, displays seventy tables, preceded by a brief explanatory text. A new edition is in preparation.

Each table lists the practice of each parliament. Areas covered are composition, organization and operation, legislative function, powers over finances and control of the executive, judicial functions and nomination of government officials and judges. Each table enables the reader to ascertain the essential similarities and differences between various parliamentary systems in respect of a given question, as well as to find detailed information concerning one or more individual Parliaments. *World Legislatures*, by John Paxton (Macmillan, 1975), claims to be limited in its aim, yet covers brief descriptions of parliaments and assemblies concerned with making laws as well as the process of electing the lawmakers worldwide. The listing is country by country A–Z, and includes regional legislatures in federal states. The last entry refers to the Parliament of the European Economic Community in Strasbourg, despite its lack of legislative authority. A brief description of the organs of government can be found in the annual country-by-country listing in the *International Yearbook and Statesmen's Who's Who* (1953– , work cited), *The Political Handbook of the World* (1927– , work cited) and the *Statesman's Year Book* (1864– , work cited).

Political parties

Political Parties: Their Organisation and Activity in the Modern State, by Maurice Duverger, translated from the French by Barbara and Robert North (Methuen, 1964) outlines the origins, the structure and membership of parties, the selection and the authority of party leaders. The party systems are treated historically with country examples; alliances, the formation of public opinion and the relationship of parties and government as participant or opposition, systems of voting are analysed. *Modern*

Governments, by Harold Zink (1962, work cited) provides a historical account of constitutional development and political systems in Great Britain, France, West Germany, Scandinavia, the Soviet Union, the Americas, Japan and India. The function of political parties and their interaction with the legislative and executive bodies are analysed. A list of the main political newspapers and periodicals follows each country chapter. A historical listing of political parties giving date of foundation, political aims and membership is included in *European Political Facts 1789–1973* (1975–1980, work cited). Up-to-date information on one thousand active political parties can be found in *Political Parties of the World*, edited by Alan J. Day and Henry W. Degenhardt (Longman, 1980). Information includes foreign name of party with English translation, date of foundation, leadership, structure, splits, aims and list of publications. The results of recent parliamentary elections with the status of each party are given. For each country a listing of minor parties not represented in parliaments is appended. This Keesing publication is in its 1st edition. The organization of the ruling party and its relationship to the state can be found by country, from Cuba to Yugoslavia, in *Marxist Governments: a World Survey* (1981, work cited). The history as well as the organization and membership of Communist parties, their relation to Soviet leadership, party press organs and dates of congresses held are given in the *Yearbook on International Communist Affairs* (1966– , work cited). Similar information in *Communist Regimes in Eastern Europe* (3rd rev. edn, 1977, work cited) is complemented by tables displaying for each country under review Communist Party membership over twenty years or more, social composition of the Party and current Party leadership. A select list of Communist Parties engaged in guerrilla warfare in Europe, Latin America, the Arab World and South-west Asia can be found at Appendix II of the *Annual of Power and Conflict* (1971–1972 to 1973–1977, work cited). Later editions of this annual include an account of the activities of extremist movements and Communist parties in the study of challenge to each established government.

World Communism: a Handbook 1918–1965, edited by Witold S. Sworakowski (Hoover Institution Press, Stanford, 1973), is a concise reference encyclopedia of the history of the international Communist movement in the nations of the world. A list of party congresses, party press organs and a bibliography accompany each country section. The Handbook provides the background information to the *Yearbook on International Communist Affairs* (Hoover Institution Press, Stanford, 1967–), which covers the years 1966 onwards. Information from primary source material in the native languages brings the history of the movement up to date.

Elections and plebiscites

Voting procedure and election results in Europe, including Turkey, from 1789 can be found in *European Political Facts* (1975, work cited). *The International Almanac of Electoral History*, compiled by Thomas T. Mackie and Rose Richard (Macmillan, 1974), provides a compilation of election results in industrial nations of Western Europe, North America, Australasia, South Africa and Japan since the beginning of competitive regular national elections. 'Countries of Latin America are excluded, so are the former colonies of the British or French Empire' (Introduction). Each chapter is preceded by a short study of the country's electoral history. *Keesing's Contemporary Archives* (1931– , work cited) covers electoral campaigns, programmes of parties, grouping of parties, results by parties with comparative figures for the previous election and distribution of seats for general elections, by-elections, municipal and other elections. An essential source is the annual *Chronicle of Parliamentary Elections and Developments* (InterParliamentary Union, Geneva). *Elections in Developing Countries: A Study of Electoral Procedures Used In Tropical Africa, South East Asia and the British Caribbean*, by Thomas Edward Smith (Macmillan, 1960), deals exclusively with electoral procedures. The material is organized functionally rather than regionally. *The World Handbook of Political and Social Indicators*, by Charles Lewis Taylor and Michael Hudson *et al.* (Yale University Press, 2nd edn, 1972) devotes a section to worldwide statistics of voters' turnout, political protest and executive change for the years 1951 to 1971.

A Monograph on Plebiscites, by Sarah Wambaugh (Oxford University Press, 1920), is a scholarly history of plebiscites and attempted plebiscites from the French Revolution onwards. Most of the volume is devoted to a collection of the pertinent documents in the original language and in parallel English translation. A chronological list from 1791 to 1905 of cases of change of sovereignty in which the right to self-determination has been recognized is appended. *Plebiscites Since the World War*, by Sarah Wambaugh (2 vols, Carnegie Endowment, Washington, 1933), lists plebiscites and attempted plebiscites in volume I. Volume II is devoted to the text of relevant documents in the original language.

United Nations General Assembly Document A/C4/351: *Plebiscites held since 1920 Under the Control or Supervision of International Organizations* (20 February 1957) analyses the organization and conduct of six plebiscites held between 1920 and 1935, the result of the vote and the decisions resulting.

Biographical sources

The Almanach de Gotha: Annuaire Généalogique Diplomatique et Statistique 1733–1944 (Perthes, Gotha, 1763–1944) is an important annual source for genealogical and diplomatic information. The reigning houses of Europe, and in later editions those outside Europe, mediatized ruling families and other princely lines are included. The *Royal Commonwealth Society Biography Catalogue of the Library of the Royal Commonwealth Society*, by Donald H. Simpson (Royal Commonwealth Society, 1961), lists all the Library's biographical material. The main sequence lists 'Individual Biographies', and is followed by 'Collective Biography and country indexes'. The preface states that 'the men and women included are in the main, those born in, or actively connected with countries of the Commonwealth and persons in the United Kingdom who have been of significance in Imperial affairs'. Books to Autumn 1960 and periodicals to the end of 1959 are included in the listing. Biographical articles on leading political figures and statesmen of the world can be found in the *Encyclopaedia Britannica* (Encyclopaedia Britannica, 15th edn, 1980) and in *Chambers' Encyclopaedia* (Chamber's Encyclopaedia, new rev. edn, 1969). The *International Encyclopedia of the Social Sciences*, edited by David L. Sills (17 vols, Collier–Macmillan, 1972) includes in the main volumes biographies of such political theorists as Karl Marx, Montesquieu and Saint-Simon. No living person is included who was born after 1890. Volume 18, *Biographical Supplement* (1979), includes nineteen further biographies of notable figures in the field of political sciences and legal theory. The most comprehensive source of current biographical information is *The International Who's Who* (Europa Publications, 1935–). The 46th edition, 1982–1983, provides up-to-date information on more than fifteen thousand personalities in the world, a considerable proportion of whom are active in the fields of international affairs, government, administration and diplomacy. *Who's Who in the World* (Marquis Who's Who 1970–) in the 5th edition (revised 1980–1981) provides brief biographical sketches of twenty-five thousand personalities, including some politicians and statesmen. Although there is considerable overlap, it constitutes a useful complementary source to *International Who's Who* (see above). *The Blue Book: Leaders of the English Speaking World* (St James's Press, 1969–1977), in the last edition published, for 1976, contains fifteen thousand entries and includes biographies of personalities in government and politics from the UK and Eire, the US, Canada, Australia and New Zealand. A selection of biographies of leaders from countries of Europe, the Middle East, the Baltic States, Scandinavia, Asia and the Far East is included in the glosssary of current world affairs at 1938 entitled *What's What and Who's Who in Some World Affairs* (J. Bale, Son and Curnow, 1938). The *Biographical Dictionary of the Comintern*, by Branko Lazitch and Milorad M. Drachkovitch (Hoover Institution Press, Stanford, 1973), lists, besides the three hundred members of the overall Directorate of the Comintern from 1919 to 1943, individuals who spoke at the Comintern congresses from 1919 to 1935 and delegates to the Executive Committee from 1922 to 1933; members and leaders of auxiliary organizations are included. The biographical entries – over seven hundred in all – are current up to April 1969 and include, besides a basic biographical resumé, a political biography of each subject as a member of the Communist Party, and an account of his participation in Comintern affairs. There is an index of the pseudonyms adopted by the secret emissaries of the Comintern and by the leaders of various national Communist parties outlawed in their respective countries. Political biographies of the current leaders in the countries reviewed follow each chapter in *Marxist Governments, A World Survey* (1981, work cited) and appear in the volume's index. Some biographies of political figures can be found in *A Dictionary of Politics*, by Florence Elliott and Michael Summerskill (Penguin, 7th edn, 1973), in *A Dictionary of Politics*, edited by Walter Laqueur *et al.* (Weidenfeld and Nicolson, 1971) and in *Dictionary of Political Science*, edited by Joseph Dunner (Littlefield Adams, Totowa, NJ, 1970). After the foundation of the United Nations in 1945, a first biographical directory of international personalities associated with the organization was published: *Who's Who Delegates to the UN* (Conference on International Organization, San Francisco, 1945). The first edition of the *Yearbook of the United Nations 1946–47* (UN, New York, 1947) also included a biographical section relating to the principal representatives to the Conference, personalities accredited to the organizations, leading officials of the UN organs and of most of the specialized agencies. *Who's Who in the United Nations and Related Agencies* (Arno, New York, 1971–) has greatly extended coverage: it includes the related agencies, data about the UN system and its personnel as well as biographical listing (at mid-year 1974 for the 1975 edition) of Secretariat staff members of rank Section Chief and above, of members of permanent missions to the UN, of members of the International Court of Justice and of bodies accredited to the UN.

Dictionaries

A Dictionary of Politics, by Florence Elliott and Michael Summerskill (1973, work cited), includes, besides political developments up to 1971, definitions of political terms, articles on countries, doctrines, policies, parties and organizations. *A Dictionary of Politics*, edited by Walter Laqueur *et al.* (1971, work cited), concentrates on post-1933 political events: entries are under countries, personalities and names of parties by acronym, with reference from the full name. *White's Political Dictionary*, by Wilbur Wallace White (World Publishing Co., Cleveland, 1947), is a popular dictionary, international in treatment, which lists terms of recent origin, names of government organizations, conferences, treaties and political events, with cross-references from abbreviations. *Polec, Dictionary of Politics and Economics*, by H. Bock *et al.* (de Gruyter, Berlin, 1967), is a general polyglot dictionary listing in one sequence sixteen thousand English, French and German terms relating to politics, government, political events, parties and treaties. *A Dictionary of Political Analysis*, by G. K. Roberts (Longman, 1971), provides definitions for the terms, listed in English, of politics and government. *The International Relations Dictionary*, by Jack Charles Plano and R. Olton (Holt Rinehart and Winston, New York, 1969), contains twelve alphabetical sequences including, 8. National Political Systems, 11. International Law and 12. International Organizations. Each brief definition of a term is followed by a subject discussion under the heading 'significance'.

The *Dictionary of Political Science*, edited by Joseph Dunner (1964, work cited) provides a listing of political terms with definitions, along with descriptions of the government of nation states. The *Dictionary of Politics: Selected American and Foreign Political and Legal Terms*, by John Walter Raymond (Brunswick Pub. Co., Lawrenceville, Va., 6th edn, 1978), also includes brief entries relating to events and phenomena of government and politics. Bibliographical sources to be consulted for additional in-depth information are listed. In the Reference Aid Series *A Guide to Political Acronyms*, compiled by the US Central Intelligence Agency (CIA, Washington, DC, October 1979) is a ten-page alphabetical listing designed to help government analysts decipher accurately daily diplomatic cables. The list, compiled with the cooperation of all divisions of the Office of Political Analysis, contains the most frequently used acronyms concerning general political developments, some foreign political parties, foreign states and such specialized areas as arms control, SALT, NATO and the European Community. An appendix contains a list of some of the most active terrorist and 'revolutionary' groups in Western Europe.

Atlases

A variety of current physical–political maps, as well as some historical maps of the world, can be found in major atlases such as *The Times Atlas of the World* (Times Newspapers and Bartholomew, 6th edn, 1980); *The New Oxford Atlas* (1st edn edited by Sir Clinton Lewis and J. D. Campbell, reprinted with revisions to date, Oxford University Press, 1970); the *Encyclopaedia Britannica World Atlas* (Encyclopaedia Britannica, 1980); and *Cassell's New Atlas of the World*, edited by Harold Fullard (Cassell, 1961). The *Historical Atlas of Modern Europe from the Decline of the Roman Empire, Comprising also Maps of Asia, Africa and the New World Connected with European History* (The Clarendon Press, 1902), displays in ninety plates, faced by explanatory texts written by specialists, the political history of the nations of Europe, their colonies and dependencies from the tenth century to the end of the nineteenth century. The *Historical Atlas*, by W. R. Shepherd (Philip, 9th edn, 1965), contains a collection of plates, printed by offset lithography from the originals destroyed in Germany, illustrating the political history of the world from 1450 BC to AD 1965. Clear if compact inset comments accompany the maps and plans. *The Times Atlas of World History*, edited by Geoffrey Barraclough (Times Books, 1979), illustrates in one hundred and thirty plates the broad movements of world politics and history, from the first civilizations to the formation of states throughout the globe, 'Imperialism and Nationalism in the 20th C', 'European Political Problems 1919–1934', 'Nationalism 1919 –1941', 'The Balance of World Forces' to 'The World in 1975: rich nations and poor nations'. A fair amount of space is devoted to post-1945 events, 1975 being the cut-off year; series of maps illustrate such topics as: the Aftermath of the War in Europe and Southern Asia since Independence 1937–1945. Each plate is accompanied by a commentary from a leading expert. There is a twelve-page chronological synopsis of the major events set out in columns under regional headings, a glossary and an index. *An Atlas of Current Affairs*, by J. F. Horrabin (Gollancz, 5th rev. edn, 1936), was not intended as a substitute for a reference atlas: its purpose was to be a short (168 pages) and simple guide to key facts and places in the pre-Second World War world. Maps illustrate key problems following the Treaty of Versailles such as Germany's eastern frontier and the Polish corridor; the 'Little Entente'; problems of Czechoslovakia, Yugoslavia and Rumania; separatism in Spain; the problems of Indian States; the Rhodesias; and Germany in Africa. *An Atlas of World Affairs*, by Clifford H. MacFadden *et al.* (Thomas Y. Crowell, New York, 1946), intended for American readership in anticipation of US post-war involvement in international affairs, presents a survey in maps, tables and diagrams of political and economic problems of the world at the onset of peace in 1945. A number of historical maps are included to illustrate changes through time and the course of wars and campaigns. Each page of maps is faced by a short essay. There are two lists of current and potential hot spots in Europe and in the rest of the world. *An Atlas of Post War Problems* (Penguin, 1943) is a slim collection of some forty maps illustrating the changes in Europe from 1919, post-First World War colonial problems in India, Africa, the Arab countries and the West Indies, and the emerging problems of poverty and under-development. *An Atlas of World Affairs*, by Andrew Boyd (Methuen, 6th edn, 1970), displays political and economic world problems in maps faced by a short text, covering the period from 1945 to the late 1960s. *The Geography of World Affairs*, by John Peter Cole (Penguin, 1959), discusses a state of world affairs dominated by the East–West struggle. The 2nd and 3rd editions, published in 1963 and 1967, reflect the increasing complexity of the world situation as China, Japan and West Germany re-emerged and economic groupings came into being. Since the 1960s increasing publicity has been given to the demographic, economic and ecological problems facing mankind, and these aspects have been considered in the 5th and latest edition (1979). This is a background reference manual, which includes a historical introduction to world affairs, studies of six selected countries, five major developed regions, six major developing regions and a section devoted to 'world affairs in the future'. There are maps, tables, diagrams and cartoons. The *Current Affairs Atlas*, edited by Donald Paneth (Macmillan, 1979), adopts a thematic approach. The nature of contemporary national issues such as the American political mood, Latin American military regimes, international problems such as arms and the superpowers, rivalry in the Indian

Ocean and terrorism are briefly analysed and illustrated by maps. The *State of the World Atlas*, by Michael Kidron and Ronald Segal (Heinemann, 1981), adopts a similar approach, aiming to demonstrate in sixty-five maps the international preoccupations of states in the 1970s which determine their groupings in opposing blocs. Under a series of arresting headings, the power of nations, the utilization of resources, the resulting industrial and military power and the consequences for society and the environment are displayed. A fourteen-page commentary corresponding to the maps precedes a subject index. Sources with dates are given for the information contained in each map.

14
The United States
R. L. Borthwick

In the case of no political system, except perhaps his own, is the British reader faced with as much information as he is with the US. In part, this reflects the accessibility of the language and the international importance of the country. More important, however, are probably the openness of the society, which facilitates examination and discussion of its political system, and the quantity and productivity of its political scientists, political journalists and politicians. Probably no other political system in the world is exposed to such thorough examination, measurement and analysis.

All of this makes the tasks of writing a chapter such as this essentially one of what to leave out rather than what to include. Accordingly, the works referred to in the following pages can make no claim to being a comprehensive coverage; such a task would require at least this whole volume rather than just a chapter in it. The most that could be claimed is that a series of signposts is offered to the traveller.

Writing on the politics of the US has been characterized not merely by its volume but also by the variety of approaches to the study of the subject. Beginning with a legal/constitutional tradition, the subject has developed through institutional, behavioural and quantitative phases. Whatever the heat generated by the proponents of these various approaches, it seems likely that none has a monopoly on light. The pursuit of theoretical purity has not been matched by explanatory clarity, and it remains true that much of the most influential and useful writing on the subject is not that couched in the most scientific language. Here, as in other areas of political science, the temptation to measure the measurable is not always matched by the importance of what is measured. In part also, the development of the subject is characterized by a faith that a value-free political science is possible. This desire to be non-judgmental, while resting on dubious philosophical premises, has always had to compete with an alternative strand – the reforming mission. Political science is inevitably uncomfortable with the latter notion since it denied desired parallels with the natural sciences, but not for long can such issues be avoided.

To exemplify what has been said about the volume of information available on the US one should begin by considering the official and quasi-official sources of information. Of material published by the American Government itself (see also Chapter 1) perhaps the best known is the text of congressional debates, the *Congressional Record* (US Congress, 1873–), although it notoriously includes (in an Appendix) material not delivered on the floor of either House. Congressional committees are the source of a vast amount of information published under the title of the committee in question as *Hearings* or *Report* (US Congress). Information on the personnel of Congress (and other parts of government) is contained in the *Congressional Directory* (US Congress). The structure of American government (particularly the executive branch) is displayed in the *United States Government Manual*, formerly the *U.S. Government Organization Manual* (National Archives and Record Service). Government publications are listed in *Monthly Catalogue of United States Public Documents* (US Government Printing Office). The decisions of the Supreme Court are published as *United States Reports* (US Government Printing Office, 1875–). Pre-1875 decisions were published under a variety of titles.

The prime non-governmental source is provided by a unique institution, the Congressional Quarterly organization (CQ). Despite its official-sounding name, it is a private organization but one which produces a vast amount of highly reliable information. The best-known of its publications is the *Congressional Quarterly Weekly Report* (1945–), which gives much useful information on all branches of government each week to its subscribers. A distillation of the weekly summaries is published twice-yearly as the *C.Q. Guide to Current American Government*. More substantial are the summaries published under the title of *Congress and The Nation*, the first volume in this series, published in 1965, covered the period 1945–1964; subsequently volumes have been issued to cover each four-year period of Presidential office. Thus Volume II, published in 1969, covers the period 1965–1968 and so on up to Volume 5, published in 1981. A great deal of factual material about Congress is made available in the *Guide to the Congress of the United States* (Congressional Quarterly, 2nd edn, 1976), while information on the legislative output of Congress is published annually in the *Congressional Almanac*. Detailed information on Members of Congress is given in *Politics in America*, edited by A. Ehrenhalt (Congressional Quarterly, 1982). In addition, the organization publishes a wide range of material on other branches of government, on elections and on issues of public policy.

Two other organizations well respected for their publications are the long-established Brookings Institution, generally regarded as a liberal 'think-tank', and the newer and allegedly more conservative American Enterprise Institute for Public Policy Research (AEI). In the case of neither body can the alleged ideological leanings be said to infringe the scholarly and reliable quality of its publications on government. One immensely useful recent publication by the American Enterprise Institute is *Vital Statistics on Congress, 1982*, by J. F. Bibby *et al.* (American Enterprise Institute, 1982).

A useful source of information on Senators and Congressmen and on their States and Districts as well as their committee assignments is *The Almanac of American Politics*, edited by M. Barone *et al.* (Dutton, 1972–). A new edition of this work is published every two years. For those struggling to cope with some of the terms used in American politics, *Safire's Political Dictionary* by W. Safire (Random House, 3rd edn, 1978), may be a source of guidance and consolation. Less idiosyncratic is *The American Political Dictionary*, by J. C. Plano and M. Greenberg (Dryden Press, 4th edn, 1976).

Journals

Foremost among the journals on American politics is the *American Political Science Review* (1906–), though some of its contents are formidably mathematical. Less intimidating on the whole are the *American Journal of Political Science* (1957–), the *Journal of Politics* (1939–) and *Legislative Studies Quarterly* (1976–). Much readable information is contained in *Political Science Quarterly* (1886–), *The Proceedings of the Academy of Political Science* (1910–) and *The Annals of the American Academy of Political and Social Science* (1891–).

Textbooks

Most students of American politics and government probably begin with a textbook on the subject. Traditionally, the market has been dominated by weighty American volumes designed for adoption in American colleges and usually going through several editions. Such volumes have sometimes been criticized for their blandness of style and a too-uncritical acceptance of the American system as the apotheosis of democracy. A superior example of this type of volume is *Government by the People*, by J. M. Burns and J. W. Peltason (Prentice-Hall, 11th edn, 1981): regular updating allows for changes in style and interpretation. More recent examples tend to reflect a greater interest in behaviouralism, as well as a more critical attitude towards the system. Fairly typical are *The Politics of American Democracy*, by M. D. Irish *et al.* (Prentice-Hall, 7th edn, 1981); *Democracy in the United States: Promise and Performance*, by R. A. Dahl (Houghton Mifflin, 4th edn, 1981); *An Introduction to American Government*, by K. Prewitt and S. Verba (Harper and Row, 2nd edn, 1976); and *A More Perfect Union*, by S. C. Patterson *et al.* (Dorsey Press, rev. edn, 1982). The last of these, by three distinguished congressional scholars, incorporates also another modern concern of the discipline – policy analysis. A textbook attempting to incorporate elements of systems analysis and structural-functionalism is *American Politics*, by S. V. Monsma (Dryden Press, 3rd edn, 1976). In textbook form but with a much more sceptical tone is *The Irony of Democracy*, by T. R. Dye and L. H. Zeigler (Duxbury Press, 5th edn, 1981). The subtitle here, 'An Uncommon Introduction to American Politics', gives a hint of the approach which is to challenge pluralist interpretations of the system with an explicitly elitist approach, though the authors are anxious to stress that this approach in itself is intended to convey neither praise nor criticism of the system. An unambiguously critical account of the system is given in *The Perverted Priorities of American Politics*, by D. Lockard (Collier–Macmillan, 2nd edn, 1976). This is a reflective essay which is lively and provocative, and to that extent a useful counterweight to some of the blander offerings. Others offering a radical approach include *The Politics of Power: A Critical Introduction to American Government*, by I. Katznelson and M. Kesselman (Harcourt Brace Jovanovich, 2nd edn, 1979) and *American Politics: Policies Power and Change*, by K. M. Dolbeare and M. J. Edelman (Heath, 4th edn, 1981).

However, British audiences also have textbooks written specifically for them. These have the obvious advantage that the writers are more aware of the needs and assumptions of British readers. Three books in particular deserve notice here: *Politics in the U.S.A.*, by M. J. C. Vile (Hutchinson, 3rd edn, 1983); *The Political System of the United States*, by J. D. Lees (Faber, 3rd edn, 1983); and one that began life as *American Government and Politics*, by A. M. Potter, but now appears under that title by three authors, A. M. Potter, P. Fotheringham and J. G. Kellas (Faber, 3rd edn, 1981). Not strictly textbooks but to be recommended as introductions to the subject are two essays on American politics: *The Nature of American Politics*, by H. G. Nicholas (Oxford University Press, 1980), and *Understanding American Politics*, by R. V. Denenberg (Fontana, 1976). Although much has changed in American politics over the past decade or two, the writing of one earlier British observer retains much of its charm and insight: *An Introduction to American Politics*, by D. W. Brogan (Hamish Hamilton, 1954), can still be read with benefit.

As an alternative to the conventional textbook there is the collection of essays. One of the most useful of these is *The New American Political System*, edited by A. King (American Enterprise Institute, 1978).

History and ideas

An obvious necessity for understanding American politics is some knowledge of American history. While it is clearly impossible to embark on detailed references here it is perhaps worth mentioning one or two of the more general works. A good starting point is *A Concise History of the American Republic*, by S. E. Morison *et al.* (Oxford University Press, 2nd edn, 1983). Of particular value in this context, because it is written for a British audience and specifically for students of politics, is *Vision and Reality: The Evolution of American Government*, by W. Simpson (John Murray, 1978). This provides a clear account of the main themes of American political history.

Two aspects of American history deserve particular attention: the creation and development of the Constitution and the development of political ideas. On the making of the Constitution, the standard account is *The Framing of the Constitution of the United States*, by M. Farrand (Yale University Press, 1913; republished 1962). A more recent account is *The Making of the American Constitution*, by M. Jensen (Van Nostrand, 1964). The development of the Constitution is covered in *A Biography of the Constitution of the United States*, by B. and L. Mitchell (Oxford University Press, 2nd edn, 1975). An innovative interpretation of the development of the American system is *The First New Nation:*

The United States in Historical and Comparative Perspective, by S. M. Lipset (Heinemann, 1964).

The classic interpretation of the values represented by the Constitution remains *The Federalist Papers*, by A. Hamilton *et al.* (Dent, 1961). Written originally to advocate ratification of the document drawn up at Philadelphia in 1787, they remain arguably the chief American claim to a contribution to political thought and certainly the best starting point for an understanding of the values of the American political system. These values have been set out in *Main Currents in American Thought*, by V. L. Parrington (Vols 1–3, Harcourt, Brace and World, 1927). More manageable, however, is the collection of essays, *The American Political Tradition*, by R. Hofstadter (Vintage Books, 1948). This remains a superb introduction to the main themes of American political thinking. Arguably the dominant strand in that thought has been liberalism, and the standard account of this is *The Liberal Tradition in America*, by L. Hartz (Harcourt Brace, 1955). Although written over a quarter of a century ago, it remains an important work; more recent and more controversial is *American Politics: the Promise of Disharmony*, by S. P. Huntington (Harvard University Press, 1981). This work raises important questions about the nature of the American experience and draws attention to the gap between American ideals and reality and the tension which this creates, especially in what the author calls 'periods of creedal passion'. Explicitly conservative approaches are dealt with in *Conservatism in America*, by C. Rossiter (Heinemann, 1955).

Much debate has taken place over the issue of elitism versus pluralism in American politics. The Constitution itself was subject to a classic quasi-Marxist interpretation in *An Economic Interpretation of the Constitution*, by C. A. Beard (Macmillan, 1913; reprinted Free Press, 1965); in turn, the classic responses to Beard are *Charles Beard and the Constitution*, by R. E. Brown (Princeton University Press, 1956), and *We the People: The Economic Origins of the Constitution*, by F. McDonald (Chicago University Press, 1958).

More recently the standard statement of the elitist interpretation of American politics has been *The Power Elite*, by C. W. Mills (Oxford University Press, 1956); this was followed by an influential article by P. Bachrach and M. Baratz, 'The Two Faces of Power', *American Political Science Review* (1962) and by *Who Rules America?*, by G. W. Domhoff (Prentice-Hall, 1967). These last two were explicit attempts to refute the pluralist interpretation set out in such works as *Who Governs?*, by R. A. Dahl (Yale University Press, 1961), and *Community Power and Political*

Theory, by N. W. Polsby (Yale University Press, 1963). For a response by Polsby, see *Community Power and Political Theory: a Further Look at Problems of Evidence and Inference*, by N. W. Polsby (Yale University Press, rev. edn, 1980). The subject of elites is considered also in *The Ruling Elites: Elite Theory, Power and American Democracy*, by K. Prewitt and A. Stone (Harper and Row, 1973).

Interest groups

The natural extension of this debate is, of course, the study of interest (or pressure) groups in American politics (see also Chapter 6). The forerunner here was *The Process of Government*, by A. F. Bentley (University of Chicago Press, 1908; republished Harvard University Press, 1967), but the modern study of the subject may be said to have begun with *The Governmental Process*, by D. B. Truman (Knopf, 1951). The subject is one that has produced much controversy; for example, *The Semi-Sovereign People*, by E. E. Schattshneider (Holt Rinehart and Winston, 1960): one provocative recent view is *The End of Liberalism*, by T. Lowi (Norton, 2nd edn, 1979). Those who view groups as central to the system have perhaps tended to overestimate the amount of balance in the system; an accusation that could not be levelled against some of the works mentioned in the previous paragraph, nor against C. E. Lindblom, in his *Politics and Markets* (Basic Books, 1977). The assumption that all voices are heard in the system is less uncritically accepted nowadays. Empirical studies have tended to concentrate on the obvious areas like business; for example, *American Business and Public Policy*, by R. Bauer *et al.* (Prentice-Hall, 1964), or trade unions; for example *Unions in American National Politics*, by G. K. Wilson (Macmillan, 1979). More recently attention has focused on the growth of public interest groups; a topic dealt with in *Lobbying for the People*, by J. M. Best (Princeton University Press, 1977), and in *Power and Protest in American Life*, by A. Barbrook and C. Bolt (Martin Robertson, 1980). More general studies of groups are *The Washington Lobbyists*, by L. W. Milbrath (Rand-McNally, 1963), *Politics, Parties and Pressure Groups*, by V. O. Key (Crowell, 5th edn, 1968), and *Pressure Groups in American Politics*, by H. R. Mahood (Scribners, 1967). Two of the most up-to-date introductions to the subject are *Interest Groups in the United States*, by G. K. Wilson (Oxford University Press, 1981), and *Interest Groups, Lobbying and Policymaking*, by N. Ornstein and S. Elder (Congressional Quarterly, 1978).

Political parties and elections

Some commentators have seen the rise of interest groups, particularly the so-called single-interest groups, as one side of a coin whose other is the decline of political parties. Even before that, however, American political parties had rarely matched up to the expectations of European, and even some American, observers. In part this was because American parties seemed to lack the ideological clarity which their European counterparts were assumed to possess, in part because they developed at local level machine-like qualities which offended some observers. One of the most celebrated expressions of American concern about their party system is contained in the American Political Science Association Report, *Towards a More Responsible Two-Party System* (American Political Science Association, 1950). The Committee of the Association which produced that Report was chaired by E. E. Scattschneider, who had made some of the same arguments about the need for disciplined parties in his *Party Government* (Rinehart, 1942). Less critical of the system have been some of the standard accounts of the party system, for example, Key (1968, work cited), *Parties and Politics in America*, by C. Rossiter (Cornell University Press, 1960), and *The American Party Systems*, edited by W. N. Chambers and W. D. Burnham (Oxford University Press, 2nd edn, 1975).

One of the factors that makes it difficult (indeed impossible) for American political parties to resemble closely their British counterparts is the system of separation of powers, or, to be more accurate, the separation of personnel between executive and legislative branches. The consequences of this separation, as viewed in the 1960s, are explored in *The Deadlock of Democracy*, by J. M. Burns (John Calder, 1964). The subtitle of this work, 'Four-Party Politics in America', gives a better clue to its thesis that each of the major parties has a presidential and a congressional wing with different attitudes, constituencies and aspirations.

Until recently it could be argued that the party system that has dominated modern American history was that created either side of 1932. Arguably, 1932 was the last great realigning election: though commentators, especially in the Republican Party, are constantly searching for the next. The elections of 1972 and 1980 from that point of view have both heralded false dawns. The idea that certain elections are 'critical' is dealt with in *Critical Elections and the Mainsprings of American Politics*, by W. D. Burnham (Norton, 1970); the topic of realignment is discussed also in *Dynamics of the Party System*, by J. L. Sundquist (Brookings Institution, 1973). Of equal concern in recent years has been the decay of parties as institutions, as evidenced in their decline as determinants of voter behaviour or candidate selection. Among the literature which covers this area is *The Party's Over*, by D. S. Broder (Harper and Row, 1971); *Curing the Mischiefs of Faction: Party Reform in America*, by A. Ranney (University of California Press, 1975); *Transformations of the American Party System*, by E. C. Ladd and C. D. Hadley (Norton, 1975); and *American Parties in Decline*, by W. J. Crotty and G. C. Jacobsen (Little, Brown, 1980).

Among the general surveys of American parties are *Party Politics in America*, by F. J. Sorauf (Little, Brown, 4th edn, 1980), and *Political Parties in American Society*, by S. J. Eldersveld (Basic Books, 1982). Reflections on some aspects of the contemporary problems of parties are contained in *Political Parties in the Eighties*, edited by R. A. Goldwin (American Enterprise Institute, 1980). A bibliography on political parties is *American Political Parties*, by L. R. Wynar (Libraries Unlimited, 1969).

Changes in the operation of political parties reflect, of course, changes in the behaviour of the electorate. The classic study of the American electorate has long been *The American Voter*, by A. Campbell *et al.* (Wiley, 1960). This study, one in a series produced by the Michigan Survey Research Center, dealt with the voter as he was behaving in the heyday of the modern party system. The changes in that behaviour are better reflected in the appropriately titled *The Changing American Voter*, by N. H. Nie *et al.* (Harvard University Press, 1976), and also in *Voters' Choice*, by G. M. Pomper (Harper and Row, 1975). Some of the factors that are important in voting are explored in *The Political Beliefs of Americans*, by L. A. Free and H. Cantril (Rutgers University Press, 1967). A discussion of the issues affecting the electorate still of interest is *The Real Majority*, by R. J. Scammon and B. J. Wattenberg (Coward-McCann, 1970).

A good general introduction to American elections is *Elections in America*, by G. M. Pomper with S. S. Lederman (Longman, 2nd edn, 1980). The process by which Americans choose their President is covered best in *Presidential Elections*, by N. W. Polsby and A. B. Wildavsky (Scribners, 5th edn, 1980). This is also the subject of *The Road to the White House*, by S. J. Wayne (St Martin's Press, 1980). These works reflect the changes that have taken place in the last decade or so in the way in which Presidential candidates are nominated and in the nature of elections generally but particularly the Presidential election, following the work of the McGovern –Fraser Committee in the Democratic Party.

There has been a significant increase in the use of primary elections for the selection of delegates to the Party Conventions and at the same time a number of other changes relating to the rules about the selection of delegates to the Conventions, as well as important changes in the financing of Presidential elections. These changes are succinctly dealt with in an article by G. M. Pomper, 'New Rules and New Games in Presidential Nominations', *Journal of Politics*, **3** (1979). The standard work on the Party Conventions themselves has traditionally been *The Politics of National Party Conventions*, by P. David *et al*. (Vintage Books, rev. edn, 1964). No aspect of the American electoral process strikes the outsider as more curious, and none is more resistant to change, than the Electoral College. Two works which explain both the rationale for the institution and arguments for change are *Voting for President: The Electoral College and the American Political System*, by W. S. Sayre and J. H. Parris (Brookings Institution, 1970), and *The Case Against Direct Election of the President*, by J. Best (Cornell University Press, 1975). As noted above, an area where change has occurred, however, is in the financing of elections; this topic is dealt with in *Financing Politics: Money, Elections and Political Reform*, by H. Alexander (Congressional Quarterly, 1976); *Parties, Interest Groups and Campaign Finance Laws*, edited by M. J. Malbin (American Enterprise Institute, 1980); and in an issue of *The Annals of the American Academy of Political and Social Science* (No.425, 1976) entitled 'Political Finance: Reform and Reality'. Another feature of recent elections is covered in *The Rise of Political Consultants: New Ways of Winning Elections*, by L. J. Sabato (Basic Books, 1981).

Within the field of elections one growth area is the study of particular elections. The modern fashion here was set in 1961 with the publication of *The Making of the President, 1960*, by T. H. White (Pocket Books, 1961). Although White produced similar volumes for each of the next three Presidential elections, none achieved quite the success of the first. A view of the Nixon campaign of 1968 that attracted much attention is *The Selling of the President, 1968*, by J. McGinnis (Trident Press, 1969). For many, no doubt, the election of 1960 must seem like ancient history, and their concern instead will be with the most recent election. Among the studies of the 1980 election are *Portrait of an Election*, by E. Drew (Routledge and Kegan Paul, 1981), which is a perceptive account drawn from the author's writings for *The New Yorker* and reflecting something of the longwindedness associated with that source; *The American Elections of 1980*, edited by A. Ranney (American Enterprise Institute, 1981); and *Change and Continuity in the 1980 Elections*, by P. Abramson *et al*. (Congressional Quarterly, 1982).

The Presidency and the executive branch

There would not be much argument that the dominant feature of modern American politics is the Presidency. It is at once the focus of attention within the country and that aspect of the system which personifies American politics to the foreign observer. The literature on the subject is indeed formidable; one convenient starting-point is *Evolution of the Modern Presidency: A Bibliographical Survey*, by F. I. Greenstein *et al.* with D. Lidtke (American Enterprise Institute, 1977).

It is perhaps as well to remember that the notion of the President as the focus of the whole political system is largely something which has developed in the last half-century. For a somewhat longer perspective, see *The President: Office and Powers 1787–1957*, by E. S. Corwin (New York University Press, 1957) and *American Presidents and the Presidency*, by M. Cunliffe (Fontana, 1972). It would not be too much to argue that the Presidency of F. D. Roosevelt saw a transformation of the office into one where the responsibility for providing a legislative programme and attempting to secure its implementation became an inescapable part of the job. Before Roosevelt, some Presidents had acted in that way but many had not; after Roosevelt, they no longer had the choice. In short, Roosevelt created the modern Presidency which has become both an object of hope and a target for blame for the American people, and as part of the transformation he helped to institutionalize the Presidency, so that the office became more than merely the extension of particular personalities. Roosevelt's own efforts are covered in *The Lion and the Fox*, by J. M. Burns (Harcourt Brace and World Inc., 1956). The flavour of the Presidency under Roosevelt's successor can be gained from Truman's own account, *Memoirs*, by H. S. Truman (Vols 1–2, Signet, 1965). The best account of the Eisenhower Presidency is now to be found in *The Hidden-Hand Presidency: Eisenhower as Leader*, by F. I. Greenstein (Basic Books, 1982).

For at least twenty years after the Second World War the Presidency was seen as the great hope of liberals who wished to achieve change in American politics. The President was seen with some accuracy as representing urban, industrial America, and this was translated as meaning that he alone represented the national interest. Yet it seemed that the President lacked much of the power which this role demanded of him. The classic statement of this view, that the power of the President was merely the power to persuade, was first published in 1960, *Presidential Power: The Politics of Leadership*, by R. E. Neustadt (Wiley, rev. edn, 1980).

What might be called the Roosevelt–Truman–Kennedy version of the Presidency and of Presidential studies was severely dented by the twin blows of the Vietnam war and Watergate. The fate of liberal intentions in relation to Vietnam is well portrayed in *The Best and the Brightest*, by D. Halberstam (Random House, 1972). The changing future of the Presidency and of perceptions of it in this period gave rise to a work which has become synonymous with a certain style of the office, *The Imperial Presidency*, by A. M. Schlesinger (Houghton Mifflin, 1973). Schlesinger was concerned to argue that the Presidency had escaped from the restrictions placed on it and that it was, in effect, out of control. While hindsight may enable us to be more optimistic, Schlesinger's view, given the circumstances of the time, made a great deal of sense. A similar view was taken by other observers, for example, *Presidential Power and Accountability: Towards a New Constitution*, by C. M. Hardin (University of Chicago Press, 1974), and *The Twilight of the Presidency*, by G. Reedy (New American Library, 1970). Mr Reedy had had the advantage of observing the Johnson Administration at close quarters. An insider from the Kennedy era produced an assessment of the Presidency in the light of Watergate, *Watchmen in the Night: Presidential Accountability and Watergate*, by T. C. Sorensen (MIT Press, 1975). The events of Watergate itself are readably described in the well-known *All the President's Men*, by B. Woodward and C. Bernstein (Quartet Books, 1974). The flavour of the Nixon White House is displayed in the transcript of the notorious recordings of conversations there, *The White House Transcripts* (Bantam Books, 1974); while the Congressional consideration of the possible impeachment of President Nixon is available in *The Impeachment Report* (New American Library, 1974).

Since the mid-1970s concern has switched from the strength of the Presidency to its apparent weakness: titles like *The Tethered Presidency*, edited by T. M. Franck (New York University Press, 1981), reflect this change. Franck's book deals with increased Congressional efforts to deal with Executive power, a topic referred to later. One of the most readable assessments of the contemporary state of the Presidency is *All Things To All Men*, by G. Hodgson (Weidenfeld and Nicolson, 1980), in which the author argues that the Presidency presents us with a paradox: an office with immense power whose holder is relatively impotent. This model of the office seemed to fit well the style of Presidents Ford and Carter; to what extent they adopted the style from choice or necessity is a matter for argument, but even President Reagan, while attempting to restore some of the lost 'imperial' style, has had to adjust to new realities. His first year in office looks likely to prove his most successful; it is described in *President and Congress, Assessing Reagan's First Year*, edited by N. Ornstein (American Enterprise Institute, 1982).

Through the vicissitudes of the Presidency some books have survived; for example, one which was first published in 1964, *The Chief Executive*, by L. W. Koenig (Harcourt Brace Jovanovich, 4th edn, 1981); while others have appeared for the first time. Among these are *The State of the Presidency*, by T. E. Cronin (Little, Brown, 2nd edn, 1980); *The American Presidency*, by R. M. Pious (Basic Books, 1979); and *Presidential Power and American Democracy*, by P. Strum (Goodyear, 1979). Among the collections of essays on the Presidency are *Perspectives on the Presidency*, edited by A. B. Wildavsky (Little, Brown, 1975) and *The Illustion of Presidential Government*, edited by H. Heclo and L. M. Salamon (Westview Press, 1981). The Vice-Presidency, long regarded in an unfavourable light by both occupants and observers, has been taken a little more seriously in recent years, and the office is dealt with in *The Modern American Vice Presidency*, by J. L. Goldstein (Princeton University Press, 1982).

Beyond the Presidency itself lies not only the Executive Office of the President (an area of great growth in modern times) but also the whole of the Federal Government. Some of the problems of the former are examined in *Organizing the Presidency*, by S. Hess (Brookings Institution, 1976) and in *The Institutionalized Presidency*, by N. C. Thomas and H. W. Baade (Oceana, 1972). The problems of the Executive branch more widely interpreted are discussed in *Politics, Position and Power*, by H. Seidman (Oxford University Press, 3rd edn, 1980) and in *A Government of Strangers*, by H. Heclo (Brookings Institution, 1977). A useful study of decision making is *The Policy-Making Process*, by C. E. Lindblom (Prentice-Hall, 1968). One aspect of administration is dealt with in *The Politics of the Budgetary Process*, by A. B. Wildavsky (Little, Brown, 3rd edn, 1979). An important feature of the modern Presidency is the Office of Management and Budget. For the rise to prominence of this, see *The Office of Management and Budget and the Presidency, 1921–1979*, by L. Berman (Princeton University Press, 1979).

One of the most crucial determinants of the success of a President is his relations with Congress. One starting point here might be *Congress and the Presidency*, by N. W. Polsby (Prentice-Hall, 3rd edn, 1976); however, a good part of this is really devoted to each institution separately. One of the most notable features of the relationship between President and Congress in recent years has been the development of a formal system of liaison; this is the subject of *Legislative Liaison: Executive Leadership in Congress*, by A. Holtzman (Rand-McNally, 1970). Relations between the two branches are discussed in *The Politics of Shared Powers: Congress and the Executive*, by L. Fisher (Congressional Quarterly, 1981). Some of the policy implications of the relationship are dealt with in *The Legislative Presidency*, by S. J. Wayne (Harper and Row, 1978); *Presidential Influence in Congress*, by G. C. Edwards (Freeman, 1980); and *Congress, The Bureaucracy, and Public Policy*, by R. B. Ripley and G. A. Franklin (Dorsey Press, 1980). A major change in the relationship in the past decade has been the greater willingness of Congress to assert its influence, a topic dealt with in *The Decline and Resurgence of Congress*, by J. L. Sundquist (Brookings Institution, 1981).

Congress

Congress itself has become the subject of a great deal of attention in recent years. As a subject of study, Congress possesses obvious advantages compared with some other aspects of the system: its work is relatively open (and has become much more so in the past fifteen years) and its members sufficiently numerous and diverse to make study of their activity rewarding. Perhaps the most famous study of Congress is *Congressional Government*, by W. Wilson (Johns Hopkins University Press, 1981). First published in 1885, it has survived remarkably well and still provides a convenient starting point for the study of the subject. Of course, Congress has changed many times in the course of the century since Woodrow Wilson wrote; a sense of some of those changes is conveyed very concisely in *The Congress and America's Future*, edited by D. B. Truman (Prentice-Hall, 2nd edn, 1973). A quite different kind of introduction to the subject is the bibliography: *The United States Congress*, by R. U. Goehlert and J. R. Sayre (Free Press, 1981).

Writing on Congress in the 1950s and 1960s tended either to be very critical of the shortcomings of the institution or more sympathetic (either explicitly or implicitly) as political scientists sought to avoid value judgements on the material they were observing. This tendency was enhanced by the fact that many of those writing did so from close-hand observation, and thus perhaps subtly became part of the same value systems they were describing. Notorious as an over-sympathetic picture, though not by a political scientist, is *Citadel: The Story of the U.S. Senate*, by W. S. White (Harper, 1957). Among the most trenchant critics of what one might call the 'old-style' Congress were some members of the institution itself, notably Senator Clark, *Congress: The Sapless Branch*, by J. S. Clark (Harper and Row, rev. edn, 1965), and Congressman Bolling, *House Out of Order*, by R. Bolling (Dutton, 1965), and *Power in the House*, by R. Bolling (Dutton, 1968).

Many of the criticisms made in works like this have been met. The changes that have taken place in the procedure, composition and ethos of Congress in the period since about 1970 have been very considerable. Among the most important of these changes has been the shift in power away from the chairmen of standing committees, particularly in the House of Representatives, towards the membership of the committee as a whole, subcommittees, the party caucus or the party leadership. At the same time, some chairmen were voted out of office by their party colleagues in the Democratic Party in the House, others were defeated in elections, while others disgraced themselves or simply became too old. The passage of time also moved more Northern Democrats into positions of power at the expense of their Southern colleagues, and there was a substantial turnover in the membership of both Houses. All these together mean that Congress today is very different from the Congress of even the late 1960s. That is not to say that it is necessarily a more effective body, merely that it behaves in a more open way and with much less regard for the old norms of deference and apprenticeship. In short, power has become much more evenly distributed within the institution.

The best picture of the Senate before the changes of recent years is in *U.S. Senators and Their World*, by D. R. Matthews (University of North Carolina Press, 1960). This remains a superb piece of work, but for more recent information on the Senate the reader should consult *The New Senate*, by M. Foley (Yale University Press, 1980). For a view of the Senate written almost midway between these two, see *Power in the Senate*, by R. B. Ripley (St Martin's Press, 1969).

Some of the most useful work on the House of Representatives has been available in the successive editions of *New Perspectives on the House of Representatives*, edited by R. L. Peabody and N. W. Polsby (Rand-McNally, 3rd edn, 1977). One of the best short introductions to Congress is *Congress: The Electoral Connection*, by D. R. Mayhew (Yale University Press, 1974). An important part of Mayhew's thesis, that the main objective of members of Congress is to secure re-election, is examined in *Congress: Keystone of the Washington Establishment*, by M. P. Fiorina (Yale University Press, 1977). An earlier taste of relations between a congressman and his constituents is given in *Member of the House: Letters of a Congressman* by C. Miller (Scribners, 1962). A more systematic study is *Home Style: House Members in their Districts*, by R. F. Fenno (Little, Brown, 1978).

The most celebrated feature of Congress is probably its committee system. Among the important studies of committees are those of the Ways and Means Committee, *The Politics of Finance*, by J. F. Manley (Little, Brown, 1970), and of the Appropriations Committees, *The Power of the Purse*, by R. F. Fenno (Little, Brown, 1966). The best study of congressional committees as a whole is *Congressmen in Committees*, by R. F. Fenno (Little, Brown, 1973). Here, Fenno convincingly demonstrates the diversity of such committees, helping thereby to undermine some of the stereotypes. Since Fenno's work much of the writing has been concerned with changes in the committees; a useful compilation of ideas about reform is contained in an issue of *The Annals of the American Academy of Political and Social Science* (No.411, 1974), devoted to 'Changing Congress: The Committee System'. The fate of some of that reform effort in the mid-1970s is examined in *Congress Against Itself*, by R. H. Davidson and W. J. Oleszek (Indiana University Press, 1977).

The legislative procedure of Congress is explained in *The Congressional Process: Strategies, Rules and Procedures*, by L. A. Froman (Little, Brown, 1967) and in *Congressional Procedures and the Policy Process*, by W. J. Oleszek (Congressional Quarterly, 1978); the problems of actually getting a bill through Congress are well portrayed in *The Dance of Legislation*, by E. Redman (Simon and Schuster, 1973). Two aspects of Congress that have attracted much criticism in the past are the seniority system and the Rules Committee. As we have seen, the seniority system has been at least dented; the system at its height is examined in *The Seniority System in Congress*, by B. Hinckley (Indiana University Press, 1971). The Rules Committee, too, has been much modified in recent years to bring it effectively under the control of the majority party leadership; the Committee is the subject of *Rulemakers of the House*, by S. M. Matsunaga and P. Chen (University of Illinois Press, 1976).

Among the most useful of the more wide-ranging work on Congress are *The New Congress*, edited by T. E. Mann and N. J. Ornstein (American Enterprise Institute, 1981); *Congress Reconsidered*, edited by L. C. Dodd and B. I. Oppenheimer (Congressional Quarterly, 2nd edn, 1981); *The United States Congress*, by C. O. Jones (Dorsey Press, 1982); and *Leadership in Congress*, by R. L. Peabody (Little, Brown, 1976).

Attention has already been drawn to the efforts made by Congress in recent years to provide a greater check on the Executive branch (see the works cited above by Ripley and Franklin, 1980, Fisher, 1980 and Sundquist, 1981). This area is dealt with also in *Congress against The President*, edited by H. C. Mansfield (Harper and Row, 1975) and in *Congress and the Administrative State*, by L. C. Dodd and R. L. Schott (Wiley, 1979). One of the topics dealt with in these two works is the change in congressional budget procedure. This is the subject of *The Fiscal Congress: Legislative Control of the Budget*, by L. T. LeLoup (Greenwood Press, 1980) and of *Congress and Money: Budgeting, Spending and Taxing*, by A. Schick (Urban Institute, 1980). These are also particular aspects of a wider issue; the exercise of Congressional oversight, a topic dealt with in *Congress Oversees the Bureaucracy*, by M. Ogul (University of Pittsburgh Press, 1976). Another important feature of change in Congress in recent years has been the enormous growth in congressional staff. Their role is discussed in *Congressional Staffs: The Invisible Force in American Lawmaking*, by H. W. Fox and S. W. Hammond (Free Press, 1977) and in *Unelected Representatives: Congressional Staff and the Future of Representative Government*, by M. J. Malbin (Basic Books, 1980).

Finally in this section a useful work of comparison is *Parliament and Congress*, by K. Bradshaw and D. Pring (Quartet, 1973). This was republished with an additional chapter (Quartet, 1982).

The Supreme Court

The esteem in which President and Congress are held by the American public has declined over recent years: cynicism about politicians has grown in the US as it has elsewhere. One branch of government has escaped this, the judicial; thereby providing the irony that its embodiment in the Supreme Court should be the most popular branch while being the only one that is not popularly elected.

A good introduction to the historical development of the Court is *The American Supreme Court*, by R. G. McCloskey (University of Chicago Press, 1960). More detail on the impact of the Court on the Constitution can be found in *The Constitution and What it Means Today*, by E. S. Corwin (Princeton University Press, 14th edn, 1978), and in *Historic Decisions of the Supreme Court*, by C. B. Swisher (Van Nostrand, 2nd edn, 1969).

Perhaps the most useful approach to the contemporary Court is through *The Politics of the US Supreme Court*, by R. Hodder-

Williams (Allen and Unwin, 1980). Other general surveys include *Courts, Judges, and Politics*, by W. F. Murphy and C. H. Pritchett (Random House, 2nd edn, 1974); *The Supreme Court in American Politics: Judicial Activism vs. Judicial Restraint*, edited by D. F. Forte (Heath, 1972); *American Constitutional Law*, by M. Shapiro and R. J. Tresolini (Macmillan, 5th edn, 1979); and *The Supreme Court*, by L. Baum (Congressional Quarterly, 1981). Some useful reflections on the Court are to be found in *The Role of the Supreme Court in American Government*, by A. Cox (Oxford University Press, 1976).

One of the most readable books dealing with the Court is *Gideon's Trumpet*, by A. Lewis (Random House, 1964). This deals with one of the many controversial cases to come before the Court in recent years. For consideration of some of the issues raised by the Warren and Burger Courts, see *The Least Dangerous Branch: the Supreme Court at the Bar of Politics*, by A. M. Bickel (Bobbs-Merrill, 1962); *Government by Judiciary*, by R. Berger (Harvard University Press, 1977); *Constitutional Counterrevolution?* by R. Y. Funston (Shenkman, 1977); *Continuity and Change: From the Warren Court to the Burger Court*, by S. L. Wasby (Goodyear, 1976); and *Politics, The Constitution and the Warren Court*, by P. B. Kurland (University of Chicago Press, 1970). Defenders of the Court have seen it as struggling to deal with social problems and issues of individual freedom which the other branches have lacked the courage to tackle. Its critics have charged it with poor legal reasoning, paying scant regard to the restraints of the Constitution and of pandering to fashionable social theories. Behind the debate lie not only arguments about activism versus restraint or liberalism versus conservatism but also a dispute about the essence of the Court's role; making law or discovering it. Among work that deals with the Court's involvement in some of these areas of controversy is *Freedom and the Court: Civil Rights and Liberties in the United States*, by H. J. Abraham (Oxford University Press, 4th edn, 1982).

The relations between the Court and the other branches of government are discussed in *Congress and the Court*, by W. F. Murphy (University of Chicago Press, 1962); *The Supreme Court and Congress: Conflict and Interaction 1945–1968*, by J. R. Schmidhauser and L. L. Berg (Free Press, 1972); *The Supreme Court and the Presidency*, by R. Scigliano (Free Press, 1971); and *The President and the Supreme Court*, by J. D. Lees (British Association for American Studies Pamphlet No.3, 1980). Finally, at the level of superior gossip is *The Bretheren*, by B. Woodward and S. Armstrong (Simon and Schuster, 1979).

State and local government

One of the most significant facts about the US is that it is a federal system. One introduction is *The Structure of American Federalism*, by M. J. C. Vile (Oxford University Press, 1961); an alternative perspective is provided in *Federalism: A View from the States*, by D. Elazar (Crowell, 2nd edn, 1972). General studies of the subject include *Understanding Intergovernmental Relations*, by D. Wright (Duxbury Press, 2nd edn, 1981), and *American Federalism*, by R. Leach (Norton, 1970). Some of the problems in the system are dealt with in *Making Federalism Work*, by J. L. Sundquist (Brookings Institution, 1969). Much rhetoric has been devoted by recent Republican Presidents to the need to adjust the federal balance in favour of the States; both Presidents Nixon and Reagan have had plans for a new federal balance. The best introduction to this debate is provided by *The New Federalism*, by M. D. Reagan and J. C. Sanzone (Oxford University Press, 2nd edn, 1981).

The standard work on the constituent parts of the federal system for a long time was *American State Politics*, by V. O. Key (Knopf, 1956). Inevitably, it is now somewhat dated. More up to date are *The Maligned States: their accomplishments, problems and opportunities*, by I. Sharkansky (McGraw-Hill, 1972) and *State and Local Government* by M. S. Stedman (Little, Brown, 3rd edn, 1982). A recent study of a particular state is *The Government and Politics of New York State*, by J. F. Zimmerman (New York University Press, 1981). American State Government has developed enormously in the post-war period. This is reflected in *Goodbye to Good-Time Charlie: The American Governor Transformed 1950–1975*, by L. J. Sabato (Heath, 1978).

The study of local politics and government has tended, for understandable reasons, to concentrate on the cities. An introduction to this field is *City Politics*, by J. Q. Wilson and E. C. Banfield (Harvard University Press, 1963). Some of the policy issues involved are discussed in *Urban Politics and Public Policy*, by R. Linberry and I. Sharkansky (Harper and Row, 1974). A useful brief discussion of some of the issues involved in urban politics is *The Metropolitan Mosaic*, by P. Davies (British Association for American Studies Pamphlet No.4, 1980). Inevitably, much of the concern of urban government is with difficult social problems. Problems of a different sort were provided by the party machines that in the past ran many of the big cities. Widely regarded as a near-extinct species, one of the last survivors is, or was, to be found in Chicago. A hostile, but very readable account of Chicago under Mayor Daley is to be found in *Boss*, by M. Royko (Paladin,

1972). A more serious and more balanced study of the same phenomenon is to be found in the splendidly titled *Don't Make No Waves – Don't Back No Losers*, by M. L. Rakove (Indiana University Press, 1975). Mention should also be made here of works cited earlier by Dahl (1961) and Polsby (1963).

Foreign policy

Particularly in the period since 1945, the content and conduct of American foreign policy has been of interest and importance to the whole world. It is not possible here to do justice to the enormous literature on the subject. The following, however, may be regarded as starting points for further exploration. A reliable introduction is provided by *American Foreign Policy Since World War II*, by J. Spanier (Holt Rinehart and Winston, 8th edn, 1980). A crucial period in the development of America's position in the world is covered in *Rise to Globalism: American Foreign Policy since 1938*, by S. E. Ambrose (Penguin, 1971). No area of modern American foreign policy has been more argued about than her part in the emergence of the Cold War; a useful study of this area is *America, Russia and the Cold War, 1945–1966*, by W. LaFeber (Wiley, 1967). An introduction to foreign policy from a different angle is provided by two works whose subject matter in each case is apparent from the titles: *The Ideas of American Foreign Policy*, by M. Donelan (Chapman and Hall, 1963) and *Architects of Illusion: Men and Ideas in American Foreign Policy*, by L. C. Gardner (Quadrangle Books, 1970).

A great deal of information about the foreign affairs of the US is provided in two annual series published by the Council of Foreign Relations: *Documents on American Foreign Relations* and *The United States in World Affairs*. The procedures for the making and control of American foreign policy are matters of some interest. The former is covered in *How American Foreign Policy is Made*, by J. Spanier and E. M. Uslaner (Holt Rinehart and Winston, 2nd edn, 1978); *The Politics of Policy Making in Defense and Foreign Affairs*, by R. Hilsman (Harper and Row, 1971); *Congress, the Executive and Foreign Policy*, by F. O. Wilcox (Harper and Row, 1971); and *Congress, the Presidency and American Foreign Policy*, edited by J. Spanier and J. Nogel (Pergamon, 1981). The process over the past twenty years has been characterized by ambiguity as to whether foreign policy was being made in, and conducted by, the State Department or by the National Security Council, and in particular the President's National Security Adviser. Control is dealt with primarily by the two Houses of Congress, who take a more active part in foreign affairs than possibly any other representative assembly. A recent study of their work in this field is *Foreign Policy by Congress*, by T. M. Franck and E. Weisband (Oxford University Press, 1979).

Americans used to be characterized by their faith in their way of life, by their moral support for their institutions and by their wealth of natural resources. They have experienced a decade or more of growing doubts about all of these things. The title of one of the most famous studies of American values, *The People of Plenty: Economic Abundance and the American Character*, by D. M. Potter (Phoenix Books, 1954), now seems to have a distinctly ironic air about it. Questions about the limited nature of natural resources and the limited nature of her power in the world have induced a mood of greater pessimism among her citizens. Some of these are reflected in D. Bell, 'The End of American Exceptionalism' in *The American Commonwealth, 1976*, edited by N. Glazer and I. Kristol (Basic Books, 1976). Yet despite all that, the US remains a resilient political system and one that retains enormous capacity to fascinate those who wish to explore it via the literature on the subject.

15
Central and Southern America
Kenneth N. Medhurst and J. Pearce

Introduction

In tackling our subject we have been mindful of a number of important considerations. First, we are conscious of the great predominance in the English-language literature of North American contributions. There are significant contributions from British scholars but the pace has frequently been set by North Americans. This partly reflects the importance of Americans within the political science community, but also the US's very real political, economic, military and cultural involvement in the Western hemisphere. We are also conscious that a substantial portion of the literature reflects and follows hard upon particular crises within the area in which the US has had specific policy interests at stake. Thus one of our themes will be the impact of these concerns upon academic debate. In addition, alternative viewpoints or interpretations often come, at least in part, as reactions to the prevailing orthodoxies within the US. Academic debate in the field proceeds through a 'dialogue' between current North American fashions and challenges to those fashions from within the US or elsewhere. For example, the Cuban revolution inspired a substantial literature as well as provoking fresh thought and activity with reference to other parts of the region. The same would be true of events following upon the Brazilian military *coup* (1964), the Peruvian military *coup* (1968), Allende's short-lived regime in Chile (1970 –1973) and recent Central American upheavals. Our discussion then trys to chart academic responses to these developments. One problem about all this is that an event such as Castro's revolution may engender such a massive literature that the question of selectivity becomes unusually acute. We have had to make our own assessment of what is most valuable and durable and what may be excluded because of its ephemeral or highly partisan qualities. Conversely, there are issues and indeed whole countries which, given the way fashions have gone, receive scant treatment.

We will, given shortage of space, focus on full-length book studies rather than articles or collected essays except where these are of special importance. However, for readers coming to the field for the first time, we would recommend the following books: *Political Forces in Latin America: Dimensions of the Quest for Stability*, edited by B. G. Burnett and Kenneth Johnson (Wadsworth, 1970); *Latin America: The Struggle with Dependency and Beyond*, edited by R. H. Chilcote and J. C. Edelstein (Schenkman, 1974); *Political Power in Latin America*, R. R. Fagen and W. A. Cornelius (Prentice-Hall, 1970); *Authoritarianism and Corporatism in Latin America*, edited by J. M. Malloy (University of Pittsburgh Press, 1977); and *The New Authoritarianism in Latin America*, edited by D. Collier (Princeton University Press, 1979).

The first relatively serious and systematic treatment of Latin American politics came in the 1940s and 1950s from a generation of primarily North American scholars who were concerned to evaluate Latin America largely in terms of its apparent inability to throw up durable liberal–democratic institutions. They assumed that North American liberal democracy constituted a norm and that their job as political scientists was to identify institutions or practices approximating to North American counterparts and explain why they were failing to match up to the Anglo-Saxon model. For example, P. A. Gomez, 'Latin American Executives: Essence and Variations', *Journal of Inter-American Studies,* **III** (1961), talks of the Executive branch in these general terms. Likewise, 'The Party Potpourri in Latin America' by R. Fitzgibbon, *Western Political Quarterly,* **10,** No.1, 3–22 (March 1957), draws from the US experience, paying special attention to political parties that were identified as necessarily positive contributors to the 'progress of democracy'. A final example might be *Church and State in Latin America: A History of Politico – Ecclesiastical Relations*, by J. Lloyd Mecham (University of North Carolina Press, 2nd edn, 1966), who wrote a 'classic' on Church–State relations based on the general assumption that the US model of the separation of the Church and the State was necessarily appropriate for a would-be democracy. These assumptions distracted attention from the distinctive historical experience from which the structures under review had sprung. For example, the study of political parties often failed fully to understand the real function of parties in Latin America, and too little attention was paid to such important local phcnomena as patron–client relationships or *personalismo*, presumably because these were deemed to be ill suited to a liberal–democratic polity. In addition, authors of this school reflected contemporary political science's preoccupations with formal institutions.

The 'modernization' approach

In response to this last problem, the next generation of North American scholars evolved the political development and/or 'modernization' school. Major figures included Gabriel Almond, James Coleman, Seymore Lipset and Samuel P. Huntingdon. Perhaps the seminal work was *The Politics of the Developing Areas*, edited by G. Almond and J. S. Coleman (Princeton University Press, 1960), which replaced a traditional emphasis on institutions with an apparently novel preoccupation with basic functions. This approach constituted a significant breakthrough because of its willingness to look at sociological factors and non-formal institutions, which earlier analyses had neglected. This approach seemed, on closer inspection, to be a more sophisticated version of earlier analysis and developments of a later decade were cruelly to underline the absence from their analyses of social and economic factors and patterns of conflict which account for the subsequent collapse of competitive politics in those countries. In Latin America, as more recent developments have made plain, domination, the exercise of power and sharp if not violent conflicts of interest seem to be very much the order of the day.

Similar problems are attached to the assumption that Latin American states are to be seen as developing along some pathway trodden by more developed and specifically Anglo-Saxon polities. Thus economic and political changes were evaluated in terms of the extent to which they pointed in this direction. It was assumed that Latin American countries were 'modernized' by adopting institutions, practices and values from developed Western nations. Such processes of diffusion were believed to exist within Latin American countries characterized by the existence of 'modern' urban and sometimes industrial sectors on the one hand, and 'backward', traditional (feudal) and rural sectors on the other. A prime example of this general approach is the important volume

Elites in Latin America, edited by S.M. Lipset and A. Solari (Oxford University Press, 1967). This volume identified and evaluated politically relevant elite groups in terms of their capacity or willingness to promote a liberal–democratic approach to political stability. 'Counter elites', not to mention mass attitudes and practices, were largely screened out of the analysis. Another contribution was *Political Development in Latin America: Instability, Violence and Evolutionary Change*, by M. Needler (Random House, 1968). The tendency to conceive of popular political involvement or political democracy in North American terms led to works such as *The Perón Era*, by R. Alexander (Columbia University Press, 1971); *Perón's Argentina*, by G. Blanksten (University of Chicago Press, 1967); and *Leader and Vanguard in Mass Society: A Study of Peronist Argentina*, by J. Kilpatrick, (MIT Press, 1971), and *Political Man, the Social Bases of Politics*, by S.M. Lipset (Doubleday–Anchor Books, 1963), which characterized Peronism as an essentially anti-democratic or even Fascist movement, despite significant evidence to the contrary.

In similar fashion, early work on Mexico was distorted by authors thinking of the ruling Mexican party as an embryonic democratic institution. Examples are *The Mexican Political System*, by V. Padgett (Houghton Mifflin, 2nd edn, 1976), and *Mexican Government in Transition*, by R.E. Scott (University of Illinois Press, 2nd edn, 1964). More generally, it was assumed that a crucial role in development belonged to middle-class groups – thus one influential work, *Political Change in Latin America: The Emergence of the Middle Sector*, by J. Johnson (Stanford University Press, 1958), was particularly concerned to identify and analyse Latin America's 'middle sectors' in these terms. The problem of his approach seems to have been insufficient attention to the specific values, loyalties and alignments of those Latin American middle classes. Analyses of Brazil suggest that whilst some portions of the middle classes may be radicalized by populist leaders, many others, in time of upheaval, take refuge in authoritarianism and support for the type of stability that the military supplies. Such general conclusions can be inferred from *Politics in Brazil: 1930 –1964*, by T.E. Skidmore (Oxford University Press, 1964); *Crisis in Brazil*, by O. Ianni (Columbia University Press, 1968); *Economic and Political Development: A Theoretical Approach and a Brazilian Case Study*, by H. Jaguaribe (Harvard University Press, 1968); and F.C. Weffort 'State and Mass in Brazil', *Studies in Comparative International Development*, **2(12)** (1966).

Early work on organized labour often approached the issue from the point of view of labour's contribution (positive or negative) to the development of democratic institutions as in, for instance, *Labour Relations in Argentina, Brazil and Chile*, by R. Alexander (McGraw-Hill, 1962), and *Organised Labor in Latin America*, by R. Alexander (Free Press, 1965). But there were some works by Americans and others less concerned with such preoccupations and more inclined to root the discussion in the context of the dynamics of local political processes. This is perhaps true of the general study *Organized Labor in Latin America*, by H. A. Spalding, Jr (New York University Press, 1977), and the more specific study *Politics and the Labour Movement in Chile*, by A. Angell (Oxford University Press, 1972). It is also perhaps true of the work *Labor Nationalism and Politics in Argentina*, by S. L. Baily (Rutgers University Press, 1967) and *Labour and Politics in Peru: The System of Political Bargaining*, by J. L. Payne (Yale University Press, 1967), where the question of political violence is treated dispassionately as a commonly anticipated feature of local political struggle.

Perhaps more significantly, discussion of the military by earlier commentators was spectacularly overtaken by events. Thus *Arms and Politics in Latin America*, by E. Lieuwen (Praeger, 1961) and *Generals versus Presidents: Neo-Militarism in Latin America*, by E. Leiuwen (Praeger, 1964), viewed the military as a 'modernizing' force contributing to 'political development' within the area.

Similarly, writers of this general outlook frequently underrated the politics of Latin America's rural areas. Thus, the countryside, its agrarian structures and its peasantry were examined in such anthropological works as *Sons of the Shaking Earth*, by E. R. Wolf (University of Chicago Press, 1959) and *Peasant Society in the Colombian Andes*, by O. Fals Borda (University of Florida Press, 1957) rather than by political analysts. Later, mainly as a result of political change and a growing preoccupation with land reform, political scientists turned their attention to these issues in, for instance, *Politics of the Altiplano: The Dynamics of Change in Rural Peru*, by E. Dew (University of Texas Press, 1976); *The Rape of the Peasantry: Latin America's Landholding System*, by E. Feder (Doubleday, 1971); *The Politics of Land Reform in Chile*, by R. R. Kaufman (Harvard University Press, 1972); *Agrarian Structures in Latin America*, edited by S. Barraclough (Heath, 1973); *Struggle in the Andes: Peasant Political Mobilization in Peru*, by H. Handelman (University of Texas Press, 1974); *The Revolutionary Potential of Peasants in Latin America*, by G. Huizer (Heath, 1972); *Latin American Peasant Movements*, edited by H. A. Landsberger (Cornell University Press, 1969); *Cultivat-*

ing Revolution: the United States and Agrarian Reform in Latin America, by J. Petras and R. La Porte (Random House, 1971); *Political Mobilization of the Venezuelan Peasant*, by J. D. Powell (Harvard University Press, 1971); *Agrarian Problems and Peasant Movements in Latin America*, edited by R. Stavenhagen (Doubleday, 1970); and *Zapata and the Mexican Revolution*, by J. Womack (Knopf, 1969). These authors took rural elites and the peasantry as serious or at least potentially serious actors upon the political stage and were concerned to see whether the peasantry conformed to its conservative image or contained some revolutionary potential. Equally, they acknowledge the explosive political potential of the land reform issue as it surfaced from the 1950s onwards.

Alternatives to the 'modernization' approach

Proponents of the conventional 'modernization' or 'developmental' schools were brought up short by political events. The Cuban revolution gave pause for thought and moves in Brazil, and other countries, toward long-term military rule questioned the assumptions and liberal–democratic optimism of influential scholars. Commentators began to look beyond practices or values of essentially North American provenance and to grapple more seriously with Latin American realities. They began to look more closely at structures, institutions, practices and values rooted within the Latin American context. Amongst economists, but having important implications for political analysis, the United Nations Economic Commission for Latin America (ECLA), led by the influential figure of R. Prebisch, developed the so-called structuralist approach to local economic problems and development. This body's work, *The Economic Development of Latin America and its Principal Problems* by R. Prebisch (United Nations, 1950), and the work of scholars influenced by or reflecting its underlying concern stressed the importance of deep-rooted local institutional or structural obstacles to economic development.

They also placed on the agenda the question of economic relations with the developed world, which were explored more fully by subsequent commentators. Elements of this approach can be found in *Economic Development of Latin America*, by C. Furtado (Cambridge University Press, 1970); *Obstacles to Development in Latin America*, by C. Furtado (Doubleday, 1970); *The Latin American Economies*, by W. P. Glade (Van Nostrand Reinhold, 1969); and *Underdevelopment in Spanish America*, by

K. Griffin (Allen and Unwin, 1969). There is also *Latin America Issues: Essays and Comments*, by A. O. Hirschman (Twentieth Century Fund, 1961), written from a political economy perspective. Finally, from a more obviously political science standpoint there is the work *Economic Change in Latin America: the Governing of Restless Nations*, by C. W. Anderson (Van Nostrand, 1967). Some of this writing coincided with a United States Alliance for Progress launched by the Kennedy Administration, which articulated a certain guarded optimism concerning Latin America's willingness or capacity to steer a 'middle course' between revolutionary challenges from the Left and military authoritarianism. Within the area, at one point, Chile appeared to offer a particularly hopeful venue for such an experiment. This is reflected in literature written by those perhaps friendly toward the experiment: *Economic Development and Reform in Chile: Progress under Frei 1964–1970*, by T. Edwards (Michigan State University, Latin American Studies Center, 1972); *The Political System of Chile*, by F. Gil (Houghton Mifflin, 1966); *The Last Best Hope: Eduardo Frei and Chilean Democracy*, by L. Gross (Random House, 1967); and *Latin American Christian Democratic Parties*, by E. J. Williams (University of Tennessee Press, 1967), as well as more radical commentators sceptical about its desirability or viability such as *Politics and Social Forces in Chilean Development*, by J. Petras (University of California Press, 1969), and *Latin America: Reform or Revolution?* edited by J. Petras and M. Zeitlin (Fawcett, 1968). Latterly, only the Venezuelan polity remains (at least in South America) as an active witness to this approach to politics. This, too, has produced its own accompanying literature, such as *The Venezuelan Democratic Revolution: A Profile of the Regime of Remulo Betancourt*, by R. J. Alexander (Rutgers University Press, 1964); *Politics in Venezuela*, by E. Blank (Little, Brown, 1973); *The Politics of Change in Venezuela*, edited by F. Bonilla and J. S. Michelana (MIT Press, 1967); *From Doctrine to Dialogue*, by J. Friedman (Syracuse University Press, 1965); *Conflict and Political Change in Venezuela*, by D. Levine (Princeton University Press, 1973); and *The Democratic Experience*, edited by J. Martz and D. Myers (Praeger, 1977).

Much recent academic debate has been conducted by varying proponents of the 'dependency' paradigm, as, for instance, in *The Political Economy of Growth*, by P. Baran (Monthly Review Press, 1957). The important works by A. G. Frank, *Capitalism and Underdevelopment in Latin America* (Monthly Review Press, 1967), and *Latin America: Underdevelopment or Revolution* (Monthly Review Press, 1969), also stressed Latin America's dependent role in the international economic division of labour and argued that its economic problems, and political dilemmas, stem from the impact of the developed capitalist world, which tended systematically to exploit the region to the detriment of its growth. One catch-phrase became the 'development of underdevelopment'.

Clearly, the literature on 'dependency' is inspired by Marxist understandings, even when some of those influenced by it are not themselves necessarily Marxist. Indeed, within Latin America itself one may safely say that academic political science, where it is able to thrive or to free itself from state control, is more influenced by Marxist approaches than any others. This is perhaps an eloquent commentary upon the conflict-laden nature of Latin American politics.

Many of the seminal contributions to the debate about 'dependency' appeared in Spanish rather than English, and any contributions in English tend to be scattered amongst journals or in edited volumes. Something of their nature can be gathered from *Theories of Underdevelopment*, by I. Roxborough (Macmillan, 1979), and *Underdevelopment & Development*, edited by H. Bernstein (Penguin, 1973), and also *Latin America: Reform or Revolution*, edited by J. Petras and M. Zeitlin (Fawcett Publications, 1968) and 'A Critical Synthesis of the Dependency Literature', by R. Chilcote, *Latin American Perspectives* (4–29, Spring (1974)). A major contribution has recently been translated as *Dependency and Development in Latin America*, by E. H. Cardoso and E. Faletto (University of California Press, 1978). A British scholar has gone so far as to suggest that this literature about 'dependency', in some measure, represents a nationalist response to extensive foreign involvement in Latin American society and politics ('Dependency: the New Nationalism?', by P. O'Brien in *Latin American Review of Books, I*, and edited by C. Harding and C. Roper, Rampart Press, 1973).

The state and challenges to its authority

Within this framework a facet of the debate, of particular interest for political scientists, has concerned the nature and role of the state. Such debate continues against the background of the authoritarian rule that now characterizes so much of the region. In discussing the contemporary state in Latin America some commentators continue to give special attention to the constraints, stemming from externally inspired economic or technological developments. This seems to be true, for example, of 'Nationalism and Capitalism in Peru', by A. Quijano, *Monthly Review* (July (1971)). Quijano seeks to grapple with the dynamics of authoritarian rule within its economic context. In particular, there has been a group of writers (not all Marxists) who explain authoritarian rule in terms of the perceived need to give priority to capital accumulation or technological innovation. According to this school of thought, military rule is invoked in the interests of a particular form of economic development, as in 'Political Crisis and Military Populism in Peru', by J. Cotler, *Studies in Comparative International Development*, **6**, No.5 (17), 95–113 (1971); 'State Power and Military Nationalism in Latin America', by I. L. Horowitz and E. K. Trimberger, *Comparative Politics*, 8, No.2, 223–244 (January 1976), and *The State and Society: Peru in Comparative Perspective*, by A. Stepan (Princeton University Press, 1978). This conception is carried further in *Modernization and Bureaucratic-Authoritarism*, by G. O'Donnell (University of California Press, 1973). O'Donnell sees contemporary military regimes as representing a new form of corporate state based on the alliance of the military and civilian technocrats, and his contribution, like that of others, seeks to balance political and economic factors. Indeed, one may say that much of the best recent scholarship has been inspired by a political economy approach to current issues.

The subject is further covered in two significant collections of essays, *The New Authoritarianism in Latin America*, edited by D. Collier (Princeton University Press, 1979), and *Authoritarianism and Corporatism in Latin America*, edited by J. M. Malloy (University of Pittsburgh Press, 1977).

Turning to individual countries, we have for MEXICO *The Mexican Profit Sharing Decision: Politics in an Authoritarian Regime*, by S. K. Purcell (University of California Press, 1975); and *Authoritarianism in Mexico*, edited by J. L. Reyna and R. Weinert (Institute for the Study of Human Issues, Philadelphia, 1977). Similarly, there are works on the more obviously relevant cases of ARGENTINA, such as *Economic Policy Making in a Conflict Society: The Argentine Case*, by R. D. Mallon and J. V. Sourrouille (Harvard University Press, 1975); *Political Forces in Argentina*, by P. Snow (Allyn and Bacon, 1971); and *Argentina in the Post War Era*, by G. Wynia (University of New Mexico Press, 1978). For BRAZIL there is *The Brazilian Corporative State and Working Class Politics*, by K. P. Erickson (University of California Press, 1977); *Dependent Development: The Alliance of Multinational State, and Local Capital in Brazil*, by P. Evans (University of Princeton Press, 1979); *Authoritarian Brazil: Origins, Policies and Future*, edited by J. Linz (Yale University Press, 1973); *Brazil: Politics in a Patrimonial Society*, by R. Roett (Praeger, 1978); *Interest Conflict and Political Change in Brazil*, by P. C. Schmitter (Stanford University Press, 1971); and *The Political System of Brazil: Emergence of a 'Modernizing' Authoritarian Regime*, by R. M. Schneider. For CHILE there is *Transitions to Stable Authoritarian–Corporate Regimes: The Chilean Case?* by R. Kaufman (Sage Professional Papers, Comparative Politics Series No. 01-060, 1976); and for PERU, *Pressure Groups and Power Elites in Peruvian Politics*, by C. A. Astiz (Cornell University Press, 1969); *Power and Society in Contemporary Peru*, by F. Bourricaud (Praeger, 1970); *The State and Economic Development: Peru since 1968*, by E. V. K. Fitzgerald (Cambridge University Press, 1976); *Economic Stress Under Peruvian Democracy*, by P. P. Kuczynski (Princeton University Press, 1977); *The Peruvian Experiment: Continuity and Change under Military Rule*, edited by A. Lowenthal (Princeton University Press, 1975); *The State and Society: Peru in Comparative Perspective*, by A. Stepan (Princeton University Press, 1978); and *Government Policy and the Distribution of Wealth in Peru, 1963–1973*, by R. C. Webb (Harvard University Press, 1978). Finally, we mention those commentators who have sought to adduce a fairly clear continuity between contemporary authoritarianism and long-established Hispanic practices; for example, *The Centralist Tradition of Latin America*, by H. Wiarda (Westview Press, 1981), and *The Continuing Struggle for Democracy in Latin America*, by H. Wiarda (Westview Press, 1980).

Literature on the radical politics of urban society is well covered from a sociological perspective in *Cities of Peasants*, by B. Roberts (Edward Arnold, 1978), which contains an extensive bibliography, and *Squatters and Oligarchs: Authoritarian Rule and Political Change in Peru*, by D. Collier (Johns Hopkins University Press, 1976); *Politics and the Migrant Poor in Mexico City*, by W. Cornelius (Stanford University Press, 1975); and *The Politics of the Barrios of Venezuela*, by T. F. Ray (University of California Press, 1969).

The Peruvian experience also throws some light on the limited capacity of determined nationalist regimes to grapple with economic interests, and in particular the multinational corporations, which historically have played such a major role in developing Latin America's mineral resources and which latterly have been in the forefront of efforts to develop advanced capital-intensive industry based on modern and generally imported technology. Some of the more general discussion of multinationals in Latin

America initially viewed them from a North American perspective, and were less concerned with their specific impact on host-countries (for example, *Sovereignty at Bay*, by R. Vernon, Basic Books, 1971). Equally, there have been works written from the 'dependency' point of view stressing the constraining effects of multinational corporations upon local polities, such as *The Nationalization of Venezuelan Oil*, by J. Petras *et al.* (Praeger, 1977). Some work, however, has hinted at a rather more complex situation, and one in which all the bargaining cards are not necessarily in the hands of economic interests. These include *The Politics of Oil in Venezuela*, by F. Tugwell (Stanford University Press, 1975); *Multinational Corporations and the Politics of Dependence: Copper in Chile*, by T. Moran (Princeton University Press, 1974); and *The Multinational Corporation as a Force in Latin American Politics: A Case Study of the International Petroleum Company in Peru*, by J. Adabberto Pinelo (Praeger, 1973). Reference above has been made to the quasi-radical military regime of an authoritarian kind experienced in Peru, but it must, of course, be noted that this particular experiment ran into the sands, and that the last years of military rule in that country were of a more clearly conservative variety. To that extent, Peru for a while fell more into line with the other military regimes which, to varying degrees, followed the model first established by the Brazilian army. (An important feature of the Peruvian situation was a relative absence of that repression which has undoubtedly characterized Brazil, Chile, Uruguay and Argentina.) This raises the whole question of the military's specific role.

The military

Some earlier writers showed an optimism about civilian institutions which has been overtaken by events. Not least, one has the cases of Chile and Uruguay which, as recently as a decade ago, were still being held up as liberal–democratic polities with civilian traditions that constituted a marked exception to Latin America's general rule. Now in those countries, as well as in the major powers of Brazil and Argentina, the military has not only overthrown elected governments but has also asserted itself as a corporate body within the governmental domain and, as an institution, assumed long-term responsibility for control of the state. They created and are sustaining that brand of rule already referred to under the heading of 'bureaucratic authoritarianism'. Such developments have obviously focused renewed attention upon the nature of the Latin American military and the special factors predisposing it to intervene in the political arena. In the relevant literature, it is perhaps possible to discern two distinct, though not necessarily mutually exclusive, emphases.

First, there are those who tend to stress the military's relationships with the wider society and, in particular, alliances with particular class interests. Particularly important amongst such commentators is Jose Nun, who made a short but perhaps seminal contribution which drew attention to possible links between the military and 'middle class' groups. The work was somewhat indiscriminating in that he tended to assume the existence of one relatively homogenous middle class and did not spell out the variety of interests that could be covered by this term. Equally, he did not clearly indicate which parts of the 'middle classes' the military were associated with, and he did not chart, in any detail, the practical consequences of such alliances in specific historical circumstances. Nevertheless, 'The Middle Class Military Coup', by Jose Nun in *Politics of Conformity in Latin America*, edited by C. Veliz (Oxford University Press, 1967), suggested ideas later to be developed and given a more general significance by authors such as O'Donnell (work cited).

Second, there are those who emphasize the military's own distinctive corporate interests, values and missions. Some have stressed the emergence of a distinctive and largely military-inspired ideology of hemispherical and national security, whereby military regimes have sought to legitimize repressive policies. Such an ideology is seen as a distinctive professional military viewpoint or interest. Particularly important work of this kind is *The Military in Politics: Changing Patterns in Brazil*, by A. Stepan (Princeton University Press, 1971), which specifically examined the army's changing understanding of its role. Similarly, *Latin American Institutional Development: Changing Military Perspectives in Peru and Brazil*, by L. R. Einaudi and A. Stepan (Rand Corporation, 1971) compares the Peruvian and Brazilian militaries.

Finally, in discussing the military, one should briefly refer to other theoretical approaches, generally of a North American origin, which seek to analyse military involvement in politics. These include *Military Rule in Latin America: Function Consequences and Perspectives*, by P. C. Schmitter (Sage, 1973) and perhaps the work of R. D. Putnam, 'Toward Explaining Military Intervention in Latin America', *World Politics,* **20** (1), October (1967). We should also mention the significant if still limited range of detailed case studies of military involvement. Classic studies under this heading have been *The Army and Politics in Argentina,*

1928–1945: Yrigoyan to Peron, by R. A. Potash (Stanford University Press, 1969); *Soldiers, Guerrillas and Politics in Colombia*, by R. Maullin (Heath, 1973); and *Chilean Politics 1920–31: The Honourable Mission of the Armed Forces*, by F. M. Nunn. At an earlier stage there has been useful introductory work on Argentina, Chile and Peru, *Civil–Military Relations in Argentina, Chile and Peru*, by L. North (Institute of International Studies: University of California, 1966); *The Military Coup d'etat as a Political Process: Ecuador 1948–1966*, by J. S. Fitch (The Johns Hopkins University Press, 1977); *The rise and fall of the Peruvian Military Radicals 1968–76*, by G. Philips (Athlone Press, 1978); and *Armies and Politics in Latin America*, edited by A. Lowenthall (Holmes and Meier, 1976), the latter being a series of case studies which, amongst other things, contains a chapter on the too little studied Mexican military.

Recent events in Argentina as well as chronic crises in Brazil, Chile and Uruguay, not to mention Peru (where at least provisionally the military has been constrained to leave the political arena), remind us of the difficulties Latin American military regimes have had in legitimizing their rule, and in securing sustained economic development and of the possibility that military governments could therefore eventually seek to shuffle off their responsibilities. The work represented in *The Breakdown of Democratic Regimes: Latin America*, edited by J. J. Linz and A. Stepan (The Johns Hopkins University Press, 1978), and the work of H. Wiarda (work cited) on the possible quest for a distinctively Latin American expression of political democracy may be relevant straws in the wind.

Revolutionary regimes and processes

In the broad sweep of Latin America's political history, Mexico had been understandably held up as the first polity to undergo upheaval of revolutionary proportions but no longer stands as the model for other Latin American radicals. Most writing in recent times has registered Mexico's general departure from ostensibly radical beginnings, for example, *The Poverty of Revolution: the State and the Urban Poor in Mexico*, by S. J. Eckstein (Princeton University Press, 1977); *Democracy in Mexico*, by P. Gonzalez Casanova (Oxford University Press, 1970); *The Politics of Mexican Development*, by R. D. Hansen (The Johns Hopkins University Press, 1971); *Mexican Democracy: A Critical Review*, by K. F. Johnson (Praeger, rev. edn, 1978); and *Labyrinths of*

Powers: Political Recruitment in Twentieth Century Mexico, by P. H. Smith (Princeton University Press, 1978).

Later, Bolivia briefly promised to offer a model of how revolutionary change might be effective in Latin America, but the 'Bolivian revolution' did not run its course and, in fact, that country collapsed into a state of chronic chaos, characterized by struggles between rival military factions and challenges from a radicalized labour movement. Regrettably, very little work is readily available in English, and much research remains to be done. But mention could be made of the background works such as *Parties and Political Change in Bolivia*, by H. Klein (Cambridge University Press, 1971); *Bolivia: the Uncompleted Revolution*, by J. Malloy (Pittsburgh University Press, 1970); *Beyond the Revolution: Bolivia since 1952*, edited by J. Malloy and R. Thorn (Pittsburgh University Press, 1971); and the specific work on the labour movement, *A History of the Bolivian Labour Movement*, by G. Lora (Cambridge University Press, 1977).

The worldwide attention focused on Castro's Cuba, and the shock waves his revolution sent through the Western hemisphere, obviously inspired a very substantial body of material. Only a relatively small portion is of a high or durable quality, and much of it is inevitably somewhat partisan. Nevertheless special mention must be made of the monumental historical work, *Cuba*, by H. Thomas (Eyre and Spottiswoode, 1971), as well as the now-dated contributions, *The Cuban Revolution and Latin America*, by B. Goldenberg (Praeger, 1965); *Guerrillas in Power*, by K. S. Karol (Hill and Wang, 1970); *Castroism, Theory and Practice*, by T. Draper (Praeger, 1965); *Cuba in Revolution*, edited by R. Bonachea and V. Valdes (Doubleday, 1972); and *Cuba: Castroism and Communism, 1959–1966*, by A. Suarez (MIT Press, 1967). Equally, we mention *Cuba in the 1970s: Pragmatism and Institutionalization*, by C. Mesa Lago (University of New Mexico Press, 1974); *Cuba Under Castro: The Limits of Charisma*, by E. Gonzalez (Houghton Mifflin, 1974); *The Rise and Decline of Fidel Castro*, by M. Halperin (University of California Press, 1972); and the specialized study of Cuban political culture in *The Transformation of Political Culture in Cuba*, by R. R. Fagen (Stanford University Press, 1970). Most of this literature covers the early period of upheaval and initial consolidation: the institutionalization of the revolution and the mechanisms for popular participation have not been the subject of much detailed or sustained investigation. The Cuban revolution helped to inspire rural guerrilla movements in other parts of Latin America, and there were theorists of revolution, associated with the Cuban upheaval, who argued in favour of the Cuban experience as a relevant model to follow, as in *Revolution in the Revolution*, by R. Debray (Grove Press, 1967), and *Reminiscences of the Cuban Revolutionary War*, by E. 'Ché' Guevara (Grove Press, 1968). However, as Guevara's own fate was to suggest, the Cuban experience did not supply an obviously successful model, and the stress, by the late 1960s, moved from rural- to urban-based guerrilla movements, of which the Uruguayan Tupamaros and the Argentine Montoneros were perhaps the most spectacular. Such urban guerrilla activities also threw up theoreticians from among their ranks, the most celebrated work being *For the Liberation of Brazil*, by C. Marighela (Penguin, 1971). Still the classic work on rural guerrillas must be *Guerrilla Movements in Latin America*, by R. Gott (Nelson, 1970), while urban guerrillas are examined in *Urban Guerrilla Warfare in Latin America*, by J. Kohl and J. Litt (The MIT Press, 1974); *Violence and Repression in Latin America*, by E. Duff and J. McLamont (Free Press, 1976); and *Critique of Arms*, by R. Debray (Penguin, 1977). Finally, mention could be made of the sharply contrasting works, *The Tupamaros*, by A. Labrousse (Penguin, 1973), who writes from a broadly sympathetic outlook, and *Urban Guerrillas*, by R. Moss (Temple Smith, 1972), written from an undisputedly conservative viewpoint.

There is a significant amount in English on the distinctive regime of Allende in Chile. We first mention two short books involving Allende himself, *Chile's Road to Socialism*, by S. Allende Gossens (Penguin, 1973), and in 1971 there appeared a record of conversations between Allende and Régis Debray. Of the academic literature written whilst Allende was still in office, arguably the best was *The Chilean Road to Socialism*, edited by J. A. Zammit (Institute of Development Studies, University of Sussex, 1973). Of more recent work, particularly important is *Allende's Chile: The Political Economy of the Rise and Fall of Unidad Popular*, by S. de Vylder (Cambridge University Press, 1976), an important exercise in political economy. Equally, there is an important work collectively written, *Chile: The State and Revolution*, by I. Roxborough *et al.* (Macmillan, 1977), which has significant things to say about the state and which takes a friendly if critical view of the 'Chilian Road to Socialism'. Finally, there is from the liberal–democratic perspective *The Overthrow of Allende and the Politics of Chile 1964–1976*, by P. E. Sigmund (University of Pittsburgh Press, 1978), as well as *The Breakdown of Democratic Regimes – Chile*, by A. Valenzuela (The Johns Hopkins University Press, 1978).

The Church

Since the collapse of Allende's experiment, forces working for radical political change have been largely driven underground and are therefore difficult to investigate. Arguably, the one major institution which in part does remain visibly committed to the cause of radical change to some extent is the Roman Catholic Church. Traditionally the Church has been seen as a conservative force, but the 1960s produced some literature which was concerned to indicate how the Church had or might become a 'modernizing' force. A particularly notable contribution is *Catholicism, Social Control and Modernization in Latin America*, by I. Vallier (Prentice-Hall, 1970), though *Catholicism and Political Development in Latin America*, by F. Turner (University of North Carolina Press, 1971), also merits a mention. Preoccupation with the changing nature of Latin American Catholicism was equally apparent in *The Church and Social Change in Latin America*, edited by H. Landsberger (University of Notre Dame Press, 1970), and *Latin American Institutional Development: The Changing Catholic Church*, edited by L. Einaudi *et al.* (Rand Corporation, 1969). By the 1970s, the Church had in some places become a more obviously radicalized institution, and there were writers who, from a relatively radical perspective, came up with critiques of the Church in politics. These include *The Political Transformation of the Brazilian Catholic Church*, by T. C. Bruneau (Cambridge University Press, 1974); *Catholic Radicals in Brazil*, by E. de Kadt (Oxford University Press, 1974); *The Church as a Political Factor in Latin America*, by D. Mutchler (Praeger, 1971); and *The Rebel Church in Latin America*, by A. Gheerbrant (Penguin, 1974). There have been more recent books charting the changing nature of debates in the Church about political matters, including *Churches and Politics in Latin America*, edited by D. H. Levine (Sage, 1979), which contains a good bibliography on this subject, and *The Church and Politics in Chile*, by B. H. Smith (Princeton University Press, 1982). Levine has also produced a significant book on the Church in the relatively more open societies of Colombia and Venezuela: *Religion and Politics in Latin America* (Princeton University Press, 1981). Finally, we mention anthropological work on religion in Latin America, which has certain limited political implications. Such a study is *The Symbolism of Subordination: Indian Identity in a Guatamalan Town*, by K. Warren (University of Texas Press, 1978).

Whilst radical Catholics are in the main committed to non-violent change, there are Catholic groups who support violent struggle. A prototype was the famous Colombian priest, Camilo Torres, in his book *Revolutionary Writings* (Harper and Row, 1972).

Central America

The question of revolutionary upheaval points to the issue of conflict in contemporary Central America. On this subject there is relatively little English-language political science material, but we mention the useful though now dated book on Guatemala, *Crucifixion by Power*, by R. Adams (University of Texas Press, 1970), and the general background works, *El Salvador*, by A. White (Benn, 1973); *El Salvador – Landscape and Society*, by D. Browning (The Clarendon Press, 1971); and *The Long War*, by J. Dunkerley (Junction Books, 1982). On Nicaragua there is the narrative work on the revolution, *Triumph of the People*, by G. Black (Zed Press, 1981), and *Nicaragua: The Sandinist Revolution*, by H. Weber (New Left Books, 1981). In conclusion, there is the radical commentary, *Under the Eagle*, by J. Pearce (Latin America Bureau, 1981), which is concerned with US involvement in Central America and the Caribbean and which contains an extensive bibliography (including materials on the rather special case of the Dominican Republic).

The international dimension

The international relationships of Latin America (see the earlier discussion of 'dependency') have two aspects, interstate dealings and foreign penetration of, or involvement in, the domestic affairs of Latin America. In reality the two can never be wholly separated.

Under the first heading, we would cite *Latin America in the International Political System*, by G. P. Atkins (Free Press, 1977); *The Hovering Giant: U.S. Responses to Revolutionary Change in Latin America*, by C. Blasier (University of Pittsburgh Press, 1974); *U.S. Foreign Policy and Latin America*, by R. R. Fagen (Stanford University Press, 1979); *Latin America and World Economy: A Changing International Order*, edited by J. Grunwald (Sage, 1978), which is mainly economic; *Latin America: The Search for a New International Role*, edited by R. Hellman and

H. J. Rosenthal (Sage, 1975); *The United States and the Southern Cone: Argentina, Chile and Uruguay*, by A. P. Whitaker (Harvard University Press, 1976); *The Alliance that Lost its Way*, by J. Levinson and J. D. Onis (Quadrangle, 1970); and *Latin America – United States Economic Interactions: Conflict, Accommodation and Policies for the Future*, edited by R. Williamson *et al.* (American Enterprise Institute, 1974). These are inevitably concerned with the dominant presence of the US in the region or, alternatively, written from a North American perspective. Two significant British contributions are *Latin America, The Cold War and the World Powers 1945–1973*, by F. Parkinson (Sage, 1974) and *The Inter-American System*, by G. Connell-Smith (Oxford University Press, 1962), written in a more historical vein. The scant literature on Soviet involvement in the area includes *The Soviet Presence in Latin America*, by J. D. Theberge (Crane, Russak, 1974). There is a recent book attempting to fill a gap, namely *The European Challenge: Europe's New Role in Latin America*, edited by J. Pearce (Latin America Bureau, 1982). Finally, with regard to Latin America's own and generally frustrated attempt to integrate, especially on the economic front, there is *The Latin American Common Market*, by S. Dell (Royal Institute of International Affairs, 1967), and the analytical work, *Latin American Economic Integration – Experiences and Prospects*, by M. Wioncsek (Praeger, 1966).

Under the second heading one is inevitably much concerned with American interests operating within Latin America and, in particular, US economic interests. There is *Capitalism and the State in U.S.–Latin American Relations*, edited by R. Fagen (Stanford University Press, 1979), which is a key study, and *Politics and Social Structure in Latin America*, by J. Petras (Monthly Review Press, 1970). Other forms of American involvement – for instance, military or intelligence activities – has also provoked discussion, particularly as these have affected the Dominican Republic and Chile. On the former we would cite *The Dominican Intervention*, by A. F. Lowenthal (Harvard University Press, 1972); *Intervention and Negotiation: the United States and the Dominican Revolution*, by J. Slater (Harper and Row, 1970); and *The Caribbean Community: Changing Societies and U.S. Policy*, by R. Crassweller (Praeger, 1972). On the latter, there is *The United States and Chile: Imperialism and the Overthrow of the Allende Regime*, by J. Petras and M. Morley (Monthly Review Press, 1975). There is also *United States' Penetration of Brazil*, by J. Black (Manchester University Press, 1977).

Single-country studies

In terms of country studies, Brazil, as one of the great powers of Latin America, has understandably been the subject of considerable scrutiny, as is shown in the bibliography in *Brazil: A Political Analysis*, by P. Flynn (Benn, 1978).

Similarly, Argentina and Mexico have attracted an arguably disproportionate share of academic attention, though even here there are large gaps, particularly for recent times, when political repression has necessarily placed major obstacles in the way of research, at least in the case of Argentina. One of the best recent books on Argentina is *Argentina in the Twentieth Century*, edited by D. Rock (University of Pittsburgh Press, 1975).

High on a list of countries neglected by political scientists are Paraguay, Uruguay, Ecuador and, to some extent, Bolivia. The Latin America Bureau has been trying to fill some of these gaps with introductory works for the non-specialist such as its brief essays on Uruguay (1980), Paraguay (1980) and Bolivia (1981), which contain basic bibliographies on these countries. Indeed, in the case of Paraguay the only real scholarly work available is of a historical, pre-Stroessner character. On Uruguay, however, there have been major new contributions, namely *A Political Economy of Uruguay Since 1870*, by H. Finch (Macmillan, 1981); *Uruguay: the Politics of Failure*, by M. Weinstein (Greenwood Press, 1975); *Uruguay in Transition*, by E. Kaufman (Transaction Books, 1978); and *Government and Politics of Uruguay*, by P. B. Taylor (Tulane University Press, 1960).

Even when Uruguay was still being held up as a model of apparently liberal–democratic rule, it was not the subject of any significant investigation by political scientists. The same is even more true of Ecuador (for bibliography on this, see Fitch, work cited) and of the most recent developments in Bolivia.

An early study of Colombia's politics is the now very dated but still highly readable *Dance of the Million*, by V. L. Fluharty (University of Pittsburgh Press, 1957). Subsequently, the country's unusual experiment in institutionalized coalition rule on the part of its two traditional dominant parties helped to inspire *Colombia: the Political Dimension of Change*, by R. H. Dix (Yale University Press, 1968), and *Colombia: A Contemporary Political Survey*, by J. Martz (University of North Carolina Press, 1962). Much more recently, there has been *Politics of Compromise: Coalition Government in Colombia*, edited by R. A. Berry *et al.* (Transaction Books, 1980), which includes a comprehensive bibliography. As the book by D. H. Levine (work cited) indicates, the Church has an unusually significant role in this society, and one aspect of this is the subject of *The Church and Labour in Columbia*, by K. Medhurst (Manchester University Press, 1984).

Under-researched subjects

Just as there are countries which have been neglected by academic investigators, so there are some important topics or themes which also have received relatively scant attention. There are certain areas which require particular research if the political map of Latin America is to be better sketched out and understood. Some of these have already been mentioned, but we would particularly indicate the following.

First, there is the whole question of political parties in Latin America. Recent neglect of this issue is perhaps understandable because of the suspension of conventional party politics in so many Latin American countries. Nevertheless, even prior to the current wave of authoritarian regimes, this seems to have been an under-studied topic. What is more, if military rule is to give way to some form of civilian government, then it is essential to understand the origins, structures, values and general dynamics of political parties. Some literature does exist, though a fair amount is scattered in articles or edited volumes. There is the work of Fitzgibbon (work cited); *Changing Latin America: New Interpretations of its Politics and Society*, edited by D. Chalmers (Academy of Political Science, New York, 1972); R. R. Kaufman in J. M. Malloy (1977, work cited); 'Dilemmas in the Study of Latin American Political Parties', by J. D. Martz, *Journal of Politics*, 509–531, August (1964) and 'Political Parties in Colombia and Venezuela: Contrasts in Substance and Style', by J. D. Martz, *Western Political Quarterly, 318–333, June (1965); 'Party Systems in Latin America', by A. Angell, Political Quarterly*, July–September (1966); 'A Two Dimensional Typology of Latin American Political Parties', by P. Ranis, *Journal of Politics*, 798–832, August (1968); and the contribution of R. Scott to *Political Parties and Political Development*, edited by J. LaPalombara and M. Weiner (Princeton University Press, 1966). The latter in particular represents the modernization approach. Full-length books on the subject fall into two main categories, namely comparative studies and case studies of individual parties. Perhaps the most notable examples of the former are *Political Parties of the Americas*, by R. J. Alexander (Greenwood Press, 1982), which is more a work of reference, as is the very useful *Guide to the Political Parties of*

South America, edited by J. P. Bernard *et al.* (Penguin, 1973). With different emphasis there is the study *Party Systems and Elections in Latin America*, by R. McDonald (Markham, 1971). Finally, there are one or two studies of parties of the left. A very early example of this is *Communism in Latin America*, by R. J. Alexander (Rutgers University Press, 1957). More recent is *International Communism in Latin America: A History of the Movement, 1917–1963*, by R. Poppino (Free Press, 1964), and *Castroism and Communism in Latin America: the Varieties of Marxist –Leninist Experience, 1959–1976*, by W. E. Ratcliff (American Enterprise Institute, 1976). Mention should also be made of *Marxism in Latin America*, by M. Aguilar (Knopf, 1968).

One other book dealing with a particular 'family' of parties is *Latin American Christian Democratic Parties*, by E. J. Williams (University of Tennessee Press, 1967). Detailed case studies of individual parties seem surprisingly few, and there is obviously an important field here for future scholars. Amongst those already extant we would cite *Acción Democratica: Evolution of a Modern Political Party in Venezuela*, by J. Martz (Princeton University Press, 1966). Apart from studies of Mexico's ruling party which have already been mentioned, the only other studies we are aware of concern the long-established Aprista party of Peru, namely H. Kantor's *The Ideology and Programme of the Peruvian Aprista Movement* (Octagon Books, 1966) and *Modernization, dislocation and Aprismo*, by H. Klaren (University of Texas Press, 1973).

If political parties have been relatively neglected by scholars so, too, have studies of such elite groups in Latin America as rural landowners and the business community. Studies of recent authoritarian trends do, of course, have much to say about the political impact of business and capital, but detailed empirical investigations are, naturally, hard to come by. One classic study of business leaders is *Los Que Mandan (Those who Rule)*, by J. L. Imaz (State University of New York Press, 1970); there are also *Elites in Latin America*, edited by S. M. Lipset and A. Solari (Oxford University Press, 1968); and a chapter by T. Cook in *Latin America: From Dependence to Revolution*, edited by J. Petras (Wiley, 1973). Other works include *Workers and Managers in Latin America*, edited by S. M. Davis and L. W. Goodman (Heath, 1972); *Enterprise in Latin America: Business Attitudes in a Developing Economy*, by A. Lauterbach (Cornell University Press, 1966); *Industrial Relations and Social Change in Latin America*, edited by W. H. Form and A. A. Blum (University of Florida Press, 1965); and work on Mexico in *Authoritarianism and Corporatism*, by J. M. Malloy (1977, work cited).

Similarly, there is a relative dearth of detailed work on the day-to-day operations of state institutions and governmental bureaucrats. Amongst existing books we note *Politics and Economic Change in Latin America: The Governing of Restless Nations*, by C. W. Anderson (Van Nostrand, 1967); *Brazilian Planning*, by R. Daland (University of North Carolina Press, 1967); *Authoritarianism and Corporatism*, by J. M. Malloy (1977, work cited); *Civil Service Reform in Brazil: Principle versus Practice*, by L. S. Graham (University of Texas Press, 1968); *Bureaucracy and Development: A Mexican Case Study*, by M. H. Greenberg (Heath, 1970); *Bureaucrats, Politicians and Peasants in Mexico*, by M. S. Grindle (University of California Press, 1977); and *Politics and Planners, Economic Development Policy in Central America*, by G. W. Wynia (University of Wisconsin Press, 1972). Furthermore any return to civilian politics may involve some thought about the rehabilitation of legislative institutions. The very limited range of materials on this subject confirms the subordinate role such bodies have habitually played in Latin America. We would simply cite *Latin American Legislatures: Their Role and Influence*, edited by W. Agor (Praeger, 1971).

We would like by way of conclusion to identify particular themes which, in the light of dramatically changing realities, seem almost bound to provoke debate in this decade and to invite academic study. First, and perhaps foremost, are changes of an economic kind having major political implications. Thus on both the agrarian and industrial fronts there are observable tendencies for capital-intensive methods of production to gain in importance, with serious implications for the nature, organization and latent political role of both the peasantry and organized labour. In the latter case the emergence of the Brazilian Workers Party (PT) points to the potentially fresh political importance of strategically placed sectors of the labour force in industries dependent on imported technology. Such developments clearly warrant close attention. Equally, in the rural sector, economic changes are tending to have the effect of creating a semi-proletarianized workforce on a historically novel scale. Developments in Central America strongly suggest that such a workforce has at least some revolutionary potential and, for that reason alone, merits study. We still need to know a great deal more about changing political values, expectations and modes of organization in the whole of Latin America's countryside.

Another important blank space on Latin America's political map is the political role of women – women having played an unusually significant part in the upheavals of Central America.

Apart from a little work on the role of the middle-class women in Chile under Allende, there is little on this subject. One exception (partially) is the doctoral thesis by M. Lombardini, *Women in the Modern Art Movement in Brazil: Salon Leaders, Artists and Musicians, 1917–1930* (University of California, Los Angeles, 1977).

Discussions of the underlying possibilities for change is clearly important in the context of military government. As already hinted, a large potential area of study is the whole question of whether, when and in what way the military may divest itself of its self-imposed governmental role. As recent events remind us, the dilemmas of the military could tempt them to divert attention from domestic problems by engaging in external military conflicts and appealing to nationalist sentiments. Argentina's recent conflict obviously reminds us that such adventures can involve Latin America's relationships beyond the Western hemisphere. Such relationships (with Western Europe, Eastern Europe, Japan and even Africa or the Middle East) are, as mentioned earlier, also important topics for research. This is even more true given that the growth of such extra-hemispherical relationships seems likely partly to offset the US' long-established dominance within the area.

Similarly, current crises are a reminder of potential international conflicts within Latin America itself. Significant numbers of unresolved border disputes and squabbles over natural resources have major implications for the politics of the region and even for the region's links with the rest of the world. The serious miscalculations lying behind the conflict between Argentina and the UK shows how important it is to grasp Latin America's contemporary political realities and just how much research in these areas needs to be encouraged.

16
Australia, Canada, New Zealand and South Africa
Michael Rush

Introduction

A bibliographical essay on politics in Australia, Canada, New Zealand and South Africa written in the early 1960s would have been short and limited in scope, but since that time there has been an enormous burgeoning of the literature in both monograph and periodical forms, with the result that the bibliographer is now faced with a much more formidable task. This growth has, however, been uneven, both between countries and within particular areas of interest: it has been greatest in Canada and least in New Zealand, whilst some areas, such as race relations in South Africa or federalism in Canada, have grown disproportionately compared with others, such as political parties in South Africa or pressure groups in all four countries. It is also the case that whilst the monograph literature on New Zealand and South African politics has expanded considerably since the early 1960s, the periodical literature has not kept pace, and this needs to be borne in mind.

All four countries have a number of features in common. Each, of course, was one of the 'white dominions' of the British Empire; each therefore has a white immigrant population, which, to varying degrees, is ethnically mixed; and each therefore inherited a political system based on that of Britain. All four countries have 'native' or non-white populations, constituting a majority, of course, in the South African case. Two of the four are federations, whilst South Africa could be said to encompass some federal characteristics and originally New Zealand adopted a much looser form of unitary government than now exists. Even so, this has not resulted in an extensive comparative literature, as the final section of this chapter shows.

There are, however, a number of journals which regularly contain articles on one or more of the four countries. Most obviously, there is the *Journal of Commonwealth and Comparative Politics* (formerly the *Journal of Commonwealth Political Studies*, (1961–) and the *Parliamentarian* (formerly the *Journal of the Parliaments of the Commonwealth*, 1920–). Many articles are also found in other political science and social science journals, other than those published in the four countries, but references to these are more appropriately traced in various bibliographies, notably the *International Bibliography of Political Science* (1953–), the *Social Science Citation Index* (1966–) and the various bibliographies cited in the country sections of this chapter. However, a useful list of books and articles on parties, elections and other aspects of politics is found in *Commonwealth Elections, 1945 –1970: a Bibliography*, by Valerie Bloomfield (Mansell, 1976). Apart from these sources, accounts of current events in the four countries can be found in *Keesing's Contemporary Archives* (1931 –) and *Current History* (1914–).

The four country sections below provide details of available bibliographies, various official publications and a selection of the monograph literature, dealing with each broad topic in the latter case in the same order in each section. In addition a list of relevant journals in political science and related subjects is included. It should be noted that in cases where there are two or more journals with the same title, the relevant journal is indicated by citing its place of publication.

Australia

Bibliographies and reference works

A number of useful bibliographical works are available, including the *Australian National Bibliography* (Australian National Library, 1961–), which is published in cumulative and annual editions, and the *Annual Catalogue of Australian Publications* (Australian National Library, 1936– , except for 1941–1945), which includes lists of official publications of the federal and state governments. The Australian Public Affairs Information Service has published a subject index of current literature since 1945 and a more specialized tool is available in the form of *Australian Social Abstracts* (SSRC of Australia, 1954–). Though now somewhat out of date, *Background to Politics: a Sourcebook of Major Documents and Statements which Affect the Course of Australian Politics*, by B. C. Fitzgerald (Cheshire, 1969), remains useful.

The *Official Yearbook of the Commonwealth of Australia* (1908 –) contains much useful information, including sections on Australian government at federal and state levels, whilst the *Australian Dictionary of National Biography* (Melbourne University Press, 1966–), which will eventually run to twelve volumes, is a useful source of information about individuals in Australian political history. The *Current Affairs Bulletin* (Sydney, 1947–) provides a useful summary of political events in Australia.

As with the UK Parliament, a wide variety of documents relating to the Australian Federal Parliament are published, including the *Journals of the Senate, Votes and Proceedings of the House of Representatives, Parliamentary Papers* (i.e. reports and other documents presented to Parliament), *Parliamentary Debates (Hansard), Notices of Motions and Orders of the Day (Notice Papers)* of the Senate and the House of Representatives, *Acts of the Commonwealth of Australia* and *Treaties*. The six state parliaments also publish details of their proceedings and various reports.

The boundaries of politics and political science are notoriously difficult to define, but no bibliographical essay dealing with them would be complete with a brief reference to wider aspects of the subject, particularly history. In the Australian case *Australia: a Short History*, by Russel Ward (Ure Smith, rev. edn, 1979) provides a good introduction, whilst much greater depth is provided by *History of Australia*, by C. M. H. Clark (4 vols, Melbourne University Press, 1978). In addition, *Contemporary Australia*, by Tony Griffiths (Croom Helm, 1977), is a useful general introduction to Australian affairs.

Politics

There has been a considerable growth in the number of general books on Australian politics since the 1960s. For long a standard work, *Australian National Government*, by L. F. Crisp (Longman, Australia, 5th edn, 1970) remains valuable, as does *Australian Government and Politics: an Introduction*, by J. D. B. Miller and Brian Jinks (Duckworth, 4th edn, 1971). *A Handbook of Australian Government and Politics, 1890–1964*, by Colin A. Hughes and

B. D. Graham (Australian National University Press, 1968) and *A Handbook of Australian Government and Politics, 1965–1974*, by Colin A. Hughes (ANU Press, 1977) provide a useful historical perspective, and several books with a variety of approaches have been published in the 1970s: *Inside Canberra: a Guide to Australian Federal Politics*, by Don Whitington and Robert Chalmers (Rigby, 1971); *Government and Politics in Australia*, by W. J. Byrt and Frank Crean (McGraw-Hill, Australia, 1972); *Australian Politics: a Third Reader*, edited by Henry Mayer (Cheshire, 1973); *The Politics of Australian Democracy: An Introduction to Political Science*, by E. V. Emy (Macmillan, Australia, 1974); *The Canberra Model: Essays on Australian Government*, by David E. Butler (Macmillan, 1974); *Stability and Change in Australian Politics*, by Don Aitkin (ANU Press, 1977); *Politics and Policy in Australia*, by Geoffrey Hawker *et al.* (University of Queensland Press, 1979); and *Government, Politics and Power in Australia: An Introductory Reader*, edited by A. Parkin *et al.* (Longman Cheshire, 1980). A number of monographs deal with particular periods in recent Australian political history: *From Curtin to Menzies and After: Continuity or Confrontation?* by Frederick Alexander (Nelson, Australia, 1973); *The Liberal Era: a Political and Economic Analysis*, by J. C. Horsfall (Sun Books, 1974); *From Bob to Bungles: People in Politics, 1966–70*, by Raymond Aitchison (Sun Books, 1970); and *From Whitlam to Fraser: Reform and Reaction in Australian Politics*, by Allan Patience and Brian Head (Oxford University Press, Australia, 1979).

The monograph literature on ideology in Australia is extremely limited, but the following are useful: *A New Britannia: an Argument Concerning the Social Origins of Australian Radicalism and Nationalism*, by H. McQueen (Penguin, Australia, 1970); *Australian Conservatism: Essays in Twentieth Century History*, edited by Cameron Hazlehurst (ANU Press, 1979); and *Socialism or Nationalism: Which Road for the Australian Labor Movement*, by Jon West *et al.* (Pathfinder Press, 1979). Of wider relevance in this area are *Equality and Authority: a Study of Class, Status and Power in Australia*, by S. Encel (Cheshire, 1970); *Elites in Australia*, by John Highey *et al.* (Routledge and Kegan Paul, 1979); and *Class Structures in Australian History: Documents, Narrative, Argument*, by Robert W. Connell and T. H. Irving (Longman Cheshire, 1980). Literature on the media is also limited, but *Mass Media in Australia*, edited by Gersh Major (Hodder and Stoughton, Australia, 1976), provides a good introduction and *Politics and the Media*, by Henry Rosenbloom (Fitzroy Scribe, rev. edn, 1978) is a more specialized work.

Constitution

There is a useful literature on the Australian constitution general-
ly, including *A Constitutional History of Australia*, by W. G.
McMinn (Oxford University Press, Australia, 1979); *The Making
of the Australian Constitution*, by J. A. La Nauze (Melbourne
University Press, 1972); *Cases and Materials on Constitutional
Law*, by Colin Howard and Cheryl Saunders (Law Books, 1979);
*Labor and the Constitution, 1972–1975: Essays and Commentaries
on the Controversies of the Whitlam Years*, edited by Gareth Evans
(Heinemann, Australia, 1977); and *Conventions, the Australian
Constitution and the Future*, by Mark Cooray (Legal Books, 1979).

Various aspects of federalism are dealt with in *Australian
Federalism*, by Russell Mathews (ANU Press, 1977); *The Australian Federation*, by Jean Holmes (Allen and Unwin, 1978); *Patterns of Australian Federalism*, by J. E. Richardson (Centre for
Research on Federal Financial Relations, ANU, 1973); *Administrative Federalism: Selected Documents in Australian Inter-
Governmental Relations*, edited by Kenneth W. Wiltshire (University of Queensland Press, 1977); and *Financing the Small States
in Australian Federalism*, by R. J. May (Oxford University Press,
Australia, 1971).

Parliament and the executive

Although there is only a small literature on the Australian
Parliament it is a subject of growing interest and, with the
formation of an Australian Study of Parliament Group, a steady
growth can be expected. Meanwhile the following provide some
useful insights: *Inside the Australian Parliament*, by David H.
Soloman (Allen and Unwin, Australia, 1978); *The Acculturation
to Political Work: New Members of the Federal Backbench*, by J.
Walter (Parliamentary Folio Monograph No.2, Australian Political Science Association Series An. 1 Parliament of Australia, 1979);
and *Influence Without Power: the Role of the Backbench in
Australian Foreign Policy, 1976–77*, by M. Indyk (Parliamentary
Folio Monograph No.1, 1979). The standard works on parliamen-
tary procedure are J. R. Odgers, *Australian Senate Practice* (Commonwealth Government Printer, 3rd edn, 1967) and J. A. Pettifer,
House of Representatives Practice (Commonwealth Government
Printer, 1981).

A curiously neglected area in Australian politics, though some-
what less so in the periodical literature, is that of the Prime
Minister and the Cabinet. The standard works at present are
Cabinet Government in Australia, by S. Encel (Melbourne Uni-

versity Press, 2nd edn, 1974) and *Mr. Prime Minister: Australian Prime Ministers, 1901–1972*, by Colin A. Hughes (Oxford University Press, Australia, 1976).

Political parties and representation

An area of Australian politics to which a good deal of attention has been paid, however, is that of political parties and elections. Certainly it was one of the areas in which some of the earlier monographs were written, as *The Australian Political Party System*, by S. R. Davis *et al.* (Angus and Robertson, 1954), *Australian Parties in a Changing Society, 1945–67*, by Louise Overacker (Cheshire, 1968), and *Australian Party Politics*, by James Jupp (Melbourne University Press, 2nd edn, 1968) illustrate, but more recent works, such as *Political Parties in Australia*, by Graeme Starr *et al.* (Heinemann, Australia, 1978) now exist. In addition, a number of books are devoted to particular parties: *Labor in Vain? A Survey of the Australian Labor Party*, by D. W. Rawson (Longman, Australia, 1966); *The Split: the Australian Labor Party in the Fifties*, by Robert Murray *et al.* (Cheshire, 1970); *The Democratic Labor Party*, by P. L. Reynolds (Jacaranda Press, 1974); *Looking at the Liberals*, edited by Raymond Aitchison (Cheshire, 1974); and *The Liberal Party: Principles and Performance*, by Peter G. Tiver (Jacaranda Press, 1978).

Australian General Elections, by Malcolm Mackerras (Angus and Robertson, 1972), and *Voting for the Australian House of Representatives, 1901–1964*, by Colin A. Hughes and B. D. Graham (ANU Press, 1974), provide general coverage of elections, whilst *Policies and Partisans: Australian Electoral Opinion, 1941–1968*, by Murray Goot (University of Sydney, 1969), and *Society and Electoral Behaviour in Australia: a Study of Three Decades*, by David A. Kemp (University of Queensland Press, 1978), deal with electoral behaviour. There are also some studies of particular elections: *Australia Votes: the 1958 Federal Election*, by D. W. Rawson (ANU Press, 1961); *Labor to Power: Australia's 1972 Election*, edited by Henry Mayer (Angus and Robertson, 1973); and *The Australian National Elections of 1977*, by Howard R. Penniman (American Enterprises Institute for Public Policy, 1979).

As in all four countries covered in this chapter, the literature on pressure groups is extremely limited and in the Australian case there is only one general book on the subject, *Interest Groups and Public Policy: Case Studies from Australian States*, edited by Roger Scott (Macmillan, Australia, 1980), but *In Union is*

Strength: a History of Trade Unions in Australia, 1788–1974, by
Ian Turner (Nelson, Australia, 1976); *Unions and Unionists in
Australia*, by D. W. Rawson (Allen and Unwin, 1978); and
Catholics and the Free Society: an Australian Symposium, edited
by Henry Mayer (Cheshire, 1961) add to the limited periodical
coverage.

State and local governments

The literature on state government in Australia has grown considerably since the 1960s, but it has dealt almost exclusively with
individual states, and there is no recent book on state government
and politics generally, so that *The Government of the Australian
States*, edited by S. R. Davis (Longman, 1960), and *Politics at State
Level in Australia*, edited by John Rorke (University of Sydney,
1970), remain the principal sources. New South Wales has the
most and Tasmania the least extensive literature, and the scope of
the coverage of each state varies markedly. On New South Wales,
for instance, there is *The Framework of Government in New South
Wales*, by L. J. Rose (Government Printer, Sydney, 1972); *New
South Wales Elections*, by Malcolm Mackerras (Department of
Political Science, ANU, 1973); *The Parliament of New South
Wales, 1856–1965*, by Geoffrey Hawker (Government Printer,
Sydney, 1971); and *The Country Party in New South Wales: a
Study of Organisation and Survival*, by Don Aitkin (ANU Press,
1972); on Queensland: *Three Decades of Queensland Political
History, 1929–1960*, by Clem Lack (Government Printer, Bris-
bane, 1962); *Images and Issues: the Queensland State Elections of
1963 and 1966*, by Colin A. Hughes (ANU Press, 1969); and
Voting for the Queensland Legislative Assembly, 1890–1964, by
Colin A. Hughes and B. D. Graham (Department of Political
Science, ANU, 1974); on South Australia: *Responsible Govern-
ment in South Australia*, by Gordon D. Combe (Government
Printer, Adelaide, 1957); *South Australia*, by Michael Page (Rig-
by, 1979); and *Playford to Dunstan: the Politics of Transition*, by
Neal Blewett and Dean Jaensch (Cheshire, 1971); on Tasmania:
Tasmania: a Century of Responsible Government, 1856–1956,
edited by F. C. Greene (Government Printer, Hobart, 1956); on
Victoria: *The Government of Victoria*, by Marjorie J. Holmes
(University of Queensland Press, 1976), and *Politics, Power and
Persuasion: the Liberals in Victoria*, by Peter Aimer (James
Bennett, 1973); on Western Australia: *The Organisation of Gov-
ernment in Western Australia*, by Martyn Forrest (University of

Western Australia, rev. edn, 1979); and *Western Australian Elections and Politics 1965–78: a Handbook and Guide*, by David Black and Michael Wood (Western Australian Institute of Technology, 1979); and on the Northern Territory: *The Government of the Northern Territory*, by A. J. Heatley (University of Queensland Press, 1979), and *Under One Flag: the Northern Territory Elections, 1980*, by Dean Jaensch and P. Loveday (Allen and Unwin, 1980).

Local government in Australia is fairly well covered in the periodical literature, but less so in book form, with *The Civic Frontier: the Origins of Local Communities and Local Government in Victoria*, by Bernard Barrett (Melbourne University Press, 1979), and *Albany to Zechar: a Look at Local Government*, by Ruth Atkins (Law Book Co., 1979), being the principal contributions.

Administration and policy studies

The most comprehensive textbook on public administration is *Government Administration in Australia*, by R. H. Spann (Allen and Unwin, Australia, 1979). There is still no adequate replacement for *Career Service: an Introduction to the History of Personnel Administration in the Commonwealth Public Service of Australia, 1901–1961*, by G. E. Caiden (Melbourne University Press, 1965), although other aspects of public administration are beginning to be covered: for example, *Politics Between Departments: the Fragmentation of Executive Control in Australia*, by Martin Painter and Bernard Carey (University of Queensland Press, 1979), and *New Bureaucracy: Reconstruction of State Government Bureaucracies to Meet the Needs and Expectations of Post-Industrial Society*, by Allan R. B. Skertchly (Government Printer, Perth, 1977).

Policy studies are a growing area in Australian political science, although this has manifested itself principally in the periodical literature to date. Nonetheless, useful monographs, such as *Public Policy in Australia*, edited by R. Forward (Cheshire, 1974), and *Welfare Politics in Australia*, by A. Graycar (Macmillan, 1979), have become available. A much more highly developed area of policy studies is that devoted to foreign affairs, and only a small selection can be cited here: *Politics and Foreign Policy in Australia*, by Henry S. Albinski (Durham University Press, NC, 1970); *Australian Foreign Policy*, by K. M. Thomson (Cassell, Australia, 1975); *Australia and the World: a Political Handbook*, by J. P. Chiddick and Max E. Teichmann (Macmillan, Australia, 1977); and *Australian External Policy Under Labor: Content, Process and the National Debate*, by Henry S. Albinski (University of Queensland Press, 1977).

The ethnic make-up of the Australian population is an important factor in Australian politics and has not been neglected in the literature. In particular the impact of post-war immigration is dealt with in *Immigrants and Politics*, by R. Paul Wilson (ANU Press, 1973). *Race Relations in Australia: Aborigines, Politics and the Law*, by C. M. Tatz (University of New England Publishing Unit, 1979); and *Racism: the Australian Experience – a Study of Racial Prejudice in Australia*, edited by F. S. Stevens (Australian and New Zealand Book Co., 1971) deal with racial policy generally as well as the policy towards Aborigines. The latter are dealt with in greater depth in *Aborigines in Australia: a Documentary History of Attitudes Affecting Official Policy on the Australian Aborigine*, edited by Sharman N. Stone (Heinemann, Australia, 1976); *Australia's Policy Towards Aborigines*, by Herbert C. Coombs (Minority Rights Group, London, 1978); and *Black and White Australians*, by Margaret A. Franklin (Heinemann, Australia, 1976).

Journals

There are a number of journals published in Australia devoted to politics and political science. These include *Politics* (Kensington, NSW, 1966–), the journal of the Australian Political Studies Association; the *Australian Journal of Politics and History* (1955 –); the *Australian Journal of Public Administration* (formerly entitled *Public Administration*, 1938–); the *Australian Journal of Social Issues* (1961–); the *Australian Municipal Journal* (1921–); and the *Australian Foreign Affairs Record* (formerly *Current Notes on International Issues*, 1936–). In addition, relevant articles are frequently found in *Historical Studies* (formerly *Historical Studies of Australia and New Zealand*, 1940–); the *Australian and New Zealand Journal of Sociology* (1965–); and in *Pacific Affairs* (1928–), whilst periodicals covering a wider range of matters, such as *Australian Outlook* (1947–) and the *Australian Quarterly* (1929–), are also useful sources.

Canada

Bibliographies and reference works

The most comprehensive bibliographic tool is *Canadiana* (1950 –), which provides a monthly list of works of Canadian interest, including federal and provincial official publications. *A Bibliography of Canadian Bibliographies*, by Raymond Tanghe (University of Toronto Press, 1960), with supplements for 1964 and 1965 by Madeleine Pellerin, published by the Bibliographical Society of Canada in 1966, is useful, though dated. More recent is *Canadian Reference Sources: A Selective Guide*, edited by Dorothy E. Ryder (Canadian Library Association, 1973). In addition, the National Library of Canada has published a list of *Canadian Theses* annually since 1960. The Canadian Department of External Affairs has published two limited but useful guides, *Canadian Studies Bibliographies* (1977), which include sections on political science, sociology, history and economics, and a *Guide to Resources for Canadian Studies in Britain*, by Valerie Bloomfield (1979). *Canada Since 1867: A Bibliographical Guide*, edited by J. L. Granatstein and Paul Stevens (Samuel Stevens and Hakkert, 2nd rev. edn, 1977), is a useful general bibliography with sections on politics, business and economic history, social and intellectual history, the regions, and foreign and defence policy. The most valuable bibliography for politics, however, is found in *The Canadian Political System*, by Richard J. Van Loon and Michael S. Whittington (McGraw-Hill–Ryerson, 3rd edn, 1981). This contains a most extensive list of monographs and of periodical literature. On political parties in particular there is *Canadian Political Parties, 1867–1968: A Historical Bibliography*, edited by Grace F. Heggie (Macmillan, Canada, 1977).

A number of official and commercial publications contain useful information on Canada and Canadian politics. These include the *Canada Yearbook* (1905– , although some years have been amalgamated), which not only includes sections on federal and provincial government, but periodically contains relevant articles on various aspects of politics. *The Canadian Almanac and Directory* (Copp Clark, 1848–) is a valuable compendium of information and the *Canadian Annual Review* (published since 1902; now published by University of Toronto Press, 1960–) contains sections on political events, Parliament, the national economy, external affairs and defence. The *Dictionary of Canadian Biography* (University of Toronto Press, 1966–), which has a projected twenty volumes, is a useful source on figures in Canadian political history, but the most useful publication for keeping in touch with political events is *Canadian News Facts* (Canadian News Facts, 1967–), which is a digest of current events culled from Canadian newspapers. A wide variety of parliamentary papers is also available: the *Official Report of Debates of the Senate* and *Debates. Official Report (House of Commons)*, the *Votes and Proceedings* of both houses, which include committee reports, *Acts of the Parliament of Canada*, and the *Treaties* series. Similar documents are available from provincial legislatures. All federal publications in Canada, including parliamentary papers, are available in the two official languages, English and French, either in separate editions or side-by-side translations. The *Canadian Parliamentary Guide* (1900–), edited and published annually by Pierre G. Normandin, provides extensive information about the Canadian government at federal and provincial levels, including election results since 1867 and biographical sketches of all current members of the Senate and the House of Commons and members of the provincial legislatures.

Politics

The growth of the literature on politics and political science since the 1960s has been greater in Canada than in any of the other three countries covered by this chapter. This is true of both monograph and periodical literature. The principal problem that this presents is therefore that of selectivity, even though some areas remain relatively neglected, especially in the monograph field. What follows therefore is only a small selection of what is available.

The Pelican History of Canada, by Kenneth McNaught (Penguin, 1969), is an excellent short history, but an extensive treatment can be found in *The Canadians, 1867–1967*, edited by J. M. S. Careless and R. C. Brown (Macmillan, Canada, 1967). In addition, *Historical Statistics of Canada*, edited by M. C. Urquhart and K. A. H. Buckley (Cambridge University Press, 1965), and *Canadian Political Facts*, edited by Colin Campbell (Methuen, Canada, 1977), are invaluable sources of information.

A variety of relevant sociological texts are available, of which *Canada: A Sociological Profile*, edited by W. E. Mann (Copp Clark, 1968), and *Canadian Society: Sociological Perspectives*, edited by B. R. Blishen *et al.* (Macmillan, Canada, 1968), are still worth reading, whilst *French–Canadian Society*, edited by Marcel Rioux and Yves Martin (McClelland and Stewart, 1964), remains invaluable, as does John Porter's classic *The Vertical Mosaic: An Analysis of Social Class and Power in Canada* (University of Toronto Press, 1965). A more recent assessment can be found in *Foundations of Canadian Political Culture: Readings in Political Socialisation in Canada*, edited by Jon H. Pammett and Michael S. Whittington (Macmillan, Canada, 1976), and *The Roots of Disunity: A Look at Canadian Political Culture*, by David V. Bell and

Lorne Tepperman (McClelland and Stewart, 1979). As in Australia, the literature on the media is limited, but the *Report of the Senate Committee on the Mass Media* (3 vols, Queen's Printer, 1971) is useful and there is a growing periodical literature.

An increasing interest has been shown in political ideology in recent years, although *A History of Canadian Political Thought*, by G. P. de T. Glazebrook (McClelland and Stewart, 1966), still remains useful. *Political Parties and Ideology in Canada: Liberals, Conservatives, Socialists, Nationalists*, by William Christian and Colin Campbell (McGraw-Hill–Ryerson, 1974). *Ideological Perspectives on Canada*, by Patricia M. Marchak (McGraw-Hill–Ryerson, 1975), and *The Language of Canadian Politics: A Guide to Important Terms and Concepts*, by J. McMenemy (Wiley, Canada, 1980), specifically relate ideology to Canadian politics.

The number of general texts on Canadian politics is now considerable, and a wide choice of approaches is available, from the institutional to the functional and from collections of readings to comprehensive textbooks. The most comprehensive textbook available is *The Canadian Political System: Environment, Structure and Process*, by Richard J. Van Loon and Michael S. Whittington (McGraw-Hill–Ryerson, 3rd edn, 1981), which, as noted above, has an excellent bibliography, and the most useful collection of readings is *Politics: Canada*, edited by Paul Fox (McGraw-Hill–Ryerson, 5th edn, 1982), which contains an excellent guide to Canadian government publications and a valuable series of select bibliographies. R. Macgregor Dawson's classic *Government of Canada* (University of Toronto Press, 5th edn, rev. by Norman Ward, 1970) is still worth reading, and the following provide a variety of approaches: *The Canadian Political Process: A Reader*, edited by O. Kruhlak *et al.* (Holt Rinehart and Winston, rev. edn, 1973); *Working Papers on Canadian Politics*, by John Meisel (McGill–Queen's University Press, rev. edn, 1973); *Government in Canada*, by Thomas A. Hockin (Norton, 1975); *Canadian Politics: An Introduction to Systematic Analysis*, by Jane Jenson and Brian W. Tomlin (McGraw-Hill–Ryerson, 1977); and *Approaches to Canadian Politics*, edited by John H. Redekop (Prentice-Hall, 1978). *Renegade in Power: the Diefenbaker Years*, by Peter C. Newman (McClelland and Stewart, 1963) and *The Distemper of Our Times: Canadian Politics in Transition, 1963–68*, by Peter C. Newman (McClelland and Stewart, 1968) are highly readable and illustrate the flavour and atmosphere of Canadian politics.

Constitution

Much of the writing on the Canadian constitution inevitably overlaps with that on federalism, but there is a very worthwhile literature on the constitution in its own right. *The Structure of Canadian Government*, by J. R. Mallory (Methuen, Canada, 1971), and *The Constitutional Process in Canada*, by R. I. Cheffins (McGraw-Hill, 1969), remain the two most useful works, whilst *Essays on the Constitution: Aspects of Canadian Law and Politics*, by F. R. Scott (University of Toronto Press, 1977), provides a more recent discussion. There are, of course, a number of specialized texts, several of which deal in particular with judicial review and the role of the Supreme Court of Canada: *Leading Constitutional Decisions*, by Peter H. Russell (McClelland and Stewart, rev. edn, 1973); *The Courts and the Canadian Constitution*, by W. R. Lederman (McClelland and Stewart, 1963); *The Judicial Committee and the British North America Act*, by G. P. Browne (University of Toronto Press, 1967); and *The Judicial Review of Legislation in Canada*, by B. Strayer (University of Toronto Press, 1969). *The Canadian Bill of Rights*, by W. S. Tarnopolsky (McClelland and Stewart, 2nd edn, 1973) is also useful.

More has probably been written about federalism than any other aspect of Canadian politics, and the output continues unabated; what follows can therefore be only a small selection. No study of Canadian federalism would be complete without some reference to the *Report of the Royal Commission on Bilingualism and Biculturalism* (commonly known as the B and B Commission) (Preliminary Report plus 4 vols, Queen's Printer, 1967), together with the many volumes of evidence and special reports prepared for it, some of which are cited below. *Evolving Canadian Federalism*, by A. R. M. Lower *et al.* (Duke University Press, 1958), and *The Future of Canadian Federalism*, edited by Paul A. Crepeau and C. B. Macpherson (University of Toronto Press, 1965), are both classic collections of essays. Pierre Trudeau, writing as a Canadian statesman, provides another view of federalism in *Federalism and the French–Canadians* (Macmillan, Canada, 1968). More recent academic writings are prolific: *Constitutional Adaptation and Canadian Federalism since 1945*, by Donald V. Smiley (prepared for the B and B Commission, Queen's Printer, 1970); *The Canadian Political Nationality*, by Donald V. Smiley (Methuen, Canada, 1971); *Canadian Federalism: Myth or Reality?* edited by Peter C. Meekison (Methuen, 3rd edn, Canada, 1977); *Canada in Question: Federalism in the Seventies*, by Donald V.

Smiley (McGraw-Hill, 2nd edn, 1976); *Divided Loyalties: Canadian Concepts of Federalism*, by Edwin R. Black (McGill–Queen's University Press, 1975); *Must Canada Fail?* edited by Richard Simeon (McGill–Queen's University Press, 1977); *Quebec and the Constitution, 1960–1978*, by Edward McWhinney (University of Toronto Press, 1979); *Regionalism in Canada: Flexible Federation or Fractional Nation*, by George A. Rawlyk *et al.* (Prentice-Hall, 1979); and *Canada Challenged: the Viability of Confederation*, edited by R. B. Byers and Robert W. Redford (Canadian Institute of International Affairs, 1979). Specialized treatment of federal –provincial relations can be found in *Federal–Provincial Diplomacy: the Making of Public Policy in Canada*, by Richard Simeon (University of Toronto Press, 1972), and *Initiative and Response: the Adaptation of Canadian Federalism to Regional Economic Development*, by A. G. S. Careless (McGill–Queen's University Press, 1977). Canadian political culture and federalism are dealt with in *Public Opinion and Canadian Identity*, by Mildred A. Schwartz (University of California Press, 1967) and regionalism and federalism in *Politics and Territory: the Sociology of Regional Persistence in Canada*, by Mildred A. Schwartz (McGill–Queen's University Press, 1974). Federalism is also dealt with in much of the literature on provincial politics, particularly that dealing with Quebec, which is covered in this section.

Parliament and the executive

The best introductory text on the Canadian Parliament is *The Canadian Legislative System*, by Robert J. Jackson and Michael M. Atkinson (Macmillan, 2nd rev. edn, Canada, 1980). The Canadian Senate has not received very much attention, which, given its relative unimportance, is not surprising, but *The Modern Senate of Canada, 1925–1963: A Reappraisal*, by F. A. Kunz (University of Toronto Press, 1965), and *The Unreformed Senate of Canada*, by Robert A. Mackay (McClelland and Stewart, 1967), remain useful, and *The Canadian Senate: A Lobby from Within*, by Colin Campbell (Macmillan, Canada, 1978), provides a more recent commentary. By far the best book on the House of Commons is John B. Stewart's *The Canadian House of Commons: Procedure and Reform* (McGill–Queen's University Press, 1977), of which a new edition is in preparation, and this is well supplemented in a behavioural approach by *Influence in Parliament: Canada*, by Allan Kornberg and William T. Mishler (Duke University Press, 1976). Two older studies worthy of mention are *The Canadian House of Commons: Representation*, by Norman

Ward (University of Toronto Press, 2nd edn, 1963), and *Bilingualism and Biculturalism in the Canadian House of Commons*, by David Hoffman and Norman Ward (prepared for the Bilingualism and Biculturalism Commission, Queen's Printer, 1970). One of the most recent additions to the literature is *Parliament, Policy and Representation*, by Harold D. Clarke *et al.* (Methuen, Canada, 1980).

The Cabinet and the Prime Minister is a neglected area in the literature, and only two major studies exist, *The Prime Minister and the Cabinet*, by W. A. Matheson (Methuen, Canada, 1976), and *The Prime Minister in Canadian Government and Politics*, by R. M. Punnett (Macmillan, Canada, 1977), although there is also a book of readings, *Apex of Power: The Prime Minister and Political Leadership in Canada*, edited by Thomas A. Hockin (Prentice-Hall, 1971). One of the Bilingualism and Biculturalism Commission studies, however, adds a useful dimension: *Cabinet Formation and Bicultural Relations: Some Case Studies*, by Frederick W. Gibson (Queen's Printer, 1970).

Political parties and representation

After federalism and Quebec, political parties and elections have probably generated a more extensive literature than any other area. *Party Politics in Canada*, edited by Hugh Thorburn (Prentice-Hall, 4th edn, 1979), is a standard set of readings and *Political Parties in Canada*, by Conrad Winn and John McMemeny (Prentice-Hall, 1979), is a useful introductory text. *Political Parties and the Canadian Social Structure* and *Canadian Political Parties: Origin, Character, Impact*, both by Frederick C. Engelmann and Mildred A. Schwartz (Prentice-Hall, 1967 and 1975, respectively), provide a more sociological approach, and a more recent discussion can be found in *Crisis, Challenge and Change: Party and Class in Canada*, by M. Janine Brodie and Jane Jenson (Methuen, Canada, 1980). There is a variety of monographs on particular parties, although minor parties tend to receive more attention than the two major parties, and in recent monograph literature the Liberal Party in particular has been largely neglected. Four studies of wider interest are *Canadian Party Platforms, 1867–1968*, edited by D. Owen Carrigan (University of Illinois Press, 1968); *Political Party Financing in Canada*, by Khayyam Z. Paltiel (McGraw-Hill, 1970); *The Selection of National Party Leaders*, by John C. Courtney (Macmillan, Canada, 1973); and *Citizen Politicians – Canada: Party Officials in a Democratic Society*, by Allan Kornberg *et al.* (Carolinas Academic Press, 1979). The Conservative Party is dealt with in *The Conservative Party in Canada, 1920*

–1949, by J. R. Williams (Duke University Press, 1956), *The Politics of Survival: the Conservative Party of Canada, 1939–45*, by J. L. Granatstein (University of Toronto Press, 1967), and, more recently, *The Tory Syndrome: Leadership Politics in the Progressive Conservative Party*, by George C. Perlin (McGill–Queen's University Press, 1980). The most recent general monograph on the Liberals is J. W. Pickersgill's *The Liberal Party* (McClelland and Stewart, 1962), although there is the more specialized *The Regional Decline of the National Liberal Party: The Liberals in the Prairies*, by David Smith (University of Toronto Press, 1981). Canada's equivalent of the British Labour Party, the New Democratic Party (formerly the Co-operative Commonwealth Federation), has been the subject of a great deal of attention: *A Protest Movement Becalmed: a Study of Change in the CCF*, by Leo Zakuta (University of Toronto Press, 1964); *Canadian Labour in Politics*, by Gad Horowitz (University of Toronto Press, 1968); *The Anatomy of a Party: the National CCF, 1932–61*, by Walter D. Young (University of Toronto Press, 1969); and *Socialism in Canada: a Study of the CCF in Federal and Provincial Politics*, by Ivan Avakumovic (McClelland and Stewart, 1978). Another minor party, Social Credit, is also prominent in the literature: *Democracy and Discontent: Progressivism, Socialism and Social Credit*, by Walter D. Young (Ryerson, 1969), is a comparison of the CCF/NDP and Social Credit; *The Rise of a Third Party: a Study in Crisis Politics*, by Maurice Pinard (Prentice-Hall, 1971), and *The Dynamics of Right-wing Protest: a Political Analysis of Social Credit in Quebec*, by Michael B. Stein (University of Toronto Press, 1973), concentrate on the Quebec wing of the national movement, whilst a number of studies mentioned below deal with Social Credit at provincial level. The Communist Party is discussed in *The Communist Party in Canada: A History*, by Ivan Avakumovic (McClelland and Stewart, 1975).

There are several general studies of Canadian elections, notably *Canada Votes: A Handbook of Federal and Provincial Elections Data*, by Howard A. Scarrow (Hauser Press, 1962); *Pendulum of Power: Canada's Federal Elections*, by J. Murray Beck (Prentice-Hall, 1968); *Voting in Canada: a Selection of Papers*, edited by John C. Courtney (Prentice-Hall, 1967); and *The Election Process in Canada*, by Terence H. Qualter (McGraw-Hill, 1976). But none is particularly recent. Similarly, there are several studies of particular elections or periods: *The Canadian General Election of 1957*, by John Meisel (University of Toronto Press, 1962); *The Diefenbaker Interlude: Parties and Voting in Canada – An Interregnum*, by Peter Regenstreif (Longman, Canada, 1965); *Papers on the 1962 Election*, edited by John Meisel (University of Toronto Press, 1962); and *Journey to Power: the Story of a Canadian Election* [1968] by Donald Peacock (Ryerson, 1968).

Although pressure groups are, as in the other three countries, a relatively neglected area, there is a growing literature on the subject in Canada: *Pressure Group Behaviour in Canadian Politics*, edited by A. Paul Pross (McGraw-Hill–Ryerson, 1975); *Elite Accommodation in Canadian Politics*, by Robert Presthus (Macmillan, Canada, 1973); *Business and Government in Canada: Selected Readings*, edited by K. J. Rea and J. T. McLeod (Holt, Rhinehart and Winston, 1969); *Silent Surrender: the Multi-National Corporation in Canada*, by Kari Levitt (Macmillan, Canada, 1970); *The Canadian Corporate Elite: An Anatomy of Economic Power*, by W. Clement (McClelland and Stewart, 1975); and *Organised Labour and Pressure Politics: the Canadian Labour Congress, 1956–1968*, by David Kwavnick (McGill–Queen's University Press, 1972). The role of labour is also covered extensively in the literature cited earlier on the CCF/NDP.

Provincial and local governments

Provincial government and politics have been the subject of growing interest, although some distinction should be drawn between this area in general and the question of Quebec in particular. There are several general texts: *Provincial Government and Politics: Comparative Essays*, edited by Donald C. Rowat (Department of Political Science, Carleton University, 2nd edn, 1973); *The Provincial Political Systems: Comparative Essays*, edited by David J. Bellamy *et al.* (Methuen, Canada, 1976); *Canadian Provincial Politics: the Party Systems of the Ten Provinces*, edited by Martin Robin (Prentice-Hall, 2nd edn, 1978); *Public Policy and Provincial Politics*, by Marsha A. and William M. Chandler (McGraw-Hill–Ryerson, 1979); *Small Worlds: Provinces and Parties in Canadian Political Life*, by David J. Elkins and Richard Simeon (Methuen, Canada, 1980); and *Representative Democracy in the Canadian Provinces*, by Allan Kornberg *et al.* (Prentice-Hall, 1982). There is also a steady stream of periodical literature. The coverage of individual provinces is uneven, and in several cases there is no recent major study: *Politics in Newfoundland*, by S. J. R. Noel (University of Toronto Press, 1971); *The Management of a Myth: the Politics of Legitimation in a Newfoundland Community*, by A. P. Cohen (Manchester University Press, 1975); *The Government of Nova Scotia*, by J. Murray Beck (University of Toronto Press, 1957); *Politics in New Brunswick*, by Hugh Thorburn (University of Toronto Press, 1961);

Gentlemen, Players and Politicians [New Brunswick], by Dalton Camp (McClelland and Stewart, 1970); *The Government of Prince Edward Island*, by Frank Mackinnon (University of Toronto Press, 1951); *The Government and Politics of Ontario*, by D. C. Macdonald (Macmillan of Canada, 1975); *Responsible Government in Ontario*, by Frederick F. Schindler (University of Toronto Press, 1969); *The Government of Manitoba*, by Murray S. Donnelly (University of Toronto Press, 1963); *Politics in Saskatchewan*, edited by Norman Ward and Duff Spafford (Longman, Canada, 1968); *Saskatchewan Government*, by Evelyn Eager (Western Producer Prairie Books, 1980); *Agrarian Socialism: the CCF in Saskatchewan – A Study in Political Sociology*, by Seymour M. Lipset (Anchor Books, rev. edn, 1968); *Prairie Liberalism: the Liberal Party in Saskatchewan, 1905–1971*, by David E. Smith (University of Toronto Press, 1975); *The Politics of Defeat: the Decline of the Liberal Party in Saskatchewan*, by Barry Wilson (Western Producer Prairie Books, 1980); *Democracy in Alberta: the Theory and Practice of a Quasi-Party System*, by C. B. Macpherson (University of Toronto Press, 1953); *The Social Credit Movement in Alberta*, by John A. Irving (University of Toronto Press, 1968); *Prairie Politics and Society: Regionalism in Decline*, by Roger Gibbins (Butterworths, Canada, 1980); and *Pillars of Profit: the Company Province, 1934–1972* [British Columbia], by Martin Robin (McClelland and Stewart, 1973).

Of all the provinces, however, Quebec has the most extensive literature in both English and French, and what follows is only a small selection of that available in English: *Quebec: Social Change and Political Crisis*, edited by K. McRoberts and D. Postgate (McClelland and Stewart, 1976); *Quebec Society and Politics: Vews from the Inside*, edited by D. C. Thomson (McClelland and Stewart, 1973); *French–Canadian Nationalism: An Anthology*, edited by Ramsay Cook (Macmillan, Canada, 1969); *Quebec in the Duplessis Era, 1935–1959: Dictatorship or Democracy?* edited by Cameron Nish (Copp Clark, 1970); *The Union Nationale: a Study of Quebec Nationalism*, by Herbert F. Quinn (University of Toronto Press, 1963); *The State of Quebec*, by P. Desbarats (McClelland and Stewart, 1965); *The Decolonisation of Quebec: An Analysis of Leftwing Nationalism*, by H. and S. Milner (McClelland and Stewart, 1973); *Quebec/Canada and the October Crisis* [1971], edited by Dan Daniels (Black Rose Books, 1973); *The Shouting Signpainters: a Literary and Political Account of Quebec Revolutionary Nationalism* (Monthly Review Press, 1972); *Bleeding Hearts – Bleeding Country: Canada and the Quebec Crisis* [1971], by Denis Smith (Hurtig, 1971); *The Rise of the Parti*

Québécois, 1967–76, by John T. Saywell (University of Toronto Press, 1977); *Politics in the New Quebec*, by H. Milner (McClelland and Stewart, 1978); *An Option for Quebec*, by René Levesque (McClelland and Stewart, 1968); *Quebec in Question*, by Marcel Rioux (James, Lewis and Samual, 1971); *White Niggers of North America*, by Pierre Vallières (McClelland and Stewart, trans. by Joan Pinkler, 1971); and *The Question of Separatism: Quebec and the Struggle over Sovereignty*, by J. Jacobs (Random House, 1980). In addition, much of the literature on federalism deals with various aspects of provincial politics in general and Quebec in particular, whilst the growth of separatist feeling in Western Canada is covered in *Western Separatism: the Myths, Realities and Dangers*, edited by Larry Pratt and Garth Stevenson (Hurtig, 1980).

Local government is a somewhat neglected area, although there is a fairly extensive periodical literature. The principal monographs are *The Politics and Government of Urban Canada*, by Lionel D. Feldman and Michael D. Goldrick (Methuen, Canada, 1968); *The Real World of City Politics* [a study of Toronto], by J. Lorimer (University of Toronto Press, 1969); *The Canadian Municipal System: Essays on the Improvement of Local Government*, by Donald C. Rowat (McClelland and Stewart, 1969); and, more recently, *Local Government in Canada: An Introduction*, by C. R. and S. Tindal (McGraw-Hill–Ryerson, 1979).

Administration and policy studies

One of the strongest areas of Canadian political science is public administration, which constitutes separate schools in a number of Canadian universities, and again only a small selection can be cited: *Public Administration in Canada*, edited by Abraham M. Willms and W. D. K. Kernaghan (Methuen, Canada, 2nd rev. edn, 1971); *The Business of Government: An Introduction to Canadian Public Administration*, by Thomas J. Stevens (McGraw-Hill–Ryerson, 1978); *Public Policy in Canada: Organisation, Process and Management*, edited by G. Bruce Doern and Peter Aucoin (Macmillan, Canada, 1979); *Canadian Public Service: A Physiology of Government, 1867–1970*, by J. E. Hodgetts (University of Toronto Press, 1973); *Public Finance in Canada: Selected Readings*, edited by A. J. Robinson and James Cutt (Methuen, Canada, 1968); *Canadian Crown Corporations*, by C. A. Ashley and R. G. H. Smails (Macmillan, Canada, 1965); and *The Regulatory Process in Canada*, edited by G. Bruce Doern (Macmillan, Canada, 1978). Policy studies are similarly extensive: *Canadian Social Policy*, edited by Shankar A. Yelaja (Wilfrid

Laurier University Press, 1978); *The Structure of Policy-Making in Canada*, by G. Bruce Doern and Peter Aucoin (Macmillan, Canada, 1971); *The Politics and Management of Canadian Economic Policy*, by Richard W. Phidd and G. Bruce Doern (Macmillan, Canada, 1978); *The Making of Canadian Foreign Policy*, by R. B. Farrell (Prentice-Hall, 1969); *Canada: a Middle-Aged Power*, by John W. Holmes (McClelland and Stewart, 1976); and *A Foremost Nation: Canadian Foreign Policy and a Changing World*, edited by Norman Hillmer and Garth Stevenson (McClelland and Stewart, 1977).

There is also a small but useful literature on Canada's non-white population, for example: *The Indian: Assimilation, Integration or Segregation*, by R. P. Bowles *et al.* (Prentice-Hall, 1973); *Canada and its People of African Descent*, by Leo W. Bertley (Bilongo Publications, 1977); and *White Canada Forever: Popular Attitudes and Public Policy Towards Orientals in British Columbia*, by Peter W. Ward (McGill–Queen's University Press, 1978).

Journals

Canada has a fairly extensive range of relevant journals, most of which accept articles in either English or French and provide an abstract in the other language. These include the *Canadian Journal of Political Science* (1968–), formerly the *Canadian Journal of Economics and Political Science* (1935–1967); *Canadian Public Administration* (1958–); the *Canadian Journal of Political and Social Theory* (1977–); and *Canadian Public Policy* (1977–). There are also a number of journals specializing in areas relevant to politics, such as the *Canadian Journal of Economics* (1968–), the *Canadian Review of Sociology and Anthropology* (1964–) and the *Canadian Historical Review* (1970–). There are other journals covering a wider range of matters, notably the *Queen's Quarterly* (1893–), *Optimum* (1970–) and the *Bulletin of Canadian Studies* (1977–), the journal of the British Association for Canadian Studies.

New Zealand

Bibliographies and reference works

The annual New Zealand National Bibliography (Government Printer, 1966–) is the principal bibliographic work available, and this is supplemented for earlier years by the *New Zealand National Bibliography to the Year 1960*, edited by A. G. Bagnall (4 vols,

Government Printer, 1970–1980) and by the annual *Index to New Zealand Periodicals* (Government Printer, 1940–) with a list of books for the years 1961–1965. *The Union List of Theses of the University of New Zealand, 1910–54* (New Zealand Library Association, 1956, plus supplements) is also a useful source. In addition, there are two relevant specialized bibliographies: *The New Zealand Labour Party, 1916–1966: A Bibliography*, by M. D. Coleman (National Library of New Zealand, 1972) and *Immigration and Immigrants: a Bibliography* (New Zealand Department of Labour, 1975).

The *New Zealand Official Yearbook* (1892–) contains chapters on the history and government of New Zealand, on international relations and other relevant matters. Proceedings of the unicameral New Zealand Parliament are available in *New Zealand Debates* and *Appendices to the Journals of the House of Representatives*, which include the annual reports of government departments and of corporations, reports of commissions, etc. and all papers presented to Parliament. *Statutes of New Zealand* and Statutory Regulations are also published. There is also a great deal of useful information in the *New Zealand Parliamentary Record, 1840 –1949*, edited by G. H. Scholefield (Government Printer, 1950) and the *New Zealand Parliamentary Record, 1950–1969*, edited by J. O. Wilson (Government Printer, 1969).

Politics

There has been a steady growth in recent years in the literature on New Zealand politics, but in size and scope it still lags behind that of at least two of the four countries covered in this chapter. The periodical literature in particular is much more limited. *The Oxford History of New Zealand*, by W. H. Oliver with B. R. Williams (Oxford University Press, New Zealand, 1981) provides an excellent account of New Zealand's development, whilst a shorter account is provided in *History of New Zealand*, by K. A. Sinclair (Allen Lane, rev. edn, 1980). *Contemporary New Zealand: Essays on the Human Resource, Urban Growth and Problems of Society*, edited by K. W. Thomson and A. D. Trlin (Hicks Smith, 1973); *New Zealand Society: Contemporary Perspectives*, edited by Stephen D. Webb and John Collette (Wiley, Australia, 1973); and *Social Class in New Zealand*, edited by David Pitt (Longman Paul, 1977), are useful on the background to New Zealand politics.

One of the undoubted growth areas has been general texts, and a number of texts and readers are now available: *New Zealand,*

Politics of Change, by W. K. Jackson (Reed, 1973); *New Zealand Politics: A Reader*, edited by Stephen Levine (Cheshire, 1975); *Politics in New Zealand: A Reader*, edited by Stephen Levine (Cheshire, 1975), *Politics in New Zealand: A Reader*, edited by Stephen Levine (Allen and Unwin, Australia, 1978); *The New Zealand Political System: Politics in a Small Society*, by Stephen Levine (Allen and Unwin, Australia, 1979); *Unbridled Power: an Interpretation of the New Zealand Constitution and Government*, by G. Palmer (Oxford University Press, 1979); and *The Politics of Utopia: New Zealand and its Government*, by Les Cleveland (Methuen, New Zealand, 1979). There are also some studies of a particular period, such as, *Labour in Power – Promise and Performance: an Evaluation of the Work of the New Zealand Government from 1972 to 1975*, edited by Ray Goldstein with Rod Alley (Price Milburn, 1975), and *The Third Labour Government: a Personal History*, by Michael Bassett (Dunmore, 1976).

Constitution

There is a limited but useful literature on the constitution, though most of it is not very recent: *The New Zealand Constitution*, by K. J. Scott (Oxford University Press, 1962); *Crown Colony Government in New Zealand*, by A. H. McLintock (Government Printer, 1958); *New Zealand and the Statute of Westminster*, edited by J. C. Beaglehole (Victoria University College, Wellington, 1944); and a monograph on New Zealand's abortive quasi-federal system, *The Provincial System in New Zealand, 1852–76*, by W. P. Morrell (Whitcombe and Tombs, 2nd rev. edn, 1964).

Parliament and the executive

A somewhat neglected area is Parliament: *Government by Party: Parliament and Politics in New Zealand*, by A. V. Mitchell (Whitcombe and Tombs, 1966); *The Parliament of New Zealand and Parliament House*, by H. N. Dollimore (Government Printer, 3rd edn, 1973); and *The New Zealand Legislative Council: a Study of the Establishment, Failure and Abolition of an Upper House*, by W. K. Jackson (University of Otago Press, 1972), being the main works available. Parliament may be neglected, but the literature on the New Zealand Cabinet and Prime Minister is virtually non-existent in monograph form, the only work being *The Making of a New Zealand Prime Minister*, by J. Eagles and C. James (Cheshire, 1973).

Political parties and representation

As is often the case, the literature on parties and elections is the most extensive, although there is still no more recent general book than R. S. Milne's *Political Parties in New Zealand* (Oxford University Press, 1966). Moreover, far more attention has been paid to the Labour Party than to its principal rival, the National Party: *Oligarchy and Democracy: the Distribution of Power in the New Zealand National Party, 1936–1949*, by Alan D. Robinson (Institute of Social Studies, The Hague, 1959); *The Rise of the New Zealand Labour: a History of the New Zealand from 1916 to 1940*, by Bruce Brown (Price Milburn, 1962); *Social Change and Party Organisation: the New Zealand Labour Party since 1945*, by Barry S. Gustafson (Sage, 1976); and *Labour's Path to Political Independence: the Origin and Establishment of the New Zealand Labour Party, 1900–1919*, by Barry S. Gustafson (Auckland University Press and Oxford University Press, 1980).

The New Zealand Voter – a Survey of Public Opinion and Electoral Behaviour, by Stephen Levine and Alan D. Robinson (Price Milburn, 1976) is a general study and there are a number of more limited studies: *New Zealand Politics in Action: the 1960 Election Campaign*, by R. M. Chapman *et al.* (Oxford University Press, 1962); *Marginals '72: an analysis of New Zealand's Marginal Electorate*, by R. M. Chapman (Heinemann, New Zealand, 1972); *The New Zealand General Election of 1975*, by Stephen Levine and Juliet Lodge (Price Milburn, 1976); and *New Zealand at the Polls: the General Election of 1978*, by Howard Penniman (American Enterprise Institute, 1980).

The literature on pressure groups is very limited. There is one general monograph, *The Anatomy of Influence: Pressure Groups and Politics in New Zealand*, by Les Cleveland (Hicks Smith, 1972). But there are some individual studies such as *Trade Unions in New Zealand, Past and Present*, by H. O. Roth (Reed, 1973); and *Against the Wind: the Story of of the New Zealand Seamen's Union*, by Conrad Bollinger (New Zealand Seamen's Union, 1968).

Regional and local government

Local government has received rather more attention as far as general texts are concerned: examples are *Local Government and Politics in New Zealand*, by G. W. A. Bush (Allen and Unwin, Australia, 1980); *Local and Regional Government in New Zealand: Functions and Finance*, by Claudia D. Scott (Allen and

Unwin, Australia, 1979); and *Local Government at the Cross-roads*, by R. Sidebotham (Whitcomb and Tombs, 1970); whilst there is a useful but limited periodical literature.

Administration and policy studies

Public administration and policy studies are undoubtedly a growth area of publication, but there has been considerably more emphasis on the latter than on the former. *Government Administration in New Zealand*, by R. J. Polaschek (New Zealand Institute of Public Administration, 1958); *The New Zealand Bureaucrat*, by Thomas B. Smith (Cheshire, 1974); *Regulation-Making Powers and Procedures of the Executive of New Zealand*, by G. Cain (Schools of Law, University of Auckland, 1973); *State Servants and the Public in the 1980s*, edited by R. M. Alley (New Zealand Institute of Public Administration, 1980); and *Establishment of the Ministry of Transport: Some Inside Views*, by M. G. Kerr (School of Political Science and Public Administration, Victoria University of Wellington, 1974), give some idea of the range of monographs in public administration. New Zealand's experience of an Ombudsman has inevitably attracted attention, notably in two studies by L. B. Hill: *The Model Ombudsman: Institutionalising New Zealand's Democratic Experiment* (Princeton University Press, 1976) and *Parliament and the Ombudsman of New Zealand* (Bureau of Government Research, University of Oklahoma, 1974).

A variety of policy studies are available, including several on foreign policy: *Social Policy and Administration in New Zealand*, by C. A. Oram (New Zealand University Press, 1969); *Social Policy and the Welfare State*, by Brian Easton (Allen and Unwin, New Zealand, 1980); *The Politics of Social Security*, by Elizabeth Hanson (Auckland University Press and Oxford University Press, New Zealand, 1980); *Trade, Growth and Anxiety: New Zealand Beyond the Welfare State*, by S. H. Franklin (Methuen, New Zealand, 1978); *The New Zealand Doctor and the Welfare State*, by J. B. Lovell-Smith (Paul, 1966); *New Zealand in World Affairs* (New Zealand Institute of International Affairs, 1977); *New Zealand Foreign Policy*, by Richard Kennaway (Hicks Smith, 1972); and *Beyond New Zealand: the Foreign Policy of a Small State*, edited by John Henderson *et al.* (Methuen, New Zealand, 1980).

There are, as might be expected, a number of studies of ethnic politics: *The Maori Population of New Zealand, 1769–1971*, by Ian D. Pool (Auckland University Press and Oxford University Press,

1977); *The Maori People in the 1960s*, edited by Erik Schwimmer (Longman Paul, 1968); *Racial Issues in New Zealand*, edited by Graham Vaughan (Akarana Press, 1972); *The Maori and New Zealand Politics*, edited by J. G. A. Pocock (Paul, 1965); and *Conflict and Compromise: Essays on the Maori since Colonisation*, by A. W. Reed (Reed, 1975).

Journals

The three major journals relating to New Zealand politics are *Political Science* (Wellington, 1948–); *Public Sector* (formerly the *New Zealand Journal of Public Administration*, 1938–), the Journal of the New Zealand Institute of Public Administration; and *New Zealand Local Government* (1965–). Other relevant journals are *Historical Studies* (formerly *Historical Studies of Australia and New Zealand*, 1940–), the *New Zealand Journal of History* (1967–), the *Australian and New Zealand Journal of Sociology* (1965–), the *New Zealand Law Journal* (1925–) and *Pacific Affairs* (1929–). Journals covering wider matters include *Landfall* (1947–), *Comment* (1959–1971, resuming publication in 1977) and the *New Zealand News Review* (1960–).

South Africa

Bibliography and reference works

The most recent bibliographic work is *South Africa Bibliography: a Survey of Bibliographies and Bibliographical Works*, by Reuben Musiker (David Philip, 2nd edn, 1980). The period to 1910 is covered by a *South African Bibliography*, by Sydney Mendelssohn (1910), which has been extended in *A South African Bibliography to the Year 1925* (Mansell, 1979). Further supplementation is available in *African Books in Print*, edited by Hans. M. Zell (2 vols, Mansell, 1978) and *African Research and Documentation* (African Studies Association (UK), 1973–). There is also a *Catalogue of Theses and Dissertations of the South African Universities* (Potchefstrom University Library, 1978) available on microfiche and a *Bibliography of South African Government Publications* (Department of Cultural Affairs, 1970). A number of more specialized bibliographies are available, including *A Bibliography for the Study of African Politics*, by Robert B. Shaw and Richard L. Sklar (African Studies Center, University of California, LA, 1973), which contains an extensive section on South Africa; *South African Politics, 1933–39*, by G. M. M. Hodge (University of Cape

Town Library, 1965); *South African Parties and Policies, 1910 –1960: a Select Source Book*, by D. W. Kruger (Human and Rouseau, 1960); and *South African Political Materials: Catalogue of the Carter-Karis Collection*, compiled by Susan G. Wynne (Southern African Research Archives Project, Bloomington, Indiana, 1977), consisting of documents used in the preparation of the four-volume series *From Protest to Challenge: A Documentary History of African Politics, 1882–1964*, by Gwendolen M. Carter and Thomas Karis (Hoover Institution Press, 1972).

The *Official Yearbook of the Republic of South Africa* (formerly the Union of South Africa) (1902–) contains much useful information, including chapters on the constitution and system of government, government departments, provincial and local government, political parties and organizations, public finance and foreign affairs (from 1913 to 1916 entitled the *Statistical Yearbook*). The *Debates, Minutes and Proceedings* and *Reports from Sessional and Select Committees* of the Senate and the House of Representatives are published regularly, and other reports appear in *Printed Annexes to Votes and Proceedings*. The *Quarterly Bulletin of the South African Library* contains lists of government publications. Official publications in South Africa are available in both English and Afrikaans.

There are a number of good histories of South Africa, but the *Oxford History of South Africa*, edited by L. Thompson and M. Wilson (2 vols, Oxford University Press, 1971), provides an exhaustive account, whilst a shorter but very readable work is *South Africa: A Modern History*, by T. R. H. Davenport (University of Toronto Press, 1977). The Afrikaner's perspective can be found in *The Afrikaner's Interpretation of South African History*, by F. A. Jaarsveld (Simondium, 1964).

Politics

Like New Zealand, there has been a marked growth in the literature on South African politics since the 1960s, but it is perhaps inevitable that much of this should revolve around South Africa's racial problems and policies and around the future of South Africa. There therefore remain important gaps in the monograph and periodical literature. The emphasis on racial issues is reflected in some of the following such as *South African Government Politics*, edited by Denis Worrall (Van Schaik, 2nd rev. edn, 1977); *South African Government*, by Anthony Hocking (Macdonald, 1977); *The Politics of South Africa: Democracy and*

Racial Diversity, by Howard M. Brotz (Oxford University Press, 1977); *Conflict and Compromise in South Africa*, edited by Robert J. Rotberg and John Barrett (Lexington Books, 1980); and *The People and Policies of South Africa*, by Leo Marquard (Oxford University Press, 4th edn, 1969).

There are few studies of particular periods, other than through biographies, and many studies concentrate on South Africa's future; for example, *How Long Will South Africa Survive?* by Richard W. Johnson (Macmillan, 1977); *Plural Democracy: Political Change and Strategies for Evolution in South Africa*, by W. H. Thomas (South African Institute of Race Relations, 1977); and *South Africa into the 1980s*, edited by Richard E. Bissell and Chester A. Crocker (Westview Press, Colorado, 1979). It is also inevitable that much of the writing on ideology deals with the question of apartheid, but there is a limited literature on other aspects: *Liberalism in South Africa, 1948–1963*, by Janet M. Robinson (Oxford University Press, 1971) and *The Liberal Dilemma in South Africa*, edited by Pierre van den Berghe (St Martin's Press, 1979), for instance. The major work on Afrikaner ideology is *The Rise of Afrikanerdom: Power, Apartheid and the Afrikaner Civil Religion*, by T. D. Moodie (University of California Press, 1975).

Constitution

The South African constitution and its development are more than adequately dealt with in the standard work, *The Union of South Africa, the Development of its Laws and Constitution*, by H. R. Hahlo and Ellison Kahn (Stevens, 2nd edn, 1965), usefully supplemented by *The New Constitution*, by Ellison Kahn (Stevens, 1962) and *Constitutional Change in South Africa*, edited by John A. Benyon (University of Natal Press, 1978).

Parliament, however, is a much-neglected subject, even in the periodical literature, as is the role of the Cabinet, the Prime Minister and the more recently established office of President.

Political parties and representation

Even political parties and elections have only a limited literature, a reflection perhaps of the nature of the party system and electoral behaviour since at least 1948: *South African Parties and Policies, 1910–1960: A Select Souce Book*, edited by D. W. Kruger (Human and Rousseau, 1960); *The Nationalists in Opposition, 1934–1948*, by Newell M. Stultz (Human and Rousseau, 1975; published as

Afrikaner Politics in South Africa, 1934–1948, University of California Press, 1974); *General Elections in South Africa, 1943 –1970*, by Kenneth Heard (Oxford University Press, 1974); and *The South African Voter: Some Aspects of Voting Behaviour with special reference to the General Elections of 1966 and 1970*, by H. Lever (Huta, 1972). Several other areas have only an extremely limited literature. There is no recent monograph on pressure groups, for instance, the most recent being *Interest Groups in South African Politics*, by P. B. Harris (University of Rhodesia Monographs in Political Science, 1968).

Provincial and local government

Local government is rather better served, with two books of readings edited by J. M. Cloete, *Provincial and Municipal Government and Administration: Selected Readings* (Van Schaik, 1978) and *Provincial and Municipal Finance: Selected Readings* (Van Schaik, 1978); *An Introduction to Local Government*, by W. A. Hammond (Witwatersrand University Press, 1977); and the now-dated *History of Local Government in South Africa*, by L. P. Green (Juta, 1957).

Administration and policy studies

Public administration, however, is little developed, with no major text other than *Administrative Law*, by G. M. Cockram (Juta, 1976), although *The Darker Reaches of Government: Access to Information about Public Administration in Three Societies – the United States, Britain and South Africa*, by A. Mathews (Juta, 1978) perhaps offers an explanation. There are no major policy studies available other than in the area of foreign policy, of which some of the more recent are *The World, the West and Pretoria*, by A. Steward (David McKay, New York, 1977); *South Africa in Africa: a Study in Ideology and Foreign Policy*, by S. C. Nolutshunga (African Publishing Co., New York, 1975); and *International Pressures and Political Change in South Africa*, edited by F. McA. Clifford-Vaughan (Oxford University Press, South Africa, 1978).

Racial problems in South Africa have, understandably, received more attention than in any other single aspect of politics, but the question of race is an excellent example of the problem of defining the boundaries of politics and political science, and only important themes can be illustrated here: *Race and Politics in South Africa*, edited by Ian Robertson and Phillip Whitten (Transaction Books,

New Jersey, 1978); *Basic Facts on the Republic of South Africa and the Policy of Apartheid*, by Julien R. Friedman (United Nations, 1978); *Class, Race and Gold: a Study of Class Relations and Racial Discrimination in South Africa*, by Frederick A. Johnstone (Routledge and Kegan Paul, 1976); *South Africa's Options: Strategies for Sharing*, by Frederick van Zyl Slabbert and David Walsh (St Martin's Press, 1979); *Modernising Racial Domination: South Africa's Political Dynamics*, by Heribert Adam (University of California Press, 1971); *Year of Fire, Year of Ash: the Soweto Revolt – Roots of a Revolution?* by Baruch Herson (Zed Press, 1979); *One Anzania, One Nation: the National Question in South Africa*, by N. Sizwe (Zed Press, 1978); *The Rise of African Nationalism, 1912–1952*, by P. Walshe (Hurst, 1970); and *Action, Reaction and Counteraction: A Brief Review of the Non-White Political Movements in South Africa*, by M. Horrell (South African Institute of Race Relations, 1971). The establishment of the black homelands has also produced a significant literature: *The African Homelands of South Africa*, by M. Horrell (South African Institute of Race Relations, 1973); *Black Homelands in South Africa*, by T. Malan (Africa Institute, 1976); *Black Perspectives: Bantustans*, edited by T. Mbanjwa (Black Community Programme, 1976); *The Transkei: South Africa's Politics of Partition*, by P. Laurence (Ravan, 1976); *Transkei's Half-Loaf – Race Separation in South Africa*, by Newell M. Stultz (Yale University Press, 1979); *Ciskei: the Economics and Politics of Dependence in a South African Homeland*, edited by Nancy Charton (Croom Helm, 1980); and *The Black Homelands of South Africa: the Political and Economic Development of Bophuthatswana and Kwazulu*, by T. Butler *et al.* (University of California Press, 1977).

Journals

Politikon (1974–), the journal of the South African Political Science Association, is the most relevant journal on South African politics, but many articles are contained in journals covering wider aspects of African affairs, such as the *Journal of Modern African Studies* (1963–), the *Journal of Asian and African Studies* (1966 –), *African Affairs* (1901–), the journal of the Royal African Society, the *Journal of Southern African Studies* (1974–), the *Journal of Southern African Affairs* (1976–), the *African Review* (1969–), *Africa Today* (1954–), the *Africa Quarterly* (1961–), *Africa Report* (1969–), *African Insight* (formerly the *South African Journal of African Affairs*, 1971–), *African Studies* (1921–) and *Ufahamu* (1970–). The *South African Journal of Sociology*

(1970–) and the *Comparative and International Law Journal of South Africa* (1968–) are also useful sources, as is *Africanus – African Notes and News* (1943–). A number of the journals published in South Africa have articles in Afrikaans, as well as English, with abstracts in the other language.

Comparative studies

There are few studies which encompass aspects of the politics of Australia, Canada, New Zealand and South Africa, although a number touch upon various combinations of two or three of the countries. Apart from the older editions of some constitutional law textbooks which deal with all four as members of the Common-wealth and later editions which deal with Australia, Canada and New Zealand in the same capacity, only the subject of race appears to have produced a fully comparative study: *Four Kinds of Dominion: Comparative Race Politics in Australia, Canada, New Zealand and South Africa*, by C. M. Tatz (University of New England, Armidale, 1972). However, *The Founding of New Societies* (Harcourt Brace, 1969), edited by Louis Hartz, contains interesting chapters on Australia, Canada and South Africa, whilst a number of studies of federalism provide a comparative dimension on Australia and Canada: these include *Federal Government* by K. C. Wheare (Oxford University Press, 4th edn, 1963); *Federalism, Finance and Social Legislation in Canada, Australia and the United States*, by A. H. Birch (Oxford University Press, 1955); and *Federalism and Constitutional Change*, by W. S. Livingstone (Oxford University Press, 1963). *Parliamentary Supervision of Delegated Legislation: the United Kingdom, Australia, New Zealand and Canada*, by John E. Kersell (Stevens, 1960) is a further example of a wide-ranging comparative work, but, these apart, most studies are limited to two of the four countries, almost exclusively Australia and New Zealand and Australia and Canada: *The Australian and New Zealand Nexus*, by A. A. and R. Burnett (Australian Institute of International Affairs, 1978); *Australian and New Zealand Relations*, edited by Ralph Hayburn (Foreign Policy School, University of Otago, 1978); *New Zealand and Australia: Foreign Policy in the 1970s*, by G. R. Laking *et al.* (Price Milburn, 1970); *Race Relations in Australia and New Zealand – a Comparative Survey, 1770s–1970s*, by K. R. Howe (Methuen, New Zealand, 1977); *Canadian and Australian Politics in Comparative Perspective*, by Henry Albinski (Oxford University Press, 1973); *Federalism in Canada and Australia: The Early Years*, by

B. W. Hodgins *et al.* (ANU, 1979); *Public Choice and Federalism in Australia and Canada*, by M. H. Sproule-Jones (Centre for Research on Federal Financial Relations, ANU, 1975); and *The Effect of Judicial Review on Federal–State Relations in Australia, Canada and the United States*, by R. E. Johnston (Louisiana University Press, 1970).

17
Western Europe
Carole Andrews

Introduction

In the space of this chapter it is possible to mention only a limited number of the many works available on political systems and political developments in the countries of Western Europe. This selection is therefore confined to English-language material covering the period since 1945 (apart from some historical works included as background reading), with the emphasis on recent and readily available publications. It does not include primary sources or periodical articles, but many of the works cited have bibliographies, containing references to other sources (including foreign-language material) which would be useful for more detailed study.

As one might expect, English-language coverage is unevenly distributed among the countries of Western Europe. Whereas there are numerous books in English dealing with politics in France and West Germany, for example, there are very few on Belgium or the Netherlands. In recent years, however, a number of general surveys or comparative studies of the political systems of several Western European countries have been published, no doubt partly in response to a growing interest in our fellow member states since the UK joined the European Community. Some of these works include chapters on politics in the smaller states and thus compensate for the lack of books in English dealing with these countries individually. The first part of this chapter is devoted to material covering Western Europe as a whole or a number of countries within the region. It includes reference works, periodicals and general political surveys, as well as comparative studies on particular topics, such as political parties, electoral systems or legislatures. It is followed by sections on individual countries or groups of countries.

Reference works

There are few basic political reference books dealing only with Western Europe. Many of the international works cited in Chapter 13 are important sources of information on the countries covered by this chapter, but those references need not be repeated here, with the possible exception of *European Political Facts 1918–73*, by Chris Cook and John Paxton (Macmillan, 1975), which, in addition to listing heads of state, prime ministers, foreign and finance ministers, with dates of office, also contains brief information on parliament, political parties, electoral system, election results, judicial system and trade unions in each country covered. The quarterly *Vacher's European Companion* (A. S. Kerswill, London, April 1972–), although mainly concerned with European Community institutions, also includes a section on each country in Western Europe, containing basic information on political structure, details of head of state, cabinet membership and composition of parliament and addresses of government ministries. Other European reference works are referred to below, according to the aspect of the political system that they cover.

General and comparative political surveys

Six European States, the Countries of the European Community and their Political Systems, by Stephen Holt (Hamish Hamilton, 1970), is a useful introduction to the political systems of France, West Germany, Italy, Belgium, Luxembourg and the Netherlands, with a comparative study of their electoral systems as an Appendix. *Government and Administration in Western Europe*, edited by F. F. Ridley (Martin Robertson, 1979), covers the same countries as Holt, with the exception of Luxembourg and the addition of the UK. It discusses the organization of central government in each country, in its administrative and political context. Designed to introduce American students to those European countries which are generally neglected in US textbooks, *The*

Other Western Europe, a Political Analysis of the Smaller Democracies, by Earl H. Fry and Gregory A. Raymond (Clio, 1980), compares Britain, France and West Germany with the less familiar countries of the Iberian, Benelux, Alpine and Scandinavian regions, covering historical background, political structure and recent political developments in the countries concerned.

In *Politics in Western Europe, a Comparative Analysis*, by Gordon Smith (Heinemann, 3rd edn, 1980), the approach is comparative rather than descriptive: most of the book examines aspects of politics and political institutions, with reference to all the Western European democracies; but a final section provides a short political profile of each country. Smith's analysis includes consideration of the former dictatorships in Greece, Portugal and Spain, as examples of non-democratic variants in Western Europe. *European Politics: a Reader*, edited by Mattei Dogan and Richard Rose (Macmillan, 1971), brings together studies of France, West Germany, Italy and Britain by various European and American authors, and aims to highlight the differences and similarities between these political systems. Each chapter deals with a particular political concept (e.g. leadership, social structure and voting alignments) and includes both country and comparative studies.

Among more specialized works is *The Failure of the State: on the Distribution of Political and Economic Power in Europe*, edited by James Cornford (Croom Helm, 1975), which examines the various ways in which East and West European governments have confronted the problematical relationship between centralized planning and regional autonomy. The chapters on Western Europe cover France, Italy, West Germany and the UK. *Trade Unions and Politics in Western Europe*, edited by Jack Hayward (Cass, 1980), examines the impact of the unions on domestic and international politics, in a series of country and comparative studies dealing with West Germany, Sweden, Italy and Britain.

Political parties

The subject of political parties in Western Europe has been well covered by recent studies. Among the most wide-ranging is *Western European Party Systems, Trends and Prospects*, edited by Peter H. Merkl (Collier Macmillan, 1980), which consists of a series of country studies, including several on the smaller European democracies, and a collection of papers on research topics relating to political parties. *Social and Political Movements in Western Europe*, edited by Martin Kolinsky and William E.

Paterson (Croom Helm, 1976), is a survey of important democratic and non-democratic movements, ranging across the whole political spectrum in France, Italy and West Germany, while *Political Parties in Europe*, by Theo Stammen (John Martin, 1979), examines the development of Western European party systems in the context of a policy of European unification, describes existing transnational links and considers the possible structure of a European party system.

Political Parties in the European Community, edited by Stanley Henig for the Policy Studies Institute (Allen and Unwin, 1979), is a sequel to *European Political Parties*, edited by Stanley Henig and John Pinder for Political and Economic Planning (Allen and Unwin, 1969); but, unlike the earlier work, which included Austria, Switzerland and the Scandinavian countries, Henig (1979) concentrates on the nine European Community states (prior to Greek membership), giving an account of the party political history of the decade since 1969 and updating the information on party membership, finance, electoral support, etc. Subsequent chapters look at party groups in the European Parliament and the development of European party federations. Two further books deal specifically with party groupings in the European Community context: *The Party Groups in the European Parliament*, by John Fitzmaurice (Saxon House, 1975), and *Transnational Party Cooperation and European Integration, the process towards direct elections*, by Geoffrey and Pippa Pridham (Allen and Unwin, 1981). *Party Politics and Pressure Groups: a Comparative Introduction*, by Maurice Duverger (Nelson, 1972), discusses both theoretical and practical aspects of parties and pressure groups in Western democracies, drawing most of its examples from Western Europe.

A number of books deal with particular political movements. Among those covering the parties of the Right is *The European Right, a Historical Profile*, edited by Hans Rogger and Eugen Weber (Weidenfeld and Nicolson, 1965), which includes essays on France, Belgium, Spain, West Germany, Austria, Italy and Finland. *The Christian Democratic Parties of Western Europe*, by R. E. M. Irving (Allen and Unwin, for the Royal Institute of International Affairs, 1979), is an important comparative study of the origins and development of Christian Democrat parties in France, Italy, West Germany, Belgium and the Netherlands, which also analyses the political philosophy of Christian Democracy and speculates on the extent to which it is possible to speak of a united European movement. The contributors to *Conservative Politics in Western Europe*, edited by Zig Layton-Henry, St

Martin's Press, (New York, 1982), examine contemporary Conservative politics in Britain, Scandinavia, West Germany, Belgium, the Netherlands, France and Italy, as well as transnational party cooperation within the European Community.

The parties of Western Europe's Centre Right are the subject of *Moderates and Conservatives in Western Europe: Political Parties, the European Community and the Atlantic Alliance*, edited by Roger Morgan and Stefano Silvestri (Heinemann, 1982). The parties covered are the 'Gaullists' and 'Giscardians' in France, the Christian Democrats in West Germany and Italy, the Conservatives in Britain and the Democratic Centre Union in Spain, as well as the Liberal parties in these countries. The studies on the various national parties are followed by comparative chapters on the development of transnational links, the measure of agreement on economic policy priorities and attitudes to NATO and East–West relations.

A History of European Socialism, by Albert S. Lindemann (Yale University Press, 1983), covers Socialism and Communism in the period since 1800, with only one chapter devoted to developments since the Second World War. *Social Democracy in Post-war Europe*, by William E. Paterson and Ian Campbell (Macmillan, 1974), gives a detailed account of structural and political changes in the major Social Democratic parties since 1945, with the emphasis on Britain, France, Italy, West Germany and Scandinavia. The approach is comparative, and topics covered include the interaction of Social Democracy and Communism, the relationships of Social Democratic parties with trade unions, and changes in party membership and electoral support. *Social Democratic Parties in Western Europe*, edited by William E. Paterson and Alastair H. Thomas (Croom Helm, 1977), is more concerned with individual party studies, including chapters on the French and Austrian Socialist Parties the British and Irish Labour Parties, the West German Social Democratic Party and Social Democracy in Italy, the Iberian Peninsula, Scandinavia, Belgium and the Netherlands. A final chapter looks at cooperation among West European Socialist parties.

In recent years, the growing strength of the major West European Communist parties and the development of the concept of 'Eurocommunism' have given rise to a large number of publications on these topics. *The Communist Parties of Italy, France and Spain, Postwar Change and Continuity: a Casebook*, edited by Peter Lange and Maurizio Vannicelli (Allen and Unwin, 1981), is a useful documentary collection of speeches, articles and manifestoes emanating from the Italian, French and Spanish Communist

Parties. The selection of texts follows the parties' post-war evolution up to 1979, and the documents are grouped so as to illustrate the parties' respective positions on five basic issues: general strategy, domestic alliances, internal organization, relations with other Communist parties and international outlook.

First published in Spanish in 1976, when the Spanish Communist Party was still illegal, *'Eurocommunism' and the State*, by Santiago Carrillo, General Secretary of the Spanish Communist Party (Lawrence and Wishart, 1977), is an important analysis, focused on Spain, of the significance of 'Eurocommunism', both in relation to domestic politics and in relation to the Soviet Union. Among the earlier British studies on 'Eurocommunism' is *The Communist Parties of Western Europe*, by Neil McInnes (Oxford University Press, for the Royal Institute of International Affairs, 1975), which explores the hypothesis that West European Communism exists as an entity, by analysing the support, structures and policies of Communist parties in Western Europe. The most wide-ranging study in terms of country coverage is *The Communist Parties of Western Europe*, by R. Neal Tannahill (Greenwood Press, 1978), which includes a section on every West European Communist party with a bibliography on each, followed by a comparative analysis of the domestic and international factors which have shaped the development of these parties. *The Changing Face of Western Communism*, edited by David Childs (Croom Helm, 1980), includes contributions on the Communist parties of Spain, Italy, France, the Nordic countries and Austria, and on the origins and various interpretations of the term 'Eurocommunism'.

Most other recent books concentrate on the major Communist parties of Italy, France and Spain, among them *'Eurocommunism', Implications for East and West*, by Roy Godson and Stephen Haseler (Macmillan, 1978); *The Politics of Eurocommunism: socialism in transition*, edited by Carl Boggs and David Plotke (Macmillan, 1980); and *In Search of Eurocommunism*, edited by Richard Kindersley (Macmillan, 1981), which brings together contributions from Communist politicians and academics in all three countries. Other works also include the Portuguese Communist Party: *Eurocommunism and Détente*, edited by Rudolf L. Tökés (Martin Robertson, for the Council on Foreign Relations, 1979); *Eurocommunism: Myth or Reality?* edited by Paolo Filo della Torre *et al.* (Penguin, 1979); and *Power and the Party: Changing Faces of Communism in Western Europe*, by Keith Middlemas (André Deutsch, 1980), which is particularly useful for its detailed account of the political development of each of these four parties.

At the opposite end of the political spectrum, two books deal with right-wing extremism in Europe. *Fascism in Europe*, edited by S. J. Woolf (Methuen, 2nd rev. edn, 1981), concentrates on the roots of Fascism and its strength in several countries during the inter-war years, but also includes a chapter on its prospects in contemporary Europe, while *The New Fascists*, by Paul Wilkinson (Grant McIntyre, 1981), is predominantly a study of Fascism in the post-war period, with particular reference to contemporary Fascist-type organizations in France, Italy, Britain, Spain and West Germany, as well as the US.

Elections and electoral systems

The International Almanac of Electoral History, by Thomas T. Mackie and Richard Rose (Macmillan, 1974), provides a record of election results in industrialized countries since the first competitive national elections. It includes all the countries of Western Europe except Greece, Spain and Portugal. The figures for each country are prefaced by a brief electoral history and a historical checklist of political parties. Since 1974, the same authors have annually reported the results of national elections in Western nations in the September issue of the quarterly *European Journal of Political Research*. The annual *Chronicle of Parliamentary Elections and Developments* (Inter-Parliamentary Union, 1967–) covers legislative elections held throughout the world during the period under review, giving details of electoral system, results and distribution of seats in Parliament. Volume I of the *International Guide to Electoral Statistics*, edited by Stein Rokkan and Jean Meyriat (Mouton, The Hague, 1969), covers 'National elections in Western Europe'. It traces the development of electoral arrangements in each country since the establishment of representative government and provides extensive bibliographies of statistical and analytical sources on each set of elections, as well as election results. *An Electoral Atlas of Europe, 1968–81: a Political Geographic Compendium including 76 maps*, by John Sallnow and Anna John (Butterworth Scientific, 1982), provides a visual and statistical record of all national and significant regional elections in Western Europe during the period covered. Each country section includes a commentary on political parties, coalitions, the electoral system and recent elections.

A Short History of Electoral Systems in Western Europe, by Andrew McL. Carstairs (Allen and Unwin, 1980), examines the electoral systems of thirteen West European countries in the context of their constitutional, political and social development. It includes chapters on Belgium and the Netherlands, Austria and Switzerland, and the Nordic countries. *Nine Democracies: Electoral Systems of the Countries of the European Economic Community*, by Enid Lakeman (The Arthur McDougall Fund, 2nd edn, 1975), gives a brief outline, in pamphlet form, of the electoral systems of the European Community states (prior to Greek membership). The same countries are covered in more detail in *European Electoral Systems Handbook*, edited by Geoffrey Hand *et al.* (Butterworths, 1979). A standard work on voting methods is *How Democracies Vote: a Study of Majority and Proportional Electoral systems*, by Enid Lakeman (Faber, 4th rev. edn, 1974), which includes sections on the various forms of party list proportional representation in Scandinavia, Switzerland, Belgium, the Netherlands, West Germany, Italy, Greece and France, and on the Single Transferable Vote system in Ireland. *Electoral Behaviour: a comparative handbook*, edited by Richard Rose (Collier Macmillan, 1974), provides a description and analysis of the relationships between social structure, political parties and electoral behaviour in a range of countries, including Ireland, Norway, Sweden, Finland, the Netherlands, Belgium, West Germany, Italy and the UK, and contains numerous statistical tables and bibliographical references. The use of the referendum and its effects on government policies and democratic institutions is the subject of *Referendums, a Comparative Study of Practice and Theory*, edited by David Butler and Austin Ranney (American Enterprise Institute for Public Policy Research, 1978), which includes studies on Switzerland, France, Scandinavia and Ireland.

Legislatures

Mention has already been made in Chapter 13 of *Parliaments of the World: a Reference Compendium*, by Valentine Herman and Françoise Mendel (Macmillan, for the Inter-Parliamentary Union, 1976, new edn in preparation), which is an indispensable source of comparative information on parliamentary procedure and practice. The first section of the annual *Chronicle of Parliamentary Elections and Developments* (1967– , work cited) summarizes developments in the organization, composition, procedures and powers of parliaments during the year covered. Parliamentary procedure in eleven West European countries is described and compared in *European Parliamentary Procedure, a Comparative Handbook*, by the Lord Campion and D. W. S. Lidderdale (Allen and Unwin, for the Inter-Parliamentary Union, 1953).

Two more recent publications deal with the role of European parliaments in economic affairs. *The Power of the Purse: the Role of European Parliaments in Budgetary Decisions*, by David Coombes *et al.* (Allen and Unwin, for Political and Economic Planning, 1976), covers Britain, France, West Germany, Italy, the Netherlands and Switzerland, while *Parliaments and Economic Affairs in Britain, France, Italy and the Netherlands*, edited by David Coombes and S. A. Walkland (Heinemann, for the European Centre for Political Studies of the Policy Studies Institute, 1980), examines parliament's influence on the determination of economic policy and the control of public expenditure.

Political Oppositions in Western Democracies, edited by Robert A. Dahl (Yale University Press, 1966), describes and compares the role of opposition parties in nine West European countries and the US.

Government

In *Presidents and Prime Ministers*, edited by Richard Rose and Ezra N. Suleiman (American Enterprise Institute for Public Policy Research, 1980), the contributors study political leadership in six European countries (Britain, France, West Germany, Italy, Norway and Franco's Spain), as well as Canada and the US. Since the Second World War, government by coalition rather than by majority party has been the norm in many West European countries. *Government Coalitions in Western Democracies*, edited by Eric C. Browne and John Dreijmanis (Longman, 1982), examines coalition behaviour in ten European states and is particularly useful for the information it contains on countries such as Belgium, Iceland and Switzerland, on which little English-language material is available.

Policy Styles in Western Europe, edited by Jeremy Richardson (Allen and Unwin, 1982), analyses the policy-making process in West Germany, Norway, Sweden, France, the Netherlands and the UK. Finally, mention should be made of two comparative studies in public administration: *The Mandarins of Western Europe: the Political Role of Top Civil Servants*, edited by Mattei Dogan (Sage, 1975), which covers nine West European countries and draws comparisons with Yugoslavia and Poland; and *Ombudsmen Compared*, by Frank Stacey (The Clarendon Press, 1978), which compares the operation of Ombudsman systems in Sweden, Denmark, Norway and France, as well as the Canadian provinces and the UK.

Periodicals

One periodical which deals specifically with political developments in Western Europe is the quarterly *West European Politics* (1978 –). Another quarterly, *European Journal of Political Research* (1973–), gives preference to articles of a theoretical or comparative nature. Articles on West European politics also appear regularly in certain journals with an international coverage, notably *World Today* (1945–), the monthly periodical of the Royal Institute of International Affairs (Chatham House), and in journals of comparative politics, such as the quarterlies *Government and Opposition* (1965–) and *Parliamentary Affairs* (1947–). More occasionally, articles on other West European countries may appear in *Public Administration* (1923–) and in *Political Quarterly* (1930–).

A relatively new journal, *Electoral Studies* (Butterworths, April 1982–), aims to contain in each issue articles on particular elections and analytical articles, often comparative in nature, as well as a 'Guide to Journal Articles' and a summary record of election results and changes in electoral systems. Reference should also be made to two periodicals which regularly reproduce useful texts. The quarterly *Constitutional and Parliamentary Information* (2nd series, 1948–) publishes English texts of new constitutions and major constitutional amendments, as well as important documents relating to Parliamentary procedures and political parties in member states of the Inter-Parliamentary Union, which publishes the journal. Also quarterly, *Communist Affairs, Documents and Analysis* (Butterworth Scientific, 1982–) publishes texts from Communist parties and related organizations, as well as articles. It contains a section on Western Europe, and the chronology in each issue has a column on developments relating to non-ruling Communist parties.

Individual countries

Austria

Two political histories of twentieth-century Austria are recommended as a background to the study of contemporary Austrian politics: *Austria*, by Karl R. Stadler (Benn, 1971), concentrates on the period from 1914 to the end of the Allied occupation, with only one chapter on developments since 1955, while *Austria, 1918 –1972*, by Elisabeth Barker (Macmillan, 1973), examines the interplay of internal and external forces which determined the course of Austrian history during the period covered.

Several books deal with Austria in the immediate post-war period. They include *The Rebirth of Austria*, by Richard Hiscocks (Oxford University Press, 1953), an account of the revival of political, economic and cultural life in post-war Austria; and *Between Liberation and Liberty: Austria in the Post-war World*, by Karl Gruber (André Deutsch, 1955), who was Austrian Foreign Minister from 1945 to 1953 and describes from first-hand experience the negotiations leading up to the Austrian State Treaty of 1955. *Austria between East and West, 1945–1955*, by William B. Bader (Stanford University Press, 1966), studies the evolution and interaction of Soviet and Western attitudes towards their role in Austria during that period, while *Building an Austrian Nation: the Political Integration of a Western State*, by William T. Bluhm (Yale University Press, 1973), examines the way in which Austria proceeded to the establishment of an independent republic after 1945.

There are relatively few English-language publications covering more recent Austrian political developments. *Politics in Austria*, by Kurt Steiner (Little, Brown, Boston, 1972), attempts to explain the change from pre-war Austrian political life to the comparative stability of the Second Republic. It includes chapters on political institutions and parties, interest groups, policy making and the bureaucracy. *Modern Austria*, edited by Kurt Steiner *et al.* (Society for the Promotion of Science and Scholarship, Palo Alto, Ca, 1981), is a more wide-ranging survey, but contains useful chapters on the constitution, political parties, public administration, elections and parliament.

The Transformation of Austrian Socialism, by Kurt L. Shell (State University of New York, 1962), is a study of changes in the ideology and policies of the Austrian Socialist Party, and *Political Parties and Elections in Modern Austria: the Search for Stability*, by Melanie A. Sully (Hurst, 1981), contains useful information on political parties and electoral politics in the post-war period. Austrian political parties are also included in some of the works cited in the first part of this chapter: Henig and Pinder (1969), Rogger and Weber (1965) and Paterson and Thomas (1977).

The Benelux countries

There are few books in English dealing specifically with politics in Belgium, the Netherlands or Luxembourg, but many of the works referred to in the above section on Western Europe include chapters on the Benelux countries, and the bibliographies in Paterson and Thomas (1977) and Henig (1979) (works cited) include references to French, Flemish and Dutch as well as English publications. *The Benelux Nations: the Politics of Small-country Democracies*, by Gordon L. Weil (Holt, Rinehart and Winston, New York, 1970), is a useful political survey of the three countries. It includes chapters on history, economy and foreign relations, but most of the book covers various aspects of politics in Belgium and the Netherlands, with one chapter on politics in Luxembourg.

Belgium, by Vernon Mallinson (Benn, 1969), and *Modern Belgium*, by F. E. Huggett (Pall Mall, 1969), remain useful as historical and political surveys of the war years and post-war developments. Mallinson concentrates on wartime Belgium, post-war reconstruction and the reign of King Baudouin, while Huggett includes chapters on the two cultures, the constitution, political parties and the administrative system. Some extremely useful material on Belgian politics has appeared in the *Memo from Belgium* series, issued periodically by the Belgian Ministry of Foreign Affairs and, until fairly recently, published in English. The following, all by Robert Senelle, are particularly worth mentioning: *The Political, Economic and Social Structures of Belgium* (Nos 122–124, 1970); *The Revision of the Constitution* (Nos 144–146, 1972); *The Belgian Constitution, Commentary* (No. 166, 1974); and *The Reform of the Belgian State* (No. 179, 1978 and no. 182, 1979). These are all fairly substantial paperback books. *The Flemings and Walloons of Belgium*, by R. E. M. Irving (Minority Rights Group, Report No. 46, September, 1980), is a concise study of the intercommunal problem, covering historical background and developments up to the 'Community pact' of 1977–1978 and beyond.

The Netherlands Ministry of Foreign Affairs publishes a useful series of booklets, under the general title of *The Kingdom of the Netherlands: Facts and Figures*. These are obtainable from the Netherlands Embassy, and are periodically updated. One deals with the constitution and another with elections and the party system. *The Modern Netherlands*, by Frank E. Huggett (Pall Mall, 1971), is a general survey of the country, which includes chapters on the constitution, the system of government and political parties. First published in 1968, *The Politics of Accommodation: Pluralism and Democracy in the Netherlands*, by Arend Lijphart (University of California Press, 2nd edn, 1975), attempts to explain the paradox of the Netherlands political system between 1917 and 1967, characterized by social cleavage and yet a notable example of stable democracy. In the 1967 elections, however, support for the major parties was lower than ever before, and the 1975 edition includes a chapter on the breakdown of the politics of accommodation. In *The Economy and Politics of the Netherlands since 1945*, edited by Richard T. Griffiths (Nijhoff, The Hague, 1980), chapters on the economy predominate, but there are also useful contributions on voting behaviour, government formation and interest groups. An authoritative early work on the Netherlands legislature is *The Parliament of the Kingdom of the Netherlands*, by E. Van Raalte (Hansard Society, 1959).

For material on politics in Luxembourg, reference should be made to the chapters on Luxembourg in various works cited above under 'Western Europe', and to French publications on Luxembourg in their bibliographies.

France

There is so much valuable material in English on the subject of French politics that this section poses particular problems of selection, so descriptive matter has been kept to a minimum in order to include as many references as possible.

A standard work on modern France is *Democracy in France since 1870*, by David Thomson (Oxford University Press, for the Royal Institute of International Affairs, 5th edn, 1969), which analyses the development of democratic ideals and institutions in the context of changing economic and social structures. *The Government and Politics of France*, by Vincent Wright (Hutchinson, 2nd edn, 1983), is an introduction to French politics in the post-war period, which is particularly useful for its analysis of presidential government. It includes an extensive bibliography and a detailed chronology of the Fifth Republic. Another useful introductory work is *Contemporary France: Politics and Society Since 1945*, by D. L. Hanley *et al.* (Routledge and Kegan Paul, 1979), which sets the French political system in its historical, social and economic context and includes an excellent bibliographical essay.

Among works dealing with the Fourth Republic (1946–1958) is *The Fourth Republic of France, Constitution and Political Parties*, by O. R. Taylor (Royal Institute of International Affairs, 1951), which describes the origins and character of the 1946 constitution, and provides a guide to post-war political parties. Two books by Dorothy Pickles also cover the new constitution and the functioning of its institutions: *French Politics, the First Years of the Fourth Republic* (Royal Institute of International Affairs, 1953) and *France, the Fourth Republic* (Methuen, 1955).

The outstanding comprehensive study of political life in the Fourth Republic is, however, *Crisis and Compromise, Politics in the Fourth Republic*, by Philip M. Williams (Longman, 3rd edn, 1964), which gives a detailed account and analysis of political parties and institutions, and assesses the strengths and weaknesses of the Fourth Republic's political system. In *Parliament, Parties and Society in France, 1946–1958*, by Duncan MacRae, Jr (Macmillan, 1967), political science techniques are used to analyse the internal political weaknesses which contributed to the fall of the Fourth Republic, while *The de Gaulle Revolution*, by Alexander Werth (Hale, 1960), is an account of the events which brought about the end of the Fourth Republic and the establishment of the de Gaulle regime.

Politics and Society in de Gaulle's Republic, by Philip M. Williams and Martin Harrison (Longman, 1971), is a political history of the period from the beginning of the Fifth Republic in 1958 up to de Gaulle's departure in 1969, covering topics such as the use of the referendum, the nature of the party system, the development of political institutions and moves towards decentralization. It closes with a discussion of the transition from de Gaulle to Pompidou and an evaluation of de Gaulle's political legacy.

Anyone studying this period in French politics must examine the causes and effects of the students' and workers' revolt of May 1968, which is the subject of several books in English, from various viewpoints: *French Revolution 1968*, by Patrick Seale and Maureen McConville (Penguin, in association with Heinemann, 1968); *Students and Workers: an Analytical Account of Dissent in France, May-June 1968*, by John Gretton (Macdonald, 1969); *The Elusive Revolution: Anatomy of a Student Revolt*, by Raymond Aron (Pall Mall, 1969); and *Reflections on the Revolution in France: 1968*, edited by Charles Posner (Penguin, 1970).

De Gaulle's own account of the early years of his Presidency is published in English as *Memoirs of Hope: Renewal, 1958–62, Endeavour, 1962–* (Weidenfeld and Nicolson, 1971). Originally intended as a trilogy, it was incomplete when he died in 1970. Biographies in English include *De Gaulle: a Political Biography*, by Alexander Werth (Penguin, 1965); *De Gaulle: a Biography*, by Aidan Crawley (Collins, 1969); *De Gaulle the Statesman*, by Brian Crozier (Eyre Methuen, 1973), which is the second of two volumes and covers the period 1946–1970; and *De Gaulle*, by Bernard Ledwidge (Weidenfeld and Nicolson, 1982).

The period in office of a more recent President is the subject of *France in the Giscard Presidency*, by J. R. Frears (Allen and Unwin, 1981), which was completed before Giscard d'Estaing's defeat in the May 1981 Presidential election. The first part of the book is an account of Giscard's previous career, his political ideology and the nature of the French Presidency; the second part analyses his performance in key policy areas. *François Mitterrand: a Political Odyssey*, by Denis MacShane (Quartet, 1982), is a biography of President Mitterrand, which traces his political development from the 1930s up to his victory in the 1981 Presidential election and the subsequent election of a Socialist government.

Among more general surveys of French politics in the Fifth Republic, a standard text is *The Government and Politics of France*, by Dorothy Pickles (2 vols, Methuen, 1972–1973). The first volume deals with institutions, political parties, the electoral system and the role of extra-parliamentary parties and interest groups, while the second examines Gaullist policies and those of the Opposition parties. Other political surveys include *Govering France, the One and Indivisible French Republic*, by Jack Hayward (Weidenfeld and Nicolson, 2nd edn, 1983), which is particularly good on the relationship between politics and administration; and two books by Jean Blondel: *Contemporary France: Politics, Society and Institutions* (Methuen, 1974) and *The Government of France* (Methuen, 2nd edn, 1974). More specialized publications include: *French Politics and Public Policy*, edited by Philip G. Cerny and Martin A. Schain (Pinter, 1980), which examines the political decision-making processes and the various areas and levels of public policy in France; and *Problems of Contemporary French Politics*, by Dorothy Pickles (Methuen, 1982), which is a commentary on party politics, foreign policy and the Presidential system in France since de Gaulle.

The French party system has undergone fundamental changes since the beginning of the Fifth Republic. This transformation, from weak multi-party coalitions to a strong government–opposition polarization, is described and analysed in *Political Parties and Elections in the French Fifth Republic*, by J. R. Frears (Hurst, 1977), which also includes studies on individual parties. The collection of essays published as *Contemporary French Political Parties*, edited by David S. Bell (Croom Helm, 1982), gives an overview of the French party system at the time of Mitterrand's victory.

The Right Wing in France: from 1815 to de Gaulle, by René Rémond (University of Pennsylvania Press, 2nd edn, 1969), is a useful introduction to the parties of the Right, supplemented by *Conservative Politics in France*, by Malcolm Anderson (Allen and Unwin, 1974), which covers the period from 1880. Two important studies of Gaullism are *The Gaullist Phenomenon, the Gaullist movement in the Fifth Republic*, by Jean Charlot (Allen and Unwin, 1971), and *Gaullism, the Rise and Fall of a Political*

Movement, by Anthony Hartley (Routledge and Kegan Paul, 1972). *Christian Democracy in France*, by R. E. M. Irving (Allen and Unwin, 1973), is particularly useful on the 'Mouvement républicain populaire' (MRP), which was a key party in governments of the Fourth Republic.

The Long March of the French Left, by Richard W. Johnson (Macmillan, 1981), and *The Left in France*, by Neill Nugent and David Lowe (Macmillan, 1982), are comprehensive studies of the historical development and conflictual relationship of the French Socialist and Communist Parties; and *Ideology and Politics: the Socialist Party of France*, by George A. Codding Jr and William Safran (Westview Press, 1979), is a history of the Socialist Party during the Fourth Republic and up to the end of the 1960s, with very little coverage of Mitterrand's period of leadership. Radicalism, which was a major force in the Third and Fourth Republics, is the subject of *The French Radical Party from Herriot to Mendès-France*, by Francis de Tarr (Oxford University Press, 1961).

In addition to the works on 'Eurocommunism' referred to in the first part of this chapter, a number of books deal specifically with the PCF, notably: *Communism and the French Left*, by Charles Micaud (Weidenfeld and Nicolson, 1963); *Communism and the French Intellectuals, 1914–1960*, by David Caute (André Deutsch, 1964); *The French Communist Party and the Crisis of International Communism*, by François Fejtö (MIT Press, 1967); *The French Communists, Profile of a People*, by Annie Kriegel (University of Chicago Press, 1972); *French Communism, 1920–1972*, by Ronald Tiersky (Columbia University Press, 1974); and *The French Communist Party in Transition: PCF–CPSU Relations and the Challenge to Soviet Authority*, by Annette E. Stiefbold (Praeger, 1977).

French Electoral Systems and Elections since 1789, by Peter Campbell (Faber, 2nd edn, 1965), is an electoral history of the period from the Revolution to the early years of the Fifth Republic, while the second part of Frears (1977, work cited) covers Presidential, parliamentary and local elections, as well as referenda, during the Fifth Republic. The essays in *French Politicians and Elections, 1951–1969*, by Philip M. Williams with David Goldey and Martin Harrison (Cambridge University Press, 1970) cover elections and major political developments in the Fourth and Fifth Republics. Studies of particular elections include *France at the Polls, the Presidential Election of 1974*, and *French National Assembly Elections of 1978*, both edited by Howard R. Penniman (American Enterprise Institute for Public Policy Research, 1975 and 1980); and *War will not take Place, the French Parliamentary Elections, March 1978*, by John R. Frears and Jean-Luc Parodi (Hurst, 1979).

The parliament of the Fourth Republic is the subject of *The Parliament of France*, by D. W. S. Lidderdale (Hansard Society, 1951), while the pamphlet *Organization and Procedure of the National Assembly of the Fifth Republic*, by Albert Mavrinac (Hansard Society, 1960), and a later book, *The French Parliament (1958–1967)*, by Philip M. Williams (Allen and Unwin, 1968), deal with the legislature of the Fifth Republic.

Government in France: an Introduction to the Executive Power, by Malcolm Anderson (Pergamon, 1970), is a useful work on the executive area of government; and French public administration is the subject of two wide-ranging studies, *Public Administration in France*, by F. Ridley and J. Blondel (Routledge and Kegan Paul, 2nd edn, 1969), and *Politics, Power and Bureaucracy in France: the Administrative Elite*, by Ezra N. Suleiman (Princeton University Press, 1974). The powers and functions of the Conseil d'Etat, the chief legal advisory body of the French government, are described and analysed in *Executive Discretion and Judicial Control, an aspect of the French Conseil d'Etat*, by C. J. Hamson (Stevens, 1954), and, more recently, in *The Administrative Functions of the French Conseil d'Etat*, by Margherita Rendel (Weidenfeld and Nicolson, 1970).

Two classic studies of French local government remain useful, in spite of their early publication dates: *Introduction to French Local Government* and *The Prefects and Provincial France*, both by Brian Chapman (Allen and Unwin, 1953 and 1955). More recent publications are *The Prefect in French Public Administration*, by Howard Machin (Croom Helm, 1977), and *Paris and the Provinces: the Politics of Local Government Reform in France*, by P. A. Gourevitch (Allen and Unwin, 1980). Finally, mention should be made of two comparative studies: *Local Government in Britain and France, Problems and Prospects*, edited by Jacques Lagroye and Vincent Wright (Allen and Unwin, 1979), and *British Dogmatism and French Pragmatism: Central–local Policy-making in the Welfare State*, by Douglas E. Ashford (Allen and Unwin, 1982).

West Germany

A useful introduction to twentieth-century Germany is *Germany since 1918*, by David Childs (Batsford, 2nd edn, 1980), which includes chapters on East Germany since 1945. Two important political histories of post-war Germany are: *Germany in Our Time, a Political History of the Post-war Years*, by Alfred Grosser (Pall Mall, 1971; Penguin, 1974), which includes a section on East

Germany and a bibliographical essay containing many German references; and *West Germany: a Contemporary History*, by Michael Balfour (Croom Helm, 1982), which begins with a survey of German history up to 1945, but concentrates on political developments in the Federal Republic, up to 1980. *The Velvet Chancellors, a History of Post-war Germany*, by Terence Prittie (Muller, 1979), traces West Germany's political history by studying the careers of the first five post-war Chancellors: Adenauer, Erhard, Kiesinger, Brandt and Schmidt.

Among political studies of particular periods is *Western Germany, from Defeat to Rearmament*, by Alfred Grosser (Allen and Unwin, 1955), which examines the period of Allied occupation, the creation of the two Germanies, and West Germany's post-war recovery. *The Origin of the West German Republic*, by Peter H. Merkl (Oxford University Press, 1963), is a detailed account of the drafting of the post-war Constitution and the rebuilding of the governmental structure into a democratic federal system, while *Democracy in Western Germany*, by Richard Hiscocks (Oxford University Press, 1957), examines the political problems of the post-war years and assesses the prospects for West German democracy. *Germany Revived, an Appraisal of the Adenauer Era*, also by Richard Hiscocks (Gollancz, 1966), is an analysis of the achievements of Adenauer's Chancellorship, and *Konrad Adenauer, 1876–1967* is a biography by Terence Prittie (Stacey, 1972).

Two convenient background texts for students of contemporary West German politics are *West Germany, an Introduction*, by Günther Kloss (Macmillan, 1976), and *West Germany: Politics and Society*, by David Childs and Jeffrey Johnson (Croom Helm, 1981), both of which deal with political, economic and social structures and policies in present-day Germany. Among recently published studies of politics and government in the Federal Republic, the following are to be recommended: *West German Politics*, by Geoffrey K. Roberts (Macmillan, 1972); *The Government and Politics of West Germany*, by Kurt Sontheimer (Hutchinson, 1972); *The Governments of Germany*, by Arnold J. Heidenheimer and Donald P. Kommers (Crowell, New York, 4th edn, 1975), which includes a section drawing comparisons with East Germany; *The German Polity*, by David P. Conradt (Longman, 1978); *Democracy in Western Germany: parties and politics in the Federal Republic*, by Gordon Smith (Heinemann, 2nd edn, 1982); and *The Political System of the Federal Republic of Germany*, by Klaus von Beyme (Gower, 1983).

The essays published in *The West German Model: Perspectives on a Stable State*, edited by William E. Paterson and Gordon Smith

(Cass, 1981), explore a range of issues central to an understanding of contemporary German politics; and *Party Government and Political Culture in Western Germany*, edited by Herbert Döring and Gordon Smith (Macmillan, 1982), is a collection of papers which examine the relationships between political culture, party system and parliamentary government in the West German political system. *Society and Democracy in Germany*, by Ralf Dahrendorf (Weidenfeld and Nicolson, 1968), is a study of twentieth-century German society, related to the history of democracy and the development of political institutions in Germany; and *Germany Transformed: Political Culture and the New Politics*, by Kendall L. Baker *et al.* (Harvard University Press, 1981), is a political science analysis, based on electoral data from 1953 to 1976, of the factors which account for the stabilization of a democratic political system in the Federal Republic.

The West German Party System: an Ecological Analysis of Social Structure and Voting Behavior, 1961–1969, by David P. Conradt (Sage, 1972), is a short study which seeks to explain the changes in the party system which led to the 1969 federal election result, when the SPD first achieved relative electoral parity with the CDU; and *Parties and Elections in West Germany: the Search for Stability*, by Tony Burkett (Hurst, 1975), examines the history of the SPD, the CDU and the minor parties, and the electoral history of the Federal Republic.

Turning to particular parties, *Adenauer and the CDU, the Rise of the Leader and the Integration of the Party*, by Arnold J. Heidenheimer (Nijhoff, The Hague, 1960), covers the immediate post-war period and the 1950s, whereas *Christian Democracy in Western Germany: the CDU/CSU in Government and Opposition, 1945–76*, by Geoffrey Pridham (Croom Helm, 1977), analyses the development of the CDU/CSU as a political force since the Second World War, in government (1949–1969) and in opposition (1969–1976), and also contains much useful information on the structure, support, organization and electoral politics of both parties. Several books deal with the post-war development of the SPD: *The Social Democratic Party of Germany, from Working-class Movement to Modern Political Party*, by Douglas A. Chalmers (Yale University Press, 1964); *From Schumacher to Brandt, the Story of German Socialism, 1945–1965*, by David Childs (Pergamon, 1966); *The SPD in the Bonn Republic: a Socialist party Modernizes*, by Harold K. Schellenger, Jr (Nijhoff, The Hague, 1968); and *The German Left since 1945: Socialism and Social Democracy in the German Federal Republic*, by William D. Graf (Oleander Press, 1976). *The Minor Parties of the Federal Republic of Germany: Toward a Comparative Theory of Minor Parties*, by Stephen L. Fisher (Nijhoff, The Hague, 1974), is a detailed study of all minor parties which participated in federal elections between 1949 and 1972; and the right-wing NPD is the subject of *The National Democratic Party, Right Radicalism in the Federal Republic of Germany*, by John D. Nagle (University of California Press, 1970).

Studies of particular elections include *German Electoral Politics, a Study of the 1957 Campaign*, by U. W. Kitzinger (The Clarendon Press, 1960); *Germany at the Polls, the Bundestag Election of 1976*, edited by Karl H. Cerny (American Enterprise Institute for Public Policy Research, 1978); and *The West German Federal Election of 1980*, by Juliet Lodge (University of Hull, Hull Papers in Politics, No. 21, 1981). Elections in the eleven 'Länder' of the Federal Republic and their impact on politics at national level is the subject of *'Land' Elections in the German Federal Republic*, by R. J. C. Preece (Longman, 1968).

German Parliaments: a Study of the Development of Representative Institutions in Germany, by Sir Stephen King-Hall and Richard K. Ullmann (Hansard Society, 1954), is a historical study with little coverage of the post-war period; but *Parliament in the German Political System*, by Gerhard Loewenberg (Oxford University Press, 1968), examines in some detail the membership, organization and functions of the Bundestag in the period 1949 –1965. The 'Upper House' of the West German Parliament is the subject of *Federalism, Bureaucracy and Party Politics in Western Germany: the Role of the Bundesrat*, by Edward L. Pinney (University of North Carolina Press, 1963); and *The West German Legislative Process: a Case Study of Two Transportation Bills*, by Gerard Braunthal (Cornell University Press, 1972), is a useful study of the legislative process, illustrated by the progress of two controversial bills.

Government in the Federal Republic of Germany: the Executive at Work, by Nevil Johnson (Pergamon, 1973), is an important work on the process of government in West Germany at federal and state level; and policy making at the national level is the subject of *Policy-making in the German Federal Bureaucracy*, by Renate Mayntz and Fritz W. Scharpf (Elsevier, 1975). *Federalism and Decentralisation in the Federal Republic of Germany*, by Nevil Johnson (Commission on the Constitution, Research Paper 1, HMSO, 1973), is a concise study prepared at the request of the UK Commission on the Constitution; and *Federalism and Judicial Review in West Germany*, by Philip M. Blair (The Clarendon

Press, 1981) examines the role of the Federal Constitutional Court in relation to the West German federal system.

Greece

The historical background to modern Greek politics is covered by two recent histories, *Modern Greece: a Short History*, by C. M. Woodhouse (Faber, 1977), and *A Short History of Modern Greece*, by Richard Clogg (Cambridge University Press, 1979), both of which contain chapters on twentieth-century developments. Two general studies of modern Greek society also make useful background reading. *Greece without Columns, the Making of the Modern Greeks*, by David Holden (Faber, 1972), and *The Metamorphosis of Greece since World War II*, by William McNeill (Blackwell, 1978), both cover, but do not concentrate on, political life, attempting rather to draw a complete picture of country and people in their historical and cultural context.

The Web of Modern Greek Politics, by Jane and Andrew Carey (Columbia University Press, 1968), is a history of political developments up to the 1967 *coup*, with the emphasis on the period since 1940; and *Politics in Modern Greece*, by Keith R. Legg (Stanford University Press, 1969), is a study of the Greek political system, which includes an account of the 1967 *coup* and its immediate aftermath. *Greece, a Political and Economic Survey, 1939–1953*, by Bickham Sweet-Escott (Royal Institute of International Affairs, 1954) and *The Struggle for Greece, 1941–1949*, by C. M. Woodhouse (Hart-Davis, MacGibbon, 1976), cover, between them, the Second World War, the subsequent Greek civil war, and the early 1950s; and *Revolution and Defeat, the Story of the Greek Communist Party*, by George Kousoulas (Oxford University Press, 1965), is a history of the Party since its foundation in 1918, with particular emphasis on its role during the German occupation and the civil war.

The Greek Passion, a Study in People and Politics, by Kenneth Young (Dent, 1969), gives an account of the events leading up to the 1967 *coup* and the aims and actions of the military government, preceded by a survey of Greek history, with the emphasis on developments since 1936. Written in exile during the Colonels' regime, *Democracy at Gunpoint: the Greek Front*, by Andreas Papandreou (André Deutsch, 1971), also deals with the events which led to the imposition of military dictatorship, from the personal viewpoint of the author, who is now Prime Minister of a Socialist government in Greece; and *Greece under Military Rule*, edited by Richard Clogg and George Yannopoulos (Secker and

Warburg, 1972), is a collection of essays which seek to demonstrate the impact of military government on Greek society. Two personal accounts of Greece under the Colonels are *Inside the Colonels' Greece*, by 'Athenian' (later identified as Rodis Rouphos, a Greek intellectual) (Chatto and Windus, 1972), and *A Piece of Truth*, by Amalia, Lady Fleming (Cape, 1972), who was imprisoned, interrogated and eventually deported by the military regime.

Surprisingly little has been published in English on political developments in Greece since the return to democracy in 1974. *Greece at the Polls: the National Elections of 1974 and 1977*, edited by Howard R. Penniman (American Enterprise Institute for Public Policy Research, 1981), is a study of the first two democratic elections, and *Political Forces in Spain, Greece and Portugal*, by Beate Kohler (Butterworth Scientific, in association with European Centre for Political Studies, 1982), offers a useful analysis of the historical development, current attitudes and future prospects of political parties in each of the three countries which emerged during the 1970s from periods of dictatorship.

Karamanlis: the Restorer of Greek Democracy, by C. M. Woodhouse (The Clarendon Press, 1982), is an important study of the political career of Constantine Karamanlis, who is now President of Greece. Based on the subject's personal archives, it is particularly useful on his two terms of office as Prime Minister (1955 –1963 and 1974–1980).

Republic of Ireland

This section deals only with the internal politics of the Republic and does not attempt to cover relations between the Republic and Northern Ireland. It does not include histories of the IRA, whose principal period of influence on the political development of the Republic pre-dates this chapter's terms of reference; but the following studies of Irish history and the evolution of Irish nationalism are a useful background to the study of contemporary Irish politics.

Ireland since the Famine, by F. S. L. Lyons (Collins/Fontana, rev. edn, 1973), is a political and social history of Ireland since 1850, while *Ireland in the Twentieth Century*, by John A. Murphy (Gill and Macmillan, Dublin, 1975), covers the period since 1918. So far, only two out of ten volumes have appeared in *A New History of Ireland*, edited by T. W. Moody *et al.* (The Clarendon Press, 1976–). One of the volumes already published is Volume VIII, *A Chronology of Irish History to 1976* (1982), which is one of three reference volumes in the series. Volume VII will be a history of the period 1921–1976. The development of Irish nationalism is examined in *Nationalism and Socialism in Twentieth-century Ireland*, by E. Rumpf and A. C. Hepburn (Liverpool University Press, 1977); *The Evolution of Irish Nationalist Politics*, by Tom Garvin (Gill and Macmillan, 1981); and *Nationalism in Ireland*, by D. George Boyce (Croom Helm, 1982). The influence of the Catholic Church on Irish politics is dealt with in *Church and State in Modern Ireland, 1923–1979*, by J. H. Whyte (Gill and Macmillan, 2nd edn, 1980).

There are few studies of particular periods in Irish politics since 1945, but one well-documented account is *De Valera's Finest Hour: in Search of National Independence, 1932–1959*, by T. Ryle Dwyer (Mercier Press, Dublin, 1982). *Eamon de Valera*, by The Earl of Longford and Thomas P. O'Neill (Hutchinson, 1970), is a major biography, based on the subject's private papers; a more concise study is *Eamon de Valera*, by T. Ryle Dwyer (Gill and Macmillan, 1980). A later period in Irish politics is the subject of *Cosgrave's Coalition: Irish politics in the 1970s*, by Brian Harvey (Selecteditions, London, 2nd edn, 1980), which explains the formation of the Fine Gael/Labour coalition and examines its period in government (1973–1977).

Three standard works on Irish government and politics are: *The Republic of Ireland, its Government and Politics*, by Morley Ayearst (University of London Press, 1971); *How Ireland is Governed*, by James D. O'Donnell (Institute of Public Administration, Dublin, 6th edn, 1979); and *The Government and Politics of Ireland*, by Basil Chubb (Longman, 2nd edn, 1982). *A Source Book of Irish government*, edited by Basil Chubb (Institute of Public Administration, 1964), is a useful selection of documents (extracts from legislation, parliamentary debates, official reports, etc.) for students of Irish politics. Each chapter deals with a particular aspect of politics and has an introduction which places the documents in context. *The Constitution and Constitutional Change in Ireland*, by Basil Chubb (Institute of Public Administration, 3rd rev. edn, 1978), is a study of the origins and working of the Irish constitution, whereas *The Irish Constitution*, by J. M. Kelly (Jurist Publishing Co., Dublin, 1980), is largely a textual commentary, with numerous references to relevant statutes and cases.

The origins of the Irish party system and the development of the major political parties are examined in *Irish Political Parties, an Introduction*, by Maurice Manning (Gill and Macmillan, 1972), which also outlines the role of smaller parties. One particular party is the subject of *The Irish Labour Party in Transition, 1957–82*, by Michael Gallagher (Manchester University Press, 1982). An early study of the Irish electoral system is *The Irish Election System, What it is and How it Works*, by J. F. S. Ross (Pall Mall, 1959), but reference should also be made to the section on the Irish system in Lakeman (1974, work cited). *Electoral Support for Irish Political Parties, 1927–1973*, by Michael Gallagher (Sage, 1976), is a brief study of the social bases of electoral support, while *Irish Elections, 1918–77: Parties, Voters and Proportional Representation*, by Cornelius O'Leary (Gill and Macmillan, 1979), examines the campaigns, results and political consequences of all general elections during the period covered, and the origins and effects of the proportional representation system in Ireland. Two studies of particular elections are *Republic of Ireland: the General Elections of 1969 and 1973*, by James Knight and Nicolas Baxter-Moore (The Arthur McDougall Fund, 1973), and *Ireland at the Polls: the Dáil Elections of 1977*, edited by Howard R. Penniman (American Enterprise Institute for Public Policy Research, 1978).

The *Founding of Dáil Éireann, Parliament and Nation Building*, by Brian Farrell (Gill and Macmillan, 1971), explains the stability of modern Irish governmental and political institutions by tracing their origins back to the first Dáil, elected in December 1918; and *Representative Government in Ireland, a Study of Dáil Éireann, 1919–48*, by J. L. McCracken (Oxford University Press, 1958), is a detailed study of the first thirty years of the Dáil, and its relations with other organs of government. More recent publications include a brief study of the functions of both Houses of the Irish Parliament, *The Houses of the Oireachtas*, by John McG. Smyth (Institute of Public Administration, 4th edn, 1979); and two books on the Senate: *The Irish Senate*, by Thomas Garvin (Institute of Public Administration, 1969), and *The Theory and Practice of the Irish Senate*, by John McG. Smyth (Institute of Public Administration, 1972).

Two studies in Irish political leadership are: *Chairman or Chief? The Role of the Taoiseach in Irish Government*, by Brian Farrell (Gill and Macmillan, 1971), in which the position of Irish Prime Minister is examined in relation to executive leadership in other countries and the performance of successive holders of the office; and *The Irish Political Elite*, by A. S. Cohan (Gill and Macmillan, 1972), which compares the social composition of two distinct generations of Irish political leaders between 1919 and 1969, identifying a transition from the 'revolutionary' to the 'management' elite. *Cabinet Government in Ireland*, by Basil Chubb (Institute of Public Administration, 1974), traces the development of the cabinet system since 1922 and discusses the cabinet's role in policy-making and administration. The duties of the Attorney-General and his relations with government and Parliament are examined in *The Office of the Attorney-General in Ireland*, by J. P. Casey (Institute of Public Administration, 1980).

The Irish Administrative System, by T. J. Barrington (Institute of Public Administration, 1980), is a survey and critique of public administration in Ireland; and *The Irish Civil Service*, by Seán Dooney (Institute of Public Administration, 1976), describes the evolution of the civil service and the role of civil servants in the policy-making process. At the local government level, P. G. Meghen's *Local Government in Ireland*, edited by D. Roche (Institute of Public Administration, 5th edn, 1975), is a brief factual guide. In addition to the many publications on Irish government and administration referred to above, the Dublin Institute of Public Administration publishes a quarterly journal, *Administration* (1953–).

Italy

Italy, by Muriel Grindrod (Benn, 1968), and *Italy since 1945*, by Elizabeth Wiskemann (Macmillan, 1971), are useful general studies of the post-war period, covering economic, social and cultural matters, as well as political developments. The former includes some coverage of Italy's previous history, with the emphasis on the period after 1890. *A Political History of Postwar Italy*, by Norman Kogan (Praeger, 1966), is a survey of the period 1945–1965, and is updated by *A Political History of Postwar Italy, from the Old to the New Center–left*, also by Norman Kogan (Praeger, 1981), which covers the years 1965–1980. *Patterns of Political Participation in Italy*, by Giorgio Galli and Alfonso Prandi (Yale University Press, 1970), is an analysis of Italian political developments from 1945 to 1963, with particular reference to the two major political parties, the Christian Democrats and the Communists. Two books deal with the significant role of the Catholic Church in Italian politics: *Church and State in Italy, 1850–1950*, by A. C. Jemolo (Blackwell, 1960) and *The Politics of the Vatican*, by Peter Nichols (Pall Mall, 1968).

Italy's economic and political regeneration in the early post-war years is the subject of *The Rebuilding of Italy: Politics and Economics, 1945–1955*, by Muriel Grindrod (Royal Institute of International Affairs, 1955), and of the essays by British and Italian contributors in *The Rebirth of Italy, 1943–50*, edited by S. J. Woolf (Longman, 1972). The next period to attract particular attention is the 1970s, a time of economic, social and political crisis. *Italy in the 1970s*, by John Earle (David and Charles, 1975), is a wide-ranging study by a Rome-based journalist, while the essays in *Italy in Transition: Conflict and Consensus*, edited by Peter Lange and Sidney Tarrow (Cass, 1980), attempt to identify the elements of permanent economic and political change to emerge from this period of crisis.

General studies of Italian politics and government include *The Government and Politics of Contemporary Italy*, by Dante L. Germino and Stefano Passigli (Harper and Row, 1968); *The Government of Republican Italy*, by John C. Adams and Paolo Barile (Houghton Mifflin, Boston, 3rd edn, 1972), and *Italy: Republic without Government?* by P. A. Allum (Weidenfeld and Nicolson, 1973). Turning to the literature on Italian political parties, *Christian Democracy in Italy, 1860–1960*, by Richard A. Webster (Hollis and Carter, 1961), concentrates on the period 1870–1945, and *The Politics of Faction: Christian Democratic Rule in Italy*, by Alan S. Zuckerman (Yale University Press, 1979), is a theoretical study which includes useful factual information on the Christian Democrats. Chapters on Christian Democracy in Italy also feature in several books mentioned in the first part of this chapter, notably Irving (1979), Layton-Henry (1982) and Morgan and Silvestri (1982) (works cited). In addition to the many works on 'Eurocommunism' already cited, several books deal specifically with the Italian Communist Party. They include: *The Italian Communist Party: the Crisis of the Popular Front Strategy*, by Grant Amyot (Croom Helm, 1981); *The Strategy of the Italian Communist Party, from the Resistance to the Historic Compromise*, by Donald Sassoon (Pinter, 1981); and *The Italian Communist Party, 1976–81, on the Threshold of Government*, by James Ruscoe (Macmillan, 1982).

Two studies of Italian elections are *Italy at the Polls: the Parliamentary Elections of 1976*, and *Italy at the Polls, 1979: a Study of the Parliamentary Elections*, both edited by Howard R. Penniman (American Enterprise Institute for Public Policy Research, 1977 and 1981). *Surviving without Governing: the Italian Parties in Parliament*, by Giuseppe Di Palma (University of California Press, 1977), is an interesting study of the impact on the Italian Parliament of the uncertain relationship between majority and opposition in Italy's fragmented party system.

The Nordic countries

Several books deal with politics and government in all five Nordic countries (Denmark, Finland, Iceland, Norway and Sweden) or with regional cooperation in Nordic Europe, particularly in the context of the Nordic Council.

Government and Politics in the Nordic Countries, by Nils Andrén (Almqvist and Wiksell, Stockholm, 1964), outlines the five political systems and identifies similarities and distinctive features. A more recent book, *The Consensual Democracies? The government and politics of the Scandinavian states*, edited by Neil Elder *et al.* (Martin Robertson, 1982), gives an account of the development and present functioning of government and politics in all five states, and assesses the extent to which they constitute a distinct group of consensual democratic systems. *The Other European Community: Integration and Cooperation in Nordic Europe*, by Barry Turner and Gunilla Nordquist (Weidenfeld and Nicolson, 1982), is not, essentially, an account of post-war efforts to institutionalize Nordic unity, as its title suggests, but rather a comparative study of modern political, economic, social and cultural developments in the Nordic countries, with particular attention to post-war social reform and the growth of Social Democracy.

Three studies of regional cooperation, with particular reference to the Nordic Council founded in 1952, are: *The Nordic Council: a study of Scandinavian Regionalism*, by Stanley V. Anderson (University of Washington Press, 1967); *The Nordic Council and Scandinavian Integration*, by Erik Solem (Praeger, 1977); and *Cooperation in the Nordic Countries, Achievements and Obstacles*, by Frantz Wendt (Almqvist and Wiksell, for the Nordic Council, 1981).

The Scandinavian Party System(s): a Comparative Study, by Sten Berglund and Ulf Lindström (Studentlitteratur, Lund, 1978), compares twentieth-century political parties and party systems in Denmark, Finland, Norway and Sweden, while *The Social Democratic Image of Society: a Study of the Achievements and Origins of Scandinavian Social Democracy in Comparative Perspective*, by Francis G. Castles (Routledge and Kegan Paul, 1978), seeks to explain the post-war prominence of the Scandinavian Social Democrat parties, and its consequences. *The Communist Parties of Scandinavia and Finland*, by A. F. Upton with contributions by Peter P. Rohde and Å. Sparring (Weidenfeld and Nicolson, 1973), concentrates on the Communist Party of Finland, with extended essays on the less significant Danish, Norwegian and Swedish parties. *Scandinavia at the Polls, Recent Political Trends in Denmark, Norway and Sweden*, edited by Karl H. Cerny (American Enterprise Institute for Public Policy Research, 1977), is a comparative analysis of the 1973 election results in the three Scandinavian countries, in relation to contemporary socio-economic developments. The quarterly journal *Scandinavian Political Studies* (1965– ; previously annual, from 1961), published in Oslo by the Nordic Political Science Association, is the major source of articles in English on politics in the Nordic countries.

There are relatively few books in English on the Nordic countries individually. Two histories of Denmark, with only brief coverage of the post-war period, are *Denmark*, by Walton G. Jones (Benn, 1970), and *The Story of Denmark*, by Stewart Oakley (Faber, 1972). *Government and Politics in Denmark*, by Kenneth E. Miller (Houghton Mifflin, Boston, 1968), is a useful introduction to the Danish political system; and *Politics in Denmark*, by John Fitzmaurice (Hurst, 1981), is a particularly valuable recent study of post-war political developments and the political system, with particular attention to parties, pressure groups and coalition government in Denmark. *Parliamentary Parties in Denmark, 1945–1972*, by Alastair H. Thomas (Survey Research Centre, University of Strathclyde, Occasional Paper 13, 1973), presents, in a reference format, a detailed collection of historical and statistical data on all Danish political parties which have sat in the Folketing.

Two useful sources on Finland's political history are *The Political History of Finland*, by L. A. Puntila (Otava, Helsinki, 1975), and *Finland in the Twentieth Century*, by D. G. Kirby (Hurst, 1979). *The Finnish Political System*, by Jaakko Nousiainen (Harvard University Press, 1971), is a detailed account of Finnish politics and government, which compares the Finnish system with those of the Scandinavian countries. Other useful works are *Communism in Finland, a History and Interpretation*, by John H. Hodgson (Princeton University Press, 1967), and *The Electoral System of Finland*, by Klaus Törnudd (Hugh Evelyn, 1968).

Two general surveys of Iceland, each of which includes a chapter on politics, are *Modern Iceland*, by John C. Griffiths (Pall Mall, 1969), and *Northern Sphinx: Iceland and the Icelanders from the Settlement to the Present*, by Sigurdur A. Magnússon (Hurst, 1977).

A History of Modern Norway, 1814–1972, by T. K. Derry (The Clarendon Press, 1973), places present-day Norwegian politics in their historical context, and *Norwegian Democracy*, by James A. Storing (Allen and Unwin, 1963), is a detailed survey of Norwegian politics and government. *Political Parties in Norway, a Community Study*, by Henry Valen and Daniel Katz (Tavistock, 1964), is basically a case study of electoral behaviour in the Stavanger area at the 1957 general election, but its introductory chapters deal with the Norwegian political system and the development of political parties. The policies of the Norwegian Communist and Labour parties are compared and contrasted in *The Soviet Communist Party and Scandinavian Communism: the Norwegian Case*, by Trond Gilberg (Universitetsforlaget, Oslo, 1973), which covers the period 1917–1970 and examines both parties' relations with the Soviet Communist Party.

The *Story of Sweden*, by Stewart Oakley (Faber, 1966), is a concise history, while *Sweden*, by Irene Scobbie (Benn, 1972), is a general survey of Swedish history, politics, culture and society. *The New Totalitarians*, by Roland Huntford (Allen Lane, 1971), is an interesting critical study of the Swedish political system. Two general studies of Swedish government and politics are *Modern Swedish Government*, by Nils Andrén (Almqvist and Wiksell, 2nd edn, 1968), and *The Government and Politics of Sweden*, by Joseph B. Board, Jr (Houghton Mifflin, Boston, 1970), whereas *The Politics of Compromise, a Study of Parties and Cabinet Government in Sweden*, by Dankwart A. Rustow (Princeton University Press, 1955), deals particularly with political parties and the cabinet system. *Swedish Social Democracy: into the 'Seventies*, by Russell Lansbury (Fabian Society, Young Fabian Pamphlet 29, 1972), is a very brief discussion of Swedish-style Socialism, and *The Parliament of Sweden*, by Elis Håstad (Hansard Society, 1957), is an authoritative, if rather dated, study of the Swedish Parliament. *Government in Sweden: the Executive at Work*, by Neil C. M. Elder (Pergamon, 1970), concentrates on the executive and administrative areas of government, and *The Swedish Institution of Ombudsman, an Instrument of Human Rights*, by Ibrahim al-Wahab (LiberFörlag, Stockholm, 1979), is an up-to-date and detailed account of a Swedish institution established in 1809, which has been imitated in other countries.

Portugal

The standard history of Portugal in English, from pre-history to the mid-1970s, is *A New History of Portugal*, by H. V. Livermore (Cambridge University Press, 2nd edn, 1976). Two general studies of the country and its people are *Oldest Ally, a Portrait of Salazar's Portugal*, by Peter Fryer and Patricia McG. Pinheiro (Dennis Dobson, 1961), and *Portugal*, by Sarah Bradford (Thames and Hudson, 1973), which are useful background reading on the period of the Salazar and Caetano regimes (1926–1974).

Two books on Portugal's period of dictatorship by opponents of the regime are *Portugal's Struggle for Liberty*, by Mário Soares

(Allen and Unwin, 1975), written in exile and completed in 1972 by the present leader of the Portuguese Socialists; and *Portugal, Fifty Years of Dictatorship*, by Antonio de Figueiredo (Holmes and Meier, New York, 1976). The biography *Salazar and Modern Portugal*, by Hugh Kay (Eyre and Spottiswoode, 1970), is broadly sympathetic to the regime.

Two studies of the origins, events and immediate aftermath of the April 1974 revolution, which overthrew the Caetano regime, are *Insight on Portugal: the Year of the Captains*, by the *Sunday Times* 'Insight' team (André Deutsch, 1975), and *The Portuguese Armed Forces and the Revolution*, by Douglas Porch (Croom Helm, 1977). *Portugal, the Last Empire*, by Neil Bruce (David and Charles, 1975), places the 1974 *coup* in historical perspective and makes a provisional assessment of the new political situation, while *Portugal in Revolution*, by Michael Harsgor (The Washington Papers, III, 32; Sage, 1976), describes the emergence of new political forces after the revolution. *Portugal, Birth of a Democracy*, by Robert Harvey (Macmillan, 1978) is an account of political developments between the overthrow of the Caetano regime and early 1978.

Two recent books are indispensable to students of Portugal's contemporary history and politics. *Contemporary Portugal: a History*, by R. A. H. Robinson (Allen and Unwin, 1979), examines the country's economic, social and political development during half a century of dictatorship, with a more detailed account of the 1974 revolution and its aftermath, up to the establishment of parliamentary democracy. In *Portugal: a Twentieth-century Interpretation*, by Tom Gallagher (Manchester University Press, 1983), the Salazar/Caetano regime is examined in the context of the periods of democracy which preceded and followed the dictatorship. It includes an analysis of Salazar's political philosophy, power structure and economic policies, an assessment of democracy in Portugal from 1974 up to the early 1980s and a very full bibliographical essay.

On political parties in Portugal, reference should be made to Kohler (1982) (work cited in the section on Greece); and the Portuguese Communist Party is included in some of the books on 'Eurocommunism' mentioned in the first part of this chapter: Tökés (1979), Filo della Torre (1979) and Middlemas (1980) (works cited).

Spain

The classic history of nineteenth- and twentieth-century Spain is *Spain, 1808–1975*, by Raymond Carr (The Clarendon Press, 2nd edn, 1982). A shorter work by the same author, *Modern Spain, 1875–1980* (Oxford University Press, 1980), concentrates on the period up to the 1930s, but has two chapters on developments since the Civil War, including one on the Juan Carlos monarchy, established in 1975. *Spain*, by George Hills (Benn, 1970), is a study of political, economic, social and religious developments in Spain since the 1930s, set against the background of Spanish history and thought; and *Spain under Franco, a History*, by Max Gallo (Allen and Unwin, 1973), is a study of the Franco regime up to 1969.

Government in Spain: the Executive at Work, by Kenneth N. Medhurst (Pergamon, 1973), examines the structure and functioning of the machinery of Spanish government against the historical, social and economic background of Franco's Spain, whereas *Franco's Political Legacy, from Dictatorship to Facade Democracy*, by José Amodia (Allen Lane, 1977), is a critical assessment of the political system under Franco and its constitutional development, with particular reference to the formula designed to secure the transition from dictatorship to monarchy. *Spain in Transition: Franco's Regime* and *Spain in Transition: Prospects and Policies*, both by Arnold Hottinger (The Washington Papers, II, 18 and 19; Sage, 1974), are two slim volumes on Franco's Spain. The first is a general survey of economic, social and political developments, while the second is an analysis of the main political forces in Spain. *Spain in Crisis: the Evolution and Decline of the Franco Regime*, edited by Paul Preston (Harvester Press, 1976), brings together research on various aspects of the regime, the forces which supported it and its opponents. Two studies of underground political opposition in Franco's Spain are *The Communists in Spain, Study of an Underground Political Movement*, by Guy Hermet (Saxon House, 1974), and *Dictatorship and Political Dissent, Workers and Students in Franco's Spain*, by José Maravall (Tavistock, 1978). Much useful material on Spain under Franco is also contained in the following major biographies: *Franco, a Biographical History*, by Brian Crozier (Eyre and Spottiswoode, 1967); *Franco, the Man and his Nation*, by George Hills (Hale, 1967); *Franco*, by Alan Lloyd (Longman, 1970); and *Franco, a Biography*, by J. W. D. Trythall (Hart-Davis, 1970).

A number of recent books deal with Spain's transition from dictatorship to democracy and the early years of the new political era, following Franco's death at the end of 1975. *The Political Transformation of Spain after Franco*, by John F. Coverdale (Praeger, 1979), is a narrative of Spanish political life between Franco's death and the adoption of the 1978 constitution. A particularly important work on this period is *Spain: Dictatorship to Democracy*, by Raymond Carr and Juan Pablo Fusi (Allen and Unwin, 1979), which begins with a study of Spain under Franco, followed by an analysis of tensions within the Franco regime and a narrative of political events, concentrated on the period from 1969 to the 1977 elections. *The Transition to Democracy in Spain*, by José Maravall (Croom Helm, 1982), is a study of the political culture and political sociology of post-Franco Spain, particularly interesting for its analysis of support for the Spanish Socialist Party, which gained an overall majority in the 1982 general election. Reference should also be made to the section on Spain in Kohler (1982) (work cited in the section on Greece).

Among the many works on 'Eurocommunism' cited earlier in this chapter, all of which cover the Spanish Communist Party, particular mention should be made of the book by its General Secretary, Santiago Carrillo (1977, work cited). A further brief study of the SCP is *Eurocommunism and the Spanish Communist Party*, by David Bell (Sussex European Research Centre, 1979).

Finally, mention should be made of some recent works on Basque and Catalan nationalism. *Basque Nationalism*, by Stanley G. Payne (University of Nevada Press, 1975), deals mainly with the period up to 1939, but developments are brought up to date by *The Basques: the Franco years and beyond*, by Robert P. Clark (University of Nevada Press, 1979), and *The Basques and Catalans*, by Kenneth Medhurst (Minority Rights Group, Report No. 9, rev. edn, July 1982).

Switzerland

It is not really possible to make a detailed study of the Swiss political system without referring to material in French or German, but the following works in English are useful as an introduction.

A Short History of Switzerland, by Edgar Bonjour *et al.* (The Clarendon Press, 1952) contains only one chapter on the period since the First World War, whereas *Why Switzerland?*, by Jonathan Steinberg (Cambridge University Press, 1976; paperback edn, 1981), covers various aspects of Swiss history (political, social, economic, religious, military and linguistic) in thematic rather than chronological order, and in relation to present-day Switzerland. It includes a chapter on political institutions and practices, illustrating the distinctive Swiss system of 'direct democracy' at all levels of government. An Appendix describes the Swiss electoral system. *Switzerland*, by Christopher Hughes

(Benn, 1975), is a general survey of the country, which includes chapters on Swiss government and institutions, political parties and pressure groups.

The Federal Constitution of Switzerland, by Christopher Hughes (The Clarendon Press, 1954), contains an English translation of the Swiss constitution and two important related documents (the law of 1902 on relations between parliament and the chief executive authority, the Federal Council; and the decree on neutrality of 30 August 1939), accompanied by a detailed commentary on each text and introductory sections on wider aspects, such as parliamentary procedure. *The Federal Government of Switzerland*, by George A. Codding (Houghton Mifflin, Boston, 1961), outlines Switzerland's constitutional history and examines the practice of 'direct democracy' as well as political institutions, parties and pressure groups. *Amicable Agreement versus Majority Rule: Conflict Resolution in Switzerland*, by Jürg Steiner (University of North Carolina Press, rev. edn, 1974), is a political science analysis of the Swiss political system, which includes some useful material on political parties and interest groups. *The Parliament of Switzerland*, by Christopher Hughes (Cassell, for the Hansard Society, 1962), is a detailed study of the Swiss parliament, illustrated by reference to particular examples and actual events.

Reference should also be made to the sections on Switzerland in certain books cited in the first part of this chapter, namely: Fry and Raymond (1980) on the political system; Henig and Pinder (1969) on political parties; Carstairs (1980) and Lakeman (1974) on the electoral system; Butler and Ranney (1978) on the referendum; and Browne and Dreijmanis (1982) on coalition government (works cited).

18
The European Community
Rohan Bolton

Bibliographies and reference works

Mansell have published a number of bibliographical guides which give very thorough coverage of information sources on the Community. Examples include *Policy Formation in the European Communities: a Bibliographical Guide to Community Documentation 1958–1978*, by Michael Hopkins (Mansell, 1981). This is an annotated description of over 650 important reports, grouped according to policy sectors. It has three useful indexes: a numerical list of documents, an alphabetical subject index and one by author and title. *A Guide to the Official Publications of the European Communities*, by John Jeffries (Mansell, 2nd edn, 1981), lists the regular publishing output of all the institutions of the Communities, including the smaller bodies such as the recently established Court of Auditors. An appendix gives selected non-official sources. *Sources of Information on the European Communities*, edited by Doris Palmer (Mansell, 1979), describes where to find legal, technical, commercial and industrial information as well as services available from government departments and HMSO. Another useful guide is *Reports of the European Communities 1952–1977: an Index to Authors and Chairmen*, by June Neilson (Mansell, 1981), which lists all the published reports of the European institutions by author or chairman's surname in one alphabetical sequence. A second part contains a subject index. A further Mansell publication is due towards the end of 1984 –

European Communities Information: its Use and Users, to be edited by Michael Hopkins.

The Encyclopedia of European Community Law is produced in 11 volumes under the editorial guidance of K. R. Simmonds (Sweet and Maxwell, loose-leaf updatings). Authoritative, comprehensive and up to date, it covers UK sources (Volume A), European Community Treaties (Volume B) and Community secondary legislation (Volume C). Less expensive is the one-volume *European Community Treaties*, also edited by K. R. Simmonds (Sweet and Maxwell, 4th edn, 1980). This includes the UK and Greek accession treaties.

General material

There are a number of good studies of the functioning of the Community, both from a historical angle and from the point of view of current developments. *West European Politics since 1945: the Shaping of the Community*, by Roger Morgan (Batsford, 1973), is unfortunately now out of print, as is *Policy Making in the European Communities*, edited by Helen Wallace *et al.* (Wiley, 1977), but a new edition of the latter is expected towards the end of 1983. *Power and Decision in Europe: the Political Institutions of the European Community*, by Stanley Henig (Europotentials Press, 1980), is a very readable account of the institutions and the practical details of the decision-making machinery. Another comprehensive introduction is *Building Europe: Britain's Partners in the EEC*, edited by Carol and Kenneth J. Twitchett (Europa, 1981), in which each EEC member state is considered in turn, giving the background to membership and attitudes of government and people since joining. The complex question of EEC finance is considered in *Budgetary Politics: the Finances of the European Community*, by Helen Wallace (Allen and Unwin, 1980).

Studies in European Politics is a series of brief and up-to-date analyses of European political issues compiled from research undertaken at the Policy Studies Institute in London by the European Centre for Political Studies. A recent example is *The European Voter: Popular Responses to the First Community Election*, by Jay G. Blumer and Anthony D. Fox (Policy Studies Institute, 1982). This analyses public opinion and the involvement of individual citizens during the 1979 direct elections. It shows how they were influenced by the media and describes the campaigns conducted by the political parties. Other books in this series are mentioned elsewhere in this chapter. Another series of academic monographs has been put out by the Sussex European Research Centre of Sussex University. *The Mediterranean Challenge* (1978 –) discusses the problems arising from the enlargement of the Community to include Greece, Spain and Portugal.

The European Community: the Practical Guide for Business and Government, by Brian Morris *et al.* (Macmillan, 1981), is a most useful starting point for any Community query. It explains in dictionary form how the Community institutions operate, how laws are made and what state individual policy areas have reached. Names and addresses are given as sources to contact for further information.

Several guides are available to help the businessman through the maze of the European Community. *Doing Business in the European Community,* by John Drew (Butterworths, 2nd edn, 1982), explains how the EEC affects business and how British exporters can make the most of the Common Market. *The Directors Guide to the EEC: a Quick Checklist of Policy and Legislation for British Business* is prepared annually by ECI services for the Institute of Directors' European Association. This is a brief factual summary of legislation in force and under discussion, giving the exact stage reached and, where possible, the future timetable plans. A comprehensive and useful guide to the grants and loans that are available from Brussels is contained in *A Guide to European Community Grants and Loans* (Euroinformation Ltd, 3rd edn, 1982). It gives full details of the resources and conditions that apply, together with examples of successful projects. Contact points within the European Community and the British Government are given at the end.

The European Parliament

A thorough survey of the powers and organizational structure of the European Parliament was prepared for the delegation of UK Members joining the Parliament in 1973. *The European Parliament: Structure, Procedure and Practice,* by Sir Barnett Cocks (HMSO, 1973), is still useful as a basic reference work, although some of the detail on procedure is somewhat out of date.

A number of books were published on the European Parliament in the period just before the first direct election in June 1979 analysing Parliament's powers and assessing the probable impact of direct elections. *The European Parliament and the European Community,* by Valentine Herman and Juliet Lodge (Macmillan, 1978), falls into this category as a readable, factual account. *The European Parliament,* by John Fitzmaurice (Saxon House, 1978), was written to try to stimulate a new impetus to the European Community through the forthcoming direct elections. *The Future of the European Parliament*, by David Coombes (Policy Studies Institute, 1979), was also written before the first direct elections and discusses the future rule of the Parliament. *The European Parliament and the National Parliaments*, by Valentine Herman and Rinus van Schendelen (Saxon House, 1979), considers the patterns of relationships between the national Parliaments and the European Parliament, especially in the newer member states, where there is great concern for democratic control. *The European Parliament: What it is, What it Does: How it Works*, by Michael Palmer (Pergamon, 1981), is an account by an official of the European Parliament of its functions, structure and method of operation. An appendix outlines recent developments including the effect of Greek accession. Another good general description is contained in *The European Parliament: the Three Decade Search for a United Europe*, by Paula Scalingi (Aldwych Press, 1980).

Political parties and representation

Much discussion and academic research is devoted to the principle of upholding an individual citizen's democratic rights within the European machinery. This is particularly so at the time of direct elections, when the differing electoral systems in each member state become apparent. Much has been published in the run-up to the second direct elections in June 1984, for example *Political Rights for European Citizens*, by Guido van den Berghe (Gower, 1982), which outlines the voting rights and right to stand as a candidate in each member country. *The European Parliament: Towards a Uniform Procedure for Direct Elections*, edited by Christopher Sasse *et al.* (European University Institute, 1981), examines the feasibility of adopting a truly uniform procedure in all the member states. A number of other books are available, each concentrating on a particular aspect of the 1979 campaign: *Europe Elects its Parliament*, by Genevieve Bibes *et al.* (Policy Studies Institute, 1980), is a comparative study by a team of French political scientists outlining the different national perspectives and preoccupations. *The Legislation of Direct Elections to the European Parliament*, edited by Valentine Herman and Mark Hagger (Gower, 1980), is a series of case studies on the passage of electoral legislation through the nine national parliaments. *Direct Elections and the European Parliament: a Community perspective*, by Juliet Lodge and Valentine Herman (Macmillan, 1982), out-lines the various information campaigns conducted throughout the Community in 1979. A definitive record of the election results in tabular form is contained in *Europe Votes 1: European Parliamentary Election Results 1979*, edited by F. W. S. Craig and T. T. Mackie (Parliamentary Research Services, 1980). Similar statistics plus biographies and photographs of MEPs and the texts of the party manifestos are published in *The Times Guide to the European Parliament*, by David Wood and Alan Wood (Times Newspapers, 1979).

There is an increasing interest in the links being formed between the various national political parties. Recent items include *Moderates and Conservatives in Western Europe: Political Parties, the European Community and the Atlantic Alliance*, edited by Roger Morgan and Stefano Silvestri (Heinemann, for Policy Studies Institute, 1982); *Political Parties in the European Community*, edited by Stanley Henig (Allen and Unwin, for Policy Studies Institute, 1979); and *Transnational Party Co-operation and European Integration: the Process Towards Direct Elections*, by Geoffrey and Pippa Pridham (Allen and Unwin, 1981). Of more historical interest is *The Party Groups in the European Parliament*, by John Fitzmaurice (Saxon House, 1975). In view of the forthcoming enlargement of the Community, *Political Forces in Spain, Greece and Portugal*, by Beate Kohler (Butterworths, 1982), is a welcome addition to the literature. Research is currently under way for a book to be published soon through the Policy Studies Institute – *European Social Democracy in the 1980s: a Comparative Study in Policy Developments*, by Giles and Lisanne Radice.

Britain and Europe

There have been a number of studies both of Britain's role in Europe and of the effect of EEC membership on Britain. A valuable historical study of Britain's accession is contained in *Terms of Entry: Britain's Negotiations with the European Community 1970–1972*, by Simon Z. Young (Heinemann, 1973). This analyses the discussions that took place on topics of controversial interest, many of which are still causing problems today, such as agriculture and the UK budgetary contribution. *The British People: Their Voice in Europe* (Saxon House, 1977) is the result of an enquiry sponsored by the Hansard Society into the effects of British membership on the British Parliament and other representative institutions. Two political commentators discuss the implications of the direct elections on the established political structure of the UK in *European Elections and British Politics*, by David Butler and David Marquand (Longman, 1981). A recent study *Can We Save the Common Market?*, by Malcolm Rutherford (Blackwell, 1982), discusses the topical questions of Britain's continuing membership of the European Community. He considers that if Britain is not to withdraw and suffer the consequences of economic, political and strategic isolation then the Community must reform its budgetary procedures and expand its political cooperation role, and Britain must generally develop a more positive role towards its Community partnership. A general survey of the problems raised by British membership is contained in *Britain in Europe*, edited by William Wallace (Heinemann, 1980). Examples of the many other books that are available on specific topics connected with British membership include *The Reluctant Party: Labour and the EEC 1961–1975*, by Lyton J. Robins (Ormskirk, 1980), and *Britons in Brussels: Officials in the European Commission and the Council Secretariat*, by Virginia Willis (Policy Studies Institute, 1983).

Periodicals

There are a number of very useful journals entirely devoted to the Common Market as well as many which feature the occasional article about Community policy. Some of the most well-known are described below.

Europe: Agence internationale d'information pour la presse is published five times each week in English from its offices in Brussels (10 Blvd St Lazare, 1030 Brussels) and provides extensive coverage of all Community events as well as some national political events. This includes many meetings that produce no public record of proceedings. It also reports frequently on forthcoming documents. Its 'Documents' supplement reproduces important Community background papers and communiqués. There is a monthly key-word index produced by computer some 3–4 months in arrears. *British Business: Weekly News from the Department of Trade and Industry* (HMSO) includes a substantial section of 'European Community News', outlining recent developments in Europe, including proposed and adopted legislation. Other features include British Parliamentary coverage of Community policies, a monthly selection of written questions from Euro MPs and a regular series giving the stage that discussion has reached on particular groups of legislation. Examples include company law and food standards harmonization. *European Report: Political, Eeconomic and Industrial News Bulletin* is published twice a week by Europe Information Service (Avenue Albert Elisabeth, 46, 1040 Brussels). This covers all aspects of the Community, both internal and external, and also produces specialized supplements, for example, *Europe Energy* and *Europe Environment*, both of which appear twice-monthly. *The Journal of Common Market Studies*, produced quarterly by Blackwell, contains about four or five readable articles in each issue, giving comment on topical issues. A serious and well-respected periodical is published by the legal firm of Sweet and Maxwell: *The European Law Review* includes one or two academic articles on particular Community policy followed by a current survey of recent judgements in the Court of Justice.

Official community publications

Material published by the Community institutions appears in the seven official Community languages, but the items to be discussed in this chapter will deal primarily with English-language documentation. Before 1973 only a small proportion of documents was printed in English, but since then, all publications have been available in English. HMSO is the main UK agent for Community publications and Alan Armstrong Associates, the specialist booksellers, have recently become sub-agents.

For users wishing to consult official documents or to obtain information about them, the European Commission has an Information Office in London and regional offices in Edinburgh, Cardiff and Belfast. There is also an Information Office for the European Parliament based in London. In addition, there is a network of forty-five European Documentation Centres, mainly housed in university and polytechnic libraries, which receive all the major official publications of the various Community institutions.

The official gazette of the Communities is the *Official Journal of the European Communities*, which appears in several different parts:

> *Series L: Legislation* (daily) publishes the finally adopted texts of all European Community legislation.
> *Series C: Information and Notices* (daily) documents the current activities of the Community institutions, such as cases referred to the Court of Justice, the Minutes of Proceedings of the sittings of the European Parliament and consultative

papers produced by the Commission. These two series are both available in microfilm.

Series S: Supplements invites tenders for contracts for public works and supply of goods and services to public bodies. This supplement is now available on-line through Euronet and other computer networks on the morning of its publication date.

A useful starting point for investigation into any aspect of Community policy is the *General Report on the Activities of the European Community* (1957–). This appears annually each February and outlines both progress so far and action planned in the immediate future. A series of glossy supplements is published in conjunction with the general report; for example, *The Agricultural Situation in the Community, Report on the Development of the Social Situation*, and *Report on Competition Policy*. These are not analytically indexed, but it should be noted that they contain useful information on policy developments in individual member states, plus statistical tables.

The Bulletin of the European Communities (1968–) is a detailed monthly summary of events in each main policy area as well as developments in the field of external relations. It also has a useful list of all recent publications produced by the Institutions and other bodies of the Community. A series of supplements, published separately, sets out important policy texts such as the annual reports on European union.

The Secretariat of the European Parliament compiles an excellent reference book outlining the legislative development of each policy area, giving bibliographical references to the main provisions in the *Treaties*, the *Official Journal*, the *Working Documents* of the European Parliament and the *Bulletin of the European Communities*. The most recent edition of this reference book is *Europe Today: State of European Integration 1982–83*.

Commission documents

From May 1983 these documents (known as Com documents) have been made available to the public on subscription. There is a choice between paper format or microfiche version, together with monthly and annual cumulative indexes. These papers include the finalized drafts of Community legislation, new policy initiatives and progress and action reports. A limited number of these items is also published in the *Official Journal* C series at a later stage.

European Parliament

The European Parliament normally meets in plenary sessions for one week in each month. Its sittings are usually held in Strasbourg, although the Secretariat is currently based in Luxembourg and Committee meetings take place in Brussels.

The records of the debates in plenary sessions are available in a number of formats. The most current version is the daily *Verbatim Report of Proceedings*, known as the 'rainbow' version because each speech appears in the language in which it was delivered. These daily issues are translated into English and later published as an *Annex to the Official Journal*. The formal record of decisions taken at each sitting, the *Minutes of Proceedings*, is published in the *Official Journal C Series*. Many of the Parliament's debates are based on documents drawn up by one of the eighteen subject committees and made available in the *European Parliament Working Documents* sequence. These are documents on a variety of topics about which the Committee hopes to stimulate Community action, and include Committee opinions on the text of legislative proposals upon which Parliament has been required to deliver an opinion. Also falling into this category of *Working Documents* are Motions for Resolutions tabled by individual MEPs. These may be discussed immediately but are normally referred to the appropriate Committee for further consideration.

The Court of Justice

Proceedings through the European Court of Justice in Luxembourg (not to be confused with the European Court of Human Rights in Strasbourg, a Council of Europe body) can be traced fairly easily through a number of sources. First, there is a weekly summary of *Proceedings of the Court of Justice of the European Communities*, which covers judgements, opinions, oral proceedings and new cases. A quarterly bulletin, *Information on the Court of Justice of the European Communities*, summarizes the most important cases appearing before the European Court and before national courts. Finally, an annual survey is produced for the legal profession, students and teachers – *Synopsis of the Work of the Court of Justice of the European Communities*.

The authentic legal text of judgements and opinions, *Reports of Cases before the Court*, is published annually. However, there tends to be some delay in publication of these volumes, and it is often necessary to rely on commercial services. The main such series is *Common Market Law Reports* (1962–), published weekly by the European Law Centre Limited.

CELEX, the Communities' legal data base set up in 1971, is a good example of the progress made by the European Community in establishing mechanized information-retrieval systems. Originally, in French, it is now available in English through Euronet Diane (Direct Information Access Network for Europe). At the moment it includes the Treaties, secondary legislation, decisions of the Court of Justice and European Parliament resolutions and questions. Eventually it is planned to include details of how national governments have implemented Community laws.

Another important Community body is the *Economic and Social Committee*, which represents the interests of employers, trades unions and consumers. It is consulted by the Commission on many legislative proposals and its activities and documentation are covered in a monthly *Bulletin of the Economic and Social Committee* (1974–). The full membership can be found in the *Directory of the Economic and Social Committee* and a self-assessment of its influence on the decision making of the Community is published in their *Annual Report* (1973–). The Committee's opinions on individual proposals are published in the *Official Journal C Series*. Other Community organizations that produce their own publications include the *European Investment Bank* and the *Court of Auditors*, both of which are based in Luxembourg, and the *Joint Research Centre* in Italy.

Eurostat

A unique and valuable set of statistics is compiled by the Statistical Office of the European Communities (SOEC), collated from data provided by the national statistical offices of each member state. *Basic Statistics of the Community* (Annual, 1958–) includes the principal statistics of the member states together with comparisons with important non-member countries such as Japan and the USA. More recent information is found in *Eurostatistics*, which appears twice-monthly, giving data on current economic trends. Other major statistical series include *Analytical Tables of Foreign Trade: NIMEXE*, which for 1979 comprised 13 volumes. There is also a monthly *External Trade Bulletin*. Examples of more specialized series include monthly bulletins on *Coal* and *Electrical Energy* and quarterly issues of *Crop Production* and *Animal Production*.

Eurostat was one of the first organizations to make use of the microfiche format for its publications, and a number of its titles including the trade statistics are available in microfiche at a fraction of the cost of the paper format. It is making increasing use of computers and the CRONOS data base, consisting of some 600 000 statistical series, is now available to the public through Euronet. Of particular note is the fact that this contains information that is much more up to date than that contained in conventional paper-format publications.

The future

The European Community has made increasing use of modern information technology in its efforts to explain policies and developments to as wide a public as possible. Originally most of its information systems were for internal use within the Institutions, but these are increasingly being made available to outside users.

Several examples of modern techniques have already been touched upon in this chapter: *CELEX*, the legal information-retrieval system, the use of microform for the Official Journal and 'Com' documents and *TED* (Tender Electronic Daily), the system that makes available online calls for tenders for public works and other contracts. In the UK, Prestel users have access to *Euronews*, which contains press releases and information on investment opportunities as well as a range of other Community news.

Progress in this field involves the use of complex and costly technologies, and the European Community is in a unique position to stimulate research and to publicize successful results in the growing European market. The first European information network, Euronet Diane, was inaugurated in 1980 on the initiative of the Commission and now consists of over 300 data bases. Much of this information is provided by non-Community sources, but the statistical data bases *CRONOS* and *CELEX* are examples of well-used data bases provided by the Community.

The Community has stimulated research into other areas of information technology which individual member states could not develop on their own both because of the high costs involved and because of the shortage of research workers and technicians. The *ESPRIT* Programme (European Strategic Programme for Research in Information Technology) is now under way with a ten-year programme envisaged. Pilot projects include advanced information processing and software technology as well as office automation and advanced microelectronics. Other areas in which Community research is being concentrated include machine translation and experimental schemes in electronic document delivery.

Developments such as these show that, as the Community becomes more mature and its interdependence increases, the rate of technological advance in information systems will undoubtedly be matched by the Commission's efforts to facilitate effective communication.

19
Eastern Europe
Richard Ware

For the student of politics, the 'Iron Curtain' remains a formidable barrier. The virtual absence beyond it of contested elections and a free press, the lack of frank memoirs and the insistence on clothing all debate in the esoteric vocabulary of Marxism–Leninism would seem to deprive the political analyst of almost all the customary sources of information.

There are some cracks in the monolith, however; conflicting interest groups still grapple with each other in the East as in the West, and the observer learns to detect signs of activity below the surface, drawing on whatever information is available. Furthermore, at infrequent intervals the system suffers a major local breakdown. Each time that this happens (Hungary in 1956, Czechoslovakia in 1968, Poland in 1980–1981), matters which are normally concealed have been exposed to public view. For a short while, political life is conducted in the newspapers, at public gatherings, on the streets, even in parliament; moreover, the new and temporary frankness sheds light on old events.

In some parts of Eastern Europe even a temporary 'opening up' seems a remote prospect. One day, perhaps, the archives of Tirana, Prague and Moscow will be thrown open to the inquisitive, but in the meantime we have to accept that our ignorance usually exceeds our knowledge, and in every serious study there is an element of guesswork; both the details and the general conclusions are always liable to correction.

Bibliography

Whatever the nature of the inquiry, it is likely to begin with an investigation of what published sources are already available. Since in the following pages it will be possible to mention only a small number of individual works, it may be useful to begin with bibliographies, and indeed with an indispensible bibliography of bibliographies. *Russian Bibliography, Libraries and Archives: A Selective List of Bibliographical References for Students of Russian History, Literature, Political, Social and Philosophical Thought, Theology and Linguistics*, by J. S. G. Simmons (Oxford, 1973), is particularly aimed at researchers in the field of Russian and Soviet Studies, but many of the items listed deal also with Eastern Europe. These range from current bibliographies of Soviet Studies to listings of periodicals and archive holdings.

According to P. L. Horecky, writing in 1969, literature on Eastern Europe in all its aspects (but without the USSR) must be selected from a potential bibliographical field of more than one million items (it would be much more now). Horecky and his collaborators narrowed the field to approximately 10 000 items for two volumes of annotated listings – *Southeastern Europe* and *East–Central Europe*, both subtitled *A Guide to Basic Publications* (both published by University of Chicago Press in 1969). Both have detailed sections on history, politics, law, etc. Similar, but limited to English publications, is S. M. Horak's *Russia, the USSR, and Eastern Europe: A Bibliographic Guide to English Publications* (Libraries Unlimited, Colorado, USA, 1978 and 1982). Two volumes have so far appeared spanning 1964–1980.

More specifically aimed at political researchers is *Current Research in Comparative Communism: An Analysis and Bibliographic Guide to the Soviet System*, by L. Whetten (Praeger, 1976). This covers the USSR and Eastern Europe (except for Albania). It is complemented by *Periodicals on the Socialist Countries and on Marxism: A New Annotated Index of English-language Publications*, by H. G. Shaffer (Praeger, 1977), which notes the scope and slant of the periodicals listed. For individual countries the bibliographical coverage is patchy and specialist bibliographies are often many years out of date. Exceptions to this are the three countries so far included in the World Bibliographical Series published by the Clio Press – Yugoslavia (1977), the USSR (1979) and Hungary (1980). There is also *Yugoslav Studies*, by G. M. Terry (A. C. Hall, 1977), an annotated listing of bibliographies and references work. Though not a bibliography as such, *Resources for Soviet, East European and Slavonic Studies in*

British Libraries, edited by G. Walker (University of Birmingham, 1981), is a very useful companion to the above since it describes the holdings of British academic libraries and suggests many other sources of information for researchers in the field.

Texts and reference books

While hard facts about the politics of Eastern Europe may be in short supply, there is no shortage of raw material on which to work. The various state and party institutions produce a constant flow of reports and resolutions; the media are clogged with 'political' comment and information. Political meetings are held in every type of institution and every college syllabus finds time for 'dialectical materialism' and 'the history of the Party'.

The obsession with formalities is nowhere more apparent than in the field of constitutional law. Basic texts and details of constitutional change may be found in *The Constitutions of the Communist World*, edited by W. B. Simons (University of Leyden, Netherlands, 1980), while texts and commentaries on the Soviet constitution alone (including the 'Brezhnev Constitution' of 1977) are in *Constitutional Development in the USSR – A Guide to the Soviet Constitution*, by A. Unger (Methuen, 1981).

The structure of such international organizations as the Council for Mutual Economic Assistance (CMEA or COMECON), the Warsaw Treaty Organization and others which link the Eastern European states and the Soviet Union is dealt with in *The System of the International Organizations of the Communist Countries*, by R. Szawlowski (Leyden, 1976), and, in much greater depth and detail, but virtually without editorial comment, in *A Sourcebook on Socialist International Organizations*, edited by W. E. Butler (Sijthoff and Noordhoff, 1978). A useful guide to official texts such as laws and formal statements of policy, is *Official Publications of the Soviet Union and Eastern Europe 1945–1980*, edited by G. Walker (Mansell, 1982), a listing which includes helpful critical annotations.

The flow of new documents, including speeches, communiqués, etc. is monitored in English translation, albeit in a very selective fashion, in *Documents in Communist Affairs*, which began publication in 1978 and, after three annual volumes (University College Cardiff Press, 1978, 1979; Macmillan, 1980), was transformed from the beginning of 1982 into a quarterly journal, edited as before by B. Szajkowski and published in London by Butterworths.

Equally important and more comprehensive for current political information and references, though lacking full texts, are the research series published in English by the US-funded Radio Free Europe and Radio Liberty, both based in Munich. Each station prepares and publishes annually about 400 reports on its target area (Eastern Europe and the Soviet Union, respectively). These consist of detailed commentaries on political developments in each country and include summaries (with extracts) of significant speeches, books and articles. Most reports are accompanied by a short abstract and there are full annual indexes. Regular features include lists of senior government and party office holders, chronologies and general surveys of the press.

In each of the Eastern European states one national newspaper stands pre-eminent as the official voice of the Communist Party, and this is always a major source of information (*Pravda* in the USSR, *Trybuna Ludu* in Poland, *Zeri i Popullit* in Albania, etc.). Other newspapers and magazines are scarcely more independent because they are also subject to the censors' scrutiny and are ultimately controlled by the Communist Party. Despite this limitation, differences of emphasis are detected and may sometimes be seen as reflecting competing interest groups. Some of the peculiarities of Eastern European journalism are discussed in *The Bureaucracy of Truth: How Communist Governments Manage the News*, by P. Lendvai (Burnett Books, 1981). The operation of the censorship is analysed in *Censorship and Political Communication: Examples from Eastern Europe*, edited by G. Schöpflin (Frances Pinter, 1982), which draws mostly on Polish sources. English abstracts of major articles in Soviet newspapers appear in the *Current Digest of the Soviet Press* (American Association for the Advancement of Slavic Studies, weekly).

An absolutely up-to-date source of information is provided by the Soviet and East European sections of the *Summary of World Broadcasts* (BBC, daily). Based on broadcasts monitored by the BBC at Caversham Park, Reading, it gives access, in instant but reliable translation, to a wide range of broadcast material. Since it is the habit of state-controlled radio stations in Eastern Europe to broadcast important political speeches in full and to read out substantial extracts from the press each day, the *Summary* includes far more than a mere transcript of news bulletins.

Documents and speeches may also be found in a version expressly designed for foreign consumption in official digests and press releases published by the various foreign ministries or their embassies abroad.

So much for the public face of the Communist polity: for what happens behind the scenes, information is much more limited. Only once has a major political archive fallen into the hands of Western scholars. In 1941 the Germans captured virtually intact the archive of the Communist Party offices in Smolensk and sent it back to Germany, whence it was removed eventually to the US. The analysis of the archive, published as *Smolensk under Soviet Rule*, by M. Fainsod (Macmillan, 1959), is fascinating. For the post-war period the nearest equivalents are the occasional memoirs of highly placed officials who have emigrated or smuggled their writings to the West.

The most striking recent example of this is *Night Frost in Prague: the End of Humane Socialism*, by Z. Mlynář (C. Hunt, 1980). Mlynář was a member of the Czechoslovak Communist Party Secretariat in 1968 and a close associate of Alexander Dubček. He migrated to Vienna in 1977. The only first-rank leader to indulge in political memoirs so far has been Khrushchev, in *Khrushchev Remembers* (André Deutsch, 1971), but although the authenticity of his text is now generally accepted, it provides disappointingly little new information.

Biographical reference books have a particular relevance in Eastern Europe, where the career profile of a middle-ranking official may yield significant information about the interplay of political forces in the system as a whole. *Who's Who in the Socialist Countries*, by B. Lewytzkyj and J. Stroynowski (K. G. Saur, 1978), is a useful starting point, and listings prepared for Western governments are sometimes released to the public, for example, by the CIA National Foreign Assessment Centre. The British Foreign and Commonwealth Office has occasionally released biographical notes: for example, Foreign Policy Document No.69 (March 1982) on 'Albanian State, Government and Party Institutions', is one of a series deposited in major British libraries. For information on personalities active in the political opposition, the *Biographical Directory of Dissidents in the Soviet Union 1956–1975*, edited by S. P. de Boer *et al.* (Nijhoff, 1982), is valuable, though it stops short in the mid-1970s.

Methods and approaches

Despite the limitations referred to above, there is now a large body of literature in English about the politics of the USSR and Eastern Europe. Inevitably, both scholars and publishers have been influenced by the changing climate of East–West relations and, as an irritated reviewer recently noted, 'Soviet Studies have always been bedevilled by the How-To-Fight-The-Russians-More-Effectively brigade' (*International Affairs*, Winter 1981–1982, p.157).

Some branches of study are unavoidably weak. For example, the political biography does not find ready material in Eastern Europe, and has been attempted only rarely in relation to post-war personalities. Communist leaders themselves promote the false impression that they lack the more interesting human characteristics. There exist informative biographies of Gomulka (by N. Bethell, Longman, 1969), Ulbricht (by C. Stern, Pall Mall Press, 1965), and Tito (by P. Auty, Longman, 1970), and there are several preliminary assessments of Brezhnev, but all are ultimately disappointing.

While the Cold War was at its height in the 1950s there was a strong emphasis on the monolithic uniformity of the Eastern polity. The USSR was perceived as a totalitarian state and the other countries merely its 'satellites'. By contrast, in the 1960s it became routine to balance the essential homogeneity of Communist Eastern Europe against the increasingly apparent signs of diversity, as is done in the influential textbook *The Soviet Bloc: Unity and Conflict*, by Z. Brzezinski (Harvard University Press, 1960, rev. edn, 1967). A number of studies emphasized the importance of 'national Communism' as it had evolved in each nation-state; for example, *Communism National and International: Eastern Europe after Stalin*, by H. G. Skilling (University of Toronto Press, 1964) and *Eagles in Cobwebs: Nationalism and Communism in the Balkans*, by P. Lendvai (Macdonald, 1969).

The recognition that each Eastern European country had after all retained a distinctive political character, which shows through the artificial uniformity, took firm hold in the 1970s and culminated in the application to the Communist world of the concept of 'political culture'. This approach took its inspiration from the theoretical work of Lucian Pye and Sidney Verba (*Political Culture and Political Development*, Princeton University Press, 1965). The key property of political culture is that it changes much more slowly than political structure. Communist institutions may have been in place now for more than thirty years (longer in the USSR), but the political culture is still made up of attitudes and values which predate them. When the imposed structure weakens, as it did in Poland in 1980, the underlying values and attitudes resurface. Even when the political structure holds firm it is influenced by the underlying culture in subtle ways. These ideas are explored in several recent studies, including *Political Culture and Political Change in Communist States*, edited by A. Brown and J. Gray (Macmillan, 2nd edn, 1979), which spans the whole of Eastern Europe, and *Political Culture and Soviet Politics*, by S. White (Macmillan, 1979). Since these appeared, a new deterioration in East–West relations has led some to re-examine the new orthodoxy, and once again voices are heard suggesting that to some extent the 'totalitarian' model was right all along, and that too much has been made of national diversity, political culture, changing generations, etc. It seems unlikely, however, that there will be a complete return to 'totalitarianism' as a means of explaining the politics of the whole region.

One reason for this is that there has been an evolution in technique which may be crudely represented as a shift from 'Kremlinology' to political sociology. The essentials of Kremlinology were to make much out of little, to trust in rumours (which abound in Eastern Europe) and, where rumours conflicted, to trust in the more interesting of them. At its best, as in *Power in the Kremlin: from Khrushchev's Decline to Collective Leadership*, by M. Tatu (Collins, 1969), Kremlinology makes absorbing and persuasive reading – but the drawbacks are obvious.

The art of Kremlinology is not dead, but in recent years scholars have tended to take a more critical attitude towards sources and to underpin the more colourful details of high politics with generalizations drawn from career analysis or arguments drawn from the theoretical study of decision making and interest-group conflict, or again to look beyond the Kremlin to the politics of the regions.

A recent example of the more sophisticated 'new' Kremlinology is *Soviet Intervention in Czechoslovakia 1968: Anatomy of a Decision*, by J. Valenta (Johns Hopkins University Press, 1979), which offers a case study in Soviet crisis management and analyses the decision-making process in Moscow as one of bargaining between rival bureaucratic elites. Though much of the detail is unsubstantiated, Valenta presents a highly plausible picture of miscalculation and shifts in the 'bureaucratic mood'. A slightly different perspective on the same problem is provided by H. Adomeit in *Soviet Risk-Taking and Crisis Behaviour: A Theoretical and Empirical Analysis* (Allen and Unwin, 1982), which seeks to apply Western models and assumptions to Soviet crisis management during the Berlin crises of 1948 and 1962.

An example of the statistical approach to Communist politics is G. Hodnett's *Leadership in the Soviet National Republics: A Quantitative Study of Recruitment Policy* (Mosaic Press, 1978), which analyses career patterns and promotion prospects in an environment complicated by national factors in the non-Russian Soviet Republics.

Since the early 1960s a small number of research students from Britain and North America have been able to work in Soviet regional centres such as Voronezh, Rostov-on-Don, Kiev and Kishinev under official exchange schemes, and to return with a view of Soviet life 'at the grass roots'. Although archives of political interest remain closed, these scholars have been able to study such sources as local newspapers (the export of which from the USSR is illegal) and sometimes to interview local officials. The outcome has been a number of books on Soviet local government and a fresh perspective. Amongst the most penetrating of these studies is *Soviet Political Elites: the Case of Tiraspol*, by R. J. Hill (Martin Robertson, 1977), which explicitly rejects the 'struggle at the top' school of Soviet studies and finds that there is, after all, some sort of political life in the Soviet provinces.

The region as a whole

We turn next to a selective survey of monographs on the political history and current politics of the USSR and Eastern Europe as a whole, followed by surveys of the individual countries.

The history of the region since the earliest times (excluding Russia, but including the Ukraine and the Baltic) is covered in the eleven volumes (not yet all published) of *A History of East Central Europe*, edited by P. F. Sugar and D. W. Treadgold (University of Washington Press, Seattle, 1974–). For most purposes, however, the student of contemporary politics will not have to go further back than the early nineteenth century, when the modern shape of Eastern Europe began slowly to emerge within the anachronistic confines of the Hapsburg, Russian and Ottoman Empires. *The Lands Between, A History of East–Central Europe since the Congress of Vienna*, by A. W. Palmer (Weidenfeld and Nicholson, 1970), is an introduction to the political development of the region since 1815. *Independent Eastern Europe: a History*, by C. A. Macartney and A. W. Palmer (Macmillan, 1962), provides an overview of the inter-war period, as does the rather more idiosyncratic *Eastern Europe between the Wars 1918–1941*, by H. Seton-Watson (Cambridge University Press, 1946; rev. edn, 1967), which has the advantage of not being burdened with hindsight.

Some works on post-war Eastern Europe have been mentioned already. The role of the Soviet-led Communist movement has been crucial everywhere. One of the few books to examine all of the Eastern European Communist Parties (including the Albanian) is *The Communist Parties of Eastern Europe*, edited by S.

Fischer-Galati (Columbia University Press, 1979). The other side of the coin is tackled in *Opposition in Eastern Europe*, edited by R. L. Tökes (Macmillan, 1979), which divides up its subject not only by countries (Czechoslovakia, Poland, East Germany and Hungary earn separate chapters), but also by social groups. The question of how the various Communist governments have fared in counteracting and deflecting criticism, by economic and social, as well as administrative, measures is central to all the essays in the book.

The quiescent and subservient role of parliaments in the region is no doubt the reason why they are so little studied in the West, but there is some evidence that they have a potential to be more than just a legitimizing rubber stamp. In Poland, for example, during the crisis of 1980–1981, genuine and lively debates took place in the Sejm. *Communist Legislatures in Comparative Perspective*, edited by D. Nelson and S. White, is a pioneering study in this field, which finds that parliaments do more generally have a role in Eastern Europe, particularly in the detailed drafting of legislation. At a humbler and more mundane level, the operation of local government in Eastern Europe, including the USSR, is surveyed in *Local Politics in Communist Countries*, edited by D. N. Nelson (Kentucky University Press, 1980).

Nationalism is still a potent force which can work for and against Communist regimes. In Romania, for example, it gives a certain, much-needed, legitimacy to Ceausescu's quasi-Peronist rule, while in multinational states like the USSR and Yugoslavia it poses the threat of disintegration and disaster. A useful survey (though excluding the USSR, about the nationality problems of which there is a considerable specialized literature) is provided by *Nationalism in Eastern Europe*, edited by P. F. Sugar and I. J. Lederer (University of Washington Press, 1969).

Individual countries

East Germany

Created out of the zone of Germany which had been occupied by the Red Army, the German Democratic Republic was long regarded as a mere Soviet appanage. *German Politics under Soviet Occupation*, by H. Krisch (Columbia University Press, 1974), and *Uprising in East Germany: June 17 1953*, by A. Baring (Cornell University Press, 1972), confirm that this was so; the emergence of the GDR in the 1960s as a major industrial (and also sporting) power led to studies like *East Germany*, by D. Childs (Ernest

Benn, 1969), which recognized that the East Germans had acquired a political character of their own.

The nature of this political character is explored in two more specialized studies: *The Changing Party Elite in East Germany*, by P. C. Ludz (MIT Press, 1972), and *East German Civil–Military Relations: the Impact of Technology, 1949–1972*, by D. R. Herspring (Praeger, 1973). The particularly compelling need for Communism in East Germany to organize the efficient production of consumer goods is one of the recurring themes of *Marxism –Leninism in the German Democratic Republic*, by M. McCauley (Macmillan, 1979).

Finally, *The Government and Politics of East Germany*, by K. Sontheimer and W. Bleek (Hutchinson, 1975), is a useful survey of the system as it operated in the 1970s.

Poland

Unlike East Germany, Poland is a nation with a long and sometimes heroic past. *God's Playground: a History of Poland*, by N. Davies (2 vols, Oxford University Press, 1981), covers the ground in 1330 pages of part-thematic and part-chronological analysis. *The History of Poland since 1863*, edited by R. F. Leslie (Cambridge University Press, 1980), gives a slightly different perspective on the modern period, and one of the contributers to this volume, A. Polonsky, has also treated the inter-war period when Poland's statehood was restored, but its democracy soon lost, in *Politics in Independent Poland* (Oxford University Press, 1972).

The Communist Party of Poland: An Outline of History, by M. K. Dziewanowski (Harvard University Press, 2nd edn, 1976), suffers from the dearth of reliable 'inside' sources and is very sketchy about developments after 1956. The gap is partly filled, for the 1970s at least, by *Background to Crisis: Policy in Gierek's Poland*, edited by M. D. Simon and R. E. Kanet (Westview Press, 1981). The intellectual opposition to both Gomulka and Gierek is recorded in *Political Opposition in Poland 1954–1977*, by P. Raina (Poets and Painters Press, 1978), which reproduces many of the relevant documents and has a useful bibliography.

The events of August 1980 and subsequent months sparked off a new interest in Poland abroad. *August 1980: the Strikes in Poland*, edited by W. F. Robinson (Radio Free Europe Research, 1980), was an 'instant' reaction to the crisis, but contains a mass of raw information, as do the very detailed chronologies subsequently published in the Radio Free Europe 'Background Report' series.

Independent Social Movements in Poland, by P. Raina (Orbis, 1981), complements the same author's earlier work (see above) and chronicles the activities of groups such as KOR (Committee for Workers' Defence) and KPN (Confederation of Independent Poland) as well as the more well-known 'Solidarity' unions. *The Polish Challenge*, by K. Ruane (BBC, 1982), is largely based on information from the BBC Monitoring Reports and covers the period from August 1980 to December 1981. *Poland: a Crisis for Socialism*, by M. Myant (Lawrence and Wishart, 1982), also takes in the declaration of martial law late in 1981, but seeks to place the events of 1980–1981 in a historical context. *Policy and Politics in Contemporary Poland: Reform, Failure and Crisis*, edited by J. Woodall (Frances Pinter, 1982), is a symposium dedicated 'to the spirit of August 1980'. Many new books on Polish politics are currently in preparation and there will no doubt be more to follow.

Czechoslovakia

There is no comprehensive history in English of the Czech and Slovak peoples, though *Czechoslovakia*, by W. V. Wallace (Ernest Benn, 1977), is a good introduction. *The Czech Renascence of the Nineteenth Century*, edited by P. Brock and H. G. Skilling (University of Toronto Press, 1970), describes the political awakening of the Czechs and their further evolution is treated in *Neo-Slavism and the Czechs 1898–1914*, by P. Vyšný (Cambridge University Press, 1977).

Zealots and Rebels: a History of the Communist Party of Czechoslovakia, by Z. L. Suda (Hoover Institution Press, 1980), analyses the Czechoslovak Communist Party from its prewar origins, while *A History of the Czechoslovak Republic 1918–1948*, edited by V. S. Mamatey and R. Luža (Princeton University Press, 1973), covers most aspects of Czechoslovak politics in the inter-war years and during the Second World War, when the Republic was occupied and dismembered.

The process by which the Communists won absolute power is described in *Socialism and Democracy in Czechoslovakia 1945 –1948*, by M. Myant (Cambridge University Press, 1981), and the grim Czechoslovak version of Stalinism is treated not only in Suda (1980, work cited) but also in the opening chapters of the indispensable *Czechoslovakia's Interrupted Revolution*, by H. G. Skilling (Princeton University Press, 1976), which focuses on the events of 1968.

Dubček's abortive attempt at 'socialism with a human face' is inevitably the focal point of most recent books. *The Czechoslovak*

Reform Movement: Communism in Crisis 1962–1968, by G. Golan (Cambridge University Press, 1971), and *The Intellectual Origins of the Prague Spring*, by V. Kusin (also Cambridge University Press, 1971) are studies of the prelude to 1968, whereas *From Dubček to Charter 77*, by V. Kusin (Q Press, 1978), is a kind of extended epilogue.

The literature on 1968 itself is large. A useful guide is *Czechoslovakia 1968–1969: Chronology, Bibliography, Annotation*, by V. Kusin and Z. Hejzlar (Garland, 1975). Almost all of the essential documents of the Dubček era are now available in English in such compilations as *The Czech Black Book*, edited by R. Littell (Pall Mall Press, 1969); *Winter in Prague*, edited by R. A. Remington (MIT Press, 1969); and *The Secret Vysočany Congress: Proceedings and Documents of the Extraordinary Fourteenth Congress of the Communist Party of Czechoslovakia, 22 August 1968*, edited by J. Pelikan (St Martin's Press, 1971). Z. Mlynař's valuable memoirs were mentioned earlier, as was J. Valenta's study of the Soviet decision to invade. The best general analytical account is that by Skilling (1976, work cited). The same author has subsequently written *Charter 77 and Human Rights in Czechoslovakia* (Allen and Unwin, 1981), which includes the texts of Charter 77 documents.

Hungary

Hungary is another of Eastern Europe's 'old' nations. A useful introduction to its political history up to 1945 is *A History of Hungary*, by D. Sinor (Allen and Unwin, 1959). The main turning point in that history during the nineteenth century is treated in *The Lawful Revolution: Louis Kossuth and the Hungarians 1848–1849*, by I. Deak (Columbia University Press, 1979), while *The Politics of Backwardness in Hungary*, by A. C. Janos (Princeton University Press, 1982), spans most of the nineteenth and the first half of the twentieth century.

In 1918–1919 Hungary was one of the first countries outside the old Russian Empire to experience its own short-lived Communist revolution – an episode described in *Bela Kun and the Hungarian Soviet Republic*, by R. L. Tökés (Praeger, 1967). Fascism also had its turn, and is the subject of *The Greenshirts and the Others. A History of Fascism in Hungary and Rumania*, by N. M. Nagy-Talavera (Hoover Institution Press, 1970). *A Short History of the Hungarian Communist Party*, by M. Molnar (Westview Press, 1978), is brief but useful.

The post-war turning point and the starting point for the 'Kadarism' of the present day was the uprising of 1956. Essential documents (including some concerned with the 'Polish October' of the same year) are contained in *National Communism and Popular Revolt in Eastern Europe*, edited by P. Zinner (Columbia University Press, 1957), and more considered analysis may be found in *Rift and Revolt in Hungary: Nationalism versus Communism*, by F. A. Vali (Harvard University Press, 1961). The international constraints on Hungary during and after the crisis are examined in *Hungary and the Superpowers: the 1956 Revolution and Realpolitik*, by J. Radvanyi (Hoover Institution Press, 1972).

Finally, the calmer and more prosperous, if more cynical, heyday of Kadarism is the subject of *The Pattern of Reform in Hungary: a Political, Economic and Cultural Analysis*, by W. F. Robinson (Praeger, 1973) and its achievements are reviewed in *Hungary: a Decade of Economic Reform*, edited by P. Hare *et al.* (Allen and Unwin, 1981).

Romania

With the partial exception of Yugoslavia, Balkan politics are not well covered in English. *Twentieth Century Romania*, by S. Fischer-Galati (Columbia University Press, 1970), is a brief study in the political history of that country and is complemented by *Oil and the Romanian State*, by M. Pearton (Oxford University Press, 1971), which, although not pretending to be a history of Romania as such, does throw a good deal of light on the pre-war period.

A History of the Romanian Communist Party, by R. R. King (Hoover Institution Press, 1980), is sound, but regrettably brief, covering almost sixty years in 140 pages of text. *Democratic Centralism in Romania: a Study of Local Communist Parties*, by D. N. Nelson (Westview Press, 1980), is based on interviews with local officials, and argues that economic modernization is making Romania's existing political system untenable. The appearance of *Romania in the 1980s*, edited by Nelson (Westview Press, 1981), may indicate, together with a recent surge of periodical literature, that academic interest in Romania is growing.

Bulgaria

A History of Bulgaria 1393–1885, by M. Macdermott (Allen and Unwin, 1962), is a substantial scholarly history. The subsequent period, including the inter-war years, is poorly covered, but *The Communist Party of Bulgaria: Origins and Development 1883 –1936*, by J. Rothschild (Columbia University Press, 1959), does partially fill the gap.

Bulgarian Communism: the Road to Power 1934–1944, by N. Oren (Columbia University Press, 1971), picks up where Rothschild ends, and a further study by the same author, *Revolution Administered: Agrarianism and Communism in Bulgaria* (Johns Hopkins University Press, 1973), takes us up to 1971. Finally, *Bulgaria under Communist Rule*, by J. F. Brown (Pall Mall Press, 1970), is based mostly on work carried out for Radio Free Europe and covers both political and economic aspects of Bulgaria during 1953–1968.

Yugoslavia

Certain aspects of Yugoslavia, such as its wartime history, the subsequent break with Stalin's Russia and, more recently, the development of a new type of Communist economy based on self-management, have been treated relatively generously in English-language publications, but Yugoslav political history, in the narrow sense, has been rather neglected. *Twentieth-Century Yugoslavia*, by F. Singleton (Macmillan, 1976), is a sound introduction which concentrates on the post-war period. The immediate pre-war years are covered in *Yugoslavia in Crisis 1934–1941*, by J. Hoptner (Columbia University Press, 1962), and more stylishly, with unhurried historical and descriptive digressions, in *Black Lamb and Grey Falcon*, by Rebecca West (Macmillan, 1942; latest reprint 1982). *The History of the Communist Party of Yugoslavia Volume I*, by I. Avakumovic (Aberdeen University Press, 1964), stops at 1941 and leaves after it a gap which has yet to be adequately filled.

The process by which Tito's party gradually extended and legitimated its hold on Yugoslav society after 1945 is described in *The Legitimation of a Revolution: the Yugoslav Case*, by B. Denitch (Yale University Press, 1976), while *The Yugoslav Experiment 1948–1974*, by D. Rusinow (Hurst, 1977) concentrates on developments since 1961. *Democratic Reform in Yugoslavia: the Changing Role of the Party*, by A. Carter (Frances Pinter, 1982), is a study of the controlled liberalization of the 1960s, but ends with Tito's tightening of political control in 1971–1972. The death of Tito in May 1980 has led to a number of reassessments of the Yugoslav system, including *The End of the Tito Era: Yugoslavia's Dilemmas*, by S. Stanković (Hoover Institution Press, 1981).

Albania

Objective and scholarly books on Albania are few, and must be supplemented on the one hand by travellers' tales and on the other by translations of Albanian works, with all their oddities. *The History of Albania*, by S. Pollo *et al.* (Routledge and Kegan Paul, 1981), is one of the latter, but may be useful on the earlier history.

The Albanian National Awakening 1878–1912, by S. Skendi (Princeton University Press, 1967), is a scholarly work, as is *Albania*, edited by the same author (Atlantic Press, 1957), which is a compendium containing virtually everything known about Albania in the West in 1956. For the inter-war period we have to turn to *King Zog's Albania* (Hale, 1937), the work of an enthusiastic journalist who had been made an honorary Commander of the Order of Skanderbeg.

Albania and the Sino–Soviet Rift, by W. E. Griffith (MIT Press, 1963), concentrates on 1960–1962 and relies on 'the intensive deciphering and analysis of esoteric Communist communications', while *Socialist Albania since 1944: Domestic and Foreign Developments*, by P. R. Prifti (MIT Press, 1978), just takes in the Albanian break with China in 1977.

The USSR

The fundamental history of the Soviet Union in its formative years is E. H. Carr's *History of Soviet Russia* (14 vols, Macmillan, 1950–1978), the slow, but massively detailed progress of which is continued by R. W. Davies in *The Industrialization of Soviet Russia* (2 vols to date, Macmillan, 1980). Further volumes by Davies are intended to carry the story forward to the mid-1930s. There are a number of single-volume introductions to Soviet political history which take in the more recent past. Among the best are *A History of Soviet Russia*, by G. von Rauch (Praeger, 6th edn, 1972), *A History of Soviet Russia*, by A. B. Ulam (Holt Rinehart and Winston, 1976), and *The Soviet Union since 1917*, by M. McCauley (Longman, 1981).

All countries have to live with their past, and this is especially true of the Soviet Union, which bears the scars not only of its dreadful travails in the twentieth century but also of the less efficient tyranny and obscurantism of its rulers before the Revolutions of 1917. There are many specialized studies of the 1920s and 1930s to which reference may be found in the works mentioned above. The continuing psychological and political effects of the 'Great Patriotic War' of 1941–1945 and the agonizingly swift return to internally imposed terror after it are less well covered, though they form part of the background to *Political Culture and Soviet Politics*, by S. White (Macmillan, 1979), which was mentioned in an earlier section. For a fuller understanding of the human significance of these events as they impinge on political behaviour today it is necessary to look to some of the many Russian sources now available in English, such as *Let History Judge*, by R. Medvedev (Spokesman, 1976), and *The Gulag Archipelago*, by A. Solzhenitsyn (3 vols, Collins, 1974–1978). A. Werth's *Russia at War* (Barrie and Rockliff, 1964) is a moving account based on the personal observations of a Russian-born journalist who also draws on the Soviet press and official histories. *Postwar Soviet Politics: the Fall of Zhdanov and the Defeat of Moderation 1946–1953*, by W. G. Hahn (Cornell University Press, 1982), covers the final grim period of Stalin's dictatorship and attempts to identify the ideological factors which became entangled in the power struggle between Stalin's henchmen.

The most exhaustive general study of the Soviet political system as it has evolved since the war is *How the Soviet Union is Governed*, by J. F. Hough and M. Fainsod (Harvard University Press, 1980). *Contemporary Soviet Government*, by L. G. Churchward (Routledge and Kegan Paul, 1968), covers much of the same ground but has an emphasis on Soviet legal and political theory. *Contemporary Soviet Politics: an Introduction*, by D. D. Barry and C. Barner-Barry (Prentice-Hall, 1978), is a useful synthesis of recent (mostly American) research.

There is a considerable specialist literature on the sociological context and social impact of Soviet politics. *Social Change in Soviet Russia*, by A. Inkeles (Harvard University Press, 1968), for example, has interesting chapters on the use of, and response to, political propaganda. *The Socialist Industrial State*, by D. Lane (Allen and Unwin, 1976), is an attempt to fit a theoretical social model to the realities of the USSR (and to a lesser degree of other East European states), which rejects both the 'totalitarian' approach and formal Marxist explanations in favour of a theoretical description of the Soviet social system as 'a state-directed form of socialist modernization'. *Political Participation in the USSR*, by T. H. Friedgut (Princeton University Press, 1979), is an empirical study which examines the involvement of Soviet citizens in local government and provides a detailed account of local elections.

The central Soviet political institution is, of course, the Communist Party, and the fundamental study of it remains *The Communist Party of the Soviet Union*, by L. Schapiro (Eyre and Spottiswoode, 2nd edn, 1970). *The Soviet Communist Party*, by R. J. Hill and P. Frank (Allen and Unwin, 1981), is a modest volume by comparison, but is more attuned to recent political theory than Schapiro. *Communist Party Membership in the USSR 1917–1967*, by T. H. Rigby (Princeton University Press, 1968), is also a basic text. It was written at a time when the rise of a new managerial elite in the USSR seemed likely to transform the role of the Communist Party – an expectation which largely failed to materialize in the Brezhnev era.

Indeed, the surface of Soviet politics changed remarkably little during Brezhnev's term of office as First, and then General Secretary of the CPSU, except that his collaborators of 1964, Kosygin and Podgorny, failed to stay the course. *The Soviet Union since the Fall of Khrushchev*, edited by A. Brown and M. Kaser (Macmillan, 2nd edn, 1978), was originally prepared for the tenth anniversary of Khrushchev's removal from office and was subsequently updated to 1977. The mentality of the Soviet elite of the 'Brezhnev generation' and the prospects for change in the future are discussed in *Stalin's Successors: Leadership, Stability and Change in the Soviet Union*, by S. Bialer (Oxford University Press, 1980), while in *Khrushchev and Brezhnev as Leaders: Building Authority in Soviet Politics* (Allen and Unwin, 1982), G. W. Breslauer examines the exercise of political leadership in the USSR, with heavy emphasis on domestic policy – another example of the new-style 'scientific' kremlinology.

The debates which have been taking place in the half-submerged world of Soviet political science are the subject of *Soviet Politics, Political Science and Reform*, by R. J. Hill (Martin Robertson, 1980). In the long term it may be that these debates and the longer-term changes which are occurring away from the centre will be just as decisive for the future of the Soviet Union as the changes in the top leadership, which are bound to continue in the next few years, but can only be a matter of speculation.

At the time of writing it is too early for considered assessments of Soviet politics in the post-Brezhnev era, but *Yuri Andropov*, edited by R. Maxwell (Pergamon, 1983), provides translations into English of the major speeches and writings of Brezhnev's immediate successor.

Conclusion

Although the USSR and Eastern Europe do present particular problems, they are no longer a 'blind spot' for the political scientist. Furthermore, though original research into the politics of a single country demands knowledge of the local language, there is ample scope now for the student of comparative politics to work from English sources only.

Naturally, there are areas where more work is needed and the limited sources of information have not been fully utilized. Hungary and Romania, for example, have each developed a unique local blend of Soviet Communism; neither is completely stable or successful and both deserve greater attention.

As ever, the past is better covered than the present. Despite the current preoccupation with Poland, for example, it is too soon to write a definitive account of the turmoil which began there in August 1980 or of the confusion of 1981. In particular, we lack reliable information on the part played in these events by pressures from the USSR and East Germany. By contrast, the 'Prague Spring' of 1968 has now retreated sufficiently into the past for a more lasting assessment to be made, and even the role of the Kremlin is no longer a total mystery.

So it will be eventually with the whole region. The lack of reliable current information is not to be seen simply as a source of frustration. It is a challenge, too, and one that begs to be accepted.

20
East Asia

A. D. S. Roberts

Introduction

The nations of East Asia are among the most populous in the world. Population growth has often outstripped the natural resources necessary for life support, and the ingenuity of their rulers has been taxed to find a solution to this problem. It must be said that all of the countries in the area have enjoyed some measure of success in tackling it. Japan, often extolled as a model of economic and technological progress, has throughout its recent history been haunted by the spectre of economic failure, and fears of this have been an ever-present factor determining the political strategy of her rulers. Previous contacts with foreign powers have left their mark on national consciousness, and outside interference has resulted in the implantation of political ideologies not always ideally adapted to the needs of the peoples of East Asia. They have shown their ingenuity in subtly tailoring imported dogmas to suit their psychological make-up and their physical requirements.

In the absence of a unifying factor such as a religion held in common or commitment to any single ideology it is not surprising that few analysts are prepared to attempt comprehensive coverage of East Asian politics. However, an important source of factual information covering the whole area should be noted. This is the annual *Far East and Australasia* (Europa Publications, 1969–). The work is normally divided into two parts. In the first of these, topics relevant to the whole area are summarized. Subjects covered are: development and population problems; recent political developments; industrial and agricultural production; and the religious situation. In part two, attention is devoted to each of the constituent nations in turn. For each, articles are provided which deal with its geography, history and economy. Detailed information is supplied about constitutions, governments, legislatures and other political and economic institutions. A final section provides a 'who's who' of prominent persons, a guide to different calendars and systems of weights and measures. As far as possible, information is kept up to date by regular postal inquiry directed to the institutions under review. For obvious reasons, the information this work provides is more reliable than that contained in the series of *Area Handbooks*, each devoted to a particular country, published by the American University.

A comprehensive history of the Far East in modern times can only serve as an introduction for the general reader and as a basis from which more specialized areas of study can be explored. *The Far East in the Modern World*, edited by F. H. Michael and G. E. Taylor (Dryden Press, 3rd edn, 1975) is such a work, with a coverage extending into the mid-1970s. Perhaps the most recent attempt to provide a digest of political activity in Asia is made in *An Introduction to Asian politics*, by C. E. Kim and L. Ziring (Prentice-Hall, 1977). Under the sections devoted to particular countries, valuable suggestions for further reading are to be found. A similar encapsulation is *The Politics of East Asia*, by J. E. Endicott and W. R. Heaton (Westview Press, 1978) in which the politics of China and Japan are treated in some detail and those of Korea in outline only. A volume under multiple authorship, edited by R. A. Scalapino, is devoted to the subject of Communism in Asia. *The Communist Revolution in Asia: Tactics, Goals and Achievements* (Prentice-Hall, 2nd edn, 1969) has, of relevance to this chapter, sections on the parties of China, Japan, Mongolia and North Korea. A most useful source of general information is *East Asia, Tradition and Transformation*, compiled by J. K. Fairbank *et al.* (Houghton Mifflin, 1973).

Perhaps the most useful and comprehensive bibliographical guide to available monographs and periodical literature both on the area as a whole and for individual countries is provided by the annual *Bibliography of Asian Studies*. Issues for the years prior to 1969 used to appear as the final fascicule in each volume published of the *Journal of Asian Studies*. After the *Bibliography* was separated from the parent journal to appear as a periodical production in its own right, it ceased to appear as promptly as hitherto, and the most recent issue seen covers the year 1978.

Another guide to periodical literature is worthy of mention, namely A. Ferguson's *Far Eastern Politics: China, Japan, Korea, 1950–1975, an Index to International Political Science Abstracts, Volumes 1–25* (International Political Science Association, 1977).

Apart from the *Journal of Asian Studies*, a number of other periodicals give general coverage to politics in East Asia. Occasional articles of relevance appear in the *American Political Science Review, Problems of Communism* and other journals of global interest. More specialized journals include *Pacific Affairs* and *Asian Survey*. The latter carries a particularly useful feature in the first issue for the year, a 'Survey of Asia', in which specialists in current affairs assess the latest situation in individual states.

The likelihood is that researchers will focus their attention on the politics of a particular country, rather than dwell on the situation in Asia as a whole. At this stage, attention must be concentrated on each country in turn, and a start will be made with the giant of them all, The People's Republic of China.

Individual countries

The People's Republic of China

The problems faced by China are no different, except perhaps in scale, from those encountered by other nations. Of particular and absorbing interest, however, is the uniquely Chinese way in which questions of authority, participation, representation, cohesion and bureaucracy are tackled. It will be noted that China's polity departs in significant ways from the norms prescribed by Soviet Communism. The reasons for this can be traced back to China's earlier history and traditions. Many recent monographs derive their inspiration from the theory of 'political culture' as adumbrated by Gabriel Almond and other scholars. This theory develops the concept of national character a stage further, to assert that political values are differently interpreted in accordance with the features of the society in which they operate, and these differences do not arise entirely from the operation of factors such as the level of economic development attained, the type of regime maintained or the social class of those in power. Certain Chinese cultural traits have been isolated: strong feelings of nationalism will be maintained even when powerful regional loyalties are displayed. An outward show of status equality is made, yet hierarchical differences are jealously preserved. The Chinese believe that morally superior persons should be recruited to hold office and that, once in power, leaders should concern themselves with the moral instruction of the people. In general, the Chinese are rather distrustful of charismatic leadership. The welfare of the group should take precedence over that of the individual. Where the reaching of decisions is concerned, the Chinese preference is that this should be arrived at by consensus. Any expression of open opposition is likely to reveal disharmony and, by extension, weakness, in government. Favours received have to be repaid equivalently, thereby removing any sense of obligation. These values are held to just as much in the province under Nationalist rule as in Communist China. It may be observed that some of the generalizations just made about Chinese political culture would be equally applicable to Japanese society, and this is in no small way due to the fact that the two nations share a common Confucianist tradition.

One problem that is encountered in any attempt to assess the resources for the study of Mainland politics is that the influence of the Communist Party pervades every sector of life in China. With 'politics in command' it is difficult to assert that any branch of study, such as economics, sociology, demography or education, does not have bearing on the political situation and can be ruled out for consideration.

To chart a way through the vast corpus of literature on the subject of contemporary China, a knowledge of the bibliographical tools available will be essential. Given the pace at which the study has developed, all the reference works in monograph form are out of date, and there is nothing more satisfactory than the *Bibliography of Asian Studies*, already referred to. *Contemporary China: a Research Guide*, compiled by P. A. M. Berton and E. Wu (Hoover Institution Press, 1967), is still the best bibliography of the modern period. Volume one of *Modern Chinese Society: an Analytical Bibliography*, compiled by G. W. Skinner *et al.* (Stanford University Press, 1973), concerns itself with publications in Western languages, 1644–1972. Its strength lies in its coverage of periodical literature as well as monographs. *China: a Resource and Curriculum Guide*, by A. Posner and A. J. de Keijzer (University of Chicago Press, 2nd rev. edn, 1976) is valuable as a critical bibliography in that it contains pithy comments on most monographs that a political researcher will need to consult. A. J. Nathan's *Modern China, 1840–1972: an Introduction to Sources and Research Aids* (Center for Chinese Studies, University of Michigan, 1973), is less useful at the elementary stage than its title might suggest, since much of the material it includes is actually in Far Eastern languages. Nevertheless, the compiler gives useful advice on methodology. In-depth study of contemporary politics has largely been made possible as the result of research work at university level, mostly carried out, it must be admitted, at institutions of higher learning in the US, though individual scholars and institutions in Western Europe, Australia and Japan have made significant contributions. F. J. Shulman brings thesis literature under bibliographic control in *Doctoral Dissertations on China: a Bibliography of Studies in Western Languages, 1945–70* (with L. H. D. Gordon, Association for Asian Studies, 1972), and its continuation, *Doctoral Dissertations on China, 1971–1975* (University of Washington Press, 1978). Theses presented at North American Universities too recently for inclusion in these works (except for those from Harvard and Chicago Universities) are described in issues of *Dissertation Abstracts* (University Microfilms, 1940–).

The soundest work on Chinese politics is done by those with sufficient linguistic knowledge to work on original sources. A command of the spoken language enables the researcher to conduct interviews with refugees from the Mainland or question important defectors in order to have the benefit of their inside knowledge of the background to important decision making. However, the absence of linguistic knowledge is not a total impediment to work in the field. Political scientists not versed in Chinese are able to base their studies on translated material of different kinds. They have access to monitored radio broadcasts produced in translation in the *Daily Report, Foreign Radio Broadcasts* (Foreign Broadcast Information Service, 1941–) and the *Summary of World Broadcasts* (BBC Monitoring Service, 1941–) published in the US and the UK, respectively. These sources necessarily convey more immediate information than that available in the translation series produced by two US agencies, the American Consulate-General in Hong Kong and the US Joint Publications Research Service. A useful listing of materials of this nature that might be found in a major library was made by J. Lust and F. Wood in their *Catalogue of Publications of Translation and Monitoring Services . . . in the Library of the School of Oriental and African Studies* (SOAS, 1974). The official Chinese version of the news appears in releases from the New China News Agency.

To this day, the People's Republic of China remains a closed society. Since unofficial contacts at personal level between Chinese citizens and outsiders are frowned upon, traditional methods of inquiry, such as the interview or dissemination of questionnaires, are usually barred, and it has only recently become possible to carry out research in the field. Inevitably, there is a place for the 'China-watcher' who is trained to interpret what

Donald Zagoria and others call 'esoteric communications'. This entails an ability to understand the hidden significance of published materials. The scholar may receive the occasional 'windfall' in the shape of important, hitherto unpublished documents which are released with the intention, perhaps, of discomfiting a political adversary or refuting an erroneous line. During the Cultural Revolution, publication of material of this nature served to shed light on events in the recent past of the Communist Party which had defied earlier analysis. The Chinese Communists frequently use the device of cloaking a message they wish to convey by the usc of analogies from the literary past. A classic example of the use of such a technique is provided in the case of the play *Hai Jui Dismissed from Office*, in which Wu Han tells the story of a Ming official who was dismissed for returning (to peasants) lands which had been taken unjustly from them. This was interpreted in radical circles as an attack on Chairman Mao for his dismissal of P'eng Te-huai in 1959. This affair served as a catalyst for the Cultural Revolution. For a description see J. R. Pusey, *Wu Han: Attacking the Present through the Past* (East Asian Research Center, Harvard University, 1969).

Certain features of Communism as practised in Mainland China are unique, none more so than the central role played by Chairman Mao. Few political theorists could, as he did, live to see their philosophy adopted as an integral part of the national constitution. The originality of Mao's 'thought' has been a matter of debate for political commentators. The consensus of opinion seems now to be that much of what he wrote is a synthesis of what was taught by earlier theorists, and that his unique contribution to the history of the Communist movement was to organize a successful revolution based on the rural peasantry. The question of the extent to which Mao can be regarded as an innovator is touched upon in a number of important studies; for example, B. I. Schwartz, *Communism and China, Ideology in Flux* (Harvard University Press, 1968); J. Hsiung, *Ideology and Practice, the Evolution of Chinese Communism* (Praeger, 1970); and C. C. Tan, *Chinese Political Thought in the Twentieth Century* (David and Charles, 1972). Another subject for debate has been the question of whether Mao was in command of the political situation to the extent that China should be regarded as a 'stable dictatorship' or whether a theory of 'constant conflict' should be accepted, whereby Mao was only *primus inter pares*, whose help would be sought and credentials used by factional interests seeking to establish the ascendancy of their cause. The object lesson of the Cultural Revolution lends credibility to the 'constant conflict' approach. Parris Chang, in *Power and*

Policy in China (Pennsylvania State University Press, 2nd edn, 1978), suggests that Mao was not always in full command of events. Experts now tend to the view that Mao's influence on the future course of Chinese politics will be less than fundamental, witness *Mao, the People's Emperor*, by Dick Wilson (Hutchinson, 1979).

The only certain way to understand what Mao taught and to assess his significance is to study what he wrote. Here, difficulty will be experienced, since the definitive edition of his writings has still to appear, and his *Selected Works* (5 vols, Foreign Languages Press, varying dates of publication) do not cover the very modern period and, in any case, are textually unreliable. Fortunately, translations of his more recent pronouncements, not always based on officially authorized texts, are made available in certain biographies or analyses of his political thought. Particularly of note in this connection are various contributions by S. R. Schram: *The Political Thought of Mao Tsê-tung* (Praeger, rev. edn, 1969); and *Mao Tsê-tung Unrehearsed, Talks and Letters, 1956–71* (Penguin, 1974). Mao's writings since 1949 are listed by J. B. Starr and N. A. Dyer in *Post-liberation Works of Mao Zedong, a Bibliography and Index* (Center for Chinese Studies, University of California, 1976).

An unusual feature of Chinese Communism is the adoption of what is termed 'the mass line'. In order to attain a desired political, economic or social objective, the ruling elite will use its cadres to awaken latent political consciousness in the broad masses. The regime will ally itself with acceptable class elements in collective action to change patterns of belief, refute erroneous lines or raise industrial and agricultural production. The history of China since the establishment of the People's Republic of China has been puncutated by a series of over seventy mass campaigns, the outward manifestations of which have been frequently dramatic and occasionally bizarre. Many Chinese date the events of their personal lives in relation to the particular campaign in course at the time. The subject of mass campaigns has been treated in a number of studies. The best introduction to it is provided by J. R. Townsend in *Political Participation in Communist China* (University of California Press, 1969). Gordon Bennett, in *Yundong: Mass Campaigns in Chinese Communist Leadership* (Center for Chinese Studies, University of California, 1976), comes to the conclusion that mass campaigns do present a genuine opportunity for democratic participation in decision making.

A number of guides to the basic principles of Chinese politics spare the researcher the necessity of spending valuable time in amassing information at the elementary level. It is impossible to mention them all, and recommendations must be based on the practical consideration that the more recent publications will be the most reliable, since important changes took place during the Cultural Revolution, not all of which were rescinded in favour of earlier practices. *China: Politics and Government*, by Tony Saich (Macmillan, 1981), takes account of happenings as recent as January 1981. *Contemporary Chinese Politics*, by J. C. F. Wang (Prentice-Hall, 1980), ends its coverage with the arrest of the Gang of Four. The earlier *China: an Introduction* of L. W. Pye (Little, Brown, 2nd edn, 1978) still has its admirers on the grounds of convenient arrangement and comprehensive coverage.

Two works are usually singled out for providing the best coverage of the laws, statutes and rules of hierarchies within the Party, the state, the army, etc. F. Schurmann has been widely commended for his *Ideology and Organization in Communist China* (University of California Press, 2nd edn, enlarged, 1968). However, critics have taken him to task for assuming that the system always works in the way that the Chinese designed it to. *Cadres, Bureaucracy and Political Power in Communist China*, by A. D. Barnett with E. Vogel (Columbia University Press, 1967), analyses Party and governmental organization at ministerial, county and commune/brigade level, on the basis of intensive interviews with cadres who had defected.

The Constitution has gone through a number of revisions, all of which may be compared in translation. The 1945 version is to be found in C. Brandt *et al.*, *A Documentary History of Chinese Communism* (Allen and Unwin, 1952). The constitutions current in 1956 and 1959 appear in *China, a Yearbook*, edited by Yuan-li Wu (David and Charles, 1973).

The Chinese published their English-language version of the 1969 constitution in *Peking Review*, **XII** (9). The very latest recension, that of 4 December 1982, has just been published by the Foreign Languages Press.

A good survey history of the Chinese Communist party will be required by all researchers. J. P. Harrison's *The Long March to Power: a History of the Chinese Communist Party, 1921–1972* (Praeger, 1972) is very strong on the period before the foundation of the People's Republic. For events after that, *The Chinese Communist Party in Power*, translated from the French of J. Guillermaz (Dawson, 1976), is essential reading. There are so many monographs concerning the history of individual campaigns that any selection is bound to be invidious. The Socialist Revolutionary Movement of 1962–1965 was launched with a view to arresting a trend back towards capitalism and decollectivization inspired by the spectacular failure of the Great Leap Forward and reasserting discipline among cadres in the rural areas. To achieve these ends, emulation of the best features of the People's Liberation Army was enjoined on the people and a large-scale transfer of cadres and intellectuals from the cities to the countryside, a programme known as *hsia fang*, took place. This Movement formed the prelude to the more fundamental Great Proletarian Cultural Revolution, and is treated in *Prelude to Revolution, Mao, the Party and the Peasant Question, 1962–66*, by R. Baum (Columbia University Press, 1975). The period leading up to the Cultural Revolution is the subject of an important three-part study by R. MacFarquhar, *The Origins of the Cultural Revolution* (Columbia University Press). Volume one was published in 1974, and volume two was published in April 1983). The Cultural Revolution is remarkable in history as an example of a totalitarian figure mobilizing the masses to undermine the fabric of the Party of which he was leader in order to ensure a state of continuing revolution. Various interpretations of the Revolution are possible, and it has been widely written about. H. Y. Lee's *The Politics of the Chinese Cultural Revolution* (University of California Press, 1978) may be cited as an example of a sound study, particularly as it is based on Red Guard sources, about which Lee has produced a research guide. The aftermath of the Revolution has received attention from a number of scholars. The extraordinary turn of events whereby Mao's chosen successor, Lin Piao, fell from grace and died in mysterious circumstances after allegedly attempting to stage a *coup* has been well described by Jürgen Domes in *China after the Cultural Revolution: Politics between Two Party Congresses* (C. Hurst, 1976). It is premature to expect the appearance of a definitive history of the very recent years in monograph form. Two lengthy articles shed considerable light on the politics of the last decade. Parris Chang's 'Chinese Politics, Deng's Turbulent Quest', *Problems of Communism*, Jan.–Feb. (1981), shows that the trend is towards the abandonment of radicalism in favour of a programme of pragmatic modernization. The goals are not in dispute, but the means to attain them are the occasion for serious differences within the ruling elite. Chang isolates the contending factions in chart form and provides a roll of membership. Similar ground is covered by M. Oksensberg and R. Bush in the September/October 1982 number of the same journal. 'China's Political Evolution, 1972–82' itemizes the events of the decade and picks out the salient features. The authors are also illuminating on the subject of factions in ruling circles, showing the geographical and institutional power bases of the individual leaders. They allude to the very Chinese concept of *kuan-hsi*, which holds factions together, defined by them as 'a sense of loyalty, mutual obligation and shared vulnerability'.

Academic treatises, valuable as they are as analyses of events, often fail to breathe life into the exciting subjects with which they deal. The student in need of inspiration may feel it necessary occasionally to consult works by non-specialists, accounts of perspicacious visitors to China or reports by well-informed journalists. The most influential of the latter type of account is Edgar Snow's *The Other Side of the River* (Random House, 1970), a valuable work after due allowance has been made for Snow's partiality in favour of his subject. The subject may also be brought to life by the consultation of well-written biographies of actors on the political scene. Stuart Schram's *Mao Tse-tung: A Biography* (Pelican, 1967) is a reliable account of the Chairman's life, taking in events during the Cultural Revolution. Hsu Kai-yu's *Chou En-lai: China's Gray Eminence* (Doubleday, 1968) is somewhat speculative in nature. Volume one of a two-part *Selected Works of Zhou Enlai* was published in 1981 by the Foreign Languages Press. No definitive biography of Liu Shao-ch'i has appeared, and it may be that it will never be possible to produce one. Details of his life, insofar as they are known, are given in Lowell Dittmer's *Liu Shao-ch'i and the Chinese Cultural Revolution* (University of California Press, 1974), which is more an analysis of the Two Line doctrinal dispute between Mao and Liu. The collected works of *Liu Shao-ch'i* (2 vols, covering the years 1945–1967, Union Research Institute, 1968/1969) is, in fact, a selection only of his more important utterances. Roxane Witke's *Comrade Chiang Ch'ing* (Weidenfeld and Nicolson, 1977) must surely be the most extraordinary biography of a recent leader, since change of circumstance dictated that the final content of the work would prove to be very different from what had been envisaged, either by the author or by the subject. D. W. Klein and A. B. Clark's excellent *Biographic Dictionary of Chinese Communism, 1921 –1965* (2 vols, Harvard University Press, 1971) is supplemented by W. Bartke's *Who's Who in the People's Republic of China* (Harvester Press, 1981), which contains material on individuals active during and after the Cultural Revolution and, rarely for such a work, contains photographs of the personalities it describes.

A recent reference work deserving of mention is *Modern China, a Chronology from 1842 to the Present*, by C. Mackerras (Thames and Hudson, 1982), which consolidates information from a number of sources, including some in Chinese.

Very up-to-date statistical information about politics, economics and social conditions will be found in *China Facts and Figures*

Annual (Academic International Press, 1978–). *The China Quarterly* (Congress for Cultural Freedom, 1960–) is an outstanding repository of articles on Chinese politics. The regime gives its official version of events in the *Beijing* (formerly, *Peking*) *Review* (1958–) and the Nationalist assessment of the situation is contained in *Issues and Studies* (Institute of International Relations, Taipei, 1964–).

Republic of China (Taiwan)

The political situation on the island remnant of Nationalist rule evokes nothing like the same interest in scholarly circles as that of the Mainland. The bibliography section in *The Taiwan Experience, 1950–1980*, edited by J. C. Hsiung (Praeger, 1981), lists some twenty-five monographs under the heading 'Domestic Politics', and, similarly, forty-seven periodical articles. The bibliography section of this book, under the headings cultural values and cultural continuity; education; economic development; social conditions and social change; law and justice; domestic politics; foreign relations; and security and defense capabilities provides the most up-to-date listing of available literature about contemporary Taiwan. It reprints useful articles and excerpts from major monographs. The extract given from Han Lih-wu's *Taiwan Today* (Institute of International Relations, Taipei, 1974) is instructive on the workings of government at central and local levels. The structure of the Kuomintang is explained in a passage from R. N. Clough's *Island China* (Harvard University Press, 1978). The same passage touches upon what is probably the most controversial issue in Formosan politics, namely, the relationship between the Mainlanders (persons who have settled in Taiwan since 1945) and the original inhabitants of the island. As long ago as February 1947 an uprising was triggered off by resentment on the part of the indigenous inhabitants against the preferment of Mainlanders for senior positions in government, which was brutally suppressed. This incident left a legacy of bitterness, and the situation was soon exacerbated by the arrival of refugees fleeing from the victorious Communists. The original islanders subsequently could expect only limited participation in the machinery of Party and government, since it was essential to stress the validity of the island administration as a government for the whole of China by the inclusion of persons originally coming from all parts of the country. The Formosan Nationalist movement antedates the arrival of Chiang Kai-Shek's army, and independence movements have been active since that time both inside and outside Taiwan. The best monograph on the subject is that of Douglas Mendel, *The Politics of Formosan Nationalism* (University of California Press, 1970). Intellectual circles have also felt dissatisfaction over some of the more repressive aspects of Kuomintang rule. Agitation by them for political reform provides the theme for Mab Huang's *Intellectual Ferment for Political Reforms in Taiwan, 1971–1973* (Center for Chinese Studies, University of Michigan, 1976). The most serious manifestation of public discontent so far has been the rioting in Kaohsiung on 10 December 1979. The trial of those allegedly responsible for the disorders is described in a recent small study by J. Kaplan, *The Court-martial of the Kaohsiung Defendants* (Institute of East Asian Studies, University of California, 1981).

If the Nationalists had been able to rule the whole of China without having to fight aggression from abroad and subversion within the country, they might have been able to achieve an economic success of the order of that achieved in Taiwan. Perhaps the 'model province' that now exists is the real monument to their leader, Chiang Kai-Shek, thought much of the credit for this is due to the brilliant success of the agrarian reform carried out by Ch'en Ch'eng. Biographies of Chiang Kai-Shek are revealing about political life on Taiwan. The concluding chapters of *Chiang Kai-Shek*, by Robert Payne (Weybright and Talley, 1969), are illuminating in this way. Two fuller and more recent biographies *The Man who Lost China*, by B. Crozier (Angus and Robertson, 1977) and *Chiang Kai-Shek, His Life and Times*, translated from the Japanese of K. Furuya (St John's University, 1981), go into considerable detail about the earlier part of his life, but add little to our knowledge of his activities during the closing years.

In recent years, Taiwan has been something of a magnet to social scientists frustrated in their wish to carry out fieldwork on Chinese society on the Mainland. A fruit of one investigation is *Local Politics in a Rural Chinese Cultural Setting: a Field Study of Mazu Township*, by J. B. Jacobs (Contemporary China Centre, Australian National University, 1980), one of the few studies of political life at local level. Jacobs has proceded from this to contribute a number of articles on other aspects of politics in Taiwan.

The most exhaustive single source of facts and figures about Taiwan is the *China Yearbook* (China Publishing Co., 1951– ; earlier issues bore the title *China Handbook*). Histories of the three parties licensed to practice in Taiwan are given and details of their organization and major activities are supplied. A whole section is devoted to the system of government, and biographical information, otherwise hard to find, is provided in another section. The constitution, essentially no different from that of pre-war China, is given in full in the appendix. Another work to be consulted with advantage is *China and the Question of Taiwan: Documents and Analysis*, edited by Hungdah Chiu (Praeger, 1973), which contains a section on political development in Taiwan contributed by Wei Yung. This provides a useful summary of the ideology of the Kuomintang and outlines government structure. It deals with the main political problems besetting the country, essentially, those of political integration and participation. There is no really good survey history of the Kuomintang in recent years such as that provided by Guillermaz on the subject of the Communist Party. For the early years, Ch'ien Tuan-sheng's *The Government and Politics of China, 1912–1949* (Harvard University Press, 1950; reprinted in paperback form, Stanford University Press, 1970) is a reliable record.

Japan

Japan has risen from the state of devastation in which she was left at the end of the Second World War to take a place among the world's leading industrial nations, with a GNP inferior only to that of the US and the USSR. In spite of this, she does not play a role on the world stage commensurate with her achievements in the economic sphere. Perhaps this is because she is prevented by her constitution from building up military forces larger than are absolutely necessary for her essential security, and cannot make her presence felt by virtue of military muscle. The same party has remained in government without interruption since its foundation in 1955, and a fissile opposition appears incapable of supplying an alternative regime to that of the Liberal Democratic Party. It may be that scholars study the politics of her giant neighbour in preference to those of Japan simply because of the relatively static situation in that country. Although studies of Japanese politics are comparatively few in number, much work in thesis form has been produced by researchers in North America, Europe and Australia. Once again, F. J. Shulman provides the necessary guide to this in successive publications: *Japan and Korea, an Annotated Bibliography of Doctoral Dissertations in Western Languages, 1877–1969* (Frank Cass, 1970); *Doctoral Dissertations on Japan and Korea, 1969–1974* (University Microfilms International, 1976); and *Doctoral Dissertations on Japan and on Korea, 1969–1979* (University of Washington Press, 1982).

An essential preliminary to the study of Japan's political system is an understanding of the historical background. This may be achieved by consulting a reliable survey history, probably the most satisfactory being that of J. W. Hall, *Japan, from Prehistory to Modern Times* (Weidenfeld and Nicolson, 1970). Another useful introduction is *Japan: the Story of a Nation*, by E. O. Reischauer (Knopf, rev. edn, 1974). Specifically devoted to the modern period is G. R. Storry, *A History of Modern Japan* (Penguin, 1960).

The political stability enjoyed by Japan in recent years is in no small measure due to the Constitution drawn up during the period of occupation by the Allied Powers. This was prepared in the amazingly short period of six days and presented in cabinet on 13 February 1946. The reasons for the speed with which the document was framed are known – the Supreme Commander was aware that a Far Eastern Commission was due to commence operations later that month and would have powers of decision about any changes in Japan's constitutional position, and SCAP was anxious to forestall it with a *fait accompli*. However, the exact means by which the predominantly American administration of the Occupation persuaded the Japanese cabinet to accept the draft are not fully understood, and political analysts differ over the question of whether the Constitution was entirely imposed on the Japanese or whether it was the outcome of consultation between them and the occupying powers. An impetus behind subsequent moves to make alterations to the Constitution has been a wish on the part of the Japanese to be governed in terms of a document drawn up without foreign intervention. The history of the Constitution is discussed by R. E. Ward in an article in the *American Political Science Review,* L(4) (1956), 'The Origins of the Present Japanese Constitution', and by T. McNelly in another, 'The Japanese Constitution, Child of the Cold War', to be found in the *Political Science Quarterly,* LXXIV (2) (1959). The most famous and controversial clause is article 9, whereby resort to war is renounced as a sovereign right and the threat or use of force as a means of settling international disputes is abjured. Although the article goes on to state that land, sea and air forces will never be maintained, its provisions have been circumvented sufficiently to allow the country to create a substantial 'Self-defence Force'. The clause is popular with the people at large who enjoy their semi-pacifist role. Politicians of the Right use it as a means to avoid inconvenient pressure from the US to shoulder a greater portion of the cost of national defence and those of the Left use its existence as a means to frustrate American defence policies in the

Far East. Studies in the *Constitution of Japan; the First Twenty Years, 1947–1967*, edited by D. F. Henderson (University of Washington Press, 1969), give information on how the constitution has worked in practice. Periodic attempts at revision have been made, but have foundered, because this would require acceptance by a majority of two-thirds in the Diet. The issue was live during the 1960s, and a Cabinet Commission reported on the subject in 1964. This is treated by R. E. Ward in 'The Commission on the Constitution and Prospects for Constitutional Change in Japan', *Journal of Asian Studies*, **XXIV** (3) (1965). During the period of *hakuchū* of the 1970s, when the Liberal Democratic party enjoyed only a small majority over the combined opposition, the issue was dormant, but since the ruling party substantially improved its position in the election of 1980, there has been some renewed pressure for constitutional change.

Other measures brought in during the Occupation were to have long-lasting effects on the political situation. Agrarian reforms served to remove grievances which had contributed in large measure to the instability of pre-war years. As a result of an inequitable distribution of constituencies in favour of the rural areas, these also had the effect of ensuring that the writ of the Liberal Democratic Party would be all-powerful outside the urban concentrations of population, and this has been a crucial factor in perpetuating that party's dominance in government. For a full understanding of the present situation, a knowledge of the history of the years of Occupation is requisite. In the absence of a definitive history, the official version of SCAP, *Political Reorientation of Japan, September 1945–September 1948* (2 vols, reprinted by the Greenwood Press, 1970) is required reading. An assessment from the Japanese point of view is provided by K. Kawai in *Japan's American Interlude* (University of Chicago Press, 1960). H. J. Passin studies the impact that measures brought in at that time were to have on future stability and economic growth in *The Legacy of the Occupation–Japan* (East Asia Institute, Columbia University, 1968).

The Occupation left Japan in the possession of a bicameral Diet not dissimilar to the British model except in one important respect, in which the influence of American constitutional thinking is apparent. A system of special and standing committees was devised, to which bills initiated by members of the Diet are referred. These committees provide the most lively forum for political debate in the parliamentary system, since it is possible for the party in government to lose control of them to the opposition, which then has the opportunity to try delaying tactics and force the government to make bargains and concessions. The parliamentary system is analysed by H. Baerwald in *Japan's Parliament, an Introduction* (Cambridge University Press, 1974).

The system for electing members of the House of Representatives has one very interesting feature. Each constituency elects between three and five members, and individual voters have a single, non-transferable vote. This has a considerable effect upon a candidate's chances of election, since, even after he has been endorsed by a party, he is dependent upon personal popularity and the nature of the backing he receives. If, for example, a party fields two candidates, it is unlikely that the party vote will divide evenly between them. The effect of the system is to encourage factionalism within political parties, since, to have any chance of success, a candidate will require the backing of a *Kóenkai* or personal support group, and to have firmly based local connections. This gives advantage to the sitting member and leads to a low turnover of membership in the Diet. The best description of electoral procedures is provided by G. L. Curtis in *Election Campaigning Japanese Style* (Columbia University Press, 1971). S. C. Flanagan and B. M. Richardson, *Japanese Electoral Behavior, Social Cleavages, Social Networks and Partisanship* (Sage, 1977) is also required reading.

Japan's constitutional arrangements have failed to bring about the alternation of rule by class-based political groupings. The country has been ruled without interruption by conservative circles in alliance with big business since 1955. The major opposition parties have too little in common with one another to establish a concerted programme for action in government and the left-wing parties are plagued by internal divisions. There is at the moment no credible alternative to rule by the Liberal Democrats and the principal political excitement is that generated by the interaction of differing factions within the party in government. The subject of factionalism is studied in articles by G. O. Totten and T. Kawakami, 'The Functions of Factionalism in Japanese Politics', *Pacific Affairs*, **XXXVIII** (2) (1965) and by M. Leiserson, 'Factions and Coalitions in One Party Japan', *American Political Science Review*, **LXII** (3) (1968). The best available studies of the Liberal Democratic Party are: H. Fukui, *Party in Power, The Japanese Liberal-Democrats and Policy Making* (Australian National University Press, 1970) and N. B. Thayer, *How the Conservatives Rule Japan* (Princeton University Press, 1969).

In terms of voting strength, the largest of the opposition parties is the Japanese Socialist Party. It has been riven by disputes between Left and Right over questions such as whether the class base might be enlarged to include lower middle-class elements, small businessmen and the poorer farmers. Early differences of opinion over the San Francisco Peace Treaty led to a formal breach between the contending wings which was subsequently healed in 1955. Its strength was once more affected in 1960, when a number of Right-wingers defected to form the Democratic Socialist Party. Its dependence on the trade union organization Sohyo has not always worked to the best advance of the JSP. The Japanese Communist Party was plagued by internal divisions during the 1950s, occasioned principally by doctrinal disputes between Moscow and Peking. Its fortunes revived in the 1960s thanks to the organizational ability of Miyamoto Kenji. Since Miyamoto became ill and was discredited, a new period of decline has set in. The standard work on the Japanese Socialist Party remains *Socialist Parties in Postwar Japan*, by A. B. Cole *et al.* (Yale University Press, 1966). For a study of the Communist movement, two works can be recommended: R. A. Scalapino, *The Japanese Communist Movement, 1920–1966* (University of California Press, 1967) and P. F. Langer, *Communism in Japan* (Hoover Institution Press, 1972).

One other political party enjoys large-scale electoral support. This is the Kōmeitō, which gathered strength in the 1960s. Its ideology is somewhat nebulous, and the Party's main concern is with cleansing the political system by attacking corruption, factionalism and tendencies towards domination by bureaucratic elements. Although it is now officially separated from its parent organization the Sōka Gakkai, a study group propagating the doctrines of Nichiren Buddhism, it remains the political arm of that grouping. The party and its source of inspiration are studied in J. W. White, *The Sōkagakkai and Mass Society* (Stanford University Press, 1970).

The most lucid and complete guide to the history of recent politics in Japan and the current situation is Arthur Stockwin's *Japan, Divided Politics in a Growth Economy* (Weidenfeld and Nicolson, 2nd edn, 1982). Frank Langdon's *Politics in Japan* (Little, Brown, 1967) is a comparative study of the 'political culture' school, which provides useful insights into the manner in which political demands are articulated by different kinds and sizes of association. The dynamics of Japanese politics are further probed in R. E. Ward's *Japan's Political System* (Prentice-Hall, 1967).

A useful series of corporate studies is deserving of mention. Published by Princeton University Press and mostly based on conference proceedings, these focus on Japan as an example of a successfully modernizing society. Particularly relevant to the study of politics are: *Political Development in Modern Japan*, edited by R. E. Ward (1968), and *Political Opposition and Local Politics in Japan*, edited by K. Steiner *et al.* (1980).

A selection in translation from the scholarly writings of eight Japanese political scientists is provided in *Japanese Politics, an Inside View*, edited by H. Itoh (Cornell University Press, 1973). The principal interest of the contributors lies in decision and policy making at national and sub-national levels and in patterns of voting behaviour.

Although there is a profusion of excellent reference works in Japanese covering the modern period, there is a singular paucity of aids in English. Bernard Silberman's *Japan and Korea, a Critical Bibliography* (University of Arizona Press, 1962) is the kind of tool which might be updated with great advantage to scholarship. An English-language biographical dictionary of the contemporary period is a reference work which is seriously required. The *Japan Biographical Encyclopedia and Who's Who* (The Rengo Press, 3rd edn, 1964) covers the whole period of Japanese history. A useful guide to scholarly work in progress is the *Newsletter of Research on Japanese Politics* (Brigham Young University).

Korea

Since the division of the peninsula at the end of the Second World War, North and South Korea have been contenders in a struggle to establish the legitimacy of their regime as an administration for the whole Korean people. They have developed independently of one another and formal contacts are reduced to ineffectual discussions about eventual reunification. The political problems of the rival regimes are quite different – those of South Korea are better known and understood, as, for all its shortcomings as a democracy, it preserves the more open society. *A Handbook of Korea* (Korean Overseas Information Service, 1978) contains a section on government and administration giving all the information that could conceivably be required in respect of the constitution, the organs of state, the bureaucracy and the political parties of South Korea. The Constitution, which, at the time of writing had already been written six times, is not actually reproduced in this volume. The constitution of the Fifth Republic, the eighth since 1948, promulgated on 27 October 1980, appears in full in the *Korea Annual 1982* (Yonhap News Agency). This may usefully be compared with só-called 'Yushin' constitution accepted after a referendum in 1972, an English version of which is given in *Korean*

Politics in Transition, edited by E. R. Wright (Royal Asiatic Society, Korea Branch, 1975). This work, with contributions by a number of different specialists, serves as a comprehensive introduction to recent and contemporary politics. The number of alterations that have been made to the constitution over the years is an indication of the instability that has plagued the Republic since its birth. Most of them had the object of ensuring the re-election of the President or removing the limits on the number of terms in office he might serve. The *Korea Annual* has a number of useful features: a chronology of events from 1901 to 1980, supplemented by a more detailed chronology of the actual year it covers; directories for the government and the diplomatic service; and an alphabetic 'Who's who'. The persistent failure of democracy to take root in South Korea has led to a series of *coups* initiated in military circles. Gregory Henderson's *Korea, the Politics of the Vortex* (Harvard University Press, 1965) traces the development of political life from its beginning until 1965. It is particularly strong in its account of the early post-war years, 1948–1961. The history of the Democratic Party government of Chang Myŏn, in office from August 1960 until it was overthrown in a *coup* led by Park Chung Hee, is the principal theme of *The Failure of Democracy in South Korea*, by Han Sungjoo (University of California Press, 1974). Political instability in the early 1960s, marked by the inability of the political parties to resolve national issues through normal democratic processes, is treated in *The Korea–Japan Treaty Crisis and the Instability of the Korean Political System*, by Kwan Bong Kim (Praeger, 1971). This work has useful sections on the formation of the Democratic Republican Party as a vehicle for the political aims of the junta and the attempt, in the establishment of the Mass Party, to unify opposition to the ROK–Japan treaty.

In *Political Participation in Korea: Democracy, Mobilization and Stability* (Clio Books, 1980) the editor, C. L. Kim, identifies three forms of citizen participation in political life: democratic participation; mobilized participation; and anomic participation. Democratic participation is the process by which educated and mature persons register a personal political preference. This process is unlikely to be followed by disadvantaged sections of society, such as women, the elderly and those living in rural areas, which will respond to direction by ruling circles. By anomic participation Kim means attempts by frustrated persons or groups to enforce attention to their political aspirations by the use of violence or unlawful action. The studies in this book make difficult reading, but the work is the first and only one to tackle the question of political participation in South Korea.

The subject of Communism in Korea has been subjected to thorough scrutiny in two important monographs, the earlier of these being Dae-sook Suh's *The Korean Communist Movement, 1918–1948* (Princeton University Press, 1967). Three years later, Suh contributed a volume of source material in translation, *Documents of Korean Communism, 1918–1948* (Princeton University Press, 1970). The history of the Korean Workers' Party is carried a stage further by R. Scalapino and Lee in a massive two-volume study entitled *Communism in Korea* (University of California Press, 1972). C. S. Lee Chong-sik has subsequently produced another volume of history, containing the information conveyed in the earlier work in condensed form, and adding some further material. His *Korean Workers' Party, a Short History* (Hoover Institution Press, 1978) may be recommended as a quick introduction to the subject.

The writings and speeches of politicians in both North and South have been translated and widely circulated without regard to cost. The *Selected Works* of Kim Il-Sung (Vols 1–7, Foreign Languages Publishing House, 1967–1978) have been followed by his *Works* (Foreign Languages Publishing House, 1980–). A hagiography by Baik Bong appeared in Japan, *Kim Il-Sung Biography* (General Federation of Koreans Resident in Japan, 1969–1970). Various works by Park Chung-hee have also been made available, notably *Our Nation's Path: the Country, the Revolution and I*; and *Major Speeches* (Hollym Corporation, 1970). A volume of speeches by President Chun Doo Hwan, *The 1980s, Meeting a New Challenge* (Korea Textbook Co., Ltd) appeared in 1981.

Area Handbooks exist for both North and South Korea, and were both published in 1969. The bibliographies these contain are very useful, since there are otherwise few bibliographical aids to the study of modern Korea. *Sources in Modern East Asian History and Politics*, edited by T. McNelly (Appleton, 1967), has references to works on Korean politics and government. The very recent *Studies on Korea, a Scholar's Guide* (University of Hawai Press, 1980), by Kim Han-Kyo, contains a list of research materials on North Korea and gives information about materials too late for inclusion in the best previous source, the bibliography in R. Scalapino and C. S. Lee (1972, work cited). This work provides all the information that any researcher will need about sources in European languages on the politics of the Korean peninsula.

Mongolia

Fundamental to an understanding of the politics of modern Mongolia is a knowledge of the historical background. This may be gained from consultation of C. R. Bawden's *The Modern History of Mongolia* (Weidenfeld and Nicolson, 1968). A view of Mongolian society from within is provided in *Mongolia's Culture and Society*, by Sechin Jagchid and P. Hyer (Westview Press, 1979), which acts to correct the misconception that Mongolian identity is being systematically destroyed by urbanization and influences from abroad. The official version of recent history is provided in *The History of the Mongolian People's Republic*, translated and annotated by W. A. Brown and Urgunge Onon (East Asian Research Center, Harvard University, 1976). R. Rupen has written on the politics of Mongolia in a number of works. The most recent of these, *How Mongolia is Really Ruled: a Political History of the Mongolian People's Republic, 1900–1978* (Hoover Institution Press, 1979), draws on Soviet sources to paint a picture of the political, social, economic and military situation during the period it covers.

21
South Asia

Qazi Mahmudul Haq

Introduction

For the purposes of this chapter, modern politics in the South Asian context has been taken to cover events since independence from the British was achieved in the 1940s. The geographical area encompassed is enormous, well over one and a half million square miles, and the population it contains amounting to over one-fifth of the world's total. It includes the Indian subcontinent, comprising India, Pakistan and Bangladesh, and the neighbouring regions of Nepal, Bhutan, Sikkim, Sri Lanka and Burma. Works dealing with South Asia as a whole and those related to various disputes resulting from the subcontinent's partition have been listed in the opening section. All but one of the subsequent sections are devoted to individual countries, the exception being that Nepal, Bhutan and Sikkim have been grouped together as the Himalayan region.

There are a number of general introductions to the politics of modern South Asia, both in the form of monographs and collections of articles. One of the finest works on the subject which, as its title indicates, also provides useful historical and cultural background is Stanley Wolpert's *Roots of Confrontation in South Asia: Afghanistan, Pakistan, India and the Superpowers* (Oxford University Press, 1982). Other studies in the field include *South Asia in the World Today*, edited by Phillips Talbot (University of Chicago Press, 1950); *Politics in Southern Asia*, edited by Saul

Rose (St Martin's Press, New York, 1963); and *Political Change in South Asia*, by Myron Weiner (Firma K. L. Mukhopadhyay, Calcutta, 1963).

Most of the recent South Asian studies seem to concentrate on individual themes. Typical of such publications are *The Security of Southern Asia*, by Donald Edward Kennedy (Praeger, 1965); *Imperialism and Revolution in South Asia*, edited by Kathleen Gough and Hari P. Sharma (Monthly Review Press, 1973); *The States of South Asia: Problems of National Integration*, edited by A. Jeyaratnam Wilson and Dennis Dalton (C. Hurst, 1982); *Radical Politics in South Asia*, edited by Paul R. Brass and Marcus F. Franda (The MIT Press, 1973); *Elections and Political Development: the South Asian Experience*, by Norman D. Palmer (Vikas, New Delhi, 1976); *Aspects of Political Mobilization in South Asia*, edited by Robert J. Crane (Syracuse University, 1976); *Rule, Protest, Identity: Aspects of Modern South Asia*, edited by Peter Robb and David Taylor (Curzon Press, 1978); *South Asian Religion and Politics*, edited by Donald Eugene Smith (Princeton University Press, 1969); *Religion and Social Conflict in South Asia*, by Bardwell L. Smith (Brill, Leiden, 1976); *Population, Politics, and the Future of Southern Asia*, edited by W. Howard Wriggins and James F. Guyot (Columbia University Press, 1973); and *Southern Asia: the Politics of Poverty and Peace*, edited by D. C. Hallmann (D. C. Heath, Lexington, Mass., 1976).

Several works are devoted to Indo–Pakistani disputes arising out of the subcontinent's partition, i.e. the future of Jammu and Kashmir, division of the Rann of Kutch and the sharing of river water. Some of the important publications in this category are Michael Brecher's *The Struggle for Kashmir* (Oxford University Press, 1952); Josef Korbel's *Danger in Kashmir* (Princeton University Press, 1954); Russell Brines' *The Indo–Pakistani conflict* (Pall Mall Press, 1968); Surya P. Sharma's *India's Boundary and Territorial Disputes* (Vikas, Delhi, 1971); and Lars Blinkenberg's *India–Pakistan: the History of Unresolved Conflicts* (Munksgaard International, Copenhagen, 1972).

The persistence of inter-state and political instability in (some parts of) South Asia, and the region's strategic importance has attracted increasing superpower interest and involvement. The subject is adequately examined in *India, Pakistan, and the Great Powers*, by William J. Barnds (Praeger, 1972); *Soviet–South Asian Relations, 1947–1978*, by Rajendra Kumar Jain (Humanities Press, Atlantic Highlands, 1979); *Soviet Russia and the Hindustan Subcontinent*, by Vijay Sen Budhraj (Somaiya Publications, Bombay, 1973); *The Soviet Union and the Indo–Pakistan Sub-*

continent, by Hasan Askari Rizvi (Progressive Publishers, Lahore, 1974); *South Asia and the United States Policy*, by Norman D. Palmer (Houghton Mifflin, 1966); *The Indian Ocean: its Political, Economic and Military Importance*, edited by Alvin J. Cottrell and R. M. Burrell (Praeger, 1972); *Politics of the Indian Ocean Region*, by Ferenc A. Vali (The Free Press, New York, 1976); *The Subcontinent in World Politics: India, its Neighbors, and the Great Powers*, edited by Lawrence Ziring (Praeger, 1978); and the relevant works listed in the section on Bangladesh.

Individual countries
India

India won her independence from the British Empire on 15 August 1947. Thanks to Prime Minister Nehru's seventeen years as the head of government, the country enjoyed much more political and administrative stability than did neighbouring Pakistan. The other important achievements of the Nehru era were the speedy integration of 550 princely states and the formulation of the nation's Constitution. However, the central objectives of Nehru's domestic policy were to improve India's economic and social conditions, and he achieved a measure of success in both. The country made significant progress in the industrial sector, although its performance in agricultural production was less than expected. The government's achievements in the field of social progress were equally uneven. Relative success in the reduction of illiteracy, as well as the improvement of the peasant farmers' position and the granting of equal legal status to women, were unmatched by any practical achievement in rooting out untouchability, and the harijans continued to be treated much as before. The salient feature of Nehru's foreign policy was the principle of non-alignment, which he refused to discard even after the Sino–Indian war of 1962.

On Nehru's death in 1964, Lal Bahadur Shastri became the prime minister. The most significant development of his term of office was the virtually indecisive India–Pakistan war over the disputed territory of Jammu and Kashmir. Shastri died early in 1966, and was succeeded by Mrs Indira Gandhi. The new prime minister's successful assertion of authority led to a split in the Congress in 1969, but left her in complete control of the ruling majority faction. Mrs Gandhi departed from her late father's tradition in two important ways. In the foreign policy sphere, she practically abandoned the path of non-alignment in 1971, and signed a treaty of friendship and cooperation with the Soviet

Union. The treaty was intended to deter China from intervening on Pakistan's behalf during India's confrontation with the latter over Bangladesh. In domestic policy, she was prepared to tackle the opposition far more firmly than her father ever did, as was shown by her imposition of the Emergency during 1975–1977. This, together with the alleged excesses of her son Sanjay, enabled the united opposition to defeat her in the 1977 elections. However, the chaotic performance and discord within the new Janata government, led by the veteran Morarji Desai, enabled her to regain power in 1980.

The volume of general introductions to politics and government in India is mounting by the year, with impressive contributions by British and American scholars. W. H. Morris-Jones' *The Government and Politics of India* (Hutchinson, 3rd edn, 1971) and *Politics mainly Indian* (Orient Longman, Bombay, 1978) are two of the best books on the subject, which is equally admirably covered by Michael Brecher's *Nehru's Mantle: the Politics of Succession in India* (Praeger, 1966); D. C. Gupta's *Indian Government and Politics* (Vikas, Delhi, 1976); Robert L. Hardgrave's *India: Government and Politics in a Developing Nation* (Harcourt Brace Jovanovich, New York, 3rd edn, 1980); and Ved Mehta's *A Family Affair: India under Three Prime Ministers* (Oxford University Press, New York, c. 1982).

Several writers have adopted a period or thematic approach, thereby analysing the subject in greater detail. Typical works in this category include *A Decade of Indian Politics, 1966–77*, by Asoka Mehta (S. Chand, New Delhi, 1979); *Indira Gandhi's India: a Political System reappraised*, edited by Henry Hart (Westview Press, 1976); and *Indira Gandhi Returns*, by Kushwant Singh (Vision Books, New Delhi, 1979).

A balanced selection of works on the Indian Constitution should include Granville Austin's *The Indian Constitution: Cornerstone of a Nation* (The Clarendon Press, 1966); D. N. Bannerjee's *Some Aspects of the Indian Constitution* (World Press, Calcutta, 1962); *The Constitution and the Parliament in India: the 25 years of the Republic*, edited by S. L. Shakdher (National Publishing House, Delhi, 1976); K. C. Markandan's *The Amending Process and Constitutional Amendments in the Indian Constitution* (International Publishing Service, New York, 1972); Somnath Roy's *Indian Politics and Constitutional Development* (Meenakshi Prakashan, New Delhi, 1976); and Kuldip Nayar's *The Judgement: Inside Story of the Emergency in India* (Vikas, New Delhi, 1977).

Constitutional position and practice in regard to a number of federal institutions and functionaries is discussed in *Parliament in*

India, by W. H. Morris-Jones (Longman, 1979); *Presidential Government or Parliamentary Democracy*, by Anirudh Prasad (Deep and Deep, New Delhi, 1981); *The Indian Prime Minister: Office and Powers*, by L. N. Sharma (Macmillan, Delhi, 1976); *Cabinet Government in India*, by R. J. Venkateswaran (Allen and Unwin, 1967); *The Indian Speaker: Crisis of Identity*, by J. N. Singh Yadav (Academic Press, Gurgaon, 1982); and *The Indian Supreme Court and Politics*, by Upendra Baxi (Eastern Books, Lucknow, 1980).

Political system and process at various levels has attracted the attention of various scholars. Some of the more important writings on this theme include *India's Political System*, edited by Richard L. Park and Bruce Bueno de Mesquita (Prentice-Hall, 1979); *Democracy and the Representative System in India*, by Rajni Kothari (Citizens for Democracy, New Delhi, *c.* 1976); *India at the Polls: the Parliamentary Elections of 1977*, by Myron Weiner (American Enterprise Institute for Public Policy Research, *c.* 1978), *Citizens and Politics: Mass Political Behavior in India*, edited by Samuel J. Elderveld and Bashiruddin Ahmad (University of Chicago Press, 1978); *Political Participation in a Developing Nation: India*, by Madan Lal Goel (Asia Publishing House, New York, 1975); *Citizens and Parties: Aspects of Competitive Politics in India*, by D. L. Sheth (Allied Publishers, Bombay, *c.* 1975); *Coalition Governments in India: Problems and Prospects*, edited by K. P. Karunnakaran (Indian Institute of Advanced Study, Simla, 1975); *The Process of Opposition in India*, by R. W. Stern (University of Chicago Press, 1970); *Preventive Detention in India: a Case Study in Democratic Social Control*, by David H. Bayley (Firma K. L. Mukhopadhyay, Calcutta, 1962); *Constitutional Crisis in the States in India*, by Meera Srivastava (Concept, New Delhi, *c.* 1980); *Opposition in a Dominant Party System: a Study of the Jan Sangh, Praja Socialist, and Socialist Parties in Uttar Pradesh, India*, by Angela S. Burger (University of California Press, 1969); *Coalitional Politics in Orissa*, by Sukadev Nanda (Sterling, New Delhi, 1979); *The Expansive Elite: District Politics and State Policy-making in India*, by Donald B. Rosenthal (University of California Press, *c.* 1977); and *Elections and Political Consciousness in India: a Case Study*, edited by S. P. Varma and C. P. Bhambhri (Meenakshi Prakashan, Meerut, 1967).

Some of the more important writings on union–state relationship and state government include *Federalism in India: a Study of Union–State Relations*, by Asok Chanda (Allen and Unwin, 1965); *State Politics in India*, edited by Myron Weiner (Princeton University Press, 1968); *Union–State Relations in India*, by Santhanam Kasturiranga Iyengar (Asia Publishing House, New York,

1961); and *State Government and Politics, Andhra Pradesh*, edited by G. Ram Reddy and B. A. V. Sharma (Sterling, New Delhi, 1979).

Some of the typical works on the administrative system and bureaucracy include Prem Lata Bansal's *Administrative Development in India* (Sterling, New Delhi, 1974); R. S. Varma's *Bureaucracy in India* (Progress Publishers, Bhopal, 1973); and C. P. Bhambhri's *Bureaucracy and Politics in India* (Vikas, Delhi, 1971).

Since independence, hundreds of political parties of all persuasions – socialist and reactionary, communal and secular – have emerged in India. However, a vast majority of these are local groupings with insignificant following. Congress remains the dominant party at the centre, and in most of the states, although it lacks much of the popular appeal it once enjoyed. Some of the more important individual or collective studies devoted to political parties include *Congress in Free India: the Nehru phase*, by K. C. Chaudhry (Neelaj Publications, New Delhi, 1980); *The Congress Crucible: Role of Indian National Congress in Indian Politics, 1966–1980*, by Satish Kumar Rastogi (Anu Publications, Meerut, 1980); *The Janata Party: a Profile*, by C. P. Bhambhri (National, New Delhi, 1980); *Bharatiya Jana Sangh: Organization and Ideology* (Sterling, New Delhi, 1980); *Jan Sangh and Swatantra: a Profile of the Rightist Parties in India*, by Motilal Janghiani (P. C. Manaktala, Bombay, 1967); *The Major Socialist Parties in India: a Study in Leftist Fragmentation*, by Lewis P. Pickett, Jr (Syracuse University, 1976); *Moscow and the Communist Party of India*, by John H. Kautsky (Wiley, 1956); and *The Naxalite movement*, by Biplab Dasgupta (Allied Publishers, New Delhi, 1974).

Understanding of political ideas and actions of some of India's influential statesmen and politicians may be usefully attempted through their biographies or memoirs, including, for instance, Michael Brecher's *Nehru: a Political Biography* (Oxford University Press, 1959); R. H. Copley's *The Political Career of C. Rajagopalachari, 1937–1954: a Moralist in Politics* (Macmillan, Delhi, 1978); Jayaprakash Narayan's *Towards Total Revolution*, edited by Brahmanand (Popular Prakashan, Bombay, 1978); Hallam Tennyson's *India's Walking Saint: the Story of Vinoba Bhave* (Doubleday, 1955); Chalpathi Rau's *Govind Ballabh Pant, his Life and Times* (Allied, New Delhi, 1981); B. K. Swamy's *Kamraj, the Man of the Masses* (Muthukumaran Publishers, Madras, 1967); Promilla Kalhan's *Jagjivan Ram and Power Politics* (Allora, New Delhi, *c.* 1980), T. V. Kunhi Krishnan's *Chavan and the Troubled Decade* (Somaiya Publications, Bombay, 1971); Morarji Desai's

The Story of My Life (Macmillan, Delhi, 1977); and Mary C. Carras' *Indira Gandhi in the Crucible of Leadership: a Political Biography* (Beacon Press, 1979).

Typical of the works on political economy are Francine R. Frankel's *India's Political Economy, 1947–1977: the Gradual Revolution* (Princeton University Press, 1978) and Pramit Chaudhuri's *The Indian Economy: Poverty and Development* (St Martin's Press, 1979). Some of the more important publications on associational pressure groups include S. A. Kochanek's *Business and Politics in India* (University of California Press, 1974); H. Crouch's *Trade Unions and Politics in India* (Manaktala, Bombay, 1966); Richard D. Lambert's *Workers, Factories, and Social Change in India* (Princeton University Press, 1963); and Myron Weiner's *The Politics of Scarcity, Public Pressure and Political Response in India* (University of Chicago Press, 1962).

There is a large number of publications on aspects of the Indian society. The more important of these include *Socialism and Nationalism in India*, by Sankar Ghose (Allied Publishers, Bombay, 1971); *The Language Controversy and Minorities*, by Gopi Nath Shrivastava (Atma Ram, Delhi, 1970); *Federalism and Linguistic States*, by Naresh Chandra Roy (Firma K. L. Mukhopadhyay, Calcutta, 1962); *Ethnic Plurality in India*, by R. A. Schermerhorn (University of Arizona Press, 1978); *Caste in Indian Politics*, edited by Rajni Kothari (Orient Longmans, New Delhi, 1970); *The Politics of Untouchability: Social Mobility and Social Change in a City of India* (Cambridge University Press, 1969); *Islam in India's Tradition to Modernity*, by M. A. Karandikar (Orient Longmans, Bombay, 1968); *India's Search for National Identity*, by Ainslie T. Embree (Knopf, 1972); *Regionalism versus Provincialism: a Study in the Problems of Indian National Unity*, by Joan V. Bondurant (University of California Press, 1958); and *The Ordeal of Nationhood: a Social History of India since Independence, 1947–1970*, by Krishan Bhatia (Atheneum, 1971).

Pakistan

Pakistan came into being on 14 August 1947, overburdened with serious handicaps. Physically it was divided into two wings, separated from each other by a thousand miles of 'hostile' foreign territory. It lacked the machinery of a central government in terms of personnel and equipment, and possessed neither a treasury nor resources. The bureaucracy and army had to be hurriedly assembled, and governmental institutions created from scratch. Above all, the new state had immediately to cater for millions of destitute refugees, contend with widespread sectarian riots and fight an undeclared war with India over Jammu and Kashmir. Had it not been for Jinnah's reassuring presence and his capacity to inspire confidence and motivate sacrifice, Pakistan might well have collapsed within a few months of independence.

Jinnah died in September 1948, leaving the struggle for survival and consolidation in the hands of his trusted confidant, the Prime Minister Liaquat Ali Khan. However, following the latter's assassination in October 1951, the country relapsed into a long era of political instability. The Muslim League's decline and the mushrooming of political parties and factions, few of them issue-oriented and most only regionally based, and the relative scarcity of popular statesmen dedicated to institution building and democracy thwarted the evolution of a national consensus and identity, as well as an orderly political system and lasting constitution. The failure of the political process accounted for one military *coup* after another, and the establishment of military-led regimes in which such other elites and power groups as the bureaucracy, big businessmen and industrialists, as well as the landed aristocracy, were coopted as partners. The system denied the country's eastern wing its due share of executive power and decision-making processes, giving an added fillip to the separatist tendency and transforming it into open revolt. India's victory in the ensuing war, and the consequential emergence of independent Bangladesh, led to the fall of the military regime in Islamabad. It was replaced by Pakistan's first democratically elected government headed by Zulfikar Ali Bhutto, under whom renewed struggle for survival was successfully accomplished, a new constitution agreed upon and several urgently needed reform programmes carried out. Unfortunately, however, he shared his predecessors' preference for personalized leadership, and, like most of them, did nothing to democratize his party's structure and organization. Thus when the opposition mounted a united campaign of relentless agitation to drive him from office, the Pakistan People's Party was in no position to confront them on the streets. The ensuing lawlessness forced the army to assume power yet again, thereby putting an end to Pakistan's short experience with democracy.

There is no dearth of general introductions to the politics of Pakistan, although most of the studies by Pakistani authors tend to be descriptive and superficial. *Pakistan*, by Ian Stephens (Benn, 1963), may be a good beginning for the interested reader. Other works in this category include *Pakistan: a Political Study*, by Keith Callard (Allen and Unwin, 1957); *Political Development in Pakistan*, by Karl von Vorys (Princeton University Press, 1965); *Gov-

ernment and Politics in Pakistan, by Mushtaq Ahmad (Space Publishers, Karachi, 3rd edn, 1970); *The New Pakistan*, by Satish Kumar (Vikas, New Delhi, 1978); *Pakistan: the Enigma of Political Development*, by Lawrence Ziring (Westview, 1980); and *Politics in Pakistan: the Nature and Direction of Change*, by Khalid B. Sayeed (Praeger, 1980).

Most of the above works also provide a useful insight into Pakistan's initial struggle for survival and consolidation. Additional material on the subject will be found in *Pakistan: the Formative Phase*, by Khalid Bin Sayeed (Pakistan Publishing House, Karachi, 1960), and *Pakistan: the Consolidation of a Nation*, by Wayne A. Wilcox (Columbia University Press, 1963).

Many writers have addressed themselves to Pakistan's quest for a lasting constitution, but the number of scholarly works on the subject is surprisingly small. These include *A Constitution for Pakistan*, by Herbert Feldman (Oxford University Press, Karachi, 1956); *Constitutional Problems in Pakistan*, by Sir Ivor Jennings (Cambridge University Press, 1957); *Constitutional Development in Pakistan*, by G. W. Choudhury (Longman, Lahore, 1959); *Legislatures in Pakistan, 1947–58*, by Muneer Ahmad (University of the Punjab, Lahore, 1960); *Pakistan: the Development of its Laws and Constitution*, by Alan Gledhill (Stevens, 2nd edn, 1967), *The Politics of Pakistan: a Constitutional Quest*, by Richard S. Wheeler (Cornell University Press, 1970); and *The Three Constitutions of Pakistan*, by Y. V. Gankovsky and V. N. Moskalenko (People's Publishing House, Lahore, 1978).

One dominant leader and a personal approach to government has been the political norm in Pakistan ever since its creation. This was presumably understandable in the case of Mahomed Ali Jinnah, and perhaps even Liaquat Ali Khan, but others from Ghulam Mohammed through to Iskandar Mirza, Ayub Khan, Yahya Khan, Zulfikar Ali and Bhutto favoured personalized government purely out of self-interest, each relying on political manoeuvre rather than democratic institutions to exercise the function of their office. Relevant works on this theme include *Jinnah: Creator of Pakistan*, by Hector Bolitho (John Murray, 1954); *Qaid-e-Azam Jinnah as I Knew Him*, by M. A. H. Ispahani (Forward Publications, Karachi, 1966); *Liaquat Ali Khan: Leader and Statesman*, edited by Ziauddin Ahmad (The Oriental Academy, Karachi, 1970); *Friends not Masters: a Political Autobiography*, by Mohammed Ayub Khan (Oxford University Press, 1967); *Bhutto: a Political Biography*, by Salmaan Taseer (Ithaca Press, London, 1979); and *State and Society in Pakistan, 1971–77*, by Shahid Javed Burki (Macmillan, 1980). The last-named is an excellent study of Bhutto's rise to virtually absolute power, his major policies and shortcomings, and ultimate downfall.

However, the failure of political parties to resist personalized government by enlisting broad support among the masses and to create a stable governmental system has yet to be fully analysed. Existing works in this category include *Political Parties in Pakistan, 1947–1958*, by M. Rafique Afzal (National Commission on Historical and Cultural Research, Islamabad, 1976); *Party Politics in Pakistan, 1947–1958*, by K. K. Aziz (National Commission on Historical and Cultural Research, Islamabad, 1976); *The Jama'at-i-Islami of Pakistan: Political Thought and Political Action*, by Kalim Bahadur (Chetana Publications, New Delhi, 1977); and *Pakistan People's Party: First Phase 1967–71*, by Hasan Askari Rizvi (Progressive Publishers, Lahore, 1973).

The phenomenon of military rule has come to be firmly associated with Pakistan. Hasan Askari Rizvi's *The Military and Politics in Pakistan* (Progressive Publishers, Lahore, 2nd edn, 1976) is probably the best study on this subject, which has also aroused considerable interest among American writers. The result is a number of fascinating, mostly regime-oriented studies, including Lawrence Ziring's *The Ayub Khan Era: Politics in Pakistan, 1958–1969* (Syracuse University Press, 1971); Herbert Feldman's *Revolution in Pakistan: a Study in the Martial Law Administration* (Oxford University Press, 1967); *From Crisis to Crisis: Pakistan in 1962–69* (Oxford University Press, 1970); and *The End and the Beginning: Pakistan 1969–1971* (Oxford University Press, 1975). Useful works on the subject by Pakistani authors include Mohammad Asghar Khan's *Generals in Politics: Pakistan 1938–1982* (Vikas, New Delhi, 1983), G. W. Choudhury's *The Last Days of United Pakistan* (Indiana University Press, 1974) and, of course Mohammed Ayub Khan's *Friends not Masters: a Political Autobiography* (work cited).

Virtually every military regime has run the country in partnership with the bureaucracy and such other powerful elites as the industrialists, big businessmen and the landed aristocracy. Studies devoted to these groups include *The Civil Servant in Pakistan*, by Muneer Ahmad (Oxford University Press, 1964); *Research on the Bureaucracy of Pakistan*, by Ralph Braibanti (Duke University Press, 1966); *Bureaucracy and Political Development in Pakistan*, by Mumtaz Ahmad (National Institute of Public Administration, Karachi, 1974); *Power and Privilege: Influence and Decision-making in Pakistan*, by Robert LaPorte (California University Press, 1975); *Elite Politics in an Ideological State: the Case of Pakistan*, by Asaf Hussain (Dawson, 1979); *Politics without Social*

Change, by Mushtaq Ahmad (Space Publishers, Karachi, 1970); *Industrial Concentration and Economic Power in Pakistan,* by Lawrence J. White (Princeton University Press, 1974); and *The Functions of International Conflict: a Socio-economic Study of Pakistan* (Royal Book Co., Karachi, 1975).

Islam is not only the religion of a vast majority of Pakistan's citizens, it was also the sole factor responsible for its very creation. Not surprisingly, politics in Pakistan has always had to adjust itself to placate religious opinion. Some of the studies devoted to this subject are *Religion and Politics in Pakistan,* by Leonard Binder (University of California Press, 1961), *Islam in the Modern National State,* by Erwin I. J. Rosenthal (Cambridge University Press, 1965) and *From Jinnah to Zia,* by Muhammad Munir (Vanguard Books, Lahore, 1979). The apparent failure of religion to forge a common identity and nationhood in Pakistan has manifested itself not only in the separation of Bangladesh (discussed in the following section), but also in serious tribal unrest in the province of Baluchistan, which is the subject of Selig S. Harrison's *In Afghanistan's Shadow: Baluch Nationalism and Soviet Temptations* (Carnegie Endowment, 1981).

Bangladesh

The most formidable problem confronting Pakistan at the time of its birth was that of national integration, especially in regard to its eastern wing. This was because the Bengalis were not merely the largest, and strikingly distinct, ethno-cultural subgroup in the country but actually constituted a majority (55 per cent) of Pakistan's total population. However, at the time of independence, they had little representation in the top echelons of the military and the civil service hierarchy, and the entrepreneurial class. As a result, the urban Panjabis and Pathans, and the migrants from northern and western India, became the national power elite of Pakistan from the outset. Whatever leverage the Bengalis were able to exercise at the centre, whether in the decision-making and the legislative process or in the formation of governments, was eliminated by the repeated introduction of martial law and the consequential dissolution of national assemblies and the suspension of political process. The denial of participation in decision making, and the continuous neglect of East Pakistan's economic development, led to the growing alienation of the Bengalis. Their frustration articulated itself in the emergence of Sheikh Mujibur Rahman's Awami League, which demanded the grant of virtually absolute autonomy as the only effective means of achieving East Pakistan's legitimate aspirations and rights. Rather than accede to these demands and settle for a loose federation, the military regime in Islamabad sought to crush the movement. In the ensuing civil war India intervened on the Bengalis' behalf. The hostilities came to an end on 16 December 1971, when Pakistani troops surrendered to India and Bangladesh achieved her independence.

The phenomenon of Pakistan's failure in integration, its ultimate dismemberment and the emergence of independent Bangladesh has attracted the attention of political analysts in every continent. Some of the most authoritative general works on the subject include Talukder Maniruzzaman's *The Bangladesh Revolution and its Aftermath* (Bangladesh Books International, Dacca, 1980); Moudud Ahmad's *Bangladesh: Constitutional Quest for Autonomy, 1950–1971* (Steiner, 1978); Kalim Siddiqui's *Conflict, Crisis and War in Pakistan* (Macmillan, 1972); and Rounaq Jahan's *Pakistan: Failure in National Integration* (Columbia University Press, 1972). Useful additional information will also be found in Kazi Ahmad Kamal's *Sheikh Mujibur Rahman and Birth of Bangladesh* (Kazi Giasuddin Ahmad, Dacca, 1972) and Anwar Iqbal Qureshi's *Mr. Mujib's Six Points: an Economic Appraisal* (Haniya Publishing House, Lahore, 1970). President Yahya Khan's efforts to bridge the gap between the Awami League and the West Pakistani leaders, especially Bhutto, and senior generals, is the subject of G. W. Choudhury's *The Last Days of United Pakistan* (work cited).

India's support for the Bengalis' cause and the role of other countries in the conflict is examined in J. A. Naik's *India, Russia, China and Bangladesh* (S. Chand, New Delhi, 1972); Krishna P. Menon's *The Indo–Soviet Treaty: Setting and Meaning* (International Publishing Service, New York, 1972); J. P. Jain's *China, Pakistan and Bangladesh* (Radiant, New Delhi, 1974); W. Norman Brown's *The United States and India, Pakistan, Bangladesh* (Harvard University Press, 3rd edn, 1972); and G. W. Choudhury's *India, Pakistan, Bangladesh, and the Major Powers* (Collier –Macmillan, 1975). Several works are largely devoted to the war itself, namely David Loshak's *Pakistan Crisis* (Heinemann, 1971) and Robert Jackson's *South Asian Crisis: India–Pakistan–Bangladesh* (Chatto and Windus, 1975).

There are a number of general introductions to the politics of Bangladesh. Talukder Maniruzzaman's *The Bangladesh Revolution and its Aftermath* (work cited) is probably the most authoritative account of political events up to and including the regime of the late President Ziaur Rahman. Other useful studies in this category include Rounaq Jahan's *Bangladesh Politics: Problems and Issues* (Dacca University Press, 1980) and Marcus Franda's *Bangladesh, the First Decade* (Universities Field Staff International, Hanover, 1981), which is a collection of essays covering the period 1971–1981. M. Rahman's *Bangladesh Today: an Indictment and a Lament* (News and Media, 1978) is, as its name indicates, a criticism of the post-independence situation in the country.

The first three works are also the most appropriate for any reader interested in Bangladesh's political and constitutional development under Sheikh Mujibur Rahman, the nation's founder. Other books on similar themes include *Politics and Bureaucracy in New Nation, Bangladesh*, edited by Mohammad Mohabbat Khan and Habib Mohammad Zafarullah (Centre for Administrative Studies, Dacca, 1980); *Bangladesh, Public Administration and Society*, by M. Anisuzzaman (Bangladesh Books International, Dacca, 1979); and *Minority Politics in Bangladesh*, by Muhammad Ghulam Kabir (Vikas, New Delhi, 1980).

Sheikh Mujibur Rahman's intolerance of political opposition and his failure to act decisively against the widespread excesses and corruption of his own partymen led to his assassination at the hands of a number of young, disgruntled army officers. This heralded an era of army *coup* and counter-*coup* in Bangladesh, and on more than one occasion civil war appeared to be virtually imminent. The situation was brought under effective control under General Ziaur Rahman, whose regime, while it lasted, gave the country much-needed political stability and economic reform. On 30 May 1981, Zia was assassinated in Chittagong by Major General Manzur Ahmed, who was killed two days later. Vice-President Abdus Sattar became acting president, but was overthrown by the Army Chief of Staff Lieutenant General H. M. Ershad. Publications covering this subject include Marcus Franda's *Bangladesh Nationalism and Ziaur Rahman's Presidency* (American Universities Field Staff, Hanover, c. 1981–) and *The Death of Ziaur Rahman* (Universities Field Staff International, Hanover, 1982) and S. S. Bindra's *Indo–Bangladesh Relations* (Deep and Deep, New Delhi, 1982).

The Himalayan region: Nepal, Bhutan, Sikkim

Until the beginning of this century relatively little was known or written about the politics of the Himalayan region. However, more recently a number of geopolitical factors, especially the Chinese annexation of Tibet, the Sino–Indian war of 1962 and the Russian involvement in neighbouring Afghanistan has changed the situation, and the region has finally received the attention of several specialist historians and political scientists. A useful general introduction to the area will be found in *The Himalayan Kingdoms: Bhutan, Sikkim and Nepal*, by Pradyumna Karen and William M. Jenkins Jr (Kentucky University Press, 1967). Foreign interest in the region as a whole is the subject of Dorothy Woodman's *Himalayan Frontiers: a Political Review of British, Chinese, Indian and Russian Rivalries* (Praeger, 1970).

On account of Nepal's strategic location between the two antagonistic Asian giants, China and India, several writings on the kingdom's politics and foreign relations reflect the mutually hostile Sino–Indian interests and policies. Typical of such works are Girilal Jain's *India Meets China in Nepal* (Asia Publishing House, New York, 1959), and *Documents on Nepal's Relations with India and China, 1949–1966*, edited by Avtar Singh Bhasin (Academic Books, Bombay, 1970). Indo–Nepalese dimensions of the problem are discussed in Agarwal Shriman Narayan's *India and Nepal: an Exercise in Open Diplomacy* (Popular Prakashan, 1970) and Pashupati S. Rana's *Trade and Transit: Nepal's Problems with her Southern Neighbour* (Centre for Economic Development and Administration, Kathmandu, 1970). Valuable information on the subject will also be found in Leo E. Rose's *Nepal: Strategy for Survival* (University of California Press, 1971) and E. B. Mihaly's *Foreign Aid and Politics in Nepal: a Case Study* (Oxford University Press, New York, 1965).

The internal politics of Nepal have been admirably analysed in a number of general studies, including Leo E. Rose's *Nepal: Government and Politics* (University of California, 1971); R. S. Chauhan's *Political Change in Nepal, 1950–70* (Associated Publishing House, New Delhi, 1971); Leo E. Rose and Margaret W. Fisher's *The Politics of Nepal: Resistance and Change in an Asian Monarchy* (Cornell University Press, 1970); Rishikesh Shaha's *Nepali Politics: Retrospect and Prospect* (Oxford University Press, New York, 1978); and Lok Raj Barel's *Oppositional Politics in Nepal* (South Asia Books, Columbia, Mo., 1978).

Useful books related to Bhutan and Sikkim include Leo E. Rose's *The Politics of Bhutan* (Cornell University Press, 1977); Ram Rahul's *Modern Bhutan* (Vikas, Delhi, 1973); Nagendra Singh's *Bhutan: a Kingdom in the Himalayas; a Study of the Land, its People and their Government* ((Thomson Press, New Delhi, 1972); Nari Rustomji's *Bhutan: the Dragon Kingdom in Crisis* (Oxford University Press, Delhi, 1978); Kapileshwar Labh's *India and Bhutan* (Sindhu Publications, New Delhi, 1974); and Vincent Herbert Coelho's *Sikkim and Bhutan* (Vikas, Delhi, 1971).

Sri Lanka (formerly Ceylon)

After independence from British rule in 1948 Sri Lanka's political system closely followed the Westminster model. Despite the occasional political upheavals and ethnic unrest, mostly involving the Tamil minority (viz. the violent events of 1983), the country claims to be one of Asia's few successful democracries, on the basis of having undergone six successive elections in which incumbent governments have handed over power to victorious opposition parties. There are a number of admirable general introductions to the politics of Sri Lanka. These include *Sri Lanka: from Dominion to Republic*, by Lucy M. Jacob (National Publishing House, New Delhi, 1973); *Sri Lanka: a Survey*, a collection of essays edited by K. M. de Silva (Hurst, 1977); *The Politics of Ceylon (Sri Lanka)*, by R. N. Kearney (Cornell University Press, 1974); *Sri Lanka: Third World Democracy*, by James Jupp (Frank Cass, 1978); and finally, the very authoritative *Politics in Sri Lanka, 1947–1979*, by A. Jeyaratnam Wilson (Macmillan, 2nd edn, 1979).

The nation's constitutional development is discussed in *The Gaullist System in Asia: the Constitution of Sri Lanka*, by A. Jeyaratnam Wilson (Macmillan, 1980). Typical of works devoted to Sri Lanka's political system, leadership and elites are *Universal Franchise, 1931–1981: the Sri Lankan Experience*, edited by K. M. de Silva (Department of Information, Ministry of State, Colombo, 1981); *The Growth of Party System in Ceylon*, by C. A. Woodward (Brown University Press, 1969); and *The Emerging Elite: a Study of Political Leadership in Ceylon*, by Marshal R. Singer (MIT Press, 1964).

The role of caste, religion and ethnology in Sri Lankan politics and society has been explored in *Caste and Family in the Politics of the Sinhalese, 1947–1976*, by Janice Jiggins (Cambridge University Press, 1979); *Religion and Politics in Sri Lanka*, by Urmilla Phadnis (Hurst, 1976); *Communalism and Language in the Politics of Ceylon*, by Robert N. Kearney (Duke University Press, 1967); and *Modern Sri Lanka: a Society in Transition*, edited by Tissa Fernando and Robert N. Kearney (Syracuse University, 1979).

Subjects like political economy and foreign policy are adequately covered in Satchi Ponnambalam's *Dependent Capitalism in Crisis: the Sri Lankan Economy, 1948–1980* (Zed Press, 1980); Peter Richards and Wilbert Goonerratne's *Basic Needs, Poverty and Government Policies in Sri Lanka* (International Labour Office, Geneva, 1980); Robert N. Kearney's *Trade Unions and Politics in Ceylon* (University of California Press, 1971); and Sheton U. Kodikara's *Foreign Policy of Sri Lanka: a Third World Perspective* (Chanakya Publications, Delhi, 1982).

Burma

The inclusion of Burma in a bibliographical survey of politics in South Asia might at first seem strange, since nowadays the country is generally regarded as a part of South-east Asia. Yet Burma, by virtue of her geopolitical location and historical past, has had close cultural, religious and political ties with the Indian subcontinent. The other factor that merits Burma being grouped with South Asia here is her colonial experience since the country was administered as a part of British India until 1937 and subsequently as a separate colony until granted independence in January 1948.

One of the most important general introductions to Burmese politics is Josef Silverstein's *Burma: Military Rule and the Politics of Stagnation* (Cornell University Press, 1977). Three of its chapters are devoted to 'Constitutional Government, 1948–1962', 'Military Rule in Burma: First Phase, 1962–1974' and 'Constitutional Dictatorship: The Second Phase of Military Rule'. Other useful accounts of the history and politics of Burma include Frank N. Trager's *Burma from Kingdom to Republic* (Praeger, 1966) and Hugh Tinker's *The Union of Burma* (Oxford University Press, 4th edn, 1967). *Southeast Asia: the Politics of National Integration*, edited by John T. McAlister, Jr (Random House, New York, 1973), contains a number of essays related to contemporary Burma. The country's ethnic problems are admirably analysed in *Burmese Politics: the Dilemma of National Unity*, by Josef Silverstein (Rutgers University Press, 1980).

22
Sub-Saharan Africa

Chris Allen

This chapter is of necessity much shorter than the writer would have liked and concentrates largely on the literature in English. As a result, something of an injustice is done not only to the vast French literature, so often neglected by anglophone scholars, but also to the growing body of material in other European languages and in Arabic. Preference has also been given to books, and to those texts which themselves provide a good guide to the relevant literature. Articles, theses and the more obscure and fugitive pieces have thus been relatively neglected, though they have often been no less influential or seminal than books. The resulting citations will be found under four major headings: an introductory survey of the development of the study of African politics; materials on the general development of African states and political systems; materials on major aspects of contemporary systems; and further reading.

The study of African politics

Scholarly concern with African politics first occurred on a large scale in the 1950s, as a result of the growth of African nationalism and impending independence, though it relied heavily on a few pioneering works, such as Thomas Hodgkin's *Nationalism in Colonial Africa* (Muller, 1956), Jean Suret-Canale's *Afrique Noire* (3 vols, Editions Sociales, 1958–1976) – the second volume of which is available in English as *French Colonialism in Tropical Africa* (Hurst, 1971) – and George Balandier's *The Sociology of Black Africa* (André Deutsch, 1970). Until then, the literature had concerned itself mainly with descriptive and apologetic accounts of colonial administration and policy, and with the applied political anthropology of what were seen as discrete 'tribes', as with M. Fortes and E. E. Evans-Pritchard, *African Political Systems* (Oxford University Press, 1940); Lord Hailey's massive *An African Survey* (Oxford University Press, 1938; rev. edn, 1957); and R. Delavignette, *Freedom and Authority in French Africa* (Oxford University Press, 1957; rev. edn, Cass, 1968). This latter 'administrative' literature remains valuable now for an understanding of the 'official mind' of colonial government and for the study of colonial administration, while its preoccupations and preconceptions can be found emerging again in the recent historial literature on decolonization.

The new Africanists of the 1950s and early 1960s were far more concerned with and sympathetic to nationalism than to colonial rule. Their work tended to focus on the process of transfer of power, with British and French scholars adopting a somewhat institutional and constitutional orientation, while American scholars, present in force for the first time, tended to look for general typologies and explanatory theories. These they derived from theories of modernization, such as those deployed in J. S. Coleman and C. G. Rosberg's collection, *Political Parties and National Integration in Tropical Africa* (University of California Press, 1964) and theories of political development, as in Aristide Zolberg's influential *Creating Political Order* (Rand-NcNally, 1967). The contrast between the two groups shows up very clearly in the differing concerns and conclusions of two studies by David Apter, his early *The Gold Coast in Transition* (Princeton University Press, 1955) and his *The Political Kingdom in Uganda* (Princeton University Press, 1961), when set beside their British counterparts, Denis Austin's *Politics in Ghana 1946–60* (Oxford University Press, 1964) and David Low's *Political Parties in Uganda 1949–62* (The Athlone Press, 1962).

The early attempts at generalization and theorization proved ineffective, as modernization approaches in particular concealed both cultural and political presuppositions, and the conclusions drawn from them proved unreliable. With the exception of Hodgkin (work cited) and – in sharply contrasting style if not sympathies – Franz Fanon's *The Wretched of the Earth* (McGibbon and Kee, 1965), there are no major general studies of African politics from this period that remain of value. The real strength of the period lay in the single-country case study, normally of a limited time span. Though these studies now seem to have concentrated too much on political parties, and to have seen nationalism as an inevitable and a homogeneous phenomenon, they remain essential reading, especially such classics as the two works already cited by David Apter, J. S. Coleman's *Nigeria: Background to Nationalism* (University of California Press, 1958); Austin (work cited); Ruth Schachter-Morgenthau's *Political Parties in French-Speaking West Africa* (The Clarendon Press, 1964); Crawford Young's *Politics in the Congo* (Princeton University Press, 1965), Aristide Zolberg's *One Party Government in the Ivory Coast* (Princeton University Press, 1964) and R. I. Rotberg's *The Rise of Nationalism in Central Africa* (Harvard University Press, 1966). Two fat compendia convey the flavour of this period, its strengths, and the contrasting approaches of British and American scholars: *Political Parties and National Integration in Tropical Africa* (University of California Press, 1964), edited by J. S. Coleman and C. G. Rosberg, and R. I. Rotberg and Ali Mazrui's *Protest and Power in Black Africa* (Oxford University Press, 1970).

The growth of single-party regimes and increasing military intervention during the 1960s forced reconsideration of the nature of African regimes and political systems, and a questioning of the scholarly characterization of nationalism and independence. Some of this stemmed from the already cited work of Fanon, with its notions of 'true' and 'false' decolonization and its scathing indictment of African nationalism and its leaders. More important was the impact of Marxism, hitherto largely confined to French anthropology. From this and other sources, notably Third World economic nationalism, arose a 'political economy' approach marked by a concern with the economic and social bases of political activity and systems, with conflict as opposed to order, and with the role of external political and economic influences conceived of as pathogenic rather than as benign. The effect of this approach can be seen in most of the important contributions of the 1970s; characteristic instances are Colin Leys' *Underdevelopment in Kenya* (Heinemann, 1975); Bjorn Beckman's *Organising the Farmers: Cocoa Politics and National Development in Ghana* (Scandinavian Institute of African Studies, 1976); Richard Joseph's *Radical Nationalism in Cameroun* (The Clarendon Press, 1977); John Dunn's collection *West African States* (Cambridge University Press, 1978); and J. F. Bayart's *L'état au Cameroun* (Fondation Nationale de Science Politique, 1979). Much of the resulting material, especially that influenced by dependency theory, was stimulating and influential, such as the materials brought together in Giovanni Arrighi and John Saul's *Essays on the Political Economy of Africa* (Monthly Review, 1973); Peter Gutkind and Peter Waterman's *African Social Studies: a Radical Reader* (Heinemann, 1977); and Peter Gutkind and Immanuel Wallerstein's *The Political Economy of Contemporary Africa* (Sage, 1976), the latter two of which contain useful bibliographical essays by Chris Allen. At the same time, the material was crudely formulated, determinist and weak in its treatment of such concepts as class and the state, as can be seen in Issa Shivji's influential *Class Struggles in Tanzania* (Heinemann, 1976); for further discussion see the commentary in Chris Allen and Gavin William's reader *Subsaharan Africa* (Macmillan, 1982).

This has encouraged radical Africanists to devote more attention to the nature of class formation and action (as in the work of Bjorn Beckman and Joel Samoff, only some of which can be mentioned in this chapter); to the nature of the state and its functions and to the relationship between classes and the state, on which there are good Zairean case studies by D. J. Gould, *Bureaucratic Corruption in the Third World* (Pergamon, 1980), and by M. G. Schatzberg, *Politics and Class in Zaire: Bureaucracy, Business and Beer in Lisala* (Africana, 1980); and to policy choice and implementation, as in *Rural Development in Tropical Africa*, edited by Judith Heyer *et al.* (Macmillan, 1982). The means chosen to examine such questions has been the monographic case study, a small selection of which is cited below. Their impact has led to sustained questioning of the political economy approach and to a partial retreat by Marxists from attempts at analytical generalization on African politics. Instead, this function has again been taken on by American scholars, both those sympathetic to but critical of political economy approaches – like Crawford Young – and those inspired by a careful appraisal of the weaknesses and strengths of older, modernisation approaches. Their work also reflects strongly – perhaps too strongly – an increasing intellectual impact of the developmental, institutional and other failures of modern African states. Of special importance is the work of Crawford Young, notably his *The Politics of Cultural Pluralism* (Wisconsin, 1976) and *Ideology and Development in Africa* (Yale University Press, 1982). There are also useful general texts by R. H. Jackson and C. G. Rosberg, *Personal Rule in Black Africa* (University of California Press, 1982), and by A. D. Smith, *State and Nation in the Third World* (Harvester Press, 1982), and a forthcoming volume on African politics by Bill Tordoff, to be published by Macmillan.

In contrast to the 1960s, institutional and official support for the study of African politics in the US and the UK is dangerously weak. Intellectually, however, the study is far stronger. The field is no longer the preserve of scholars from the old colonial metropoles and the US. Instead, African scholars now make major contributions, despite the pressures under which they work, discussed among other matters in Y. Barongo's collection *Political Science in Africa* (Zed Press, 1983). So also do Scandinavian, South African, and Canadian scholars. Marxist and non-Marxist scholars are less doctrinaire and more inclined to learn from each other instead of scoring debating points or simply ignoring rival approaches. There exists now a considerable body of detailed empirical studies covering a much wider range of subjects and parts of Africa than even ten years ago, providing a much sounder base both for analytical accounts of particular political systems and phenomena and for more general studies of both regional and continental scope.

Historical development of contemporary states and systems

Colonial rule

The best introduction to the nature and impact of the colonial period is provided by Basil Davidson, especially in *Africa in Modern History* (Allen Lane, 1978) and in the latest of his many books, *Modern Africa* (Longman, 1983). General histories of the colonial period are common; the best to consult are volumes 6 to 8 of the new *History of Africa*, edited by John Fage and Raymond Oliver (Cambridge University Press, 1978–1983), and – though the editorial touch is somewhat perverse – L. H. Gann and P. Duignan's *Colonialism in Africa* (5 vols, Cambridge University Press, 1969–1973). The differing colonial practices of France and Britain are covered in P. Gifford and W. R. Louis, *France and Britain in Africa* (Yale University Press, 1971), of Belgium in Young (1965, already cited) and that of Portugal by Gerry Bender in *Angola under the Portuguese* (Heinemann, 1978) and Leroy Vail and Landeg White's *Capitalism and Colonialism in Mozambique* (Heinemann, 1981). Less well covered is the political impact of colonial development policy, though John Iliffe's massive study *A Modern History of Tanganyika* (Cambridge University Press, 1979) is good on this as on everything else, and it is worth consulting J. M. Lee's *Colonial Development and Good Govern-*

ment (Oxford University Press, 1967), and Mike Cowen's chapter in M. Fransman (ed.), *Industry and Accumulation in Africa* (Heinemann, 1982).

Decolonization

Decolonization has recently been much studied, as the archives are opened; R. D. Pearce, *The Turning Point in Africa* (Cass, 1982) is typical of the virtues and quirks of this literature. Volume 8 of the Cambridge *History of Africa* (work cited) and R. Gifford and W. R. Louis's *The Transfer of Power in Africa* (Yale University Press, 1982) provide excellent surveys of and bibliographic guides to new work. Fanon (work cited) remains the most seminal piece on nationalism (except perhaps Hodgkin, work cited), while Joseph (work cited) is the most detailed and thoughtful of the individual studies of the postwar radical–nationalist movements. The classics of the early 1960s, mentioned above, are all relevant here of course, especially on party building, as is Iliffe (work cited), while Xavier Yacono provides a still helpful and brief survey of decolonization in francophone Africa, in *Les étapes de la decolonisation* (Que sais-je?, 1971). Two specialized studies are worth mention here also, for their quality: K. W. J. Post and G. D. Jenkins, *The Price of Liberty: Personality and Politics in Colonial Nigeria* (Cambridge University Press, 1973) is one of the few good African political biographies, while the best on colonial labour policy is A. Clayton and D. Savage, *Government and Labour in Kenya 1895–1961* (Cass, 1974).

Clientelism and *coups*

The development of parties and of political support around independence in the 1956–1964 period was marked particularly by the politicization of ethnicity, as described in C. Young (1976, work cited), Nelson Kasfir's *The Vanishing Political Arena* (University of California Press, 1976) and John Saul's *State and Revolution in Eastern Africa* (Monthly Review, 1979). It was also marked by the elaboration of clientelist relations between leaders and followers, at local and national levels. The tension between clientelist demands by followers on the elite, and the latter's desire to monopolize resources and thus strengthen themselves as individuals and as classes, led to the breakdown of political order and to military intervention. The best accounts of clientelism remain case studies, such as Donal O'Brien, *Saints and Politicians* (Cambridge University Press, 1975) and C. S. Whitaker, *The Politics of*

Tradition (Princeton University Press, 1970), while the forthcoming study of Zambia for Zed Press by Morris Szeftel and Carolyn Baylies will be particularly useful on the degeneration of clientelism into a politics of spoils. Also helpful are M. A. Ekpo's collection *Bureaucratic Corruption in Subsaharan Africa* (University Press of America, 1979), several of the country studies in John Dunn (work cited) and the articles by Medard and Clapham in *Private Patronage and Public Power* (Frances Pinter, 1982), edited by C. Clapham.

Still the most vivid account of *coups* and their origins is that by the late Ruth First, in *The Barrel of a Gun* (Allen Lane, 1970), which is best read in combination with J. M. Lee's *African Armies and Civil Order* (Chatto and Windus, 1969), Robin Luckham's excellent case study *The Nigerian Military* (Cambridge University Press, 1971) and T. S. Cox, *Civil–Military Relations in Sierra Leone* (Harvard University Press, 1976). The rest of the literature on *coups* and military regimes is well surveyed in Roger Charlton's article, 'A Review of Two Decades of Theoretical Analyses of African *coups d'état*', *Cultures et Développement*, **13** (1/2), 27–62 (1981). Such regimes may differ very little from their predecessors, as can be seen from the discussion in S. Decalo, *Coups and Army Rule in Africa* (Yale University Press, 1976) and W. E. Gutteridge, *Military Regimes in Africa* (Methuen, 1975), and there is a general trend towards the militarization of political life in Africa, succinctly analysed by Robin Luckham in 'Armament, Underdevelopment and Demilitarisation in Africa', *Alternatives*, **6** (2), 179–245 (1980). Those regimes that do differ markedly are best seen as military versions of bureaucratic–authoritarian states (as with Zaire or Benin), though whether Ethiopia is likewise best lumped in with other 'socialist' states is more open to doubt; the question is discussed in Yanni Markakis and Nega Ayele, *Class and Revolution in Ethiopia* (Spokesman, 1978) and in Fred Halliday and Maxine Molyneux, *The Ethiopian Revolution* (New Left Books, 1981). Other valuable case-studies on military regimes include K. Panter-Brick (ed.), *Soldiers and Oil* (Cass, 1978) on Nigeria, Dennis Austin and Robin Luckham (eds), *Soldiers and Politicians in Ghana 1966–72* (Cass, 1975), and Naomi Chazan's *An Anatomy of Ghanaian Politics 1969–82* (Westview, 1983).

Bureaucratic–authoritarian states

An alternative response to the contradictions of clientelist politics, with its intensification of conflict over resources and spoils, and its tendency towards repression and violence, has been to attempt to

contain and control both resource competition and political participation through the partial displacement of the party and other
representative institutions by bureaucratic institutions, and the
creation of a powerful executive presidency, among other measures. This process is well described, though less well interpreted
in Kasfir (work cited) and in B. Selassie's *The Executive in African
Government* (Heinemann, 1974), and is best studied through the
individual cases mentioned below. The degree and role of political
participation in such systems is analysed in G. Hermet *et al.*
(eds), *Elections without Choice* (Macmillan, 1978), and the role and style
of leadership in Jackson and Rosberg (work cited). It is also worth
consulting Ruth Collier's examination of the role of elections since
1945, in *Regimes in Tropical Africa* (University of California
Press, 1982), and Naomi Chazan's more limited study, 'The New
Politics of Participation in Tropical Africa', *Comparative Politics,*
14 (2), 169–189 (1982). Among individual country studies, the
most enlightening are: J. F. Bayart (work cited) on Cameroun;
E. J. Schumacher *Politics, Bureaucracy and Rural Development in
Senegal* (University of California Press, 1975); Y. A. Faure and
J. F. Medard *Etat et bourgeoisie en Côte d'Ivoire* (Karthala, 1982);
and Bill Tordoff's two collections, *Politics in Zambia* and *Administration in Zambia* (both Manchester University Press, 1974 and
1980). As can be seen from the case of Zaire, well described in G.
Gran (ed.), *Zaire* (Praeger, 1979), such systematic changes only
increase the chance of stability; they do not protect it from the
ravages of class conflict, external intervention, greed, and incom-
petence at the top.

Liberation through armed struggle

In contrast to the politics of peaceful decolonization and to the
political systems arising from it, are the politics and systems that
result from armed liberation struggle (well and sympathetically
described in Basil Davidson, *The People's Cause*, Longman,
1981), though it is easy to make too sharp a distinction, as do both
Fanon (work cited) and John Saul in Chapter 8 of Arrighi and Saul
(work cited). Mass participation, including that of women, is an
essential element of guerrilla political practice, described in studies of Guinea-Bissau by Lars Rudebeck, *Guinea-Bissau: a Study
in Political Mobilisation* (Scandinavian Institute of African Studies, 1974) and Patrick Chabal, *Amilcar Cabral* (Cambridge
University Press, 1983), and of Mozambique by Barry Munslow,
Mozambique (Longman, 1983), and Barbara and Alan Isaacman,
Mozambique (Gower, 1983). Since the wars the ruling parties

have been faced with problems of external intervention, economic failure, the setting of developmental priorities and the growth of class divisions and class ambitions among the bureaucracy and political leadership. These problems, analysed generally in Young (1982, work cited) and in D. and M. Ottaway, *Afrocommunism* (Schenkman, 1981), have led to increasingly centralized and authoritarian government in Angola (sympathetically described in Michael Wolfers and Jane Bergerol, *Angola in the Frontline*, Zed Press, 1983) and to a *coup* in Guinea-Bissau, analysed by Lars Rudebeck in his pamphlet *Problème de pouvoir populaire et développement: transition difficile en Guine-Bissau* (Scandinavian Institute of African Studies, 1982). This brings into question the extent to which these regimes will differ in future from other African regimes, and the feasibility of socialist strategies in Africa (see further below).

Aspects of contemporary political systems

This section covers only some of the possible topics; the criteria for omission have been the lesser significance of certain phenomena such as interest articulation or local government within African political systems, coverage elsewhere, or the relative weakness of the literature.

Political sociology

This field has expanded remarkably over the last decade as the range of material presented or cited in Allen and Williams (work cited) shows. The use of class categories and even of class analysis has become common, displacing earlier elite/mass characterizations; compare, for example, Peter Lloyd's *Power and Independence* (Routledge and Kegan Paul, 1974) with another study of the same area in Nigeria by Adrian Peace, *Choice, Class and Conflict* (Harvester Press, 1979). The discussion of the theoretical and methodological problems arising from this remains weak, as Lonsdale points out in his long and useful survey 'States and Social Process in Africa', *African Studies Review,* **24** (2/3), 139–225 (1981); see also Joel Samoff's 'Class, Class Conflict and the state in Africa', *Political Science Quarterly,* **97** (1), 105–127 (1982), and C. Young, 'Patterns of Social Conflict: State, Class and Ethnicity', *Daedalus,* **111** (2), 71–98 (1982). Among individual classes, the **African bourgeoisies** are relatively poorly studied despite their political importance and the speed and extent of the social transformation which brought them into existence. Early work saw them primarily as an educated elite, necessarily dominating politics but requiring little distinct analysis, while Marxist scholars found difficulty in fitting so rapidly developing a group into rigid class categories, as can be seen in Shivji (work cited); for a survey of such early Marxist work, see S. Katz, *Marxism, Africa and Social Class* (Centre for Developing Area Studies, Montreal, 1980). Some insight into their origins can, however, be found in the classic country studies, notably Sklar (work cited) and in such work as Colin Ley's seminal *Underdevelopment in Kenya* (Heinemann, 1975), Gavin Kitching's *Class and Economic Change in Kenya* (Yale University Press, 1980) and the articles in Dunn (work cited). The more recent development of African capitalism has provoked a lively debate and a more coherent literature, including Nicola Swainson, *The Development of Corporate Capitalism in Kenya 1918–1977* (Heinemann, 1980); Fransman (work cited); Bjorn Beckman, 'Imperialism and the National Bourgeoisie', *Review of African Political Economy*, **22**, 5–19 (1981) and 'Whose State? State and Capitalist Development in Nigeria', *Review of African Political Economy*, **23**, 37–51 (1982); and C. Baylies and M. Szeftel, 'The Rise of the Zambian Capitalist Class in the 1970s', *Journal of Southern African Studies*, **8** (2), 187–213 (1982).

A more intensively studied category is the **working class.** The best introduction to both workers and the urban poor in general is Dick Sandbrook's oddly titled *The Politics of Basic Needs* (Heinemann, 1982), while his briefer joint study with Jack Arn, *The Labouring Poor and Urban Class Formation: the Case of Greater Accra* (Centre for Developing Area Studies, Montreal, 1977), is also well worth attention. The relationship between urban life, the labour process, union organization and class consciousness is analysed in fine case studies by Peace (work cited) and Michael Burawoy, whose *The Colour of Class on the Copperbelt* (Institute of African Studies, Lusaka, 1972) is carried further by his recent 'Labour Process and the State in Zambia', *Politics and Society*, **11** (2), 123–166 (1982). There are useful collections on workers, unions and politics edited by Dick Sandbrook and Robin Cohen, *The Development of an African Working Class* (Longman, 1975), and by Peter Gutkind et al., *African Labour History* (Sage, 1980), plus a very helpful literature guide by Jean Copans, 'Les classes ouvrières d'Afrique noire', *Cahiers d'études africains*, **81/83**, 405 –430 (1981). Industrial relations are less well discussed, with the best of a weak choice U. K. Damachi (ed.), *Industrial Relations in Africa* (Macmillan, 1979).

Peasants and rural politics can be explored through a vast and uneven literature, but there is still no good overall account of the development of peasantries and their characteristic forms of consciousness and action. A good start can, however, be made with Gavin Williams' article in Gutkind and Wallerstein (work cited), F. Cooper, 'Peasants, Capitalists and Historians', *Journal of Southern African Studies*, 7 (2), 284–314 (1981), R. H. Bates' *Essays on the Political Economy of Rural Africa* (Cambridge University Press, 1983), and Martin Klein (ed.), *Peasants in Africa* (Sage, 1980). For peasant life and economy there is Polly Hill's classic *Rural Hausa* (Cambridge University Press, 1972) and Keith Hart's analytical survey *The Political Economy of West African Agriculture* (Cambridge University Press, 1982), though these deal with only one of Africa's regions, and have little to say on labour migration, so important in the South, as Colin Murray shows in *Families Divided: the Impact of Migrant Labour in Lesotho* (Cambridge University Press, 1981). Peasant politics can take numerous forms, as is shown by J. D. Y. Peel's excellent and vivid case study *Ijeshas and Nigerians: the Incorporation of a Yoruba Kingdom 1890–1970* (Cambridge University Press, 1983). The more conservative varieties, based on patron–client relationships and often involving religious ties, are discussed in several monographs, notably O'Brien and Whitaker (both works cited). Resistance to state exaction and intervention, which is probably the most frequently studied form of rural political activity, has been analysed from differing perspectives in Bates, and Vail and White (both works cited), and by Goran Hyden, *Beyond Ujamaa in Tanzania* (Heinemann, 1980); Chris Beer, *The Politics of Peasant Groups in Western Nigeria* (University of Ibadan Press, 1975); and Henry Bernstein, 'Notes on State and Peasantry: the Tanzanian Case', *Review of African Political Economy*, 21, 44–62 (1981). Far rarer is peasant revolt, discussed in several of the articles in Rotberg and Mazrui (work cited), in Benoit Verhaegen's *Rebellions au Congo* (Centre de Recherche et d'Informations Socio-Politique, Brussels, 2 vols, 1967–1969) and Robert Buijtenhuijs' review of the literature on Mau Mau, *Contributions to Mau Mau Historiography* (African Studies Centre, Leiden, 1982), and Terry Ranger's forthcoming work on peasant politics in twentieth-century Zimbabwe.

Amidst all this scholarly activity one major social group still suffers neglect, especially by male scholars. Though **women** play a crucial role in social life and production, and have been deeply involved in African politics, the literature on all these aspects remains relatively thin and unintegrated, with the best work done very largely by women. General surveys occur in Allen and Williams (work cited) and in Margaret Strobel, 'African Women',

Signs, **8** (1), 109–131 (1982), and a good discussion of some key methodological issues as well as Southern African material in Belinda Bozzoli, 'Marxism, Feminism and South African Studies', *Journal of Southern African Studies*, **9** (2), 139–171 (1983). The role of women in armed liberation struggles is treated in several good case studies, such as those by Stephanie Urdang, *Fighting Two Colonialisms: Women in Guinea-Bissau* (Monthly Review, 1979) and R. E. Lapchick and S. Urdang, *Oppression and Resistance: the Struggle of Women in Southern Africa* (Greenwood, 1982). Their subsequent role is less readily discerned, however, with B. Isaacman and J. Stephens' *Mozambique: Women, the Law and Agrarian Reform* (UN Economic Commission for Africa, 1980) being virtually alone in the field; fortunately it is both sympathetic and revealing. Women's part in the nationalist movements has to be teased out of other accounts, or constructed from minor case studies, while women in independent states have usually been portrayed, when they are studied at all, as politically constrained and repressed. Though somewhat one-sided, this is a largely accurate judgement, as witness Audrey Wipper, 'The Maendeleo ya Wanawake Movement in Kenya', *African Studies Review*, **18** (3), 99–120 (1975) and Irma Schuster, *New Women of Lusaka* (Mayfield, 1979), among others.

The state

Despite the importance of this concept in Marxist political analysis, it remains highly problematic and unsatisfactorily studied in the political economy literature on Africa, with John Lonsdale's survey (work cited) a partial exception, with its breadth of reference and historical insight. Some help can be gained from policy studies (discussed below) but the field remains principally occupied by more or less descriptive and institutional accounts, such as Selassie (work cited) on the chief executive's role, or B. O. Nwuabeze, *Presidentialism in Commonwealth Africa* (Hurst, 1974) and *The Presidential Constitution of Nigeria* (Hurst, 1982). Other aspects of constitutional development and analysis are best covered by consulting such journals as the *Journal of African Law* (Butterworths, London, 1957–) and the French *Revue Juridique et Politique* (Paris: Institut Internationale de Droit d'expression francaise, 1947–) and *Penant* (Paris). The interaction between law and politics has inspired several valuable studies, including Yash Ghai and J. Macauslan's influential *Public Law and Political Change in Kenya* (Oxford University Press, 1970), Bob Seidman's *The State, Law and Development* (Croom Helm, 1978) and most recently Francis Snyder's work on Senegal: *Capitalism and Legal Change* (Academic Press, 1981). Snyder has also written a helpful bibliographic article on this field' 'Law and Development in the Light of Dependency Theory', *Law and Society Review*, **14** (3), 723–804 (1980).

The literature on **administration** is large in extent but modest in quality, and less touched by political economy insights than other fields, even in the case of development administration discussed in D. Hirschmann, 'Development or Underdevelopment Administration', *Development and Change*, **12** (3), 459–479 (1981). Good recent studies include a general text by Ladipo Adamolekun, *Public Administration* (Longman, 1983), and case studies by Tordoff (1980, work cited) and Gould (work cited). There are characteristically lively critiques of administration, civil and development, by Goran Hyden, *No Short Cuts to Progress: African Development Management in Perspective* (Heinemann, 1983); D. K. Leonard, *Reaching the Peasant Farmer: Organisation Theory and Practice in Kenya* (Chicago University Press, 1977); and by M. G. Schatzberg (work cited). Other relevant material includes a massive study of bureaucratic control by J. H. Breton: *Le controle d'état sur le continent africain* (Librarie Generale de Droit et Jurisprudence, 1978) and R. M. Price's *Society and Bureaucracy in Contemporary Ghana* (University of California Press, 1975). Despite the importance of the **military** in African politics there is surprisingly little on African armies other than the material cited on *coups*; there is also little on the **police**, though Otwin Marenin provides a starting point in his 'Policing African States', *Comparative Politics*, **14** (4), 379–396 (1982).

Policy

Given the authoritarian nature of African political systems, and the difficulties encountered in implementing policy, it is not surprising that the study of the political aspects of policy making has been inhibited. Much of the available material, especially that on planning and the economy, is technical or only narrowly critical, and it is very rare to find general or comparative studies with political insight. One such is the collection edited by Joel Barkan and John Okumu, *Politics and Public Policy in Kenya and Tanzania* (Praeger, 1979). Urban policy is – as so often – covered best by case studies, notably M. A. Cohen *Urban Policy and Political Conflict in Africa: a Study of the Ivory Coast* (Chicago University Press, 1974) and Richard Stren, *Housing the Urban Poor: Policy, Politics and Bureaucracy in Mombasa, Kenya* (Insti-

tute of International Studies, Berkeley, 1979). The modern literature on education policy in Africa is not often directed towards
political scientists, but there are a number of good and enlightening contributions, including D. B. Abernethy, *The Political Dilemma of Popular Education* (Stanford University Press, 1969); D.
Court and K. Kinyanjui, *Development Policy and Educational
Opportunity: the Experience of Kenya and Tanzania* (International
Institute for Educational Planning, Paris, 1978); and O. Le Brun,
'Education and Class Conflict' in *Dependence in Senegal*, edited by
R. C. O'Brien (Sage, 1979, pp. 175–208). Two further areas –
rural development and foreign policy – stand out for their signifi-
cance for political scientists. The best single volume on **rural
development policy** is Heyer *et al.* (work cited), while similar
ground is covered from a less political economy stance by R. H.
Bates and M. Lofchie, in *Agricultural Development in Africa:
Issues of Public Policy* (Praeger, 1980). Goran Hyden's study
(1980, work cited) generalizes from Tanzania's problems with
rural policy to a broad critique of both policy and implementation.
On **foreign policy**, competent accounts exist for most individual
African states, the best being D. Anglin and T. Shaw, *Zambia's
Foreign Policy* (Westview, 1979), O. Aluko, *Essays in Nigerian
Foreign Policy* (Allen and Unwin, 1981) and T. Shaw and O.
Aluko (eds), *Nigerian Foreign Policy* (Macmillan, 1983). For more
general coverage see T. Shaw and O. Aluko (eds), *The Political
Economy of African Foreign Policy* (Gower, 1983) and G. A.
Nweke, *Harmonisation of African Foreign Policies 1955–75* (Afri-
can Studies Centre, Boston, 1980); for further insights consult the
material on foreign intervention discussed below.

Religion and ideology

Religion has been as great an influence on African political
behaviour and consciousness as class or ethnicity, yet no general
analysis of this influence exists. Due to its recent prominence, such
analyses do exist for the impact of Islam, with general surveys by
Guy Nicolas, *Dynamique de l'Islam au sud du Sahara* (Publications orientalistes de France, 1981), and D. Westerlund, *From
Socialism to Islam? Notes on Islam as a Political Factor in
Contemporary Africa* (Scandinavian Institute of African Studies,
1982), and a particularly good case study by John Paden, *Religion
and Political Culture in Kano* (University of California Press,
1973). The nearest counterpart to these on Christianity is Adrian
Hasting's *A History of African Christianity 1950–75* (Cambridge
University Press, 1979). One common outcome of the influence of
religion on politics is the millennarian movement, discussed gener-

ally by Thomas Hodgkin in Gutkind and Waterman (work cited), but perhaps better approached through case studies, such as Wim van Binsbergen's splendid *Religious Change in Zambia* (Routledge and Kegan Paul, 1981), Verhaegen (work cited), or Audrey Wipper's *Rural Rebels* (Oxford University Press, 1978). **Ideology** has otherwise been a weak influence until recent years – South Africa excepted – as Yves Benot made clear in *Ideologies des independances africaines* (Maspero, 1969). Of the many collections on African political thought the best is Jabez Langley, *Ideologies of Liberation in Black Africa 1856–1970* (Rex Collings, 1979), and there are good accounts of the role of ideology in Young (1982, work cited) and in Wyatt MacCaffey's survey article, 'African Ideology and Belief', *African Studies Review*, **24** (2/3), 227–274 (1981).

Socialism is habitually studied in the context of its supposed practice, despite the peculiarity of some claims to socialist status made by African heads of state. The most valuable general discussions are by Crawford Young (1982, work cited) and the Ottaways (work cited). These can be supplemented by the country studies in C. G. Rosberg and T. Callaghy (eds), *Socialism in Subsaharan Africa* (Institute of International Studies, Berkeley, 1979), and those in B. Szajkowski, *Marxist Governments* (4 vols, Macmillan, 1981); the latter collection is to be expanded into a set of country volumes, to be published by Frances Pinter from 1984. Among the numerous and increasingly critical individual case studies, one can learn most from Chabal and Rudebeck (work cited) on Guinea-Bissau; Isaacman (work cited) on Mozambique; Markakis and Ayele and Halliday and Molyneux (work cited) on Ethiopia; and – to but sample a vast pile of writing on Tanzania – Andrew Coulson, *Tanzania: a Political Economy* (The Clarendon Press, 1982), Joel Samoff, 'Crises and Socialism in Tanzania', *Journal of Modern African Studies*, **19** (2), 279–306 (1981), and Bernstein (work cited).

External relations

Inter-state relations are of growing importance in Africa, whether manifest in continental cooperation, as in the OAU (described in M. Wolfers, *Politics in the Organisation of African Unity*, Methuen, 1976), or in regional conflict, described in B. H. Selassie and others (eds), *Conflict and Intervention in the Horn of Africa* (Monthly Review, 1980) and T. Callaghy (ed.), *South Africa in Southern Africa* (Praeger, 1982). The most significant external relations of African states remain, however, those with states and agencies outside Africa. There are good brief introductions in

James Mayall's 'Africa in the International System', *Government and Opposition*, **14** (3), 349–362 (1979) and Gerard Chaliand's *The Struggle for Africa* (Macmillan, 1982); further references can be had from M. W. Delancey's bibliography, *African International Relations* (Westview, 1981). There are no outstanding studies of British involvement, but several on French intervention, including D. G. Lavroff (ed.), *La politique africaine du General de Gaulle* (Pedone, 1980), and – on French military influence – Robin Luckham, 'French Militarism in Africa', *Review of African Political Economy*, **24**, 55–84 (1982). Of the non-colonial powers, Cuba and China are covered respectively by W. M. Leogrande, *Cuba's Policy in Africa 1959–80* (Institute of International Studies, Berkeley, 1980) and Bruce Larkin, *China and Africa 1949–70* (University of California Press, 1971). The bulk of the literature deals, however, with the two major powers. In recent years, the emphasis in studies of US involvement has been the apparent decline of American influence, a major theme in J. S. Whitaker (ed.), *Africa and the United States* (New York University Press, 1978) and the annual surveys by different authors in *Foreign Affairs* (Council on Foreign Relations, New York, 1922–). Earlier periods are dealt with in F. S. Arkhurst, *United States Policy Toward Africa* (Praeger, 1975); S. Weissman, *American Foreign Policy in the Congo 1960–64* (Cornell University Press, 1974), and – fascinating but unscholarly – E. Ray (ed.), *Dirty Work 2: the CIA in Africa* (Zed Press, 1980). C. A. Stevens' *The Soviet Union and Black Africa* (Macmillan, 1976) remains the best general account. It can be updated with H. Bienen, 'Soviet Political Relations with Africa', *International Security*, **6** (4), 153–173 (1982), and an African perspective can be obtained from O. Ogunbadejo, 'Ideology and Pragmatism: the Soviet Union and Nigeria 1960–77', *Orbis*, **21** (4), 803–830 (1978). Finally, some particular case studies call for mention. Richard Sklar, *Corporate Power in an African State* (University of California Press, 1975) and Ronald Graham, *The Aluminium Industry and the Third World* (Zed Press, 1982) supply rare accounts of the role of foreign capital, while R. T. Libby, 'External Cooptation of an LDC's Policy Making: Ghana', *World Politics*, **29** (1), 67–89 (1976) is a succinct analysis of the IMF influence, also discussed in Gran (work cited).

Further reading and sources

There is no good select bibliography on African politics, the nearest being the uneven and uncritical listing by T. M. Shaw and R. L. Sklar, *A Bibliography for the Study of African Politics*

(African Studies Centre, UCLA, 1973), which has been updated to the mid-1970s in A. C. Solomon, *A Bibliography for the Study of African Politics*, Vol. 2 (Crossroads, 1977). Individual country bibliographies are published by the Clio Press of Oxford, in their *World Bibliography* series, and by the Scarecrow Press of Metuchen, New Jersey, in their *African Historical Dictionary* series. Both cover more than politics and are very uneven in quality, though the former's annotations are helpful. The Gower Press series on individual African states (*African Profiles* series) may well prove to be a more useful initial source than either of the above; publication began in 1983. Various items already cited in this chapter, such as Allen and Williams, are themselves good guides to the literature. Keeping track of new material is easier, for several good current bibliographies exist. The best of the annotated listings are *International Political Science Abstracts* (International Political Science Association, Paris, 1951–) whose coverage of Africa is, however, weak, and the Leiden Afrikastudiecentrum's *Documentatieblad* (1969–), which covers the social sciences and history. Of the listings which lack annotation, the *International African Bibliography* (Mansell, London, 1971–) does give a general indication of the discipline or field of the items listed. Its coverage is more reliable but less comprehensive than the author's own listing in the *Review of African Political Economy* (The Review, Sheffield, 1972–), which includes theses and is limited to the social sciences and colonial history.

Monitoring recent events is most easily done for Southern Africa, as numerous news digests and magazines exist for this region, together with the comprehensive annual *Survey of Race Relations* produced by the Institute of Race Relations in Johannesburg since 1957. Of the other regions, only the West is specifically covered, by the weekly *West Africa* (West Africa Publishing Company, London, 1917–), but there are several monthlies and annuals covering the whole continent. The best by a small margin are *New African* (International Communications, London, 1968 –), *Africa Now* (Pan-African Publications, London, 1981–) and *Jeune Afrique* (Groupe Jeune Afrique, Paris, 1960–) for reportage and commentary; the monthly *Africa Research Bulletin* (Africa Research Ltd, Exeter, 1964–) for news digests; and the annual *Africa Contemporary Record* (Africana, New York, 1968 –), which provides extensive accounts of recent events at continental and state level, and is strong on international relations.

23
The Middle East and North Africa
Peter Colvin

The enormous expanse covered by the Middle East and North Africa stretches from the Atlantic coast of Africa to the borders of the Indian subcontinent and China. Although it is a comparatively thinly populated region, it is overcrowded with the ruins of former civilizations and empires, whose traditions still survive, and it is the birthplace of three great world religions, whose adherents still come into sharp conflict. The peoples of the region are in general very conservative, but at the same time economic changes, in particular, oil money, and world events have introduced developments that cause great tensions within the societies of the area. Any valid generalizations about the politics of the whole area are difficult, if not impossible, because of the great differences in political development of different parts of it. Some of the more traditional areas are more amenable to study by the methods of the anthropologist than the political scientist. In practically all cases the obtaining of hard data is difficult, as most are what would be considered from a Western point of view as closed societies. Techniques like questionnaires and examining voting patterns are often considered with suspicion by the regimes in power, and by the people they have power over. Understanding the political dynamics of the area, therefore, must take into account the historical background, ethnographic features and regional peculiarities more than would be the case in studying the politics of the more developed parts of the world. Without this knowledge even the political discourse of the area, in which modern events are justified in terms of historical events of 1500 and 2000 years ago, will be totally incomprehensible. Perhaps the nearest approach in our immediate experience to this explosive mixture of sectarian and tribal loyalties, in which the past is constantly drawn upon to justify the present, is Northern Ireland. In the attempt to understand the very different politics of the Middle East and North Africa it may be useful to remember that particular part of our own political system.

Introductory texts

There are a number of general introductions to the politics of the area which present the basic facts about the political configurations of the countries without attempting any interpretation. An indispensible reference work which keeps up with the bewildering changes is the annual *The Middle East and North Africa, 1981–82* (Europe Publications, 28th edn, 1981). General articles on the area, and developments in the Arab–Israeli conflict, are followed by individual country articles, with updated information on the historical, political and economic situations.

The Government and Politics of the Middle East and North Africa, edited by David E. Long and Bernard Reich (Westview Press, Boulder, Colorado, 1980), is a collection of articles of varying quality on the different countries of the area by American scholars, followed by short bibliographies. Perhaps constraints on length accounts for the blandness and surface treatment by some of the contributors. Two recent books, that make no more claims than to be textbooks, make good introductions to the subject. *Comparative Politics of the Middle East: an Introduction*, by B. M. Borthwick (Prentice-Hall, 1980), consists of a general section with more detailed introductions to Israel, Lebanon, Egypt, Iran and Turkey. *Politics in the Middle East*, by James A. Bill and Carl Leiden (Little, Brown, 1979), presents the outlines of modernization and political development over the whole region.

William Zartman's article on political science in *The Study of the Middle East: Research and Scholarship in the Humanities and the Social Sciences*, edited by Leonard Binder (Wiley, 1976), presented a detailed report on the state of the art at that time. He showed how the two seminal works *The Passing of Traditional Society*, by Daniel Lerner (The Free Press, 1958), and *The Politics of Social Change in the Middle East and North Africa*, by Manfred Halpern (Princeton University Press, 1963), set the trends which most scholarship in the subject followed. These were the study of the effects of modernization, the development of modern political structures and the emergence of a new elite class, educated and qualified in Western science and technology, leading the process of modernization. Typical of such works are *Political Elites in the Middle East*, edited by George Lenczowski (American Enterprise Institute, 1975), *Political Elites and Political Development in the Middle East*, edited by Frank Tuchau (Schenkman, 1975), *Political Dynamics in the Middle East*, edited by P. Y. Hammond and S. S. Alexander (American Elsevier, 1972), and *The Economics and Politics of the Middle East*, by Abraham Becker *et al.* (American Elsevier, 1975). One of the finest works in this tradition is *Arab Politics: the Search for Legitimacy*, by Michael Hudson (Yale University Press, 1977). Hudson categorizes the governments of the area, dividing them into revolutionary republics, traditional patriarchal rulers and bourgeois republics; and gives an account of how these regimes manipulate certain key issues in order to supply themselves with some legitimacy in the eyes of their peoples, who have a minimal or no share in choosing their rulers. Although he limits his study to the Arab world, many of his conclusions could be extended to Turkey, Iran and Afghanistan.

However, the revolution in Iran, and the emergence of Khomeini as its leader, the Iran–Iraq war, the murder of Sadat by members of the Muslim Brotherhood and the war that the Brotherhood is fighting with the regime in Syria are the most arresting manifestations of the re-emergence in the politics of the area of a force that much of Western scholarship had concluded was slowly fading from the political scene, and has upset many of its other assumptions about the progress of modernization.

Particular aspects

Islam

The presence of Islam as the religion of the vast majority of the population is one of the most characteristic features of the whole area, although, of course, the Islamic world extends beyond its boundaries, and the most populous Muslim countries lie outside it. Nevertheless the Middle East is the historic heartland of Islam, and it is very important to understand the very central part that this religion plays in the life of society.

Unlike Christianity and other major world religions, Islam has always provided a complete way of life for its devotees, and as a result there is no separation of the secular from the religious. In its golden age Islam was both a religion and a political system, and the prophet Muhammad was not only a spiritual leader, but also an extremely able political leader who united the Arab tribes and sent them off on their enormous conquests. The desire to reinstate Islam as the political system has never completely died out, and the Muslim Brotherhood has been a significant force in Egypt since the 1930s. But a general return to Islam has been accelerating in the whole region since 1973, and the Iranian revolution has led to a flurry of journalistic writing attempting to account for this phenomenon. *Militant Islam,* by G. H. Jansen (Pan Books, 1979) gives a popular account of recent trends. *The Politics of Islamic reassertion*, edited by Muhammed Ayoob (Croom Helm, 1981), *Islam and Power*, edited by Alexander S. Cudsi and Ali E. Hillal Dessouki (Croom Helm, 1981), and *Islam in the Political Process*, edited by James P. Piscatori (Cambridge University Press, 1983), consist of collections of studies that stress the immense variety of ways in which Islam can be used to express feelings of protest and disillusion, varying according to place. Indeed, Islam is exploited at the same time by 'reactionary' regimes like Saudi Arabia and 'progressive' ones like Qaddafi's Libya. The most important party of Sunni fundamentalism is the Muslim Brotherhood, which although founded in Egypt, has spread its influence to all neighbouring countries. It has been studied in a number of monographs, including *The Society of the Muslim Brothers*, by Richard Mitchell (Oxford University Press, 1969); *Nationalism and Revolution in Egypt*, by Christina Phelps Harris (Mouton, 1964); and *The Moslem Brethren*, by Ishak Musa Husaini (Khayat's, Beirut, 1952). The centre of the other major, but smaller branch of Islam, Shi'ism, is Iran, and it is best to mention works on it in the section on that country. But it is worth noting that a large Shi'ite minority in Lebanon is becoming increasingly prominent.

Arab nationalism

Throughout its war with Iran, which declares itself the force of true Islam, and with increasing urgency as the tide has turned against it, the regime in Iraq of Saddam Husain has appealed to the other important supranational ideology of the area, Arab Nationalism, or Arabism (al-'Urūbah). In contrast to Western Europe, nationalism is a very recent and alien growth in the Middle East. As expressed in its classic exposition, *Caravan, the Story of the Middle East*, by Carleton Coon (Henry Holt, 1951), the traditional pattern of society was of a patchwork quilt of cities loosely dotted over a vast rural expanse of villages and uncultivated areas, in which loyalty was to the city, or village, or tribe; and wider loyalty was usually to a religious group: for the majority, the nation of Islam. Albert Hourani in *Arabic Thought in the Liberal Age* (Oxford University Press, 1970) shows how Arabism started with a revival of interest in the Arabic language and literature, and developed as a political movement as a reaction to Ottoman Turkish nationalism; itself a reaction to Balkan nationalisms. It has continued to grow under the pressure of the conflict with the Jewish nationalist movement of Zionism. As Hudson's book *Arab Politics* (work cited) shows, this has placed the Arab–Israeli conflict at the centre of those issues to which no Arab regime can afford not to pay at least lip-service. *Arab Nationalism: an Anthology*, edited by Sylvia Haim (University of California Press, 1962), is a useful collection of documents. Studies that have plotted the appeal of this movement to the intelligentsia of the area are *Political Trends in the Arab World: the Role of Ideas and Ideals in Politics*, by Majid Khadduri (Johns Hopkins Press, 1970), and *The Ideological Revolution in the Middle East*, by Leonard Binder (Wiley, 1964). *The Crisis of the Arab Intellectual*, by Abdulla Laroui (University of California Press, 1976) and *The Arab Predicament: Arab Political Thought and Practice since 1967*, by Fouad Ajami (Cambridge University Press, 1981), discuss the diminishing appeal of the movement in the face of military defeats. There have been two main contenders for the leadership of the Arab Nationalist movement: one was Nasser, who took over the one Arab country with an indigenous nationalism of its own, and tried to make it the leader of the whole Arab world as the most populous country within it; and the other was the Ba'th Party. Studies on Nasserism will be mentioned in the section on Egypt. Studies on the Ba'th Party will be considered in the sections on the two countries with an official Ba'thist ideology: Syria and Iraq. Patrick Seale's *The Struggle for Syria: a Study of Post-war Arab Politics, 1945–1958* (Oxford University Press, 1965), and *The Arab Cold War: Gamal Abd al-Nasir and Rivals, 1958–1970*, by Malcolm H. Kerr (Oxford University Press, 3rd edn, 1971), chronicle the struggles between Cairo and Damascus for the leadership of the Arabs. *The Arab left*, by Tereq Y. Ismael (Syracuse University Press, 1976) is a summary of the various currents of the left, including Ba'thism, Nasserism and the New Arab left.

Whether as a cause or effect of Arab nationalism, Arabs feel a solidarity and interest in each other that transcends their national boundaries, and is similar to, but stronger than, the feeling of solidarity within the 'Anglo-Saxon' world'. Despite this, attempts at formalized unity have been singularly unsuccessful. *The League of Arab States*, by Robert W. Macdonald (Princeton University Press, 1965), examines the chief institution of Arab unity.

Elites

The approach to understanding political dynamics through the study of the groups that wield power has been attempted in the Middle East. Two collections edited by Lenczowski and Tuchau were cited above, and consist of studies of individual countries. *Elites in the Middle East*, edited by I. William Zartman (Praeger, 1980), gives the papers of a workshop assessing the validity of this approach, with particular reference to the Middle East. An excellent study of a particular group that may point the way for future studies, is *Lawyers and Politics in the Arab World, 1880 –1960*, by Donald M. Reid (Bioliotheca Islamica, 1981). Lawyers led the independence movements in the Arab world, and continued to enjoy political leadership until they lost out to the military in the 1950s.

The military

The phenomenon of rule by military men is such a common one in the area that a number of general studies have been devoted to it. However, in contradistinction to Europe and Latin America, military revolutions in the Middle East often are, or claim to be, progressive left-wing movements. Thus the Turkish army has twice intervened in order to restore democracy and Kemalist ideals, and the Egyptian, Iraqi, Syrian and Libyan armies intervened to introduce socialism. In practice a 'Praetorian state' is often the result, as shown in the following studies: *Political Roles and Military Rulers*, by Amos Perlmutter (Frank Cass, 1981); *Middle-East Politics: the Military Dimension*, by J. C. Hurewitz (Praeger, 1969); and *Army Officers in Arab Politics and Society*, by Eliezer Be'eri, translated by Dov Ben-Abba (Praeger, 1969).

Communism

Up to now, Communism has been surprisingly unsuccessful in gaining political power in the area, although it exercises a strong influence on sections of the intellegentsia. The only Arab country to declare itself officially Marxist is the People's Democratic Republic of Yemen, and the only other Islamic country in the region to do so is Afghanistan: two of the most undeveloped countries in the entire area, both politically and economically. Fred Halliday's *Arabia without Sultans* (Penguin, repr. 1979) gives a well-informed account of the rise and fall of the radical movement in the Arabian Peninsula. *Communism and Nationalism in the Middle East*, by Walter Laqueur (Praeger, 1956), covers the whole region. *The Communist Movement in Iran*, by S. Zabih (University of California Press, 1966), and *The Origins of Communism in Turkey*, by G. Harris (Stanford University Press, 1967), consider two countries with large Communist parties.

The Arab–Israeli conflict

The conflict caused by the setting up of Israel, and the turning of the greater part of Palestine, which was 90 per cent Arab at the turn of the century, into a predominantly Jewish state, by immigration from the rest of the world, as well as from within the region itself, has been central to Arab Nationalism, as well as having an enormous effect on neighbouring countries, and international relations with the area. It has engendered a huge literature, and exercised a baneful influence on scholarship by turning scholars into apologists for one side or the other. Purely political studies will be considered under the sections on Israel, the Palestinians and other countries.

Individual countries of the Middle East

Turkey

The only two countries in the area to have developed pluralistic democratic governments of a type familiar to Western political scientists, and therefore readily amenable to the application of Western political concepts, are Turkey and Israel. Turkish society exhibits a somewhat schizophrenic character, in which some elements consider themselves European, while others regard themselves as wholly Islamic and Oriental. It is the successor state to the huge Ottoman Empire, but owes its very existence to the resistance led by Kemal Ataturk, who refused to allow the victorious allies to dismember what remained after the First World War. Kemal turned Turkey into a secular state, and endowed it with a philosophy named after him, which embraced a number of strands, including democracy and étatism. Most of these ideas had already been present in Ottoman political thought, as shown in *The Emergence of Modern Turkey*, by Bernard Lewis (Oxford University Press, 2nd edn, 1968). *Democracy and Development*, by C. H. Dodd (Eothen Press, 1979), points to elements remaining from the Ottoman past, as well as the others that make up the complex political scene. *Turkey's Politics, the Transition to a Multi-party System*, by K. H. Karpat (Princeton University Press,

1964), *The Turkish Political Elite*, by F. W. Frey (MIT Press, 1965), and *Social Change and Participation in Turkey*, by Ergun Ozbudun (Princeton University Press, 1976), cover aspects of Turkish politics. Jacob Landau's *Radical Politics in Modern Turkey* (Brill, 1974), describes one of the causes of the periodical breakdowns in the Turkish political system, which have led to interventions by the army to restore Kemalism. These are considered in *The Role of the Military in Recent Turkish Politics*, by Ergun Ozbudun (Harvard University Press, 1966). A recent study by Binnaz Toprak, *Islam and Political Development in Turkey* (Brill, 1981), discusses the role of religion and shows how far Kemalism has altered Turkey in relation to other Muslim countries.

Israel

The other highly developed political system in the area, in Western terms, is Israel. It also occupies an extremely anomalous position. In the eyes of its neighbours it is an alien entity, founded and sustained by forces from outside the area, at the expense of the Palestinians. In fact, Zionism, as a political expression of Jewish nationalism, was a response to European nationalist movements and European persecution of Jews. The socialist ideals that inspired the Kibbutz and Moshav movements, and the people who compose the political elite, are also of European provenance. But just over half the population is composed of Oriental Jews who immigrated to Israel after its founding in 1948, with very different political cultures, and this is having its effect on the resulting fusion. The most obvious feature of the Israeli political system is an amazing multiplicity of parties, leading to a highly fractionalized, and apparently chaotic, situation. But as *Party and Politics in Israel: Three Visions of a Jewish State*, by Rael Jean Isaac (Longman, 1981) points out, there is great stability under the shifting surface. The political parties can be divided into three blocs: a labour bloc, a religious bloc, and a national–liberal bloc. Because of the constant need to form coalitions, smaller parties, like the extreme religious parties, often achieve greater influence than would be expected from their voting power. Other studies of the role of parties in general and of particular parties include *Political Parties in Israel: the Evolution of Israeli Democracy*, by David M. Zohar (Praeger, 1974), *Mapai in Israel: Political Organization and Government in a New Society*, by Peter Y. Medding (Cambridge University Press, 1972), and *The Israeli Communist Party*, by Dunia Habib Nahas (Croom Helm, 1976). The unsuccessful attempt to create a written constitution is partly covered by

Israel's Emerging Constitution, 1948–51, by Emanuel Rackman (Columbia University Press, 1955), and its legislative assembly is the subject of *Knesset: the Parliament of Israel*, by Asher Zidon (Herzl Press, 1967). The important role played by the army in integrating the society is considered in two books by Amos Perlmutter: *Military and Politics in Israel* (Frank Cass, 1969) and *Politics and the Military in Israel 1967–1977* (Frank Cass, 1978).

Egypt

Egypt is one of the oldest political units in the world, and in modern times is the one Arab country which developed a nationalist ideology before the rise of Arab nationalism. *The Intellectual Origins of Egyptian Nationalism*, by Jamal Mohammed Ahmed (Oxford University Press, 1960), and *Egypt in Search of Political Community: an Analysis of the Intellectual and Political Evolution of Egypt, 1804–1952*, by Nadav Safran (Harvard University Press, 1961), give the background of this movement. However, despite an unbroken succession of Pharoahs and other strong rulers since the earliest times, from the Persian conquest in the sixth century BC up to the 1952 revolution, Egypt had never been ruled by a native Egyptian. Naturally, therefore, the figure and revolution of Nasser loom large in the literature on modern Egypt. Nasser's conscious taking on of the role of the leader of the Arabs, placed Egypt at the head of the Arab world; a position which its population nearly twice the size of the next most populous Arab country, partly justified. Nasser's own account of his revolution, *Egypt's Liberation: the Philosophy of the Revolution* (Public Affairs Press, Washington, 1955) is a good starting point, as are two biographies: *Nasser*, by Anthony Nutting (Constable, 1972), and *Nasser, a Political Biography*, by Jean Lacouture, translated by Daniel Hofstadter (Knopf, 1973). The Egyptian brand of socialism, anti-imperialism and Arab nationalism is considered in *Nasserist Ideology: its Exponents and Critics*, by Nissim Rejwan (Wiley, 1974), and *Arab Socialism*, by Abdel Moghny Said (Blandford Press, 1972). Despite the great influence of Nasser's charisma and oratorical power, and the undoubted tendency of Egyptians to obey their leaders (in contrast to other Arabs), the regime that Nasser headed was a military one, and the following studies examine this fact, and assess the extent to which significant changes were made in Egyptian society: *Egypt, Military Society: the Army Regime, the Left and Social Change under Nasser*, by Anouar Abdel-Malek, translated by Charles Lam Markmann (Random House, 1968); *Egypt, the Praetorian State*, by Amos

Perlmutter (Transaction Books, 1974); and *The Egyptian Army in Politics: Pattern for New Nations?*, by P. J. Vatikiotis (Indiana University Press, 1961). The last-named author has attempted to sum up the Nasserite experiment in *Nasser and his Generation* (Croom Helm, 1978). The turning away from the socialist aspects of Nasser's rule by Sadat, and his gamble on Western support and a settlement with Israel, are still too recent for scholarly assessment. The biography *Sadat*, by David Hirst and Irene Beeson (Faber and Faber, 1981), attempts an early summing up, and an explanation for the indifference of the Egyptians, and jubilation of the rest of the Arabs, when he met his sudden and violent end.

Much work remains to be done on the deeper analysis of Egyptian political society, and especially the vast and ubiquitous bureaucracy which has always run Egypt. Two important works have shown the way: *Bureaucracy and Politics in Contemporary Egypt*, by Nazih N. M. Ayubi (Ithaca Press, 1980), and *Egypt: Burdens of the Past, Options for the Future*, by John Waterbury (Indiana University Press, 1978).

Iran

Like Egypt, Iran has had an identity as a separate country that stretches back into antiquity, but it has nothing like the same continuity of strong centralized rule. It also lacks Egypt's homogeneity of population: in fact, only about half the population belongs to the dominant Persian-speaking group. The large minorities placed round the edges of the country have always shown strong fissiparous tendencies. The important fact of the adherence of the majority of the Iranians to the Shi'ite branch of Islam is owing to the deliberate policy of the Safavid dynasty in the sixteenth and seventeenth centuries. Two important features distinguish Shi'ism from the Sunni branch of Islam; one is the importance of the religious classes, who have developed some of the characteristics of the Christian clergy, and the other is a strong tradition of revolt against the civil authority, which goes back to its earliest history in struggles against the Ummayad caliphs in the first century of Islam. Also of importance today is the fact that half the population of Iraq, and an important minority in Lebanon, also adhere to Shi'ism.

The modern state of Iran owes its present shape to the late Shah's father, Riza Pahlavi, who was a military strong man, in the Ataturk mould, with similar anti-clerical feelings. From his seizure of power in 1921 to his exile in 1941, forced on him by the allied powers Britain and Russia, Riza Shah sought to turn Iran into a strong, centralized and modernized state with himself in firm command. *The Modernization of Iran, 1921-1924*, by Amin Banani (Stanford University Press, 1961), and *Nationalism in Iran*, by Richard W. Cottam (University of Pittsburg Press, 2nd edn, 'updated through 1978', 1979), give the historical background. After early struggles against the nationalist leader Musaddiq, Muhammad Riza Pahlavi carried on his father's tradition. He enjoyed two advantages over his father: the enormous and ever-increasing oil revenues (more of which came to the government than previously) and the active support of the US, who regarded him as their chief ally in the region after Israel. The highly centralized and ruthlessly controlled regime that ensued, in which the middle class accepted political impotence in exchange for economic bribes, has been described in *The Political Elite of Iran*, by Marvin Zonis (Princeton University Press, 1971); *The Politics of Iran: Groups, Classes and Modernization*, by James Bill (Charles Merill, 1972); and *Iran: Political Development in a Changing Society*, by Leonard Binder (University of California Press, 1962). Two books written shortly before the revolution pinpointed the weaknesses of this system, with its repression of all forms of opposition, and lopsided economic development resulting from centralized planning to realize the Shah's ambitions: *Iran, Dictatorship and Development*, by Fred Halliday (Penguin, 1979), and *Iran, the Illusion of Power*, by Robert Graham (Croom Helm, 1978).

The revolution of 1978/1979 took the world and the Shah himself by surprise, and the new political system is still being created. It must be borne in mind that clerical rule is a completely new phenomenon in the Middle East. Khomeini's own political theory, published in a hostile American translation under the title *Islamic Government* (Manor Books, 1979), is by no means accepted by all his fellow clerics. Nikki Keddie's *Roots of Revolution: an Interpretative History of Modern Iran* (Yale University Press, 1981), and *Modern Iran: the Dialectics of Continuity and Change*, edited by M. E. Bonine and N. R. Keddie (State University of New York Press, 1981), attempt respectively to present the historical antecedents of the revolution, and its effects down through different layers of society.

Syria

Up to the time of the collapse of the Ottoman Empire at the end of the First World War, the area called Syria included present-day Lebanon, Israel and Jordan. After being divided up in a number of ways by the Mandated powers, Britain and France, and various rebellions, the rump that constitutes modern Syria achieved full independence only in 1943. For a time Syria was notorious for the instability of its governments, and *coup* followed *coup* with bewildering rapidity. The books of Seale and Kerr cited above, *The Struggle for Syria* and *The Arab Cold War*, and *Syrian Politics and the Military: 1945–1958*, by Gordon H. Torrey (Ohio State University Press, 1964), chronicle the changes of government, and the struggle between the Ba'this and the Nasserites for the control of the area and the leadership of the Arab world, that led to the brief union with Egypt, and its rapid dissolution. The party that finally managed to retain power in Syria in alliance with the military is considered in *The Arab Ba'th Socialist Party: History, Ideology, and Organization*, by Kemal Abu Jaber (Syracuse University Press, 1966), and *Syria under the Ba'th, 1963–1966: the Army–Party Symbiosis*, by Itamar Rabinovich (Halsted Press, 1972). A feature of the Ottoman Empire that has left a legacy that has bedevilled Syria and its neighbours was the Millet system, or the organization of groups on a confessional basis. The Ba'th regime that has been led by Hafiz al-Asad since 1970 is dominated by the heterodox Alawite sect, and its bitter rivalry with the Sunni Muslim Brotherhood has recently led to bloodshed.

A political party that never achieved political power but has been influential intellectually was founded by a Syrian called Farah Antun, who worked in both Syria and Lebanon. It was based on the idea of Greater Syria, secular, and opposed to pan-Arabism. Two studies have been devoted to the party: *The Syrian Social Nationalist Party: an Ideological Analysis*, by Labib Zuwiyya Yamak (Harvard University Press, 1966), and *The Odyssey of Farah Antun: a Syrian Christian's Quest for Secularization*, by Donald M. Reid (Bibliotheca Islamica, 1975).

Lebanon

Lebanon has one of the most complicated political systems in the world, as perhaps befits a tiny country with a great number of religious sects represented among its population. The modern state of Lebanon emerged independent from French mandate authority in 1943, as a state dominated by the largest single group, the Maronite Christians, who had long enjoyed French protection. However, an elaborate system was agreed upon based on confessionalism, in which a division of power was made among the various Christian and Muslim groups on the basis of the numbers revealed by a census carried out in 1932. As in Israel, political parties are paramount in this system, but parties of a very different type. Here they represent a religious group, and are led by political bosses who resemble feudal barons, being the *de facto* rulers of their own fiefs, backed by the force of their own armed retainers, and eventually militias.

Central government has always been weak, and has evolved through shifting alliances among the party bosses. The best expositions of this system are probably *The Precarious Republic: Political Modernization in Lebanon*, by Michael C. Hudson (Random House, 1968); *Political Parties in Lebanon*, by Michael W. Suleiman (Cornell University Press, 1967); and *Modernization without Revolution: Lebanon's Experience*, by Elie A. Salem (Indiana University Press, 1973). One party that has slowly emerged as the chief expression of right-wing Christian sentiment is studied in *Pluralism and Party Transformation in Lebanon: al-Katā'ib 1936–1970*, by John P. Entelis (Brill, 1974). Great demographic and economic changes within Lebanese society began to exert pressures on this system of comparative equilibrium. In addition, all the currents sweeping the Arab world found echoes in Lebanon, and other Arab countries all backed Lebanese parties, as did ultimately Israel. Lebanon was dragged into the Arab–Israeli conflict through the presence of large numbers of Palestinians, who in turn were dragged into Lebanese conflicts. All these pressures led to the bloody civil war of 1975–1976, which conflict has still not been resolved. A host of books have appeared on it, among the better of which are: *Lebanon in Strife: Student Preludes to the Civil War*, by Halim Barakat (University of Texas Press, 1977); *Crossroads to Civil War: Lebanon 1958–1976*, by Kemal Salibi (Caravan Books, 1976); *Lebanon in Crisis: Participants and Issues*, edited by P. Edward Haley and Lewis W. Snider (Syracuse University Press, 1979); and *Death of a Country: the Civil War in Lebanon*, by John Bullock (Weidenfeld and Nicolson, 1977). The Syrian intervention, which continues to the present, is considered in *Syria and the Lebanese Crisis*, by Adeed I. Dawisha (Macmillan, 1980).

Jordan

The complete name of this state, The Hashemite Kingdom of Jordan, previously Transjordan, points to its salient feature. King Husain is the last surviving ruler of the ill-fated Hashemite clan, which, while occupying the position of Sharifs of Mecca, and with British encouragement, led the Arab revolt against the Turks in the First World War. These events, and the conflicting promises made by the British to their French allies, the Arabs and the Jews, are presented in *The Arab Awakening: the Story of the Arab Revolt*, by George Antonius (Hamish Hamilton, 1938). After the war, the British placed one of the sons of the Sharif of Mecca, 'Abd Allah, in the position of Amir of the tribes of the Trans-Jordan area. The form of Kingdom that 'Abd Allah developed, and bequeathed to his grandson King Husain, was of the classical paternalistic Arab ruler whose position depends on the personal loyalty of Bedouin tribesmen. The latter were trained into a formidable army by British officers, among them Glubb Pasha. The central role of the army in Jordanian politics has been explored in *Politics and the Military in Jordan: a Study of the Arab Legion, 1921–1957*, by P. J. Vatikiotis (Frank Cass, 1967). The problem that has threatened the very existence of the state goes back to the annexation in 1950 of the parts of Palestine that had not become Israel. Although thereafter forming the largest part of the population, the Palestinians owed little loyalty to the Hashe-mites, and often detested their Bedouin army power base. Husain was obliged to settle with the armed Palestinian resistance in 1970, when he turned his army on the Fedayeen.

Two general studies of Jordan are *The Kingdom of Jordan*, by Raphael Patai (Princeton University Press, 1958), and *Jordan: a Political Study, 1948–1957*, by A. H. H. Abidi (Asia Publishing House, 1965). A study of local level politics is *Politics and Change in al-Karak*, by Peter Gubser (Oxford University Press, 1973).

Iraq

After an attempt to make the elder son of the Sharif of Mecca, Faisal, king of Syria, which was halted by the French, the British found a kingdom for him in Iraq. This, however, has traditionally been a politically unruly area, and while not perhaps having as many sects as Syria, it has its own causes of division. Over half the population is Shi'ite, and some of the most sacred places of Shi'ism are in southern Iraq, while the ruling elite has tended to come from the minority Sunni Arabs. A large section of the population of the northern part of the country are not Arabs at all, but Kurds, for whom Arab Nationalism in general, and the ideology of the ruling Ba'th party in particular, hold little attraction. The modern political history of Iraq divides into three sections usefully covered by three books by Majid Khadduri: *Independent Iraq: a Study in Iraqi Politics from 1932 to 1958* (Oxford University Press, 1961); *Republican Iraq: a Study in Iraqi Politics since the Revolution of 1958* (Oxford University Press, 1969); and *Socialist Iraq: a Study in*

Iraqi Politics since 1968 (Middle East Institute, Washington, 1978). *Iraq: International Relations and National Development*, by Edith and E. F. Penrose (Benn, 1978), covers the whole span. The revolution of 1958 that swept away the Hashemite kings was led by General Qasim, and his regime is the subject of *Iraq under Qassem*, by Uriel Dann (Praeger, 1969). Some more analytical works are beginning to appear, and among them are *The Old Social Classes and the Revolutionary Movements of Iraq: a Study of Iraq's Old Landed and Commercial Classes and of its Communists, Ba'thists, and Free Officers*, by Hanna Batatu (Princeton University Press, 1978), and *The Integration of Modern Iraq*, edited by Abbas Kelidar (Croom Helm, 1979).

The Arabian Peninsula

The vast area known in English as the Arabian Peninsula is known to the Arabs themselves as the 'Jazirat al-'Arab', or Island of the Arabs, as it is bound on three sides by water and the fourth by desert. It is the homeland of the Arab race, but except for the brief moment when, under the prophet Muhammad and the early Caliphs, Mecca became the capital of the whole Islamic Empire stretching from Morocco to the borders of China, it has been essentially an inward-looking area, intensely conservative, and peripheral even to Middle Eastern affairs. Only the coastal areas became involved in the designs of European colonial expansion. But the twentieth century has revealed that the area contains the largest known reserves of petroleum in the world, and with it new wealth that is bringing enormous social changes, so the area will never again be out of the world's attention. Few studies treat the whole area, but *The Arabian Peninsula: Society and Politics*, edited by Derek Hopwood (Allen and Unwin, 1972), is a collection of articles ranging over the whole area, and Halliday's book *Arabia without Sultans* (work cited) gives a left-wing view of it.

Saudi Arabia

The state that has grown to become the dominating power in the Peninsula, and through its immense oil wealth, one of the leading voices of the Arab world, is largely the creation of the skill, daring and energy of one man, 'Abd al-Aziz ion Sa'ud. Although descended from a princely family that had united the tribes of eastern Arabia under the banner of an extreme puritanical revivalist sect of Islam called Wahhabism, and had conquered large parts of the Peninsula in the last century, at the turn of this century Ibn

Sa'ud was in exile in Kuwait with a handful of supporters. In 1902 he recaptured Riyadh from the local rival dynasty, and defeated them finally in 1922. By 1926 he had captured the western part of the Peninsula, the Hijaz, expelled the Hashemites and declared himself king of Saudi Arabia. Meanwhile in 1929 he had been forced to repress the religious Ikhwan fighters who had been instrumental in his conquests. Although based on the same classic patriarchal pattern of Arab rule as Jordan, the Saudi dynasty is more securely based by virtue of its sheer size: all the important positions in the state are in the hands of the very large Saudi clan, and the present king is the fourth son of 'Abd al-'Aziz to occupy the throne. Again like the Jordanian monarch, the power base of the regime is an army composed of Bedouin tribesmen with a personal loyalty to the regime. The ideology of the state is based on the puritanical Wahhabi ethic, but the growth of oil revenues and the resulting economic development has finally defeated the attempt to keep out the modern world. With its conservative policies, Saudi Arabia is a natural ally of the US, whose companies extract and market its petroleum, and it came into violent conflict with the Nasserite regime in Egypt in the Yemeni civil war. However, its religious stance makes it strongly anti-Israeli, and the shattering defeat of 1967 caused Egypt and Saudi Arabia to bury their differences. The 1973 Arab–Israeli war was made possible by a pact between Egypt, Syria and Saudi Arabia, with the last supplying the finance, and wielding the oil weapon. There are relatively few studies of Saudi Arabia. A recent journalistic account is the *The Kingdom*, by Robert Lacey (Hutchinson, 1981). More serious studies are *A House Built on Sand: a Political Economy of Saudi Arabia*, by Helen Lackner (Ithaca Press, 1978), which considers the political structure in the context of the economic development of the country, and *State, Society and Economy in Saudi Arabia*, edited by Tim Niblock (Croom Helm, 1982).

The Gulf States

The political pattern of the Gulf States differs little from the Saudi Arabian model of patriarchal dynastic rulers. However, unlike the inward-looking desert kingdom, these states have long histories of trading relations with India and Africa, as well as long-standing relations with the Persian shore of the Gulf. None of them had independent existences as separate countries, and all came under British protectorate status. When Britain finally cast them adrift it endeavoured to unite them into larger units. The whole area is considered in *The Persian Gulf: an Introduction to its Peoples, Politics and Economy*, by David Long (Westview Press, rev. edn, 1978). The oldest and most complex of the city states is Kuwait, covered by *Kuwait, Prospect and Reality*, by Zahra Freeth and Victor Winestone (Crane and Russak, 1972). *Arab States of the Lower Gulf: People, Politics, Petroleum*, by John Duke Anthony (Middle East Institute, Washington, 1975), talks about Bahrain, Qatar and the United Arab Emirates. Bahrain's political development has gone the furthest of these states, due to a larger and more mixed population, as shown in *Bahrain: Political Development in a Changing Society*, by Emile Nakhleh (Lexington Books, 1976). Although primarily a history, *The Creation of Qatar*, by Rosemarie Said Zahlan (Croom Helm, 1979), gives the background to the refusal of this emirate to join the United Arab Emirates and its present political system.

Yemen and Oman

The two areas that form the north-eastern and south-eastern corners of the Peninsula have many features in common. Both occupy very strategic positions: Oman at the narrow entry to the Persian Gulf and Yemen at the entry to the Red Sea. Both are dominated by mountainous areas that have been the strongholds of heterodox Islamic sects, from whose tribes the Imams have emerged who have ruled the countries. In both, tribalism remains strong, and tribal leaders doggedly resist attempts to impose central government authority. But outside influences have caused the two areas to develop very differently.

In Oman, the cycle in which dynasties of Ibadi imams appeared from the interior to take over the coastal areas until they fell in their turn, was interrupted when the British backed the Al Bu Sa'd dynasty and supported them against further claimants; though in the process the dynasty changed into one of secular Sultans. After its golden age when it ruled an empire in Zanzibar and parts of present-day Pakistan, Oman sank into poverty and obscurity. British residents directed policy, and militarily shored up the dynasty until the 1960s, when the revolt in Dhofar was put down. But the British found it necessary to support the *coup* in which the conservative Sultan Sa'id bin Taimur was replaced by his modernizing son Qabus, who was prepared to spend some of the new oil wealth on development. Two studies chart these changes: *Oman in the Twentieth Century: Political Foundations of an Emerging State*, by J. E. Peterson (Croom Helm, 1978), and *Oman, the Making of a Modern State*, by John Townsend (Croom Helm, 1977).

In Yemen, on the other hand, British influence acted to detach Aden and its tribal hinterland, and the Hadramaut region, from the influence of the northern mountainous area. Although there is strong desire on the part of Yemenis to reunite the region, in practice two countries have emerged with bitterly opposed ideologies and interests, which have led to armed conflicts in 1972 and 1979.

The part often referred to as North Yemen is officially entitled The Yemen Arab Republic. It has always been dominated by its northern mountain heartland whence the elected leader of the Zaidi Shi'ite tribes, the Imam, emerged to rule over the Shafi'i Sunni population of the lowlands. The boundaries of the present state were established by a vigorous dynasty of Imams called the Hamid al-Din, who managed to impose a rudimentary form of government on the tribes, in which all the major positions were in the hands of the ruling family. In order to sustain this traditional form of rule, great efforts were made to exclude foreigners and the modern world. In 1962 a revolution overthrew the Imamate and established a republic, which was supported by Nasser's Egypt. A civil war ensued, in which the royalists were supported by the Saudis. Ultimately a reconciliatory settlement was achieved by which the country is a republic, but as *Yemen, the Search for a Modern State*, by J. E. Peterson (Croom Helm, 1982), shows, many of the features of the pre-revolutionary era continue. Government remains centred on one powerful figure, whose rule normally ends violently. Military rulers have replaced religious ones, but tribal leaders still retain a lot of power. Great changes are taking place in the society, but the regime has a basically conservative stance, and North Yemen has been drawn into the Saudi Arabian sphere of influence.

South Yemen's political development has taken a very different turn. Aden was a directly administered British possession, but its hinterland was left undeveloped in the hands of its traditional tribal rulers. With the approach of independence the British attempted to cobble together a federation of South Arabian emirates. After a turbulent period as independence approached in 1967, and a short and sharp civil war, the radical National Liberation Front emerged victorious to create the People's Democratic Republic of Yemen. This is the only Marxist regime in the Arab world, and it is supported by the Soviet Union. It attempted to export its revolution to Dhofar, but it was checked by the military assistance of Britain and the Shah of Iran. These events are described in Halliday's *Arabia without Sultans* (work cited). The only monograph on recent developments is *South Yemen: a Marxist Republic in Arabia,* by W. Stookey (Croom Helm, 1982).

Afghanistan

Like the other mountain states of Yemen and Oman, Afghanistan has remained one of the most conservative countries in the Middle East. Although religiously homogeneous, with the great majority belonging to Sunni Islam, and a small minority of Shi'as, the population is made up of a great variety of different tribes belonging to various racial groups and speaking different languages. But, as the name of the country suggests, the dominant section has been the Afghan tribes, speaking Pushtu, who make up about half the population. However, about as many again live over the border in Pakistan, and this has led to irredentist claims by the Afghans for the North West Fronter Province of Pakistan, which they call Pashtunistan. From the creation of the country in 1747 up to 1973, the ruler had been from the same Afghan clan, and even during the republican phase from 1973 up to the Marxist *coup* of 1978, the presidency was in the hands of the former king's uncle. Significantly, the only gap in this succession was in 1928, when a modernizing monarch, King Aman Allah, ran up against conservative resistance to his reforms. Even more significantly, the different branch of the same family that restored the monarchy the following year did so with the help of tribal armies from the frontier area. Tribalism has remained the chief force resisting attempts to impose central government. After the Marxist revolution of 1978, and still more after the Soviet invasion of December 1979 which was ostensibly to save the revolution, the same tribal-based conservative Islamic resistance has conducted an armed struggle against the Kabul regime. A reference work that gives a lot of historical background and anthropological information is *Afghanistan*, by Louis Dupree (Princeton University Press, 1973). Most studies of this country with such a rudimentary political system have been from a historical angle, but *The Politics of Afghanistan*, by Richard S. Newell (Cornell University Press, 1972), is an exception to this rule. The 1978 Marxist takeover and the Soviet invasion have inspired a large number of works, most of little permanent value. An attempt to piece together the scanty information available is made in *The Struggle for Afghanistan*, by Nancy Peabody Newell and Richard S. Newell (Cornell University Press, 1981). An interesting defence of the shortlived Marxist leader, Hafiz Allah Amin, is made by Beverley Male in *Revolutionary Afghanistan: a Reappraisal* (Croom Helm, 1982). A collection of articles giving an Indian perspective is *Afghanistan in Crisis*, edited by K. P. Misra (Croom Helm, 1981).

Minorities

The problems associated with the break-up of multi-ethnic dynastic empires like the Hapsburg and Ottoman empires are well enough known in European history to have given rise to the term 'Balkanization'. The problems are if anything more acute in the Middle East, with its greater confusion of religions and sects, in addition to the patchwork quilt of ethnic and linguistic groups. The whole area is littered with the ruins of former powerful states based on this or that group. The two-edged weapon of nationalism has been used by governments to try to knit peoples into modern states, the boundaries of which are often historical accidents or the results of external forces. Invariably, the appeal is made to past glories, but the national myths of one group frequently offend the historical myths of the others. Perhaps the most typical minority groups of the whole area are the Jews and the Gypsies. The former, through an aggressive nationalism of their own, have united in Israel to become the majority, creating a Palestinian minority both within their own borders and in the neighbouring countries. The dominant nationalism of the whole area, Arab nationalism, runs into opposition in all the countries on the borders of the Arab religion with large numbers of non-Arabs: Iraq, Sudan and the Maghreb countries. In Turkey, Iran and Afghanistan, the same opposition by minorities to the dominant nationalisms are encountered. Within wholly Arab countries, minority religious groups rule, to the annoyance of the majorities, but the attempt by Lebanon to institutionalize the sharing of power in a nation of minorities has ended in signal failure. *The Political Role of Minority Groups in the Middle East*, edited by R. D. Mclaurin (Praeger, 1979), is a collection of articles on this important issue.

Palestinians

The problem of the Palestinians has given rise to an enormous literature. Whatever the final outcome of their struggle, the Palestinians have achieved the changing of their status of 1947 of mere refugees into a widespread recognition of their existence and rights as a people, with its highpoint of Yasser Arafat's address to the United Nations in 1974. It is probably true to say that every book on any aspect of the Arab–Israeli conflict is to some extent partisan. One of the more objective introductions is *The Palestinian Movement in Politics*, by Paul A. Jureidini and William E. Hazen (Lexington Books, 1976). A detailed but hostile study is

PLO: Strategy and Politics, by Aryeh Y. Yodfat and Yuval Arnon-Ohanna (Croom Helm, 1981). Among the books on the Palestinians in Israel are *The Arabs in Israel*, by Sabri Jiryis (Monthly Review Press, 1976); *The Arabs in Israel*, by Jacob M. Landau (Oxford University Press, 1969); and *Arabs in the Jewish state: Israel's Control of a National Minority*, by Ian Lustick (University of Texas Press, 1980).

Kurds

The difficulties facing minorities, and those studying them, are exemplified by the case of one of the biggest groups in the Middle East without a nation state of their own. Even the most basic fact of their number is impossible to know accurately. In *People without a Country: the Kurds and Kurdistan*, by A. R. Ghassemlou *et al.*, edited by Gerard Chaliand (Zed Press, 1980), they are called a 'community of over 15 million persons'. In *Muslim Peoples: a World Ethnographic Survey*, edited by Richard V. Weekes (Greenwood Press, 1978), (a useful reference work on minority groups), after a warning on the unreliability of official statistics, 'a fairly conservative estimate' is offered of 'nearly 7.6 million'. At all events, Kurds make up a significant percentage of the populations of Turkey, Iraq and Iran, and are far from insignificant in Syria. Ghassemlou's book (1980, work cited) is probably the most accessible introduction to the subject, but it is written by Kurds and is presenting their case, and this must be borne in mind. The strengths of the Kurds are also their weaknesses: their inaccessible homeland, their strong adherence to tribalism and traditional social patterns, etc., make it difficult for them to evolve an effective national consciousness. Each of the countries that Kurdistan straddles feels threatened by Kurdish nationalism and has tried hard to suppress it. In Turkey, military repression has been largely successful in denying the Kurds any political power. In Iraq, Kurdish revolts have on several occasions fought the government to a standstill, and although the most recent, led by Mulla Barzani, was defeated when the Shah of Iran suddenly withdrew his support in 1975, some kind of autonomy for Kurdistan has been wrested from the regime in Baghdad. Two recent studies of this conflict which has been a running sore for the Arab nationalist Ba'thi regime are *Iraq and the Kurdish Question, 1958–1970*, by Sa'd Jawad (Ithaca Press, 1981), and *The Kurdish Question in Iraq*, by Edmund Ghareeb (Syracuse University Press, 1981). The Kurds in Iran, who are mostly Sunnies, are involved in a conflict with the revolutionary Shi'ite regime of Khomeini.

North Africa

The three states that make up what the Arabs call the Maghrib, or West, and is often called North Africa in English, show certain features in common that differentiate them from the rest of the Arab world, but also show a great deal of variety between themselves. Geographically they share a pattern of fertile coastal plain backed by inaccessible mountains giving way to the Sahara desert. The population of all three states is made up of a Berber base, which has been steadily Arabized since the Muslim conquests by influxes of Arab tribes, refugees from Muslim Spain and most recently by government educational policy. This process has left the mountain and desert areas of Morocco and Algeria with large numbers of Berber-speaking tribesmen, and the coastal areas with the cities speaking Arabic. In strong contrast to the Eastern Arab world, religion is a unifying factor, and the vast majority of the population adheres to the Maliki school of Sunni Islam. Finally, all have shared the same dislocating experience of French colonialism, though in different degrees. At the same time the political structures show examples of the three typical types of Middle Eastern government, from Morocco's patriarchal monarchy to Tunisia's bourgeois republic, via Algeria's revolutionary socialism.

A useful basic introduction to the area is *Comparative Politics of North Africa*, by John P. Entelis (Syracuse University Press, 1980). More detailed studies are: *Politics in North Africa: Algeria, Morocco, and Tunisia*, by Clement Henry Moore (Little, Brown, 1970); *Leadership and National Development in North Africa: a Comparative Study*, by Elbaki Hermassi (University of California Press, 1972); and *Man, State and Society in the Contemporary Maghrib*, edited by I. William Zartman (Praeger, 1973).

Individual countries of North Africa

Algeria

The country that experienced the harshest and most total form of European colonialism in the area was Algeria. From the French conquest in 1830 until the bloody war of independence, very well described in Alisdair Horne's *A Savage War of Peace: Algeria 1954–1962* (Penguin, 1979), the Algerians were the victims of a determined effort to destroy their social institutions and cultural identity, and to turn their country into a department of France. To this end, large numbers of European settlers were imported and settled on the best land, that had been confiscated. The last in a long series of revolts was led by the FLN (National Liberation Front), who evolved a revolutionary socialist ideology in the course of the struggle. The war finally completed the dislocation of the Muslim society by spreading to the remotest regions where the peasantry were forcibly resettled in concentration camps. Frantz Fanon's observations made during this bitter struggle led him to his influential theories of peasant revolt, expressed in such books as *The Wretched of the Earth* (Grove Press, 1963). As the end of the war approached the French terrorist OAS's excesses frightened the European settlers into mass flight, leaving a yawning gap in the infrastructure of the new state. Perhaps the only bonus for the newly independent country was the developing oil industry, although this factor had lengthened the war by increasing France's reluctance to leave. Theoretically Algeria is a one-party state, the FLN continuing in the new order. In practice, under the flamboyant leadership of Ben Bella, and then of the withdrawn Boumedienne and his successor Chedli Benjedid, military men, in alliance with technocrats, have ruled Algeria, and the party has been pushed into the background. *The Algerians*, by Pierre Bourdieu (Beacon Press, 1962), is a good introductory study. *Revolution and Political Leadership: Algeria, 1954–1968*, by William B. Quandt (MIT Press, 1969); *Algeria, a Revolution that Failed – a Political History since 1954*, by Arslan Humbaraci (Praeger, 1966); and *Algeria, the Politics of a Socialist Revolution*, by David and Marina Ottoway (University of California Press, 1970), all try to elucidate the politics of this highly secretive society.

Morocco

The traditional system of government in Morocco had been of a balance between a part directly ruled by the Sultan, called the Bled al-makhzan, and a part in a permanent state of ferment, called the Bled al-siba. French and Spanish colonialism did little to disturb the traditional structures beyond imposing a military peace on the whole area, and, in the case of the French, putting the powers of the Sultan in the hands of a resident, with a small and predominantly French administrative machine. During the Second World War demands for independence began to be enunciated by the Istiqlal party. In the course of the struggle for independence, the Sultan, Muhammad V, became the symbol of the nation, and after independence, he became the constitutional monarch. Within five years the king had taken the real power in the country, and his son Hasan, in twenty years of a stormy reign, has continued to develop the power of the monarchy. On the surface still a constitutional monarchy with several parties and a national assembly, Morocco is ruled through ministers directly responsible to the monarch, who manipulates the various parties to prevent any one being a challenge to his power. A very fine study of the system is *The Commander of the Faithful: the Moroccan Political Elite: a Study in Segmented Politics*, by John Waterbury (Columbia University Press, 1970). Earlier studies include two by I. William Zartman, *Morocco: Problems of New Power* (Atherton Press, 1964), and *Destiny of a Dynasty: the Search for Institutions in Morocco's Developing Country* (University of South Carolina Press, 1964), and *Political Change in Morocco*, by Douglas E. Ashford (Princeton University Press, 1961). King Hasan has used foreign issues to unite the nation behind him, the most recent being his incorporation of the former Spanish Sahara into his dominions, following the 'Green March'. However, this has involved him in a long war with the Polisario guerrillas, backed by Algeria.

Tunisia

Enjoying the greatest homogeneity of population of the three Maghrib countries, and the longest history of centralized government and therefore the greatest national consciousness, Tunisia also experienced a much less disruptive colonial presence than Algeria. As was the case in Morocco, the French left many traditional structures intact, but unlike that country, Tunisia had seen some modernization under the Beys before the French arrived. The struggle leading up to independence was led by the Destourian Socialist Party headed by Habib Bourguiba. The system since independence has been a one-party state dominated by Bourguiba. He has chosen to ignore the pan-Arabism of Nasser's Egypt and Qaddafi's Libya, the socialism of Algeria and the Islamic traditionalism of Morocco. Rather, Bourguibism stresses a humanistic socialism and Tunisian nationalism, which, from a Western perspective, leads to 'moderate' positions on most issues. This unique polity is studied in *Tunisia since Independence, the Dynamics of One-party Government*, by Clement Henry Moore (University of California Press, 1965); *Party and People: a Study of Political Change in Tunisia*, by Lars Rudebeck (Praeger, 1969); and *Tunisia: the Politics of Modernization*, by Charles Micaud, with Leon Carl Brown and Clement Henry Moore (Praeger, 1964).

Libya

Libya is perhaps the only country in the world to have come into existence primarily through a resolution of the General Assembly of the United Nations. The country comprises three provinces with rather loose historical connections: in many ways Tripolitania belongs to the Maghrib, Cyrenaica has many associations with Egypt, and Fezzan in the south looks to black Africa and the Sudan. Unity was partly owing to the common experience of Italian colonization, which, especially in its last Fascist phase, was particularly brutal and disruptive. Another unifying factor was the widespread influence of the Islamic religious order of the Sanusiyah. How this became the soul of the resistance to the Italians is described in *The Sanusi of Cyrenaica*, by E. E. Evans-Pritchard (Oxford University Press, 1968). After the Second World War the victorious allies were unable to agree on the future of the area, at that time one of the poorest in the world, and the matter was referred to the UN. In 1951 a constitutional monarchy was set up, a process described by the UN commissioner in Libya, Adrien Pelt, in *Libyan Independence and the United Nations: a Case of Planned Decolonization* (Yale University Press, 1970). The system was a federal one up to 1963, when a unitary government was announced. The structure of the kingdom was examined in *Modern Libya: a Study in Political Development*, by Majid Khadduri (Johns Hopkins University Press, 1963). Libya became projected to the forefront of Arab politics by the unexpected military *coup* of 1969 which brought Qaddafi to power. Qaddafi considers himself the inheritor of the mantle of Nasser and actively backs pan-Arab and revolutionary movements in the rest of the world. He has also tried unsuccessfully to unite his country with his Arab neighbours, but his convictions and tone have tended to alienate other Arab leaders. His own political theory has been published in translation as *The Green Book: Part One, the Solution to the Problem of Democracy 'the Authority of the People'*, by Muammar al-Qadhafi (Martin Brian and O'Keefe, 1976). He calls it the third theory; that is, neither capitalism nor Communism. It is an Islamic socialism with a stress on direct democracy through people's congresses, without the intermediary of representatives and parties. *Libya, the Elusive Revolution*, by Ruth First (Penguin Books, 1974), attempted an early assessment. *Political Development and Social Change in Libya*, by Omar I. El Fathaly and Monte Palmer (Lexington Books, 1980), and *Political Development and Bureaucracy in Libya*, by Omar I. El Fathaly *et al.* (Lexington Books, 1977), are more recent studies using the techniques of political sociology.

Sudan

Sudan is the part of the Arab world that reaches down into black Africa. The dominant section of the population who live in the north are Arabic-speaking and Muslim, while the southern tribes, like the Shilluk and Dinka, have more in common with their neighbours to the south, and are for the most part animist or Christian. The history and politics of the north are closely connected with those of Egypt. In the nineteenth century the area was conquered by the Egyptians, but they were ejected by the famous Mahdi, who established a theocratic state which lasted from 1881 until 1898. Britain reconquered the area, and although it was theoretically an Anglo-Egyptian condominium, it was effectively a British colony. Up till 1947 the southern territories were administered separately, but as independence began to loom, the two areas were united. After the Sudanese had chosen not to be united with Egypt, and independence ensued in 1955, the relations between the north and south have proved a great problem. The southerners have considered themselves under threat from the north as it tried to impose Arabic and Islam on the whole country, and this led to open military conflict, which was in turn a factor in northern political instability. The years 1955 to 1958 and 1965 to 1969 were periods of parliamentary democracy, with the military rule of General Abboud in between. Since 1969, and despite a number of attempted *coups*, General Ja'far al-Nimeiry has kept power firmly in his own hands. He began his presidency by settling the southern problem by granting regional autonomy. The Sudan is a one-party state (the Sudanese Socialist Union) with a president and a people's assembly. But real power resides with the president. Studies of the Sudanese political scene are sparse. *Politics in the Sudan: Parliamentary and Military Rule in an Emerging African Nation*, by Peter K. Bechtold (Praeger, 1976), considers the whole country. Among the more numerous studies of the southern problem are *The Southern Sudan: the Problem of National Integration*, edited by Dunstan M. Wai (Frank Cass, 1973), and two books by Mohamed Omer Beshir, *The Southern Sudan: Background to Conflict* (Hurst, 1968), and *The Southern Sudan: from Conflict to Peace* (Hurst, 1975).

Bibliographies and further references

This survey has limited itself to English-language studies, with an emphasis on the more recent ones up to the beginning of 1982. Many of the books cited have bibliographies which will lead to further studies. There are many bibliographies both on the area in general and on specific countries. One of the best of the general ones is *The Contemporary Middle East 1948–1973: a Selective and Annotated Bibliography*, by George N. Atiyeh (G. K. Hall, 1975). Two indexes to periodical articles that come out regularly are *Index Islamicus* (1958–) and *Bibliography of Periodical Literature on the Near and Middle East*, by the staff of the *Middle East Journal* (1947–).

24
International organizations
Peter D. Griffiths

The concept of international organization is familiar to many, and most people would be able to name an intergovernmental organization. The fact that they would probably name the same one – the United Nations – belies the complexity of such organizations and the problems of their definition, description and categorization. These may vary according to the economic, political or other standpoint of the commentator, and a number of groupings are possible. For the purposes of this survey, intergovernmental organizations will be considered as multi-purpose bodies that provide a political forum for sovereign nation states to meet as equals to discuss and resolve problems of mutual concern. To propose such a description is not to ignore the wealth of debate on the theoretical aspects of the subject but merely to adopt a working definition.

The 19th edition of the *Yearbook of International Organizations* (1908–) appeared in 1981 with 14 784 entries for international bodies; it is clear that many bodies are therefore excluded by the definition adopted. An examination of the *Yearbook* will nevertheless show many of the different types of body in existence, and its preface will hint at some of the problems of definition. A thorough survey of the many ways of examining intergovernmental organization is found in *The Concept of International Organization*, edited by Georges Abi-Saab (UNESCO, 1981). This includes contributions from all viewpoints – legal and political, and from both sides of the East–West and North–South divides – and has

many references including much non-English-language material.
International Organization: Principles and Issues, by A. Leroy
Bennett (Prentice-Hall, 3rd edn, 1984) is a theoretical and historical survey based largely on the United Nations. Its approach
provides a wealth of material but risks exclusion or misinterpreta-
tion of forms of international organization which do not conform
to the United Nations pattern.

United Nations

There is, of course, a wide range of literature examining the prime
intergovernmental organization, the United Nations. *The United
Nations: How it Works and What it Does*, by Evan Luard
(Macmillan, 1979), is a useful introduction to the UN system by a
British politician who is strongly committed to the cause of the UN
and who in this book counters criticisms that the UN has failed.
The book explains in some detail what the UN's activities are and
justifies them within the context of present-day international
politics, showing in particular that the present UN is the result of
an evolutionary process from the immediate post-war organization, and that this process will continue to meet the challenge
presented by future conditions. A number of difficulties are
identified, and countered. These include various aspects of relations between the great power blocs, in which Luard argues that
the UN can provide a forum for 'manufactured' negotiated
settlements of disputes between the powers, and can act as a
longstop to discourage aggressive acts within the spheres of
influence of the powers in which the other would hesitate to
intervene. There is, too, a role for the UN in apparently internal
disputes in which it is powerless under its charter to act; this is
amply demonstrated by the observer and peacekeeping forces set
up during internal conflicts in Cyprus, the Congo, Yemen and
other places. Luard argues that the UN should provide the
initiative for change within itself to meet the challenge of new
areas of interest such as pollution, resources, terrorism or the
population crisis; but he considers that if the resolutions of the
General Assembly are to carry authority, especially with the larger
powers, then a weighted system of voting is required to counteract
the voting ability of the many emergent nations which is disproportionate to their population, and to their influence in the case of
the smallest states. Returning to his constant emphasis, Luard
warns that 'unless it evolves significantly [the UN] may find that
governments increasingly look elsewhere for the solution of the
problems they face'.

The United Nations system has often been referred to as a family. This characteristic is one which is found in inter-governmental organizations of both regional and global scale, and appears with the creation of specialist agencies entrusted with particular responsibilities within the overall programme of the organization. In the case of the UN the characteristic is particularly well developed, and is displayed in both regional organizations and in worldwide agencies, many of which have their headquarters remote from the centres of administration of the UN itself. The UN has in addition established institutes which are now autonomous, such as the Asian and African Development Banks. Information on these bodies is widely spread, but basic data on the entire range of the bodies associated with the UN can be found in the *United Nations Handbook* (1961–), which is published by the New Zealand Ministry of Foreign Affairs. (The title until 1968 was *United Nations and Specialised Agencies Handbook* and from 1968 to 1972 was *United Nations and Related Agencies Handbook*.) Here can be found basic information on the General Assembly, the Security Council and the Economic and Social Council – the provisions of the Charter which created them and provide their authority, their composition and structure – and brief resumés of the activities of the special bodies and what are here termed the intergovernmental agencies, including the development banks as well as such obvious candidates as UNESCO, UNCTAD and the others.

The UN itself also provides basic information in *Everyone's United Nations* (United Nations, 9th edn, 1979). This edition is designed to be read in conjunction with the eighth edition, which was published under the title *Everyman's United Nations* in 1968. The 9th edition describes the structure and activities of the UN and its seventeen related intergovernmental agencies, concentrating on their work up to 1977/1978. The earlier edition gives a more detailed account of the activities and evolution of the UN in its first twenty years. Taken together, the two volumes are designed to provide a basic history of the UN, but a far more detailed picture is given by the *Yearbook of the United Nations* (1947–). Early volumes carried the title *United Nations Year Book*. A full account is given of issues debated in the General Assembly and the Security Council and the resolutions considered during the year reported, whilst appendices contain the full text of the charter and various agreements.

A record of the activities of the UN and its related agencies is provided by the *UN monthly chronicle* (May 1964–). It states itself to be designed to advance public understanding of all aspects of UN work, aiming to be factual and comprehensive. From the outset the periodical has included articles of note, beginning in the first issue with two essays by U Thant, 'The League of Nations and the United Nations' and 'The Strengthening of the United Nations', and an article 'Trends at the Trade Conference'. In more recent issues a more journalistic tone has appeared, whilst its coverage has widened to include discussions of international issues from viewpoints more general than those of the officials of the UN.

It is evident that the organization of UN documentation is complex, not least because there are so many issuing bodies within the system. Many commentaries and several copious explanatory volumes are available which will permit the reader to construct or to decipher document symbols with comparative ease, but there remains at the end a welter of publications in which the problem is not so much how to describe easily obtained publications but how to discover the existence of many of the more obscure documents which have not achieved wide distribution. This is fortunately a problem to which the UN's own libraries and documentation centres have turned their attention and to which the latest computer-assisted methods of bibliographic control and information retrieval are now being applied.

In *Documentation of the UN system: a Survey of Bibliographic Control and a Suggested Methodology for an Integrated UN Bibliography*, prepared by John Clews (IFLA International Office for UBC, 1981, Occasional papers; no. 8), existing documentation of the UN system is described – documents, official records, sales publications and public information material, together with microform editions of this and other material – and the problems of bibliographic control and research through existing systems are explored. The paper recommends the creation of an integrated UN bibliographic system which would contain details of all publications of the UN and of all the specialized agencies: the operation would be computer assisted and the bibliographic format compatible with current cataloguing standards.

Although the paper is most obviously aimed at the library and documentation community, it serves to point out the shortcomings of the present system to those wishing to use UN publications as a primary source of research. Not the least of the present bibliographic control systems is the United Nations Bibliographic Information System, or UNBIS. This is based in a number of UN libraries and documentation centres and attempts to combine comprehensive coverage of UN documentation and external materials required for UN activities, compatibility with other bibliographic information systems and solutions to the particular problems encountered in servicing the UN where some conventional bibliographic approaches are unsuitable for the material being handled. (Consider the difficulty of retrieving a treaty signed by thirty nations which could be sought by any of those nations as the primary signatory.) The system is described in 'The United Nations Bibliographic Information System (UNBIS)', by Surjit Singh, *Unesco Journal of Information Science, Librarianship and Archives Administration*, **2,** No. 4, 220–226, October/December 1980). The article also includes in concise form information on the monthly *UNDOC: Current Index*, which provides a listing of UN documents and publications together with official records and sales publications, and a number of indexes to assist their retrieval. The list has appeared since 1979 and will cumulate. It replaces earlier indexes, *UN Documents Index* (1950–1973) and the three series of *UNDEX* (1970–1978), A: subjects, B: countries and C: list of documents issued.

In 1978 a conference at Indiana University considered the documentation of intergovernmental organizations, and its proceedings were published in *Government publications Review,* **6,** No. 2 (1979). Of particular note in the present context were papers by Elva Levy, including 'Patterns of UN Documentation', which provides details of the General Assembly, Security Council, Economic and Social Council, Trusteeship Council, Secretariat and the International Court of Justice. Two recent studies in greater detail which also assist in understanding the structure of the UN are *Documentation of the United Nations System: Coordination in its Bibliographic Control*, by Luciana Marulli (Scarecrow, 1979), and *Guide to United Nations Organization, Documentation and Publishing for Students, Researchers and Librarians*, by Peter I. Hajnal (Oceana, 1978). These provide general descriptions of the system sufficient for those who intend to use UN documentation as their primary source for study.

UN agencies

The UN has a large number of subsidiary bodies, some of a purely regional nature such as the Economic and Social Council for Asia and the Pacific (to name but one of many), some of an international nature but controlled more or less directly by the United Nations (such as the United Nations Development Programme), and yet others, numbering about fifteen, which are themselves independent intergovernmental organizations such as the World Health Organization and the Food and Agriculture Organization.

The last group find their origins in resolutions and activities of the UN and have been established as a direct result of some action of the UN. Of this group, often referred to as the United Nations family, one organization, the International Labour Organization (ILO), may be distinguished as the most senior; it of all the family predates the parent, having been established as a subsidiary of the League of Nations by the peace settlement of 1919. Following the failure of the League, the ILO continued in existence and became a specialized agency of the UN upon its creation. The headquarters are in Geneva, where its permanent staff form the International Labour Office. The creation of the ILO marked the first international efforts to improve conditions of employment; the compilers of the peace treaties wished to create conditions which would bring about lasting peace and identified employment as a field in which their efforts were required. As the longest-established of the specialized agencies, the ILO has been described in many books; many of the historical descriptions were issued at the time of the celebration of its fiftieth anniversary. One of the most easily accessible histories is the *History of the International Labour Organisation*, by Anthony Alcock (Macmillan, 1971). The ILO is itself a prolific publisher both of monographs and serial titles. A regular report of developments in the field of labour appears in *Social and Labour Bulletin* (1975–), whilst ILO activities and labour developments are described in popular style in *ILO Information* (1965–).

There are various long-established serials: the *ILO Official Bulletin* (1920–) and the *International Labour Review* (1921–) both appear in English-, French- and Spanish-language editions. There are also regular *Minutes of the Governing Body* (1920–) and a *Legislative Series* (1919–). Details of ILO monographs are found in *ILO Publications* (1969–), which supplements the extensive catalogue of ILO publications, is published annually and includes a list of the ILO's sales agencies in various countries.

Besides the subsidiary bodies of the UN and the specialized agencies there are a number of organizations which operate at an intergovernmental level within a restricted geographical area. A number of these have interests in a broadly political sphere, even if this political interest is as a result of some other purpose, often that of defence. Within Europe, a number of countries, including the UK, are members of several organizations; the differing memberships allow contact in an international forum with other states which may be precluded from membership of, for example, those groupings with primarily a defence interest in common.

The Council of Europe and the Western European Union

The Council of Europe represents 21 member governments from Western Europe, including Turkey and the Nordic countries. The headquarters are in Strasbourg, where sessions of the Parliamentary Assembly, the deliberative organ of the Council of Europe, take place three times each year. The foreign ministers of member states meet twice a year and their deputies meet monthly. The Council was established by statute in 1949 to achieve unity in order to hasten social and economic progress in Europe. Although many of its committees and subsidiary bodies are social in their nature, the Council is responsible for the European Court and the Commission in Human Rights. A range of publications includes the quarterly *Council of Europe Forum* and an annual list of publications; the Secretary-General also produces an annual report.

The Western European Union represents seven member governments, coinciding with the original European Economic Community countries together with the UK. It was brought into being following a conference held in London late in 1954 after the breakdown of negotiations to form a proposed European Defence Community. This same conference agreed the entry of the Federal Republic of Germany into NATO. The legal basis of the Union is the Brussels Treaty of 1948, which was modified by the 1954 conference to include provision for collaboration in economic, social and cultural matters and collective self-defence. The Union has particularly strong objectives in the field of defence but has played a role in the political and economic development of Europe, for example by providing a forum where contacts could be maintained between the UK and the EEC countries following the suspension in 1963 of negotiation for UK accession to the Treaty of Rome. The Western European Union has as its main organs a Council which meets at ministerial level in various European locations and an Assembly which is located in Paris. Its Secretariat is based in London, whilst an Armaments Control Agency is in Paris. The Assembly produces an annual report.

NATO

The Brussels Treaty powers of Europe were soon associated with the US by the North Atlantic Treaty and through it the creation of NATO. Although primarily a defensive grouping, NATO has a political aspect both in terms of the political cooperation required to maintain a common defensive policy and in the wider international political issues of concern to its members. The history of NATO is described in *The Birth of NATO*, by Sir Nicholas Henderson (Weidenfeld and Nicolson, 1982), or in *NATO: the Next Thirty Years: the Changing Political, Economic and Military Setting*, edited by Kenneth A. Myers (Westview; Croom Helm, 1980). Current issues are examined in the *Atlantic Community Quarterly* (1963–).

The alliance was established by the signature of the North Atlantic Treaty on 4 April 1949, and now has its headquarters in Brussels; they were earlier in London and then Paris. The main organ is the Council, which sits in permanent session at the headquarters. *NATO Review* (formerly *NATO Letter*, 1953–) appears four or six times a year in each of nine languages, and a handbook is available. *NATO's Fifteen Nations* (1956–) contains articles of a general defensive or political nature, often written by prominent persons within NATO. The North Atlantic Assembly is an interparliamentary body founded in 1955 and now linked to NATO with membership drawn from all fifteen member countries of NATO; the Assembly's Secretariat-General is also located in Brussels and it publishes the *North Atlantic Assembly News*.

Organization of American states

Besides its links with Europe through NATO, the US is linked with other countries on its own continent through other regional intergovernmental organizations. The Organization of American States was established as the International Union of American Republics at the first International Conference of American States on 14 April 1890. From its original commercial intentions it has come to serve to strengthen the peace and security of the American continent, to provide a forum for the settlement of disputes and to encompass the political, juridicial and economic fields. Its General Assembly meets annually whilst specific problems are considered by Meetings of Consultation of Ministers of Foreign Affairs. Twenty-eight governments from South America and the Caribbean together with the US are members, whilst Canada, Guyana and a number of European, Asian and African countries hold observer status.

There is a range of OAS publications. The magazine *Americas* (1949–) is produced monthly in three editions corresponding to the three official languages of the OAS, English, Spanish and Portuguese. The *OAS Chronicle* (1965–) appears quarterly in English and Spanish, whilst the Secretary-General (whose Secretariat is the central organ of the OAS) produces an annual report in all three languages. The history of the OAS is described in *The Inter-American System*, by Gordon Connell-Smith (Oxford University Press, for the Royal Institute of International Affairs, 1966), and in *The Organization of American States: an Introduction*, by Carlos O. Stoetzer (Praeger, 1965). Some more recent issues are considered in *The Americas in the 1980s: an Agenda for the Decade Ahead*, by Alejandro Orfila (University Press of America, 1980).

The seat of the Organization is in Washington, DC, in a building also occupied by the Union's commercial bureau, the Pan American Union. The body's charter is to be found in *Charter of the Organization of American States signed at the Ninth international conference of American States, Bogota, 1948* (Pan American Union, 1962). This was later amended by the Protocol of Buenos Aires and reprinted in 1970 as OAS Treaty Series NO. 1-C. A recent general and diplomatic history is available in Spanish, *Origines y evolucion del sistema interamericano*, by Ismael Moreno Pino (Secretaria de Relaciones Exteriores (Mexico), 1977).

Organization of African Unity

Similarly, there is a regional African intergovernmental organization, the Organization of African Unity, which has as its members forty-nine African governments with a base in Addis Ababa, where the Organization was founded in May 1963. The aim of the Organization is the promotion of unity and international peace and cooperation. Development is emphasized, as is the process of decolonization. Members' interests are taken account of in a wide range of fields including diplomacy, defence, education, economics, health and welfare, technology and science. Heads of state meet in an annual assembly whilst two meetings take place each year of foreign ministers of member governments. There is a Secretariat together with subsidiary commissions to deal with various specialized interests. The history of the OAU is to be found in *Politics in the Organization of African Unity*, by Michael Wolfers (Methuen, 1976); a more radical view is taken in *Pan-African or Neo-Colonialism: the Bankruptcy of the OAU*, by Elenga M'Buyinga (Zed Press, 1982).

World Bank and the IDA

International bodies in the financial and economic sphere also inevitably find a political aspect to their work; this applies in particular to the International Bank for Reconstruction and Development, which was set up following the Bretton Woods Conference. With its affiliate, the International Development Association (established in 1960), the IBRD is often referred to as the World Bank. The institutions' object is to channel resources from developed to developing nations to help raise productivity and living standards, but it is clear that it is increasingly difficult to separate this economic purpose from the international political relationships embodied in the Bank. The Institutions have in any case a non-financial role in the provision of policy analysis when assessing particular projects and their relationship to a given country's economy.

The IBRD was established in 1945 and is owned by the countries which have subscribed to its capital: in 1981 these totalled 139. Countries' subscriptions are related to their assessed economic strength, which in turn is measured by their quota in the International Monetary Fund, of which all IBRD subscribers are members. The IDA assists poorer developing countries by providing financial assistance on less stringent terms than those of the IBRD's loans.

The historical position of the Bank is located in a long and detailed history of international economic relations since 1919, *International economic Cooperation and the World Bank*, by Robert W. Oliver (Macmillan, 1975). In this, the Bretton Woods Conference and the establishment of the Bank form the conclusion rather than the beginning of the story; this provides the political and historical context as well as the economic. Professor Oliver is a long-time student of the Bank, and his earlier paper *Early Plans for a World Bank* (Department of Economics, Princeton University, 1971) provides further detail of the same period. Professor Oliver was at one time associated with the Brookings Institution, from which appeared *The World Bank since Bretton Woods*, by Edward S. Mason and Robert E. Asher (Brookings Institution, 1973). This work includes a section relating the Bank to other bodies, 'The Bank in the realm of international diplomacy': there is also an analysis of the Bank's role in three international political affairs of the 1950s, the Iranian oil crisis, the Indus waters dispute and the Egyptian High Dam project. Although they conclude that in retrospect the Bank's action displayed some naïveté, they provide a useful description of the political role played by the

Bank in international affairs. A more recent critical study is *The World Bank and the Poor*, by Aart van de Laar (Nijhoff, 1980), which examines the IBRD and IDA activities before concluding with an examination of the structure and organization of the Bank.

The Bank is itself a prolific publisher and produces a wide range of papers on economics as well as analyses of sectors of activity and the economies of particular countries. A catalogue of publications is produced annually and lists all publicly available and in-print materials, both priced and free. Among the free publications are two describing *The World Bank* (1981) and *The IDA* (1978), which give outline details of projects, lending and finance as well as short histories of the institutions. *IDA in Retrospect: the First Two Decades of the International Development Association* (Oxford University Press, for the World Bank, 1982) is a recent history of the IDA which examines the amounts and kinds of financing and the effectiveness of its assistance. The book also looks at the varying political support for IDA and its relations with other aid programmes. The Bank produces an annual report (1946– ; the first report appeared as part of the report of the annual meeting of Governors), and a further publication, the *World Development Report* (1978–) is published as a 'series of reports providing a comprehensive assessment of global development issues'. It is primarily concerned with the analysis of policy on the international political and economic scale and so does not detail Bank activity and involvements.

The Commonwealth

It was suggested earlier that empirical studies of international organization based on a study of the UN risked excluding other possible forms of international grouping simply because they did not conform to the UN pattern. Many regional groups exist for economic, defence or political reasons, but one organization offers an interesting comparison with the UN on a global scale (even though it is consigned by Bennett to being a regional group, a strange description for a group of over forty-five members on all five continents). This is the Commonwealth. Although the view is often put forward that it merely serves to illustrate the remaining constitutional and legal links between the UK and its members and is therefore essentially a constitutional organization without a political will or authority of its own, the Commonwealth has many of the characteristics identified in intergovernmental organizations, and has produced a number of agencies whose form and activities parallel those of the UN specialized agencies. However, some of the Commonwealth bodies, not least the Secretariat based in London, were formed much later than the organization itself, so that the history of its development and of its international role is quite different from that of the UN. The Commonwealth has demonstrated itself to have a political will which is independent of that of its individual members, and indeed its views have, on occasion, run counter to the interests of what might have been considered its prime member, the UK. Yet so little has the Commonwealth become a reflection of the constitutional link that it could be seriously suggested in the debate on links with South Africa that the UK might be suspended from membership.

The Commonwealth shows many parallels with the UN. It, too, is an organization which brings together nations with populations which range from a few thousands to several hundreds of millions on an equal footing in its forum, be they monarchies or republics, developed or developing, or indeed multi-party or one-party states. The Commonwealth has the distinction of achieving this with a membership approaching one-third of that of the UN, all in a voluntary association based eventually on their common past. It is based on the constitutional relationship between the Dominions which was arrived at in the closing stages of the First World War and later expressed in the Balfour Declaration: 'They are autonomous communities within the British Empire, equal in status, in no way subordinate to one another in any aspect of their domestic or external affairs, though united by a common allegiance to the Crown and freely associated as members of the British Commonwealth of Nations'. A legal status was given to this formula by the Statute of Westminster (1931), which established the independence of the Dominions and their relationship to the UK and to one another, and unconsciously provided the yardstick by which the Commonwealth could arrange itself. A further development was the emergence of the Sovereign as a symbol of the free association of the member states and therefore as head of the Commonwealth, quite separately from being the sovereign monarch of the UK and of many of the independent monarchies. This role arose from the creation of independent republics within the Commonwealth, beginning with India. Nor does the Commonwealth represent every former British colony: the terms of association were couched in such a way that the decision of Burma not to become a member on reaching independence, and the withdrawal of a number of states which formerly were members, including Pakistan and the Republic of South Africa, were quite admissible within the terms laid down.

The view of the Commonwealth as an intergovernmental organization is effectively argued in *The 'Open' Commonwealth*, by M. Margaret Ball (Duke University Commonwealth Studies Center, 1971). The term 'open' is used to denote that the Commonwealth does not demand the exclusive or prime allegiance of its members – that is, no member is precluded from belonging to any other political, economic or defensive grouping of states. The book details the growth of organs which parallel those of bodies generally described as IGOs, and it is argued that although there are some deviations from the pattern usually found within these organizations (for example, there is no written constitution), the Commonwealth can no longer be seen as a constitutional or quasi-constitutional body whose existence and form depends on the present or former nature of the links between member countries and the UK. A chapter on 'Political consultation' provides a summary of the political and diplomatic processes which have taken place at the times of various crises. Commonwealth attitudes to issues in the international arena are considered, and the author concludes that whilst the Commonwealth forms an alternative forum for discussion outside the UN, it does not necessarily agree or act in concert upon such issues.

A more recent study, 'Is the Commonwealth an International Organisation?', by William Dale (*International and Comparative Law Quarterly*, **31**, 451–473 (1982)), considers this question from a legal standpoint. Dale attempts to find a suitable definition of an international – that is, an inter-governmental – organization, and then considers in turn the elements of the Commonwealth association, the role of the Sovereign, the organs of the Commonwealth and the various privileges which the employees of those organs enjoy compared with those of the employees of other intergovernmental organizations, and the legal substructure. The overall conclusion is, once more, that the Commonwealth is indeed an intergovernmental organization, but one of an extraordinary nature having qualities not possessed by other IGOs – and, one might add, sometimes lacking other qualities often found in IGOs.

Much information on the Commonwealth can be gathered from British official sources. A primary reference tool is the *Yearbook of the Commonwealth* (1969–), which is edited within the Foreign and Commonwealth Office and appears annually. It sets out much historical and constitutional detail on the development of the Commonwealth and includes much information on the member countries, including economic, geographical and climatic, historical and constitutional descriptions, and lists ministers and other office holders. The history of the *Yearbook* goes back to 1862 when the *Colonial Office List (1862–1925)* began as a private venture. With the creation of the Secretaryship of State for the Dominions in 1925 the list became the *Dominions Office and Colonial Office List (1926–1940)*.

Publication was suspended during wartime, and when it resumed with the reappearance of the *Colonial Office List* in 1946 it was for the first time as an official work of reference published by His Majesty's Stationery Office. The *Commonwealth Relations Office List (1951–1965)* continued to provide the considerable detail of its predecessors (and its contemporaries) but, as the first edition under its later title, the *Commonwealth Relations Office Yearbook 1966* (HMSO, 1966), pointed out, the *List* always provided information about the Commonwealth considerably in excess of that about the staff which it listed. With the separate appearance of the *Diplomatic Service List* the title of the *Yearbook* was again changed: it was the *Commonwealth Office Yearbook* in 1967 and 1968, and from 1969 *A Yearbook of the Commonwealth*, the present title. A number of articles on the Commonwealth appeared in various editions of the *List*, and in chapter 59 of the 1966 *Yearbook* a complete list of these articles is to be found. They include articles on the development of the constitutional relationship between members of the Commonwealth (1953 edition) and an article, 'The Modern Commonwealth', by the then Secretary of State for Commonwealth Relations, Duncan Sandys (*CRO List*, 1963). This latter also appeared as an illustrated booklet (HMSO, 1962). In his essay the Secretary of State attempts to identify the elements which set the Commonwealth apart from other organizations – its common institutional forms, its function as a means of political contact, the association of peoples, the use of the English language and a common sentiment between its peoples. Problems, too, are considered – economic (such as the relationship between EEC and the Commonwealth) and social (such as immigration into Britain). Sandys concluded that the Commonwealth acted as a force for world peace by 'showing the way to other nations, proving that a group of such dissimilar states could nevertheless agree and act in concern on questions of mutual importance'.

Sandys' essay is further interesting in that it argues against the establishment of a Commonwealth secretariat comparable with the UN Secretariat on the grounds that it would cut across the direct personal relations between Ministers and officials in Commonwealth countries, whilst bodies had already been set up to assist cooperation in those fields where they were needed, such as economics and agriculture. But the argument over a secretariat is much older than this. Its history is described in an essay 'The Secretariat: Born in the Nick of Time', by Derek Ingram in his *The Imperfect Commonwealth* (Rex Collings, 1977), which illustrates the growth of the Commonwealth Secretariat as an instrument of international diplomacy and emphasizes in particular its separation from Britain. Indeed, this independence from Britain is underlined in the account of pressure brought to bear by the Secretariat against the UK over the questions of Rhodesia and arms sales to South Africa, where Ingram argues that without the Secretariat the Commonwealth would have disintegrated.

The Imperfect Commonwealth contains, besides the piece on the Commonwealth Secretariat, a number of articles written for newspapers at the time of conferences and other events which have somehow touched the Commonwealth either directly or through their international repercussions. The book's overall conclusion is that the Commonwealth has a crucial role to play in the economic sphere, in the relationship between the developed and the developing countries, in the racial question, and in particular in the area of coalescence of the economic and racial problems in Southern Africa. The Commonwealth must evolve and promote a unified position representative of all its members in order to act as a mediator between East and West. The implication is that the Commonwealth, being derived from the former colonial status of the countries of that region, is better suited to understand and solve the region's problems than is the UN.

The Commonwealth: a New Look, by Andrew Walker (Pergamon, 1978), is a brief descriptive work which sets out the evolution and the international role of the Commonwealth before going on to describe in a number of succinct chapters many of its associated activities and related bodies. These include the Commonwealth Parliamentary Association, which forms a link between members of the national and state legislatures of Commonwealth countries, and publishes a quarterly journal, *The Parliamentarian* (1966–), (as the *Journal of the Parliaments of the Commonwealth*, 1950–), which reports parliamentary developments in member countries; another chapter describes the role of the Commonwealth Heads of Government Meetings (CHoGMs), formerly Commonwealth Prime Ministers' Meetings, which take place every two years in one or other of the Commonwealth countries. The CHoGM provides a means for a review of Commonwealth affairs and the coordination of a policy for the Commonwealth until the next meeting. Many far-reaching decisions have emerged from these meetings, including the 1971 Declaration of Commonwealth Principles, the establishment of the Commonwealth Fund for Technical Cooperation and the Commonwealth Youth Programme, and the plan to provide independence for Zimbabwe under democratic rule. The final communiqués of the CHoGMs are published, both by the Secretariat and, in the United Kingdom, by HMSO as a Command paper; the proceedings themselves are not made public.

Some of the most passionate writing about the Commonwealth has come from those closely connected with it, especially in an official capacity. *The Commonwealth*, by Patrick Gordon Walker (Secker and Warburg, 1962), is written by a former Commonwealth Secretary and traces the history of the Commonwealth to 1960. The opening chapters, 'Transformation of British imperialism' and 'The rise of the Commonwealth nations' provide a very readable account of the development of the British Empire, the creation of the Dominions and the emergence of the Commonwealth as an association of former colonies of settlement. Above all in this account there springs from the page a tremendous enthusiasm for the Commonwealth idea and an emphasis of the totally unique character of the Commonwealth grouping of states. In *The Commonwealth Office 1925–68*, by Joe Garner (Heinemann Educational, 1978), Lord Garner, who was Head of the Diplomatic Service from 1965 to 1968, provides a comprehensive account of the British Government department concerned with the Dominions and later the Commonwealth in which he spent his career. Apart from an account of the historical and constitutional basis of the Commonwealth, the book details the structure of British administration. In particular, the Imperial Conferences of 1926 and 1930 and the passing of the Statute of Westminster are considered in detail in a chapter 'Dominion status and its consequences'.

It is perhaps fortunate that we have recently seen published volumes by both the first Secretary-General of the Commonwealth Secretariat and by the first director of the Commonwealth Foundation. *Stitches in Time: the Commonwealth in World Politics*, by Arnold Smith with Clyde Sanger (André Deutsch, 1981), describes the setting up of the Commonwealth Secretariat and its role during its first ten years, 1965 to 1975, when Arnold Smith was Secretary-General. The history of the Commonwealth Foundation, which has several broad aims in the field of the professions, is contained in *The Unofficial Commonwealth*, by John Chadwick (Allen and Unwin, 1982), in which the author describes how the Foundation was set up under his direction and helped to set up centres for the exchange of professional opinion and expertise.

Numerous other bodies and institutions are concerned with a wide range of activities within the Commonwealth. Until the mid-1970s these were listed in the *Yearbook of the Commonwealth*, but their details now appear in *Commonwealth Organisations: a Handbook of Official and Unofficial Organisations Active in the Commonwealth* (Commonwealth Secretariat, 2nd edn, 1979).

A range of periodicals is concerned with the Commonwealth, many with a long history. *Commonwealth* (1970–) was until 1981 (after which it became an independent commercial publication) a publication of the Royal Commonwealth Society, and had as its earlier titles *Journal of the Royal Commonwealth Society* (1958 –1960) and *Commonwealth Journal*. The journal under its various guises has included both comment and feature reports on economic and political matters of Commonwealth concern as well as news. The topics cover a wide range, from immigration issues to detailed examination of conditions in particular countries. *Round Table* (1910–) was by 1934 calling itself 'a quarterly review of the politics of the British Commonwealth', but its scope was wider than might be implied by this title, since it viewed the role of the Commonwealth within the wider context of international affairs. Thus during the 1930s the journal was considering topics such as 'Germany and Europe' and 'Power Politics in the Pacific', which accurately foreshadowed the effects of the ascendency of Japan and Germany on all members of the Commonwealth – as indeed did the article 'Foreign Affairs: Anglo-German Rivalry' in the very first issue in 1910. This wider range of interest was later shown in the change of the subtitle to 'The Commonwealth Journal of International Affairs'. Recent issues have considered several aspects of the role of the Commonwealth in the 1980s. The *Journal of Comparative and Commonwealth Politics* (1974–) includes scholarly articles on aspects of politics in Commonwealth countries. It was earlier known as the *Journal of Commonwealth Political Studies* (1961–1973), and from the outset included articles on the Commonwealth in the world context; the first volume, for example, included articles comparing the Commonwealth and the UN, and discussing the origin of the Balfour Declaration, whilst Patrick Gordon Walker described the office and work of the Commonwealth Secretary. In a recent volume, political considerations in countries as diverse as Nigeria, India and Barbados have been discussed in their local and international contexts, whilst an appreciation of Earl Mountbatten was included in a historical article on the independence of Burma.

Recent progress in the Commonwealth is charted in the bimonthly *Commonwealth Currents*, which is published by the Commonwealth Secretariat. This is part of a prolific output of priced and free publications which form a comprehensive survey of the activities of the Commonwealth; it includes short descriptive folders as well as substantial books on topics from agriculture through law and politics to medicine or bibliography. The list of these titles (which is updated at intervals) provides a key to these, but also serves to illustrate the wide area of Commonwealth activity.

The Commonwealth provides a valuable example of international organization to set against the UN. With a membership composed of one quarter of the population of the world and with representatives of both rich and poor countries from every continent, it is second only to the UN in world importance. Yet is has proved its ability to act by consensus to provide solutions to problems which have defeated the UN, notably the question of independence for Zimbabwe. It demonstrates the possibility of progress through an entirely voluntary organization, with consultation and cooperation rather than conflict being the means of negotiation within the organization. It shows finally that a theory of intergovernmental organization which relies solely on observations of the UN and its associated bodies is one which excludes the ever-present possibility of alternative organizations coming into existence, and can therefore tell only half the story.

Index